13-14 18, 39, 89
95 168   178 206
213, 217 224 268
273 275 282 289
291   367 369

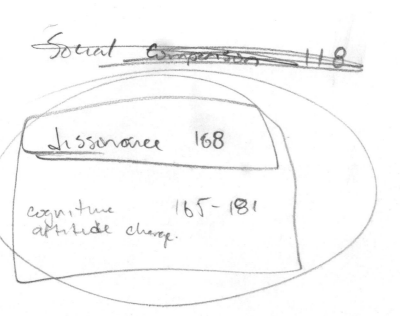

~~Social Comparison~~ 118

Dissonance 168

cognitive   165-181
attitude change.

Volume 1

Small Groups and Social Interaction

Volume 1

Small Groups and Social Interaction

Edited by

Herbert H. Blumberg
University of London Goldsmiths' College

A. Paul Hare
Ben-Gurion University of the Negev, Israel

Valerie Kent
University of London Goldsmiths' College

and

Martin F. Davies
University of London Goldsmiths' College

JOHN WILEY & SONS

Chichester · New York · Brisbane · Toronto · Singapore

Library of Congress Cataloging in Publication Data:

Main entry under title:

Small groups and social interaction.

   Includes index.
    1. Small groups—Addresses, essays, lectures.
2. Social interaction—Addresses, essays, lectures.
3. Interpersonal relations—Addresses, essays, lectures.
4. Social change—Addresses, essays, lectures.
5. Personality—Addresses, essays, lectures.
I. Blumberg, Herbert H.
HM133.S65   1983   302.3′4   82-8558

ISBN 0 471 10242 3

British Library Cataloguing in Publication Data:

Small groups and social interaction.
   1. Social interaction
I. Blumberg, Herbert H.
   302   HM291

ISBN 0 471 10242 3

Typeset by Pintail Studios Ltd, Ringwood, Hampshire.
Printed by Page Bros., Norwich.

Acknowledgements

We would like to thank those colleagues and students who kindly read portions of the proposals and manuscript and offered suggestions—in particular, Paul Webley, Duncan Cramer, and a number of the represented authors.

For the translation of papers into English we wish to thank Gordon Davies, Andrew Sutton, and an anonymous translator.

Acknowledgements for permission to reprint various extracts are shown at the relevant places in the text.

We especially wish to thank our publishers—particularly Celia Bird, Linda Burden, Amanda Gray, and Wendy Hudlass for their advice and help in a variety of major and minor matters.

Contributors to Volume 1

Irwin Altman, *University of Utah, USA*
Michael Argyle, *University of Oxford, England*
Joel Aronoff, *Michigan State University, USA*
Elliot Aronson, *University of California at Santa Cruz, USA*
Carlfred B. Broderick, *University of Southern California, USA*
John T. Cacioppo, *University of Iowa, USA*
Aaron V. Cicourel, *University of California, San Diego, USA*
James E. Driskell, *University of South Carolina, USA*
Fred E. Fiedler, *University of Washington, USA*
James J. Gange, *University of Missouri, USA*
Russell G. Geen, *University of Missouri, USA*
Janet R. Goktepe, *University of Maryland, USA*
John M. Gottman, *University of Illinois, Urbana-Champaign, USA*
J. Richard Hackman, *Yale University, USA*
Stephen G. Harkins, *Northeastern University, Boston, Massachusetts, USA*
Tamar Heller, *University of Illinois, Chicago Circle, USA*
Robert A. Hinde, *M.R.C. Unit on the Development and Integration of Behaviour,
    Madingley, Cambridge, England*
Edwin P. Hollander, *State University of New York at Buffalo, USA*
Carol Nagy Jacklin, *Stanford University, USA*
Yoram Jaffe, *Bar-Ilan University, Israel*
Irwin Katz, *Graduate Center of the City University of New York, USA*
Valerie Kent, *University of London Goldsmiths' College, England*
R. L. Krichevskii, *Scientific Research Institute of General and Pedagogic Psy-
    chology of the USSR Academy of Pedagogic Sciences, Moscow, USSR*
Lowell J. Krokoff, *University of Illinois, Urbana-Champaign, USA*
Ellen J. Langer, *Harvard University, USA*

M. Powell Lawton, *Philadelphia Geriatric Center, USA*
Eleanor E. Maccoby, *Stanford University, USA*
Valerie Melburg, *State University of New York at Albany, USA*
Lawrence A. Messé, *Michigan State University, USA*
John Metcalf, *Yale University, USA*
Stanley Milgram, *City University of New York, USA*
Charles G. Morris, *University of Michigan, USA*
Serge Moscovici, *École des Hautes Études en Sciences Sociales, Paris, France*
Lucille Nahemow, *West Virginia University, USA*
Charlan Nemeth, *University of California, Berkeley, USA*
Theodore M. Newcomb, *University of Michigan, USA*
Geneviève Paicheler, *École des Hautes Études en Sciences Sociales, Paris, France*
Richard E. Petty, *University of Missouri, USA*
Earl H. Potter, III, *US Coast Guard Academy, USA*
Judith Rodin, *Yale University, USA*
Zick Rubin, *Brandeis University, Waltham, Massachusetts, USA*
John Sabini, *University of Pennsylvania, USA*
Glenn S. Sanders, *State University of New York at Albany, USA*
Craig Eric Schneier, *University of Maryland, USA*
Marvin E. Shaw, *University of Florida, USA*
Susan K. Solomon, *Yale University, USA*
Robert Sommer, *University of California, Davis, USA*
R. Timothy Stein, *A. T. Kearney, Inc., Chicago, USA*
(The late) Henri Tajfel, *University of Bristol, England*
Dalmas A. Taylor, *University of Maryland, USA*
James T. Tedeschi, *State University of New York at Albany, USA*
Murray Webster, *University of South Carolina, USA*
John P. Wilson, *Cleveland State University, USA*
Suzanne Yates, *University of California at Santa Cruz, USA*
Yoel Yinon, *Bar-Ilan University, Israel*
Carolyn Zahn-Waxler, *National Institute of Mental Health, Bethesda, Maryland, USA*
Philip G. Zimbardo, *Stanford University, USA*

Contents

Preface xiii

Part I   The Situation and Things that People Bring with Them
Introduction   3

1. Physical Situation

    1.1 *Robert Sommer*. Spatial Behavior   9
    1.2 *Dalmas A. Taylor and Irwin Altman*. Environment and
        Interpersonal Relationships: Privacy, Crowding, and Intimacy   17
    1.3 *Judith Rodin, Susan K. Solomon, and John Metcalf*. Role of
        Control in Mediating Perceptions of Density   43

2. Personality, Social Characteristics, and Group
    Composition

    2.1 *Murray Webster and James E. Driskell*. Processes of Status
        Generalization 57
    2.2 *Charlan Nemeth*. Sex Differences and Decision Making in Juries   69
    2.3 *Joel Aronoff, Lawrence A. Messé, and John P. Wilson*.
        Personality Factors in Small Group Functioning   79
    2.4 *Marvin E. Shaw*. Group Composition   89

3. Impressions of the Group

    3.1 *Irwin Katz*. The Process of Stigmatization   99
    3.2 *Henri Tajfel*. Experiments in Intergroup Discrimination   . . 109

3.3 *Elliot Aronson and Suzanne Yates.* Cooperation in the Classroom: the Impact of the Jigsaw Method on Inter-ethnic Relations, Classroom Performance, and Self-esteem . . . 119

Part II Influence of Others
Introduction 133

4. Presence of Others

4.1 *Russell G. Geen and James J. Gange.* Social Facilitation: Drive Theory and Beyond 141

4.2 *Glenn S. Sanders.* Attentional Processes and Social Facilitation: How Much, How Often, and How Lasting? 155

4.3 *Richard E. Petty, John T. Cacioppo, and Stephen G. Harkins.* Group Size Effects on Cognitive Effort and Attitude Change . 165

5. Social influence

5.1 *Stanley Milgram and John Sabini.* On Maintaining Social Norms: a Field Experiment in the Subway 185

5.2 *Ellen J. Langer.* The Mindlessness/Mindfulness of Social Cognition 195

5.3 *Theodore M. Newcomb.* Coercion and Resentment in Juvenile Correctional Institutions 199

5.4 *Serge Moscovici and Geneviève Paicheler.* Minority or Majority Influences: Social Change, Compliance, and Conversion . . 215

6. Helping and Hurting

6.1 *Valerie Kent.* Prosocial Behaviour and Small Group Processes 227

6.2 *Carolyn Zahn-Waxler.* Maternal Child Rearing Practices in Relation to Children's Altruism and Conscience Development 243

6.3 *James T. Tedeschi and Valerie Melburg.* Aggression as the Illegitimate Use of Coercive Power 255

6.4 *Yoram Jaffe and Yoel Yinon.* Collective Aggression: The Group–Individual Paradigm in the Study of Collective Antisocial Behavior 267

7. Friendship and Attraction

7.1 *Lucille Nahemow and M. Powell Lawton.* Similarity and Propinquity: Making Friends with 'Different' People 279

7.2 *Zick Rubin.* The Skills of Friendship 293

7.3 *Carlfred B. Broderick.* Men and Women 303

Part III Nature of the Group: Structure and Function
Introduction 315

8. Social Interaction and Task

    8.1 *Michael Argyle*. Five Kinds of Small Social Group 321
    8.2 *J. Richard Hackman and Charles G. Morris*. Group Tasks, Group Interaction Process, and Group Performance Effectiveness 331
    8.3 *Lowell J. Krokoff and John M. Gottman*. The Structural Model of Marital Interaction 347

9. Roles and Relationships

    9.1 *Robert A. Hinde*. Dyadic Relationships 361
    9.2 *Aaron V. Cicourel*. Interpreting Normative Rules in the Negotiation of Status and Role 371
    9.3 *Carol Nagy Jacklin and Eleanor E. Maccoby*. Social Behavior at 33 Months in Same-Sex and Mixed-Sex Dyads 379
    9.4 *Philip G. Zimbardo*. Transforming Experimental Research into Advocacy for Social Change 383

10. Leadership

    10.1 *R. Timothy Stein and Tamar Heller*. The Relationship of Participation Rates to Leadership Status: A Meta-Analysis . 401
    10.2 *Fred E. Fiedler and Earl H. Potter, III*. Dynamics of Leadership Effectiveness 407
    10.3 *Craig Eric Schneier and Janet R. Goktepe*. Issues in Emergent Leadership: The Contingency Model of Leadership, Leader Sex, and Leader Behavior 413
    10.4 *Edwin P. Hollander*. Women and Leadership 423
    10.5 *R. L. Krichevskii*. The Phenomenon of the Differentiation of the Leadership Role in Small Groups 431

Name Index 437

Subject Index 451

Preface

Most of the papers in this book have been specially prepared. When we set out to edit a new revision of *Small Groups*, it quickly became clear that there has been so much major material since the mid-1960s that it would be best to let the 1965 revision—edited by Hare, Borgatta, and Bales—stand as a collection of main work up to that time and to compile a new work, with virtually no overlap of actual content. After preparing a 'draft anthology' as described below, we invited the represented authors to contribute new papers, consolidating their present perspectives. It is these new papers that constitute the bulk of the present volumes. In some cases, though, we have simply reprinted existing work from journals and books.

As was true even for the 1965 edition, probably most of the articles have to do with social interaction in general or with the individual in a social situation, rather than being limited to the small group. However, the results are all applicable to the analysis of behaviour in small groups.

For an overview and extensive bibliography, readers might like to refer to Hare's (1976) *Handbook of Small Group Research*. To identify current works in this field, one could also use the sources from our own search, described below. For example, one could look under 'small groups' (and, for longer lists, 'social psychology' and the other headings described by Blumberg, 1977) in the *Subject Guide to Books in Print* and (for longer lists) the other sources noted in (d), below, plus the Library of Congress cumulative subject catalogues. See also the *Annual Review of Psychology*, for example, the chapters on intergroup relations and group research in Volume 33 (1982).

The present work was planned, in its initial stages, by Paul Hare and Herbert Blumberg, who were then joined by Valerie Kent and Martin Davies. All major decisions have been made jointly. The primary responsibilities for selecting and editing were as follows: Volume 1—Part I, MD; Parts II and III, VK (Chapters 7 and 8, MD); Volume 2—Parts I and II HB; and Part III, VK and APH.

In proposing selections for the present work, we have used various criteria and carried out a number of searches. We have tried to give coverage to the entire field—including major developments and areas that have 'remained active'—since the early 1960s. (However, social behaviour among non-human primates is among topics not dealt with here—see, for example, Chalmers, 1979.) We have tried for a reasonable mix (both within and among papers) of theory, review, empirical studies, and applications. In preparing shortlists of authors, papers, and topics, we paid special attention to a number of sources, some of which were: (a) authors and specific items heavily cited in any two of the following three—Hare (1976), relevant topics in Middlebrook (1980) (a particularly recent and comprehensive text), and the 1978 *Social Sciences Citation Index* (for this set of names, the results would not have been substantially different if, for example, the 1980 SSCI or the 1971–75 SSCI 5-year cumulation had been used instead of 1978)—to look at particularly 'seminal' work; (b) 1977–79 *Psychological Abstracts* to 'update' the searches; (c) about 15 key journals, especially 1979, plus various convention programmes, also for 'updating'; (d) scan of all books on social psychology (and selected other topics) in various reference libraries and bookshops, and of listings in the *Subject Guide to Books in Print*, *Subject Guide to Forthcoming Books*, and *British National Bibliography*; (e) work cited in Blumberg (1976 and also 1977—works which were themselves compiled on the basis of various literature searches); and (f) a variety of personal recommendations and miscellaneous notices, etc. (Also, in retrospect, virtually all of the names heavily cited by Wrightsman and Deaux, 1981, came to notice in the course of the foregoing search.)

On the basis of these various searches we compiled a 'draft anthology' and where possible, as noted above, invited the represented authors to contribute new or specially revised selections for the current book. As some other editors once said of a work, 'We are happier about what is included than about what is left out.' It might have been easier to edit two works than one.

The overall organization of the volumes roughly follows the simple rationale of progressively 'bringing more things on stage,' starting in Volume 1 with the physical space (Chapter 1), then the backgrounds and personalities that people bring with them (Chapter 2), and members' impressions of the group and the fact of being part of it (Chapter 3). Part II deals with influence: the mere presence of other people (Chapter 4), effects of interacting with them (Chapter 5) and, especially, positive and negative interaction (Chapter 6) and the formation of close relationships (Chapter 7). Part III focuses on social interaction itself and broad differences among groups (Chapter 8); social interaction often shows specialization into roles (Chapter 9), and particular attention may be devoted to 'leadership' roles (Chapter 10). In Volume 2 complex processes are dealt with explicitly in Part I: group decision making (Chapter 1) plus a special focus on cooperation and conflict resolution (Chapter 2) and on interpersonal negotiations treated in a systematic quantified way (Chapter 3). By this point, complete, functioning groups are now 'on stage.' In Part II some general concerns of this work are explicitly highlighted: personal growth (Chapter 4), living together in harmony (Chapter 5) and social action and change (Chapter 6)—as these emerge from, or are manifest in, experience in small groups. Various theoretical approaches comprise Part III. We were not sure whether to place these at the beginning or end of the volumes (or perhaps between the lines of the other sections!), since a knowledge of theory would be helpful in understanding the other parts and vice versa. Since most of the selections in the volumes could in any event be read independently—and many refer to various theoretical orientations—readers may wish to cover Part III (of Volume 2) after they have read some but not all of the other parts.

References

Blumberg, H. H. (1976). 'Group processes', in *A Textbook of Human Psychology* (Eds. H. J. Eysenck and G. D. Wilson), Ch. 13, MTP, Lancaster, Lancashire.

Blumberg, H. H. (1977). 'Bibliographic guide', in *Liberation without Violence: A Third Party Approach* (Eds. A. P. Hare and H. H. Blumberg), pp. 288–341, Rex Collings, London.

Chalmers, N. (1979). *Social Behaviour in Primates*, Edward Arnold, London.

Hare, A. P. (1976). *Handbook of Small Group Research*, Second Edition, Free Press/Collier-Macmillan, New York and London.

Hare, A. P., Borgatta, E. F., and Bales, R. F. (eds.) (1965). *Small Groups: Studies in Social Interaction*, Revised Edition, Knopf, New York.

Middlebrook, P. N. (1980). *Social Psychology and Modern Life*, Second Edition, Knopf, New York.

Wrightsman, L., and Deaux, K. (1981). *Social Psychology in the 80s*, Third Edition, Brooks/Cole, Monterey, CA.

Part I

The Situation and Things that People Bring with Them

Introduction

The papers in Chapter 1 deal with aspects of the physical situation and environment which influence group and interpersonal functioning. Although the physical setting of a group may be regarded as a 'background' feature, research in environmental psychology attests to the pervasiveness of its impact on social interaction (see, for example, Altman, 1975; Proshansky, *et al.*, 1976; Stokols, 1978). Of particular interest in the study of groups are the ways in which the environment affects the spacing and distribution of group members, and how such spatial factors influence group processes.

Sommer's paper (sub-Chapter 1.1) describes some of the major determinants and consequences of human spatial behaviour, focusing on interpersonal distance, invasions of personal space, spatial arrangements, and propinquity. Much of this research has been carried out in a variety of settings and mileux apart from the psychology laboratory, and owes a debt to the author's original investigations of spatial behaviour in naturalistic surroundings (Sommer, 1969).

Taylor and Altman's paper (sub-Chapter 1.2) considers the important role the environment plays in social exchange and social penetration processes. Stemming from these authors' own work on human ecological and territorial behaviour, such processes are examined in terms of boundary-control and privacy-regulation mechanisms. This analysis is expanded to include crowding, viewed here as a lower-than-desired level of privacy. Finally, the authors discuss related ideas of intimacy equilibrium and intimacy arousal in accounting for recent research on crowding and interpersonal spacing.

In recent years, the assumption that high density invariably leads to negative experiences of crowding has been questioned by investigators such as Rodin, Solomon, and Metcalf (see also Taylor and Altman). These authors suggest in their paper (sub-Chapter 1.3) that the relation between crowding and density is dependent on perceived control; people feel crowded when density reduces feelings of personal control. The importance of the concept of perceived control is evidenced by its appearance in explanations of a wide range of psychological phenomena (see Perlmuter and Monty, 1979).

Further research on topics related to those described in Chapter 1 can be found in Altman and Haythorn (1967), Baum and Epstein (1978), Edney (1974), Hayduk (1978), Henley (1977), Knowles (1980); Paulus (1980); Russell and Ward (1982); Schmidt and Keating (1979); Stockdale (1978); White (1979).

The papers in Chapter 2 are more concerned with the 'personal environment' of the group—those characteristics of each individual group member, such as age, sex, ethnicity, personality, and ability.

Owing in part to the diversity of individual-difference variables, there exists a certain lack of unity among the findings in this area. The paper by Webster and Driskell (sub-Chapter 2.1) is welcome therefore in that it proposes a means and a model for integrating the effects of these variables according to their status characteristics.

The increased concern in Western societies about the equalities of men and women highlights the relevance of sex differences in group phenomena. Nemeth's paper (sub-Chapter 2.2), as well as research described by Webster and Driskell, shows that even where there are no discernible performance differences between males and females, females are still not accorded the same (high) status and expectations as males, although Nemeth notes some improvement in this state of affairs since the 1950s.

With respect to personality differences, as long ago as 1959, Mann (1959) catalogued over 500 different measures of personality employed in research on groups. Not all these personality variables contribute equally to group behaviour; indeed, some would argue that very few are important since variations in 'situational' characteristics are paramount. For some time now, personality and social theorists (see Endler and Magnusson, 1976) have realized that the personality-situation antinomy neglects the contribution of the interaction between the two in accounting for social behaviour. Aronoff, Messé, and Wilson's paper (sub-chapter 2.3) represents one of the few attempts to investigate this interaction between personality and situation in group functioning. These authors show how personality differences can affect group behaviour by influencing the structure of the group (i.e. the 'situation').

A different kind of interaction is described in Shaw's paper (sub-Chapter 2.4) on group composition. This is concerned with the *relation* between individual characteristics of group members—such as their compatibility—rather than with the individual characteristics *per se*.

Further research on personality and social variables related to Chapter 2 can be found in: Altman and Haythorn (1967); Berger *et al.* (1972); Booth (1972); Hall and Williams (1971); Haythorn (1968); Kagan and Madsen (1971); Meeker and Weitzel-O'Neill (1977); Reis *et al.* (1980); Ruhe and Eatman (1977).

Chapter 3 presents a different set of variables which individuals bring to the group—their perceptions of the group and group members. Most of the research on this issue has been concerned with intergroup relations, stereotyping, and prejudice. This research is obviously related to that described in Chapter 2 since social variables such as age, sex, and ethnicity are not only directly associated with differences in social interaction and performance in groups, but also indirectly through their influence on members' perceptions of and reactions to each other according to these social categories.

Katz's paper (sub-Chapter 3.1) has as its unifying theme the idea of stigmatization—the process whereby people who are different are denigrated. Katz's analysis, however, emphasizes the differences in psychological mechanisms that underlie the process of stigmatization.

Tajfel's paper (sub-Chapter 3.2) demonstrates that mere classification into groups can produce discrimination against the outgroup even where the basis of such a classification is trivial.

Finally, Aronson and Yates (sub-Chapter 3.3) offer some hope for the reduction of intergroup discrimination through the use of a classroom intervention strategy. The reader may wish to compare their 'Jigsaw' method with the strategies mentioned in Webster and Driskell's paper.

Further research on topics related to those of Chapter 3 can be found in Allen and Wilder (1975), Austin and Worchel (1979), Campbell (1967), Kanter (1977), Levine and Campbell (1972), and Tajfel (1978, 1982).

References

Allen, V. L., and Wilder, D. A. (1975). 'Categorization, belief similarity, and intergroup discrimination,' *Journal of Personality and Social Psychology*. **32**, 971–977.

Altman, I. (1975). *The Environment and Social Behavior*, Brooks-Cole, Monterey, California.

Altman, I., and Haythorn, W. F. (1967). 'The ecology of isolated groups', *Behavioral Science*, **12**, 169–182.

Austin, W. G., and Worchel, S. (eds.) (1979). *The Social Psychology of Intergroup Relations*, Brooks-Cole, Monterey, California.

Baum, A., and Epstein, Y. (eds.) (1978). *Human Response to Crowding*, Erlbaum, Hillsdale, NJ.

Berger, J., Cohen, R., and Zelditch, M. (1972). 'Status characteristics and social interaction', *American Sociological Review*, **37**, 241–255.

Booth, A. (1972). 'Sex and social participation,' *American Sociological Review*, **37**, 185–192.

Campbell, D. T. (1967). 'Stereotypes and the perception of group differences,' *American Psychologist*, **22**, 817–829.

Edney, J. J. (1974). 'Human territoriality,' *Psychological Bulletin*, **81**, 959–975.

Endler, N. S., and Magnusson, D. (1976). *Interactional Psychology and Personality*, Hemisphere Publishing Corp., Washington, DC.

Hall, J., and Williams, M. S. (1971). 'Personality and group encounter style,' *Journal of Personality and Social Psychology*, **18**, 163–172.

Hayduk, L. A. (1978). 'Personal space: An evaluative and orienting overview,' *Psychological Bulletin*, **85**, 117–134.

Haythorn, W. W. (1968). 'The composition of groups: A review of the literature,' *Acta Psychologica*, **28**, 97–128.

Henley, N. M. (1977). *Body Politics: Power, Sex, and Nonverbal Communication*, Prentice-Hall, Englewood Cliffs, NJ.

Kagan, S., and Madsen, M. C. (1971). 'Cooperation and competition of Mexican, Mexican-American, and Anglo-American children of two ages under four instructional sets,' *Developmental Psychology*, **5**, 32–39.

Kanter, R. M. (1977). 'Some effects of proportions on group life: Skewed sex ratios and responses to token women', *American Journal of Sociology*, **82**, 965–990.

Knowles, E. S. (1980). 'An affiliative conflict theory of personal and group spatial behavior,' in P. B. Paulus (ed.), *Psychology of Group Influence*, pp. 133–188, Erlbaum, Hillsdale, N.J.

Levine, R. A., and Campbell, D. T. (1972). *Ethnocentricity: Theories of Conflict, Ethnic Attitude, and Group Behavior*, Wiley, New York.

Mann, R. D. (1959). 'A review of the relationship between personality and performance in small groups,' *Psychological Bulletin*, **56**, 241–270.

Meeker, B. F., and Weitzel-O'Neill, D. A. (1977). 'Sex roles and interpersonal behavior in task-oriented groups,' *American Sociological Review*, **42**, 91–105.

Paulus, P. B. (1980). 'Crowding,' in P. B. Paulus (ed.), *Psychology of Group Influence*, pp. 245–290, Erlbaum, Hillsdale, NJ.

Perlmuter, L. C., and Monty, R. A. (eds.) (1979). *Choice and Perceived Control*, Erlbaum, Hillsdale, NJ.

Proshansky, H. M., Ittleson, W. H., and Rivlin, L. G. (eds.) (1976) *Environmental Psychology: People and Their Physical Settings*, 2nd edn, Holt, New York.

Reis, H. T., Nezlek, J., and Wheeler, L. (1980). 'Physical attractiveness in social interaction,' *Journal of Personality and Social Psychology*, **38**, 604–617.

Ruhe, J., and Eatman, J. (1977). 'Effects of racial composition on small work groups,' *Small Group Behavior*, **8**, 479–486.

Russell, J. A., and Ward, L. M. (1982). 'Environmental psychology,' *Annual Review of Psychology*, **33**, 651–688.

Schmidt, D. E., and Keating, J. P. (1979). 'Human crowding and personal control: An integration of the research,' *Psychological Bulletin*, **86**, 680–700.

Sommer, R. (1969). *Personal Space: The Behavioral Basis of Design*, Prentice-Hall, Englewood-Cliffs, NJ.

Stockdale, J. (1978). 'Crowding: Determinants and effects', in L. Berkowitz (ed.), *Advances in Experimental Social Psychology*, Vol. II, pp. 198–247, Academic Press, New York.

Stokols, D. (1978). 'Environmental psychology', *Annual Review of Psychology*, **29**, 253–295.

Tajfel, H. (ed.) (1978). *Differentiation Between Social Groups: Studies in the Social Psychology of Intergroup Relations*, Academic Press, London.

Tajfel, H. (1982). 'Social psychology of intergroup relations,' *Annual Review of Psychology*, **33**, 1–39.

White, W. P. (ed.) (1979). *Resources in Environment and Behavior*, American Psychological Association, Washington, DC.

Reference Note

The reader may wish to consult the following papers in other Parts of Volumes 1 and 2 which seem particularly relevant to the chapters in Part 1:–

Chapter 1. See Volume 1: Nahemow and Lawton (7.1).
    See Volume 2: Kanter (5.1).
Chapter 2. See Volume 1: Hackman and Morris (8.2), Cicourel (9.2), Stein and Heller (10.1), Schneier and Goktepe (10.3), Hollander (10.4).
    See Volume 2: Tindale and Davis (1.1), Penrod (1.3).
Chapter 3. See Volume 2: Deutsch (2.1), Schmitt and Marwell (2.2), McClintock and Keil (3.2), Harrison and McCallum (7.3).

1 Physical Situation

Small Groups and Social Interaction, Volume 1
Edited by H. H. Blumberg, A. P. Hare, V. Kent and M. Davies
© 1983 John Wiley & Sons Ltd

1.1 Spatial Behavior

Robert Sommer   *University of California, Davis*

The relationship between people and the physical environment is so broad a topic that a researcher has to choose an audience as well as specific problem areas. Over the years, I have had three different audiences in mind. The first consisted of social scientists for whom the necessity of including environmental variables in theories of personality and society was emphasized. Anthropologists were interested in this approach from the standpoint of space usage as an aspect of non-verbal communication. Because I want to change the world, I also write articles for architects, landscape designers, and city planners. The third audience has been groups such as hospital administrators, airport managers, teachers, and office managers who are directly responsible for space allocation and utilization. It is noteworthy that animal biologists and ethologists, whom I have never tried to reach directly, are the people to whom I am most indebted for my theoretical orientation and concepts.

Human relationships are frequently described in spatial terms. We talk about being close to people we love, looking up to those we respect and looking down on those we do not. Anthropologist Edward Hall (1959) describes space as a silent language of human communication. Hall has identified four interaction zones. *Intimate distance*, the closest zone, varies from 0 to 18 inches, and involves intense sensory cues from the other person. When selected voluntarily, it is usually reserved for people with whom we are having a close intimate relationship, but it can also result from involuntary crowding in a public location. When people are tightly packed together in an elevator or bus, they are likely to make their bodies rigid, avoid eye contact, and treat others as non-persons to avoid communicating with strangers at too close a distance. *Personal distance* which ranges from $1\frac{1}{2}$ to 4 feet is used with friends but not intimates. It allows for good conversation and visual encounter, but little touching. *Social distance*, extending from 4 to 12 feet, is involved in impersonal encounters in public locations. People seated in an airport or hospital waiting room will maintain this distance unless density makes it impossible for them to do so. *Public distance* ranges anywhere from 12 to 25 feet and is reserved for formal occasions such as public speeches. One would not want to talk to a friend or even an acquaintance at this distance.

When people interact, their spacing is regulated by many factors, including their relationship, amount of previous contact, their backgrounds, the activities in which they are engaged, and environmental factors including the size and layout of the room, noise, lighting levels, and other sources of background stimulation (Altman, 1975; Sommer, 1969). Because it is non-verbal and public, spatial behavior lends itself to a variety of research methods. Although there is some divergence among the results of individual studies using different methods, which is hardly unexpected in dealing with a creature as variable and complex as *Homo sapiens*, there are general findings that have held up with replication. All of them, however, must be qualified by the sorts of factors mentioned earlier, including arrangement of furniture, the task in which the people are engaged, background stimulation, etc.

General findings

Interaction distance is directly related to familiarity and liking. Those whom we know and like are encouraged to come closer (Evans and Howard, 1973; Heshka and Nelson, 1972; Little, 1965). Interaction distance varies with social distance. Those of a higher or lower status are kept further from us than our peers (Lott and Sommer, 1967). Women tend to use smaller conversational distances than men (Heshka and Nelson, 1972; Willis, 1966).

There are cultural differences in space usage, with people from Latin countries generally using smaller interaction distances than people from Anglo-Saxon nations (Hall, 1959). Children tend to use smaller interaction distances than adults (Meisels and Guardo, 1969). Interaction distance is inversely related to the level of background stimulation (Nesbitt and Steven, 1974). Eye contact plays an important and complex role in regulating the distance between two people in an encounter (Argyle and Dean, 1965).

Three other lines of research will be mentioned at this point. The first concerns the work on spatial invasions, or violations of customary spacing distance; the second concerns work on spatial arrangements in groups; and the third concerns the effects of propinquity on interpersonal attraction and communication. Personal space is the emotionally charged zone immediately surrounding a person's body. It has also been described as a 'body buffer zone' or 'space bubble.' It is portable, and not attached to a fixed geographic location, and has invisible boundaries. Typically the space bubble has larger distances in front than at the sides. People can tolerate the unwanted close presence of others at their sides more readily than they can directly in front of them. Because its boundaries are both invisible and social, a common way for researchers to investigate personal space has been to use an invasion technique. This has been done both in the laboratory and in natural settings. In the laboratory, the researcher slowly approaches the subject and says, 'Tell me when I am coming too close,' or conversely, the experimenter remains stationary and asks the subject to 'Approach me to a point when it starts to become uncomfortable.' Researchers have also deliberately invaded people's personal space in natural settings by coming too close and observing the outcome. Since the original article by Felipe and Sommer (1966) describing spatial invasions in a college library and a mental hospital, investigators have applied the technique in a variety of public settings, including street corners (Knowles, 1973), a gym locker room (Duncan, in press), a men's restroom (Middlemist et al., 1976) and a prison (Kinzel, 1970). These studies have shown that the unwanted close presence of a stranger in a public setting increases negative affect, physiological arousal, and produces blocking and escape behaviors. Kleck (1970) found that the close presence of another person increased self-manipulative behaviors indicative of arousal and anxiety such as hair pulling, scratching, and hand rubbing. Ratings of people become more negative with the intruder's increased physical proximity (Fisher and Byrne, 1975). Men drying themselves in a gym locker room following a shower departed more rapidly when another nude man entered and stood excessively close. The speed of departure was directly related to the physical closeness of the invader (Duncan, in press). The excessive closeness of another person at urinals in a men's room produced longer delays at onset and decreased duration of urination, both of which suggest increased stress (Middlemist et al., 1976).

The goal of this research was not to find new ways to make people uncomfortable, but just the reverse. The studies were intended to learn under natural conditions the kinds of spatial intrusions that people found uncomfortable so that these might be minimized or eliminated in the design and layout of public spaces. It is becoming increasingly more difficult for people to find space to be alone or maintain a close relationship. This makes it more critical to design buildings that will minimize the intrusive effects of the unwanted close presence of other people. Researchers interested in the effects of spatial invasions should consider using laboratory simulations or paper and pencil tests which yield results reasonably similar to those obtained with actual staged invasions (Kuethe, 1964).

A sensitive administrator, like the experienced host, knows that the placement of people at a conference will affect their participation and the group atmosphere. A poor arrangement can result in the dissolution of the larger group into factions, with some people feeling left out entirely. Seating arrangement has also been found to influence the likelihood of a leader emerging in a group. People are more likely to interact with others they can see directly. If three people were seated on one side of a rectangular table and two were seated on the other, those seated on the two-person side of the table would have a potential audience of three, and those seated on the three-person side would be limited to only two. It was predicted, therefore, that persons seated on the two-person side would be more likely to emerge as leaders, and this is what occurred (Howells and Becker, 1962).

Seating preference depends on: (1) the social background of those involved; (2) the environmental setting, including levels of background noise and movement; and (3) the activity that the group is performing. High levels of background noise and activity are likely to bring a group physically closer so that people can be heard. People are also likely to sit or stand closer to one another in a large room rather than in a small room. Conversational distance in your living room is probably longer than it is in a dormitory lounge, an airport, or any other public location where strangers might overhear, interrupt, or walk through the area. The size and shape of a table also make a difference in group interaction. In one study, 63% of the students polled preferred to sit in adjacent seats for conversing at a round table, but only 11% preferred this arrangement at a rectangular table (Sommer, 1969). Smaller round tables are excellent for interaction but once they become too large, people must sit virtually in a side-by-side arrangement which is poor for conversation.

What a group plans to do has a major impact on seating preferences. In one study people were asked to choose the seating arrangement they wanted for themselves and for another person from diagrams showing a number of different possibilities at a rectangular table. For casual conversation people chose either a corner-to-corner or face-to-face arrangement. For cooperative activity, they preferred side-by-side seating to make it easier to share materials, and for competition with another person, a face-to-face arrangement so that each person could keep track of how the other was doing. For separate activities that involve no interaction with the other person (co-acting), diagonal seating across the table was preferred (Sommer, 1969).

The head seat at a table is usually seen as the leadership position. At a round table the emergence of a leader is less likely and predictable (Leavitt, 1951). In an experimental study of simulated juries at rectangular tables, there was an overwhelming tendency for the jurors to pick a person sitting at the head position to be the foreperson. The jurors felt that the leader 'belonged' at the head position, and for anyone else to be elected would be a rejection of the person at the head position. Analysis of the jury deliberations showed that people at the head locations participated more than people at other locations and were rated by the other jurors as having had the greatest influence on the verdict. However, the initial selection of the seats had not been random. It was found that people who already possessed higher status—managers and professional people—gravitated towards the head seats as they entered the room (Strodtbeck and Hook, 1961). People tend to choose locations in accordance with their status or role and these places in turn reinforce that status or role. This is why people in organizations become so sensitive about the size of their offices, the depth of the carpet, and the width of the desk. Such items have symbolic meaning over and above their functional value, in suggesting status, not only to themselves but to others as well. People who are competing for a leadership role are likely to be competing also for the physical manifestations of that role, and this will emerge more clearly in competition for spatial locations.

In contrast to the work on personal space, which involves portable interaction zones, research on propinquity tends to involve larger fixed geographic spaces. The general conclusion from this line of research is that proximity has a strong effect on communication and interpersonal attraction. Whyte (1956) found that residents of suburban housing tracts had more contact with occupants of adjoining houses, particularly if there were a shared driveway, than with people across the street. The level of noise and traffic on the street was found to affect the amount and direction of contact among neighborhood residents (Appleyard and Lintell, 1972). In a housing project for married college students, Festinger (1951), found that the two major determinants for friendship were (1) the sheer distance between the houses and (2) the direction in which a house faced. Friendships developed more readily between next door neighbors, less frequently between people whose houses were separated by another house, and so on. As the distance between houses increased, the amount of friendship decreased so rapidly that it was rare to find a friendship between people who lived more than four houses away from one another. Small architectural features, including the location of mailboxes and of stairways, affected the social life of the project.

Among employees working in a large office, there was more contact within rows of workers than between rows, more interaction between workers in adjacent rows than in distant rows, and more interaction within a row between people with adjacent desks than between those separated by one or more desks (Gullahorn, 1952). College students living in residence halls interacted more with those in adjacent rooms than with those in distant rooms, and more with those living on the same floor than with those on other floors (Priest and Sawyer, 1967). While proximity has been found to be one of the strongest variables in interpersonal attraction, communication, and friendship, it is itself an outcome of other important processes. People's location in space is not a random event. In most situations, they choose to be close to those who are like them and with whom they want to communicate, and remain distant from those who are unlike them and with whom they do not want to communicate.

Frequent criticisms have been voiced about the atheoretical nature of much of the research upon spatial behavior (Altman, 1975). This resulted from the applied bent of much of the early studies which had been motivated by a desire to obtain knowledge that would help improve the design of public spaces. Such researchers attempted to link their findings to work in architecture, interior design, and city planning. Those researchers of a naturalistic bent investigated spatial behavior as a phenomenon in its own right, much as a zoologist would study territoriality among deer or bison with the goal of finding regularities and correlations, rather than confirming or disputing a general theory. Those who studied spatial behavior in the laboratory using various simulation procedures were more interested in fitting their findings into a general theoretical framework such as Argyle and Dean's intimacy–equilibrium theory, Hall's theory of proxemic behavior, or Patterson's (1973) arousal–attribution model. The task of integrating research from naturalistic and experimental studies has not yet been accomplished.

Another application of research on spatial behavior has been in the area of non-verbal communication. People can be taught to 'read' environments according to the arrangement of people in the setting. Whyte (1941) recorded the spatial groupings of gang members on prepared floor plans. He recorded who sat with whom and in what parts of the room. Through an analysis of such maps, he was able to place most of the members into various subgroups. The same approach can be used in a variety of public settings. Walking by a classroom, it is easy to see that something is wrong when an instructor sits at a desk in the front and the first four rows are vacant with students sitting dejectedly in the rear of the room. One can also tell many things about the relationship between two people by the way they sit or stand together (Heshka and Nelson, 1972). Used in this way, spatial behavior becomes one of several important nonverbal indicators of human relationships.

References

Altman, I. (1975). *The Environment and Social Behavior*, Brooks/Cole, Monterey, CA.

Appleyard, D., and Lintell, M. (1972). 'The environmental quality of city streets,' *Journal of the American Institute of Planners*, **38**, 84–101.

Argyle, M., and Dean, J. (1965). 'Eye contact, distance, and affiliation', *Sociometry*, **28**, 289–304.

Duncan, Birt L. (In press). 'Personal space invasions in the locker room', *Environment and Behavior*.

Evans, G. W., and Howard, R. B. (1973). 'Personal space,' *Psychological Bulletin*, **80**, 334–344.

Felipe, N. J., and Sommer, R. (1966). 'Invasions of personal space,' *Social Problems*, **14**, 206–214.

Festinger, Leon (1951). 'Architecture and group membership,' *Journal of Social Issues*, **7** (1&2), 152–163.

Fisher, J. D., and Byrne, D. (1975). 'Too close for comfort', *Journal of Personality and Social Psychology*, **32**, 15–21.

Gullahorn, J. (1952). 'Distance and friendship as factors in the gross interaction matrix,' *Sociometry*, **15**, 123–134.

Hall, E. T. (1959). *The Silent Language*, Doubleday, Garden City, NY.

Heshka, S., and Nelson, Y. (1972). 'Interpersonal speaking distance as a function of age, sex, and relationship,' *Sociometry*, **35**, 481–498.

Howells, L. T., and Becker, S. W. (1962). 'Seating arrangement and leadership emergence,' *Journal of Abnormal and Social Psychology*, **64**, 148–150.

Kinzel, A. F. (1970). 'Body buffer zone in violent prisoners,' *American Journal of Psychiatry*, **127**, 59–64.

Kleck, R. E. (1970). 'Interaction distance and non-verbal agreeing responses,' *British Journal of Social and Clinical Psychology*, **9**, 180–182.

Knowles, E. S. (1973). 'Boundaries around group interaction,' *Journal of Personality and Social Psychology*, **26**, 327–332.

Kuethe, J. L. (1964). 'Pervasive influence of social schemata,' *Journal of Abnormal Social Psychology*, **68**, 248–254.

Leavitt, H. J. (1951). 'Some effects of certain communication patterns on group performance,' *Journal of Abnormal and Social Psychology*, **46**, 38–50.

Little, K. B. (1965). 'Personal space,' *Journal of Experimental Social Psychology*, **1**, 237–247.

Lott, D., and Sommer, R. (1967). 'Seating arrangement and status,' *Journal of Personality and Social Psychology*, **7**, 90–95.

Meisels, M., and Guardo, C. J. (1969). 'Development of personal space schematas,' *Child Development*, **40**, 1167–1178.

Middlemist, R. D., Knowles, E. F. and Matter, C. F. (1976). 'Personal space invasions in the lavatory,' *Journal of Personality and Social Psychology*, **33**, 541–546.

Nesbitt, P. D., and Steven, G. (1974). 'Personal space and stimulus intensity at a southern California amusement park,' *Sociometry*, **37**, 105–115.

Patterson, M. (1973). 'Compensation in Nonverbal Immediacy Behaviors: A Review', *Sociometry*, **36**, 237–252.

Priest, R. F., and Sawyer, J. (1967). 'Proximity and peership,' *American Journal of Sociology*, **72**, 633–649.

Sommer, R. (1969). *Personal Space: The Behavioral Basis of Design*, Prentice-Hall, Englewood Cliffs, NJ.

Strodtbeck, F. L., and Hook, L. H. (1961). 'The social dimensions of a twelve-man jury table,' *Sociometry*, **24**, 397–415.

Whyte, William F. (1941). 'Corner boys: A study of cliques behavior,' *American Journal of Sociology*, **46**, 647–664.

Whyte, William H. (1956). *The Organization Man*, Simon & Schuster, New York.

Willis, F. N. (1966). 'Initial speaking distance as a function of the speaker's relationship,' *Psychonomic Science*, **5**, 221–222.

Small Groups and Social Interaction, Volume 1
Edited by H. H. Blumberg, A. P. Hare, V. Kent and M. Davies
© 1983 John Wiley & Sons Ltd

1.2 Environment and Interpersonal Relationships: Privacy, Crowding, and Intimacy

Dalmas A. Taylor *University of Maryland*

and

Irwin Altman *University of Utah*

Introduction

Some years ago (1973) we introduced the term 'social penetration' to account for (1) overt interpersonal behaviors which take place in social interaction, and (2) internal subjective processes which precede, accompany, and follow these overt exchanges. The term includes verbal, nonverbal, and environmentally oriented behaviors as they function as part of a coherent ecological system.

Environmentally oriented behaviors include spatial and personal distance between people, gestures, limb and head movements, facial expressions such as smiling, eye gaze, and so on. An important aspect of the social penetration process involves the reciprocity of exchange between individuals. Does disclosure intimacy or spatial proximity increase the probability that others will reciprocate with more openness, increased eye contact, more touching—or retreat? Early studies of reciprocity within a social penetration framework exhibited support for the notion of reciprocity. Later attempts to identify the conditions under which reciprocity operates identified new mechanisms that explained inconsistencies in the literature. The most general conclusion we were able to reach at that time was that reciprocity of exchange was not the sole determinant of mutual disclosure, and we needed a better understanding of underlying conditions residing in the individual actors, the topic of exchange, and the situational context.

In 1973 we attempted to weave together divergent research findings regarding interpersonal behaviors in the areas of verbal and cognitive–motivational functioning, social–emotional functioning, person perception, and nonverbal communication through the use of space and the physical environment. Our goal was to establish a common framework within which we could describe different levels of social interaction. Advances in theory and research since that time compel a re-examination of our model. In this chapter we will integrate two lines of theorizing and research concerned with the development and management of interpersonal relationships from casual acquaintanceship to intimacy, and crowding and privacy as boundary regulation processes.

The environment and interpersonal relationships

The physical environment can be viewed from two perspectives—as a determinant of behavior and as an aspect of behavior (Altman, 1971, 1975). Not only does interpersonal exchange occur within an environment milieu which affects its course and character, but social interaction involves active use of the environment. In effect, there is a mutual relationship between person and environment. With the exception of studies by Roger Barker and his colleagues (Barker, 1963, 1968; Barker and Gump, 1964; Barker and Wright, 1955) there was, until recently, little research on environment and interpersonal behavior. The picture is now very different. There is a sizeable body of literature on various aspects of environment and interpersonal behavior (Altman, 1970, 1973b, 1975, 1976, 1977; Freedman, 1975; Newman, 1972; Stokols, 1972; Stokols et al., 1973; Worchel and Teddlie, 1976).

Past research emphasized the environment as an independent variable or as a determinant or cause of behavior. Much of this research was restricted to an examination of the effects of lighting, color, temperature, and other physical factors on cognitive and motor behaviors. The environment and interpersonal relationships have been studied in the context of proximity and interaction (Caplow and Forman, 1950; Deutsch and Collins, 1951; Festinger et al., 1950), microspace design and friendship (Blake, et al., 1956), classroom seating arrangements and participation (Sommer, 1967, 1969) and social isolation (Altman et al., 1971). Environmental design arrangements, especially proximity, seem to be consistently associated with friendship formation, dynamics of attraction and rejection, and mutual openness.

The environment can also be viewed from a behavioral perspective. People actively use the environment in interpersonal relationships analogous to the use of words, gestures, body movement, and facial expressions. The environment, then, can be viewed as an extension of the self. More simply, the environment can be described as consisting of space, objects (distance), and areas (complexes of objects in space). There have been few theories about why these variables have the effects they do. Later in the chapter we will see how theoretical summaries facilitate our understanding of the relationship between environment and a number of social and psychological behaviors.

Territoriality, privacy, and crowding

Early studies on social penetration processes indicated that individuals actively use environmental objects and areas in regulating their interactions. Altman and

Haythorn (1967) studied self-disclosure and the use of space objects in pairs of men socially isolated for 10 days. Experimentally created compatible and incompatible dyads lived and worked in sound-attenuated small rooms with no contact with the outside world. Isolates in general, and those incompatible on need dominance and need achievement experienced more subjective stress, emotional symptomatology, and interpersonal conflict than non-isolates and compatible dyads. These same groups also performed with reduced effectiveness on team tasks. Isolated pairs also disclosed more to each other than did control pairs, especially in intimate topical areas. In some respects their level of disclosure was comparable to that achieved between close friends.

Territoriality

An index of territorial behavior was obtained by systematically sampling which of two chairs men sat in, which bed they used, and which side of the table they preferred. In humans, territoriality refers to occupancy and control of areas and objects in the physical environment, and sometimes includes defense in response to intrusion. Data were also collected on how often men did things *together* (talking, playing cards), *alone* (reading, writing), or were in bed *asleep*.

Different forms of incompatibility were associated with different modes of environment use. Men incompatible on need dominance (where both men were high on desire to control and dominate others) became very territorial over time in their use of the environment and were also highly interactive. These were volatile groups who had great difficulty in the situation (two of the three groups who could not complete the isolation period came from these conditions) and men were literally 'at each other's throats.' Eventually, they divided the room and claimed territories, as reflected in the exclusive use of chairs, beds, and sides of the table. Thus they tended not to use the environmental sector of the other, although they interacted with one another in a very active, and often competitive way. Compatible dyads, on the other hand, exhibited high territoriality immediately. Gradually, territorial behaviors decreased over time as the men began to share each other's space and objects. It is clear from these data that the premature relaxing of interpersonal boundaries corresponded with an inability to establish an effective social unit, whereas effective social bonding occurred in dyads who observed interpersonal boundaries initially but were able to relax them over time. Parallel findings were obtained for verbal exchanges. Men, who had positive relationships gradually eliminated interpersonal barriers and increased their disclosure intimacy over time.

In a second isolation study, three aspects of the environment were varied in a $2 \times 2 \times 2$ factorial design: availability of privacy, expected length of social isolation, and degree of stimulation from the outside (Altman *et al.*, 1971). In a 'no privacy' condition pairs of men lived and worked in the same room for 8 days; 'privacy' groups had a two-compartment chamber with each man living in connected, but separate rooms. Two levels of outside stimulation were created via communications, from a control center, that were either verbal or electronic signals. The third variable involved was effected by informing half the groups that their length of stay would be 4 days; the other groups were instructed that their length of stay would be 20 days. The actual length of stay for all groups was 8 days.

In several facets of behavior, members of unsuccessful or abort groups (those who left the situation prior to termination of the study) were ineffective in building a viable group experience. This was evident in their social interaction and in their use of the physical environment during the first day or two of isolation. For example, during the early days of the isolation experience members of unsuccessful (abort) groups spent less time together, talking or doing things as a pair, than the groups that ultimately completed the experience. Seemingly, it is interpersonally adaptive to begin developing a *modus vivendi* with another person, even a stranger, if one is to be confined with that individual for an extensive period of time. One might also attempt to learn about the other person, to determine his/her living and work habits, and to begin working out a pattern of life that would be interpersonally viable. The aborters did not do this. The data indicate that completers did indeed work out a *modus vivendi*, which perhaps explains their ability to establish an effective social unit. The inattention to early group formation by aborters is also reflected in their use of the environment in terms of territorial behavior.

On all three measures of territorial behavior—beds, chairs, and sides of a table—members of abort groups were lower than completers early in the isolation experience. Thus, they not only failed to interact socially, they did not establish interpersonal identities in terms of use of the environment. These findings correspond to those from the Altman and Haythorn (1967) study discussed above in which incompatible groups compared to compatible groups exhibited very low territorial behavior early in the isolation experience. With the passage of time in isolation, this pattern reversed itself. Completers dropped in territorial behavior and aborters showed an increase. Boundaries between members of successful groups were slowly eliminated and those between ineffective groups increased. This was especially true for the dependent measures chair and side of table (see Figure 1). These data provide additional support for the idea that use of the physical environment reflects and is part of the process of management of an interpersonal relationship.

The data from these two studies of men functioning in socially isolated environments indirectly suggest that facets of the physical environment are actively used in the social penetration process in essentially the same way as verbal behavior. Developing interpersonal relationships, especially compatible ones, involves the gradual elimination of physical interpersonal boundaries as the actors literally begin to use one another's 'places' and 'things.'

Altman and Taylor (1973) emphasize the way in which the development of a social bond involves environmentally oriented responses such as *interpersonal*

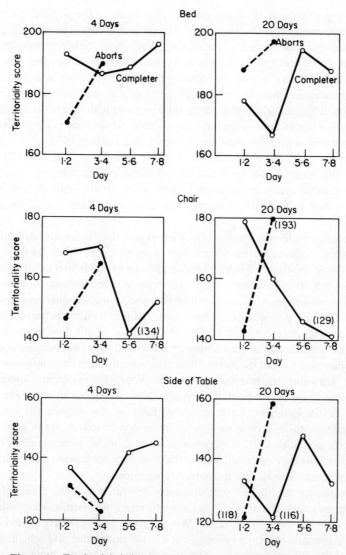

Figure 1 Territorial behavior of abort and completer groups. (From Altman *et al.*, 1971. Reprinted from *Journal of Applied Social Psychology* with permission from Scripta Publishing Co.)

distance, anticipatory selection, structuring of the physical environment, and *reactive ongoing use of the environment.* (Interpersonal distance is discussed in Sommer, sub-Chapter 1.1.) Anticipatory selection and structuring of the environment involve arrangements of environments (e.g. layout of furniture, adjustment of lighting, choice of meeting room, arrangement of seats in a classroom).

Reactive ongoing use of the environment refers to use of the physical environment (e.g. establishment of territories, use of objects and areas). The preceding studies emphasized dynamic, ongoing use of the environment. Other investigators have confirmed these findings in their observations of married couples who exhibit more territorial behavior than co-habiting couples (Rosenblatt and Budd, 1975); of basketball teams who win a greater proportion of home games than road games (Worchel and Sigall, 1976); of students who perform better on tasks and felt more comfortable when in familiar surroundings (Edney, 1976); and of individuals who argue more persuasively on their own territory (Martindale, 1971).

The following studies by Taylor *et al.* (1969), Taylor and Altman (1975), and Page (1968) demonstrate how the environment is selected and structured in advance of social exchange. In many respects these studies indicate how forecasts of future rewards and costs become translated into active use of the physical environment.

The procedures for the Taylor *et al.* (1969) and the Taylor and Altman (1975) studies were essentially the same. Sailors participated in a lengthy session, ostensibly with another sailor who was actually an experimenter confederate. Subjects were led to believe that they had been selected for an important navy program in which pairs of men would live and work together in an undersea capsule for a long period. Each subject was told that he and his partner had been assigned to work together (they had no choice about whom their teammate would be), that the partner was in another room, and that they would become acquainted over an intercom system. Subjects interacted verbally with the confederate, freely choosing personal statements concerning biography, religion, interests and hobbies, and so on from a pool of items prescaled for topical intimacy (Taylor and Altman, 1966). Following each self-description by the subject, the confederate told about himself in such a way as to create one of four types of interpersonal reward/cost conditions: (1) continuous positive; (2) later positive; (3) continuous negative; and (4) later negative. This verbal exchange took place over four interaction periods, each lasting approximately 45 minutes.

Following the exchange, subjects evaluated architectural plans of a two-compartment undersea capsule. They were to select the capsule design which they felt would be best for their team. We expected that subjects would select a physical environment which reflected their prior experience and which would set the stage for future exchange. They were presented with three plans: (1) a 'separate territorial' arrangement in which each man's bed and equipment were in a separate compartment connected by a door; (2) a 'joint territorial' arrangement in which men lived together in one room and worked in the other room, with the layout of furniture and equipment clearly indicating which side of the room belonged to each man; (3) a 'joint random' plan where the men lived in one room but where the furniture, equipment, and facilities of both were intermingled, with neither man having an area of the room clearly demarcated as his own.

The data from the two studies were pooled since there were no differences in responses between them. Hardly any subjects chose the joint random arrangement, not surprising since most people probably prefer living areas identified as their own. As can be seen in Table 1, those who had positive relationships with the confederate more often chose to live in the joint territorial arrangement (together, 73%; apart, 27%) as compared with those in the incompatible situation (together, 36%; apart, 64%). However, the live-together preference held primarily for those who experienced a continuous positive relationship, suggesting that any degree of negative experience led to a desire to live apart. Furthermore, there were no differences between later and continuous negative conditions. This is especially interesting in view of the fact that subjects in the later positive condition and the continuous positive condition reported 'liking' the confederate to the same degree. Yet, men in the later positive condition seemed unwilling to extend this expressed degree of liking into a sharing of the environment. Thus, subjects seemed to have integrated their reward/cost experiences into a general affective judgment about the other man and then projected this upon the environment in an anticipation of a continued relationship. Continuously 'good' experiences yielded a profile of verbal openness, positive feelings, and a willingness to continue the relationship in an intimate environment. Predominantly favorable (but initially negative) experiences led to verbal accessibility and a positive feeling, but there was also some reluctance to embed the relationship in a close environment.

In order to manipulate expectations about the length of time subjects would be

Table 1 Architectural design preference as a function of interpersonal reward/cost experiences. Reproduced by permission of Irwin Altman and Dalmas A. Taylor (1981)

| | | Living arrangement preference | | |
		Together	Apart	Total
Positive				
(a)	Continuous	22 (88%)	3	25
(b)	Later	13 (56%)	10	23
(a + b)		35 (73%)	13	48
Negative				
(c)	Continuous	9 (36%)	16	25
(d)	Later	8 (36%)	14	22
(c + d)		17 (36%)	30	47

$(a - b)$	$\chi^2 = 6.01, p < .02$
$(a - c)$	$\chi^2 = 14.35, p < .001$
$(b - d)$	$\chi^2 = 1.84, ns$
$(c - d)$	$\chi^2 = <1\ ns$
$(a + b) - (c + d)$	$\chi^2 = 11.50, p < .001$

committed to the relationship, half the subjects were told they would be confined for a period of 6 months, the other half were told their missions would be for 3 weeks. The results reported above held primarily for the short-term condition, with no difference in design preferences where men perceived a long-term tie to their partner. It may be that it was easier to make a commitment to or reject another individual in a short-term situation, whereas long-term situations created ambivalences. One might like another individual and want to be close but simultaneously recognize the need for privacy during a 6-month period. Contrariwise, dislike for another accompanied by the desire to be physically separated may give way to the realization that the other individual is the only source of human stimulation.

Page (1968) reported similar feelings among a college student population. Students were asked to select dormitory designs for two- and three-person rooms after they had participated in discussion groups under various reward/cost conditions. Architectural plans differentiated between *alone* and *together* arrangements, and between *living* and *study* functions. Thus, there were four combinations of room layouts: (1) study together–live together; (2) study apart–live together; (3) study together–live apart, and (4) study apart–live apart. Most subjects desired joint living arrangements in two-person groups and separate living arrangements in three-person groups. However, there were differential preferences for study arrangements as a function of reward/cost compatibility. Those in positive reward/cost conditions in contrast to subjects in negative conditions preferred plans involving joint study arrangements. Subjects in all of the varying negative conditions expressed a preference for separate study plans. Also, as before, any amount of negative experience resulted in preferences for separate environments.

Thus far, we have considered how the physical environment—space, objects, and areas—is actively used in the social penetration process. Essentially we demonstrated how territorial behaviors are used to regulate social interaction. Territoriality is not a simple concept in that it can serve as an expression of: (1) motives or need states, such as mating or eating; (2) geographical features, such as size or location; (3) social units, such as individuals, groups, or large social systems; (4) temporal duration, with some territories temporary (such as a seat on a bus) and others relatively permanent (such as a home); and (5) response repertoires, or behaviors used to mark territories, and defensive reactions in response to intrusion (Altman, 1975). We have focused on territories as preventive markers used in a variety of relationships in a way to express ownership and to signal to others the boundary conditions of the relationship. Markers have involved both symbolic and actual physical barriers.

Three types of methodological strategies have been used in studies of territorial behavior. *Observational* studies have examined intact social groups in naturalistic environments. These studies have used little or no experimental manipulation but report findings compatible with the social penetration analysis using psychiatric patients in a hospital ward (Esser *et al.*, 1965); boys in a rehabilitation center

(Sundstrom and Altman, 1974); students in a college seminar (DeLong, 1970, 1971, 1973); and individuals in private homes and public beaches (Edney, 1972; Edney and Jordan-Edney, 1974).

A second methodological approach in studies of territoriality is analogous to personal-space simulation studies. Authors have used questionnaires, interviews, and other *self-report techniques* to study table seating arrangements (Sommer and Becker, 1969) to assess effectiveness of various markers in libraries (Becker, 1973; Worchel, 1978) and to study people as markers of occupancy (Barefoot *et al.*, 1972). These studies consistently found that personal markers such as coats, books, and other personal items left on a table were effective in preventing others from using 'another's' space.

The studies reported above on social isolation and social penetration processes used experimental strategies in examining territorial behaviors (Altman and Haythorn, 1967; Altman *et al.*, 1971). Other studies have systematically manipulated indices of territoriality in libraries and other settings (Becker, 1973; Becker and Mayo, 1971; Hoppe *et al.*, 1972; Sommer and Becker, 1969). Territorial markers have been effective in preventing invasions by would-be intruders. Unlike animals, however, when a territory is invaded humans seldom use confrontation. Instead, they often retreat and find a new territory.

All of the research discussed above points to the way in which territorial behaviors help to stabilize social systems by defining possession of space and objects, and through the use of markers that regulate the degree or extent of social intercourse. An additional function of territoriality is the achievement of privacy.

Privacy

By and large the concept of privacy has been neglected by behavioral and social scientists. Empirical research on the concept is virtually nonexistent. Yet the concept is important to an understanding of interpersonal boundary control. Elsewhere we have likened privacy regulation to the shifting permeability of a cell membrane (Altman, 1975). Persons and groups regulate access to themselves by being receptive to outside inputs on some occasions, and closing off contact with the outside environment of others. Accordingly, Altman (1975) defined privacy as:

> ... an *interpersonal boundary process* by which a person or group regulates interaction with others. By altering the degree of openness of the self to others, a hypothetical personal boundary is more or less receptive to social interaction with others. Privacy is, therefore, a dynamic process involving selective control over a self-boundary, either by an individual or by a group (p. 6).

Privacy represents another mechanism whereby individuals control the amount of interaction they choose to have with others. As regards social penetration, self-disclosure and a number of nonverbal behaviors (e.g. eye contact, smiling, body orientation) can be used to regulate the input and output of information to and from the self. The ability to control or exercise choice over the amount of disclosure about oneself to others determines the extent to which an individual can achieve privacy. If others can influence or control what we divulge about ourselves, or what inputs we let in from the outside, our degree of privacy has been compromised. Derlega and Chaikin (1977) have described this process in their analysis of privacy and self-disclosure in social relationships. They view self-disclosure as an example of the regulation of two boundaries. A 'dyadic boundary' is seen as protecting the disclosure from leaking beyond the target person to others. This boundary establishes the unit relationship within which self-disclosure may occur without fear of passing to uninvited third parties. The 'self-boundary' represents the act of disclosure (the boundary is open) or nondisclosure (we erect a barrier between ourselves and the other person). Regulation of the self-boundary contributes to our feelings or perceptions about our environments, and the kinds of relationships we wish to maintain.

Two important aspects of privacy are implicated in boundary regulation—*desired privacy* and *achieved privacy* (Altman, 1975). Desired privacy is a subjective statement of an ideal level of interaction with other individuals. Achieved privacy, on the other hand, is the actual degree of contact that results from interaction with others. If the desired privacy is equal to the achieved privacy, an optimum state of privacy exists. If achieved privacy is lower or higher than desired privacy, a state of imbalance exists (see Figure 2). As can be seen in Figure 2 the balance between privacy and contact with others is an ideal, an internal subjective state, which regulates the desire for certain levels of input and output to and from others. The resultant levels of interaction can be high or low and can shift over time, as situations and interpersonal relationships change. Past experience, personal style, and situational determinants contribute to the range of mechanisms employed by individuals and groups in attempts to achieve the desired level of privacy.

As pointed out earlier, there has been little research directed at an understanding of privacy behaviors. Spinner (1978) tested Derlega and Chaikin's (1977) hypothesis that self-disclosure, as a form of privacy maintenance, is more intimate when the unit boundary is secure and there is little chance of the disclosed information being passed on to others. The results indicated that security of the unit boundary is a necessary, but not sufficient condition for intimate self-disclosure between strangers. Spinner (1978) manipulated (1) whether or not the discloser expected to remain anonymous, (2) the number of targets (three or one) to whom the subject expected to disclose, and (3) the likelihood that the target(s) would have access to the discloser's friends and acquaintances. Subjects were less willing to make intimate disclosures where the unit boundary was least secure (nonanonymous three target conditions) than in the more secure unit boundary

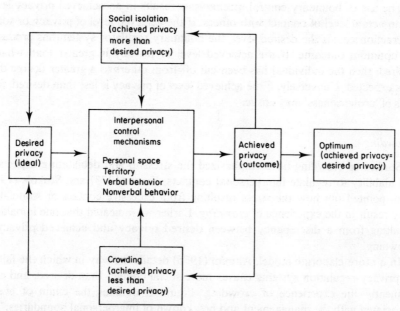

Figure 2 Overview of relationships among privacy, personal space, territory, and crowding. (From *The Environment and Social Behavior* by I. Altman. Copyright © 1975 by Wadsworth Publishing Company, Inc. Reprinted with permission of Brooks/Cole Publishing Co., Monterey, California.)

conditions (nonanonymous one target and anonymous three targets). However, unexpectedly, in one of the conditions where the unit boundary was most secure (anonymous one target condition), subjects were relatively unwilling to disclose. A similar pattern of results was obtained when boundary control was manipulated by telling subjects that the target person would be a classmate (open) or a student from another university (closed). Other authors (Jones and Archer, 1976; Rubin, 1975) have also reported that subjects were more likely to disclose when they believed that intimate communications were addressed to them, or prepared exclusively for them, than when they believed the information would be shared more widely. Jones and Archer's subjects, however, not only disclosed when they were the exclusive recipients of disclosure intimacy, but also when they knew the information had been revealed to two other individuals but not to them. While these findings are not without problems, they do confirm the notion that knowledge of the potential impact of disclosure intimacy on the security of the unit or dyadic boundary is an important consideration of an individual's willingness to modify his or her self-boundary. Findings reported by Taylor *et al.* (1979) provide further support for viewing self-disclosure as a mechanism useful in regulating interpersonal boundary properties.

The use of boundary control mechanisms results in an achieved privacy level, or an actual level of contact with others. If the achieved level of privacy or social interaction equals the desired level, the boundary regulator system has produced an optimum outcome. If the achieved level of privacy is greater than what is desired, then the individual has been cut off from others to a greater degree than was expected. Conversely, if the achieved level of privacy is less than desired, feelings of 'crowdedness' may ensue.

Crowding

Studies of crowding have emphasized the stressful and debilitating aspects of the inability to regulate interpersonal contacts. Esser (1973) and Stokols (1978) each pointed out how the stress resulting from excessive contact or stimulation may result in the experience of *crowding*. Earlier we indicated that one imbalance resulting from a discrepancy between desired privacy and achieved privacy is crowding.

In a more elaborate model, Altman (1975) details the way in which the failure of privacy-regulation systems causes more social contact than desired, and consequently the experience of crowding. Figure 3 outlines the chain of events associated with the management and breakdown of interpersonal boundaries. The successful regulation of interpersonal boundaries through verbal and nonverbal mechanisms results in the desired degrees of privacy or social contact. When we experience less social contact than desired, social isolation exists. On the other hand, more social interaction than desired leads to the experience of crowding. Thus crowding occurs when there is disequilibrium or interpersonal-boundary regulation failure.

As can be seen in Figure 3, the sequence of events begins with the expression of some desired level of privacy (situation definition) that includes expectations about what is good, acceptable, or appropriate. Personal characteristics (personality, past history, etc.) and situational factors (decor, layout of environment, furnishings, etc.) collectively contribute to the definition of the desired level of privacy. The various boundary control mechanisms, which are also a key to the social penetration process, such as level of disclosure, territorial behaviors, and other facial and body gestures, are set in motion to achieve the desired goal. The next step in the model involves an assessment of the effectiveness of the various mechanisms employed to achieve the desired outcome. Was the desired outcome actually achieved? Was the level of achieved privacy equal to, less than, or greater than the level of desired privacy? If the level of achieved privacy equals the level of desired privacy, the boundary control mechanisms worked, and everything is fine. If the reverse occurred and more interaction than desired obtained, then crowding would be experienced.

As indicated in Figure 3, the discrepancy between desired and achieved levels of privacy produces a state of stress. Consistent with theorizing by Stokols (1978)

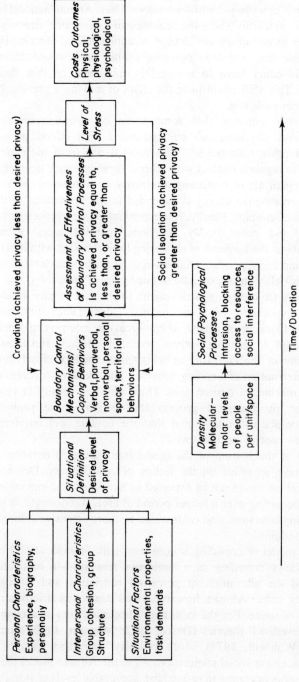

Figure 3 A model of crowding. (From *The Environment and Social Behavior* by I. Altman. Copyright © 1975 by Wadsworth Publishing Company, Inc. Reprinted with permission of Brooks/Cole Publishing Co., Monterey, California.)

and Esser (1973) the stress state motivates the person or group to attempt an adjustment in their boundary control behaviors. Thus, Altman's model (see Figure 3) is a feedback system in which the sequence of assessment–stress–adjustment cycles repeatedly as circumstances change, or until a desired outcome is obtained. It is also possible that a desired outcome cannot be achieved, in which case individuals could either learn to accept this imbalance, or shift their level of desired privacy. This shift could have the effect of making a previously undesirable outcome a desirable one.

The model also indicates that some levels of costs/outcomes (physical, psychological, and physiological) are associated with efforts at establishing satisfactory self–other boundaries. These costs derive from the expenditure of efforts required to regulate contact with others. Personal space maintenance often involves the *physical* act of protecting a territory, or movement toward or away from others. *Psychological* energy is expended in the assessment of the level of appropriateness of contact. Finally, internal *physiological* processes (endocrine, cardiovascular, and other bodily functions) parallel social exchanges as individuals go about the business of regulating their relations with others. Altman *et al.* (1971) found corresponding changes in these three behavioral modes in their analysis of territoriality among socially isolated pairs of men.

A final aspect of the crowding model relates to physical density which is seen as increasing the possibility of some form of disturbance (intrusion, social interferences, or blocking of access to resources) in interpersonal behaviors as individuals attempt to achieve optimal levels of contact. Intrusion refers to unwanted invasion of one's territory or being approached too closely; interference is simply the interruption of ongoing behavior, and blocking involves preventing someone from reaching a desired goal. Thus, physical density is viewed as an interpersonal or psychological process that increases the probability that interpersonal contact will occur, and that the contact will interfere with the various boundary control mechanisms.

As indicated at the bottom of the model (see Figure 3) duration or time is postulated to have an effect on the feeling of crowdedness. Dense conditions under short duration would not be expected to have the same impact as the same circumstances occurring over a longer period of time. Accordingly, it is predicted that stress, coping behaviors, and costs would be more extensive in long-term than in short-term conditions.

The Altman model of crowding is consistent with Stokol's (1972) equilibrium model which views crowding as a subjective reaction—'a motivational state directed toward the alleviation of perceived restriction and infringement ...' (p. 276). Stokols, unlike Altman, however, views density as strictly a measure of people per unit of space. For the most part Altman's theory of crowding is most analogous to 'overload' theories (Desor, 1972; Milgram, 1970; Simmel, 1950; Wirth, 1938; Wohlwill, 1974) which postulate crowding as the receipt or experience of excessive social stimulation. As in the Altman model these theories postulate a consequent coping to re-establish acceptable levels of stimulation.

Greenberg and Firestone (1977) tested Altman's model of crowding in a questionnaire assessment of perceived crowdedness. Subjects participated in an interview in which for half the subjects two confederates were present in the room during the interview (surveillance). The other subjects were alone with the interviewer for the entire session (no surveillance). These conditions were crosscut by an intrusion manipulation in which the experimenter maintained eye gaze with half the subjects and touched the subject's knee. For the other half there was no intrusion. The hypothesis that surveillance and intrusion would be perceived as an invasion of privacy and create feelings of crowdedness was confirmed. The highest level of crowding occurred in the surveillance–intrusion condition, and the lowest level occurred in the no surveillance–no intrusion condition. Interestingly, from the standpoint of social penetration, subjects engaged in the least amount of self-disclosure in the surveillance–intrusion condition. Consistent with the equilibrium notion in the Altman model, the reduced level of privacy in the surveillance–intrusion condition was countered by the withholding of personal information.

Other aspects of the Altman model have been confirmed by experimental studies on dormitory residents living in crowded rooms (Valins and Baum, 1973; Baum and Valins, 1973, 1977), high- and low-density play situations (Loo, 1973a, 1973b), and situations involving high and low access to toys (Rohe and Patterson, 1974). In the Valins and Baum studies dormitory residents who lived under crowded conditions were compared with those in uncrowded conditions. As subjects in an experiment they were directed to a waiting room where a confederate was seated. The subjects from crowded dormitory settings sat farther apart from the confederate and spent less time looking at or talking with him than did subjects from the uncrowded situations. More direct evidence for the cost aspect of crowdedness was found by Rohe and Patterson (1974) and Loo (1973a, 1973b). In these studies low access and high density respectively led to increased aggression and other forms of social interference.

Other studies have failed to find effects of density and crowding, or findings have been mixed. Sundstrom (1973) had pairs of subjects work on a self-disclosure task in either a large or small room. Subjects working in the high-density condition experienced feelings of crowdedness but did not experience any stress. Ross et al. (1973), on the other hand, found evidence for greater feelings of crowdedness in a small room compared to a large one, but only weak indications of personal or physical discomfort. In two separate experiments Freedman et al. (1972) failed to find any effects of density. Freedman (1975), who defines high density as crowding, hypothesized that density intensifies the individual's typical reactions to the situation. If the situation is perceived as positive, increasing the density will make it seem better; if the situation is perceived as negative, high density will make it seem worse. This 'density–intensity' notion (Freedman, 1975) challenges ideas that high density is a stressor or produces arousal.

In summary, there seems to be evidence, although mixed, that the lack of privacy does lead to the experience of crowding, which in turn causes efforts to modify the boundary control mechanisms in the interpersonal process. This part of the model explicates an important aspect of the social penetration process. Earlier, we hypothesized that openness, within limits, increases the probability of establishing healthy human relationships (Altman and Taylor, 1973). Studies and theories of personal space, territoriality, and crowding have largely focused on the virtues of people closing themselves off from others. An integration of these two perspectives now leads us to hypothesize that, while some relationships generally proceed toward greater openness, they also probably have cycles or phases of closedness. People not only make themselves accessible to one another, they shut themselves off to greater or less degrees, break off contact, and engage in more distant styles of interaction. Thus, privacy regulation and crowding, as discussed above, represent a dialectic interplay of oppositional forces to be open and closed (see Altman *et al.*, 1981, for a more complete discussion of this point).

Intimacy equilibrium

A common finding from the literature on personal space, territoriality, and crowding is that individuals react negatively to overly close approaches by others, especially strangers (Altman and Vinsel, 1977). Privacy regulation, as presented above, represented an attempt to describe more completely the boundary regulation process for openness and closedness in interpersonal relations. One deficiency in the privacy regulation theory is the absence of an explanation why crowding as opposed to some other behavior is experienced when achieved privacy is less than desired privacy or why the experience is stressful. Worchel and his colleagues (Worchel, 1978; Worchel and Teddlie, 1976; Worchel and Yohai, 1978) developed an attributional model of crowding with the hope of identifying these issues. They speculated that arousal, created by personal space invasion leads to an attribution. Earlier, Schachter and Singer (1962) found that arousal caused individuals to search their environments for the 'appropriate' attribution of its origin. Cues in the environment formed the basis for labeling the arousal. Worchel's two-factor theory of crowding follows closely the reasoning of Schachter and Singer in that the arousal resulting from personal space invasion is labeled crowding when others are perceived as being too close. If arousal is attributed to some other factor, the underlying feeling will be labeled something other than crowding. This explanation seems to satisfy the requirement of needing to account for instances when personal space invasion is neither stressful nor labeled as crowding.

Some preliminary tests of the theory indicate that individuals do experience crowding due to their negative labeling of the arousal following personal space invasion (Worchel and Teddlie, 1976; Worchel and Yohai, 1978). It is not clear, however, when the arousal will result in a negative interpretation versus a positive one. Further research is clearly needed to clarify this issue. More importantly for our purpose here, the Worchel two-factor model bears a striking resemblance to the theorizing of Argyle and Dean (1965) who proposed that social interaction involves an interplay of approach (positive) and avoidance (negative) forces that propel people toward or away from each other. Approach forces include the desire for social feedback and the satisfying of affiliative needs. Avoidance forces include the fear of rendering oneself vulnerable or being rejected. Mehrabian (1969) cited many of the same behaviors in his review of nonverbal communication. He coined the term immediacy to refer to a limited number of dimensions such as eye contact, touch, distance, and body lean and orientation.

Argyle and Dean's (1965) 'intimacy equilibrium' model is an example of openness–closedness of interpersonal boundary processes. According to the model, if intimacy exceeds a desired amount anxiety will be aroused. The heightened anxiety prompts a need to decrease the intensity of some correlative behavior (eye contact, body proximity, self-disclosure) in order to decrease the excessive intimacy. Argyle and Dean (1965) tested this hypothesis and demonstrated that reduced eye contact was an effective compensation in coping with too much intimacy resulting from physical closeness. Amount of eye contact during an interview was positively related to the distance between interactants. Exline *et al.* (1965) provided support for the intimacy equilibrium theory by manipulating topical intimacy during an interview and measuring resultant changes in eye contact. They found reduced eye contact when persons disclosed intimate information—as if they were opening a verbal channel to the self but holding a nonverbal one closed. Similar findings on the relationship between eye contact and interview intimacy were reported by Carr and Dabbs (1974) and Schulz and Barefoot (1974). Coutts and Schneider (1976) also obtained support for the theory in their examination of such immediacy cues (Mehrabian, 1969) as individual gaze, mutual gaze, and smiling. A large number of studies document the inverse relationship between distance and eye contact (Argyle and Ingham, 1972; Goldberg *et al.*, 1969; Patterson, 1973b; Schulz and Barefoot, 1974; Stephenson *et al.*, 1972), and decreased body orientation with increased proximity (Aiello and Jones, 1971; Felipe and Sommer, 1966; Mehrabian and Diamond, 1971; Patterson, 1973b; Patterson *et al.*, 1971; Pellegrini and Empey, 1970; Watson and Graves, 1966).

Breed (1972) attempted to test the intimacy equilibrium hypothesis without success. Breed manipulated three levels of intimacy by varying a confederate's degree of eye gaze, body lean, and orientation. Contrary to the intimacy equilibrium hypothesis, subjects tended to match the confederate's behavior. Increases in intimacy led to reciprocal increases in eye gazes and forward leans on the part of the subjects. Other contradictory evidence has been provided by Jourard and Friedman (1970), Kleinke *et al.* (1975), and Thayer (1969).

A number of studies designed to test the intimacy equilibrium theory report equivocal findings. Aiello (1972) found the effect for male subjects only. The studies by Carr and Dabbs (1974) and McDowell (1973) failed to find a relationship with eye contact. Finally, Russo (1975) interpreted her findings as negative because proximity did not relate to length of eye contact.

Despite the mix of findings on the intimacy equilibrium hypothesis, a large number of studies provide good support for a compensatory process involving distance, angle of orientation, eye gaze, and other behaviors (see Patterson, 1973a). The clearest support comes from the relationship between distance and eye contact. As individuals approach each other their eye contact decreases; contrariwise increased eye contact occurs when distances are increased. Both behaviors work together as a system, presumably to maintain a desired level of intimacy.

More recently, Patterson (1976) has suggested that arousal may be critical to understanding the contradictory findings regarding equilibrium theory. Specifically, Patterson proposed that variations in interpersonal intimacy can produce changes in arousal level. The changed arousal constitutes a mediating mechanism for adjustments in reciprocated intimacy. Depending on the type of relationship, setting, and so on, the arousal results in a labeling of the consequent feeling, which, in turn, influences the type of intimacy changes that occur—compensation or reciprocity (see Figure 4).

Patterson (1976) described the model in the following manner:

The basic proposition of the model . . . is that in a dyadic interaction, sufficient changes in the intimacy behaviors of one person will produce arousal changes in the other person. It seems likely that

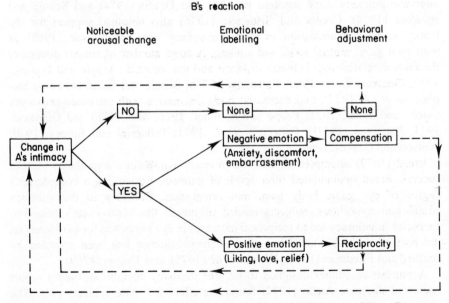

Figure 4   Diagram of the arousal model of interpersonal intimacy. (From Patterson, 1976. Copyright 1976 by the American Psychological Association. Reprinted/adapted with permission of the publisher and author.)

relatively small increases or decreases in one person's intimacy behavior relative to another would not produce proportionate changes in the other's arousal level. Rather, a type of difference threshold in behavioral intimacy may have to be exceeded before an arousal change is noted. In other words, the appropriate or comfortable level of intimacy can probably be conceptualized in adaptation-level terms as a range over which arousal changes would not occur (Patterson, 1973a). Further, it seems likely that such a range of comfortable intimacy may be a function of individual differences, type of relationship, and setting characteristics. If we start with some changes in the intimacy initiated by Person A, the two possible consequences for Person B are either arousal change or no arousal change (p. 239).

If an increase in intimacy produces a feeling-state that is given a negative label (e.g. anxiety, discomfort, embarrassment), a compensatory reaction in the form of reduced eye contact or withdrawal can be instrumental in decreasing the intimacy to a comfortable or appropriate level. On the other hand, changes in intimacy that lead to a positively labeled feeling-state (e.g. liking, love, relief) will result in the intimacy being returned—reciprocity.

Elsewhere we have argued that Patterson's arousal model can be made applicable to the self-disclosure intimacy dynamics of social penetration theory (Taylor, 1979). Patterson has extended his model to what might be described as an intimacy arousal model of crowding (Patterson, 1977). The extension of the model to explain the experience of crowding is based on the assumption that increased density raises the probability of increased interpersonal intimacy through nonverbal behaviors such as touching, eye contact, and so on. The increased frequency of these nonverbal behaviors is postulated to lead to arousal which is, in turn, labeled positively (e.g. pleasure, fun) or negatively (e.g. crowding). This extension of the intimacy arousal model to crowding highlights the resemblance of the model to Worchel and Teddlie's (1976) two-factor theory of crowding. The Patterson model is more general, however, in that it is not restricted to spatial components of intimacy.

The components of arousal and cognitive labeling in both versions of the Patterson model (Patterson, 1976, 1977) provide an important bridge to the privacy regulation and boundary maintenance mechanisms discussed earlier. Theory and data now confirm that there is a compensatory process involving various nonverbal behaviors. Strong evidence comes from studies dealing with distance and eye contact, body lean, smiling, and angle of orientation. These behavioral systems appear to be central in a person's attempts to maintain a desired level of interaction. Altman (1975) hypothesized that 'a subjective state of stress accompanies over- or undershooting of the mark . . . (which) . . . motivates the person or group to readjust boundary-control behaviors' (p. 156). The intimacy arousal model gives a more detailed understanding to the postulated stress and the subsequent motivational behaviors. Namely, the arousal is viewed as an adaptation phenomenon in which a difference threshold would have to be exceeded before an arousal change is noted. Secondly, differential outcomes in adjusted intimacy are predicted to result from the valence attached to the felt emotion. Specifically, negative emotional reactions precipitate compensatory behaviors; positive emotional reactions precipitate a reciprocation of the original intimacy behavior.

One possible shortcoming in applying the intimacy arousal model to social penetration theory is that, with few exceptions, research derived from the model has principally centered on nonverbal behaviors. This is the case for both Argyle and Dean's equilibrium theory (1965) and the intimacy arousal theories proposed by Patterson (1976, 1977). However, nonverbal behaviors are less direct than verbal behaviors and may be more automatic, as with autonomic behaviors (e.g. blushing, pupil dilation). Consequently self-disclosure intimacy may be more amenable to individual control, and therefore more responsive to the dynamics of the arousal model. In Altman's (1973a) model of reciprocity differential predictions were made for intimate and nonintimate disclosure, suggesting that individuals are sensitive to differences in disclosure levels and control their disclosure responses accordingly. The intimacy arousal model offers the possibility of explaining or accounting for a larger range of findings regarding disclosure intimacy, and will hopefully broaden our understanding of the motivational dynamics operative in verbal behaviors. Whether or not arousal mediates subsequent disclosure intimacy, consistent with nonverbal reactions, is a question that awaits future research.

Conclusion

The goal of this chapter was to integrate research and theory on privacy regulation and crowding with the conceptualizations of self-disclosure intimacy in social penetration theory. Ultimately, we tied the concepts of crowding and intimacy to notions of arousal and labelling.

In social penetration theory we posited rewards and costs as important motivational ingredients of developing relationships. Reciprocation of social exchanges occurs so long as individuals mutually experience a favorable reward/cost balance. Since these exchanges occur in situational contexts, we have described how environments affect their course and character, and how social interaction involves active use of the environment. Social penetration theory has generally dealt with the dynamics that describe how individuals close themselves off from others, and how they avoid being overly exposed and vulnerable.

Active use of the environment through territorial behaviors is an effective way of regulating interpersonal interactions. Research on the social penetration process has confirmed this. In this chapter this dynamic was expanded to include theories and research on privacy regulation and crowding. As in territorial behaviors, privacy regulation is the active control over interpersonal boundaries in order to regulate the amount of interaction with others. Regulation of the self-boundary contributes to feelings or perceptions about environments and the kind of relationship desired. The level of desired privacy is a subjective statement of an ideal amount of interaction. On the other hand, achieved privacy is the actual degree of contact resulting from interactions with others. When desired privacy equals achieved privacy an optimum state exists. If achieved privacy is lower or higher than desired privacy, a state of imbalance exists. Too much privacy creates feelings of isolation, whereas too little privacy produces feelings of crowdedness. This explanation of crowdedness is consistent with other approaches that define crowding as a subjective labeling phenomenon. It is also consistent with the equilibrium dynamics of Argyle and Dean posited in connection with nonverbal behaviors.

Finally, an equilibrium model of intimacy is discussed. Variations in interpersonal intimacy can produce changes in arousal level. The change in arousal level can produce either a positive or negative feeling-state. When the outcome is a positive feeling-state, intimacy will be reciprocated. If a negative state is produced, compensatory behaviors are evoked, e.g. reduced eye contact or withdrawal. This model was extended to an intimacy arousal model of crowding. The intimacy arousal model gives a more detailed understanding of the postulated stress associated with poor boundary maintenance, and the subsequent motivational behaviors employed to restore equilibrium.

References

Aiello, J. R. (1972). 'A test of equilibrium theory: Visual interaction in relation to orientation, distance and sex of interactants,' *Psychonomic Science*, **27**, 335–336.

Aiello, J. R., and Jones, S. E. (1971). 'Field study of the proxemic behavior of young school children in three subcultural groups,' *Journal of Personality and Social Psychology*, **19**, 351–356.

Altman, I. (1970). 'Territorial behavior in humans: An analysis of the concept,' in L. Pastalan and D. H. Carson (eds.), *Spatial Behavior of Older People*, The University of Michigan–Wayne State University Press, Ann Arbor.

Altman, I. (1971). 'Ecological aspects of interpersonal functioning,' in A. H. Esser (ed.), *Behavior and Environment: The Use of Space by Animals and Men*, pp. 291–306, Plenum Press, New York.

Altman, I. (1973a). 'Reciprocity of interpersonal exchange,' *Journal for the Theory of Social Behavior*, **3**, 249–261.

Altman, I. (1973b). 'An ecological approach to the functioning of social groups,' in J. E. Rasmussen (ed.), *Human Behavior in Isolation and Confinement*, Aldine Press, Chicago.

Altman, I. (1975). *The Environment and Social Behavior: Privacy, Personal Space, Territory and Crowding*, Brooks/Cole, Monterey, California.

Altman, I. (1976). 'Environmental psychology and social psychology,' *Personality and Social Psychology Bulletin*, **2**, 96–113.

Altman, I. (1977). 'Privacy regulation: Culturally universal or culturally specific?' *Journal of Social Issues*, **33**(3), 66–84.

Altman, I., and Haythorn, W. W. (1967). 'The ecology of isolated groups,' *Behavioral Science*, **12**, 169–182.

Altman, I., and Taylor, D. A. (1973). *Social Penetration: The Development of Interpersonal Relations*, Holt, Rinehart and Winston, New York.

Altman, I., Taylor, D. A., and Wheeler, L. (1971). 'Ecological aspects of group behavior in social isolation,' *Journal of Applied Social Psychology*, **1**, 76–100.

Altman, I. and Vinsel, A. M. (1977). 'Personal space: An analysis of E. T. Hall's proxemics framework,' in I. Altman and J. F. Wohlwill (eds.), *Human Behavior and Environment: Advances in Theory and Research*, Vol. 2, Plenum, New York.

Altman, I., Vinsel, A. M., and Brown, B. B. (1981). 'Dialectic conceptions in social psychology: An application to social penetration and privacy regulation,' in L. Berkowitz (ed.), *Advances in Experimental Social Psychology*, Vol. 14, Academic Press, New York.

Argyle, M., and Dean, J. (1965). 'Eye-contact, distance and affiliation,' *Sociometry*, **28**, 289–304.

Argyle, M., and Ingham, R. (1972). 'Gaze, mutual gaze and proximity,' *Semiotica*, **6**(1), 32–50.

Barefoot, J. C., Hoople, H., and McClay, D. (1972). 'Avoidance of an act which would violate personal space,' *Psychonomic Science*, **28**, 205–206.

Barker, R. G. (ed.) (1963). *The Stream of Behavior*, Appleton-Century-Crofts, New York.

Barker, R. G. (1968). *Ecological Psychology*, Stanford University Press, Stanford, CA.

Barker, R. G., and Gump, P. (1964). *Big School, Small School*, Stanford University Press, Stanford, CA.

Barker, R. G., and Wright, H. T. (1955). *Midwest and Its Children*, Harper & Row, New York.

Baum, A., and Valins, S. (1973). 'Residential environments, group size and crowding,' *Proceedings of the 81st Annual Convention of the American Psychological Association*, 211–212.

Baum, A., and Valins, S. (1977). *Architecture and Social Behavior: Psychological Studies in Social Density*, Lawrence Erlbaum Associates, Inc., Hillsdale, NJ.

Becker, F. D. (1973). 'Study of spatial markers,' *Journal of Personality and Social Psychology*, **26**, 439–445.

Becker, F. D., and Mayo, C. (1971). 'Delineating personal distance and territoriality,' *Environment and Behavior*, **3**, 375–381.

Blake, R. R., Rhead, C. C., Wedge, B., and Mouton, J. S. (1956). 'Housing architecture and social interaction,' *Sociometry*, **19**, 133–139.

Breed, G. (1972). 'The effect of intimacy: Reciprocity or retreat?' *British Journal of Social and Clinical Psychology*, **11**, 135–142.

Caplow, T., and Forman, R. (1950). 'Neighborhood interaction in a homogeneous community,' *American Sociological Review*, **15**, 357–366.

Carr, S. J., and Dabbs, J. M., Jr. (1974). 'The effects of lighting, distance and intimacy of topic on verbal and visual behavior,' *Sociometry*, **37**, 592–600.

Coutts, A. M., and Schneider, F. W. (1976). 'Affiliative conflict theory: An investigation of the intimacy equilibrium and compensation hypothesis,' *Journal of Personality and Social Psychology*, **34**, 1135–1142.

DeLong, A. J. (1970). 'Dominance-territorial relations in a small group,' *Environment and Behavior*, **2**, 190–191.

DeLong, A. J. (1971). 'Dominance-territorial criteria and small group structure,' *Comparative Group Studies*, **2**, 235–265.

DeLong, A. J. (1973). 'Territorial stability and hierarchical formation,' *Small Group Behavior*, **4**(1), 56–63.

Derlega, V. J., and Chaikin, A. L. (1977). 'Privacy and self-disclosure in social relationships,' *Journal of Social Issues*, **33**, 102–115.

Desor, J. A. (1972). 'Toward a psychological theory of crowding,' *Journal of Personality and Social Psychology*, **21**, 79–83.

Deutsch, M., and Collins, M. E. (1951). *Interracial Housing: A Psychological Evaluation of a Social Experiment*, University of Minnesota Press, Minneapolis, MN.

Edney, J. J. (1972). 'Property, possession and permanence: A field study in human territoriality,' *Journal of Applied Social Psychology*, **3**(3), 275–282.

Edney, J. J. (1976). 'Human territories: Comment on functional properties,' *Environment and Behavior*, **8**, 31–47.

Edney, J. J., and Jordan-Edney, N. L. (1974). 'Territorial spacing on a beach,' *Sociometry*, **37**(1), 92–103.

Esser, A. H. (1973). 'Cottage fourteen: Dominance and territoriality in a group of institutionalized boys,' *Small Group Behavior*, **4**, 131–146.

Esser, A. H., Chamberlain, A. S., Chapple, E. D., and Kline, N. W. (1965). 'Territoriality of patients on a research ward,' in J. Wortis (ed.), *Recent Advances in Biological Psychiatry*, Plenum, New York, pp. 37–44.

Exline, R., Gray, D., and Schuette, D. (1965). 'Visual behavior in a dyad as affected by interview content and sex of respondent,' *Journal of Personality and Social Psychology*, **1**, 201–209.

Felipe, N. J., and Sommer, R. (1966). 'Invasion of personal space,' *Social Problems*, **14**, 206–214.

Festinger, L., Schachter, S., and Back, K. (1950). *Social Pressures in Informal Groups: A Study of Human Factors in Housing*, Harper, New York.

Freedman, J. (1975). *Crowding and Behavior*, Freeman, San Francisco.

Freedman, J. L., Levy, A. S., Buchanan, R. W., and Price, J. (1972). 'Crowding and human aggressiveness,' *Journal of Experimental Social Psychology*, **8**, 528–548.

Goldberg, G. N., Kiesler, C. A., and Collins, B. E. (1969). 'Visual behavior and face-to-face distance during interaction,' *Sociometry*, **32**, 43–53.

Greenberg, E. I., and Firestone, I. J. (1977). 'Compensatory responses to crowding: Effects of personal space, intrusion, and privacy reduction,' *Journal of Personality and Social Psychology*, **35**, 637–644.

Hoppe, R. A., Greene, M. S., and Kenney, J. W. (1972). 'Territorial markers: Additional findings,' *Journal of Social Psychology*, **88**, 305–306.

Jones, E. E., and Archer, R. L. (1976). 'Are there special effects of personalistic self-disclosure?' *Journal of Experimental Social Psychology*, **12**, 180–193.

Jourard, S. M., and Friedman, R. (1970). 'Experimenter-subject "distance" and self-disclosure,' *Journal of Personality and Social Psychology*, **15**, 278–282.

Kleinke, C. L., Staneski, R. A., and Berger, D. E. (1975). 'Evaluation of an interviewer as a function of interviewer gaze, reinforcement of subject gaze and interviewer attractiveness,' *Journal of Personality and Social Psychology*, **31**, 115–122.

Loo, C. M. (1973a). 'Important issues in researching the effects of crowding on humans,' *Representative Research in Social Psychology*, **4**(1), 219–227.

Loo, C. M. (1973b). 'The effect of spatial density on the social behavior of children,' *Journal of Applied Social Psychology*, **2**(4), 372–381.

McDowell, K. V. (1973). 'Accommodations of verbal and nonverbal behaviors as a function of the manipulation of interaction distance and eye contact,' *Proceedings of the 81st Annual Convention of the American Psychological Association*, **8**, 207–208. (summary)

Martindale, D. A. (1971). 'Territorial dominance behavior in dyadic verbal interactions,' *Proceedings of the Annual Convention of the American Psychological Association*, **6**, 305–306.

Mehrabian, A. (1969). 'Significance of posture and position in the communication of attitude and status relationships,' *Psychological Bulletin*, **71**, 359–373.

Mehrabian, A., and Diamond, S. G. (1971). 'Seating arrangement and conversation,' *Sociometry*, **34**, 281–289.

Milgram, S. (1970). 'The experience of living in cities,' *Science*, **167**, 1461–1468.

Newman, O. (1972). *Defensible space*, Macmillan, New York.

Page, J. (1968). 'Social penetration processes: The effects of interpersonal reward and cost factors on the stability of dyadic relationships,' Unpublished doctoral dissertation, The American University, Washington, DC.

Patterson, M. L. (1973a). 'Compensation in nonverbal immediacy behaviors: A review,' *Sociometry*, **36**, 237–252.

Patterson, M. L. (1973b). 'Stability of nonverbal immediacy behaviors,' *Journal of Experimental Social Psychology*, **9**, 97–109.

Patterson, M. L. (1976). 'An arousal model of interpersonal intimacy,' *Psychological Review*, **83**, 235–245.

Patterson, M. L. (1977). 'An intimacy-arousal model of crowding,' in P. Suedfeld, J. A. R. Russell, L. M. Wood, F. Szigeti, and G. Davis (eds.), *The Behavioral Basis of Design (Book 2)*, Dowden, Hutchingson, & Ross, Stroudsberg, PA.

Patterson, M. L., Mullens, S., and Romano, J. (1971). 'Compensatory reactions to spatial intrusion,' *Sociometry*, **34**, 114–126.

Pellegrini, R. J., and Empey, J. (1970). 'Interpersonal spatial orientation in dyads,' *Journal of Psychology*, **76**, 67–70.

Rohe, W., and Patterson, A. H. (1974). 'The effects of varied levels of resources and density on behavior in a day care center,' Paper presented at Environmental Design Research Association, Milwaukee, Wisc.

Rosenblatt, P. C., and Budd, L. G. (1975). 'Territoriality and privacy in married or cohabiting unmarried couples,' *Journal of Social Psychology*, **97**, 67–76.

Ross, M., Layton, B., Erickson, B., and Schopler, J. (1973). 'Affect, facial regard, and reactions to crowding,' *Journal of Personality and Social Psychology*, **28**, 69–76.

Rubin, Z. (1975). 'Disclosing oneself to a stranger: Reciprocity and its limits,' *Journal of Experimental Social Psychology*, **11**, 233–260.

Russo, N. F. (1975). 'Eye contact, interpersonal distance, and the equilibrium theory,' *Journal of Personality and Social Psychology*, **31**, 497–502.

Schachter, S., and Singer, J. E. (1962). 'Cognitive, social and physiological determinants of emotional state,' *Psychological Review*, **69**, 379–399.

Schulz, R., and Barefoot, J. (1974). 'Non-verbal responses and affiliative conflict theory,' *British Journal of Social and Clinical Psychology*, **13**, 237–243.

Simmel, G. (1950). 'The metropolis and mental life,' in K. W. Wolff (ed. and trans.), *The Sociology of George Simmel*, The Free Press, New York.

Sommer, R. (1967). 'Small group ecology,' *Psychological Bulletin*, **67**, 145–152.

Sommer, R. (1969). *Personal Space: The Behavioral Basis of Design*, Prentice-Hall, Englewood Cliffs, New Jersey.

Sommer, R., and Becker, F. D. (1969). 'Territorial defense and the good neighbor,' *Journal of Personality and Social Psychology*, **11**, 85–92.

Spinner, B. (1978). 'Privacy and self-disclosure,' Paper presented at the annual meeting of the American Psychological Association, Toronto, Ontario, Canada. 28 August–1 September.

Stephenson, G. M., Rutter, D. R., and Dore, S. R. (1972). 'Visual interaction and distance,' *British Journal of Psychology*, **64**, 251–257.

Stokols, D. (1972). 'On the distinction between density and crowding: Some implications for future research,' *Psychological Review*, **79**, 275–278.

Stokols, D. (1978). 'A typology of crowding experiences,' in A. Baum and Y. Epstein (eds.), *Human Response to Crowding*, Lawrence Erlbaum, Hillsdale, NJ.

Stokols, D., Rall, M., Pinner, B., and Schopler, J. (1973). 'Physical, social, and personal determinants of the perception of crowding,' *Environment and Behavior*, 5(1), 87–117.

Sundstrom, E. (1973). 'A study of crowding: Effects of intrusion, goal blocking and density on self-reported stress, self-disclosure and nonverbal behavior,' Unpublished doctoral dissertation, University of Utah.

Sundstrom, E., and Altman, I. (1974). 'Field study of dominance and territorial behavior,' *Journal of Personality and Social Psychology*, 30, 115–125.

Taylor, D. A. (1979). 'Motivational bases of self-disclosure,' in G. J. Chelune (ed.), *Self-Disclosure*, Jossey Bass, San Francisco.

Taylor, D. A., and Altman, I. (1966). 'Intimacy-scaled stimuli for use in studies of interpersonal relations,' *Psychological Reports*, 19, 729–730.

Taylor, D. A., and Altman, I. (1975). 'Self-disclosure as a function of reward/cost outcomes,' *Sociometry*, 38, 18–31.

Taylor, D. A., Altman, I., and Sorrentino, R. (1969). 'Interpersonal exchange as a function of rewards and costs and situational factors: Expectancy confirmation–disconfirmation,' *Journal of Experimental Social Psychology*, 5, 324–339.

Taylor, R. B., DeSoto, C. B., and Lieb, R. (1979). 'Sharing secrets: Disclosure and discretion in dyads and triads,' *Journal of Personality and Social Psychology*, 37, 1196–1203.

Thayer, S. (1969). 'The effect of interpersonal looking duration on dominance judgments,' *The Journal of Social Psychology*, 70, 285–286.

Valins, S., and Baum, A. (1973). 'Residential group size, social interaction, and crowding,' *Environment and Behavior*, 5(4), 421–440.

Watson, O. M., and Graves, T. D. (1966). 'Quantitative research in proxemic behavior,' *American Anthropologist*, 68, 971–985.

Wirth, L. (1938). 'Urbanism as a way of life,' *American Journal of Sociology*, 44, 1–24.

Wohlwill, J. F. (1974). 'Human adaptation to levels of environmental stimulation,' *Human Ecology*, 2(2), 127–147.

Worchel, S. (1978). 'The defense of human territory,' Unpublished manuscript, University of Virginia, Charlottesville, Va.

Worchel, S., and Sigall, H. (1976). 'There is no place like home, unless . . .' *The ACC Basketball Handbook*, VMI Publication, Charlotte, NC.

Worchel, S., and Teddlie, C. (1976). 'The experience of crowding: A two-factor theory,' *Journal of Personality and Social Psychology*, 34, 30–40.

Worchel, S., and Yohai, S. (1978). 'The role of attribution in the experience of crowding,' *Journal of Experimental Social Psychology*, 15, 91–104.

Small Groups and Social Interaction, Volume 1
Edited by H. H. Blumberg, A. P. Hare, V. Kent and M. Davies
Published by John Wiley & Sons Limited, 1983.

1.3 Role of Control in Mediating Perceptions of Density*

Judith Rodin, Susan K. Solomon, and John Metcalf

Yale University

Crowding, as we all know, is almost always experienced as a negative psychological state (see, for example, Altman, 1975; Stokols, 1972). But it has been demonstrated that crowding and density are not the same thing: People in dense settings do not always feel crowded, do not always act as if they are crowded, and do not always report that they are in crowded spaces (Freedman, 1975; Stokols, 1972). When does density result in the experience of crowding? When are density and crowding unrelated? One possibility is that objectively defined conditions of density map onto a psychological state of crowding when density produces a restriction in one's *sense of personal contact* (see Baron & Rodin, 1979; Rodin & Baum, 1978). If one lone person prevents me from sitting in my favorite seat on the bus, I may feel crowded. But if my favorite seat is still available on a loaded bus of 40 people, I do not feel crowded. The colloquialism 'Don't crowd me' clearly points to the commonly experienced association between perceived crowding and loss of control.

Control does appear to be a central feature to much of human behavior. Adler (1930) has described the need to control one's personal environment as 'an intrinsic necessity of life itself' (p. 398). Perceived or actual control reduces the negative valuation of aversive stimuli (Corah & Boffa, 1970; Glass & Singer, 1972; Klemp & Rodin, 1976; Pervin, 1963), increases level of performance (Monty, Rosenberger, & Perlmuter, 1973; Stotland & Blumenthal, 1964), and may contribute to health and a general sense of well-being (Langer & Rodin, 1976; Rodin & Langer, 1977). Most relevant to present concerns, when chronic

*Abridged from Judith Rodin, Susan K. Solomon, and John Metcalf (1978). 'Role of control in mediating perceptions of density,' *Journal of Personality and Social Psychology*, **36**, 988–999. Copyright 1978 by the American Psychological Association. Reprinted by permission.

home crowding produces diminished feelings of control, it is associated with greater expectancies for failure, lessened ability to overcome frustration, and fewer efforts at self-control (Rodin, 1976).

We assumed that variations in density may be especially likely to influence feelings of control and thus lead to the experience of crowding. First, by their very nature, high physical and social density often constitute a constraint on behavior. Coordination and surveillance of the activities of other people are often increasingly more difficult with increasing density. Second, too little space as well as too many people are very salient attributional cues. Thus, they may be invoked to 'explain' a reduced sense of control—even when the explanation is a misattribution and is not the real cause for the loss in control. Consequently, people may label a dense setting as crowded because their feelings of control have been affected. This line of reasoning further suggests that even independently of density, feelings of control may influence feelings of crowding.

Sherrod (1974) explicitly manipulated the control variable in a study of crowding; he adapted the Glass and Singer (1972) paradigm comparing the consequences of exposure to controllable versus uncontrollable noise. Glass and Singer found that loud noise did not inhibit task performance during periods of experimentally induced noise; but the prior exposure to noise did affect performance on subsequent, noise-free tasks. More important to the present point, subjects who believed that they were able to terminate the initial, experimentally induced noise did not show these negative aftereffects. Sherrod found that density produced the same negative aftereffects as noise for some tasks—effects that were eliminated when subjects believed they could control (terminate) the high density. The Sherrod (1974) study does establish that high density can be a stressor that control helps to alleviate. But it leaves unanswered an even more basic question: Does a reduction in personal control produce feelings of crowding, especially but not exclusively under conditions of high density? . . .

In this study, we crafted an experimental context that simulated, insofar as possible, a primary environment (see Stokols, 1976). We assumed that apparent restriction and enhancement of personal control would have greater impact in a primary setting where people perform relatively important behaviors over an extended period of time.

The first hypothesis stated that those subjects who can control the group's activities will feel less crowded than those who can not exercise control, especially in a high-density setting. The second hypothesis dealt with the type of control possible. We reasoned that differences in the type of setting and nature of the task demands would influence the value of different kinds of control options. To test this notion, one subject in each group was instructed to control the onset and organization of the group's activities and another to control the termination of the group's activities. One reason to expect a difference is that these roles afford different opportunities to exercise actual control during the course of the interaction. In addition, for other potential stressors such as shock, onset control has been found to lessen the initial aversive impact of a stimulus (Staub, Tursky & Schwartz, 1971), while termination control is associated with less experienced aversiveness over time (Averill, 1973; Lazarus, 1968).

Method

Overview

Two subjects in each group were assigned roles at random that allowed them to assume control over the group and its activities. A group discussion and a physical interaction task were conducted, and subjects expected that several more 'group process' tasks would follow and that additional sessions on subsequent days were likely. Subjects completed questionnaires, and their behavior was observed and recorded.

Subjects

Seventy-one male Yale undergraduates participated in the study in groups of six. In one group, a confederate participated as a sixth subject, thus making 12 groups.

Independent variables

Density. The first independent variable was density, which was manipulated by varying the size of the room. Two room sizes were used. In the high-density condition, the room measured 5.94 m², whereas the room for the low-density condition measured 14.04 m². In fact, the high-density room was created by closing off half of the low-density room by means of a sliding wall. The experimental rooms had one-way glass on one wall, and the other walls were bare. The floors were carpeted, and subjects sat on the floor. Both rooms contained a video camera.

Control. The second independent variable involved a manipulation of control. This was achieved by randomly assigning roles to two people in the group that gave them the opportunity to exert different kinds of control within the group. Functions that allowed him to exert onset control were given to a person labeled the *coordinator*. He was to be responsible for initiating and facilitating the group processes, for assigning certain tasks to various group members as necessary, for dealing with procedural disputes, and for relaying materials and instructions to the group. He was also told that after the first two tasks had been completed, he was to be responsible for deciding how the group would perform the next projects.

For the group discussion task, the coordinator distributed the problem to the group members, and in all cases, he read it aloud, although he had not been specifically instructed to do so. He also distributed the questionnaires and read aloud directions for their completion. During the spatial interaction task, he decided the order in which the group members would be blindfolded and served as their guide during the task.

A second controlling role, which focused primarily on completing each task, was assigned to the *terminator*. He was told that his job was to decide when the group should finish a task and go on to a new one. Should a task call for a group solution, he would be responsible for the ultimate decision. It was also the terminator's job to stop a task if he felt that any of the group's interactions had become too stressful. When the experimenter interrupted the group discussion to ask members to complete the first set of questionnaires, he specified that after they finished, it would be up to the terminator to decide whether to continue the discussion or to begin the second task. All terminators went on to the second exercise, and none ever signaled the experimenter that help was needed.

Subjects were assigned at random to sitting positions on the floor, and then the control roles were assigned to two who were in previously designated positions. The subject sitting next to the box of materials became the coordinator, and the subject seated to the left of the experimenter was designated as the terminator. The remaining four subjects were not assigned roles, and they formed the *no-control* group.

Measures

Before entering the experimental rooms, subjects completed a perceived locus of control scale (Rotter, 1966) and a biographical information questionnaire designed primarily to elicit data about the density of their present and former living conditions.

In the experimental room, subjects' behavior was monitored by video cameras and scored on line, at 30-sec intervals, by six trained observers who did not know the experimental hypotheses or which subjects had been assigned to the controlling roles. Pairs of observers rated a randomly selected subject when a buzz, occurring every 30 sec, signaled them to begin. On a checklist of items, they evaluated the person's spatial position, verbal behavior, gaze, attention-seeking behavior, mood, and the content and tone of his speech.

After the first task, participants completed two short questionnaires asking them to respond to a set of 9-point semantic differential items. In the first questionnaire, 25 9-point semantic differential items were grouped into three subscales. The first asked for the subject's 'general impression of the present experimental situation so far.' The second asked the subject to 'assess your reaction to the room in which you are working.' The third asked the subject to indicate how 'you personally feel in this situation thus far.' Subjects also judged the size of the room and the number of people the room could comfortably hold. The second questionnaire asked them to rate every other person in the group on nine semantic differential items. Questionnaires also included open-ended items about general feelings. The final measure was the length of time each group continued doing the physical interaction task.

Procedure

Subjects who had been recruited for an experiment on group interaction processes waited in a 5.04 m² anteroom for their group of six to form. The size of the waiting room was determined by the arrangement of space in the laboratory and was not chosen for any conceptual reason. After filling out preliminary questionnaires, the subjects were escorted into the experimental room by a male experimenter and seated in a circular arrangement on the carpeted floor. They were asked to wear name tags that would identify them by first names and were also asked to remove their watches. The experimenter explained that the group was being conducted in an effort to investigate the formation of relationships in group settings. He indicated the videotape equipment and the room's one-way mirror and explained that the session would be videotaped as well as monitored occasionally through the mirror. The experimenter told the group that they would be working on group formation exercises and would be interrupted from time to time and asked to complete some questionnaires. It was emphasized that the subjects would probably find the group interesting, since they might gain ways to better understand themselves and their fellow members. The experimenter then introduced the roles that defined the experimental manipulation of control. When this had been completed, he announced that in order to encourage a more intimate level of interaction, they would begin by having each group member say something about himself. The purpose of this procedure was to make salient the cover story that the group members were participants in a study on the formation of personal relationships.

The experimenter started off the exercise, talking about his school background, his hobbies, his reasons for studying groups, and often expressing some small doubts about his chosen career. Then each subject in turn introduced himself, usually taking 2 or 3 min. The experimenter then gave a brief description of the first two tasks that the group would perform and left, indicating that the instructions for the remaining tasks would be available later. This ambiguity was created so that subjects would be unsure of the length of the first session.

The first task was a group discussion about censorship. A few questions were presented to provide an initial framework for the discussion, which was otherwise unstructured. After the group had discussed the problem for 15 min, the experimenter interrupted over a loudspeaker and asked subjects to fill out some questionnaires that had been left in the experimental room. If the group finished its discussion in less than 15 min, which occurred only once, the participants were asked to continue discussing the problem until 15 min had passed.

After completing the questionnaires, the group proceeded to a 'physical interaction' task. The group members first formed a circle. The goal of the task was described as an attempt to increase trust and contact among the group members. Each participant was to stand in the center and move around in the circle, blindfolded, without touching anyone or any object. The coordinator served as his guide, with verbal instructions about his location. The terminator had the job of deciding when each group member had been in the circle long enough. When either the coordinator or terminator was the blindfolded person, the other controller performed both roles. At the conclusion of this task, subjects were informed that the experiment was over, and the hypotheses and procedure were explained.

Results

Questionnaire data reduction and design of statistical analyses

On the interpersonal impressions scale, the semantic differential items were collapsed into two indexes, one for control (directing/following; in control over situation/lacking control over situation; in control over others/lacking control over others) and the other for interpersonal evaluations (relaxed/tense; friendly/unfriendly; aggressive/retiring; secure/insecure; warm/cold, likable/not likable).

Five composite indexes were devised from the three subscales of the task and setting scale. A general impression index included all the items asked under the *general impression subscale* except crowding. These were interesting/ boring; easy/difficult; cooperative/competitive; well defined/ambiguous; pleasant/ unpleasant; and comfortable/uncomfortable. The evaluation of crowding was embedded in the *general impression subscale* to mask somewhat our explicit interest in this variable. This item was analyzed with three items from the *reaction to room subscale* that were also intended to assess perceived crowding somewhat less reactively. These items were uncramped/cramped; large/small; and open/closed. The remaining items on the *reaction to room subscale* were intended to measure room ambience and were combined into a single index. These items were good/bad; pleasant/unpleasant; calm/agitated; inviting/hostile; friendly/ unfriendly; private/public; and liberating/constraining. Finally, the items on the *personal reactions subscale* were combined into two indexes. One measured feelings of control (directing/following; in control over situation/lacking control over situation; in control over others/lacking control over others). The other measured personal state (relaxed/tense; predictable/unpredictable; happy/sad; free/ restricted; secure/insecure). On all indexes, the lower the score, the more favorable the response. . . .

Interpersonal impression scale

Subjects assigned the controlling roles ($M = 4.62$) were seen as having greater control (by all other participants in this situation) than subjects who were not assigned controlling roles $(M = 5.19)$. This difference was significant, $F(1, 10) = 6.66$, $p < .05$. However, it is clear from the significant difference between coordinators $(M = 4.01)$ and terminators $(M = 5.22)$, $F(1, 10) = 6.062$, $p < .05$, that it was primarily the coordinators who were seen as exercising high levels of control relative to the other participants. Density had no significant effect on ratings of the exercise of control.

An ANOVA on the interpersonal evaluations index showed no significant effects of density on liking and no effects of the role of those doing or receiving the ratings. . . . [See the original article for the data which support these assertions.]

Task and setting scale

Density. As might be expected from the manipulation of room size, estimates of the room area and maximum number of people that the room could accommodate were significantly lower for subjects in the smaller room. In addition, the two indexes that evaluated reactions to the room were significantly affected by density. The small room was perceived both as being more crowded and as having a less pleasant ambience than the large room. The density manipulation did not significantly affect either the more general measure of reactions to the situation or the more personal measure of feelings about oneself.

Control. As predicted, subjects assigned a controlling role judged the rooms to be significantly less crowded than did subjects not assigned controlling roles, $F(1, 10) = 23.786, p < .001$. The means in Table 1 indicate that these differences were more pronounced in the small room, and a significant Density × Controllers versus Noncontrollers interaction, $F(1, 10) = 8.563, p < .05$, was obtained.

The type of control assigned also had important effects. In most instances, terminators rated the room and their own feelings more positively than coordinators

Table 1 Comparisons among coordinators, terminators, and noncontrollers on task and setting scale variables

| | Density | | | | | |
| | High | | | Low | | |
Variable	Coordin-ator	Termin-ator	No control	Coordin-ator	Termin-ator	No control
General impressions	6.71	5.96	6.97	5.42	6.54	5.91
Perceived crowding	6.00	5.96	10.06	3.79	5.62	5.00
Room ambience	5.67	4.85	5.71	4.69	5.33	4.65
Personal state	5.03	4.37	4.41	3.70	4.53	4.20
Control	4.06	4.50	4.69	4.06	4.61	4.72

Note. On all indexes, the lower the score, the more favorable the response. The scale anchors were 1 and 9.

in the small room and more negatively than coordinators in the large room. There was a significant Density × Coordinator versus Terminator interaction on the room ambience index, $F(1, 10) = 5.40$, $p < .05$, and on evaluation of personal state, $F(1, 10) = 6.39$, $p < .05$. The general impressions and perceived crowding indexes yielded nonsignificant interactions, but the means were in the same direction. There was no significant effect for ratings of one's own feeling of control. Since subjects veridically evaluated the extent to which others had control, as indicated by the results on the control index of the interpersonal impressions scale discussed above, we may assume that the weakness of the findings on the personal feelings of control index reflect a reluctance in communicating one's own feelings of control on a numerical scale. Open ended responses, to be discussed below, gave a clearer picture of subjects' feelings of their own control.

Observer ratings

Observers rated the gestures, body movement, and ocular activity of a pre-designated group member at 30-sec intervals. Overall, there were no reliable differences among group members as a function of role in the amount they contributed to the substance of the group discussion. There were also no reliable differences in affective reactions or spatial behavior such as stretching to define a territory.

Measures after Task 2

The actual length of time spent on the physical interaction task was to be determined by the terminators, and the task was to be directed by the coordinators. Observers' ratings indicated that during this task, both coordinators and terminators controlled the length of time each individual spent in the circle. Density apparently influenced these decisions: In the small room, the task lasted an average of 6 min, 13 sec and in the large room, 10 min, 20 sec, $t(1, 10) = 2.58$, $p < .05$.

Discussion

Unlike subjects in other studies (e.g., Griffitt & Veitch, 1971), participants in the present study did not rate one another more negatively in the small than in the large room. In other studies, however, subjects often interacted very little or on a more impersonal level. Thus, they may have lacked sufficient information or incentive to judge their fellow participants carefully and consequently may have made judgments on the basis of the affective tone generated by the physical environment. By contrast, participants in the present study found themselves in a more personal, encounter-group-type situation. This may have encouraged them to make more discriminative, personal assessments.

On the other hand, when subjects were asked to evaluate the setting, their responses were highly differentiated as a function of both density and control. The results, consistent with some previous studies (e.g., Epstein & Karlin, 1975; Sundstrom, 1975), showed that density influenced how crowded participants felt and their evaluation of the room's ambience. More important are the data that answered the two basic experimental questions that we addressed with regard to control. First, is control a variable that influences the perception of crowding? The results strongly support this hypothesis. Participants without control felt that the room was more crowded than subjects with control, especially the small room. Thus it appears that the experience of crowding is directly related to having or lacking control, especially under high-density conditions.

Our second hypothesis considered whether different types of control activities would produce different effects in different density situations. Again, the answer was yes. The small room was seen as more pleasant by terminators than coordinators, and they rated themselves as feeling better in it. Precisely the opposite was true for the large room, where terminators' judgments were even less favorable than those of subjects with no control. Why should these differences have occurred?

In the large room, all subjects reported feeling less crowded, and they reacted more positively to the environment than their counterparts in the denser setting. When subjects were relaxed, observers noted that the group's activities progressed smoothly. This allowed coordinators to regulate the task efficiently and thus presumably to feel that they had exercised their control effectively. If this is true, it is not surprising that coordinators were the most positive in their praise of the low-density setting. By contrast, any expectancy that the terminator had of an effective use of his role must have been unfulfilled in the less stressful setting. If the role of terminator in such a situation seemed to be superfluous to its incumbent, this may have colored his reaction to the situation. As a result, he reported feeling less comfortable than his companions and saw the setting in the least positive light.

Now let us consider the small, high-density room. Since density was related to increased crowding stress in the small room, the terminator's role potential may have increased as the interaction progressed. If feelings of actual or anticipated control increase feelings of effectiveness and positive affect (White, 1959), his positive state might also be reflected in more positive reactions to the setting, such as those which were obtained. In addition, when aroused by high density, these subjects with offset control may have reappraised the setting as less negative because they were able to set the limits of exposure (Averill, 1973; Lazarus, 1968).

Thus, the benefit of control may depend on one's appraisal of the likelihood of being able to use it as well as an assessment of how effective one has been or will be. In essence, our manipulations of onset and termination control led to differences in actual and anticipated exercise of control as a function of differences in density. . . .

A differentiated treatment of the concept of personal control (see Baron & Rodin, 1979) provides a starting point for deriving the conditions under which high density will or will not have a range of adverse effects. In addition to being implicated in the instigation of crowding effects, issues of personal control are also involved at many points in the coping process. Control in this sense appears relevant for understanding how one may prepare for a stressor, how one actually copes, given the actual encounter with a stressor, and finally, control appears to be a critical feature of the delayed effects or cumulative costs of coping (cf. Glass & Singer, 1972; Sherrod, 1974).

References

Adler, A. (1930). 'Individual psychology,' in C. Murchinson (ed.), *Psychologies of 1930*, Clark University Press, Worcester, Mass.

Altman, I. (1975). *The Environment and Social Behavior*. Brooks/Cole, Monterey, Calif.

Averill, J. R. (1973). 'Personal control over aversive stimuli and its relation to stress,' *Psychological Bulletin*, **80**, 286–303.

Baron, R., and Rodin, J. (1979). 'Personal control and crowding stress: Processes mediating the impact of spatial and social density.' In A. Baum, J. E. Singer and S. Valins (eds.), *Advances in Environmental Psychology: Volume 1, The Urban Environment*. Erlbaum, Hillsdale, New Jersey.

Corah, N., and Boffa, J. (1970). 'Perceived control, self observation, and response to aversive stimulation,' *Journal of Personality and Social Psychology*, **16**, 1–4.

Epstein, Y., and Karlin, R. A. (1975). 'Effects of acute experimental crowding,' *Journal of Applied Social Psychology*, **5**, 34–53.

Freedman, J. (1975). *Crowding and Behavior*, Freeman, San Francisco.

Glass, D. C., and Singer, J. E. (1972). *Urban Stress*, Academic Press, New York.

Griffitt, W., and Veitch, R. (1971). 'Hot and crowded: Influences of population density and temperature on interpersonal affective behavior,' *Journal of Personality and Social Psychology*, **17**, 92–98.

Klemp, G., and Rodin, J. (1976). 'Effects of uncertainty, delay, and focus of attention on reactions to an aversive stimulus,' *Journal of Experimental Social Psychology*, **12**, 416–421.

Langer, E., and Rodin, J. (1976). 'The effects of choice and enhanced personal responsibility for the aged: A field experiment in an institutional setting,' *Journal of Personality and Social Psychology*, **34**, 191–198.

Lazarus, R. S. (1968). 'Emotions and adaptation: Conceptual and empirical relations,' in W. S. Arnold (ed.), *Nebraska Symposium on Motivation* (Vol. 16), University of Nebraska Press, Lincoln.

Monty, R., Rosenberger, M., and Perlmuter, L. (1973). 'Amount and locus of choice as sources of motivation in paired-associate learning,' *Journal of Experimental Psychology*, **97**, 16–21.

Pervin, L. (1963). 'The need to predict and control under conditions of threat,' *Journal of Personality*, **31**, 570–585.

Rodin, J. (1976). 'Crowding, perceived choice, and response to controllable and uncontrollable outcomes,' *Journal of Experimental Social Psychology*, **12**, 564–578.

Rodin, J., and Baum, A. (1978). 'Crowding and helplessness: Potential consequences of density and loss of control,' in A. Baum and Y. Epstein (eds.), *Human Responses to Crowding*, Erlbaum, Hillsdale, NJ.

Rodin, J., and Langer, E. (1977). 'Long-term effects of a control-relevant intervention with the institutionalized aged,' *Journal of Personality and Social Psychology*, **35**, 897–902.

Rotter, J. B. (1966). 'Generalized expectancies for internal versus external control of reinforcement,' *Psychological Monographs*, **80** (1, Whole No. 609).

Sherrod, D. R. (1974). 'Crowding, perceived control, and behavioral aftereffects,' *Journal of Applied Social Psychology*, **4**, 171–186.

Staub, E., Tursky, B., and Schwartz, G. (1971). 'Self-control and predictability: Their effect on reactions to aversive stimulation,' *Journal of Personality and Social Psychology*, **18**, 157–162.

Stokols, D. (1972). 'On the distinction between density and crowding: Some implications for future research,' *Psychological Review*, **38**, 72–83.

Stokols, D. (1976). 'The experience of crowding in primary and secondary environments,' *Environment and Behavior*, **8**, 49–86.

Stotland, E., and Blumenthal, A. (1964). 'The reduction of anxiety as a result of the expectation of making a choice,' *Canadian Review of Psychology*, **18**, 139–145.

Sundstrom, E. (1975). 'Toward an interpersonal model of crowding,' *Sociological Symposium*, **14**, 129–144.

White, R. (1959). 'Motivation reconsidered: The concept of competence,' *Psychological Review*, **66**, 297–333.

Further note

[The original article also describes an experiment in which 'the positioning of four confederates in an elevator maneuvered a naive subject to a place in front of or on the opposite front side to the panel of floor selection buttons. Subjects standing in front of the "control" panel felt significantly less crowded and saw the elevator as significantly larger than subjects in the opposite position.']

2 Personality, Social Characteristics, and Group Composition

Small Groups and Social Interaction, Volume 1
Edited by H. H. Blumberg, A. P. Hare, V. Kent and M. Davies
© 1983 John Wiley & Sons Ltd

2.1 Processes of Status Generalization

Murray Webster, Jr and 'James E. Driskell, Jr
University of South Carolina

Small groups as a subfield of sociology has a long history. In fact, the earliest textbook of social psychology was written by the sociologist E. A. Ross in 1908. In recent times, the major intellectual figure has been Robert Freed Bales, whose perspective and accomplishments have influenced more than a generation of his students and other scholars. During the 1950s when the first edition of this book was published, the term 'small groups' was widely identified with the kinds of problems Bales and his students investigated, and with their methods of research. Scholars influenced by Bales later went on to pursue diverging lines of inquiry, such as Theodore Mills's investigations of self-analytic discussion groups, Frederick Strodtbeck's studies of individual interaction styles, and Philip Slater's attempts to find parallels between changing social structures and human isolation. One additional line of inquiry stimulated by Bales's early work has developed into studies of status generalization, to be described in this chapter.

Development of the theory

Background: performance expectations and interaction inequality

Status generalization is the process by which the status of actors external to a particular situation is 'imported' and used to determine the subordinate/superordinate features of that interaction. The tradition of research presented in this chapter can be traced to the work of R. F. Bales beginning in the late 1940s. Bales (1970) studied small discussion groups of college students. A striking feature of these groups was that they regularly developed marked patterns of inequality after the first few minutes of interaction. The inequality is manifested in the following: amount of talking; amount each individual is talked to; acceptance or rejection of influence; perceived and actual leadership of the group; amount of agreement and positive evaluations received from others; and interaction style (some individuals were heavily proactive and task oriented, while others were mostly reactive and focused on emotions and feelings).

That emergent inequality marks the starting point for Joseph Berger's (1958) theory of 'performance expectation states,' which is the foundation for contemporary theories of status generalization. Berger explained the inequality as being the result of performance expectation states—ideas about the relative task-performance ability of each group member—which develop during the initial phases of interaction. The reasoning is as follows. When previously unacquainted individuals come together to work on a task, one of their 'subtasks' is to decide who has high ability to help the group and who has only low ability. The reason for this is to be able to take advantage of the good ideas of a high-ability member, while not being misled by the poor ideas of a low-ability member. Thus, at the outset, individuals use any available cues, such as clothing or manner, to infer who has high ability and who has low ability. Once high expectations are formed for a specific individual, he or she is encouraged to talk more, is perceived as having good ideas, is less likely to encounter disagreement, and is more likely to exert influence. In other words, when expectations have formed for every person in the group, the character of interaction changes noticeably, such that those for whom high expectations are held become more likely to receive all measured types of inequality in the group, and those for whom low expectations are held will receive less of all types of group rewards. Individuals come to be treated unequally *because* they are thought to have unequal task-relevant abilities.

Status characteristics and the burden of proof

Members of the early groups studied by Bales began interaction as status equals, that is, they were all white, male, high SES (socioeconomic status) college students. At the same time, there were abundant data from other studies in both natural and laboratory settings to show that groups of people who start out as status *unequals* develop a power and prestige structure consistent with members' external status positions. In these groups it seems as though the 'subtask' of figuring out whose ideas are good gets fulfilled almost immediately, so that external status differentiation determines actors' expectations and behavior from the very beginning of their interaction. Then interaction inequality is based upon members' external status.

In one example of this early research Strodtbeck and Mann (1956) reported that women usually deferred to men during jury deliberations. Perhaps this result would not be surprising if we knew, for instance, that most men contribute better ideas on juries than most women. But in fact we do not know that; it would be more reasonable to conclude that the external status characteristics of individuals are irrelevant to the quality of their contributions to the groups. But the fact remains that in most cases individuals seem to treat the status *as if* it gave very reliable cues to the quality of future contributions.

These cases and many others were explained by the first theory of status characteristics and expectations states (Berger *et al.*, 1966). According to this theory, interaction studies involving such characteristics as race, sex, occupation, and military rank are related in that they all involve *status characteristics*. Status characteristics operate to define interaction situations through a generalization principle called 'burden of proof,' and determine group behavior through an expectation state process. The burden of proof principle states that, unless the relevance or applicability of an external status characteristic is challenged, actors will *infer* task-specific performance expectations on the basis of any discriminating status characteristics they possess. Such inferences occur *regardless of the actual relevance* of the status characteristics to the task at hand. In other words, individuals act as if the burden of proof were placed upon demonstrating that the status characteristic is *not* relevant rather than demonstrating it is relevant to the task at hand.

Combining multiple characteristics

Multicharacteristic situations include Hughes's (1945) classic dilemma (for the male patient) of seeking medical treatment from a female physician: is she to be treated deferentially as befits her occupational status, or does the patient expect her to act like a deferential woman?

These situations usually contain two different types of status characteristics, *diffuse* (to be called D's) and *specific* (C's). D's such as race, sex, and age, carry ability expectations without explicit limit: in our culture, males are widely thought to be more intelligent, logical, sensible, mechanical, strong, athletic, etc., than women. C's are limited to specific abilities and specific situations: we expect a physician to be highly skilled at treating illness, but not necessarily at changing a tire. Despite the difference in scope of the two types of characteristics, they both function similarly in status generalization.

How multiple items of status are processed has received considerable attention. One early line of thought held that people would simplify complex situations cognitively by attending only to one 'master status;' for example, 'No matter how good my ideas are, they still treat me as just another (woman, black person, child).' However, most evidence shows that all available status information is utilized. So the doctor in Hughes's example is treated less deferentially than a male doctor would be, but more deferentially than a woman without the medical degree would be. This 'combining process' is used in interventions to overcome undesirable effects of status characteristics such as race and sex.

The theory of status characteristics and social interaction*

Below is a formal statement of the most recent version of the theory of status generalization (adapted from Berger *et al.*, 1977).

Scope conditions

We assume a situation containing at least two actors p and o (for person and other), certain D and C status characteristics, task outcome states T+ (success) and T− (failure), and the specific characteristic C* (C*+ and C*−) which the actors believe is relevant to successful or unsuccessful task completion.

The theory applies to groups of individuals who meet two conditions, task orientation and collective orientation. Task orientation means that the members' purpose in meeting is to solve some problem, rather than simply to enjoy each other's company. Thus, a jury or a committee is task oriented, while people at a cocktail party are not. Collective orientation means that members consider it legitimate and necessary to consider every individual's ideas. Thus, members of a planning session are collectively oriented, while students taking a final examination ordinarily are not.

Notice that the scope of the theory is broader than the small group setting from which it emerged. Status generalization is a process which can occur in any face-to-face interaction, in large or small groups, in natural settings as well as in the small-groups laboratory.

Definitions

1. C is a specific status characteristic if and only if: (a) C possesses at least two states which are differentially evaluated in the culture; and (b) to every state of C there are associated specific performance expectations.

2. D is a diffuse status characteristic if and only if it meets both conditions (a) and (b) and in addition: (c) to every state of D there are associated general performance expectations without limit as to scope.

Assumptions

1. (Salience)   All D or C characteristics which are already considered by the actor p to be linked to outcome states of T become salient in the situation, and all D or C characteristics which discriminate between actors will also become salient in the situation.

2. (Burden of proof)   If any D or C characteristic is salient in the situation,

---

*This section is rather technical. Some readers may wish to read it lightly now and come back to it later.

then: (a) for each D characteristic, its associated general expectation state (Γ) will also become salient, and will become relevant to a similarly evaluated state of C*; and (b) for each C characteristic, its relevant task outcome state (τ) will become salient, the (τ) will become relevant to a similarly evaluated state of abstract task ability (Υ), and (Υ) will become relevant to the similarly evaluated state of T.

3. (Sequencing of interaction) A given structure will become fully connected through the saliency and burden of proof processes. If actors leave or enter the situation afterwards, all parts of the structure previously completed will remain for later interactions.

4. (Forming aggregate expectations) If any actor p is connected to outcome states T+ and T− in a completed graph, then p's aggregated expectations e_p may be represented by:

$$e_p^+ \text{ for positive paths, } e_p^- \text{ for negative paths,}$$

where

$$e_p^+ = (1 - (1 - f(i)) \ldots (1 - f(n))), \text{ and}$$

$$e_p^- = -(1 - (1 - f(i)) \ldots (1 - f(n))), \text{ and}$$

$$e_p = e_p^+ + e_p^-.$$

5. (Basic expectation assumption) Given that p has formed aggregated expectation states for self and other, p's power and prestige position relative to o will be a direct function of p's expectation advantage over o.

In reading the assumptions, it is helpful to imagine a diagram containing the actors p and o, the T+ and T− outcome states, and the associated relevant ability states C*+ and C*−. Such a figure is reproduced as Fig. 1. Elements given by the structure of the situation are shown in white, with given connections between them. The elements and relations in the shaded portion of Figure 1 are those induced, produced by the burden of proof process of assumption 2. Essentially the theory describes a process of structure completion in which individuals see links which already exist (such as recognizing that possessing C*+ is relevant to attaining T+), and infer elements and relations that do not previously exist through the burden of proof process.

For example, if p is a man (D+) and o is a woman (D−), while o possesses very high mechanical skill (C+) and p possesses low mechanical skills (C−), assumption 1 tells us that both those characteristics will become salient in the situation because they discriminate the actors. Assumption 2 tells us that each status characteristic will induce various inferential characteristics, which also will become relevant to the C* and T elements of the structure, and that the actors will infer relevance bonds which connect themselves to the outcome states.

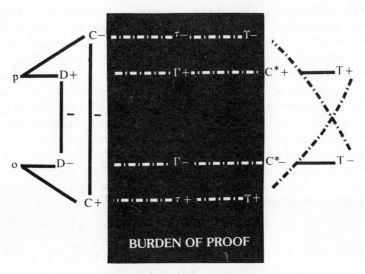

Figure 1   Given and inferred relations of status elements

We defer discussion of assumption 3 because it deals with complex situations where actors leave and enter an ongoing group. Without going into details, assumption 4 says that the aggregate expectations associated with each actor are: (1) a direct function of the number of paths connecting that actor to a particular state of T; (2) an inverse function of the length of those paths; and (3) a direct function of the consistency of value of that actor's status elements. Those claims are proved in Humphreys and Berger (1981).

Assumption 5 is the basic expectation assumption, which says that all features of inequality in the group, such as those enumerated earlier, are produced by the pattern of expectations associated with each group member.

In Figure 1, p has links to T+ through D+ and links to T− through C−, while o has the exact opposite pattern. Thus p's 'expectation advantage' over o is zero. If those actors recognized a third status characteristic which differentiated them, such as race, then the person with the higher state of race would have a positive expectation advantage over the other.

Some applications of the theory

Race as a status characteristic

Mixed-race interaction has long occupied the attention of sociologists and social psychologists. Often the goal has been to find interventions which can reduce or eliminate the 'interaction disability' faced by members of racial minority groups (such as American blacks) in interaction with members of the majority group (such as American whites).

Some early studies by Katz and associates (see Katz, 1970) identified the specific types of interaction disability, and demonstrate some difficulties in attempts to redress them. In biracial problem-solving groups (black and white) of college age men from varying geographical and SES backgrounds, whites dominated group interaction—they talked more, exerted more influence, and were perceived by both blacks and whites as having greater ability to solve the group's problems. Furthermore, several interventions designed to increase inter-racial harmony did not affect the interaction patterns. Other studies showed that neither intellectual ability (IQ) nor authoritarianism (F-scale) was a cause of the interaction inequality. Finally, interventions which gave blacks assertiveness training before the group session did increase their participation rates somewhat (though not up to the level of whites), but they also aroused considerable hostility and downgrading of blacks by whites.

To interpret those results, we begin by noting that race is a diffuse status characteristic in America, with white being the preferred state. Race functions through the burden of proof process to produce low expectations for blacks (held by both blacks and whites). These expectation differences produce differential participation rates and influence, both favoring whites. The assertiveness training may well have raised blacks' expectations for themselves, but whites' expectations were unaffected in those studies, so what ensued was a 'status struggle' comparable to that seen in some of Bales's groups. From the whites' point of view, the blacks behaved inappropriately—they were 'uppity'. From the blacks' point of view the whites, refusing to acknowledge their equal abilities, behaved inappropriately—they were racists.

Elizabeth G. Cohen and colleagues (see Cohen, 1982) explicitly adopted the perspective developed here, and built upon Katz's work in several ways. These investigators were successful in overcoming the effects of the race characteristic in groups of schoolchildren by 'adding on' additional status, high for blacks and low for whites. The technique was to give black boys special training at a separate task and to show that they were successful at it (C+), and then designate them 'teachers' and the white boys 'learners' while blacks show whites how to do a task. The relative superiority of blacks at C was emphasized by showing all boys a video tape of those training sessions, with an experimenter pointing out instances of blacks' superior knowledge.

Notice that this successful intervention requires demonstrating superiority of blacks over whites, and demonstrating it to both groups of boys, thus altering both sets of expectations in complementary fashion. Blacks must be superior at C to balance the effects of the social definition of race (D). Notice also that, as the theory predicts, all status information is combined in producing aggregate expectations. If race were eliminated as a factor here, Cohen's techniques would surely have produced strong interaction inequality favoring blacks.

The first direct test of the 'combining' aspects of the theory as presented above, which also tests the analyses of mixed-race interaction situations, was a laboratory experiment conducted by Webster and Driskell (1978). Subjects, white women volunteers who were students at the University of South Carolina, interacted with black women college students at a variety of tasks. Results showed that status generalization occurred on the basis of race when that was the only salient characteristic, but that addition of contradictory specific status characteristics (specific abilities at which the black women exceeded the white women) could overcome the effects of race. In a three-condition experiment, the amount of influence subjects accepted from their (black) partners was ordered as predicted by assumption 5 of the theory. In further analyses using assumption 4 to predict exact values for the influence measure, all observed and predicted values were within 1% of each other. This experiment provides confirmation of the process of status generalization as described, support for the intervention techniques developed with the guidance of the theory, and evidence for the exact combining function of assumption 4 which describes in detail how status information is processed in forming performance expectations.

Sex as a status characteristic

Important as it is, race is only one of the status characteristics which affect people's lives. Another is sex. In a large number of cases, the interaction disability faced by women in mixed-sex groups is similar to that faced by members of racial minority groups in mixed-race groups.

Meeker and O'Neill (1977) reviewed a large number of studies of mixed-sex task-oriented groups. Their main concern was to assess the relative merits of two differing explanations for sex differences in interaction styles. The first explanation is the more familiar one to many people; we will call this the sex role socialization approach. Essentially this view says that men and women (or boys and girls) behave differently because they have been trained since early childhood to behave differently. Males are taught (rewarded) to be proactive, task oriented, rational, logical, and assertive. Females are taught to be reactive, social–emotional, and passive.

But an alternative explanation, status characteristics/expectation states, says that all the behaviors above are in the repertoire of almost all humans. When a person finds himself or herself in a social situation of low relative status (compared to others in that situation), he or she activates the reactive, passive, social–emotional aspects of the repertoire. When the same person is in a position of high relative status, he or she activates the proactive, assertive, task-oriented aspects of the repertoire. Thus, this second line of explanation says that it is the expectation states, produced by status differences, which account for most of the interaction differences between men and women in task-oriented groups.

Meeker and O'Neill conclude from their review of studies that in many cases, the evidence favors an interpretation that sex differences in behavior are the result of the individual's relative status in a particular situation, rather than a learned, trans-situational interaction style. Particularly persuasive was a study by Lockheed and Hall (1976) which found, in mixed-sex groups of high school students, girls who previously had been members of all-female groups and had experience of being high interactors, proactive, task oriented, etc., were more likely to act in the same manner among boys than girls who had not had such experiences. But note also that those girls, who had been dominant in the all-female groups, were most likely to occupy the number 2 position in mixed-sex groups, with a boy in the number 1 position. Again, this shows the situationality of relative status positions.

In terms of interventions to reduce women's interaction disabilities, the status/expectation approach offers considerably more hope than the sex role socialization approach. If the interaction problems women face really are the result of lifetime socialization, then the treatment required is a long-term changing of the child rearing patterns of hundreds of millions of people. But if it is a status characteristic problem, then relatively quick treatments of the sort developed for mixed-race interaction should be effective.

Meeker and O'Neill suggested that women who would be dominant in mixed-sex groups face an additional problem not faced by men; namely, that they must take steps to defuse the potential status struggle which could be activated if they simply claim competence and act assertively (comparable to what Katz found in mixed-race groups). An ingenious experiment by Ridgeway (1982) confirms that suggestion. Ridgeway conducted mixed-sex groups of college students, with a pre-instructed confederate in each one. The confederate was instructed to act in one of two ways: (1) to say, in effect, 'I know how to do this sort of problem, and I don't really care whether the rest of you want to use my ideas or not;' or (2) to say 'I really care about helping this group, and I have some ideas which I think may do some good in helping us all.' The first interaction style was very effective for male confederates; it virtually guaranteed they would dominate all aspects of group discussion. But when female confederates tried it, the other group members quickly acted to consign them to the bottom position in their groups.

On the other hand, strategy (2) was a highly successful one for women. In mixed-sex groups where women first proclaimed their loyalty and commitment to the group, and then displayed their knowledge, they attained either the top or the second position in their group's power and prestige structures. Thus it appears true that women have to do something—in this case, to profess their modesty and desire to cooperate—in addition to revealing their expertise. A skillful man is seen as 'helpful, valuable;' a skillful woman, unless she takes steps to defuse the men's status anxiety, risks being seen as 'pushy.' Notice that the techniques Ridgeway developed allow women to overcome the effects of the sex characteristic without treating the expectations men hold for women. Unlike earlier intervention strategies (for example, those developed by E. G. Cohen), this one does not depend upon first changing the status generalization men are likely to do when they interact with women.

An intervention study by Pugh and Wahrman (1982) shows that demonstrations of ability need not be repeated for every different partner a person finds herself or himself with. Rather, a woman who has once experienced superiority to men on some status dimension will retain a memory of that experience in later interactions with other men. That persistence of previous status structures is predicted by assumption 3 of the theory, and gives important leads for intervention strategies.

Lockheed (1983) reviewed many studies bearing upon interaction styles of males and females in mixed-sex groups, and found some clear patterns in the results. Even with wide variety of subject populations, specific settings, and types of group tasks, the types of status generalization we have already seen are pervasive. When there is no evidence about specific competences (C's) of any of the group members, male dominance of the groups—which is based upon expectations produced by the D—always appears. When there is evidence of male–female *equality* on one or two C's, then female dominance of the group appears in a significant minority—about 40%—of the groups. When there is evidence of female *superiority* on one or two C's, female dominance appears in the majority—about 75%—of the groups. Notice that this is just the pattern of results we would expect from status generalization which is based upon the cultural definition of male as the preferred state of sex, and a process which combines all available status information in producing aggregate expectations.

Summary and conclusions

The theory of status generalization is intended to provide a way to understand status-related phenomena in a very wide range of situations. It shows how and why a number of cases of inequality in face-to-face interaction are produced as actors 'import' their external status characteristics into problem-solving groups. Thus, a structural feature of a culture—that status characteristics are differentially evaluated and carry performance connotations—is linked to specific task expectations through a social psychological process—burden of proof—and affects the structure of small groups and the behavior of individuals within them.

An important feature of this theoretical approach is its abstract nature, the search for similarities between status characteristics which differ in their concrete manifestations. This contrasts sharply with older views of status characteristics such as race and sex, which have focused on their unique features (thus, giving rise to distinctive bodies of literature on race relations and sex roles, for instance). We do not claim that the *only* important thing about, say, race or sex is that it is a diffuse status characteristic. We do claim that by conceptualizing them this way we can use the theory to understand certain widely recognized problems, and also to guide interventions to change certain of those consequences which are undesirable.

References

Bales, Robert Freed (1970). *Personality and Interpersonal Behavior*, Holt, Rinehart and Winston, New York.

Berger, J. (1958). 'Relations between performance, rewards, and action-opportunities in small groups,' Unpublished Ph.D. dissertation. Harvard University, Cambridge, Mass.

Berger, J., Cohen, B. P., and Zelditch, Jr, M. (1966). 'Status characteristics and expectation states,' in J. Berger, M. Zelditch, Jr, and B. Anderson (eds.), *Sociological Theories in Progress*, 1, pp. 29–46, Houghton Mifflin Co., Boston, Mass.

Berger, J., Fisek, M. H., Norman, R. Z., and Zelditch, Jr, M. (1977). *Status Characteristics and Social Interaction: An Expectation States Approach*, Elsevier, New York.

Cohen, E. G. (1982). 'Expectation states and interracial interaction in school settings,' *Annual Review of Sociology*, 8, 209–235.

Hughes, E. C. (1945). 'Dilemmas and contradictions of status,' *American Journal of Sociology*, 50, 353–359.

Humphreys, P., and Berger, J. (1981). 'Theoretical consequences of the status characteristics formulation,' *American Journal of Sociology*, 86, 953–983.

Katz, I. (1970). 'Experimental studies in Negro–white relationships,' in L. Berkowitz (ed.), *Advances in Experimental Social Psychology*, 5, 71–117, Academic Press, New York.

Lockheed, M. E. (1983). 'Sex and Social Influence: A Review,' in J. Berger and M. Zelditch, Jr, (eds.), *Status, Attributions and Rewards*, Jossey-Bass, San Francisco.

Lockheed, M. E., and Hall, K. (1976). 'Conceptualizing sex as a status characteristic: Applications to leadership training strategies,' *Journal of Social Issues*, 32(3), 111–124.

Meeker, B. F., and Weitzel-O'Neill, P. A. (1977). 'Sex roles and interpersonal behavior in task-oriented groups,' *American Sociological Review*, 43, 91–105.

Pugh, M. D., and Wahrman, R. (1983). 'Neutralizing sexism in mixed-sex groups: Do women have to be better than men?' *American Journal of Sociology*, 88, 4.

Ridgeway, C. (1982). 'Status in groups: The importance of motivation,' *American Sociological Review*, 47, 76–88.

Strodtbeck, F. L., and Mann, R. D. (1956). 'Sex role differentiation in jury deliberation,' *Sociometry*, 19, 3–11.

Webster, Jr, M., and Driskell, Jr, J. E. (1978). 'Status generalization: A review and some new data,' *American Sociological Review*, 43, 220–236.

Small Groups and Social Interaction, Volume 1
Edited by H. H. Blumberg, P. Hare, V. Kent and M. Davies
© 1983 John Wiley & Sons Ltd

2.2   Sex Differences and Decision Making in Juries

Charlan Nemeth   *University of California, Berkeley*

The history of trial by jury is difficult to chronicle since it has been with us in various forms over the centuries, finding expression in Greek and Roman law, tribal Germanic justice, practices under the Carolingian kings, etc. However, the form of trial by jury which bears most resemblance to that practiced in both England and the United States is generally traced to the reign of Henry II during the twelfth century. (See Cornish, 1968; Holdsworth, 1938; Howe, 1939; Nemeth, 1981; Pope, 1961.)

Throughout the history of trial by jury, there has often been a tension between wanting representation of the community and also wanting people relatively well educated and capable of 'the onerous duties of jury service.' (Cornish, 1968, p. 25.) The concern over competence of laymen to render just decisions to complex issues has been frequently voiced as a criticism of trial by jury. Thus, there have always been qualifications for jury service.

The question then becomes: 'Who is qualified to serve?' Male property holders seem to be the favored category, this qualification being found in most historical antecedents of trial by jury. Pope (1961) argues that 'every historical experiment which foreshadowed the modern jury required jurors to possess certain minimum qualifications [and from] the beginning, jurors had to be freemen, had to own property and had to come from the vicinity of the dispute' (p. 437). Until this century, both England and the United States barred women from jury service and until quite recently, England still had a property qualification for service.

In the United States, some states gave women the right to serve on juries when they were given the right to vote. Other states, however, still barred women from jury service. The battle against such discrimination became more difficult since the courts did not see fit to interpret the 14th Amendment of the Constitution as prohibiting the exclusion of women. Thus, it was a state-by-state battle and, as recently as the mid-1960s, four states still barred women from jury service. Today, women are not specifically barred from service in either England or the United States but both countries still allow excuses from service based on such sex-linked reasons as care for children or the elderly. As a result, our juries are not representative with regard to sex (or to other categories as well). Most studies on the composition of juries have found women to be under-represented (Levine and Schweber-Koren, 1976; Simon, 1975; Mills, 1969; Alker and Barnard, 1978). The picture that is painted from these studies is that the jury represents middle America. The groups that are under-represented tend to be black, female, both lower and upper class, both lowly and highly educated, both very young and very old (see Alker and Barnard, 1978; Nemeth, 1981). In England, the picture is very similar. Lord Devlin described juries there as 'male, middle aged, middle minded and middle class' (Pope, 1961, footnote 10).

The courts in recent years have been responsive to discrimination against women on juries. However, many opinions have been revealing about the images and stereotypes that are presumed of female jurors. In 1961, the court in *Hoyt* v. *Florida* ruled that requiring registration by women before they would be selected for jury service (while no such registration was required for men) was constitutional because it was based on a reasonable classification.

> Despite the enlightened emancipation of women from the restrictions and protections of bygone years, and their entry into many parts of community life formerly considered to be reserved to men, woman is still regarded as the center of home and family life. We cannot say that it is constitutionally impermissible for a State, acting in pursuit of the general welfare, to conclude that a woman should be relieved from the civic duty of jury service unless she herself determines that such service is consistent with her own special responsibilities. (*Hoyt* v. *Florida*, pp. 61–62)

It should be mentioned, however, that more recent decisions have ruled that women may not be systematically excluded (e.g. *Taylor* v. *Louisiana*, 1975; *Duren* v. *Missouri*, 1979.)

The notion that women are not capable of the onerous duties of jury service goes hand in hand with the more chivalrous phrasing and protectionism illustrated by the Hoyt court and the folklore of most lawyers. The persistent portrayal of female jurors by lawyers is that they are emotional, submissive, passive, and envious (Appleman, 1952; Darrow, 1936; Goldstein, 1935).

Such portrayals fit even further with the popular stereotypes of women held by both males and females over the years. The stereotype of males, as found by Bardwick and Douvan (1971) is one of aggressiveness, competitiveness, task orientation, independence, objectivity, and stoicism. Females, on the other hand, are seen as passive, interpersonally oriented, sensitive, submissive, and intuitive.

Such sex-linked traits are also found in the masculinity/femininity scales such as those developed by Spence and Helmreich (1972).

The notion that males are task oriented and active and females are interpersonally oriented and passive has also found expression in empirical work on juries by Strodtbeck and Mann (1956). In their study investigating deliberation processes in the 1950s, each comment was coded in terms of the Bales (1970) categories. Their analyses found males to be higher in categories 4 (giving suggestions), 5 (giving opinions), and 6 (giving information) whereas females were higher in categories 1 (showing friendliness, solidarity), 2 (tension release), and 3 (agreement). Both Strodtbeck *et al.* (1957) and James (1959) report that males talk more than do females, a practice that is linked to influence.

Such differences pose two theoretical issues. One is the way in which such differences are interpreted. The other is whether or not such differences found in the 1950s persist into the 1970s and 1980s, these two decades being quite important given the strength of the women's movement and the entry of many women into occupations and positions previously occupied almost solely by men. Let us first consider the interpretation aspect.

In keeping with popular stereotypes of males and females, Strodtbeck and Mann argue that the male usage of categories 4, 5, and 6, as found in their study, is a reflection of the fact that males proact, i.e. 'they initiate relatively long bursts of acts directed at the solution of the task problem' (p. 9). The female usage of categories 1, 2, and 3, they argue, means that females react 'to the contributions of others' (p. 9). Such a phrasing implies that males are task oriented and females are socio-emotionally oriented and it further suggests that it is the males who are contributing substantively to the solution of the issue at hand.

For those who have used Bales categories, it should be clear that such interpretations are open to criticism. In our studies (Nemeth, 1977; Nemeth *et al.*, 1976), we often found two individuals trading comments in category 5, for example. Rather than this being a substantive contribution to the solution of the jury's decision, it consisted of stubborn adherence to an opinion which took the form of 'I think he did do it' (i.e. commit the crime) v. 'I think he did not do it.' Further, the giving of information (category 6) can be a statement of the obvious. It also may have little to do with the discussion at hand.

Perhaps more significantly, we have been relatively unsuccessful as researchers in delineating influence based on 'right and reason' from that created by dominance, manipulation, and various machinations. Substantive contribution to a decision need not relate to amount of talking or to certain categories of talking. It may be a quiet though profound reflection at the appropriate time. Our coding systems do not reflect such subtleties and, as such, we are in danger of interpreting available categorizations in the light of our own stereotypes. Thus, the interpretation of sex differences in amount of talking or specific Bales categories must be made cautiously and need not support the prevailing stereotypes of women.

The other aspect which bears some attention is the historical one. In a very interesting review article, Eagly (1978) collated studies conducted before 1970 with those conducted since 1970 on male v. female influenceability, group conformity, and conformity without surveillance. Of the 62 studies conducted on 'influenceability,' Eagly reports that 7 of the 22 studies (32%) published before 1970 'yielded greater influenceability among females' (p. 96) whereas only 3 of the 40 studies (8%) 'published in the 1970s yielded this finding' (p. 96). The comparable percentages for group conformity studies is 43% showing more conformity by females in the period prior to 1970 whereas only 21% of the studies showed this finding during the 1970s. For the third category of studies, conformity without surveillance, she reports 22% of the pre-1970 studies showing more conformity by females while 0% of the 13 studies in the 1970s show such a finding.

Thus, there is evidence for less conformity and suggestibility by females in the post-1970 period than prior to this time. This may reflect a real change in conformity or it may result from a methodological awareness on the part of researchers. Such a methodological awareness occurred in the early 1970s with studies such as that conducted by Sistrunk and McDavid (1971) who suggested that earlier studies may have used stimulus materials relatively unfamiliar to women and, as such, biased the results in the direction of showing more conformity by females. In their study, Sistrunk and McDavid sorted a large number of items in terms of whether men were more familiar with them, whether females were more familiar with them, or whether both sexes were equally familiar. When both sexes were equally familiar with the topic, the sexes did not differ in the degree of conformity exhibited. When either sex was unfamiliar with the topic, that sex was more likely to conform.

Such historical changes can also be found with regard to sex differences in participation rates, Bales categories, and influence in face-to-face decision-making groups. Recently we (Nemeth et al., 1976) conducted two studies simulating juries in deliberation. These studies allowed for a comparison with the Strodtbeck and Mann (1956) data since we analyzed the deliberations in terms of Bales categories as well as a number of other dependent variables. In the first study, we used a controlled experimental design. Groups were constructed so that they would split 4 : 2 on a criminal case involving a charge of first degree murder. Seventeen groups had the majority (4) favoring 'guilty' with the minority (2) favoring 'not guilty.' Eleven groups had the reverse, i.e. the majority favored 'not guilty' while the minority favored 'guilty.' In each of these groups, at least two persons of each sex was present. There were 14 groups consisting of 4 males and 2 females, 12 groups consisting of 3 males and 3 females, and 2 groups consisting of 2 males and 4 females. These groups of 6 deliberated the same case, the facts for which were presented in written form.

Results from this study showed no sex differences in verdict. As can be seen in Table 1, however, males made more comments in general and specifically gave more suggestions (category 4), opinions (category 5), and information (category

Table 1 Mean frequency of Bales communication acts (Study 1 sample). Reprinted from Nemeth, Endicott, and Wachtler, 1976 (Table 3) by permission of the American Psychological Association

Category	Initiator		F	Target			F
	Male	Female	df = 1/144	Male	Female	Group	df = 2/144
1. Seems friendly	.328	.213	1.62	.268	.298	.246	.22
2. Dramatizes	.703	.576	.45	.485a	.420a	1.013b	4.75**
3. Agrees	2.512	2.787	.60	3.961a	2.909b	1.079c	21.94**
4. Gives suggestion	1.568a	1.034b	5.26**	1.093a	.628a	2.182b	15.24**
5. Gives opinion	13.779a	9.989b	5.81**	11.526a	8.203a	15.924b	8.03**
6. Gives information	9.718a	6.142b	8.73**	7.507a	5.627a	10.656b	5.88**
7. Asks for information	.811	.722	.62	.664a	.532a	1.104b	7.33**
8. Asks for opinion	1.227	1.085	.54	1.225	.884	1.359	1.86
9. Asks for suggestion	.053	.046	.13	.029a	.006a	.113b	7.86**
10. Disagrees	1.131	1.230	.05	1.857a	1.363a	.321b	6.59**
11. Shows tension	1.864	2.288	1.15	1.197a	.954a	4.077b	26.75**
12. Seems unfriendly	4.495	4.018	.23	6.860a	4.951a	.958b	13.25**
13. Total acts	38.189a	30.132b	3.02**	36.673a	26.776b	39.033a	2.64*

Note: Subscripts in common indicate that the means are not different at the .05 level (two-tailed test).
*$p < .10$; **$p < .06$.

6) than females. In contrast to studies of two decades ago, there were no sex differences in comments of friendliness (category 1), dramatization (category 2), or agreement (category 3). It is apparent from the table, however, that males are addressed more than females in practically every Bales category.

We also assessed the effectiveness of males v. females by comparing their initial judgment with the final verdict of their group. No sex differences were found with regard to effectiveness. In fact, the trend of the means was that females were more likely to prevail. Yet, the males were seen as significantly more 'intelligent, influential, independent, confident, rational, strong, courageous, aggressive [and] as more of a leader' (Nemeth et al., 1976, p. 299) than were females.

A second study was conducted in which trials were simulated in an actual courtroom. Rather than using written summaries of evidence as in Study 1, this study had live attorneys, a real judge and a 2 hour trial with witnesses, direct testimony, cross-examination, closing arguments, etc. Six mixed sex groups of 6 persons each participated in this study. Two groups deliberated a criminal case involving murder and the other 4 groups deliberated civil cases involving personal injury, contract default, and slander. Nineteen subjects were female and 17 were male. Two groups were composed of 4 females and 2 males; 3 groups were composed of 3 females and 3 males; 1 group was composed of 4 males and 2 females.

As with Study 1, there were no significant differences in initial verdict between the sexes. In contrast with Study 1 (see Table 2) there were no significant differences between males and females in giving comments in *any* Bales category nor even in total number of comments. Consistent with Study 1, the sexes did not differ in effectiveness. Yet, consistent with Study 1, males were seen as more 'influential, rational, strong, independent, confident, aggressive and as more of a leader than were females' (Nemeth et al., 1976, pp. 300–302).

One of the issues raised by these studies is the historical context in which sex differences occur. For example, we found little support for the notion that males give opinions and information while females give agreement and expressions of solidarity as argued in the 1950s. Study 1, i.e. when the materials were written and available to all, showed findings consistent with the former but no support for the latter findings. In Study 2, i.e. where the facts were in the minds and memories of the 'jurors,' no support was found for either set of generalizations. No significant sex differences were found on any Bales category. Such findings raise serious questions about the generalizations made by the Strodtbeck and Mann (1956) and Strodtbeck et al. (1957) studies of the 1950s. Further, as stated earlier, it is difficult to interpret the usage of the Bales categories. The fact that males gave more 'information' in Study 1 must be viewed in the context of the fact that such information was written and in front of each person. Thus, it became a statement of the obvious. Rather than this necessarily reflecting a substantive contribution, it may well reflect an assumption of leadership and an exhibition of self-confidence.

Recent authors have pointed to the tendency for males to manifest self confidence and assume a leadership role. Maier (1970), for example, reports that

Table 2 Mean frequency of Bales communications act (Study 2 sample). Reprinted from Nemeth, Endicott, and Wachtler, 1976 (Table 6) by permission of the American Psychological Association

	Initiator			Target			
	Male	Female	F	Male	Female	Group	F
1. Seems friendly	.086	.162	NS	.174	.156	.042	NS
2. Dramatizes	.765	.303	NS	.531	.329	.743	NS
3. Agrees	1.387	1.597	NS	2.285_a	1.942_a	$.250_b$	14.29 ($p < .01$)
4. Gives suggestion	1.101	.799	NS	.602	.881	1.368	NS
5. Gives opinion	5.117	3.835	NS	5.120	4.294	4.014	NS
6. Gives information	3.275	3.825	NS	3.918	3.691	3.042	NS
7. Asks for information	.345	.424	NS	.358	.316	.479	NS
8. Asks for opinion	.812	.715	NS	.884	.481	.924	NS
9. Asks for suggestion	.068	.009	NS	.083	.032	0.00	NS
10. Disagrees	.421	.539	NS	.655	.589	.194	NS
11. Shows tension	1.060	1.115	NS	.936	.566	1.771	NS
12. Seems unfriendly	2.049	1.711	NS	3.122_a	2.462_a	0.56_b	7.94 ($p < .01$)
13. Total acts	16.486	15.033	NS	18.668	15.729	12.882	NS

Note: Subscripts in common indicate that the means are not significantly different at the .05 level.

females are persuasive and tactful when given a solution to a problem. When no solution is given, they tend to exhibit less self-confidence and, thus, achieve less acceptance. Baird (1976) suggests that such sex differences in self-confidence may relate 'to stereotypical expectations of male and female differences in task abilities' (p. 191). In other words, females are not expected to do well and thus exhibit little self-confidence. This lack of self-confidence further fosters negative stereotypic expectations in problem-solving situations. When confidence is exhibited, however, females tend to be better received (Spence and Helmreich, 1971).

Thus, one can see the spiralling paralysis created by some of the sex-linked stereotypes. Rather than assuming that women *are* passive, emotional, submissive, etc., one might well see such perceptions as creating a self-fulfilling prophecy. If females fill the prophecy of such passivity, not only they but also the group in which they are participating lose. It appears that such a spiral is being broken in the last decade. This is perhaps a tribute to the women's movement. Our studies (Nemeth *et al.*, 1976) tend to show that females are not exhibiting such passivity, particularly when their recollections and judgments are needed. They are taking their place, along with males, for contributing opinions and information to the task at hand. However, the studies also indicate quite clearly that, even then females do not behave differently from males on any of the Bales categories, and even when they are as influential as males in having their opinions prevail, they are still seen in stereotypic terms. Though we could detect no behavioral differences, it was the males who were accorded the perceptions of being independent, active, persuasive, and leaders. This of course makes it difficult for females who still need to resist a self-fulfilling prophecy fostered by such stereotypic expectations. Yet, they appear to be resistant and, as such, to contribute quite similarly to males in jury deliberations. They have yet to achieve equal recognition for equal behaviors, however.

References

Alker, H. R. Jr, and Barnard, J. J. (1978). 'Procedural and social biases in the jury selection process,' *The Justice System Journal*, **3**, 220.

Appleman, J. A. (1952). *Successful Jury Trials: A Symposium*, The Bobbs-Merrill Co., Indianapolis.

Baird, J. E. Jr (1976). 'Sex differences in group communication: A review of relevant research,' *Quarterly Journal of Speech*, **62**, 179–192.

Bales, R. F. (1970). *Personality and Interpersonal Behavior*, Holt, Rinehart and Winston, New York.

Bardwick, J., and Douvan, E. (1971). 'Ambivalence: The socialization of women,' in V. Gornick and B. Moran (eds.), *Women in Sexist Society*, pp. 225–241, Basic Books, New York.

Cornish, W. R. (1968). *The Jury*, Allen Lane, (Penguin) London.

Darrow, C. (1936). 'Attorney for the defense,' *Esquire Magazine*, pp. 36–37, 211–213.

Duren v. *Missouri*, 439 US 357 (1979).

Eagly, A. H. (1978). 'Sex differences in Influenceability,' *Psychological Bulletin*, **85**, 86–116.

Goldstein, I. (1935). *Trial Technique*, Callaghan and Co., Chicago.

Holdsworth, Sir Wm. (1938). *A History of English Law*, **IX**, Little, Brown and Co., Boston.

Howe, M. D. (1939). 'Juries as judges of criminal law,' *Harvard Law Review*, **52**, 582–616.

Hoyt v. *Florida*, 368 US 57 (1961).

James, R. M. (1959). 'Status and competence of jurors,' *The American Journal of Sociology*, **64**, 563–570.

Levine, A. G., and Schweber-Koren, C. (1976). 'Jury selection in Erie County: Changing a sexist system,' *Law and Society Review*, **11**, 43–55.

Maier, N. (1970). 'Male vs female discussion leaders,' *Personnel Psychology*, **23**, 455–461.

Mills, E. S. (1969). 'A statistical profile of jurors in a United States district court,' *Law and the Social Order*, 329–339.

Nemeth, C. J. (1977). 'Interactions between jurors as a function of majority vs unanimity decision rules,' *Journal of Applied Social Psychology*, **7**, 38–56.

Nemeth, C. J. (1981). 'Jury trials,' in L. Berkowitz (ed.), *Advances in Experimental Social Psychology*, Vol. 13, Academic Press, New York.

Nemeth, C. J., Endicott, J., and Wachtler, J. (1976). 'From the '50s to the '70s: Women in jury deliberations,' *Sociometry*, **39**, 293–304.

Pope, J. (1961). 'The jury', *Texas Law Review*, **39**, 426–448.

Simon, C. K. (1975). 'The juror in New York City: Attitudes and experiences,' *American Bar Association Journal*, **61**, 207–211.

Sistrunk, F., and McDavid, J. (1971). 'Sex variable in conforming behavior,' *Journal of Personality and Social Psychology*, **17**, 200–207.

Spence, J. T., and Helmreich, R. (1971). 'Who likes competent women? Competence, sex-role congruence of interests and subjects attitudes toward women as determinants of interpersonal attraction,' *Journal of Applied Social Psychology*, **2**, 455–461.

Spence, J. T., and Helmreich, R. (1972). 'The attitudes toward women scale: An objective instrument to measure attitudes toward the rights and roles of women in contemporary society,' JSAS *Catalog of Selected Documents in Psychology*, **2**, 66.

Strodtbeck, F. L., James, R. M., and Hawkins, C. (1957). 'Social status in jury deliberations,' *American Sociological Review*, **22**, 713–719.

Strodtbeck, F. L., and Mann, R. D. (1956). 'Sex role differentiation in jury deliberations,' *Sociometry*, **19**, 3–11.

Taylor v. *Louisiana*, 419 US 522 (1975).

Small Groups and Social Interaction, Volume 1
Edited by H. H. Blumberg, P. Hare, V. Kent and M. Davies
© 1983 John Wiley & Sons Ltd

2.3   Personality Factors in Small Group Functioning[1]

Joel Aronoff, Lawrence A. Messé   *Michigan State University*

and

John P. Wilson   *Cleveland State University*

Throughout the history of social psychology there has been extensive discussion of the role that personality factors play in determining complex social behavior. A half century of research on small group behavior has generated a consensus that both personality characteristics and conditions of the social context can influence social events (e.g. Endler and Magnusson, 1976; McGrath and Altman, 1966; Shaw, 1981). However, less agreement has evolved with regard to the relative impact that the two classes of variables have on interpersonal functioning. While some social psychologists have argued that situational factors are the most important, others have proposed models of social behavior that rest primarily on dimensions of personality (cf. Bales, 1970; Collins and Raven, 1969). Given that evidence can be cited to support both positions, it appears best to assume that each position is valid; the key issue, then, is to specify the conditions that moderate the relative strength of personality and contextual variables. Exploration of this issue calls for an integrative approach that identifies more precisely the relevant factors of each type that structure social events.

This paper summarizes two studies from a program of research that has adopted this more integrative approach in studying the relationship between individual motivation and social structure in task-oriented groups. In this research we have tried to clarify the relationship between personality variables and the degree of hierarchy in the social structure of a group—a topic that has been of great interest to social psychologists since the original work of Lewin and Lippitt (1938). Our assumption has been that individual motivation leads the members of a group to seek specific types of rewards from group processes and outcomes. Thus, individual motives determine the extent to which group members enjoy and work effectively under one type of social structure, or are frustrated and feel threatened by having to work under a different type of structure. In the absence of strong situational, task, or group pressures, motives should cause group members to structure their group in ways that are most compatible with the characteristics of the motives. In the presence of strong constraints from external factors, individual motives should lead to optimum functioning when these factors generate conditions that are congruent with the motives of the individuals who comprise the group; in contrast, external determinants of group functioning should lead to strong 'process losses' (as defined by Steiner, 1972) when these factors generate conditions that are incongruent with the motives of the group members.

Within this framework, we expected that two of the motives described by Maslow (1970), safety and esteem needs, should influence strongly the degree of hierarchy in the emergent social structure of a group, as well as mediate the effects of imposed social structures on the functioning of members in such groups. The constellation of motives that Maslow characterized as safety needs centers around the requirement for a predictable and orderly world. Individuals primarily concerned with safety needs feel insecure, incompetent, and dependent, and are uncertain of their ability to cope with social relationships, tasks, or personal feelings. Within a group setting these individuals should be motivated to evolve a hierarchical social structure in which the leadership functions tend to be concentrated in a few members who will take responsibility for them. The constellation of motives that Maslow characterized as esteem needs centers around the individual's strong concern to demonstrate his or her competence and achieve respect from others. Esteem-oriented persons should be motivated to use their participation in the group to demonstrate their competence to themselves and others, and thus not allow any group member to dominate their activities. Within a group setting, these individuals should develop a group in which all members share the leadership functions.

If different motivational orientations generate different emergent social structures, then it is reasonable to conclude that a hierarchical social structure is most compatible with safety orientation, since it should reduce role uncertainty, provide external direction, and decrease the level of risk and responsibility needed in performing the group's task. In contrast, an egalitarian social structure appears most compatible with esteem orientation, since it offers the opportunity for multiple inputs into the task and, thus, should provide greater opportunities for individual displays of competence. Steiner (1972) proposed that the actual productivity of a group is equal to potential productivity minus losses due to faulty group processes. The arguments cited above suggest that the degree of incongruence between motive and structure is one source of faulty group process and, thus, should lower group productivity.

Two experiments from our program demonstrate these relationships between personality and social structure. Experiment 1 examines the effect on emergent social structure of groups composed entirely of safety-oriented or esteem-oriented people in the absence of a strong (and restrictive) imposed social structure.

Experiment 2 examines the mediating role of these motives on the productivity of such groups when safety- and esteem-oriented members are required to work under a hierarchical or egalitarian social structure—in other words, to work under conditions that were either congruent or incongruent with the nature of members' predominant motivational orientation.

Experiment 1

Experiment 1 sought to extend and clarify results of two field studies (Aronoff, 1967, 1970) which found that safety-oriented persons worked in groups with hierarchical social structures while esteem-oriented people worked in groups with egalitarian social structures. While these studies provided preliminary evidence of the relationship between personality and social structure, continued investigation was necessary, since the direction of the effect could not be established clearly in that naturalistic setting.

In Experiment 1, we sought to examine in a quantitative manner motivational influences on those dimensions of social structure related to task-oriented behaviors. Social structure (the organization through which a group carries out its functions) can be defined operationally in terms of the distribution of task-oriented communicative acts across group members. Moreover, the social structure of groups can be ordered with respect to the degree to which they are hierarchical. At one extreme, in the egalitarian social structure, such acts are distributed equally. At the other extreme, in the most hierarchical social structure, one member emits all such acts.

The research used the categories of task-oriented acts first identified by Bales (1951), and later modified by Borgatta (1962): gives a procedural suggestion; suggests solution; gives opinion; gives orientation; draws attention, repeats, clarifies; and, asks for opinion. These categories were examined separately in order to measure more precisely the extent to which personality characteristics differentially influenced their expression across members. The behaviors of group members also were coded for the frequency of the remaining, non-task-oriented acts in order to separate the effect of personality on task-related behavior from that of activity level in general. We examined two types of experimental groups, one composed entirely of safety-oriented persons and the other composed entirely of esteem-oriented persons, and predicted that the distributions of task-oriented acts would be more hierarchical, as defined above, in safety-oriented groups than in esteem-oriented groups.

Method

Approximately 200 male subjects were recruited through an advertisement in the university newspaper and given a sentence completion test previously shown to distinguish reliably between safety- and esteem-oriented individuals (Aronoff,

1967, 1970). Based on responses to this test, 25 high-safety and 25 high-esteem subjects were selected and scheduled to comprise a set of five-man groups, with each group composed only of subjects who were strongly concerned with one motive. Thus, there were five groups of each type.

The experiment was conducted in a room that was equipped with video- and audio-equipment which permitted recording of the entire session. When the five subjects appeared for the experiment they were brought to the room and seated in a semicircle at a round table facing the remote-controlled camera. Group members were asked to work on two major tasks during the 2 hour session. These sessions provided the opportunity to observe and record a number of types of activity: independent work; group discussion; gross physical activity; and social, as well as task-oriented, behavior. More specifically, subjects were asked to work through a sequence of eight tasks: (a) preliminary behavior (e.g., filling out tax forms and reading instructions); (b) work on individual plans for designing a living–learning dormitory; (c) discussion of the individual plans and reaching a common solution; (d) drawing the group's plan; (e) coffee break; (f) work on individual plans for designing a community; (g) discussion of individual plans and reaching a common solution; and (h) drawing the group's plan.

The videotapes made of each 2 hour session provided the basis for the measurement of group social structure. Two coders, unaware of the nature of the study, were trained in the use of Interaction Process Scores (IPS) (Borgatta, 1962). They were then instructed to observe the videotapes of all 10 groups and code the interaction for the frequency of appearance of each of the seven categories of task-oriented acts listed in Table 1. Raters also coded the frequency of non-task-

Table 1   Mean deviation scores for safety- and esteem-oriented groups

	Group	
IPS Category	Safety-oriented	Esteem-oriented
Task-oriented acts		
Gives procedural suggestion	.33	.20**
Suggests solution	.29	.24
Gives opinion	.30	.17***
Gives orientation	.30	.25*
Draws attention	.34	.25*
Integrates past communication	.34	.21**
Asks for opinion	.35	.31
Residual non-task-oriented acts	.28	.26

*p < .10
**p < .05
***p < .01

oriented behaviors in the remaining IPS categories to establish that the results reported below were not due simply to differential amounts of activity.

Results

The proportion of each member's contribution to his group's total score for a task-oriented category was tabulated for each of the eight task segments. Then, for each group member, the mean proportion over the eight tasks was computed. The expected mean proportion if all members contributed equally to the total score (i.e. .20) was subtracted from each of these values, and the resultant deviation scores were summed across members, disregarding sign. Note that the more a given absolute deviation score approaches zero, the more the acts in that category are evenly distributed over the group's members. On the other hand, the greater this score, the more some members were differentially higher in the emission of these acts. Thus, the greater the score, the more the group had a hierarchical social structure.

Table 1 presents the means of these deviation scores for each type of group for the seven task-oriented and the residual non-task-oriented categories. Three differences between safety groups and esteem groups—for the acts of 'gives procedural suggestion', 'gives opinion', and 'integrates past communications'—were statistically significant, and two differences were marginally significant—for 'gives orientation' and 'draws attention'. The difference between types of groups on the distribution of non-task-oriented behavior, as expected, did not approach significance. Thus, safety-oriented groups had a more hierarchical task structure than did esteem-oriented groups. More generally, these results support the position that individual motivation influences the development of group structure, at least under fairly non-restrictive conditions.

Experiment 2

If the interactive effects of personality factors and properties of group structure can be conceptualized as being a function of the degree of congruence between these two types of variables, then such interaction effects should appear when the products of these groups are examined. Experiment 2 used the relationships between structural and motivational states found in Experiment 1 to examine the hypothesis that the degree of congruence between imposed social structures and members' motivational characteristics affects the productivity of the group.

In Experiment 2, homogeneous three-man groups of safety- or esteem-oriented persons were formed and subjected to an experimental manipulation that had them work within either hierarchical or egalitarian social structures. It was predicted that neither motive nor structure alone would control task productivity; instead, there would be an interaction between motive and social structure, with lower group productivity shown when the predominant motivational orientation of group members was incongruent with the imposed group structure.

Method

Again, male subjects were recruited through an advertisement in the university newspaper and given the same sentence completion test of motive orientation that was used in Experiment 1. Based on scores on this measure, 72 subjects, 36 who were strongly safety-oriented and 36 who were strongly esteem-oriented, were selected to participate in the study. Subjects were studied in 24 three-man groups that were homogeneous with regard to motivational orientation (either safety or esteem). There were 12 groups of each motivational orientation, with 6 groups assigned to work under a hierarchical social structure and 6 groups to work under an egalitarian social structure. Thus, examination of these independent variables required a factorial design whose dimensions were 2 (motivational orientation: safety or esteem) × 2 (type of social structure imposed: hierarchical or egalitarian).

The task that subjects were asked to perform was the construction of a model of a building. Each group was given an $8\frac{1}{2}$ × 11 inch photograph of a modern-style office building and told to study it in detail. Their job was to work as a team to construct in 1 hour as much as possible of a model of the building that was pictured in the photograph. Materials for the model were arranged on a side table. These materials consisted of about 1,000 small interlocking pieces of plastic; white and clear-colored blocks, doors, windows, etc.

Group structure was manipulated through instructions to the group. For half of the groups (the hierarchical condition), members were told that, based upon the results of the assessment interview, it was best for one of them (a subject who, in fact, had been chosen at random) to assume the role of leader and take command of the group. The other groups (the egalitarian condition) were told that, based upon their interviews, it would be best to share equally the leaders's role by directing each other's work equally and making sure that no one 'took over' the group.[2]

The subjects who comprised a work group were randomly seated around three sides of a rectangular table. The experimenter then explained the nature of the task to the subjects and informed them of the social structure under which they were to work. Subjects were told to look over the photograph carefully, discuss their ideas for about 10 minutes, and then spend the remainder of the hour actually constructing the model. The experimenter then left the room and did not return until 60 minutes had expired.

Results

Experiment 2 tested the hypothesis that congruence between social structure and member motivation positively affects group productivity. This prediction was

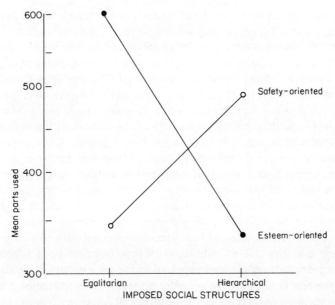

Figure 1   Group productivity as a function of group structure
and members' psychological motivation

tested through a 2 × 2 (Motivation × Social Structure) analysis of variance of the
number of parts used in completing the group's task, a measure of productivity
that is similar to those used in much research of this type (cf. Steiner, 1972). The
results of this analysis indicated that, as expected, neither motive nor structure
alone affected the productivity of the group; rather, only the Motivation ×
Structure interaction was significant ($F = 5.68$, $p < .05$.). Figure 1, which displays
the cell means that underlie this effect, indicates (and individual comparisons confirmed) that differences were as predicted: groups with egalitarian social
structures were significantly ($p < .05$) more productive when their members were
esteem-oriented; conversely, groups with hierarchical structures tended ($p < .10$)
to produce more when their members were safety-oriented.

Discussion

The results of the experiments presented in this paper support the view that
both personality and situational factors must be considered in developing a comprehensive model of small group behavior. These studies were focused on specific
questions—i.e. how motivation can affect emergent social structure and how
motive–structure congruence can affect productivity—and do not address many

other important issues that are related to the more complex model that we are advocating.

However, additional results from other research bear on one of these issues, and are noted here briefly, in order to give a more full understanding of the basic dynamics involved in these particular experiments. The variables that determine the selection of the leader in these groups (especially the leader of safety-oriented groups) were not examined in Experiment 1. In a subsequent study (Messé *et al.*, 1972), we proposed that motivation moderates the salience of the various potential determinants of emergent roles in task-oriented groups. A group presents an array of potential cues to the individuals involved: personal attributes such as task competence, external attributes indicating level of status in larger organizations, as well as a variety of situational factors—the simplest of which is seating position. This study showed that safety-oriented individuals, influenced by their high levels of interpersonal insecurity, utilized attributes of external status in selecting their leader while esteem-oriented individuals, concerned with receiving recognition for their abilities, utilized indications of task competence in selecting their leader. Safety-oriented people also appeared to use the external situational factor of seating position in selecting their leader. A series of related studies in the areas of person perception (Assor, *et al.*, 1981), prosocial behavior (Wilson, 1976), and compliance in decision-making (Ward and Wilson, 1980) all showed the task-competence concerns of the esteem-oriented group member and the dependence of safety-oriented people on sets of external situational and member attributes of the group.

The history of mixed results on group phenomena seems to call for a more complex formulation of the variables that are hypothesized to influence social activity. Thus, there have been an increasing number of suggestions to focus investigations of many aspects of group performance on the joint influence of these several classes of variables. However, fairly complex models that have attempted to outline the relationships among variables considered significant in determining group performance (e.g. Collins and Raven, 1969) have explicitly excluded personality factors. Yet, these models have distinguished between a number of different potential sources of rewards—for example, those that can be gained from the task and those that are generated by interpersonal relations—and thus indirectly introduce personality considerations. All rewards are not alike, and so directing attention to the different rewards gained from types of member behavior, modes of group process, and group outcomes seems to imply that personal characteristics of group members underly and mediate these possible outcomes.

The more complex framework for the study of groups, which is advocated here and elsewhere, likely will lead to the discovery of a variety of interactive mechanisms, of which the present characteristic is but one. It is likely that through the discovery of the array of such specific mechanisms, and the nature of their interrelations, that a highly integrated theory of group functioning may come to be realized.

Notes

1. The research summarized in this chapter was published originally as two papers, Aronoff and Messé (1971) 'Motivational determinants of small-group structure,' *Journal of Personality and Social Psychology*, **17**, 319–324, and Wilson, Aronoff, and Messé (1975). 'Social structure, member motivation and group productivity,' *Journal of Personality and Social Psychology*, **32**, 1094–1098. Copyright 1971 and 1975, respectively, by the American Psychological Association. Reprinted by permission. Space limitations preclude a full presentation of these studies. Readers should consult the original papers for methodological details, as well as additional results, manipulation checks and tests of alternative hypotheses. The research was supported by a National Science Foundation Institutional Grant for Science, the United States Air Force Office of Scientific Research (F 44620-69-C-0 114) and by National Institute of Mental Health Grant MH 22163.

2. A key manipulation check, presented fully in the original paper, needs to be mentioned here. The behavior of subjects in each group was scored, following all the procedures described in Experiment 1, to insure that the manipulation actually created groups with social structures as intended. This analysis on the deviation scores showed that groups in the hierarchical condition had significantly higher scores $(M = .45)$ than did those in the egalitarian condition $(M = .30)$.

References

Aronoff, J. (1967). *Psychological Needs and Cultural Systems*, Van Nostrand, Princeton, NJ.

Aronoff, J. (1970). 'Psychological needs as a determinant in the formation of economic structures,' *Human Relations*, **23**, 123–138.

Assor, A., Aronoff, J., and Messé, L. A. (1981). 'Attribute relevance as a moderator of the effects of motivation on impression formation', *Journal of Personality and Social Psychology*, **41**, 789–796.

Bales, R. F. (1950). *Interaction Process Analysis*, Addison-Wesley, Reading, Mass.

Bales, R. F. (1970). *Personality and Interpersonal Behavior*, Holt, Rinehart and Winston, New York.

Borgatta, E. F. (1962). 'A systematic study of Interaction Process Scores, peers and self-assessments, personality and other variables,' *Genetic Psychology Monographs*, **65**, 269–290.

Collins, B. E., and Raven, B. H. (1969). 'Group structure, attraction, coalitions, communication, and power', in G. Lindzey and E. Aronson (eds.), *Handbook of Social Psychology*, 2nd edn, Vol. IV, pp. 102–204, Addison-Wesley, Reading, Mass.

Endler, N. S., and Magnusson, D. (1976). *Interactional Psychology and Personality*, Hemisphere Publishing Co., Washington, DC.

Lewin, K., and Lippitt, R. (1938). 'An experimental approach to the study of autocracy and democracy: a preliminary note,' *Sociometry*, **1**, 292–300.

McGrath, J. E., and Altman, I. (1966). *Small Group Research*, Holt, Rinehart and Winston, New York.

Maslow, A. H. (1970). *Motivation and Personality*, 2nd edn, Harper & Row, New York.

Messé, L. A., Aronoff, J., and Wilson, J. P. (1972). 'Motivation as a mediator of the mechanisms underlying role assignment in small groups,' *Journal of Personality and Social Psychology*, **24**, 84–90.

Shaw, M. E. (1981). *Group Dynamics*, McGraw-Hill, New York.

Steiner, I. D. (1972). *Group Processes and Productivity*, Academic Press, New York.

Ward L., and Wilson, J. P. (1980). 'Motivation and moral development as determinants of behavioral acquiescence and moral action,' *Journal of Social Psychology*, **112**, 271–286.

Wilson, J. P. (1976). 'Motivation, modeling and altruism: a person × situation analysis,' *Journal of Personality and Social Psychology*, **34**, 1078–1086.

Small Groups and Social Interaction, Volume 1
Edited by H. H. Blumberg, A. P. Hare, V. Kent and M. Davies
© 1983 John Wiley & Sons Ltd

2.4   Group Composition[1]

Marvin E. Shaw   *University of Florida*

Groups are composed of individuals, each having his or her own unique characteristics and ways of behaving. Although these idiosyncratic factors influence group interaction independently of the actions of others in the group, the more important effects are those produced by the *relationships* among the characteristics of group members. We will be concerned, then, with the effects of each member's characteristics when considered in relation to the characteristics of other group members. Historically, group composition effects have been studied under at least three different labels: cohesiveness, compatibility, and homogeneity/heterogeneity of group membership. We will try to summarize the findings in each of these areas of research.

Group cohesiveness

Group cohesiveness refers to the degree to which the group 'hangs together' as a unit. Although cohesiveness has been defined and measured in many different ways, the definition proposed by Festinger is probably the most widely accepted one: group cohesiveness is 'the resultant of all the forces acting on the members to remain in the group' (Festinger, 1950, p. 274). Obviously, many 'forces' may act on an individual to influence him or her to remain in the group, but the force most commonly studied in research is interpersonal attraction. In this sense, cohesiveness may be represented by the number, strengths, and patterns of interpersonal attractions within the group. Research on the consequences of cohesiveness for group process has revealed several important effects. These will be presented and discussed in terms of plausible hypotheses, i.e. hypotheses that appear to be valid in view of the evidence currently available.

Hypothesis 1   *Intragroup communication is more extensive in high-cohesive than in low-cohesive groups*

It is not surprising that persons who like each other engage in more verbal interaction than persons who dislike each other. Research findings are consistent in showing that the amount of interaction is greater in groups composed of individuals who are highly attracted to the group than in groups composed of members who are less attracted to or are repelled by the group (Back, 1951; Lott and Lott, 1961).

Hypothesis 2   *Interactions are more positively oriented in high-cohesive than in low-cohesive groups*

Members of highly cohesive groups tend to be friendly and cooperative, and to engage in behaviors that facilitate group integration. Members of low-cohesive groups tend to function as individuals rather than as group members, and when they do enact group-oriented behaviors they tend to be aggressive and uncooperative (Back, 1951; Shaw and Shaw, 1962).

Hypothesis 3   *High-cohesive groups exert greater influence over their members than do low-cohesive groups*

Interpersonal attraction is a source of social power; consequently, members of high-cohesive groups may be expected to have more power over others in the group and therefore more influence over each other. Evidence supporting this expectation derives from several studies which show that: (a) members of high-cohesive groups respond to attempted influence by other group members more than members of low-cohesive groups (Berkowitz, 1954; Schachter *et al.*, 1951); (b) members of high-cohesive dyads change their opinions in the direction of the opinion of others more than do members of low-cohesive dyads (Back, 1951); and (c) members of high-cohesive groups conform to majority judgments more than members of low-cohesive groups (Bovard, 1951; Lott and Lott, 1961; Wyer, 1966). However, one study found that cohesive groups conform more than low-cohesive groups only when conformity facilitates group effectiveness (Sakurai, 1975).

Hypothesis 4   *High-cohesive groups are more effective than low-cohesive groups in achieving their respective goals*

The relationship between cohesiveness and group performance has been widely investigated, but the findings have been less than completely consistent. Laboratory studies have typically shown only small increments in favor of high-cohesive groups (Hoogstraten and Vorst, 1978; Schachter *et al.*, 1951) or no difference in the productivity of high- and low-cohesive groups (Berkowitz, 1954), whereas results of field studies generally show that high-cohesive groups are more effective than low-cohesive groups (Goodacre, 1951; Van Zelst, 1952a, b). Still other studies show that cohesiveness may be associated with either high or low productivity, depending on the extent to which group members have adopted high productivity as a goal for the group (Seashore, 1954; Shaw and Shaw, 1962). The best interpretation seems to be that high-cohesive groups are more effective than low-cohesive groups in achieving whatever goals group members have established or accepted for the group.

Hypothesis 5   *Members of high-cohesive groups are usually better satisfied with the group than are members of low-cohesive groups*

Members of high-cohesive groups are motivated to interact with others in the group and to achieve group goals; therefore, their efforts should increase group functioning and high member satisfaction. Research data from both field studies (Gross, 1954; Van Zelst, 1952b) and laboratory experiments (Exline, 1957) support the proposition that members of high-cohesive groups are better satisfied with the group and its products than members of low-cohesive groups.

Group compatibility

Group compatibility has been analyzed most completely by Schutz (1958). In his words 'compatibility is a property of a relation between two or more persons, between an individual and a role, or between an individual and a task situation that leads to mutual satisfaction of interpersonal needs and harmonious coexistence' (p. 105). Compatibility may be linked to cohesiveness, but not necessarily so. Typically, compatibility is estimated by means of the six interpersonal need scales developed by Schutz. These scales measure the extent to which a person desires to express inclusion, control, and affection needs toward others, and the degree to which the person wants others to express those needs in his or her presence. Two persons are compatible when the expressed behaviors of each are in accord with the wanted behaviors of the other. Theoretically, compatible groups should be more productive and their members better satisfied than incompatible groups. Research data generally support these expectations.

Hypothesis 6   *Compatible groups are more effective in achieving group goals than incompatible groups*

Although there have been some failures to find a significant difference between compatible and incompatible groups, the bulk of the evidence indicates that groups that are compatible with respect to interpersonal needs function more smoothly, devote less of their time to group maintenance, and are therefore more effective than incompatible groups (Reddy and Byrnes, 1972; Sapolsky, 1960; Schutz, 1958).

Hypothesis 7   *Members of compatible groups are better satisfied with the group than members of incompatible groups*

The studies cited to support hypothesis 6 also support hypothesis 7. Other studies indicate that members of incompatible groups experience greater anxiety and more general dissatisfaction with their group than members of compatible groups (Cohen, 1956; Fry, 1965; Smelser, 1961).

Homogeneity/heterogeneity

Group compositions investigated under the heading 'homogeneity/heterogeneity' differ from the types we have considered thus far in that the relation under consideration is similarity/dissimilarity. Again, homogeneity/heterogeneity may be linked to cohesiveness and/or compatibility, but these types of group composition are not necessarily correlated. For instance, persons who are similar with respect to amount of interaction or exchange that each desires are compatible, but persons who are dissimilar with respect to control needs (desires to control others or to be controlled by others) are also compatible.

Obviously, members of a group may be homogeneous or heterogeneous with respect to many different characteristics, and the degree to which group process is affected by this aspect of group composition may depend on the particular characteristic(s) being considered. The effects of homogeneity/heterogeneity have been investigated in at least the following areas: abilities, sex, race, and personality.

Abilities. Interest in ability grouping probably derived initially from educational concerns, revealed most clearly in the long-standing controversy about the merits of homogeneous ability grouping in the classroom. This controversy continues even today, although the evidence seems to support the proposition that students learn more in heterogeneous ability groups (Goldberg *et al.*, 1966). More carefully controlled research on small groups suggests the following hypothesis.

Hypothesis 8   *Other things being equal, groups composed of members having diverse abilities that are relevant to the task perform more effectively than groups composed of members having similar abilities*

Group performance usually calls for diverse activities, each of which requires specific abilities that are more likely to be found in heterogeneous ability groups.

Hypothesis 8 is generally supported by research data (Goldman, 1965; Laughlin et al., 1969).

Sex. Stereotypes concerning the characteristics and behavior of men and women suggest that sex composition should be an important determinant of group behavior, and the controversy over the Equal Rights Amendment provided an impetus for research in this area. Several studies support the following hypothesis.

Hypothesis 9 *The interaction styles of men and women are affected differently by the sex composition of the group*

Research data reveal that men are more personally oriented, address individuals more often (as opposed to group), and speak about self more frequently in mixed-sex than in same-sex groups, whereas women become less dominant in mixed-sex groups (Aries, 1976). It has also been found that same-sex and mixed-sex dyads are affected differently by social context (face-to-face v. apart) in bargaining situations (Vallacher et al., 1979). Mixed-sex dyads reached agreement more quickly when they bargained face-to-face than when they bargained apart, whereas same-sex groups were not affected by the social context. Presumably, members of mixed-sex groups are less certain about their partner's expected responses and need cues about the other person that can be derived from face-to-face interaction.

Hypothesis 10 *Mixed-sex groups are more effective than same-sex groups*

Direct evidence for this hypothesis derives from a study by Ruhe (1978). He attributed this difference in effectiveness to differences in the leader's behavior. In the same-sex groups, the amount of disagreement and antagonistic behavior displayed by the leader was inversely related to group effectiveness, whereas no such relationship was observed in the mixed-sex groups. This interpretation appears to be consistent with the finding that leaders of both sexes address more directive behavior toward members of their own sex (Eskilson and Wiley, 1976).

Hypothesis 11 *Group members conform more in mixed-sex than in same-sex groups*

Members of mixed-sex groups appear to be more concerned about interpersonal relations than the task, whereas members of same-sex groups are more concerned about the task. Since conformity usually means decreased accuracy with respect to the task, members of same-sex groups are less likely to conform to group pressure. Research data generally support the hypothesis (Reitan and Shaw, 1964), although there are some inconsistent findings (Tuddenham et al., 1958).

Race. The question of racial composition of groups has become more significant with the advent of desegregation and affirmative action, but there still are relatively few reliable data on its effects. However, the following hypothesis is plausible.

Hypothesis 12 *Racial heterogeneity elicits interpersonal tension which is reflected in the feelings and behaviors of group members*

Research findings indicate that in racially mixed groups blacks talk less than whites, they often are less assertive, reveal a greater expectancy of failure, and are sometimes less efficient than whites (Delbecq and Kaplan, 1968; Katz *et al.*, 1965; Lefcourt and Ladwig, 1965; Ruhe and Allen, 1977; Ruhe and Eatman, 1977). These behaviors may or may not affect group performance.

Personality. Although homogeneity/heterogeneity of group membership with respect to personality characteristics may be expected to have important consequences for group interaction, reliable research is very limited. However, available data support the following hypothesis.

Hypothesis 13 *Groups composed of members who are heterogeneous with respect to personality profiles perform more effectively than groups composed of members who are homogeneous with respect to personality profiles*

Two experiments involving a variety of tasks revealed that heterogeneous groups performed better, both quantitatively and qualitatively, than homogeneous groups, where homogeneity/heterogeneity was based on the Guilford–Zimmerman Temperament Survey (Hoffman, 1959; Hoffman and Maier, 1961).

References

Aries, E. (1976). 'Interaction patterns and themes of male, female, and mixed groups,' *Small Group Behavior*, **7**, 7–18.

Back, K. W. (1951). 'Influence through social communication,' *Journal of Abnormal and Social Psychology*, **46**, 9–23.

Berkowitz, L. (1954). 'Group standards, cohesiveness, and productivity,' *Human Relations*, **7**, 509–519.

Bovard, E. W. (1951). 'Group structure and perception,' *Journal of Abnormal and Social Psychology*, **46**, 398–405.

Cohen, A. R. (1956). 'Experimental effects of ego-defense preference on interpersonal relations', *Journal of Abnormal and Social Psychology*, **52**, 19–27.

Delbecq, A. L., and Kaplan, S. J. (1968). 'The myth of the indigenous community leader within the war on poverty,' *Academy of Management Journal*, **11**, 11–25.

Eskilson, A., and Wiley, M. G. (1976). 'Sex composition and leadership in small groups,' *Sociometry*, **39**, 183–194.

Exline, R. V. (1957). 'Group climate as a factor in the relevance and accuracy of social perception,' *Journal of Abnormal and Social Psychology*, **55**, 382–388.

Festinger, L. (1950). 'Informal social communication,' *Psychological Review*, **57**, 271–282.

Fry, C. L. (1965). 'Personality and acquisition factors in the development of coordination strategy,' *Journal of Personality and Social Psychology*, **2**, 403–407.

Goldberg, M. L., Passow, A. H., and Justman, J. (1966). *The Effects of Ability Grouping*, Teachers College Press, New York.

Goldman, M. (1965). 'A comparison of individual and group performance for varying combinations of initial ability,' *Journal of Personality and Social Psychology*, **1**, 210–216.

Goodacre, D. M., III (1951). 'The use of a sociometric test as a predictor of combat unit effectiveness,' *Sociometry*, **14**, 148–152.

Gross, E. (1954). 'Primary functions of the small group,' *American Journal of Sociology*, **60**, 24–30.

Hoffman, L. R. (1959). 'Homogeneity of member personality and its effect on group problem-solving,' *Journal of Abnormal and Social Psychology*, **58**, 27–32.

Hoffman, L. R., and Maier, N. R. F. (1961). 'Quality and acceptance of problem solutions by members of homogeneous and heterogeneous groups,' *Journal of Abnormal and Social Psychology*, **62**, 401–407.

Hoogstraten, J., and Vorst, H. C. M. (1978). 'Group cohesion, task performance, and the experimenter expectancy effect,' *Human Relations*, **31**, 939–956.

Katz, I., Roberts, S. O., and Robinson, J. M. (1965). 'Effects of difficulty, race of administrator, and instructions on Negro digit-symbol performance,' *Journal of Personality and Social Psychology*, **2**, 53–59.

Laughlin, P. R., Branch, L. G., and Johnson, H. H. (1969). 'Individual versus triadic performance on a unidimensional complementary task as a function of initial ability level,' *Journal of Personality and Social Psychology*, **12**, 144–150.

Lefcourt, H. M., and Ladwig, G. W. (1965). 'The effect of reference groups upon Negroes' task persistence in a biracial competitive game,' *Journal of Personality and Social Psychology*, **1**, 668–671.

Lott, A. J., and Lott, B. E. (1961). 'Group cohesiveness, communication level, and conformity,' *Journal of Abnormal and Social Psychology*, **62**, 408–412.

Reddy, W. B., and Byrnes, A. (1972). 'The effects of interpersonal group composition on the problem solving behavior of middle managers,' *Journal of Applied Psychology*, **56**, 516–517.

Reitan, H. T., and Shaw, M. E. (1964). 'Group membership, sex-composition of the group, and conformity behavior,' *Journal of Social Psychology*, **64**, 45–51.

Ruhe, J. A. (1978). 'Effect of leader sex and leader behavior on group problem-solving,' *Proceedings of the American Institute for Decision Sciences, Northeast Division*, May, pp. 123–127.

Ruhe, J. A. and Allen, W. R. (1977). 'Differences and similarities between black and white leaders,' *Proceedings of the American Institute for Decision Sciences, Northeast Division*, April, pp. 30–35.

Ruhe, J. A. and Eatman, J. (1977). 'Effects of racial composition on small work groups,' *Small Group Behavior*, **8**, 479–486.

Sakurai, M. M. (1975). 'Small group cohesiveness and detrimental conformity,' *Sociometry*, **38**, 340–357.

Sapolsky, A. (1960). 'Effect of interpersonal relationships upon verbal conditioning,' *Journal of Abnormal and Social Psychology*, **60**, 241–246.

Schachter, S., Ellertson, N., McBride D., and Gregory, D. (1951). 'An experimental study of cohesiveness and productivity,' *Human Relations*, **4**, 229–238.

Schutz, W. C. (1958). *FIRO: A three dimensional theory of interpersonal behavior*, Rinehart, New York.

Seashore, S. E. (1954). *Group cohesiveness in the industrial work group*, University of Michigan Press, Ann Arbor.

Shaw, M. E., and Shaw, L. M. (1962). 'Some effects of sociometric group upon learning in a second grade classroom,' *Journal of Social Psychology*, **57**, 453–458.

Smelser, W. T. (1961). 'Dominance as a factor in achievement and perception in cooperative problem solving interactions,' *Journal of Abnormal and Social Psychology*, **62**, 535–542.

Tuddenham, R. D., MacBridge, P., and Zahn, V. (1958). 'The influence of the sex composition of the group upon yielding to a distorted norm,' *Journal of Psychology*, **46**, 243–251.

Vallacher, R. R., Callahan-Levy, C. M., and Messé, L. A. (1979). 'Sex effects of bilateral bargaining as a function of interpersonal context,' *Personality and Social Psychology Bulletin*, **5**, 104–108.

Van Zelst, R. H. (1952a). 'Sociometrically selected work teams increase production,' *Personnel Psychology*, **5**, 175–186.

Van Zelst, R. H. (1952b). 'Validation of a sociometric regrouping procedure,' *Journal of Abnormal and Social Psychology*, **47**, 299–301.

Wyer, R. S., Jr (1966). 'Effects of incentive to perform well, group attraction, and group acceptance on conformity in a judgmental task,' *Journal of Personality and Social Psychology*, **4**, 21–26.

Note

1. A more extensive consideration of group composition effects may be found in M. E. Shaw (1981). *Group Dynamics*, 3rd edn, McGraw-Hill, New York.

3   Impressions of the Group

Small Groups and Social Interaction, Volume 1
Edited by H. H. Blumberg, A. P. Hare, V. Kent and M. Davies
© 1983 John Wiley & Sons Ltd

3.1 The Process of Stigmatization

Irwin Katz   *Graduate Center of The City University of New York*

There are many groups in the United States that are not fully accepted by the main society—e.g. blacks; former mental patients; the aged; persons with physical disabilities, deformities, and chronic diseases; behavioral deviants such as criminals, drug addicts, alcoholics, and prostitutes. Individuals in these categories are perceived by the majority as having attributes that do not accord with prevailing standards of the normal and good. They are often denigrated and avoided—openly in the case of known criminals and other transgressors, or covertly and even unconsciously, as seems to happen when the disdained person is an innocent victim of misfortune (e.g. a paraplegic).

To account for people's negative reactions to those who are different, social scientists have proposed a whole host of causal factors, some specific to particular minority groups and others more general in their application. What is presently lacking is a single overall perspective for viewing all of these factors in relation to one another. In the interest of such unification some writers (e.g. Goffmann, 1963) use the term *stigma* to denote the common aspect of all socially disqualifying attributes, however different they may be in other respects. But there is much vagueness in the way the term has been employed. To clarify the matter, I should like to examine the notion of *stigmatization* as a general process whereby those who do not possess a certain attribute denigrate individuals who do, and exercise various forms of discrimination against them. Goffman mentions this process, but does not attempt to describe it in detail. His discussion implies that the reaction of the majority group observer has two main components: (a) the perception of a negative characteristic and (b) the global disvaluation of the possessor. Logically speaking, there are three possible ways that the two elements, a and b, can be causally related to each other: a can be the cause of b, b can be the cause of a, and a and b can be causally independent. Each of these possibilities points to a particular theoretical view of the stigmatization process, for which there is a relevant empirical literature. Thus, the first suggests a negative-attribute model of stigmatization, the second a scapegoat model, and the third a labeling perspective. There is a certain amount of overlap among these notions, and one should not try to differentiate them too sharply. But I believe they can provide potentially useful guides in analyzing the stigmatization process as it operates in different situations. Each view will be discussed below.

Models of the stigmatization process

Attribute as sufficient cause

According to this model, certain negative qualities or traits have the power to discredit, in the eyes of others, the whole moral being of the possessor. The discrediting attribute could be any feature of the person's physical makeup, social behavior, or familial heritage that arouses in observers strong feelings of repugnance, disdain, fear, etc. It is assumed that certain behavioral characteristics (such as might be associated, e.g. with mental retardation or a career of criminal violence) are so central in most people's conceptions of personality, that attribute and possessor are seen essentially as one and the same. Presumably, this perceptual bonding can occur even when the offending trait is physical, and possession of it involuntary. Thus Wright (1960), Goffman (1963) and others have written about the secretly hostile and subordinating attitudes toward handicapped people that normals are revealed to have when interviewed in depth or covertly observed in mixed situations.

The attribute-as-sufficient-cause model also makes the assumption that basic cognitive–perceptual tendencies can strengthen the linkage between recognition of an aversive characteristic and rejection of the possessor. Heider's (1944) principles of naive perception are relevant. His notion of cognitive balance suggests that a stranger who displays a strongly negative attribute will tend to be seen as having other negative attributes as well. Allport (1954) invoked a similar principle when he stated that visible differences between people are 'almost always thought to be linked with deeper lying traits than is in fact the case.' Heider also proposes that things which always appear together tend to be perceived as causally related, from which it follows that normal observers might have a bias toward perceiving the involuntary possessor of a negative attribute (e.g. a permanent disability or chronic illness) as in some way to blame for having the characteristic.

A more extreme version of the attribute-as-cause model has been put forth by Freedman and Doob (1968). They maintain that if someone is different enough from others on any dimension, even one that is generally evaluated positively, he will be considered a deviant and rejected. The nature of the attribute determines how large a discrepancy from the norm will be required to produce stigmatization, but regardless of the particular way in which a person is different, stigmatization will result. Freedman and Doob did a series of experiments in which small groups of college or high school students were given ambiguous, ostensibly nonevaluative personality tests. In one part of the procedure, subjects were given feedback that their own scores were average, but that another person had scores which deviated markedly from the group means. When subjects were later put to work at a group task it was found that the partners with unusual personality scores were discriminated against in the allotment of punishments (electric shocks) and rewards (monetary bonuses). This finding, while suggestive, does not un-equivocally support the notion that mere difference can cause stigmatization. Because there was no check on the subject's perception of the meaning of unusual test scores, the possibility remains that they were seen as being indicative of abnormality.

More recently, Tajfel and associates have shown that even minimal differences between people can give rise to discriminatory behavior, when the differences are used as a basis for categorization. In one study, Tajfel and Billig (1974) assigned schoolboys to two categories, according to how they responded to a seemingly trivial perceptual task. Each boy was told which group he was in, but he did not know who else was in his group and who was in the other group. Subjects then had to allot points worth money to their fellow subjects, knowing only their group membership. Most boys, it was found, awarded more money to anonymous ingroup members than to anonymous outgroup members, despite the fact that such responses had no utilitarian value for the boys themselves.

As yet, other measures of ingroup favoritism have not been taken, so that the generality of the effect is still in question. Further, it has recently been shown by Wilder (1978) that intergroup discrimination decreases when the outgroup is individuated by appearing to be in a state of disunity. Nonetheless, Tajfel and Billig's results are striking. The phenomenon apparently reflects the strength of a basic disposition, acquired early in life, to assign people to categories and then attach evaluative labels to groupings. In studies of young children's perceptions of foreign nations, Tajfel and Jahoda (1966) found that subjects could agree more about which countries they liked and disliked than about virtually any facts concerning the countries. That there is a fundamental human tendency to evaluate is supported by the extensive investigations of Osgood et al. (1957), who found that the categories used to classify objects or people have connotative meanings which are primarily evaluative in nature. Any classification label will elicit feelings that may be placed somewhere along a 'good–bad' or 'pleasant–unpleasant' dimension.

Another line of inquiry which is consistent with the mere difference hypothesis is associated with Hebb's (1949) proposition that discrepancies between expectation (i.e. adaptation level) and perception give rise to primary unlearned affect, the sign of which will depend upon the size of the discrepancy. Relatively small discrepancies from expectation are supposed to yield positive or pleasant affect, whereas large discrepancies are supposed to result in negative affect or unpleasantness. These predictions have been upheld for judgments of taste, temperature, saturation of colors, hue, area of the stimulus, sequence of stimulus, and other dimensions (reviewed by Cofer and Appley, 1964).

The scapegoat model

According to this conception, a defect may be ascribed to a group primarily as an expression of animosity arising from other causes. As the process is described by Campbell (1967), certain characteristics of the group seem to the observer to fully justify the hostility and rejection he shows it, when in fact the negative reaction came first, generated perhaps by real threat, by ethnocentrism, or by displacement. In the service of this hostility, various differences are opportunistically interpreted as despicable. Campbell discusses this type of causal misperception as it is manifested in cultural stereotypes. But the same point can be made with respect to the stigmatizing of noncultural groups within a society. Thus Ryan (1971) writes about the majority's tendency to assign traits of personal inadequacy to the poor, the black, the ill, the jobless, and other economically disadvantaged groups as a means of defending the prevailing belief that the American economic system is fair and adequate. He suggests that in order to reconcile self-interest with the promptings of humanitarian impulses, the majority are prone to perceive these victims of deprivation as special deviant cases—persons who for good reasons or bad are unable to adapt themselves to the system.

That people will often denigrate those for whose suffering they feel responsible has been demonstrated in several experiments in which subjects were induced to harm another person (cf. review by Berscheid and Walster, 1978). The usual interpretation of this finding is that the disparagement is an attempt on the part of the harm-doer to reduce moral discomfort by lowering the worth of the victim. Research by Lerner and associates (cf. Lerner, 1970) indicates that even passive observers of harm-doing may denigrate victims, presumably as a means of defending a belief in a just world.

Another type of evidence that is consistent with the scapegoat model, as here presented, comes from the experiments of Sherif and Sherif (1953) on competition-induced hostility between groups of boys: highly derogatory beliefs about the personal qualities of outgroup members emerged as a consequence, rather than cause, of rivalrous antipathy.

Research on displacement of aggression also provides some support for the scapegoat model. Experiments by Berkowitz and others (Berkowitz, 1962) indicate that members of groups for whom some dislike already exists tend to be preferred substitute-targets of frustration-induced hostility; further, the animosity can be manifested both through overt aggression and the attribution of negative characteristics to the stimulus person.

The labeling perspective

According to this model, deviation from a societal norm is perhaps a necessary, but not a sufficient, condition of stigmatization. It corresponds to a point of view (rooted in the symbolic interactionist tradition in sociology) which holds that individuals are disvalued and isolated less because they display attributes that violate accepted standards, than because the majority choose to regard these persons as deviant. Whether a given act or personal quality will be labeled by others as deviant will depend primarily upon contextual variables—particularly, the power or resources of the individual, the social distance between the labeler and the labelee, the tolerance level in the community, and the visibility of the deviant behavior or characteristic (cf. Gove, 1975). This perspective, as developed by Lemert (1951), Becker (1963), Kitsuse (1962), Schur (1965), and others, has been a major influence in sociological discussions of social marginality since the 1950s. (Of special interest has been the question of how being typed pejoratively affects the behavior of those so typed; for example, Szasz (1960), Sarbin (1972), Goffman (1961), and Scheff (1966) have argued that much of the symptomatic behavior shown by mental patients is actually a form of adjustment to being classified and treated as mentally ill.)

Some advocates of the labeling approach limit its application to social deviance—i.e. to acts of law- or rule-breaking such as are classified under delinquency, criminality, addiction, homosexuality, mental illness, etc.—whereas other theorists include such groups as blacks and cripples, whose deviation from societal standards may not involve rule-breaking behavior. How appropriate, then, is the labeling conception with respect to each of Goffman's (1963) three kinds of stigma—bodily, characterological, and tribal? First, the labeling interpretation would seem to be more apt in the case of characterological than of physical defects, because the former tend to be more ambiguous. An ugly facial scar or the bizarre bodily movements of cerebral palsy can function as highly aversive visual stimuli, dominating the perceptual field of the observer. By contrast, a moral flaw may exist only as an idea, an inference drawn from the discrepancy between an imputed act and a societal standard of conduct. Moreover, whether a transgression has occurred at all is often difficult to establish; as Becker (1963) has noted, norms tend to be very broad abstractions which are difficult to apply to specific situations involving real actors. Not only do norms tend to be ambiguous, but there may be several conflicting norms that seem to be relevant to a given situation. Hence, Becker concludes that the characteristics of the audience will be more important than the behavior of the individual in determining whether the latter will be typed as a deviant. It would seem, then, that the labeling perspective might be more useful for understanding characterological than bodily stigmas, because of the greater ambiguity and lesser salience, on average, of moral attributes as compared with physical ones.

Next, the labeling notion would seem to have a different meaning in the case of

Goffman's tribal stigma, particularly of the racial variety, than it has with respect to stigmas of the bodily or characterological variety. For characterological deviance (e.g. criminality) the labeling issue is whether or not the actor will be so typed by society. To some extent the same question will arise for the person who is injured or ill. (Scott, 1969, has described the social and institutional factors that can determine whether one who is visually impaired will be categorized as blind or sighted.) With regard to blacks, however, the usual issue in this country is not whether a person will be assigned to that racial group, but whether being perceived as black increases one's chances of being assigned a range of other labels, such as criminal, mentally retarded, unemployable, etc.

The labeling position has been criticized for neglecting the functional role of norms in a society, which dictates that certain personal attributes and behaviors must *a priori* be typed as deviant, regardless of who displays them, if the society is to remain stable. Indeed, sociological research to date does not provide unequivocal support for labeling hypotheses. A book edited by Gove (1975) reviews evidence on the influence of demographic characteristics like race, sex, marital status, and socio-economic status on the likelihood of an individual being given various deviant labels, when the nature of the deviating behavior or characteristic is systematically controlled. Also considered is the question of whether labeling causes or strengthens deviance. On the whole, the findings on both questions prove to be inconclusive for all of the categories reviewed. But it should be noted that most of the research dealt with legal and quasi-legal processes of classification as they occur in courts, hospitals, social agencies, and the like. The labeling perspective may be more relevant for informal stigmatization processes.

Some implications

To summarize, the first (attribute as cause) model of stigmatization that was presented holds that hostile rejection of persons who have a particular characteristic results when the attribute has a strongly negative valuation. Next, the scapegoat notion suggests a process whereby hostility—resulting from threat, displacement, etc.—occurs prior to, and is the cause of, the perception of severe defects in members of a given social category. According to the third (labeling) perspective, possession of a strongly negative quality may be a necessary condition of being rejected, but it is not a sufficient one; contextual variables play an essential role.

As mentioned earlier, there is a certain amount of overlap among these notions, and one should not try to differentiate them too sharply. They should be regarded as potentially useful guides in analyzing the stigmatization process as it operates in different situations. Further, they are not mutually exclusive in application to a particular group. Two or perhaps all three of the causal models described above may be relevant to the majority's treatment of a particular group. Blacks, for example, may have physical traits that tend to be 'inherently' aversive to whites (cf.

Gergen's, 1967, discussion of skin color and race relations), yet there is ample evidence that the relatively low power position of blacks in this society makes them prime targets for pejorative labeling by the dominant racial group, labeling that may be an expression of hostility induced by threat factors.

Thus the likelihood is that there is no single causal process underlying stigmatization phenomena, but a number of processes classifiable into three major types. This fact sharply limits the extent to which simple generalizations can be drawn from observations of a single stigma group or interaction situation, though behavioral commonalities across groups and situations no doubt exist.

If indeed stigmatization involves a relationship between two response elements, it follows that in order to examine this relationship one must be able to measure the two response elements independently of one another. As yet, few if any studies have been successful in this regard. In some investigations of people's reactions to someone having an anomalous characteristic, only one type of behavior was measured. For example, Piliavin et al. (1975) reported that subjects gave less aid to a male stranger who collapsed in a subway car when he had a facial disfigurement (a large birthmark) than they gave when his appearance was normal. Clearly, the birthmark was an aversive stimulus. However, since avoidance was the only response measure obtained, there is not unequivocal evidence from this study that the birthmark functioned as a stigma, as the authors assumed. If by stigma one means a characteristic which is not merely aversive, but which is deeply discrediting, then the term should be used only when there is good reason to believe that the person possessing the trait is disvalued by normal observers.

A similar problem of interpretation arises when acceptance–rejection of a stimulus person is assessed by means of verbal evaluations. A number of investigators have reported that when subjects are asked to form impressions of handicapped and nonhandicapped individuals they tend consistently to report a more favorable impression of the former (e.g. Ray, 1946; Barker et al. 1953; Kleck, 1968; Carver et al. 1978). From these results and similar findings of their own, Langer et al. (1976) concluded that physical disability is not stigmatizing. Other evidence, however, suggests a more complex reality. Barker et al. (1953), Wright (1960), Goffman (1963), and other writers have inferred from clinical interviews, behavioral observations and content analyses of popular fiction, etc., that deep, unverbalized feelings about the handicapped are often hostile and subordinating. Further, Katz, et al. (1977) showed that when made to feel responsible for the suffering of another, subjects were more willing to denigrate a physically handicapped victim than a normal one. A strong tendency to conceal negative racial attitudes has been observed in white subjects who were required to evaluate black stimulus persons while on or off the bogus pipeline (Carver et al., 1978; Sigall and Page, 1971). When subjects were led to believe that their true attitudes would be revealed through physiological measurements they expressed more negativity against blacks than they did in a no-pipeline control condition. It appears that sentiments about the disabled, blacks, and probably members of many other minority categories are a complicated mixture of positive and negative elements, requiring for their measurement the use of devices that tap both the conscious and unconscious levels of response. A program of research based upon an ambivalence model of attitudes toward minorities has been presented by Katz (1981).

For each of the causal models of stigmatization that were discussed above there already exist suitable experimental paradigms, capable of modification for the purposes of new research. Thus for the attribute-as-cause model there are the Freedman and Doob (1968) and Tajfel (e.g. Tajfel and Billig, 1974) procedures for studying the effects of perceived differentness and group assignment on social interactions. Further work could include explorations of the boundary conditions of the effects, along the lines of Wilder's (1978) individuation study.

As regards the labeling approach to stigmatization, a recent study of stereotyping by Taylor et al. (1978) is suggestive both for its findings and for the methods used. Subjects were exposed to slide and tape shows of interacting small groups that were of mixed sex or mixed race. There was perceptual exaggeration of between-category differences and minimization of within-category differences (i.e. stereotyping along lines of race and sex), which varied as a function of contextual factors, such as the size and composition of the groups observed. Using the same experimental setup, additional contextual variables, including status and power differences among the stimulus persons, could be fed in, and effects observed on the tendency to impute negative characteristics to members of socially marginal groups.

There are also research designs that are suitable for examining aspects of the scapegoat model. There are a number of useful procedures for investigating displaced aggression phenomena (cf. Berkowitz, 1962). Also, one can assess the effect of threat on a perceiver's tendency to denigrate a source person who is a member of a particular social category. Different types of threat—value and belief, competitive, involvement in another's dependency, etc.—can be manipulated in laboratory and field settings. As another example, the paradigm that was used by Katz et al. (1973, 1977) for studying post-harm-doing denigration of black and handicapped victims can be used to study harm-doer's responses to victimized members of various other groups.

References

Allport, G. W. (1954). *The Nature of Prejudice*, Addison-Wesley, Cambridge, Mass.

Barker, R. G., Wright, B. A., Meyerson, L., and Gonick, M. R. (1953). *Adjustment to Physical Handicap and Illness: A Survey of the Social Psychology of Physique and Disability.* Social Science Research Council, New York.

Becker, H. S. (1963). *Outsiders: Studies in the Sociology of Deviance*, Free Press, New York.

Berkowitz, L. (1962). *Aggression: A Social Psychological Approach*, McGraw-Hill, New York.

Berscheid, E., and Walster, E. H. (1978). *Interpersonal Attraction*, Addison-Wesley, Reading, Mass.

Campbell, D. T. (1967). 'Stereotypes and the perception of group differences,' *American Psychologist*, 22, 817–829.

Carver, C. S., Glass, D. C., and Katz, I. (1978). 'Favorable evaluations of blacks and the handicapped,' *Journal of Applied Social Psychology*, 8, 97–106.

Cofer, C. N., and Appley, M. H. (1964). *Motivation: Theory and Research*, Wiley, New York.

Freedman, J. L., and Doob, A. N. (1968). *Deviancy: The Psychology of Being Different*, Academic Press, New York.

Gergen, K. J. (1967). 'The significance of skin color in human relations,' *Daedalus*, 96, 390–406.

Goffman, E. (1961). *Asylums*, Doubleday, Garden City, NY.

Goffman, E. (1963). *Stigma*, Prentice-Hall, Englewood Cliffs, NJ.

Gove, W. R. (1975). *The Labeling of Deviance*, Wiley, New York.

Hebb, D. O. (1949). *The Organization of Behavior*, Wiley, New York.

Heider, F. (1944). 'Social perception and phenomenal causality,' *Psychological Review*, 51, 358–374.

Katz, I. (1981). *Stigma; A Social Psychological Analysis*, Erlbaum, Hillsdale, New Jersey.

Katz, I., Glass, D. C., and Cohen, S. (1973). 'Ambivalence, guilt, and the scapegoating of minority group victims,' *Journal of Experimental Social Psychology*, 9, 423–436.

Katz, I., Glass, D. C., Lucido, D. J., and Farber, J. (1977). 'Ambivalence, guilt and the denigration of a physically handicapped victim,' *Journal of Personality*, 45, 419–429.

Kitsuse, J. I. (1962). 'Societal reactions to deviant behavior,' *Social Problems*, 9, 247–256.

Kleck, R. (1968). 'Physical stigma and nonverbal cues emitted in face-to-face interaction,' *Human Relations*, 21, 19–28.

Langer, E. L., Fiske, S., Taylor, S. E., and Chanowitz, B. (1976). 'Stigma, staring, and discomfort: A novel stimulus hypothesis,' *Journal of Experimental Social Psychology*, 12, 451–463.

Lemert, E. M. (1951). *Social Pathology*, McGraw-Hill, New York.

Lerner, M. J. (1970). 'The desire for justice and reactions to victims,' in J. Macauley and L. Berkowitz (eds.), *Altruism and Helping Behavior*, pp. 205–229, Academic Press, New York.

Osgood, C. E., Suci, G. H., and Tannenbaum, P. H. (1957). *The Measurement of Meaning*, University of Illinois Press, Urbana, Ill.

Piliavin, I. M., Piliavin, J. A., and Rodin, J. (1975). 'Costs, diffusion, and the stigmatized victim,' *Journal of Personality and Social Psychology*, 32, 429–438.

Ray, M. H. (1946). 'The effect of crippled appearance on personality judgment,' Unpublished Masters thesis. Stanford University.

Ryan, W. (1971). *Blaming the Victim*, Pantheon, New York.

Sarbin, T. (1972). 'Stimulus/response: Schizophrenia is a myth, born of metaphor, meaningless,' *Psychology Today*, 6 (June), 18–27.

Scheff, T. J. (1966). *Being Mentally Ill: A Sociological Theory*, Aldine, Chicago.

Schur, E. M. (1965). *Crimes without Victims*, Prentice-Hall, Englewood Cliffs, NJ.

Scott, R. A. (1969). *The Making of Blind Men*, Russell Sage, New York.

Sherif, M., and Sherif, C. W. (1953). *Groups in Harmony and Tension*, Harper, New York.

Sigall, H., and Page, R. (1971). 'Current stereotypes: A little fading, a little faking,' *Journal of Personality and Social Psychology*, 18, 247–255.

Szasz, T. S. (1960). 'The myth of mental illness,' *American Psychologist*, 15, 113–118.

Tajfel, H., and Billig, M. (1974). 'Familiarity and categorization in intergroup behavior,' *Journal of Experimental and Social Psychology*, **10**, 159–170.
Tajfel, H., and Jahoda, G. (1966). 'Development in children of concepts about their own and other countries,' *Symposium*, **36**, 17–33.
Taylor, S. E., Fiske, S. T., Etcoff, N. L., and Ruderman, A. J. (1978). 'Categorical and contextual bases of person memory and stereotyping,' *Journal of Personality and Social Psychology*, **36**, 778–793.
Wilder, D. A. (1978). 'Reduction of intergroup discrimination through individuation of the out-group,' *Journal of Personality and Social Psychology*, **36**, 1361–1374.
Wright, B. A. (1960). *Physical Disability; a Psychological Approach*, Harper & Row, New York.

Small Groups and Social Interaction, Volume 1
Edited by H. H. Blumberg, A. P. Hare, V. Kent and M. Davies
Published by John Wiley & Sons Limited, 1983.

3.2 Experiments in Intergroup Discrimination*

Henri Tajfel   *University of Bristol*

Can discrimination be traced to some such origin as social conflict or a history of hostility? Not necessarily. Apparently the mere fact of division into groups is enough to trigger discriminatory behavior.

Intergroup discrimination is a feature of most modern societies. The phenomenon is depressingly similar regardless of the constitution of the 'ingroup' and of the 'outgroup' that is perceived as being somehow different. A Slovene friend of mine once described to me the stereotypes—the common traits attributed to a large human group—that are applied in his country, the richest constituent republic of Yugoslavia, to immigrant Bosnians, who come from a poorer region. Some time later I presented this description to a group of students at the University of Oxford and asked them to guess by whom it was used and to whom it referred. The almost unanimous reply was that this was the characterization applied by native Englishmen to 'colored' immigrants: people coming primarily from the West Indies, India, and Pakistan.

The intensity of discrimination varies more than the nature of the phenomenon. In countries with long-standing intergroup problems—be they racial as in the US, religious as in Northern Ireland or linguistic-national as in Belgium—tensions reach the boiling point more easily than they do elsewhere. In spite of differing economic, cultural, historical, political and psychological backgrounds, however, the *attitudes* of prejudice toward outgroups and the *behavior* of discrimination against outgroups clearly display a set of common characteristics. Social scientists have naturally been concerned to try to identify these characteristics in an effort to understand the origins of prejudice and discrimination.

*This paper was revised and abridged (by the author) from H. Tajfel (November 1970). 'Experiments in intergroup discrimination,' *Scientific American*, **223** (5), pp. 96–102. Reprinted with permission. Copyright © 1970 by Scientific American, Inc. All rights reserved. Professor Tajfel died in May 1982.

The investigative approaches to this task can be roughly classified into two categories. Some workers stress the social determinants of prejudice and discrimination. Others emphasize psychological causation. In *The Functions of Social Conflict*, published in 1956, Lewis A. Coser of Brandeis University established a related dichotomy when he distinguished between two types of intergroup conflict: the 'rational' and the 'irrational.' The former is a means to an end: the conflict and the attitudes that go with it reflect a genuine competition between groups with divergent interests. The latter is an end in itself: it serves to release accumulated emotional tensions of various kinds. As both popular lore and the psychological literature testify, nothing is better suited for this purpose than a well-selected scapegoat.

These dichotomies have some value as analytical tools but they need not be taken too seriously. Most cases of conflict between human groups, large or small, reflect an intricate interdependence of social and psychological causation. Often it is difficult, and probably fruitless, to speculate about what were the first causes of real present-day social situations. Moreover, there is a dialectical relation between the objective and the subjective determinants of intergroup attitudes and behavior. Once the process is set in motion they reinforce each other in a relentless spiral in which the weight of predominant causes tends to shift continuously. For example, economic or social competition can lead to discriminatory behavior; that behavior can then in a number of ways create attitudes of prejudice; those attitudes can in turn lead to new forms of discriminatory behavior that create new economic or social disparities, and so the vicious circle is continued.

The interdependence of the two types of causation does not manifest itself only in their mutual reinforcement. They actually converge because of the psychological effects on an individual of his sociocultural milieu. This convergence is often considered in terms of social learning and conformity. For instance, there is much evidence that children learn quite early the pecking order of evaluations of various groups that prevails in their society, and that the order remains fairly stable. This applies not only to the evaluation of groups that are in daily contact, such as racial groups and mixed environments, but also to ideas about foreign nations with which there is little if any personal contact.

In studies conducted at Oxford a few years ago my colleagues and I found a high consensus among children of six and seven in their preference for four foreign countries. The order was America, France, Germany and Russia, and there was a correlation of .98 between the preferences of subjects from two different schools. As for adults, studies conducted by Thomas F. Pettigrew in the late 1950s in South Africa and in the American South have shown that conformity is an important determinant of hostile attitudes toward blacks in both places (above and beyond individual tendencies toward authoritarianism, which is known to be closely related to prejudice toward outgroups).

These studies, like many others, were concerned with attitudes rather than behavior, with prejudice rather than discrimination. Discrimination, it is often said, is more directly a function of the objective social situation, which sometimes does and sometimes does not facilitate the expression of attitudes; the attitudes of prejudice may be socially learned or due to tendencies to conform, but they are not a very efficient predictor of discriminatory behavior. According to this view, psychological considerations are best suited to explaining and predicting the genesis and functioning of attitudes; the facts of intergroup discrimination are best related to, and predicted from, objective indexes of a social, economic and demographic nature.

Although I have no quarrel with this view, I am left with a nagging feeling that it omits an important part of the story. The fact is that behavior toward outgroups shows the same monotonous similarity as attitudes do, across a diversity of socioeconomic conditions. This apparent diversity may, of course, obscure an underlying common factor of 'rational' conflict, of struggle to preserve a *status quo* favorable to oneself or to obtain an equitable share of social opportunities and benefits. Another kind of underlying regularity is nonetheless common to a variety of social situations and is an important psychological effect of our sociocultural milieu. It is the assimilation by the individual of the various norms of conduct that prevail in his society.

Social categorization (in its sense of the 'subjective' division of people into groups) is, by definition, an inherent and inescapable feature of all intergroup situations. Although we know a great deal about various factors which enhance intergroup discrimination, competitiveness, and hostility, the effects on social behaviour of social categorization *per se* have never been systematically studied in their own right. This was simply so because social categorization is *always* there when social groups interact, and therefore the possibility that it produces certain discriminatory effects in its own right has been overlooked. This possibility needed to be taken seriously, since the psychological functions served by social categorizations include helping the individuals to find their subjective location in their social world, and thus contributing to their definitions of themselves. This self-definition may often be *comparative*, in the sense that it may include the existence or the creation of positively valued *differences* from other groups. It is therefore fully possible that a simple division into groups, even based on flimsy criteria, and initially not associated with any other differences between the groups, may lead by itself to some forms of behaviour aiming at the creation of intergroup differentiation. The aim of the present experiments was to explore this possibility.

At the University of Bristol, in collaboration with Claude Flament of the University of Aix-Marseille, R. P. Bundy and M. J. Billig, I have conducted experiments designed to test this prediction and others that follow from it. The main problem was to create experimental conditions that would enable us to assess the effects of intergroup categorization *per se*, uncontaminated by other variables, such as interactions among individuals or pre-existing attitudes. We aimed, moreover, to look at the behavior rather than the attitudes of the subjects toward their own group and the other group, to ensure that this behavior was of some importance to them and to present them with a clear alternative to discriminating against the outgroup that would be a more 'sensible' mode of behavior.

Perhaps the best means of conveying the way these criteria were met is to describe the procedure we followed in the first experiments and its variants in subsequent ones. Our subjects were 64 boys 14 and 15 years old from a state, or 'comprehensive,' school in a suburb of Bristol. They came to the laboratory in separate groups of eight. All the boys in each of the groups were from the same house in the same form at the school, so that they knew each other well before the experiment. The first part of the experiment served to establish an intergroup categorization and in the second part we assessed the effects of that categorization on intergroup behavior.

In the first part the boys were brought together in a lecture room and were told that we were interested in the study of visual judgments. Forty clusters of varying numbers of dots were flashed on a screen. The boys were asked to estimate the number of dots in each cluster and to record each estimate in succession on prepared score sheets. There were two conditions in this first part of the experiment. In one condition, after the boys had completed their estimates they were told that in judgments of this kind some people consistently overestimate the number of dots and some consistently underestimate the number, but that these tendencies are in no way related to accuracy. In the other condition the boys were told that some people are consistently more accurate than others. Four groups of eight served in each of the two conditions.

After the judgments had been made and had been ostentatiously 'scored' by one of the experimenters, we told the subjects that, since we were also interested in other kinds of decision, we were going to take advantage of their presence to investigate these as well, and that for ease of coding we were going to group them on the basis of the visual judgments they had just made. In actuality the subjects were assigned to groups quite at random, half to 'underestimators' and half to 'overestimators' in the first condition, half to 'better' and half to 'worse' accuracy in the second one.

Instructions followed about the nature of the forthcoming task. The boys were told that it would consist of giving to others rewards and penalties in real money. They would not know the identity of the individuals to whom they would be assigning these rewards and penalties since everyone would have a code number. They would be taken to another room one by one and given information as to which group they were in. Once in the other room they were to work on their own in separate cubicles. In each cubicle they would find a pencil and a booklet containing 18 sets of ordered numbers, one to each page. It was stressed that on no occasion would the boys be rewarding or penalizing themselves; they would always be allotting money to others. At the end of the task each boy would be brought back into the first room and would receive the amount of money the other boys had awarded him. The value of each point they were awarding was a tenth of a penny (about a tenth of a US cent). After these instructions were given, the boys were led individually to their cubicles to fill out their booklets.

On each page in the booklet there was one matrix consisting of 14 boxes containing two numbers each. The numbers in the top row were the rewards and penalties to be awarded to one person and those in the bottom row were those to be awarded to another. Each row was labeled 'These are rewards and penalties for member No. _ of your group' or '... of the other group.' The subjects had to indicate their choices by checking one box in each matrix. On the cover of each booklet and at the top of each page was written: 'Booklet for member of the ____ group.'

There were six matrices [see Figure 1] and each of them appeared three times in the booklet—once for each of three types of choice. There were ingroup choices, with the top and the bottom row signifying the rewards and penalties to be awarded to two members of the subject's own group (other than himself). Then there were outgroup choices, with both rows signifying the rewards and penalties for a member of the other group. Finally there were intergroup, or 'differential,' choices, one row indicating the rewards and penalties to be awarded to an ingroup member (other than himself) and the other the points for an outgroup member. (The top and bottom positions of ingroup and outgroup members were varied at random.)

The results for the intergroup choices were first scored in terms of ranks of choices. In each matrix Rank 1 stood for the choice of the term that gave to the member of the ingroup the minimum possible number of points in that matrix; Rank 14, at the opposite extreme of the matrix, stood for the maximum possible number of points. Comparable (but more complex) methods of scoring were adopted for the other two kinds of choice, the ingroup choices and the outgroup ones, and for comparison of these choices with those made in the differential situation.

The results were striking [see Figure 2]. In making their intergroup choices a large majority of the subjects, in all groups in both conditions, gave more money

1	2	3	4	5	6	7	8	9	10	11	12	13	14
14	13	12	11	10	9	8	7	6	5	4	3	2	1

18	17	16	15	14	13	12	11	10	9	8	7	6	5
5	6	7	8	9	10	11	12	13	14	15	16	17	18

Figure 1 Examples of the matrices used in the first experiment. (The interested reader should consult the original article for details of the complete set of matrices.)

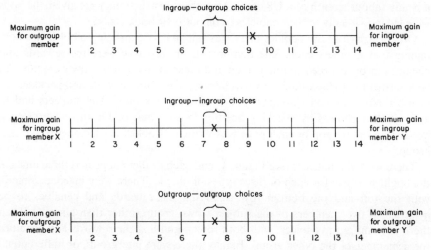

Figure 2   Results were scored by ranking choices from 1 to 14 depending on which box was checked. The end of the matrix at which the ingroup member got the minimum number of points (and the outgroup member the maximum) was designated 1; the other end, giving the ingroup member the maximum, was 14. The mean choices (marked by crosses) are shown. In the intergroup situation the subjects gave significantly more points to members of their own group than to members of the other group. In the intragroup situations, however, the means of the choices fell at Rank 7.5, between the choices of maximum fairness

to members of their own group than to members of the other group. All the results were—at a very high level of statistical significance—above both Rank 7.5, which represents the point of maximum fairness, and the mean ranks of the ingroup and outgroup choices. In contrast the ingroup and outgroup choices were closely distributed about the point of fairness. Further analysis [see Figure 3] made it clear that intergroup discrimination was the deliberate strategy adopted in making intergroup choices.

Before continuing, let us review the situation. The boys, who knew each other well, were divided into groups defined by flimsy and unimportant criteria. Their own individual interests were not affected by their choices, since they always assigned points to two other people and no one could know what any other boy's choices were. The amounts of money were not trivial for them: each boy left the experiment with the equivalent of about a dollar. Inasmuch as they could not know who was in their group and who was in the other group, they could have adopted either of two reasonable strategies. They could have chosen the maximum-joint-profit point of the matrices, which would mean that the boys as a total group would get the most money out of the experimenters, or they could choose the point of maximum fairness. Indeed, they did tend to choose the second alternative when their choices did not involve a distinction between ingroup and outgroup. As soon as this differentiation was involved, however, they

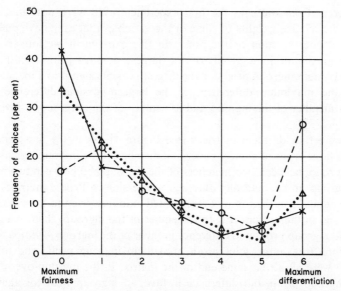

Figure 3 Intergroup discrimination was a deliberate strategy in the ingroup–outgroup choices (dashed line) and fairness a deliberate strategy in the ingroup–ingroup (dotted) and outgroup–outgroup (unbroken line) choices. This is indicated by the fact that the frequencies of intergroup choices differed significantly from those of the intragroup choices only at the extreme points of the distribution, the points of maximum fairness and of maximum discrimination. (For this analysis the two fairest choices in each matrix, the two middle ones, were ranked together as 0 and departures in either direction were scored from 1 to 6.)

discriminated in favor of the ingroup. The only thing we needed to do to achieve this result was to associate their judgments of numbers of dots with the use of the terms 'your group' and 'the other group' in the instructions and on the booklets of matrices.

The results were at a very high level of statistical significance in all eight separately tested groups of eight boys. In view of the consistency of the phenomenon we decided to analyze it further and also to validate it with a different criterion for intergroup categorization. We tested three new groups of 16 boys each, this time with aesthetic preference as the basis of the division into two groups. The boys were shown 12 slides, six of which were reproductions of paintings by Paul Klee and six by Wassily Kandinsky, and they were asked to express their preference for one or the other of these two 'foreign painters.' The reproductions were presented without the painter's signature, so that half of the subjects could be assigned to random to the 'Klee group' and half to the 'Kandinsky group.'

The matrices that confronted the boys subsequently in their individual cubicles were different from those in the first experiment. We were now interested in assessing the relative weights of some of the variables that may have pulled their decisions in one direction or the other. In this experiment we looked at three variables: maximum joint profit, or the largest possible joint award to both people; maximum ingroup profit, or the largest possible award to a member of the ingroup, and maximum difference, or the largest possible difference in gain between a member of the ingroup and a member of the outgroup in favor of the former.

There were four different matrices [see Figure 4]. As in the first experiment, there were three types of choice: between a member of the ingroup and a member of the outgroup, between two members of the ingroup and between two members of the outgroup. In the outgroup-over-ingroup version of Type *A* matrices (that is, where the numbers in the top row represented amounts given to a member of the outgroup and in the bottom row to a member of the ingroup) the three gains—joint profit, ingroup profit and difference in favor of the ingroup—varied together; their maxima (maximum joint profit, maximum ingroup profit and maximum difference) were all at the same end of the matrix. In the ingroup-over-outgroup version, ingroup profit and difference in favor of ingroup went together in one

Type A

	MD MIP												MJP	
Matrix 1	19	18	17	16	15	14	13	12	11	10	9	8	7	[Ingroup]
	1	3	5	7	9	11	13	15	17	19	21	23	25	[Outgroup]

													MD MIP MJP	
Matrix 2	23	22	21	20	19	18	17	16	15	14	13	12	11	[Outgroup]
	5	7	9	11	13	15	17	19	21	23	25	27	29	[Ingroup]

Type B

	MD												MIP MJP	
Matrix 3	7	8	9	10	11	12	13	14	15	16	17	18	19	[Ingroup]
	1	3	5	7	9	11	13	15	17	19	21	23	25	[Outgroup]

													MD MIP MJP	
Matrix 4	11	12	13	14	15	16	17	18	19	20	21	23	25	[Outgroup]
	5	7	9	11	13	15	17	19	21	23	25	27	29	[Ingroup]

Figure 4 Matrices used in the second experiment.
MD = maximum difference in favor of the ingroup;
MIP = maximum ingroup profit;
MJP = maximum joint profit.
(These symbols did not appear on the matrices presented to subjects.)

direction and were in direct conflict with choices approaching maximum joint profit. In the Type *B* matrices outgroup-over-ingroup versions again represented a covariation of the three gains; in the ingroup-over-outgroup versions, difference in favor of ingroup varied in the direction opposite to joint profit and ingroup profit combined.

A comparison of the boys' choices in the various matrices showed that maximum joint profit exerted hardly any effect at all; the effect of maximum ingroup profit and maximum difference combined against maximum joint profit was strong and highly significant; the effect of maximum difference against maximum joint profit and maximum ingroup profit was also strong and highly significant. In other words, when the subjects had a choice between maximizing the profit for all and maximizing the profit for members of their own group, they acted on behalf of their own group. When they had a choice between profit for all and for their own group combined, as against their own group's winning *more* than the outgroup at the sacrifice of both of these utilitarian advantages, it was the maximization of *difference* that seemed more important to them.

Evidence leading in the same direction emerged from the other two types of choice, between two members of the ingroup and between two members of the outgroup: the ingroup choices were consistently and significantly nearer to the maximum joint profit than were the outgroup ones—and this was so in spite of the fact that giving as much as possible to two members of the outgroup in the choices applying solely to them presented no conflict with the ingroup's interest. It simply would have meant giving more to 'the others' without giving any less to 'your own.' This represented, therefore, a clear case of gratuitous discrimination. We also included in the second experiment some of the original matrices used in the first one, with results much the same as before. Again all the results in this experiment were at a high level of statistical significance.

In subsequent experiments we tested the importance of fairness in making the choices, the effect on the choices of familiarity with the situation and the subjects', ideas about the choices that others were making. Fairness, we found, was an important determinant; most of the choices must be understood as being a compromise between fairness and favoring one's own group. We found that discrimination not only persisted but also increased when the entire situation became more familiar to the subjects. With familiarity there was also an increase (when the boys were asked to predict the other subjects' behavior) in their expectation that other boys were discriminating.

The problem we have is therefore that, in these experiments, there were no elements of an 'objective' conflict of interest between the groups, and yet discrimination did occur. A good deal of work has been done since the time these studies were conducted to elucidate the psychological processes which may be underlying the results we obtained. The general conclusions seem to be that, *in addition* to an explicit conflict, intergroup discrimination may be determined by an interaction of three variables: categorization into groups; social identity; and social comparison.

Once people have categorized themselves as members of one group or another, there are certain conditions when group membership contributes, positively or negatively, to their image of themselves. It is this group contribution to the self-image which is referred to here as an individual's 'social identity.' In turn, the positive or negative connotations of such an identity are mainly derived from selected comparisons of one's own group with other groups which are salient to the individual. In other words, individuals will tend to achieve or preserve their positive social identity by selecting or *creating* certain comparisons with other groups. In our experiments, only one possibility existed for the creation of positive comparisons: the establishment of a difference on the matrices in favor of one's own group. This is exactly what the subjects did, while at the same time general ideas about fairness still intervened in their choices. In less artificial situations, the distinctive and positive 'identity' of their group plays a very much more important role in people's behavior. There is no difficulty in finding many examples of this process in the large number of ethnic and national movements which exist round the globe today and in the social and industrial conflicts in which 'differentials' play an important role.

Small Groups and Social Interactions, Volume 1
Edited by H. H. Blumberg, A. P. Hare, V. Kent and M. Davies
© 1983 John Wiley & Sons Ltd

3.3 Cooperation in the Classroom: The Impact of the Jigsaw Method on Inter-ethnic Relations, Classroom Performance, and Self-esteem

Elliot Aronson and Suzanne Yates

University of California at Santa Cruz

> Oh, the white folks hate the black folks,
> And the black folks hate the white folks,
> All of my folks hate all of your folks,
> It's as American as apple pie.

While the lyrics of Tom Lehrer's satirical song are meant to be sung with tongue at least partly in cheek, they encompass a sad but profound truth: every distinguishable group is prejudiced against some other group and no group has ever escaped being the target of someone else's scorn. While prejudice is ordinarily defined as being either positive or negative in nature, in social psychological research it is most commonly used to signify the presence of a negative bias against a person or group of persons which is based on faulty and inflexible generalizations. The word 'inflexible' is critical in this definition because it distinguishes this bias from a simple misconception. Rather, prejudice is a highly emotional, deeply rooted set of attitudes. The prejudiced person does not correctly readjust beliefs in the light of new, conflicting evidence. On the contrary, such a person actively resists the new evidence by distorting or ignoring it. As a result, once accepted a prejudiced belief is extremely difficult to change. Historically, informational campaigns and rational arguments have had little impact on the problem.

In what has been applauded as one of the single most important efforts to reduce racial prejudice in America, the Supreme Court ruled, in 1954, to outlaw school desegregation (*Oliver Brown* v. *the Board of Education of Topeka, Kansas*). This decision reversed the *Plessy* v. *Ferguson* ruling of 1896 which held that racial segregation was permissible as long as equal facilities were provided for both races. In the *Brown* case the court held that psychologically there could be no such thing as 'separate but equal.' The mere fact of separation implied to the minority group in question that its members were considered inferior to those of the majority. Hence, the court and the supporters of the decision implied that instituting desegregation in the schools would improve minorities' self-esteem and raise their academic aspirations. Further, it was hoped that the intermingling of races in classrooms would afford white children the opportunity to correct negative stereotypes based on misinformation.

The effects of desegregation

How justified were the high hopes of 1954? Since then many have attempted to determine and evaluate the impact of the Court's ruling. The results are not encouraging. In 1975, after reviewing 120 studies, St John (who had been a strong advocate of desegregation) was forced to conclude that desegregation:

> is apparently not detrimental to the academic performance of black children, but it may have effects on their self-esteem ... not merely academic self-concept ... but also general self-concept ... desegregation apparently lowers educational and vocational aspirations ... [and] white racism is frequently aggravated by mixed schooling. (St John, 1975, pp. 119–120)

The expectation that school desegregation would raise the educational achievement of minority children, enhance their self-esteem, and improve race relations was based, in part, on the testimony of social scientists in an *amicus curiae* brief filed in the *Brown* case. Was the testimony misleading? We think not. Commentators (St John, 1975; Stephan, 1978; Cook, 1979; Clark, 1979) point out that the social scientists did not mean to imply that the expected benefits would accrue automatically. Simply producing a statistical mix of children from different racial backgrounds was not thought to be sufficient for creating true integration. Certain preconditions must be met. These have been most articulately summarized by Gordon Allport in his classic text, *The Nature of Prejudice*. Allport observes:

> Prejudice ... may be reduced by equal status contact between majority and minority groups in the pursuit of common goals. The effect is greatly enhanced if this contact is sanctioned by institutional supports (i.e. by law, custom, or local atmosphere), and provided it is of a sort that leads to the perception of common interests and common humanity between members of the two groups. (Allport, 1954, p. 281)

Sanction by authority

What went wrong? An examination of the typical desegregated classroom makes it clear that the necessary preconditions were never met. Consider the need for sanction by authority. Local authorities have differed widely in their willingness to accept and enforce desegregation rulings. Some have responded positively and quickly, while others have acted in open defiance of the law. Most have adopted a policy of gradualism and minimal compliance with only the letter of the law.

As the classroom's main authority figure, the role of the teacher must be considered as well. Teachers, by their example and policies, can encourage a smooth intermixing of the races or they can effectively thwart integration efforts. Unfortunately, evidence (Gerard and Miller, 1975) indicates that teachers have not always acted in favor of the former. Clearly, sanction by authority has not always been present.

Equal status contact

Determining the degree to which students enjoy equal status contact is a complex issue. Status can not be assumed equal for all children simply because they are in the same grade in the same school, thereby having the same 'occupational' status. Status is affected by many other factors as well—such as, the child's socio-economic background, academic, physical, and social abilities, and the evaluation of superiors.

Most minority children come from socio-economic backgrounds which are lower than their white classmates. Potentially, this places the minority child at a social disadvantage. If, because of an inferior education (prior to desegregation) or because of language difficulties, black or Mexican–American students perform poorly in the classroom, this can also lower status among peers (St John, 1975). Quite naturally, we would expect status inequities generated by these background differences to have a detrimental effect on the self-esteem of minority children. Students with low self-esteem tend to develop lower aspirations: they come to expect failure. Background inequalities, self-esteem, achievement, and social status all feed into one another in a vicious cycle. It is not astonishing, in retrospect, then, that the gulf between the races in a traditionally desegregated classroom might broaden, not lessen over time.

The teacher also has tremendous power to affect a child's status. If the teacher is prejudiced against minorities, he or she may treat them less fairly than he or she treats whites. Gerard and Miller (1975) have documented instances of overt prejudice on the part of teachers. Classes taught by these teachers display clear differences in the student's status that are correlated with their ethnicity. Detrimental effects, however, can occur even when the teacher has the best of intentions! In order to spare a child who has language or academic difficulties, a teacher may avoid calling on him/her. Unfortunately, such behavior is soon noticed by classmates who interpret it as proof that, 'This is a stupid classmate.'

The teacher has the power to affect status and self-image in yet another way. Until very recently, little or no effort was made to teach students (and hence our current teachers) about the contributions of minorities and women to our intellectual, social, and economic heritage. As a result, teachers by way of the examples they cite, interpretations they render, and the readings they assign are apt to create the impression that the only truly valuable and capable members of our society have always been (and will always be) white males.

Elizabeth Cohen (1972) has uncovered another set of factors which further complicate this issue. While Allport (1954) predicted that positive interactions will result if cooperative equal status contact is achieved, expectation theory, as developed by Cohen, holds that even in such an environment biased expectations by both blacks and whites may lead to sustained white dominance. Cohen reasoned that both of these groups accept the premise that the majority group's competence is the reason for its dominance and superior achievement.

According to Cohen, a temporary exchange of majority and minority roles is required to reverse these unconscious expectations. For example, in one study (Cohen and Roper, 1972), black children were instructed how to build radios and how to teach this skill to others. Then some of the black children taught white children how to construct radios while others taught a black administrator. Equal status interactions were found in the groups where blacks had taught the whites. The other groups demonstrated the usual white dominance.

In pursuit of common goals

At first glance, one may be tempted to conclude that all fifth graders (for example) are working in pursuit of a common goal: they are each working to become sixth graders. But this description is simplistic and deceptive. When one examines the process governing most classroom activities it becomes apparent that this is not an accurate characterization. During the past several years, we and our colleagues have systematically observed scores of elementary school classrooms, and have found that the vast majority are ruled by a highly competitive process. In spite of surface appearances, children in the typical American classroom are almost never engaged in the pursuit of common goals.

Indeed, the average classroom provides us with a powerful illustration of Spinoza's comments on the nature of competition. Spinoza (in Heider, 1958) describes competition as a situation in which two individuals appear to have the same goal but, in reality, have different goals. That is, it may *seem* that Peter and Paul both want X but, in fact 'Peter wants Peter to have X and Paul wants Paul to have X.' Further, Deutsch (1949) notes that the critical difference between a competitive and a cooperative situation lies in the nature of the relationship which develops between the participants as a function of the interaction. If we are cooperating, our outcome goal is the same. When you win, I win. The situation encourages us to watch out for each other's welfare. Such an interaction is highly conducive to developing friendships and feelings of mutual respect and trust. In competition, on the other hand, we both want the prize but we cannot both have it. The closer you come to achieving your goal, the further away I am from achieving mine. If you win, I lose. This situation obviously mitigates against the likelihood of establishing friendships and creates an environment in which hostilities can flourish.

It is certainly true that competitive teaching practices are not confined to desegregated classrooms. These dynamics make up the daily life of almost every school age child in America. But, in a newly desegregrated school, all other things being equal, this atmosphere can only exacerbate whatever prejudice existed prior to desegregation. Indeed, the relationship between prejudice and competition in other settings has been well documented (Dollard, 1949; Greeley and Sheatsley, 1971; Sherif, 1956).

In the now classic 'Robber's Cave' experiment, Muzafer Sherif and his colleagues (1956) encouraged intergroup competition between two teams of boys at a summer camp. Hostilities and expressions of anger which were initially confined to situations involving direct competitive confrontations soon began erupting in previously benign, non-competitive circumstances—such as watching a movie. Further, Sherif warns that once hostilities between groups have been established, the simple removal of the competitive goal structure will not eliminate the problem. Positive relations between the groups in Sherif's experiment were ultimately achieved only after both groups were required to work cooperatively to solve a common problem. One lesson made clear here is that instituting special tutoring programs for minorities or establishing self-paced learning units in classrooms may not be sufficient to remedy unsuccessful desegregation attempts. Rather, we believe that groups need to engage in mutually interdependent projects if they are to learn to like and respect one another.

The Jigsaw Cooperative Learning Method

In response to a call for help from the Austin, Texas, school system during the early 1970s, Aronson and his colleagues set out to design an intervention strategy that would make desegregation work and which could easily be implemented by teachers in their day-to-day classroom activities. In accordance with the analysis that has been presented here, the Jigsaw Cooperative Learning Method (Aronson, 1972) was devised and introduced to a sample of fifth grade classrooms in the area.

In a jigsaw classroom, small student-directed groups replace the teacher-dominated lecture method; students serve as the principal sources of information and reinforcement for one another. Students are placed in small groups of five or six for about an hour each day. The day's lesson is divided up into as many segments as there are group members and each student is given a unique part. Each member is then responsible for learning the assigned segment well enough to teach it to the others. Since group members can only learn a lesson in its entirety by pooling all their knowledge, interdependence is established.

An important feature of the jigsaw method is the use of 'expert groups.' In order to ensure that all students—even non-readers—master their sections, students from all the different jigsaw groups who have been assigned the *same* part prepare their presentations together before returning to their jigsaw groups and making their final presentations. In the 'expert groups' students are given time to discuss the material and to practice presenting it. This step is essential because it insures that all students will enter their groups as well trained, competent consultants.

When the children reassemble in their six-person jigsaw group, they are given a certain amount of time to teach each other all the information. Then they are tested on the entire unit. While the children are evaluated individually, it is very clear that in order to master the entire task they must help one another, teach one another, and learn from one another. No child's contribution can be overlooked. Through this process, children begin to learn two important lessons: first, none of them could do well without the aid of every other person in the group; and second, each member has a unique and essential contribution to make.

Experimental evidence and underlying mechanisms

What happens when traditionally run, competitive classrooms are broken up into small interdependent learning groups for part of the day? The experimental results are quite consistent. Compared to children who remain in traditional classrooms, students who spend part of their time in jigsaw groups come to like one another more, develop more positive inter-racial attitudes, improve in their general attitudes toward school, acquire more positive self-concepts, develop a stronger sense of having an internal locus of control, become more empathic, and do as well or better academically (Blaney *et al.*, 1977; Lucker *et al.*, 1977; Geffner, 1978; Gonzalez, 1979; Bridgeman, in press). For a more extensive discussion of these findings the reader is referred to *The Jigsaw Classroom* (Aronson *et al.*, 1978).

Increased participation through peer tutoring

Without a doubt, the jigsaw method is highly successful. We think that some of its success is due to the fact that the method is, in a sense, a highly structured form of group tutoring. As such, it requires class members to become actively involved in the learning process under conditions of reduced anxiety. Reviews of peer tutoring programs (Gartner *et al.*, 1971; Allen, 1976) as well as laboratory research (Benware, 1975) provide overwhelming support for the fact that we learn something better if we learn it in order to teach someone else. Moreover, evidence indicates that peers are frequently able to teach their classmates more effectively than specially trained experts (Fisher, 1969). Sarbin (1976) speculates that this finding may be due to the fact that peers tend to employ less formal teaching styles. In addition to creating a situation which is probably less threatening or anxiety provoking, Sarbin maintains that the kinds of reward and the style of feedback used by peers differ radically from those used by professionals. Low achieving students may not accept or understand the communication style used by nonfamiliar adults. Such an analysis explains the finding that minorities and low achievers do well in the jigsaw classroom. Further, it has been demonstrated (Rosen *et al.*, 1977) that the greatest gains in academic performance and satisfaction occur when tutors and tyros exchange roles at some point. Clearly, the jigsaw method incorporates the best features of a successful peer tutoring program. Students learn material to teach other children, low achieving students are given an opportunity to learn in a relatively non-threatening atmosphere from peers who employ a communication system which is familiar to them, and teachers and learners trade roles.

Increases in empathic role-taking

In order to engage in effective social interactions with another, Piaget (1932) observed that the child must learn to modify his/her intended behavior in anticipation of the other's reaction. As the child gains a broader range of experiences in the world he or she begins to recognize the differences between his/her own preoccupation and the concerns of others. Hence, he posits that egocentrism and role taking are negatively correlated in a child's development.

When children engage in a cooperative rather than a competitive process, the nature of their interactions should increase their ability to take another's perspective. For example, suppose that Kathy and Pedro are in a jigsaw group. Pedro is reporting and Kathy is having difficulty following him. She doesn't quite understand because his presentation style is different from what she is accustomed to. Not only must she pay close attention, but in addition, she must find a way to ask Pedro questions which he will understand and which will elicit the information she needs. To do this, Kathy must now get to know Pedro; she must put herself in his shoes and try to see the world as he does. This process of learning to take the role of another should lead to increased sensitivity and understanding. Jigsaw students, as part of their daily curriculum, are being encouraged to empathize with their peers.

Following this line of reasoning, Bridgeman (in press) tested the hypothesis that participation in the jigsaw process produces greater role-taking abilities. Bridgeman compared students who had been in classes using the jigsaw method for 8 weeks with students who had received traditional instruction. At the end of the 8 week period, students were administered a revised version of Chandler's (1973) role-taking cartoon series. Each of the cartoons in the Chandler test depicts a central character caught up in a chain of psychological cause and effect, such that the character's subsequent behavior is shaped by, and fully comprehensible only in terms of, the events preceding them. Midway in each sequence, a second character is introduced who witnesses the resultant behavior of the principal character, but who has clearly *not* been exposed to the earlier causal events. Thus, the subject is in a privileged position relative to the second story character. The cartoon series measures the degree to which the subject is able to set aside facts known only to himself/herself and adopt the perspective of the second character in the story.

After 8 weeks, students in the jigsaw classrooms were better able to put themselves in the bystander's place than students in the control classrooms. Their answers were less egocentric. They demonstrated a more developed ability to role-take both rational thought (the logical perspective of another) and affective thought (the emotional perspective of another).

Ego-enhancing attributions for others as well as self

It has long been observed that individuals tend to attribute success to their own abilities and failure to situational factors (Jones and Davis, 1965). Stephan *et al.* (1977a) have shown that when a child beats a friend in a competitive situation, the usual ego-enhancing attribution process is reversed; subjects who beat friends are *more* likely than losers to attribute their performance on the task to luck. Similarly, Stephan *et al.* (1977b) found that subjects in cooperative conditions made ego-enhancing attributions about their partners' success or failure as well, regardless of the fact that the partner was not a friend before the study. In the competitive conditions, however, the subject attributed the other's success to luck and his failures to a lack of skill. These results appear to indicate that competitive processes encourage people to derogate the accomplishments of others and to capitalize on their failures. Cooperation, on the other hand, encourages people to treat others as friends and with the same care and regard that they would accord themselves.

The interactive nature of all these processes

There is little doubt that each of the underlying mechanisms described here interacts with and augments the other processes described. For example, evidence shows that academic achievement and self-esteem are linked in a two-way causal relationship (see Covington and Beery, 1976; Purkey, 1970). Children who experience a drop in self-esteem do not perform as well as others whose self-esteem remains intact (Giby and Giby, 1967). Conversely, Franks and Marolla

(1976) argue that situations which allow the child to display expertise produce increases in self-esteem. Indeed these two factors are so entwined that Lamy (1965) found that first graders' reading ability could be predicted as accurately by their self-esteem scores as they could be by their IQ scores.

Other applications

Mainstreaming

The jigsaw process was developed to address the problem of racial prejudice in the schools. As Goffman (1963) has pointed out, however, prejudices are not limited to racial dislikes. Many different groups are stigmatized. A classroom made up only of white children is not guaranteed to be free of prejudice. Different cultural and religious heritages often set one group against another. Accents, marks of wealth, style of dress, religious observances, physical handicaps, homeliness, obesity, and emotional difficulties can all serve in the place of skin color to set people apart. While the grounds for prejudice are many, the process remains the same. A method that works to reduce prejudice in one situation, therefore, should be of use in another. The mechanisms described here are sound and can be used by teachers to help children overcome interpersonal barriers of any sort.

The process of integrating children from special classes and schools back into regular classrooms is generally called mainstreaming. Teachers involved in the mainstreaming of the physically handicapped, for example, should find the strategy outlined here well suited to their needs. Working in jigsaw groups would allow physically impaired children to contribute in equal and important ways to classroom activities. Nonhandicapped children would be given experiences that counteracted misconceptions about the mental and personal capacities of these children. In short, the principles set forth in this paper apply to any circumstance which depends upon people's ability to abandon misleading stereotypes and work together for a common good.

Traditional settings

We have been discussing the benefits of the jigsaw method in relation to its ability to reduce prejudice. The method, however, makes good pedagogical sense in any classroom. Children like school better when they work together for part of the day in interdependent groups. They learn important communication skills and are made active participants in their own learning process. These experiences serve to raise children's self-esteem, increase their sense of inner control, and help them to become more empathic. Unlike the open classroom, however, there is no need to neglect teaching basic skills. Indeed, weaker students improve academically while gifted students continue to do as well. The method does not require school systems to purchase special equipment or books. Jigsaw lessons are based on the standard materials used by teachers in standard settings. We would hope that the success demonstrated in the special and difficult situations described here will encourage all teachers to re-evaluate their classroom dynamics and consider instituting some cooperative teaching practices.

Special subjects

The jigsaw method promises to be an effective method for conveying information to individuals when traditional systems fail. For example, let us look at the problem of unwanted pregnancies among American teenagers. In spite of having sat through sex education courses, a great many teenagers remain ignorant of the factors which cause and prevent conception. It has been argued (Bridgeman and Aronson, 1980) that sex education courses have not been as effective as they might because, in part, teenagers tend to distrust information conveyed by adults about illicit pleasures (e.g. sex and marijuana). Indeed, it has been shown that most of the sex information and misinformation held by teenagers comes from their peers (Roberts et al., 1978). Accordingly, if accurate and complete information about contraception were delivered by peers as part of a structured learning experience, such information would have greater impact and be a natural way to refute peer-generated myths.

Furthermore, the jigsaw process is more than an effective way to learn information; it also produces increases in self-esteem, in the internal locus of control, and in empathic role-taking ability. All of these help arm young people with values, skills, and information which should help reduce the incidence of unintended pregnancy among teenagers. Again, there is no reason to limit the analysis to this problem. Information about drugs, educational planning and so on would almost certainly benefit from this analysis.

References

Allen, V. (1976). *Children As Teachers: Theory and Research on Tutoring*, Academic Press, New York.

Allport, G. (1954). *The Nature of Prejudice*, Addison-Wesley, Reading, Mass.

Aronson, E. (1972). *The Social Animal*, W. H. Freeman, San Francisco, Calif.

Aronson, E., with Blaney, N., Stephan, C., Sikes, J., and Snapp, M. (1978). *The Jigsaw Classroom*, Sage Publications, California.

Benware, C. (1975). 'Quantitative and qualitative learning differences as a function of learning in order to teach another,' Unpublished manuscript, University of Rochester, as cited in E. L. Deci, *Intrinsic Motivation*, Plenum Press, New York.

Blaney, N., Stephan, C., Rosenfield, D., Aronson, E., and Sikes, J. (1977). 'Interdependence in the classroom: A field study,' *Journal of Educational Psychology*, **69**, 121–128.

Bridgeman, D. (In press, 1981). 'The influence of cooperative, interdependent learning on role taking and moral reasoning: A theoretical and empirical field study with fifth-grade students,' *Journal of Experimental Social Psychology*.

Bridgeman, D., and Aronson, E. (1980). 'The use of jigsaw learning toward the reduction of unintended pregnancy,' Unpublished manuscript. University of California at Santa Cruz.

Brown v. *The Board of Education of Topeka* 347 US 483 (1954).

Chandler, M. (1973). 'Egocentrism and antisocial behavior: The assessment and training of social perspective-taking skills,' *Developmental Psychology*, **9**, 326–332.

Clark, K. B. (1979). 'The role of social scientists 25 years after Brown,' *Personality and Social Psychology Bulletin*, **5**, 477–481.

Cohen, E. (1972). 'Interracial interaction disability,' *Human Relations*, **25** (1), 9–24.

Cohen, E., and Roper, S. (1972). 'Modification of interracial interaction disability: An application of status characteristics theory,' *American Sociological Review*, **6**, 643–657.

Cook, S. W. (1979). 'Social science and school desegregation: Did we mislead the Supreme Court?' *Personality and Social Psychology Bulletin*, **5**, 420–438.

Covington, M. V., and Beery, R. G. (1976). *Self-worth and School Learning*, Holt, Rinehart and Winston, New York.

Deutsch, M. (1949). 'A theory of cooperation and competition,' *Human Relations*, **2**, 129–152.

Dollard, J. (1949). 'Hostility and fear in social life,' *Social Forces*, **17**, 15–26.

Fisher, R. B. (1969). 'An each one–teach one approach to music notation,' *Grade Teacher*, **86** (6).

Franks, D. D., and Marolla, J. (1976). 'Efficacious action and social approval as interacting dimensions of self-esteem: A tentative formulation through construct validation,' *Sociometry*, **39**, 324–341.

Gartner, A., Kohler, M. C., and Riessman, F. (1971). *Children Teach Children: Learning by Teaching*, Harper and Row, New York.

Geffner, R. (1978). 'The effects of interdependent learning on self-esteem, inter-ethnic relations, and intra-ethnic attitudes of elementary school children: A field experiment,' Unpublished Doctoral Dissertation, University of California at Santa Cruz.

Gerard, H., and Miller, N. (1975). *School Desegregation*, Plenum, New York.

Giby, R. G., Sr, and Giby, R. G., Jr (1967). 'The effects of stress resulting from academic failure,' *Journal of Clinical Psychology*, **23**, 35–37.

Goffman, E. (1963). *Stigma*, Prentice-Hall, Englewood Cliffs, NJ.

Gonzalez, A. (1979). 'Classroom cooperation and ethnic balance,' Unpublished Doctoral Dissertation, University of California at Santa Cruz.

Greeley, A. M., and Sheatsley, P. B. (December 1971). 'Attitudes toward racial integration,' *Scientific American*, **225** (6), 13–19.

Heider, F. (1958). *The Psychology of Interpersonal Relations*, Wiley, New York.

Jones, E., and Davis, K. (1965). 'From acts to dispositions,' in L. Berkowitz (ed.), *Advances in Experimental Social Psychology, Vol. 2*, Academic Press, New York.

Lamy, M. W. (1965). 'Relationship of self-perceptions of early primary children to achievement in reading,' in I. J. Gordon (ed.), *Human Development: Readings in Research*, Scott, Foresman, & Co., Chicago.

Lehrer, T. (*c.* 1965). 'National Brotherhood Week,' [*That Was The Year That Was: TW3 Songs & Other Songs of the Year*, Reprise (Warner Brothers Records), R6179.]

Lucker, G., Rosenfield, D., Sikes, J., and Aronson, E. (1977). 'Performance in the interdependent classroom: A field study,' *American Educational Research Journal*, **13**, 115–123.

Piaget, J. (1932). *Judgement and Reasoning in the Child*, Harcourt and Brace, New York.

Plessy v. *Ferguson* 163 US 537 (1896).

Purkey, W. W. (1970). *Self-Concept and School Achievement*, Prentice-Hall, Englewood Cliffs, New Jersey.

Roberts, E., Kline, D., and Gagnon, J. (1978). 'Family life and sexual learning: A study of the role of parents in the sexual learning of children,' *Population Education Inc.*, Vol. 1.

Rosen, S., Powell, E. R., and Schubot, D. B. (1977). 'Peer-tutoring outcomes as influenced by equity and type of role assignment,' *Journal of Educational Psychology*, **69**, 244–252.

St John, N. (1975). *School Desegregation: Outcomes for Children*, John Wiley and Sons, New York.

Sarbin, T. R. (1976). 'Cross-age tutoring and social identity,' in V. L. Allen (ed.), *Children as Teachers: Theory and Research on Tutoring*, Academic Press, New York.

Sherif, M. (November 1956). 'Experiments in group conflict,' *Scientific American*, **195** (5), 1–10.

Stephan, C., Kennedy, J., and Aronson, E. (1977a). 'The effects of friendship and outcome on task attribution,' *Sociometry*, **40**, 107–111.

Stephan, C., Presser, N., Kennedy, J., and Aronson, E. (1977b). 'Attributions to success and failure on cooperative, competitive, and interdependent interactions,' *European Journal of Social Psychology*, **8**, 269–274.

Stephan, W. (1978). 'School desegregation: An evaluation of predictions made in Brown *vs.* the Board of Education,' *Psychology Bulletin*, **85**, 217–238.

Part II
Influence of Others

Introduction

In this section we look at some of the ways in which people are influenced by others. We begin with the effects of the presence, real or implied, of someone who may be audience or co-actor. After looking at social influence when people are interacting, we end with the effects of particular others—children's friendships and relationships between men and women.

It might seem that the most simple question that could be put by, or to, social psychologists is 'What is the effect on behaviour of the presence of another person?' but as can be seen from the three papers which comprise Chapter 4, the question has turned out to be very complex. Although the work in this area is often styled 'social facilitation', the presence of others may sometimes detract from performance, rather than making it better. Zajonc (1965) proposed that the mediating variable was drive, which enhanced dominant responses and thus facilitated well-learned behaviour but inhibited poorly-learned responses. The drive approach has been extremely influential, but there are different explanations for the increase in drive when others are present. These are reviewed in the papers by Geen and Gange (sub-Chapter 4.1) and Sanders (sub-Chapter 4.2), the former paper favouring the idea that drive is a consequence of anticipating negative outcomes from others, the latter stressing the role of attentional processes in increasing drive. Manstead and Semin (1980) report a series of experiments which, they argue, cast doubt on the mediating role of drive. Their interpretation comes close to the conclusions of both papers here, but emphasizes the cognitive rather than drive aspects of evaluation apprehension and attentional conflict.

The effect of the presence of others may be a consequence of the perceived implications of numbers. For example, do greater numbers mean that each person feels a little less responsible for a joint outcome? This appears to be the case for physical tasks; the material on 'social loafing' is briefly reviewed by Petty, Cacioppo and Harkins (sub-Chapter 4.3). The main part of this paper is devoted to their research on the effects of group size on cognitive tasks, which has fascinating implications for the study of attitude change.

For further material related to this chapter, see Latané and Nida (1980); Zajonc (1980); Williams *et al.* (1981); Glaser (1982).

Social influence has sometimes been seen as the essential feature of social psychology (see, for example, Harvey and Smith, 1977, p. 3). Each of the four papers in Chapter 5 highlights a different issue, and provides a different perspective on social influence processes. The chapter cannot, of course, provide full coverage of the many complex and diverse issues, for which the reader might first consult a general text such as Middlebrook (1980), Wrightsman and Deaux (1981) or Hollander (1981).

Milgram and Sabini (sub-Chapter 5.1) discuss the subtle ways in which implicit norms, or 'residual rules', influence our everyday behaviour by shaping our social reality, although we are unaware of this until they are challenged. This paper reports on their research into the effects of transgressing against such a rule on the New York subway. (See also Schwartz, 1981; Garfinkel, 1967; Cicourel, sub-Chapter 9.2, this volume.)

Langer's paper (sub-Chapter 5.2) serves to emphasize the general point that social influence is not merely something intentionally exerted by one person or agency, and received by another, information-processing individual. Langer's argument that actions are often 'mindless', following 'scripts', suggests that one form of influence is neither normative nor informational, but arises when one person, intentionally or otherwise, triggers off another's script. The idea is somewhat reminiscent of Jones and Gerard's (1967) notion of 'cue control', although the theoretical ramifications of each are very different. From Langer's paper we can see that people may affect each other quite unwittingly, by eliciting each other's scripted behaviour. However, deviations from what is expected might provoke deliberate influence from the other. Equally, awareness of the inadequacy of one's scripted behaviour might render one susceptible to social influence, particularly informational influence. For a further discussion of the concept of 'script', see Abelson (1981).

There is no doubt that some deviations from what is expected provoke unambiguous attempts to influence. Newcomb (sub-Chapter 5.3) discusses his study of the competing social influences in correctional institutions, and his idea that resentment can mediate between coercion attempts and inmate behaviour.

Yet if all social influence processes operated in such a way that deviants were led, or brought themselves, back into line with already established norms (implicit or explicit), how could we explain social change? How could one person convince others of the value of new ideas, theories, evidence? Moscovici (sub-Chapter 5.4) argues for an approach to social influence in which it is possible to account for social change as well as conformity. He briefly describes his theory and some of the supporting research on minority influence.

The chapter on *Helping and Hurting* looks more specifically at the relationship between social influence and the ways in which people may treat each other. Kent (sub-Chapter 6.1) discusses the value of relating the study of prosocial behaviour to work on small group processes. Zahn-Waxler (sub-Chapter 6.2) describes one of the studies on the prosocial behaviour of very young children carried out in collaboration with Radke-Yarrow and their colleagues. They have used a multi-faceted research strategy to look at the relationship between children's altruistic and reparative behaviour and mothers' caregiving.

For further reviews and readings in this field, see Rushton and Sorrentino, 1981; Mussen and Eisenberg-Berg, 1977; Wispé, 1978; Lickona, 1976; Radke-Yarrow et al. (in press); Eisenberg, 1982.

The second part of this chapter is focused on aggression. It is a slippery concept, usually defined in terms of both the intentions of the actor and the consequences for someone else, for example, 'Aggression is the intentional injury of another' (Berkowitz, 1980, p. 337). Tedeschi and Melburg (sub-Chapter 6.3) cast the notion into an entirely different framework, by regarding it as the use of coercive power. This approach has promise both for the extension of research, and for the integration of aggression with other areas of social psychology—so often it is presented as a 'special topic'.

Jaffe and Yinon (sub-Chapter 6.4) have studied the differences between individuals and groups in their use of retaliation and aggression. While it might be argued that this research reflects another instance of the group polarization effect (see Burnstein and Schul, sub-Chapter 1.4, Volume 2), it is equally true to say that such a conclusion would place the work, like the previous paper, in the broader context of social psychological processes. Such a development is likely to enhance our understanding of the nature of aggression. For further reading on aggression see Geen and O'Neal, 1977; Berkowitz, 1980, Ch. 12.

People join groups not only because the group's activities may be rewarding, but also because they are attracted to members of the group and value the companionship and friendship which a group can provide. In addition to these aggregating effects, attraction and friendship can influence the functioning and stability of a group through their contributions to group cohesiveness (see Shaw, sub-Chapter 2.4). A great deal of research has been carried out into the determinants and consequences of interpersonal attraction and friendship, and, although not derived specifically from group contexts, the general principles revealed by this research are relevant to intragroup situations (see, for example, Berscheid and Walster, 1978; Duck, 1977; Huston, 1974; Levinger and Snoek, 1972).

Two frequently cited determinants of attraction and friendship are propinquity and similarity. Nahemow and Lawton's paper (sub-Chapter 7.1) examines the influence of these two variables in a field study of the friendship network among residents of an urban housing project.

Rubin's paper (sub-Chapter 7.2) deals with children's friendships particularly the skills required to make and maintain them. As well as documenting the kind of naturally occurring strategies involved in the formation of such friendships, Rubin also discusses research aimed at improving friendship skills.

Broderick's paper (sub-Chapter 7.3) is concerned with relationships between man and woman as 'grown-ups'. Although societal influences constrain the pattern and form of interactions between adult males and females, his review indicates that marriage is just one of a number of possible arrangements for living together in Western society.

Further research on friendship and attraction can be found in: Derlega *et al.* (1976); Krebs and Adinolfi (1975); Lewis and Rosenblum (1974); Schiffenbauer and Schiavo (1976); Segal (1979).

References

Abelson, R. F. (1981). 'Psychological status of the script concept,' *American Psychologist*, **36**, 715–729.

Berkowitz, L. (1980). *A survey of Social Psychology*, 2nd edn, Holt, Rinehart and Winston, New York.

Berscheid, E., and Walster, E. (1978). *Interpersonal Attraction*, 2nd edn, Addison-Wesley, Reading, Mass.

Derlega, V. J., Wilson, M., and Chaikin, A. L. (1976). 'Friendship and disclosure reciprocity,' *Journal of Personality and Social Psychology*, **34**, 578–582.

Duck, S. (ed.) (1977). *Theory and Practice in Interpersonal Attraction*, Academic Press, London.

Eisenberg, N. (ed.) (1982). *The Development of Prosocial Behavior*, Academic Press Inc., New York.

Garfinkel, H. (1967). *Studies in Ethnomethodology*, Prentice-Hall, Englewood Cliffs, New Jersey.

Geen, Russell G., and O'Neal, E. C. (1967). *Perspectives on Aggression*, Academic Press, New York.

Glaser, A. N. (1982). 'Drive theory of social facilitation: A critical reappraisal,' *British Journal of Social Psychology*, **21**, 265–282.

Harvey, J. H., and Smith, W. P. (1977). *Social Psychology: An Attributional Approach*, The C. V. Mosby Co., Saint Louis.

Hollander, E. P. (1981). *Principles and Methods of Social Psychology*, 4th edn, Oxford University Press, New York and Oxford.

Huston, T. (ed.) (1974). *Foundations of Interpersonal Attraction*, Academic Press, New York.

Jones, E. E., and Gerard, H. B. (1967). *Foundations of Social Psychology*, John Wiley and Sons, New York.

Krebs, D., and Adinolfi, A. A. (1975). 'Physical attractiveness, social relations, and personality style,' *Journal of Personality and Social Psychology*, **31**, 245–253.

Latané, B., and Nida, S. (1980). 'Social impact theory and group influence: A social engineering perspective', in P. B. Paulus (ed.), *Psychology of Group Influence* L. Erlbaum Associates, Hillsdale, NJ.

Levinger, G., and Snoek, J. D. (1972). *Attraction in Relationships: A New Look at Interpersonal Attraction*, General Learning Press, Morristown, NJ.

Lewis, M., and Rosenblum, L. A. (eds.) (1974). *Friendship and Peer Relations*, Wiley, New York.

Lickona, T. (ed.) (1976). *Moral Development and Behavior: Theory, Research and Social Issues*, Holt, Rinehart and Winston, New York.

Manstead, A. S. R., and Semin, G. R. (1980). 'Social facilitation effects: Mere enhancement of dominant responses?', *British Journal of Social and Clinical Psychology*, **19**, 119–136.

Middlebrook, P. N. (1980). *Social Psychology and Modern Life*, 2nd edn, Knopf, New York.

Mussen, P., and Eisenberg-Berg, N. (1977). *Roots of Caring, Sharing, and Helping: The Development of Prosocial Behavior in Children*, W. H. Freeman, San Francisco.

Radke-Yarrow, M., Zahn-Waxler, C., and Chapman, M. (In press). 'Prosocial dispositions and behavior' in P. Mussen (ed.), *Manual of Child Psychology*, (volume on personality and social development) John Wiley and Sons, New York.

Rushton, J-P., and Sorrentino, R. M. (eds.) (1981). *Altruism and Helping Behavior*, Erlbaum, Hillsdale NJ.

Schiffenbauer, A., and Schiavo, S. R. (1976). 'Physical distance and attraction: An intensification effect,' *Journal of Experimental Social Psychology*, **12**, 274–282.

Schwartz, H. (1981). 'Phenomenology and Ethnomethodology', in M. Rosenberg and R. H. Turner (eds.), *Social Psychology: Sociological Perspectives*, Basic Books, New York.

Segal, M. W. (1979). 'Varieties of interpersonal attraction and their relationship in natural groups,' *Social Psychology Quarterly*, **42**, 253–261.

Williams, K., Harkins, S., and Latané, B. (1981). 'Identifiability as a Deterrent to Social Loafing: Two Cheering Experiments,' *Journal of Personality and Social Psychology*, **40** (2), 303–311.

Wispé, L. (ed.) (1978). *Altruism, Sympathy and Helping: Psychological and Sociological Principles*, Academic Press, New York.

Wrightsman, L., and Deaux, K. (1981). *Social Psychology in the 80s*, 3rd edn, Brooks Cole, Monterey, Calif.

Zajonc, R. B. (1965). 'Social Facilitation,' *Science*, **149**, 269–274.

Zajonc, R. B. (1980). 'Compresence', in P. B. Paulus (ed.), *Psychology of Group Influence*, L. Erlbaum Associates, Hillsdale, NJ.

Reference Note

The reader may wish to consult the following papers in other Parts of Volumes 1 and 2 which seem particularly relevant to the chapters in Part 2:–

Chapter 5. See Volume 1: Cicourel (9.2), Zimbardo (9.4).
See Volume 2: Tindale and Davis (1.1), Janis (1.2), Burnstein and Schul (1.4), Murton (6.7).

Chapter 6. See Volume 2: Burnstein and Schul (1.4), Chapter 2, Zander (7.6).

Chapter 7. See Volume 1: Sommer (1.1), Taylor and Altman (1.2), Aronson and Yates (3.3), Hinde (9.1), Jacklin and Maccoby (9.3).
See Volume 2: Kanter (5.1), Gorman (5.2), Shepher and Tiger (5.3).

4 Presence of Others

Small Groups and Social Interaction, Volume 1
Edited by H. H. Blumberg, A. P. Hare, V. Kent and M. Davies
© 1983 John Wiley & Sons Ltd

4.1   Social Facilitation: Drive Theory and Beyond

Russell G. Geen and James J. Gange   *University of Missouri*

Although the phenomenon of social facilitation has a long history beginning with the research of Triplett (1898), current interest in the subject dates from 1965, when Zajonc analyzed the effects of audiences and coactors on performance in terms of drive theory. Briefly stated, Zajonc's argument was that the presence of others increases the actor's level of drive, thereby energizing dominant responses at the expense of subordinate ones in accordance with the Hull–Spence equation, $E = H \times D$ (Excitatory potential, i.e. likely strength of a particular response = Habit strength multiplied by general Drive level). The result is social facilitation of performance on easy tasks, in which correct responses are dominant, and social inhibition of performance on difficult tasks, in which dominant responses are more likely to be incorrect. Using this formulation, Zajonc was able to explain many of the contradictions in the older literature on social facilitation by taking into account the nature of the tasks used. Virtually all research on social facilitation since 1965 has been influenced in some way by Zajonc's hypothesis, either supporting it, extending it, or rejecting it in favor of various alternative viewpoints. At the present time three different varieties of the drive theory of social facilitation are discernible. One stresses the 'mere presence' of others as a stimulus for increased drive (Zajonc, 1980). Another describes socially induced drive as the product of apprehension and anxiety over being evaluated by others (Cottrell, 1972; Geen, 1976b). The third treats drive as the outcome of distraction and attentional conflict caused by the presence of others (Sanders *et al.*, 1978). Because the distraction/conflict viewpoint is the subject of another paper in this volume (sub-Chapter 4.2), we will confine our discussion to the mere presence and evaluation apprehension hypotheses, with emphasis primarily on the latter.

Evidence of socially induced drive

Studies showing the drive-inducing quality of social settings have involved both behavioral and physiological indicators of drive. The earliest tests of Zajonc's hypothesis required a choice of dependent variables that allowed the identification of dominant and subordinate responses. This requirement led to the use of several different experimental tasks, some of which involved the creation of habit-strength hierarchies (e.g. Zajonc and Sales, 1966) and others of which assumed that such hierarchies would be manifest in differential performance across levels of a task (e.g. Cottrell *et al.*, 1967). Still another demonstration of drive increments in social settings was provided by experiments in which the presence of others was shown to facilitate the emission of well-learned responses but to hamper the acquisition of new ones (Hunt and Hillery, 1973; Zentall and Levine, 1972; Levine and Zentall, 1974). Other investigators have sought to discover socially induced drive in experiments involving outcomes other than energization of dominant responses. Geen (1973) showed that female subjects who were observed by an evaluative experimenter showed poor short-term recall but enhanced long-term recall relative to nonobserved subjects, a finding consistent with other evidence that drive facilitates reminiscence in this manner (Walker and Tarte, 1963). Similar findings among male subjects have been reported by Deffenbacher *et al.* (1974) and by Walker and Borden (1976).

Several investigators have tested the hypothesis of socially induced drive by measuring psychophysiological correlates of autonomic activity in audience settings. The most commonly reported measure has been the Palmar Sweat Index. This has been shown to be related to the presence of an audience during test situations, with observed subjects showing either an increase or maintenance of level of palmar sweat relative to nonobserved subjects (Martens, 1969a, 1969b, 1969c; Cohen and Davis, 1973; Droppleman and McNair, 1971; Lipper and McNair, 1972; Geen, 1976b, 1977). Evidence from studies using measures other than palmar sweat has yielded only partial support for the notion of socially produced drive. Chapman (1974) reported higher levels of muscle action potential in subjects who listened to a recording in the presence of an experimenter than in subjects who listened alone. Cardiac acceleration has been found to be a correlate of social arousal in both rats (Latané and Cappell, 1972) and humans (Singerman *et al.*, 1976). In a study involving measurement of skin conductance, Henchy and Glass (1968) found no change as a function of observation by audience. However, Geen (1979) found evidence of increased conductance among observed subjects who had just failed at a prior task (see below). Thus, there appears to be some evidence that socially induced drive can be detected through several psychophysiological indicators, even though few studies have obtained multiple psychophysiological measures within a single experiment. Recent research has demonstrated that a concept of unified physiological arousal does not adequately describe autonomic functioning, because the various autonomic measures are weakly correlated at best. Multiple measures are therefore necessary to specify the psychophysiological effects of socially induced drive. In addition, few studies have combined both behavioral and physiological measures, and none to date has reported any correlation between the two types of measure.

Mere presence and evaluation apprehension

The question of whether the 'mere' presence of others is sufficient to produce the social facilitation effect[1] or whether the others must elicit some feelings of apprehension has been debated almost from the time of Zajonc's review. In the first study designed to distinguish between the two views, Cottrell et al. (1968) found that the presence of two attentive observers facilitated the emission of dominant responses whereas the presence of two blindfolded and inattentive people did not. Cottrell and his associates concluded that apprehension over being observed and implicitly judged by the observers was the immediate antecedent of social facilitation. Evaluation apprehension is a learned drive acquired through a history of being exposed to evaluative situations. Out of such a history the person develops generalized expectancies of either positive or negative outcomes following performance in social settings. Anticipation of negative outcomes leads to fear, anxiety, or anticipatory frustration, whereas anticipation of positive outcomes is an incentive that has strong drive properties.

Several studies have supported the findings and general position of Cottrell and his colleagues. As we have noted elsewhere (Geen and Gange, 1977), an adequate test of the evaluation apprehension hypothesis would require three conditions: one in which subjects performed alone; a second in which performance occurred in the presence of others not regarded as a source of evaluation; and a third in which the audience is both present and evaluative. Studies using this basic design or some variation of it have given considerable support to the notion that evaluation apprehension is a necessary condition for social facilitation (e.g., Henchy and Glass, 1968; Paulus and Murdoch, 1971; Geen, 1974; Sasfy and Okun, 1974; Bray and Sugarman, 1980). However, other experiments have shown that the presence of others may be arousing without eliciting any demonstrable evaluation apprehension. Zajonc et al. (1969) have reported what appear to be both coaction and audience effects in cockroaches, a species to which the attribution of evaluation apprehension seems implausible. Moreover, recent research on human subjects also indicates that the mere presence hypothesis may still be viable (Chapman, 1974; Haas and Roberts, 1975; Markus, 1978; Rajecki et al., 1977; Rittle and Bernard, 1977). At least two explanations of the mere presence effect have been suggested. One is that the company of others creates uncertainty over what those others may do, and uncertainty increases arousal level. This possibility, first noted by Zajonc (1980) has not been tested experimentally. Another possibility is that the presence of nonevaluative others may provide cues for conditioned evaluation apprehension. A history of experiences with evaluative social settings may produce an association of such settings with judgment even on occasions in which no judgment is being made. Cottrell (1972) has suggested such a possibility, as have Crandall (1974) and Rittle and Bernard (1977).

For the time being we must conclude that the mere presence v. evaluation apprehension debate has not been resolved. Evidence can be cited for both hypotheses. Furthermore, probably no advocate of the mere presence viewpoint would deny the importance of evaluation apprehension in social facilitation when conditions produce it. We shall therefore turn our discussion to an analysis of the latter view, with specific reference to Cottrell's (1972) argument that apprehension arises from anticipation of both positive and negative outcomes.

The nature of evaluation apprehension

Audience settings

In the first study designed to test Cottrell's hypothesis, Good (1973) informed some subjects that their performance on a task would be evaluated immediately by an observer, and others that the evaluation would be delayed. Half the subjects in each condition were led to believe that they would do well on the task and half were told that they should expect to do poorly. Good found a social facilitation effect among subjects who were informed that they would be judged immediately and who also expected to do well on the task. No such effect was found among subjects who expected to do poorly. Good's study thus supports the idea that anticipation of a positive outcome leads to social facilitation, but gives no such support in the case of anticipation of negative outcomes. There is mounting evidence, however, that social facilitation occurs only when subjects expect that the outcome of evaluation by others will be negative, a position first articulated by Weiss and Miller (1971). In a series of studies in our laboratory we have sought to create situations in which subjects are evaluated by observers, but are led to believe that the outcome of the judgment will be positive. In our earlier studies we informed some of the observed subjects that the purpose of the observation (by the experimenter) was to provide information to the latter that would allow her to give some help to the subject on a subsequent task. Other subjects were observed and evaluated, but not told that the purpose of the evaluation was to establish the basis for future help. In one study (Geen, 1977), performance on a complex anagram task was hindered less by the presence of a potentially helpful observer than by the presence of a merely evaluative one, even though the helpful observer was associated with poorer performance than that shown by subjects working alone. Thus the anticipation of a positive outcome did not entirely eliminate the social 'facilitation' effect, but it did reduce that effect in comparison to what happened when there was an expectation of a negative outcome. In a second study (Geen, 1976b), the provision of a promise of future help reduced social facilitation of paired-associates' learning, thus further supporting the idea that expectation of a positive outcome does not have the same effect as expectation of a negative one.

More recently, some attempts have been made to create anticipation of positive and negative outcomes through informing subjects that they have either succeeded or failed on a task preliminary to the one during which they are observed. The experimental induction of failure has been shown to exacerbate the social facilitation effect. Lombardo and Catalano (1978) found that subjects who had been led to believe that they had done poorly on an initial task showed a more drastic breakdown in performance on a subsequent complex problem during observation than did subjects who had not been given the first task. Seta and Hassan (1980) expanded upon this finding by showing that subjects who had supposedly failed a preliminary task did worse later on another task while supposedly observed than when working alone, whereas subjects who had ostensibly enjoyed prior success showed no difference in performance as a function of being observed or left alone. This study calls into serious question the assumption that anticipation of positive outcomes elicits evaluation apprehension. Geen (1979) has, in fact, reported that whereas prior failure is followed by the expected audience effects on performance, preliminary success at a task may even reverse the usual audience effect and lead to better performance on a difficult task during observation than during isolation. This social *facilitation* of performance on a difficult task is found only when the preliminary task and the main task are highly similar in nature. More recently, Geen (1980a) has suggested that such a facilitation effect may be due to a greater expenditure of effort among observed subjects following success than is shown by similarly successful, but isolated, subjects. It was proposed that the behavior of successful subjects was influenced by a desire to create a favorable impression upon the audience.

Coaction settings

The evaluation apprehension hypothesis evolved from experiments in which subjects were observed by audiences. We may ask what might be the counterpart of such audience evaluation apprehension in the coaction setting. The answer most usually given is that coacting subjects become aroused through fear of failure at competition. Such reasoning, of course, merely restates the idea of evaluation apprehension in another form. In the coaction situation subjects perceive themselves to be in competition, with the implication that one will perform better than the other and hence will 'win' at competition while the other 'loses'. We suggest that the significance of all this for the subject is that the winner attains a higher level of approval, at least implicitly, from the experimenter or anyone else present than does the loser, given the fact that winning is highly valued in our culture. Thus, to be in coaction (and hence competition) with another is in fact to experience apprehension over evaluation that will inevitably follow the outcome.

The role of competition in social facilitation under coaction conditions is suggested by several findings. Both Carment (1970) and Van Tuinen and McNeel (1975) found that the insertion of specific instructions indicating competition enhanced the social facilitation effect among coactors. Others have shown that when instructions are given that induce a cooperative and noncompetitive attitude among coactors, social facilitation effects are attenuated (e.g. Seta *et al.*, 1976). It should also be true that if implicit competition underlies social facilitation in coactors, conditions that reduce the possibility of competitiveness should reduce the coaction effect. For example, Seta *et al.* (1977) found that social facilitation was significantly reduced when members of coacting pairs worked on different tasks, compared to pairs in which members worked on the same task. Other studies have shown that providing coactors with information about performance that could sharpen feelings of rivalry may enhance social facilitation effects (Klinger, 1969; Martens and Landers, 1972; Innes, 1972; Beck and Seta, 1980).

Finally, we should note that Carment and Latchford (1970) found that the presence of the experimenter increased social facilitation in coactors, possibly by providing explicit cues for evaluation apprehension. This study suggests that audience and coaction conditions may interact. It therefore supports the line of reasoning stated above. The presence of an evaluating experimenter could heighten feelings of rivalry in coactors by reminding the latter of the payoffs associated with winning or losing in competition. Geen (1980c) has discovered some support for this contention in a survey of coaction studies reported in the literature. After reviewing 15 experimental studies on coaction reported between 1969 and 1978, Geen noted that in 9 of the 15 it was clearly stated whether or not the experimenter was present during coaction. Adopting the working hypothesis that the effects of coaction on performance are due to evaluation apprehension brought on by fear of failing before the experimenter, Geen found that 6 of the 9 studies supported the hypothesis whereas 3 disconfirmed it.

Individual differences and social facilitation

Some investigators have studied possible effects of individual difference variables on arousal produced by the presence of others. Often such attempts have failed to reveal effects due to personality, and at other times significant effects have proven to be difficult to interpret (e.g. Kohfeld and Weitzel, 1969). One reason for this is that much of the study of individual difference effects has not been guided by firm theoretical positions relating the individual difference in question to the audience situation. In some cases, however, such theoretical rationales have been formulated, and in each case important individual difference effects in social arousal have been found.

Trait anxiety

To the extent that evaluation apprehension is involved in the generation of arousal by audiences, individual differences in trait anxiety might be thought of as predictors of the magnitude of the anxiety state that the audience elicits (cf. Spielberger, 1972). Unfortunately, the situation is made ambiguous by the fact that at least six measures of trait anxiety have been reported in studies that also involve several different tasks. Some of these studies have reported no significant interaction between the trait measure and audience presence (Quarter and Marcus, 1971; Alpert and Haber, 1960; Berkey and Hoppe, 1972; Martens and Landers, 1969; Wankel, 1977). However, studies in which the trait measure used was the Test Anxiety Scale (Sarason, 1972) have reported significant anxiety-by-audience interactions (Ganzer, 1968; Geen, 1977). In addition, extensive research by Paivio and his colleagues (e.g., Paivio, 1965) has shown that when trait anxiety is quantified in terms of a specific scale of audience anxiety, it is a particularly reliable predictor of state anxiety in audience situations. Thus, whether or not trait anxiety interacts with the audience variable to affect arousal and performance depends to a large extent on the degree of congruence between the individual difference measure and the nature of the audience situation.

Achievement and affiliation motives

Atkinson (1974) has devised a model for human performance that has some implications for effects of test anxiety and audience presence. Briefly stated, his argument is that: (1) the total strength of a motivational tendency in a test situation is the sum of (a) tendencies to seek success, (b) tendencies to avoid failure, and (c) other relevant extrinsic motives such as need for social approval; and also that (2) the strength of the motivational tendency thus derived is related to performance by an inverted U according to the Yerkes–Dodson Law. This approach thus adds achievement and affiliation motivation to test anxiety as determinants of overall motive strength. Need for affiliation is especially important to the study of social facilitation because it contributes to overall motive strength only when the opportunity to receive approval is present, as in audience settings. Several studies testing Atkinson's viewpoint have been reported, and the evidence has been generally supportive (e.g., Entin, 1974; Kawamura-Reynolds, 1977; Sorrentino and Sheppard, 1978).

The Type A pattern

A recent study by Gastorf et al. (1980) has related performance in coaction settings to the Type A coronary-prone behavior pattern. The latter describes individuals who are driven by intense competitive pressures and show an exaggerated sense of time urgency. In the Gastorf et al. experiment, Type A persons were found to perform better at a simple task under coaction conditions than in isolation, but worse at a complex task during coaction than when alone. No such differences across the alone–coaction variable were found among the more relaxed and less competitive Type B subjects. The performance of the Type

A subjects is identical to the coaction effect most commonly reported (e.g., Hunt and Hillery, 1973), and suggests again the possible importance of perceived competition in coaction-induced social facilitation. The behavior of the Type A subjects is consistent with the distraction hypothesis of Sanders *et al.* (1978), in that Type A subjects showed evidence of being less attentive than Type B subjects. It is also possible that Type A subjects manifested the social facilitation effect because they were more apprehensive over being evaluated than the Type B subjects, a possibility in line with Gastorf and Teevan's (1980) finding that Type A subjects express greater fear of failure than Type B subjects.

Some new directions

As we proposed in an earlier review, it would seem safe to conclude at the present time that the bulk of the evidence to date still favors a drive-theoretical explanation of social facilitation, particularly if we define drive in terms of learned tendencies to become apprehensive in testing situations (Geen and Gange, 1977). Nevertheless, certain recent developments that have grown out of the drive approach suggest that processes other than drive induction take place in social facilitation. We shall conclude by citing two of these developments.

Test anxiety and cue utilization

Evaluation apprehension may be an anxiety response to a test situation that influences behavior through its effects on cognitive arousal (worry). One effect of such arousal may be an inward direction of attention and a consequent inattention to external stimuli, such as those associated with testing. The result may be a narrowing of the range of cues utilized in problem solving (e.g. Wine, 1971; Mueller, 1975; Geen, 1980b). This formulation may account for the finding that the presence of an audience or group of coactors facilitates performance on simple tasks but hinders performance on complex ones. Socially induced anxiety, by narrowing the range of cues utilized, may help focus the subject's attention on a small number of central cues that provide most or all of the information needed for solving a simple problem, while at the same time eliminating the influence of peripheral cues necessary for the solution of more difficult problems (Bruning *et al.*, 1968; Geen, 1976a). The study of social facilitation may therefore have important links with the emerging and important study of test anxiety.

Impression management

Some findings on social facilitation can be explained by concluding that a potentially threatening social setting enhances a person's tendency to be conservative in his or her behavior (e.g., Zajonc *et al.*, 1970). For instance, socially facilitated tendencies to emit common word associates (Matlin and Zajonc, 1968), usually viewed as evidence of the energization of habitual responses by drive, may actually represent conservatism in responding. Blank *et al.* (1976) have argued that the presence of an audience inhibits emission of idiosyncratic word associations (hence fostering emission of common ones) because such inhibition allows subjects to present themselves in the best possible light. It is reasonable to suppose that a person who feels uncomfortable in a social setting, and who anticipates evaluation and judgment, may be motivated to avoid doing anything that appears strange or undesirable. Support for this notion has recently been offered by Berger and his associates (Berger and Hecken, 1980; Berger *et al.*, 1980), who have shown that the presence of an audience inhibits overt practice during learning, such as talking to oneself, counting on the fingers, or reading aloud. Lack of such practice may be especially damaging to the encoding of material necessary for solution of difficult problems. On the other hand, inhibition of overt practice may compel the person to resort to more covert and imaginal encoding, which in turn could be of help in the learning of simpler material. This analysis is an alternative to the drive-theoretical accounts of social facilitation and inhibition of learning offered previously (e.g. Cottrell *et al.*, 1967), and is consistent with the idea that people are motivated to make a good impression on the audience. Furthermore, when such a need for good impression management is clearly present, the results of being observed can even be opposite to those predicted by the drive theory of social facilitation (Dua, 1977). As we have already noted, the creation of a strong expectancy of success may represent one such set of conditions (Geen, 1979, 1980a).

Summary

Since 1965, theory and research on social facilitation have been dominated by Zajonc's drive theory analysis. According to various versions of the drive theory, social facilitation is engendered by the mere presence of others, by distraction associated with that presence, or by feelings of evaluation apprehension elicited by the others. This chapter has reviewed primarily studies pertinent to the latter, and stated the conclusion that evaluation apprehension elicited by an audience or coactors is the result of anticipation of negative outcomes. When conditions reduce the value of others as a stimulus for such anticipations, the social facilitation effect is reduced or eliminated. Some recent studies suggest that social facilitation research may be extended through a consideration of certain non-drive mechanisms, such as cognitive arousal in evaluative settings and cognitive impression management. These studies promise some new theoretical departures in the study of social psychology's oldest empirical problem.

Note

1. Unless otherwise indicated by the context in which it is discussed, the term 'social facilitation' is used in this review to refer to the general effect of audiences or coactors on performance, whether that effect is facilitatory or inhibitory. Most of the time, in the

interests of clarity, we use the more cumbersome construction 'social facilitation effect' to describe the same process.

References

Alpert, R., and Haber, R. N. (1960). 'Anxiety in academic achievement situations,' *Journal of Abnormal and Social Psychology*, **61**, 207–215.

Atkinson, J. W. (1974). 'Strength of motivation and efficiency of performance,' in J. W. Atkinson and J. O. Raynor (eds.), *Motivation and Achievement*, Winston, Washington.

Beck, H. P., and Seta, J. J. (1980). 'The effects of frequency of feedback on a simple co-action task,' *Journal of Personality and Social Psychology*, **38**, 75–80.

Berger, S. M., Hampton, K. L., Carli, L. L., Grandmaison, P. S., Sadow, J. S., and Donath, C. H. (1980). 'Audience-induced inhibition of overt practice during learning,' Unpublished paper, University of Massachusetts.

Berger, S. M., and Hecken, M. H. (1980). 'Observer mediation and learning in the presence of a stranger,' Paper presented at the annual meeting of the Eastern Psychological Association, Hartford, Connecticut, April.

Berkey, A. S., and Hoppe, R. A. (1972). 'The combined effect of audience and anxiety on paired-associates learning,' *Psychonomic Science*, **29**, 351–353.

Blank, T. O., Staff, I., and Shaver, P. (1976). 'Social facilitation of word associations: Further questions,' *Journal of Personality and Social Psychology*, **34**, 725–733.

Bray, R. M., and Sugarman, R. (1980). 'Social facilitation among interacting groups: Evidence for the evaluation-apprehension hypothesis,' *Personality and Social Psychology Bulletin*, **6**, 137–142.

Bruning, J. L., Capage, J. E., Kozuh, J. F., Young, P. F., and Young, W. E. (1968). 'Socially induced drive and range of cue utilization,' *Journal of Personality and Social Psychology*, **9**, 242–244.

Carment, D. W. (1970). 'Rate of simple motor responding as a function of coaction, competition, and sex of the participants,' *Psychonomic Science*, **19**, 340–341.

Carment, D. W., and Latchford, M. (1970). 'Rate of simple motor responding as a function of coaction, sex of the participants, and the presence or absence of the experimenter,' *Psychonomic Science*, **20**, 253–254.

Chapman, A. J. (1974). 'An electromyographic study of social facilitation: A test of the 'mere presence' hypothesis,' *British Journal of Psychology*, **65**, 123–128.

Cohen, J. L., and Davis, J. H. (1973). 'Effects of audience status, evaluation, and time of action on performance with hidden-word problems,' *Journal of Personality and Social Psychology*, **27**, 74–85.

Cottrell, N. B. (1972). 'Social facilitation,' in C. G. McClintock (ed.), *Experimental Social Psychology* Holt, Rinehart & Winston, New York.

Cottrell, N. B., Rittle, R. H., and Wack, D. L. (1967). 'The presence of an audience and list type (competitional or noncompetitional) as joint determinants of performance in paired-associates learning,' *Journal of Personality*, **35**, 425–434.

Cottrell, N. B., Wack, D. L., Sekerak, G. J., and Rittle, R. H. (1968). 'Social facilitation of dominant responses by the presence of an audience and the mere presence of others,' *Journal of Personality and Social Psychology*, **9**, 245–250.

Crandall, R. (1974). 'Social facilitation: Theories and research,' in A. Harrison (ed.), *Explorations in Psychology*, Brooks-Cole, Monterey, Calif.

Deffenbacher, K. A., Platt, G. J., and Williams, M. A. (1974). 'Differential recall as a function of socially induced arousal and retention interval,' *Journal of Experimental Psychology*, **103**, 809–811.

Droppleman, L. F., and McNair, D. M. (1971). 'An experimental analog of public speaking,' *Journal of Consulting and Clinical Psychology*, **36**, 91–96.

Dua, J. K. (1977). 'Effect of audience on the acquisition and extinction of avoidance,' *British Journal of Social and Clinical Psychology*, **76**, 207–212.

Entin, E. (1974). 'Effects of achievement-oriented and affiliative motives on private and public performance,' in J. W. Atkinson and J. O. Raynor (eds.), *Motivation and Achievement*, Winston, Washington.

Ganzer, V. J. (1968). 'The effects of audience presence and test anxiety on learning and retention in a serial learning situation,' *Journal of Personality and Social Psychology*, **8**, 194–199.

Gastorf, J. W., Suls, J., and Sanders, G. S. (1980). 'Type A coronary-prone behavior pattern and social facilitation,' *Journal of Personality and Social Psychology*, **38**, 773–780.

Gastorf, J. W., and Teevan, R. C. (1980). 'Type A coronary-prone behavior pattern and fear of failure,' *Motivation and Emotion*, **4**, 71–76.

Geen, R. G. (1973). 'Effects of being observed on short- and long-term recall,' *Journal of Experimental Psychology*, **100**, 365–368.

Geen, R. G. (1974). 'Effects of evaluation apprehension on memory over intervals of varying length,' *Journal of Experimental Psychology*, **102**, 908–910.

Geen, R. G. (1976a). 'Test anxiety, observation, and range of cue utilization,' *British Journal of Social and Clinical Psychology*, **15**, 253–259.

Geen, R. G. (1976b). 'The role of the social environment in the induction and reduction of anxiety,' C.D. Spielberger and I. G. Sarason (eds.), *Stress and Anxiety*, Vol. 3, Hemisphere, Washington, DC.

Geen, R. G. (1977). 'The effects of anticipation of positive and negative outcomes on audience anxiety,' *Journal of Consulting and Clinical Psychology*, **45**, 715–716.

Geen, R. G. (1979). 'Effects of being observed on learning following success and failure experiences,' *Motivation and Emotion*, **3**, 355–371.

Geen, R. G. (1980a). 'Effects of being observed on persistence at an insoluble task,' Unpublished manuscript, University of Missouri.

Geen, R. G. (1980b). 'Test anxiety and cue utilization,' in I. G. Sarason (ed.), *Test Anxiety: Theory, Research, and Applications*, L. Erlbaum Associates, Hillsdale, NJ.

Geen, R. G. (1980c). 'The effects of being observed on performance,' in P. B. Paulus (ed.), *Psychology of Group Influence*, L. Erlbaum Associates, Hillsdale, NJ.

Geen, R. G. and Gange, J. J. (1977). 'Drive theory of social facilitation: Twelve years of theory and research,' *Psychological Bulletin*, **84**, 1267–1288.

Good, K. J. (1973). 'Social facilitation: Effects of performance anticipation, evaluation, and response competition on free association,' *Journal of Personality and Social Psychology*, **28**, 270–275.

Haas, J., and Roberts, G. C. (1973). 'Effect of evaluative others upon learning and performance of a complex motor task,' *Journal of Motor Behavior*, **7**, 81–90.

Henchy, T., and Glass, D. C. (1968). 'Evaluation apprehension and the social facilitation of dominant and subordinate responses,' *Journal of Personality and Social Psychology*, **10**, 446–454.

Hunt, P. J., and Hillery, J. M. (1973). 'Social facilitation in a coaction setting: An examination of the effects over learning trials,' *Journal of Experimental Social Psychology*, **9**, 563–571.

Innes, J. M. (1972). 'The effect of presence of co-workers and evaluative feedback on performance of a simple reaction time task,' *European Journal of Social Psychology*, **2**, 466–470.

Kawamura-Reynolds, M. (1977). 'Motivational effects of an audience in the content of imaginative thought,' *Journal of Personality and Social Psychology*, **35**, 912–919.

Klinger, E. (1969). 'Feedback effects and social facilitation of vigilance performance: Mere coaction versus potential evaluation,' *Psychonomic Science*, **14**, 161–162.

Kohfeld, D. L., and Weitzel, W. (1969). 'Some relations between personality factors and social facilitation,' *Journal of Experimental Research in Personality*, **3**, 287–292.

Latané, B., and Cappell, H. (1972). 'The effects of togetherness on heart rate in rats,' *Psychonomic Science*, **29**, 177–179.

Levine, J. M., and Zentall, T. R. (1974). 'Effect of a conspecific's presence on deprived rats' performance: Social facilitation vs. distraction/imitation,' *Animal Learning and Behavior*, **2**, 119–122.

Lipper, S., and McNair, D. M. (1972). 'Simulated public speaking and anxiety,' *Journal of Experimental Research in Personality*, **6**, 237–240.

Lombardo, J. P., and Catalano, J. F. (1978). 'Failure and its relationship to the social facilitation effect: Evidence for a learned drive interpretation of the social facilitation effect,' *Perceptual and Motor Skills*, **46**, 823–829.

Markus, H. (1978). 'The effect of mere presence on social facilitation: An unobtrusive test,' *Journal of Experimental Social Psychology*, **14**, 389–397.

Martens, R. (1969a). 'Effect of an audience on learning and performance of a complex motor skill,' *Journal of Personality and Social Psychology*, **12**, 252–260.

Martens, R. (1969b). 'Effect on performance of learning a complex motor task in the presence of spectators,' *Research Quarterly*, **40**, 733–737.

Martens, R. (1969c). 'Palmar sweating and the presence of an audience,' *Journal of Experimental Social Psychology*, **5**, 371–374.

Martens, R., and Landers, D. M. (1969). 'Coaction effects on a muscular endurance task,' *Research Quarterly*, **40**, 733–737.

Martens, R., and Landers, D. M. (1972). 'Evaluation potential as a determinant of co-action effects,' *Journal of Experimental Social Psychology*, **8**, 347–359.

Matlin, M. W., and Zajonc, R. B. (1968). 'Social facilitation of word associations,' *Journal of Personality and Social Psychology*, **10**, 455–460.

Mueller, J. H. (1975). 'Anxiety and cue utilization in human learning and memory,' in M. Zuckerman and C. D. Spielberger (eds.), *Emotions and Anxiety: New Concepts, Methods, and Applications* Lawrence Erlbaum Associates, Potomac, Md.

Paivio, A. (1965). 'Personality and audience influence,' in B. Maher (ed.), *Progress in Experimental Personality Research*, Vol. 2, pp. 127–173, Academic Press, New York.

Paulus, P. B., and Murdoch, P. (1971). 'Anticipated evaluation and audience presence in the enhancement of dominant responses,' *Journal of Experimental Social Psychology*, **7**, 280–291.

Quarter, J., and Marcus, A. (1971). 'Drive level and the audience effect: A test of Zajonc's theory,' *Journal of Social Psychology*, **83**, 99–105.

Rajecki, D. W., Ickes, W., Cororan, C., and Lenerz, K. (1977). 'Social facilitation of performance—mere presence effects,' *Journal of Social Psychology*, **102**, 297–310.

Rittle, R. H., and Bernard, N. (1977). 'Enhancement of response rate by the mere physical presence of the experimenter,' *Personality and Social Psychology Bulletin*, **3**, 127–130.

Sanders, G. S., Baron, R. S., and Moore, D. L. (1978). 'Distraction and social comparison as mediators of social facilitation effects,' *Journal of Experimental Social Psychology*, **14**, 291–303.

Sarason, I. G. (1972). 'Experimental approaches to test anxiety: Attention and the uses of information,' in C. C. Spielberger (ed.) *Anxiety: Current Trends in Theory and Research*, Vol. 2, pp. 381–403, Academic Press, New York.

Sasfy, J., and Okun, M. (1974). 'Form of evaluation and audience expertness as joint determinants of audience effects,' *Journal of Experimental Social Psychology*, **10**, 461–467.

Seta, J. J., and Hassan, R. K. (1980). 'Awareness of prior success or failure: A critical factor in task performance,' *Journal of Personality and Social Psychology*, **39**, 70–76.

Seta, J. J., Paulus, P. B., and Risner, H. T. (1977). 'The effects of group composition and evaluation on task performance,' *Bulletin of the Psychonomic Society*, **9**, 115–117.

Seta, J. J., Paulus, P. B., and Schkade, J. K. (1976). 'Effects of group size and proximity under cooperative and competitive conditions,' *Journal of Personality and Social Psychology*, **34**, 47–53.

Singerman, K. J., Borkovec, T. D., and Baron, R. S. (1976). 'Failure of a "misattribution therapy" manipulation with a clinically relevant target behavior,' *Behavior Therapy*, **7**, 306–313.

Sorrentino, R. M., and Sheppard, B. H. (1978). 'Effects of affiliation-related motives on swimmers in individual versus group competition: A field experiment,' *Journal of Personality and Social Psychology*, **36**, 704–714.

Spielberger, C. D. (1972). 'Anxiety as an emotional state,' in C. D. Spielberger (ed.), *Anxiety: Current Trends in Theory and Research*, Vol. 1, pp. 23–49, Academic Press, New York.

Triplett, N. (1898). 'The dynamogenic factors in pacemaking and competition,' *American Journal of Psychology*, **9**, 507–533.

Van Tuinen, M., and McNeel, S. P. (1975). 'A test of the social facilitation theories of Cottrell and Zajonc in a coaction situation,' *Personality and Social Psychology Bulletin*, **1**, 604–607.

Walker, E. L., and Tarte, R. D. (1963). 'Memory storage as a function of arousal and time with homogeneous and heterogeneous lists,' *Journal of Verbal Learning and Verbal Behavior*, **2**, 113–119.

Walker, J. W., and Borden, R. J. (1976). 'Influence of self-observation versus other-observation on immediate and delayed recall,' Paper presented at annual meeting of American Psychological Association, Washington, September.

Wankel, L. M. (1977). 'Audience size and trait anxiety effects upon state anxiety and motor performance,' *Research Quarterly*, **48**, 181–186.

Weiss, R. F., and Miller, F. G. (1971). 'The drive theory of social facilitation,' *Psychological Review*, **78**, 44–57.

Wine, J. (1971). 'Test anxiety and direction of attention,' *Psychological Bulletin*, **76**, 92–104.

Zajonc, R. B. (1965). 'Social facilitation,' *Science*, **149**, 269–274.

Zajonc, R. B. (1980). 'Compresence,' in P. B. Paulus (ed.), *Psychology of Group Influence*, L. Erlbaum Associates, Hillsdale, NJ.

Zajonc, R. B., Heingarner, A., and Herman, E. M. (1969). 'Social enhancement and impairment of performance in the cockroach,' *Journal of Personality and Social Psychology*, **13**, 83–92.

Zajonc, R. B., and Sales, S. M. (1966). 'Social facilitation of dominant and subordinate responses,' *Journal of Experimental Social Psychology*, **2**, 160–168.

Zajonc, R. B., Wolosin, R. J., Wolosin, M. A., and Loh, W. D. (1970). 'Social facilitation and imitation in group risk-taking,' *Journal of Experimental Social Psychology*, **6**, 26–46.

Zentall, T. R., and Levine, J. M. (1972). 'Observational learning and social facilitation in the rat,' *Science*, **178**, 1220–1221.

Small Groups and Social Interaction, Volume 1
Edited by H. H. Blumberg, A. P. Hare, V. Kent and M. Davies
© 1983 John Wiley & Sons Ltd

4.2 Attentional Processes and Social Facilitation: How Much, How Often, and How Lasting?

Glenn S. Sanders   *State University of New York at Albany*

Social facilitation refers to certain consequences of being in the presence of other people, as opposed to being alone. In particular, the shift from an isolated to a populated environment often improves performance on simple or well-learned tasks, and impairs performance on complex or unfamiliar tasks. Essentially, the presence of others tends to make easy chores even easier, and to make difficult jobs even harder. Zajonc (1965) assumed that both the improvement and impairment effects reflect the fact that other people increase the probability of ('facilitate') dominant task responses, via raising the performer's drive level. The dominant response on a simple task is typically an appropriate, 'correct' one, and facilitation thus results in improvement (more correct responses). In contrast, the dominant response on a complex task is typically an inappropriate, 'incorrect' one, and facilitation in these cases results in impairment (more incorrect responses). Considerable support for these assumptions is reviewed by Geen and Gange (1977) [and see preceding paper, this volume], and attention is now being focused on a refinement of Zajonc's hypothesis. In this paper we will consider three closely related issues concerning social facilitation: (1) when will the presence of other people produce facilitation of dominant tendencies? (2) what are the long-term effects of working in populated v. isolated environments? and (3) what is the practical significance of social facilitation?

Facilitation—when and why

Sanders *et al.* (1978) and Sanders (in press) have outlined three distinct explanations of social facilitation, each of which specifies different necessary conditions for its occurrence. The *mere presence* (MP) position advocated by Zajonc (1980) attributes facilitation to a reflex-like alertness response. According to the

MP position, the presence of others creates the possibilities of unpredictable and meaningful events, to which the individual responds by automatically increasing vigilance and preparedness for sudden action. Therefore, social facilitation—a byproduct of heightened alertness—should reflexively and invariably occur, although it may be overshadowed by other elements of the situation. The *learned drive* (LD) position, espoused by Cottrell (1972), proposes facilitation to result from a classical conditioning process. Under certain conditions, the presence of others is posited to serve as a conditioned stimulus signalling the likelihood of drive-relevant positive and negative events, such as praise or unsuccessful competition. Therefore, the conditioned emotional response of increased drive—and social facilitation—should result if and only if the presence of others leads to the anticipation of significant events (usually linked to competition or evaluation). Finally, the *distraction/conflict* (D/C) position, outlined by Thibaut and Kelley (1959) and extended and formalized by Sanders and Baron (1975) and Sanders *et al.* (1978), traces facilitation to the distracting influence of others' presence. When in a populated environment, attention to task requirements is often placed in conflict with attention to others' activities, and this attentional conflict is hypothesized to raise the performer's drive level. According to the D/C position, social facilitation should occur only when the presence of others attracts the performer's attention, and when attending to others is incompatible with task performance.

In summary, then, the MP position predicts that social facilitation will always result from the presence of others; the LD position proposes that others must signal impending significant events to produce facilitation; and the D/C approach specifies that others must create attentional conflict in the performer if facilitation is to occur. Each of these positions has substantial empirical support, but when placed in head-to-head competition, the D/C hypothesis seems to emerge most successfully (cf. Sanders, in press). For example, consider two studies reported by Sanders *et al.* (1978). In Study I, one set of instructions informed subjects that they were in a pilot study, and that the experimenter was interested in obtaining their reactions concerning the difficulty and interest level of tasks to be used in future research. These 'task-orientation' instructions were intended to focus attention on the task, and minimize the desire to assess relative performance via distracting orientations to the coactor. Under these conditions, the presence of others led to nonsignificantly *lower* drive than the level of isolated subjects (contradicting the MP position). A second set of instructions emphasized that persistent and rapid performance was a measure of the ability to delay gratification. These 'comparison-orientation' instructions were intended to create curiosity about relative performance, and maximize the desire to engage in distracting comparisons with coactors. Under these conditions, typical social facilitation effects occurred. It is noteworthy that the mere change from an evaluatively neutral 'task orientation' to an evaluative 'comparison-orientation' did not affect the drive level of isolated subjects (contradicting the LD position). Only when the evaluative-competitive orientation was combined with the distracting presence of others was an increase in drive observed. Of course, as in all social facilitation research, drive is a hypothetical construct, and hence must be inferred from performance levels on tasks for which the dominant response has been established empirically or theoretically. Thus, an increase in the probability of dominant responses is assumed to reflect an increase in drive level.

Study II manipulated the ability of subjects to obtain comparison information from coactors. Subjects in all coactor conditions were told their performance would be compared with national norms. They were also told, in the Same-Task condition, that their performance would be compared with that of the coactor, who was performing the same task as the subject. In the Different-Task condition, they were told that their ability to exceed national norms for their task would be compared to the coactor's ability to exceed national norms for his task, which was different from the subject's task. Relative to Alone controls, coactors increased the subject's drive level in the Same-Task but not in the Different-Task condition. This was expected on the basis that subjects in the Different-Task condition could not evaluate their performance by distracting comparisons with the coactor's progress, since relative progress on two different tasks is uninformative. Therefore, they should experience no attentional conflict and no increase in drive. Thus, in both Studies I and II, social facilitation only occurred when subjects had some motivation to attend to coactors during ongoing task activity, a result fully consistent with the D/C hypothesis. In contrast, neither the mere physical presence of others, nor signals of impending significant events (competition and evaluation) created increased drive in and of themselves.

Another example of the superior explanatory power of the D/C position arises from research on reactions to stress. Epley (1974) reviews a number of studies which agree that the presence of others reduces the aversive and drive-induction properties of threatening environments. That is, although the presence of others often *increases* drive in normal task performance situations, populated environments seem generally to *reduce* drive caused by threats. This reversal of social facilitation in some stressful settings does not follow from the MP or LD approaches, but is predictable by the D/C position. It is clearly the case that the less one attends to and processes stress-provoking stimuli, the less one should experience stress. The presence of others, by attracting attention and interfering with the reception of arousing stimuli, should therefore reduce stress and, presumably, drive. This stress-reduction function of distraction would serve to counter the drive increment produced by response conflict. Consequently, social facilitation, as manifested in the performance of simple and complex tasks, would not be observed.

The best test of the above reasoning involves comparing situations which vary in terms of the difficulty of ignoring the stressful stimuli. When these stimuli are difficult to ignore, the presence of others will produce a drive-increasing attentional conflict, but will produce little stress-reducing diversion of attention. On an overall basis, then, social facilitation should result. When these stimuli are easy to ignore, the distracting presence of others will produce a stress-reducing diversion of attention, but will produce little drive-increasing attentional conflict, since the conflict will be quickly 'lost' by the easily ignored stimuli. On an overall basis, drive reduction should be observed. The studies of the effects of species-mate presence in stressful settings reviewed by Epley (1974) reveal just such a pattern of results. When the source of stress is very difficult to ignore (i.e. the direct application of painful stimuli), the simple physical presence of others increases drive (e.g. Zajonc et al., 1969). When the source of stress is easier to ignore (i.e. anticipation and threats of pain), the presence of others either has no effect on drive level or tends to reduce it (e.g. Kiesler, 1966). And when the source of stress is very easily ignored (e.g. unfamiliar surroundings), the simple physical presence of others reliably reduces drive (e.g. Latané, 1969). Thus, the D/C hypothesis neatly accounts for the frequent failures to observe social facilitation in stressful settings, and direct empirical support for the role of distraction in reducing stress-related drive is now available (Moore et al., in press).

Sanders (in press) reviewed a number of other research efforts that generally support the proposition just illustrated—that is, the D/C position currently provides the best basis for predicting when social facilitation will follow from the presence of others. Of course, there is substantial room for improvement. As formulated, Distraction/Conflict theory does not explain why other people are so often able to tempt individuals to divert attention from task requirements. More importantly, the D/C position does not allow for the a priori specification of those properties of other people, of tasks, of the performer, and of the context that maximize the probability of attentional conflict. Thus, predictions as to when others will be somewhat distracting (but not so distracting that they completely disrupt task performance) must be made on an intuitive, hit-or-miss basis.

A possible remedy for these shortcomings is presented in Sanders (in press). In that paper I proposed an Attentional Processes model of social facilitation, which is essentially a synthesis of the MP, LD, and D/C positions. The model assigns to the MP position the task of explaining why other people are especially good diverters of attention (i.e. because they are capable of many acts that might require some preparatory action or thought by the task performer). The LD position is given the job of specifying conditioning histories that affect the probability of attentional conflict for specific combinations of performers, tasks, and observers/coactors (i.e. when will the initial attentional orientation explained by the MP position lead to sustained conflict with task requirements?). For example, working in the presence of an evaluative audience should lead to prolonged attentional conflict because the performer has been conditioned to expect useful or interesting feedback on performance quality from such an audience. Since the performance changes over time, so too might the nature of observers' reactions, leading to sustained interest in monitoring audience information. Finally, the D/C position explicates the mechanism by which sustained attentional conflict is translated into social facilitation. Rather than treating the three positions as

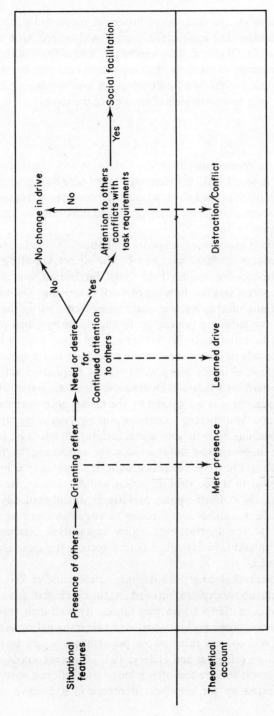

Figure 1 The Attentional Processes model of social facilitation

explanatory competitors, the Attentional Processes model links them together to form a more compreher.sive explanation than would be provided by any single position (see Figure 1). Of course, this does not, in and of itself, solve the problem of *a priori* specification of when facilitation will occur, but the synthesis does provide a framework for guiding future research and organizing its results (cf. Sanders, in press, for a more complete discussion of the model).

Long-term effects

Virtually all of the considerable theory and data on social facilitation have been derived from very abstract tasks in extremely limited time frames (typically 1 hour or less). Consequently, it is not known whether the observed effects will generalize to long-term performance on tasks common in and important to various types of individuals and organizations.

The Mere Presence explanation proposes that social facilitation results from a reflex-like preparedness response triggered by the simple knowledge that one is not alone. This orientation implies that social facilitation will always occur, regardless of the context and the duration of work experience. The Learned Drive explanation maintains that changes in performance created by the presence of others are due to the tension produced by feelings of competition or evaluation. This approach predicts that social facilitation will not occur when it is clear to the performer that the others present are not in a position to compete or evaluate. However, when these elements are present, social facilitation should continue indefinitely. The third explanation, Distraction/Conflict, argues that socially-induced performance changes are caused by the tendency of others to attract the performer's attention and thereby create tension by interfering with task concentration. This position suggests that social facilitation would be limited to settings in which the others present are in some sense 'interesting' to the performer. Even in these settings, however, evidence indicates that over a long duration, performers can learn to divide their attention without influencing their performance (Hirst *et al.*, 1980). Furthermore, performers should gradually habituate to the presence of others and have less reason to attend to them as they become more familiar. Thus, the Distraction/Conflict explanation predicts that social facilitation effects should tend to weaken as time spent in the same setting with the same task is extended.

Three further theoretical points are relevant to the issue of long-term effects. First, all three of the above explanations rest in part on Hullian drive theory. This theory would predict that as workers gain familiarity with their tasks over time, initially difficult tasks whose performance would be impaired by the presence of others would evolve into easy tasks whose performance would be facilitated by the presence of others (cf. Hunt and Hillery, 1973). In other words, to the extent that social facilitation is still in effect after a long period of time, most tasks should eventually be affected by the presence of others in a positive way. Second, although none of the explanations reviewed above would predict that social facilitation will become stronger with the passage of time, this remains an empirical possibility that would have important implications for current theory. Third, performing tasks in isolation has not been found to have any negative effects on satisfaction or output in the short time periods used in laboratory research. Yet being isolated for large portions of the standard work week may induce problems in concentration or morale that are at least as important as the effects of being in the presence of others. That is, isolated performance may provide a neutral baseline for a brief interval, but it could have its own meaningful psychodynamics over extended periods.

Practical significance

Social facilitation refers to measurable changes in the quantity and quality of work performance. Consequently, it would seem to be of more than academic interest. Individuals can very often choose to work in either isolated or populated environments, and the phenomenon of facilitation may deserve to play an important part in their decision. Moreover, large organizations of all descriptions have the power to impose or inhibit isolation in the environment of their work forces. The degree to which task performers are made aware of each other's presence may be an easily manipulable factor that can result in large gains in efficiency.

Three basic types of information are needed to determine the overall practical significance of social facilitation—that is, to determine how important it is for individuals and organizations to consider facilitation phenomena when creating task environments. First, the intensity of the phenomenon should be established, preferably in percentage terms. For example, what is the average percent increase in errors when performance of a complex task is impaired by the presence of others? What is the percent savings in time expended when performance of a simple task is improved via social facilitation? Thus, the intensity factor describes the impact of facilitation when it occurs and for as long as it occurs. Second, the breadth of the phenomenon needs delineation. As mentioned above, facilitation has usually been studied in reference to very abstract tasks—conceptually clear for theoretical inferences but obscure as to everyday significance. It is possible that many, or even most tasks that people commonly perform are 'immune' to social facilitation for a variety of reasons—the task may be neither very simple nor very complex (e.g. clerical jobs), in which case an increase in drive will not have systematic effects; the task may be so absorbing (e.g. athletic skills) that others cannot function to divert the performer's attention; or the tasks may be simple but so well practiced that there is no room for socially facilitated improvement (e.g. assembly-line routines). Therefore, it should not be taken for granted that social facilitation is a broadly applicable phenomenon. Third, the depth of facilitation needs to be determined. By depth, I refer to the question of duration raised in the previous section. If facilitation only lasts a few minutes or hours, its practical significance will obviously be quite limited.

In general terms, the degree to which facilitation should be considered when planning or evaluating work environments is a multiplicative function: intensity × breadth × depth. The multiplicative nature of the function is dictated by the fact that as the value of any of the three relevant variables approaches zero, the practical significance of facilitation also approaches zero. As far as the actual values of these variables are concerned, our knowledge itself approaches zero. In the very short time periods typically studied, the shift from baseline performance (i.e. intensity) produced by a populated environment centers in the range of 10% to 30%. This figure is neither so large as to make facilitation a top priority issue, nor so small as to discourage further research. However, an intensity value of 10% to 30% should not be taken for granted. It could well shift in either direction when more meaningful, everyday tasks are studied. Furthermore, the sign as well as the absolute value of the intensity variable needs to be considered. That is, does facilitation of dominant tendencies more often tend to favor task improvement or task impairment? The Distraction/Conflict hypothesis, as explicated in Sanders *et al.* (1978), suggests that the conditions leading to improvement require a delicate balance of level of distraction and degree of task simplicity, and thus improvement might be relatively infrequent. In any event, the practical significance of social facilitation will be strongly colored by the mix of positive and negative task outcomes.

Although little is known about the intensity of social facilitation, even less is known about the values of the breadth and depth variables, as suggested previously in this chapter. Hopefully, systematic attempts to expand, test, and disconfirm the Attentional Processes model will begin to erase our ignorance in these critical areas (cf. Sanders, in press, for some research possibilities). It is time to determine whether the substantial attention paid to facilitation by academic laboratories is matched by its impact on commonplace activities.

References

Cottrell, N. B. (1972). 'Social facilitation,' in C. G. McClintock (ed.), *Experimental Social Psychology*, Holt, Rinehart & Winston, New York.

Epley, S. W. (1974). 'Reduction of the behavioral effects of aversive stimulation by the presence of companions,' *Psychological Bulletin*, **81**, 271–283.

Geen, R. G., and Gange, J. J. (1977). 'Drive theory of social facilitation: Twelve years of theory and research,' *Psychological Bulletin*, **84**, 1267–1288.

Hirst, W., Spelke, E., Reaves, C., Caharack, G., and Neisser, U. (1980). 'Dividing attention without alternation or automaticity,' *Journal of Experimental Psychology: General*, **109**, 90–117.

Hunt, P. J., and Hillery, J. M. (1973). 'Social facilitation in a coaction setting: An examination of the effects of learning over trials,' *Journal of Experimental Social Psychology*, **9**, 563–571.

Kiesler, S. B. (1966). 'Stress, affiliation and performance,' *Journal of Experimental Research in Personality*, **1**, 227–235.

Latané, B. (1969). 'Gregariousness and fear in laboratory rats,' *Journal of Experimental Social Psychology*, **5**, 61–69.

Moore, D. M., Byers, D. A., and Baron, R. S. (In press). 'Socially mediated fear reduction in rodents: Distraction, communication, or mere presence?' *Journal of Experimental Social Psychology*.

Sanders, G. S. (In press). 'Driven by distraction: An integrative review of social facilitation theory and research,' *Journal of Experimental Social Psychology*.

Sanders, G. S., and Baron, R. S. (1975). 'The motivating effects of distraction on task performance,' *Journal of Personality and Social Psychology*, **32**, 956–963.

Sanders, G. S., Baron, R. S., and Moore, D. L. (1978). 'Distraction and social comparison as mediators of social facilitation effects,' *Journal of Experimental Social Psychology*, **14**, 291–303.

Thibaut, J. W., and Kelley, H. H. (1959). *The Social Psychology of Groups*, Wiley, New York.

Zajonc, R. B. (1965). 'Social facilitation,' *Science*, **149**, 269–274.

Zajonc, R. B. (1980). 'Compresence,' in P. Paulus (ed.), *Psychology of Group Influence*, Erlbaum, Hillsdale, NJ.

Zajonc, R. B., Heingartner, A., and Herman, E. M. (1969). 'Social enhancement and impairment of performance in the cockroach,' *Journal of Personality and Social Psychology*, **13**, 83–92.

Small Groups and Social Interaction, Volume 1
Edited by H. H. Blumberg, A. P. Hare, V. Kent and M. Davies
© 1983 John Wiley & Sons Ltd

4.3 Group Size Effects on Cognitive Effort and Attitude Change

Richard E. Petty   *University of Missouri-Columbia*

John T. Cacioppo   *University of Iowa*

and

Stephen G. Harkins   *Northeastern University*

Although the study of attitudes and persuasion has long been viewed as a central focus of social psychology (Allport, 1935), relatively little attention has been paid to two basic features of the persuasion situation—the number of people receiving a persuasive message, and the number of people delivering a communication.[1] The typical analysis of social influence considers one source presenting a message to one recipient, and the *number* of sources and recipients has not been viewed as an important factor on its own. This lack of systematic attention to group effects by persuasion researchers is unfortunate given the large number of naturalistic situations in which we are in the company of others when exposed to persuasion attempts, and are the targets of persuasion by multiple sources. For example, at political rallies, numerous speakers advocate the same position to a large group of people whose individual opinions will be combined (on election day) to determine the outcome. In the criminal justice system, multiple witnesses testify about the character of a defendant to a group of people who must form a collective judgment. In this paper, we present a brief outline of a program of research we have initiated on the effects of presenting a message to multiple recipients rather than to just one, and then we address the effects of receiving a message from multiple sources rather than from just one.

Number of message recipients

As we noted above, when a juror listens to the persuasive evidence presented in a courtroom, he or she knows that there are 11 other people who are listening to and evaluating the same evidence. When a person listens to a political candidate make a speech on television, he or she knows that there are millions of others who are also listening to and evaluating the same speech. What is the effect of knowing that the responsibility for evaluating a persuasive message is shared with others? The only experimental research directly relevant to the effects that the number of message recipients have on persuasion that we have located was conducted by Knower almost half a century ago. Knower (1935, 1936) reported that oral and written presentations were more persuasive when they were presented to individuals than when presented to groups. These findings have neither been replicated nor adequately explained. Much more recently, Latané (1976) and Newton and Mann (1980) reported correlational investigations of naturally formed crowds of different sizes and persuasion. In these studies, increasing crowd size was sometimes associated with enhanced and sometimes with diminished persuasion. Of course, in these naturalistic correlational investigations, crowd size may be confounded with many other variables (e.g. weather, speaker enthusiasm, etc.), and thus interpretation is rather difficult.

Even though there has been relatively little attention to how the number of message recipients affects persuasion, there has been a considerable amount of research on how the number of people available to perform some *physical task* affects performance on that task. A brief review of this research will be instructive.

Group size and physical tasks

There is now considerable evidence that in many situations in which a group is responsible for a physical task, the real or perceived presence of other people produces *social inhibition*. That is, people are less likely to respond, or respond with less effort than they would have if they had been alone. Perhaps the most well-known social inhibition effect is Latané and Darley's (1970) demonstration that the real or implied presence of other people inhibits individuals from rendering help to a victim in distress. This social inhibition effect is not limited to emergency situations, however. Later research has documented that when other people are present or available to respond, individuals are less likely to help pull hard on a rope (Ingham *et al.*, 1974), shout or clap loudly upon request (Latané *et al.*, 1979; Harkins *et al.*, 1980), pick up coins in an elevator (Latané and Dabbs, 1975), or answer an intercom for someone else (Levy *et al.*, 1972).

Interestingly, this social inhibition effect is not confined to situations in which one's physical efforts are aimed at helping someone else. To see if social inhibition might also operate when the physical effort required by a task might help oneself, Petty *et al.* (1977b) gave elevator riders an opportunity to help themselves to a coupon redeemable for a free sandwich at a local fast-food restaurant. The coupon was revealed to riders as the elevator doors closed, and was attached to a large sign that said 'FREE McDONALD'S BURGER'. Riders were free to help themselves to the coupon during their brief ride in the elevator. After they left the elevator, an experimenter would board, record whether the coupon was gone, and attach another coupon if necessary.

Of the 56 people who entered the elevator alone, 26 were randomly allowed to ride by themselves, 16 were joined by an informally dressed student (confederate), and 14 were joined by 2 confederates. When the coupon came into view, the confederate(s) looked at the free offer, but did not react. Single individuals were far more likely to help themselves to the coupon (81%) than were people who rode with either one (38%) or two (14%) other people. The response rates of individuals with one or two confederates present, though not differing ($p > .20$), were both significantly lower than those of riders who were alone ($ps < .01$).

Although these results are consistent with the view that social inhibition occurs even in situations in which the physical response brings an immediate reward to oneself, these results may have also been obtained in part because subjects in groups wanted to avoid taking the only coupon and thus avoid appearing selfish to the other rider(s). To see if the social inhibition effect would also emerge when the latter process could not operate, a second experiment was conducted. In this second study, two coupons were clearly visible when the elevator doors closed. Fourteen riders were randomly allowed to ride by themselves, and 13 were joined by a confederate. Overall, 86% of those individuals who were alone took at least one coupon, with 43% helping themselves to both. In comparison, only 31% of those with one other person present helped themselves to even one coupon, and no one took two, $\chi^2(1) = 8.4$, $p < .01$. These data are very similar to the comparable proportions of 81% and 38% obtained when there was only one coupon, and suggest that the social inhibition effect does not appear to be due to subjects not wanting to appear selfish to the other riders. Selfishness is not an issue in the second study because riders in pairs could have taken one coupon, leaving the other for their fellow rider.

Clearly then, the research that we have briefly summarized above indicates that across a wide variety of situations, persons appear to inhibit or reduce their physical responses when they are members of a group faced with a physical task. It is reasonable to suspect, therefore, that *cognitive* responses might likewise be inhibited when people are members of a group faced with an effortful cognitive task.

Group size and cognitive tasks

Experiment 1

To provide an initial test of the hypothesis that group responsibility for a cognitive task inhibits the cognitive effort devoted to the task, Petty *et al.* (1977a) asked undergraduates to evaluate a poem and an editorial ostensibly written by fellow students. The student evaluators were led to believe that they were either the only one, one of four, or one of 16 evaluators. All subjects actually read the same two communications, and after exposure to each stimulus were asked three questions designed to measure their perceived effortful involvement in the task (e.g. to what extent were you trying hard to evaluate the communication?), and four questions designed to provide a general measure of attitude toward the communication (e.g. to what extent did you like the communication?). Scores on the first set of questions were summed to form a general 'effort index,' and scores on the second set of questions were summed to form a general 'attitude index.'

The results from this study were quite straightforward. Individual evaluators reported putting more effort into evaluating the communications than did group evaluators ($F(1, 72) = 4.65$, $p < .05$) who did not differ according to group size. These data indicate that persons in groups felt less compelled to work at assessing the communications than individuals and provide support for our hypothesis that group responsibility for a cognitive task inhibits cognitive effort. The general attitude measure revealed that individuals who thought that they alone were responsible for rating the communications were significantly more favorable toward them than evaluators who thought they were rating in groups ($F(1, 72) = 6.01$, $p < .05$) which again did not show a significant difference according to size. Furthermore, a significant within-cell correlation between the perceived effort index and the general attitude index ($r = +.48, p < .01$) suggested that the enhanced effort of individual over group evaluators may have directly contributed to the enhanced attitude ratings that individual evaluators provided for the communications.

There are several theoretical mechanisms that might account for the relationship between effort and evaluation (e.g. commodity theory—Brock, 1968; deindividuation theory—Zimbardo, 1970). One of the most developed is Jones and Gerard's (1967) 'effort justification' hypothesis derived from Festinger's (1957) dissonance theory. This formulation states, 'If a person expends effort that is not readily justified by the amount of reinforcement received, he tends to create reinforcements out of the stimuli in the immediately surrounding environment' (p. 89). Thus, individual evaluators may have justified their increased efforts by overvaluing the communications (see also Cohen, 1959; Wicklund et al., 1967).

An alternative explanation would contend that increasing cognitive effort accentuates the perceived features of a stimulus, leading to discovery and increased liking of a good communication's virtues and disliking of a poor communication's flaws. In a series of studies on basic persuasion processes, we have shown that by either increasing a person's motivation (Petty and Cacioppo, 1979a, 1979b) or ability (Cacioppo, 1979; Cacioppo and Petty, 1979) to think about a persuasive message, more polarized attitudes result. Specifically, we have shown that with greater ability and/or motivation to process the arguments in a communication, more favorable thoughts are generated to high quality arguments yielding more positive evaluations, but more unfavorable thoughts are generated to low quality arguments yielding more negative evaluations (see Petty and Cacioppo, 1981, Chs. 8 and 9 for a review). In our initial investigation on the effects of number of evaluators on cognitive effort and attitudes (Petty et al., 1977a), group evaluators liked the communications (i.e. rated them above the midpoint on the attitude scales) and individual evaluators liked them even more. This is the result that would be expected if individual evaluators were motivated to do more thinking about the positive stimuli then group evaluators were.

Experiment 2

In order to assess these various alternative explanations, Petty et al. (1980) conducted a second experiment on group size and attitudes. In this experiment, all subjects were told that their task was to evaluate critically an editorial. The subjects, all university students, were led to believe that they were assisting the journalism school at their university evaluate its programs by providing peer feedback on the writing abilities of students in the school. Subjects were told either that they were the only person who would evaluate the editorial or that they were 1 of 10 people who would evaluate the editorial. Thus, some subjects believed that they bore the full responsibility for the evaluation, whereas others believed that they shared the responsibility with other members of a group.

Subjects read one of three editorials. Each message argued that seniors be required to pass a comprehensive exam in their declared major prior to graduation, but the editorials differed in their presentation of eight key arguments. One message was designed to contain points that were logically sound, defendable, and compelling (strong arguments message). These arguments (e.g. schools with the exams attract larger and more well-known corporations to recruit students for jobs) were shown in a pretest to elicit primarily favorable thoughts. A second message contained arguments that were designed to be more open to refutation and skepticism (moderate arguments message). These (e.g. adopting the exams would allow the university to be at the forefront of a national trend) were shown to elicit a mixture of unfavorable and favorable thoughts in a pretest. The third message contained arguments that were quite easy to counterargue and was designed as an extremely negative stimulus (weak arguments message). These arguments (e.g. the risk of failing the exam was a challenge most students would welcome) elicited primarily unfavorable thoughts in a pretest.

After reading the appropriate message, subjects completed the same communication evaluation measures as employed in the initial experiment, and the same perceived effort measures. In addition, subjects were given $2\frac{1}{2}$ minutes to list the thoughts that occurred to them while reading the editorial. This measure was employed to reflect the 'actual' in contrast to the 'perceived' amount of cognitive effort expended in the task (see Cacioppo et al., 1981). After subjects had listed their thoughts, they were instructed to go back and rate their ideas as + (something favorable or good about the editorial), − (something unfavorable or bad about the editorial) or 0 (neither in favor of nor opposed to the editorial).

The major results from this study are presented in Table 1. As in the first experiment, subjects who believed that they were the only evaluator of the editorial reported more cognitive involvement with the task on the 'perceived

Table 1 Effects of group size and editorial quality on cognitive effort and editorial evaluation

Measure	Strong arguments		Moderate arguments		Weak arguments	
	Individual	Group	Individual	Group	Individual	Group
Perceived effort index	8.81_a	7.63_b	7.81_{ab}	7.04_b	8.58_a	8.10_{ab}
Unfavorable thoughts	$.86_a$	1.40_a	1.90_{ab}	1.86_a	3.80_c	2.53_b
Favorable thoughts	3.76_a	2.83_b	2.00_b	2.20_b	$.96_c$	1.76_{bc}
Communication evaluation index	9.30_a	7.64_b	6.83_b	7.17_b	4.03_c	5.85_d

Note Means in the same row without a common subscript are significantly different at the .05 level by the Newman–Keuls procedure. Table adapted from Petty *et al.* (1980).

effort index' $(M = 8.4)$ than did subjects who believed that they were 1 of 10 evaluators $(M = 7.6)$, $F(1, 168) = 9.66$, $p < .002$. Importantly, significant main effects for the Argument Quality manipulation on the measures of favorable thoughts $F(2, 168) = 20.08$, $p < .001$, and unfavorable thoughts, $F(2, 168) = 23.02$, $p < .001$, attested to this manipulation's success. Subjects generated the most favorable thoughts to the strong arguments $(M = 3.3)$, next most to the moderate $(M = 2.1)$, and least to the weak arguments $(M = 1.3)$. Similarly, subjects generated the most unfavorable thoughts to the weak arguments $(M = 3.2)$, next most to the moderate $(M = 1.9)$, and least to the strong arguments $(M = 1.1)$. In addition to these main effects on the thought production measures, two significant Group Size × Argument Quality interactions $(ps < .05)$ emerged. These interactions indicated that increasing the number of evaluators inhibited the production of unfavorable thoughts to the weak message, and inhibited the production of favorable thoughts to the strong message.

The pattern of results on the measure of attitude toward the communications followed the thought measures quite closely. A main effect for the Argument Quality manipulation, $F(2, 168) = 59.93$, $p < .001$, revealed that subjects reading the editorials with strong arguments provided the most favorable evaluations $(M = 8.5)$, followed by subjects reading the moderate arguments $(M = 7.0)$, and then subjects reading the weak arguments $(M = 4.9)$. Of most interest, however, was a significant Group Size × Argument Quality interaction, $F(2, 168) = 16.11$, $p < .001$, which clearly indicated that individual evaluators had more favorable attitudes toward the strong argument editorial but less favorable attitudes toward the weak editorial than did group evaluators. The group size manipulation had no effect on attitudes toward the moderate editorial.

Finally, an analysis of the average within-cell correlations among the attitude and cognitive effort measures indicated that within the strong message cells, the more cognitive effort subjects perceived themselves to exert, the more favorably they evaluated the editorial ($r = +.43, p < .05$), but within weak message cells, the more cognitive effort subjects perceived themselves to exert, the less favorably they evaluated the editorial ($r = -.34, p < .05$). The pattern within all cells was that the more favorable thoughts actually generated by subjects, the more positively they evaluated the editorials ($r = +.35, p < .05$), and the more unfavorable thoughts they generated, the more negatively they evaluated the editorials ($r = -.40, p < .05$).

Limitations and implications

The results of the two studies we described above provide clear support for the view that group responsibility for a cognitive task can lead to an inhibition of cognitive effort on that task. Both experiments showed that group evaluators reported less cognitive involvement in the task on a measure of *perceived* cognitive effort, and Experiment 2 showed that group evaluators *actually* generated fewer thoughts consistent with the quality of the stimulus than did individual evaluators. People are apparently less willing to engage in effortful cognitive activity when they share the responsibility for a task with others than when they alone are responsible for the cognitive work. This may provide one explanation for why numerous political surveys show that voters are often quite uninformed about important national issues (Campbell *et al.*, 1964). When millions are responsible for making a collective decision about whom to elect for President, each individual bears only a small fraction of the responsibility for evaluating the candidates, and thus individual cognitive effort is minimal.

The two studies on group size and cognitive effort also indicated how cognitive effort is translated into an overall evaluation or attitude. Specifically, attitudes were tied to the amount of cognitive effort expended and the quality of the stimulus to be evaluated. The more cognitive effort expended, the more favorable the evaluation when the stimulus was of high quality, but the more negative the evaluation when the stimulus was of low quality. The added cognitive effort expended by individual evaluators apparently renders them better able to discover and appreciate the virtues of a positive stimulus and the flaws of a negative one. This finding, of course, suggests that the link between cognitive effort and evaluation is a result of information processing activity rather than dissonance reduction.[2]

We suspect that several of the conditions found in our two studies are necessary for group diffusion of cognitive effort to occur: the task should be clearly identified as a cooperative group project and involve costly effort, responsibility should inhere in the group as a whole and not in specific members, rewards to individuals should not be contingent on identifiable individual output, and group interaction should be minimal. When group interaction is permitted, other processes may become important. For example, the sharing of information in a group can lead group evaluators' opinions to become more *extreme* than the initial opinions of the individuals composing the group (see Burnstein and Vinokur, 1977). This group polarization phenomenon, of course, provides a direct counterpoint to the group moderation phenomenon (group evaluators expressing less extreme evaluations of a stimulus than individual evaluators) that we have described above. It appears that knowing that a group will have responsibility for an ultimate decision leads to opinion moderation in the stage of opinion formation (because group evaluators are less diligent in thinking about the stimulus to be evaluated), but actual group discussion may lead to opinion polarization (because group members share information and arguments they have individually generated). Some group decisions occur without much formal discussion among group members (e.g. election decisions) and thus cognitive inhibition and opinion moderation may be the prepotent process, but many other group decisions involve both an initial information gathering and opinion formation stage prior to discussion, and then an actual group discussion (e.g. jury decisions). In these situations, both processes will operate in direct conflict such that the larger the group that is assigned responsibility for the task, the greater the likelihood for moderation of opinion prior to discussion, but the greater is the likelihood for polarization as a result of the discussion.

Number of message sources

Just as there are many real-world situations in which groups rather than individuals are responsible for evaluating a persuasive advocacy, there are many situations in which an advocacy on a particular subject is received from several sources rather than just one. There are numerous reasons to suspect that the more people who advocate a particular view, the more persuasion that will result. First, it has been well documented that *conformity* pressures increase simply as a result of learning that others endorse a contrary view even if the reasons for the endorsements are not known (e.g. Asch, 1951; Krech *et al.*, 1962; White, 1975). Generally, conformity is thought to occur because of the implicit assumption on the part of conformers that behaving like others will elicit approval, whereas dissimilar behavior will bring about negative consequences (Allen, 1965; Kiesler and Kiesler, 1969). Another reason that multiple sources might produce more persuasion than a single source in naturalistic contexts is that multiple sources might generate more arguments than a single source, and research indicates that increasing the number of arguments associated with a position enhances agreement with that position (e.g. Calder *et al.*, 1974; Insko *et al.*, 1976). Finally, exposure to multiple sources might lead to the repetition of certain arguments. A moderate number of repetitions of relatively complex arguments appears to enhance their persuasiveness (e.g. Cacioppo and Petty, 1979, 1980). Since we were interested in whether there were any persuasive effects of multiple sources that did *not* depend on conformity pressures, multiple arguments, or message repetition, we designed an exploratory study that allowed independent assessment of these processes.

Experiment 1

In the initial study, Harkins and Petty (1981) told university students that a faculty committee was soliciting student opinions on the institution of senior comprehensive exams at their university. All of the students were told that the investigators had recently videotaped three students who were asked to give three of their thoughts about the proposed exams. All subjects were told that the first three students who were videotaped favored the exam idea, and that they would be shown a short randomly selected portion of the tapes made so far to obtain their reactions. Subjects then saw a brief segment of videotape in which either (a) one source presented one argument, (b) three different sources presented variations of the same basic argument, (c) one source presented three different arguments, or (d) three different sources gave three different arguments (one each). The segments were constructed from a master tape consisting of three males, each of whom gave three arguments in favor of the exams. Although each speaker made each of the three arguments on the master tape, each speaker's version of the argument was somewhat different.[3] The selection of speaker, argument, pairing of speaker and argument, and order of presentation was determined randomly in the appropriate conditions. Each subject saw a different randomly determined segment of videotape constructed in this way.

In addition to these four experimental conditions, two control conditions were conducted. In the *conformity-control* group, subjects read the same instructions as subjects in the experimental groups, but were told that we would like to have them answer a few questions *prior* to viewing the videotape. They, in fact, never saw the tape since this condition was designed to assess the effects of simply knowing that three fellow students who were in favor of the exams had each generated three arguments to which they might be exposed. In the *no-information* control group, the subjects simply read a brief description of the comprehensive exam proposal and were asked for their opinions on it. These subjects were unaware of the existence of the three students who generated three arguments.

To measure subjects' own attitudes about the comprehensive exams, all of them responded to four 9-point semantic differential scales (e.g. good/bad) on which they rated the exam proposal, and to one 11-point scale on which they rated their extent of agreement with the proposal. These responses were converted to standard scores and averaged to form a measure of attitude toward the position advocated in the editorial. In addition, subjects were given $2\frac{1}{2}$ minutes to list their thoughts about the exam proposal, and they responded to several ancillary questions.

The major results from this study are presented in Table 2. An analysis of the standardized attitude measure revealed a significant effect for experimental condition, $F(5, 96) = 15.4$, $p < .01$. A Newman–Keuls analysis on this measure showed the following. First, students in the conformity control condition expressed significantly more agreement with the comprehensive exam proposal than students in the no-information control condition. This indicates that simply

Table 2   Effects of multiple sources and multiple arguments on
attitudes and thought generation

Experimental condition	Attitude	Favorable thoughts
Three sources–three arguments	1.88_a	3.75_a
Three sources–one argument	$.30_b$	2.20_b
One source–three arguments	$.04_b$	1.85_b
One source–one argument	$.03_b$	1.50_b
Conformity control	$.12_b$	1.95_b
No-information control	-2.38_c	$.70_c$

Note Means in each column without a common subscript are sig-
nificantly different at the .05 level by the Newman–Keuls procedure.
Attitudes are expressed in standardized scores. Table adapted from
Harkins and Petty (1981).

knowing that others have endorsed the proposal was sufficient to increase agreement even though no arguments were actually heard (a conformity effect). The
experimental cells provide information about the effects of actual exposure to the
multiple sources and arguments. Subjects in all of the experimental cells showed
significantly more agreement with the exam proposal than subjects in the no-
information control group, but subjects in only one of the experimental groups
showed more agreement than subjects in the conformity control condition—multiple sources presenting multiple arguments. The enhanced persuasion
in this group cannot be attributed to the information included in the arguments
alone, to the number of speakers alone, nor to the simple additive combination of
these factors, since neither arguments nor speakers manipulated singly resulted in
reliably more persuasion than a single speaker presenting a single argument,
$ps > .20$. The 2 (one or three arguments) × 2 (one or three sources) interaction
contrast suggested by this non-additive pattern of means was reliable, $F(1, 96) =$
5.07, $p < .05$.[4]

Harkins and Petty suggested that there were two viable interpretations for the
multiple source–multiple argument effect. One explanation contends that subjects
in the different experimental conditions made differential attributions about the
number of good arguments that existed in support of comprehensive exams. That
is, the knowledge that several sources each independently generated different, yet
convincing arguments may have led subjects to infer that there was a large pool of
reasonable arguments in favor of the exam proposal. This inference might lead to
enhanced agreement since if a large number of reasonable proarguments exist, the
proposal must be worth supporting. A second plausible interpretation would
contend that subjects in the multiple source–multiple argument condition devoted
more cognitive effort to evaluating the message than subjects in the other conditions, and that this enhanced thinking led to more polarized attitudes. This

interpretation argues that each time a new source is introduced, the subject 'gears up' to process the message. If it is a new speaker, and a new argument, the recipient thinks about the argument's implications. However, if the same speaker appears again, even though with new arguments, the recipient puts minimal effort into processing the argument because this source has been heard already. Likewise, if new speakers are presented, but all give the same relatively simple argument, little additional thought takes place, because the recipient has heard this argument already. Consistent with this reasoning, Harkins and Petty found that subjects in the multiple source–multiple argument condition generated more favorable thoughts about the issue than subjects in any other condition (see Table 2).

Experiment 2

A second experiment was conducted to assess the two viable accounts for the multiple source–multiple argument effect. All subjects in this study were told that 100 students had been videotaped giving their opinions about raising the driving age to 21, and that 91% of the students favored the proposal. As in the first experiment, subjects were told that they would view a randomly selected sample of the videotapes. Three experimental conditions were constructed. In one condition, subjects saw one fellow student present four cogent arguments for raising the driving age. In a second condition, subjects saw four different students each present a different argument for raising the driving age. This condition replicates the multi-speaker, multi-source condition of the previous study. Finally, a third group of subjects saw four different students each present a different argument, but these subjects were told that 'although there were different wordings, when we boiled down all of the arguments generated by the 100 students . . . we found that there were essentially four different favorable arguments . . . you will hear all four.' Thus, the argument pool was specified at four arguments for these subjects. After viewing the appropriate videotape, subjects completed measures similar to those described in the previous experiment.

If the argument pool interpretation of the multiple source–multiple argument effect is correct, then subjects who see multiple persons deliver multiple arguments but think that these arguments exhaust the pool should be no more persuaded than subjects who see only one speaker deliver these four arguments. In fact, they might even be less persuaded since subjects who see only one speaker believe that the *lower* limit on the argument pool is four. On the other hand, the cognitive effort interpretation would expect that specifying the size of the argument pool would not eliminate the effect since enhanced processing in the four-speaker, four-argument case should still occur, even if the arguments presented exhausted the argument pool.

The results of this study favored the cognitive effort hypothesis. The extent of agreement with raising the driving age to 21 was the same in both conditions where four speakers were heard ($F < 1$) even though subjects had differential perceptions about the number of good arguments that existed in support of the driving age proposal. Of subjects in the condition where the argument pool was specified, 80% believed that five or fewer good arguments existed in support of the proposal, whereas only 35% of subjects in the other two conditions believed this. Also, consistent with the cognitive effort hypothesis, the four-speaker conditions produced significantly more agreement than the one-speaker condition, $F(1, 27) = 9.10$, $p < .05$. The measure of favorable thought generation showed that subjects hearing four speakers present the four arguments generated more positive thoughts ($M = 1.85$) than subjects hearing one speaker present the same four arguments ($M = .4$), $F(1, 27) = 8.4$, $p < .05$. This pattern of results argues strongly against the argument pool interpretation.

Experiment 3

One interesting implication of the cognitive effort interpretation of the multiple-source, multiple-argument effect is that if the arguments presented by multiple sources were weak rather than compelling, there would be less persuasion the more speakers who endorsed the proposal. In a test of this hypothesis, Harkins and Petty (1981) had subjects read three compelling arguments about the senior comprehensive exam issue that were attributed to either one or three people, or three weak arguments that were attributed to one or three people. The same cover story used in Experiment 1 was employed, and as in the other studies, background information about the number of people and arguments that existed in support of the advocacy was held constant. The same dependent measures as employed in the previous studies were also used.

A significant Argument Quality $\times$ Number of Sources interaction on the attitude measure, $F(1, 96) = 11.1$, $p < .001$, provided strong support for the cognitive effort hypothesis. As predicted, subjects exposed to three compelling arguments purportedly produced by three different people expressed more agreement with the exam proposal ($M = 1.08$) than subjects who read the same high-quality arguments presumably generated by one person ($M = .05$); but, subjects who read the three weak arguments purportedly generated by three different people expressed less agreement with the exam proposal ($M = -1.24$) than subjects who read the same weak arguments presumably generated by one person ($M = .11$). The latter effect is especially intriguing because it provides one instance in which the more people who endorse a particular position, the *less* influence that results. Finally, the thought generation data provided further support for the cognitive effort hypothesis: subjects having the arguments presented by three different sources generated more favorable thoughts when the arguments were strong and more unfavorable thoughts when the arguments were weak than subjects having the arguments presented by a single source.

Limitations and implications

The results of the three studies described above provide strong support for the view that the number of sources who provide arguments in support of an advocacy appears to have an effect on persuasion over and above that which would be expected based on previous research on conformity, number of message arguments, and message repetition. This 'extra' effect appears to be due to the fact that the different arguments receive greater thought when they come from multiple sources rather than from a single source. All three studies showed that subjects receiving novel arguments from multiple sources generated more thoughts consistent with the quality of the arguments presented than subjects receiving the same novel arguments from a single source. People are apparently more willing to engage in effortful cognitive activity when the information they receive comes from multiple sources rather than from a single source.

Of course, future research will be directed at determining the limiting conditions of the multiple-source effect. For example, in the research reported here all of the sources presented arguments on the same topic. If the topics were switched, then subjects might be motivated to engage in further thought about the information presented by a single source because the subject would not have heard the source's view on the second topic. This would eliminate the multiple-source effect by motivating more processing of information presented by single sources. Another way to eliminate the multiple-source effect would be to reduce motivation to process the information from many sources. For example, Wilder (1977) has shown that conformity was reduced by subjects' perceptions that the sources of influence were not independent. This suggests that to the extent that the multiple speakers' arguments are not seen as independently generated, their persuasive impact may be reduced. Thus, if subjects were told that the arguments were generated by a committee, members of which would be presenting them, we might expect that multiple speakers presenting multiple arguments would elicit no more persuasion than that found with single sources.

Summary and conclusions

The research that we have presented in this chapter delineates the effects of two basic, yet largely ignored, features of the persuasion setting: the number of message recipients and the number of message sources. The data from these studies are consistent with the notion that under certain conditions, the same process (i.e. idiosyncratic thought about the appeal) mediates the effects of number both of recipients and sources. These studies suggest the following:

1. When subjects are the targets of a communication and are individually responsible for evaluating the message, they put more effort into processing

the arguments than subjects who share the responsibility for the evaluation with other people.
2. When subjects are the targets of a communication presented by multiple sources, they put more effort into processing the arguments than subjects who are targets of the same communication presented by a single source.
3. Depending on the quality of the arguments in the message, modifications in the amount of cognitive effort expended can lead to enhanced or diminished persuasion. If the arguments in the message are normally convincing, then increasing cognitive effort leads to the discovery of the merits of the arguments and enhanced persuasion; if the arguments are unconvincing, increasing the cognitive effort expended leads to the discovery of the message flaws and diminished persuasion.

These findings suggest that the number of sources and the number of recipients of persuasive messages, relatively ignored variables, can play an important role in persuasion, and that this role is mediated by the amount of cognitive effort the recipients devote to cognitively elaborating (thinking about) the content of the message. The cognitive responses produced by expending effort (favorable or unfavorable thoughts) then mediate the direction and amount of attitude change produced.

Notes

1. Of course there are some well-known exceptions to this general statement (e.g. conformity research) which we address later in the chapter.
2. Dissonance theory would expect that increased effort would be associated with more favorable attitudes for all messages, since for each message individual evaluators would have to justify their enhanced effort. Commodity Theory would similarly expect all three messages to show enhanced value with increasing effort. Deindividuation theory would expect all group evaluators to exert the least effort and to give the least favorable evaluations since their individual responses are anonymously hidden in the group evaluation. None of these formulations can account for more effort (by individual evaluators) being associated with *less* favorable evaluations as was the case for the weak message.
3. For example, using the quality of education argument, Speaker A stated: 'My brother went to NU and didn't really learn anything. If he had known all along that he would have to take comprehensive exams, he would have tried harder as he went along and would have learned something.' Speaker B's version of this argument was: 'We have all heard about how students graduated from high school without really knowing how to read and write. Senior comprehensive exams would make sure that students couldn't graduate from NU without the basic skills.'
4. There are also a number of other accounts that cannot explain the pattern of data. Differential recall of the arguments cannot account for the results because subjects hearing the three arguments presented by one person recalled the same number of arguments as subjects hearing the arguments presented by three persons. Differential inferences about the number of people who endorsed the proposal cannot account for the results because subjects in all experimental cells made the same inferences about the number of others who endorsed the proposal (see Harkins and Petty, 1981, for further

details on these measures). Message repetition is also not a viable explanation for the potent effect of three sources presenting one unique argument each because in this condition no argument was repeated. Furthermore, even in the three source–one argument condition where one argument was repeated three times, enhanced persuasion did not result. As noted earlier, we had hoped to avoid repetition effects in this study and were apparently successful in doing so by employing short and simple arguments that were easily understood the first time they were presented. It is likely that a repetition effect would have emerged if longer or more complicated arguments had been presented (Harrison, 1977; Sawyer, 1981).

References

Allen, V. L. (1965). 'Situational factors in conformity,' in L. Berkowitz (ed.), *Advances in Experimental Social Psychology*, Vol. 2, Academic Press, New York.

Allport, G. W. (1935). 'Attitudes,' in C. Murchison (ed.), *Handbook of Social Psychology*, Vol. 2, Clark University Press, Worcester, Mass.

Asch, S. E. (1951). 'Effects of group pressure upon the modification and distortion of judgment,' in H. Guetzkow (ed.), *Groups, Leadership and Men*, Carnegie, Pittsburgh.

Brock, T. C. (1968). 'Implications of commodity theory for value change,' in A. Greenwald, T. Brock, and T. Ostrom (eds.), *Psychological Foundations of Attitudes*, Academic Press, New York.

Burnstein, E., and Vinokur, A. (1977). 'Persuasive argumentation and social comparison as determinants of attitude polarization,' *Journal of Experimental Social Psychology*, **13**, 315–332.

Cacioppo, J. T. (1979). 'Effects of exogenous changes in heart rate on facilitation of thought and resistance to persuasion,' *Journal of Personality and Social Psychology*, **37**, 489–498.

Cacioppo, J. T., Harkins, S. G., and Petty, R. E. (1981). 'The nature of attitudes and cognitive responses and their relationships to behavior,' in R. E. Petty, T. M. Ostrom, and T. C. Brock (eds.), *Cognitive Responses in Persuasion*, Erlbaum, Hillsdale, NJ.

Cacioppo, J. T., and Petty, R. E. (1979). 'Effects of message repetition and position on cognitive responses, recall, and persuasion,' *Journal of Personality and Social Psychology*, **37**, 97–109.

Cacioppo, J. T., and Petty, R. E. (1980). 'Persuasiveness of communications is affected by exposure frequency and message quality,' in J. Leigh and C. Martin (eds.), *Current Issues and Research in Advertising, 1980*, University of Michigan, Ann Arbor.

Calder, B. J., Insko, C. A., and Yandell, B. (1974). 'The relation of cognitive and memorial processes to persuasion in a simulated jury trial,' *Journal of Applied Social Psychology*, **4**, 62–93.

Campbell, A., Converse, P., Miller, W., and Stokes, D. (1964). *The American Voter: An Abridgement*, Wiley, New York.

Cohen, A. R. (1959). 'Communication discrepancy and attitude change: A dissonance theory approach,' *Journal of Personality*, **27**, 386–396.

Festinger, L. (1957). *A Theory of Cognitive Dissonance*, Row, Peterson, Evanston, Ill.

Harkins, S. G., Latané, B., and Williams, K. (1980). 'Social loafing: Allocating effort or taking it easy?', *Journal of Experimental Social Psychology*, **16**, 457–465.

Harkins, S. G., and Petty, R. E. (1981). 'The effects of source magnification of cognitive effort on attitudes: An information processing view,' *Journal of Personality and Social Psychology*, **40**, 401–413.

Harrison, A. A. (1977). 'Mere exposure,' in L. Berkowitz (ed.), *Advances in Experimental Social Psychology*, Vol. 10, Academic Press, New York.

Ingham, A. G., Levinger, G., Graves, J., and Peckham, V. (1974). 'The Ringelmann effect: Studies of group size and group performance,' *Journal of Experimental Social Psychology*, **10**, 371–384.

Insko, C. A., Lind, E. A., and LaTour, S. (1976). 'Persuasion, recall, and thoughts,' *Representative Research in Social Psychology*, **7**, 66–78.

Jones, E. E., and Gerard, H. B. (1967). *Foundations of Social Psychology*, Wiley, New York.

Kiesler, C. A., and Kiesler, S. B. (1969). *Conformity*, Addison-Wesley, Reading, Mass.

Knower, F. H. (1935). 'Experimental studies of change in attitude: I. A study of the effect of oral arguments on changes of attitudes,' *Journal of Social Psychology*, **6**, 315–347.

Knower, F. H. (1936). 'Experimental studies of changes in attitudes: II. A study of effect of printed arguments on changes in attitudes,' *Journal of Abnormal and Social Psychology*, **30**, 522–532.

Krech, D., Crutchfield, R., and Ballachey, E. (1962). *Individual in Society*, McGraw-Hill, New York.

Latané, B. (1976). 'A theory of social impact,' Paper presented at the 21st International Congress of Psychology, Paris, July.

Latané, B., and Dabbs, J. (1975). 'Sex, group size, and helping in three cities,' *Sociometry*, **38**, 180–194.

Latané, B., and Darley, J. (1970). *The unresponsive bystander: Why doesn't he help?* Appleton-Century-Crofts, New York.

Latané, B., Williams, K. D., and Harkins, S. G. (1979). 'Many hands make light the work: The causes and consequences of social loafing,' *Journal of Personality and Social Psychology*, **37**, 822–832.

Levy, P., Lundgren, D., Ansel, M., Fell, D., Fink, B., and McGrath, J. (1972). 'Bystander effect in a demand without threat situation,' *Journal of Personality and Social Psychology*, **24**, 166–171.

Newton, J. W., and Mann, L. (1980). 'Crowd size as a factor in the persuasion process: A study of religious crusade meetings,' *Journal of Personality and Social Psychology*, **39**, 874–883.

Petty, R. E., and Cacioppo, J. T. (1979a). 'Effects of forewarning of persuasive intent and involvement on cognitive responses and persuasion,' *Personality and Social Psychology Bulletin*, **5**, 173–176.

Petty, R. E., and Cacioppo, J. T. (1979b). 'Issue involvement can increase or decrease persuasion by enhancing message-relevant cognitive responses,' *Journal of Personality and Social Psychology*, **37**, 1915–1926.

Petty, R. E., and Cacioppo, J. T. (1981). *Attitudes and Persuasion: Classic and Contemporary Approaches*, Wm. C. Brown, Dubuque, Iowa.

Petty, R. E., Harkins, S. G., and Williams, K. D. (1980). 'The effects of group diffusion of cognitive effort on attitudes: An information processing view,' *Journal of Personality and Social Psychology*, **38**, 81–92.

Petty, R. E., Harkins, S. G., Williams, K. D., and Latané, B. (1977a). 'The effects of group size on cognitive effort and evaluation,' *Personality and Social Psychology Bulletin*, **3**, 579–582.

Petty, R. E., Williams, K. D., Harkins, S. G., and Latané, B. (1977b). 'Social inhibition of helping yourself: Bystander response to a cheeseburger,' *Personality and Social Psychology Bulletin*, **3**, 575–578.

Sawyer, A. (1981). 'Repetition and cognitive responses,' in R. E. Petty, T. M. Ostrom, and T. C. Brock (eds.), *Cognitive Responses in Persuasion*, Erlbaum, Hillsdale, NJ.

White, D. (1975). 'Contextual determinants of opinion judgments: Field experimental probes of judgmental relativity boundary conditions,' *Journal of Personality and Social Psychology*, **32**, 1047–1054.

Wicklund, R. A., Cooper, J., and Linder, D. (1967). 'Effects of expected effort on attitude change prior to exposure,' *Journal of Experimental Social Psychology*, **2**, 416–428.

Wilder, D. (1977). 'Perception of groups, size of opposition and social influence,' *Journal of Experimental Social Psychology*, **13**, 253–268.

Zimbardo, P. G. (1970). 'The human choice: Individuation, reason, and order, versus deindividuation, impulse and chaos,' in W. Arnold and D. Levine (eds.), *Nebraska Symposium on Motivation, 1969*, Vol. 17, University of Nebraska Press, Lincoln.

5 Social Influence

Small Groups and Social Interaction, Volume 1
Edited by H. H. Blumberg, A. P. Hare, V. Kent and M. Davies
Published by John Wiley & Sons Limited, 1983.

5.1 On Maintaining Social Norms: A Field Experiment in the Subway*

Stanley Milgram *Graduate Center: The City University of New York*

and

John Sabini *University of Pennsylvania*

The general question that motivated this research was: How are social norms maintained? Our focus was on the type of norm described by Garfinkel (1964) as 'routine grounds of everyday activity,' norms which regulate everyday activity and which are neither made explicit nor codified. Scheff (1960) refers to this class of norms as 'residual rules,' residual in the sense that they are the restraints on behavior that persist after the formal social norms have been sorted out of the analysis. Scheff isolates these rules on the basis of two criteria: (1) people must be in substantial agreement about them; and (2) they are not noticed until a violation occurs. These rules have been likened to the rules of grammar in that one can follow them without an explicit knowledge of their content and yet notice a violation immediately.

The fact that these residual rules are usually unexpressed creates a serious obstacle to their study: We are virtually inarticulate about them. When compared with formal laws, for example, which have been explicitly codified, residual rules have been left unarticulated by the culture.

An important distinction between these residual rules and laws can be drawn in terms of enforcement. The mechanism for the maintenance of laws is obvious. The entire law enforcement establishment is charged with the responsibility of keeping behavior within the law. Society is quite explicit about the consequences of breaking the law and about who should administer punishment. But who is charged with maintaining residual rules? What consequences should the residual rule breaker expect? Scheff posits a negative feedback system through which the rule

*This article is reprinted, with slight modifications by the authors, from A. Baum, J. E. Singer, and S. Valins (eds.) (1978). *Advances in Environmental Psychology*, 1, *The Urban Environment*, Lawrence Erlbaum Associates, Hillsdale, New Jersey.

breaker is returned to the straight and narrow, but he does not elaborate on the feedback process itself. Scott (1971), in an analysis of social norms from the point of view of the operant conditioning paradigm, defines social norms as 'patterns of sanctions' and sanctions as the 'reinforcing effect of interaction (p. 85).' In this formulation, norms are maintained by the negative consequences of the violation. If this is the case, it should be possible to identify the negative consequences that are supposed to befall the violator. This, then, determined our strategy: we would violate a residual rule and observe the consequences to the violator.

The idea of studying this class of norms by their violation was introduced by Garfinkel (1964); his accounts contain qualitative evidence about the consequences of norm violation. The present research goes further in measuring the effects of violating a residual norm; it centers on a discrete and measurable response to the rule-breakers's action. We are thus able to quantify how people react to violated norms and by systematically changing features of the encounter, to treat the matter experimentally.

The residual rule selected for study was a rule of social behavior on the New York City subway system. The requirements of appropriate social behavior on the subway are, on the face of it, simple. People get on the subway for a very clear and specific reason: to get from one place to another in a brief period of time. The amount of interaction among the riders required for this purpose is minimal and the rules governing this interaction are widely adhered to. One rule of subway behavior is that seats are filled on a first-come, first-served basis. Another implicit rule is one that discourages passengers from talking to one another. Even though riders are often squeezed into very close proximity, they are rarely observed to converse. The experimenters in this study violated these rules by asking people for their seats. This procedure allowed for discrete, measurable responses: people could either give up their seats or refuse to do so.

Several notions about the outcome of such a request may be formulated:

1. Scott's analysis predicts that such a violation would result in 'negative consequences.'
2. Scheff suggests that a possible outcome of a residual rule violation is a process of 'normalization.' Normalization is the attribution of a meaning to the violation that would make it seem not to be a violation at all. The attribution—'the experimenter is asking because he is sick'—would be such a 'normalization.'
3. Most of the experimenters expected not only refusal but some form of active rebuke.
4. Common sense suggests that it is impossible to obtain a seat on the subway simply by asking for it.

Harold Takooshian obtained data on this last point. He asked 16 people to predict what percentage of requests would result in the offer of a seat. Answers ranged from 1% to 55%; the median prediction was that 14% of those who were asked would give up their seats.

Before we describe the experimental procedure, it is worth pointing out some things that the procedure was *not*. The procedure was not an attempt to obtain seats by demanding that riders give them up. Experimenters were instructed to be sure to phrase their requests, not as demands. The procedure was not designed to question the subjects' right to their seats. The subjects' right to their seats was affirmed in the request; you do not request things from people which they do not rightfully possess. The procedure does *not* involve some momentous or unreasonable request. Nothing of any great or lasting value was requested from the subjects. It is, in fact, the observation that this request is so reasonable and yet so rare that suggests the operation of some strong inhibitory social force.

Procedure

The experimenters were six male and four female graduate students. One woman was black; the other experimenters were white. Experimenters worked in pairs; as one performed the manipulation, the other recorded the data and observations.

The passengers on several mid-town routes of the New York City subway system formed the subject pool for the experiment. Experimenters were free to select their own subjects under the following constraints: Each experimenter asked one passenger from each of the following categories: man under 40 (by experimenter's approximation), woman under 40, man over 40, woman over 40. One member of each category was approached by each experimenter in each of the three conditions described in the following. Experimenters approached members of their own race only.

1. In the first condition (no justification), the experimenter approached a seated subject and said, 'Excuse me. May I have your seat?' The observer recorded the age and sex of the subject, whether or not the subject gave up the seat, and other reactions of the subjects and other passengers. Information about the time of day, subway line, and nearest station was also recorded.

As Table 1 shows, 56% of the subjects got up and offered their seats to the experimenters. An additional 12.3% of the subjects slid over to make room for the experimenter. (Experimenters had been instructed to ask for seats only if all of the seats in a car were taken, but it sometimes occurred that, although there did not appear to be any seats, room could be generated if the passengers squeezed together.) If these two responses are combined, we see that 68.3% of the subjects obtained seats by asking for them.

2. A second condition tested the hypothesis that subjects gave up their seats because they assumed the experimenters had some important reason for requesting it. In order to rule out this assumption, experimenters were instructed to say

Table 1   Subway experiments: responses in each experimental condition[a]

No Justification Condition $n = 41$	
Subjects who gave up their seats	56.0%
Subjects who slid over to make room for E	12.3%
Subjects who did not give up their seats	31.7%
Trivial Justification Condition $n = 43$	
Subjects who gave their seats	37.2%
Subjects who slid over to make room for E	4.7%[b]
Subjects who did not give up their seats	58.1%
Overheard Condition $n = 41$	
Subjects who gave up their seats	26.8%
Subjects who slid over to make room for E	9.8%[c]
Subjects who did not give up their seats	63.4%
Written Condition $n = 20$	
Subjects who gave their seats	50.0%
Subjects who slid over to make room for E	0.0%[d]
Subjects who did not give up their seats	50.0%

[a]Overall chi square for four conditions collapsing subjects who gave up their seats with those who slid over $= 9.44, df = 3, p < .05$.
[b]Z test between No Justification and Trivial Justification conditions (collapsing as above): $Z = 2.3, p < .05$.
[c]Z test between No Justification and Overheard condition (collapsing as above): $Z = 2.7, p < .05$.
[d]Z test between No Justification condition and Written condition (collapsing as above): not significant.

'Excuse me. May I have your seat? I can't read my book standing up.' The experimenter stood holding a paperback mystery. It was expected that by supplying this trivial reason, experimenters would receive fewer seats. The expectation was confirmed; experimenters received significantly fewer seats (41.9% of the requests, $z = 2.3, p < .05$). In Scheff's terms, the trivial justification prevented the process of 'normalization;' subjects could not as easily create some adequate justification for the request.

3. A third condition was included because we believed that subjects might have been so startled by the request that they didn't have time to formulate an adequate reply.[1] It seemed that they might have surrendered their seats because it was easier to do so than to figure out how to refuse in the brief time allowed. This condition was, therefore, designed to allow more time to formulate a reply.

To do this, it was necessary to alert the passenger that a seat might be requested. An experimenter and confederate entered the subway car from different doors and converged in front of the subject. They then engaged in the following conversation, while giving the impression that they were strangers: E to confederate, 'Excuse me. Do you think it would be alright if I asked someone for a seat?' The confederate replied, 'What?' E repeated, 'Do you think it would be alright if I asked someone for a seat?' The confederate replied, noncommitally, 'I don't know.'

This conversation was enacted in a sufficiently loud voice so that the passengers seated in front of the pair would definitely overhear it. The seated passengers would be alerted to the possibility that one of them might be approached with a request to surrender his or her seat. It gave the seated passengers time to formulate a response to the request, eliminating the startle component of the earlier conditions.

Thus, after acting out the foregoing exchange, the experimenter paused for approximately 10 seconds, then turned to the nearest seated passenger, and requested his or her seat. In this condition, experimenters received seats only 36.5% of the time, compared to 68.3% in Condition 1. The additional time between the overhearing of the conversation and the direct request was used to advantage. Subjects were better prepared to turn down the request.

4. Finally, we wished to separate the content of the request from the oral manner in which it was delivered. An orally delivered question directed to a person seems to demand an immediate oral response. We wondered whether a written message would reduce the demand for an immediate and obliging response. Accordingly, in this condition, the experimenter stood in front of the subject and wrote the following message on a sheet of notebook paper: 'Excuse me. May I have your seat? I'd like very much to sit down. Thank you.' The experimenter then passed the message to the subject, saying, 'Excuse me.' We expected fewer seats than in the basic variant, as the request on paper seemed less direct and somewhat more distant, expecially since the subject was not forced to engage the experimenter in eye contact as he formulated a reply. Our expectation was wrong. Experimenters received seats 50.0% of the time, a nonsignificant decrease from the initial condition. (Each experimenter carried out this procedure twice rather than four times; the overall n equaled 20.) The reason for this result is not clear. This method seemed to add a touch of the bizarre to the procedure, perhaps adding to the subject's eagerness to end the whole interaction by simply giving up his seat.

Observers also recorded other aspects of the subjects' reactions. Subjects often had a vacant and bewildered facial expression. Of the subjects who gave up their seats in the initial condition, 70% did so without asking, 'Why?'[2] Other subjects responded by simply saying, 'No.' Some subjects didn't seem to be distressed at all. Subjects who attributed sickness to the experimenter were often very concerned and comforting.

Information was also gathered about the reactions of other passengers who witnessed the incident. On a few occasions, other passengers openly chided a subject who had given up a seat. A more common reaction was for one rider to turn to another and say something such as, 'Did you see that? He asked for a seat!' Such a comment points to the abnormal nature of the event and invites criticism of it. Witnesses to the exchange often turned and stared at the experimenter as he or she left the car.

The effects of the sex and age of experimenters and subjects are noted in Tables 2 and 3. Although these variables yield substantial differences in results, they are somewhat tangential to our main thesis and are not discussed in detail here.

An important aspect of the maintenance of social norms is revealed in the emotional reaction of the experimenters. Most students reported extreme difficulty in carrying out the assignment. Students reported that when standing in front of a subject, they felt anxious, tense, and embarrassed. Frequently, they were unable to vocalize the request for a seat and had to withdraw. They sometimes feared that they were the center of attention of the car and were often unable to look directly at the subject. Once having made the request and received a seat, they sometimes felt a need to enact behavior that would make the request appear justified (e.g. mimicking illness; some even felt faint).

We introduced our study partly in terms of the operant conditioning paradigm

Table 2 Effect of sex of experimenter and subject on acceding to request (for all conditions)

Sex of experimenter	Sex of subject	No. of subjects (n)	Responses		
			Got up (% of n)	Didn't get up (% of n)	Slid over (% of n)
M	M	45	40.0	53.3	6.7
	F	40	30.0	65.0	5.0
Total	(M + F)	85	35.3	58.8	5.9
F	M	30	66.7	26.7	6.7
	F	29	34.5	51.7	13.8
Total	(M + F)	59	50.8	39.0	10.2

Table 3 Effect of experimenter sex and subject age on acceding to request (for all conditions)

Age of of subject	Sex of experimenter	No. of subjects (n)	Responses		
			Got up (% of n)	Didn't get up (% of n)	Slid over (% of n)
Under 40	M	42	54.7	42.8	2.5
	F	30	63.3	30.0	6.7
Total	(M + F)	72	58.3	37.5	4.2
Over 40	M	43	27.9	62.9	9.2
	F	29	37.9	48.2	13.9
Total	(M + F)	72	31.9	57.0	11.1

by Scott as a framework for the understanding of social norms. What implications do our results have for this position? The answer depends on how one interprets 'patterns of sanctions' which Scott holds maintain social norms. If this phrase is interpreted in its most simple and direct sense, and in a way consistent with the operant paradigm, it means the objectively specifiable response of the social environment to the violation. If we use this interpretation, the operant analysis does not work. The response on the part of others to a request for a seat is usually to grant the request. The 68.3% rate with which experimenters received seats corresponds to a variable ratio schedule of positive reinforcement (VR2). Skinner (1953) has found that behavior reinforced under this schedule is enhanced rather than discouraged. If we take 'patterns of sanctions' to include the internal, emotional effects of the request which are not produced by the environment but which are direct accompaniments of the experimenters' behavior, the analysis has some merit, but it leads directly to the question: Why does the act of making this simple request cause such an acute emotional response?[3]

One might approach this question by focusing on the content of the request; after all, the experimenters did ask for a seat from someone when they had no clear right to do so. But this focus on the seat seems misguided. The intensity of the emotion the experimenters experienced is incommensurate with the small cost involved in the subjects' giving up their seats. The significance of the request lies not in the seat (that is not the heart of the matter), but in the redefinition of the immediate relationship between experimenters and subjects that the request involves. Since it is this disruption of relationships that constitutes the essence of the violation, it can better be understood as a breach of a structure of social interaction than as merely a violation of rules of equity in interaction.

One analysis of the structure of social interaction that may help us to understand the sources of this effect has been provided by Goffman (1959). His description of the breakdown of interaction that results when an actor discredits his role fits well the description our experimenters gave of their experiences:

> At such moments the individual whose presentation has been discredited may feel ashamed while the others present may feel hostile, and all the participants may come to feel ill at ease, nonplussed, out of countenance, embarrassed, experiencing the kind of anomy that is generated when the minute social system of face-to-face interaction breaks down (p. 12).

One might argue with some cogency that the experimenters were playing a social role, that of a subway rider, and that they discredited it by asking for the seat. But this use of 'role' and 'discrediting' seems strained and forced. Our results indicate, rather, that this 'anomy' is a more general phenomenon resulting directly from doing something that 'just isn't done' in a particular setting, whether it is related to the performance of any important social role or not.

This interpretation is consistent with Berger and Luckmann's argument (1967, cf. pp. 53–67) that the primary and essential means of social control is the sheer objectivity of the social world. They argue that it is the immediate and unreflective perception by actors of 'the way things are done' which stabilizes individual conduct and *ipso facto* the social order. Under this perspective, both the sanctions that Scott considers and the discrediting of identity that Goffman has explored are secondary; that is, they are derivative of this basic means of control.

To be sure the concept of 'those things that just aren't done' is itself a complex one, containing both a statistical proposition (such actions *do not* occur) and a normative proposition (such actions *ought not* to occur). Moreover, there remains the problem of specifying the precise content of those things that 'just aren't done,' a discussion we shall not develop here.

The results of our experience in doing something that 'just isn't done' suggest that knowledge of the objective social order controls behavior not only cognitively (people may simply never have thought of asking for a seat), but emotionally: actions outside of understood routine paths appropriate to the social setting, at least in this case, give rise to an intense, immediate, inhibitory emotion. This emotion[4] restricts individual action to the routine patterns that constitute the stable background of everyday life.[5]

Notes

1. Although it might seem to be a simple matter to say 'No' to the request, as Goffman (1971) points out, requests demand either compliance or an 'accounted denial.' That is, one does not merely say 'no' to a polite request, one gives a justification for saying 'no.' It takes time to realize that a justification is not required in this case or to construct one. Many subjects may have given up their seats simply because they didn't know how *not* to.

2. If subjects asked, 'Why?', experimenters were instructed to respond, 'I'm very tired.' If the subject proposed a reason. 'Are you sick?', the experimenter was to agree.

3. Even if we allow this more liberal interpretation of 'patterns of sanctions' (more liberal, probably, than Scott intended), an operant analysis of the problem is not without its problems. Such an analysis would be required to argue either that all of our experimenters had been severely traumatized by asking for a seat in the subway in the past (an improbable assumption, especially for those experimenters new to the city), or that the emotion results from 'stimulus generation' from similar experiences. This notion of generalization is both vague and, as Chomsky (1959) has pointed out, mentalistic.

4. The exact nature of this inhibitory emotion is open to further inquiry. It might be argued that the affect produced was *guilt* over either taking the seat or bothering the passenger. But the seat is not a very important matter, nor were the riders lastingly disturbed. Further, the emotion was confined to the subway car itself. As soon as experimenters left the car they felt thoroughly at ease. This emotion, rooted in the situation, seems closer to embarrassment than guilt.

Harold Takooshian (1972) has proposed an empirical test. He has suggested that the procedure be changed such that an experimenter stands before a confederate (preferably an older woman) and bluntly ask her for her seat, which she reluctantly surrenders. She is then to stand in front of the experimenter as he makes himself comfortable in her seat. The question is whether the experimenter would feel great tension even though there is absolutely no reason for him to feel guilt. The experimenter may find himself feeling embarrassed nonetheless sitting there in the sight of the other passengers.

5. A question remains as to whether this inhibition against substantial interaction among riders is functional. On the one hand, this inhibition simplifies the situation considerably for users of the subway. Since it is common knowledge that everyone minds his own business on the subway, a rider is free to assume a passive posture with regard to other riders. He need not be prepared to respond to demands from all those who surround him either for his attention or for more substantial involvement. On the other hand, daily contact with the by now clichéd 'faceless masses' of fellow riders may contribute to the alienation and anonymity often associated with urban life.

References

Berger, P., and Luckmann, T. (1967). *The Social Construction of Reality*, Doubleday Anchor, New York.

Chomsky, N. (1959). 'Review of *Verbal Behavior*,' *Language*, Jan.–Mar., **35**, 26–58.

Garfinkel, H. (1964). 'Studies of the routine grounds of everyday activity', *Social Problems*, Winter, **11**, (3), 225–250.

Goffman, E. (1959). *The Presentation of Self in Everyday Life*, Anchor Doubleday, New York.

Goffman, E. (1971). *Relations in Public*, Harper, New York.

Scheff, T. (1960). *Being Mentally Ill: A Sociological Theory*, Aldine, Chicago.

Scott, J. F. (1971). *Internationalization of Norms*, Prentice-Hall, Englewood Cliffs, N.J.

Skinner, B. F. (1953). *Science and Human Behavior*. Macmillan, New York.

Takooshian, H. (1972). 'Report on a Class Field Experiment,' Unpublished manuscript.

Small Groups and Social Interaction, Volume 1
Edited by H. H. Blumberg, A. P. Hare, V. Kent and M. Davies
© 1983 John Wiley & Sons Ltd

5.2   The Mindlessness/Mindfulness of Social Cognition

Ellen J. Langer   *Harvard University*

Similar actions can be accompanied by vastly differing degrees of cognitive activity. Indeed much of human activity that appears thoughtful is in fact conducted in what has been called a mindless fashion. Whether an activity is executed in a mindless or mindful state has critical consequences for adaptive human functioning (Langer, 1978, 1981, in press). Mindlessness may be defined as a state of reduced cognitive activity in which the individual processes cues from the environment in a relatively automatic manner without reference to potentially novel (or simply other) aspects of these cues. Mindfulness, on the other hand, is a state in which environmental cues are consciously manipulated, and the individual is engaged in actively constructing his or her environment. This is in marked contrast to the mindless state in which one deals with an already constructed environment.

Mindless information processing may arise either after many repetitions of a particular experience, or in certain instances, after a single exposure. In the former case, as an individual's experience with certain situations accumulates, a cognitive structure of the situation is formed which represents its underlying 'semantics.' The appearance of similar cues on subsequent occasions will then trigger a mindless sequence of behaviors. Once an activity becomes mindless the underlying semantics may no longer be available for conscious cognitive manipulation or even for examination.

In the latter, single exposure case, reduced cognitive activity does not result from reliance on cognitive structures built up over time, but from reliance on a cognitive structure that one has appropriated from another source. When this occurs the individual does not sufficiently scrutinize the information available at the time and, therefore, does not have that information available for later scrutiny. If on a subsequent occasion adaptive behavior requires examination of the information, the individual may be incapable of this.

Mindlessness is pervasive. In fact, for the typical individual, *mindfulness* is expected to occur only in the following circumstances: (1) when significantly more effort is demanded by the situation than was originally demanded; (2) when the external factors in the situation disrupt initiation of the mindless sequence; (3) when external factors prevent the completion of the behavior; or (4) when negative or positive consequences are experienced that are sufficiently discrepant with the consequences of prior enactments of the same behavior (Langer, 1978).

Although research by others has addressed reduced levels of cognitive activity (e.g. automaticity, preattentive processing, and overlearning), a new theory and a new term are called for, for several reasons. First, mindlessness suggests a more molar unit of analysis than has been examined in the past. Second, mindlessness may come about with, as well as without, repeated exposure. Third, mindlessness and mindfulness appear to be qualitatively different, rather than just quantitatively different. (For example, that which has been processed mindlessly may no longer be available for active conscious cognitive work.) And fourth, other researchers studying automaticity, for example, have focused on the adaptive function automatic processing serves in freeing conscious attention. While this is certainly true, all of the research we have conducted thus far suggests that it also may be quite maladaptive.

My students and I have pursued the study of mindlessness in several domains: its consequences for competent performance, for the perception of deviance, for the course of physical disease, and its implications for the very study of social psychological processes. Each aspect will be considered, briefly, in turn.

Research (Langer *et al.*, 1978; Langer and Weinman, 1981) has revealed that whether interactions between people were face to face or through written communications, whether they were semantically sound or senseless, they occasioned behavior that appeared mindless as long as the structure of the interaction triggered some overlearned sequence of behavior. With respect to potentially relevant information, people failed to hear what was said and to read what was written.

Since with each repetition of an activity the individual components of the activity progressively drop out, the result is that not only is the individual responding to some abstracted structure but also that the steps of the task become relatively inaccessible. Thus, in other research (Langer and Imber, 1979), we found that counter to an analysis that ignores the mindless/mindful distinction, a great deal of practice at a task may render the individual *more* vulnerable to external factors that bring competence into question. Groups that were moderately practiced at a task were able to supply the steps of the task as evidence of competence and therefore did not show performance decrements, while no-practice and overpracticed groups could not supply the components of the task and therefore showed clear debilitation.

Regarding the perception of deviance, we reasoned, first, that deviance (novelty) breeds mindfulness. If people are typically mindless *vis-à-vis* normal individuals, then the people who are deviant in any respect may be perceived as deviant in many respects (and therefore labeled, avoided, etc.) not so much because of their deviance but because of the thorough scrutiny that is prompted by the mindful state. Such a close examination of any individual would lead one to notice characteristics that typically go unnoticed and to the inappropriate judgment of these characteristics as extreme or unusual. As predicted, we found that the perception of the deviant was accurate but the typical characteristics and gestures that were noticed were evaluated as extreme and unusual. This occurred whether the deviance was positive (e.g. millionaire) or negative (e.g. ex-mental patient) but did not occur when the same stimulus person was unlabeled (Langer and Imber, 1980).

In work on mindlessness upon initial exposure, we found that when the individuals were initially given information (symptoms of a disorder) that was apparently irrelevant to them (in contrast to groups who were encouraged to think about the information) they became vulnerable at a later time when the information became relevant (they discovered they had the disorder). Groups that initially were encouraged to process the information mindfully did not show the debilitation (Chanowitz and Langer, 1980). It is currently unclear how many symptoms of physical diseases result from initial mindless acceptance of information about the disease and how many are a natural consequence of the disease itself. We are currently exploring this with respect to alcoholism and intend to pursue the investigation into other diseases such as cancer.

In past research (Langer and Rodin, 1976; Rodin and Langer, 1977), we have found that encouraging decision making in nursing home residents resulted in these residents being happier, healthier and more alert. In the follow-up study we also found that they lived longer than comparison groups. Initially we conceived of the experimental group as a group for whom we had induced a sense of control and responsibility. Since the elderly, especially the institutionalized elderly, are a group for whom routine is the rule, where there is very little to think about, the experimental group might be better seen as a thought-encouraged group, which would suggest that mindfulness may be necessary for survival. Current work is aimed at teasing these two explanations apart and preliminary data provide support for the mindfulness explanation. Control is very important. However, its primary effectiveness in health-related issues may be due to its ability to provoke mindfulness (cf. Langer et al., 1975, and see Chanowitz and Langer, 1981, for a discussion of the relationship between perceived control and mindfulness/mindlessness). When an individual perceives control there is reason to consider alternatives and to make plans. These activities most often are, of course, mindful.

Psychological researchers have typically conceived of their experimental subjects as thinking people. Given that people may at any point be either mindless or mindful, the generalizability of most experimental results that have failed to consider the distinction becomes questionable. Experimental situations, because of their novelty for subjects, typically *do* occasion mindful responding. However, experimenters may then be in the uncomfortable position of generalizing their findings from mindful subjects to a world of mindless individuals without assurance of any correspondence between the two (see Langer, 1978; Langer and Newman, 1979).

Thus research in this area has yielded a wealth of results spanning a number of diverse issues—all unified by a common theme: the consequences of reduced cognitive activity. The findings thus far suggest that mindlessness/mindfulness is a central dimension in human functioning, the study of which may perhaps even yield basic laws of human behavior.

References

Chanowitz, B., and Langer, E. (1980). 'Knowing more (or less) than you can show: understanding control through the mindlessness/mindfulness distinction,' in J. Garber and M. Seligman (eds), *Human Helplessness*, Academic Press, New York.

Chanowitz, B., and Langer, E. (1981). 'Premature cognitive commitments: Causes and consequences,' *Journal of Personality and Social Psychology*, 41, 1051–1063.

Langer, E. (1978). 'Rethinking the role of thought in social interaction', in J. Harvey, W. Ickes., and R. Kidd (eds.), *New Directions in Attribution Research*, Vol. II, Lawrence Erlbaum, New Jersey.

Langer, E. (In press). 'Playing the middle against both ends: the usefulness of adult cognitive activity as a model for cognitive activity in childhood and old age,' in S. Yussen (ed.), *The Development of Reflection*, Academic Press, New York.

Langer, E. (1981). 'Old age: An artifact? in *Aging, Biology, and Behavior*, Academic Press, New York.

Langer, E., Blank, A., and Chanowitz, B. (1978). 'The mindlessness of ostensibly thoughtful action: The role of placebic information in interpersonal interaction,' *Journal of Personality and Social Psychology*, 36, 635–642.

Langer, E., and Imber, L. (1979). 'When practice makes imperfect: debilitating effects of overlearning,' *Journal of Personality and Social Psychology*, 37, 2014–2025.

Langer, E., and Imber, L. (1980). 'The role of mindlessness in the perception of deviance,' *Journal of Personality and Social Psychology*, 39, 360–367.

Langer, E., Janis, I., and Wolfer, J. (1975). 'Effects of a cognitive coping device and preparatory information on psychological stress in surgical patients,' *Journal of Experimental Social Psychology*, 11, 155–165.

Langer, E., and Newman, H. (1979). 'The role of mindlessness in a typical social psychological experiment,' *Personality and Social Psychology Bulletin*, 5, 295–298.

Langer, E., and Rodin, J. (1976). 'The effects of choice and enhanced personal responsibility for the aged,' *Journal of Personality and Social Psychology*, 34, 191–198.

Langer, E., and Weinmann, C. (1981). 'When thinking disrupts intellectual performance: Mindfulness on an overlearned task,' *Personality and Social Psychology Bulletin*, 7, 240–243.

Rodin, J., and Langer, E. (1977). 'Long-term effects of a control-relevant intervention with the institutionalized aged,' *Journal of Personality and Social Psychology*, 35, 897–902.

Small Groups and Social Interaction, Volume 1
Edited by H. H. Blumberg, A. P. Hare, V. Kent and M. Davies
© 1983 John Wiley & Sons Ltd

5.3 Coercion and Resentment in Juvenile Correctional Institutions

Theodore M. Newcomb   *University of Michigan*

What does it feel like to be an inmate in a juvenile correctional institution? Even though many studies of such populations have been made, there are few, if any, systematic reports of inmates' responses to this question. Even if such responses have been recorded, their authenticity might be suspect, since respondents might fear that true responses might be used against them. In the absence of trustworthy information, it is possible to suggest certain conclusions based upon known facts of incarceration, and upon certain common psychological processes.

First, every inmate is an inmate by external coercion. He or she has (presumably) broken the law, and has been institutionalized by legal procedures, without his or her assent. Certain consequences may be inferred from the sheer fact of coercion. There are of course many overt ways of adapting to coerced incarceration, but behavioral adaptation does not necessarily correspond to internal feelings.

Second, perceived coercion is likely to be accompanied by internal resentment, defined by Webster as 'indignant displeasure'. The following discussion considers some psychological processes by which resentment can be aroused and/or maintained in correctional institutions.

Third, we must recognize that individuals differ in their degrees of resentment (although no measuring scales exist), in their changes over time, and in their overt expression of it. All of these differences are presumably related to the varying effects of institutionalization. There are ways in which inmates' resentment may be decreased. For example, they might discover that staff members really *want* to help them, or they might simply adapt to the new regime, gradually taking it for granted. But this is not a how-to-do-it treatise. It is mainly a review of selected data concerning inmates' offenses, and of some of the psychological processes by which resentment can serve as a mediating variable between coercion and inmate behavior.

Surveillance and punishment

Inmates not only are sent to institutions by coercion, but they find various forms of it after their arrival, mostly having to do with rules and regulations, about what must and what must not be done. Selo (1976), in a study of a national sample of institutions (as distinguished from smaller and less regimented programs), reports that 56% of all inmates indicate that their belongings are searched; 69% that their persons are searched; 68% report that their incoming mail and 46% that their outgoing mail is inspected. Only 44% assert that 'I can be alone when I want.' These frequencies indicate that coercive surveillance is common, though not universal.

Youths' reports (which tend to exceed frequencies of staff reports) of punishments for *first-time* misconducts are that the most frequent 'punishment' (about two-thirds) is *talking to offenders*, 'followed by taking away points' (about half); 'separation from others,' (about 40%); and 'keeping youth longer' (40% by youth and 16% by staff). Other punishments are less frequent. Repeated violations are usually punished more severely. Punishments and rumors of punishment are almost everyday events in institutions.

Serious offenses in this large sample are fairly frequent. For inmates of intermediate length of stay (4 to 11 months), about half of all respondents report that 'within the last month' they have 'fought with other youths'; one-third report 'illegal use of drugs;' and more than a quarter say that they have 'stolen something.' Since such offenses, and also their punishments, are typically well known by the offenders' peers, it may be concluded that the threat of punishment is very much on their minds.

Post-entry offenses

It is hardly surprising that many youths who are incarcerated because of previous offenses ('breaking the law') continue to commit offenses. Such behavior may be regarded as sheer habituation: they continue their previous behaviors, though not necessarily in the same ways. But it may also represent ways of fighting back at the system which sent and kept them there—a form of retaliation that presupposes resentment.

By way of indicating some of the conditions associated with post-entry offenses, I have tested the following hypotheses: the data consist of responses by nearly 2,000 youths in 40 institutions that constitute a representative sample of all such institutions in the United States (see Vinter *et al.*, 1976; and Newcomb, 1978). The hypotheses deal either with characteristics of inmates or of institutions, or both.

1. The behavior and attitudes of youth in large institutions, which tend to be bureaucratic and security conscious, will tend to be more contracultural than those in small institutions.

Table 1 Percentages of respondents who report one or more serious offenses

Categories	Number of Respondents	Pre-entry (%)	Post-entry (%)	Post-/pre-correlations
4 large programs,* many veterans	446	43	41	.95
4 large programs, few veterans	558	30	29	.97
9 small programs, many veterans	279	29	20	.69
13 small programs, few veterans	242	31	20	.64

*Henceforth I shall use the term 'institution' in an inclusive sense, and 'program' for particular kinds of institutions. Veterans are inmates who have been in their programs 10 months or more.

Table 1 presents findings of frequencies of subjects' self-reported responses to questions about pre- and post-entry offenses committed. The table frequencies represent responses of the same individuals concerning five serious offenses that they have committed before and five after entering their institutions (the particular offenses listed are not identical for the pre- and post-entry responses). Only in the small programs are post-entry frequencies significantly less than pre-entry responses ($p = .001$).

2. Homogeneity of subjects' responses of various kinds will vary inversely with population size. I have assumed: (a) that subgroups tend to develop norms; (b) at least some of these normative influences will be related to the variables measured; and (c) that the greater the number of subgroups the greater the likelihood that some of the subgroups' influences upon their members will be in approved and some in disapproved directions. Thus there should be greater population-wide homogeneity in small than in large programs. Standard deviations of responses to six questions, selected as diverse and as including both attitudes and behaviors, were compared. Distributions appear in Table 2, and the hypothesis is supported.

3. If, as commonly assumed, correctional institutions are 'schools of crime,' then offense levels should increase with length of stay. As shown in Table 3, this is true for all three categories of programs, but particularly for large programs including many veterans. Neither size alone, nor length of stay alone, accounts for the increases. The small programs have almost exactly the same proportion of veterans (long-time inmates in their present programs) as the large ones with many veterans.

4. Among sub-populations of entering youths who are very similar in pre-entry offense levels, those who enter large and those who enter small programs will *diverge*, becoming more like the programs that they enter, in post-entry levels of offense. Using four different measures of both pre- and post-offense levels I compared the post-entry offense levels of each of 34 pairs of programs—in each case

Table 2

SD levels	Numbers* and percentages in small programs	Numbers* and percentages in large programs	Total
$\geqslant 1.3$	37 (24%)	45 (35%)	82
1.0–1.2	43 (27%)	59 (46%)	102
$\leqslant .9$	76 (49%)	24 (19%)	100
Total	156 (100%)	128 (100%)	284

$X^2 = 27.66, p \leqslant .001, 2$ df

*The selected questions required a choice of one of six scaled responses; since SDs vary with numbers of alternatives, questions must offer the same numbers of them. Questions dealt with topics ranging from recent offenses, attitudes toward staff, and hopes and fears about the future. Numbers represent individuals in samples of both large and small programs who answered all of the selected questions. SDs were computed for the distributions of scores, ranging from one to six in all small and in all large programs.

Table 3   Mean indexes of post-entry offense levels

Length of stay	Large programs/ many veterans	Large programs/ few veterans	All small programs/many veterans
Short ($\leqslant 2$ months)	30	26	20
Intermediate	41	29	24
Long ($\geqslant 12$ months)	50	37	29
Percent increase at $\geqslant 12$ months	67	42	45

one large and one small program that were virtually identical in pre-entry levels. Divergence did in fact occur. The average percentages of respondents who reported *pre*commitment offenses were almost identical: 24% in large and 23% in small programs. Averages of postcommitment offenses, by the same individuals, differed greatly: 32% and 17% respectively. Offenses increased in the large programs and decreased in the small ones.

5. The *convergence* hypothesis was that sets of entering youths whose pre-entry offense levels were different but who entered programs having similar post-entry offense levels will become more similar. Each set of programs was rank-ordered in terms of pre-entry level so that both programs in all pairs compared differed by the same number of ranks of offense levels (e.g. Ranks 1 and 5, Ranks 2 and 6, and so on). The convergence hypothesis was also supported, both within and between large and small programs. The mean pre- and post-entry differences were, in index points, 17 and 8, respectively, in the large programs, and 14 and 3 in the small ones. For each of the nine programs compared, without exception, the post-entry pair difference was less than the pre-entry difference. These tests of the

hypotheses of divergence and convergence indicate that there is a consistent tendency for youths to take on the offense characteristics prevailing in the program they enter. This effect is a consequence of various differences between small and large programs, not of initial offense levels.

6. Offense rates will vary directly with proportions of veterans. There are at least two reasons for this prediction. First the longer their stay the more opportunity they have to learn and to commit offenses. Second, it is often the practice, especially in large institutions, to punish offenders by extending their length of stay. Tables 3 and 4 indicate that offenses increase with length of stay in all categories of institutions, but most conspicuously in large programs in which there are many veterans. These findings imply that 'learning to break the law' is associated with large proportions of veterans, regardless of population size, but in terms of final outcomes ('the bottom line') it is in the large programs with many veterans that most long-time 'learning' is reported. In Table 4, increase in 'learning to break the law' is, in percentage terms, very high in small programs, simply because the short-time level was very low.

7. Veterans will be more influential than non-veterans in promoting offenses on the part of the others. Veterans are apt to be older than most of their peers, and to 'know their way around'—in short, to be more sophisticated about coping. But the evidence for this proposition is indirect and not substantial. The most relevant evidence available appears in Table 5, in which 'negative' responses about

Table 4   Percentages of the response 'I have learned to break the law in many ways since I've been here'

Length of stay	Large programs/ many veterans	Large programs/ few veterans	All small programs/many many veterans
Short	21	21	6
Intermediate	39	21	15
Long	57	34	23
Percent increase	171	62	283

Table 5   Mean percentages of responses to selected questions about leaders

| Type of question | Large programs, many veterans | | | All small programs | | |
	By vets	By nonvets	By all	By vets	By nonvets	By all
'Positive'	26	42	35	46	46	46
'Negative'	48	39	43	31	25	27
Difference	−22	+3	−8	+15	+21	+19

'leaders' refer to questions about leaders' antagonism toward staff and the 'positive' to questions about leaders' interests in 'straightening out' other youth or 'helping to keep other youth out of trouble.' Veterans in the large, heavily veteran institutions saw leaders as predominantly 'negative' significantly more often than did respondents in the other three categories. Insofar as these findings imply influence, the veterans' influence in small programs contributes less to the criminalization of youths than that of the large heavily veteran institutions, in spite of the fact that there were about equal proportions of veterans in the four large institutions and in the small programs.

The final propositions are *ex post facto*.

8. No single variable accounts for differences in postcommitment offense levels. The small institutions have about the same proportions of veterans as do the heavily veteran large programs, but the former are distinctly lower than the latter in postcommitment offenses. The two largest sets of programs are similar in size but different in postcommitment offense levels, as shown in Table 6.

9. Levels of postcommitment offenses correspond rather closely to actual numbers of veterans, rather than to their proportions. Apparently a critical mass of veterans in institutions is a necessary condition for high levels of postcommitment offense, as shown in Table 7. The average numbers of veterans in the three categories of program size are 35, 8, and 6, respectively. A rationale for the assumption that a critical mass (actual number) rather than a high proportion of veterans as a predictor of postcommitment offenses might be somewhat as follows: (a) not all veterans have the personal characteristics that are associated

Table 6   Combinations of levels of four variables in three types of programs

	Size	Veterans	Precommitment offense	Postcommitment offense
Veteran programs	Large	Many	High	High
Newcomer programs	Large	Few	Not high	Intermediate
Smaller programs	Small	Many	Not high	Low

Table 7   Combinations of variables as predictors of postcommitment offense levels*

Programs	Size	Critical mass?	Precommitment level	Postcommitment	Sums of Predictor Variables
Veteran	Large (2)	Yes (2)	High (2)	High	6
Newcomer	Large (2)	No (1)	Not high (1)	Intermediate	4
Smaller	Small (1)	No (1)	Not high (1)	Low	3

*The larger the number in parentheses, the larger the score on that variable.

with influencing peers—the more veterans there are, the greater the probability of influential individuals; (b) The larger the number of veterans, the more probable it is that each of them will receive social support for offensive behavior and attitudes, and also longer acquaintance with other individuals who share long histories of resentment, and are likely to form cliques that may be described as contracultural.

Psychological processes associated with resentment

Although no measures of resentment have been developed, it is hardly to be doubted that youths who have been incarcerated feel some degree of it. Few people really want to be committed to a correctional institution, and so it can be assumed that resentment is almost universal. All inmates have been subjected to coercion, and presumably all experience resentfulness, typically continuing for some hundreds of days.

There is no single explanation of why many inmates continue to commit offenses after repeated punishments for previous ones. One reasonable answer to the question is that such individuals, more than others, are obsessed by constant resentment. Violating the rules is a form of retaliation, getting even, and it is worth the risks. They live with 'indignant displeasure,' as do most inmates at varying levels. Their thresholds for violating the rules are low, and even minor annoyances can arouse them to cross the threshold. The mere existence of rules is a denial of freedom and dignity.

One possible expression of resentment is illustrated by the fact that about a third of all inmates in a national sample of institutions report fairly serious offenses after entering their programs (Newcomb, 1978). How does it happen that youths who are being punished (by incarceration) continue their punishable behavior?

Among possible answers to this question are the following: (1) they are simply continuing their precommitment behavior—they are habituated; (2) they are expressing their resentment at being imprisoned. I know of no data that demonstrate the relative importance of these two sources. The latter one is consistent with the finding, previously noted, that inmates' post-entry offense levels are influenced by the kinds of programs that they enter. Their habits can be changed.

There are several psychological principles that help to answer the above question. All of these principles can contribute to the resentment that is felt by imprisoned people.

The most obvious of these principles is that of aggression (most simply defined as behavior designed to harm or annoy other persons) as related to frustration (feelings of being prevented from doing or having desirable things). Dollard *et al.* (1939) demonstrated that aggression is often preceded by frustration. This notion (modified by Miller, 1941) is that while overt aggression does not always follow frustration, frustration does always *instigate a tendency* to aggression, which may or may not actually occur, depending on attendant circumstances. Since commitment to an institution is always frustrating, it will sometimes be followed by actual as well as instigated aggression. The target of aggression is not necessarily the source of frustration; as Dollard *et al.* note, the targets may be persons who are 'available' but not at all responsible for the frustration.

The notion of 'reactance' also deals with such conditions (Brehm, 1966); when free behavior is threatened or prevented, the forbidden behavior becomes more desirable. Jones and Gerard (1967, p. 500) point out that 'it is possible for coercion to boomerang ... [the coerced person] will react by attempting to regain his freedom.' This psychological process, which must be fairly common in correctional institutions, is very likely to be accompanied by resentment.

Miller (1944) has studied 'approach–avoidance conflict.' Using animals who were placed at various distances from attractive and from aversive stimuli, he found that avoidance behavior became 'stronger' with increasing nearness to aversive stimuli than did approach behavior to increasing closeness to pleasant stimuli. Nearness to danger increases avoidance more than pleasant conditions increase approach (analogies can be found in human behavior). Within correctional institutions this principle would tend to minimize forbidden behavior, but at the cost of continued frustration.

When such conflict, or reactance, or frustration has to do with persons or groups (as is usually the case in these institutions) resentment is more likely to be felt and/or expressed when the conditions creating it continue, day after frustrating day.

Another important psychological theory, labeled by its author (Festinger, 1957) 'cognitive dissonance,' helps to explain why so many incarcerated youths continue behaviors for which they know they may be punished. An important part of this theory is 'self-justification' (see Aronson, 1972). Loosely stated, the self-justifier convinces himself that he was 'right the first time,' and that he must have had good reasons for his offenses, and those reasons are still justifiable. Offenders are not alone in taking this position; we are all self-justifiers in some ways, whether or not these ways include breaking the law.

As a matter of fact, all these theoretical ideas can apply to all of us. The circumstances, and the nature of the behaviors that are justified can of course differ widely.

Coping with resentment

Here are some fairly common ways by which inmates can try to deal with their resentment:

1. Self-assurance of never being committed again ...
       by being inconspicuous
       by committing no offenses, thus earning early release
       by making plans for going straight after release

2. Convincing themselves that a minor risk is preferable to endless boredom . . .
    by offending only when there is little risk of being caught, or
      when punishment is known to be trivial
    by taking the risk of being caught for a serious offense
3. Relying on support of friends if one is accused . . .
    by making friends who applaud offenses
4. Determining to get even with staff and cops . . .
    by making plans for offenses before and after release

If a good many individuals repeat serious offenses and are repeatedly punished, they must find some satisfaction in so doing, i.e. some form of self-reinforcing. For example, not all offenses are known to authorities; 'getting away with it' may be highly rewarding. Or punishment may be preferred to pleasing the authorities by conforming behavior.

Are the commonly reported increases in offenses during youths' lengthening stay in their programs accompanied by increases in resentment, in the manner of a positive feedback system in which an increase in either leads to an increase in the other? Helson's (1964) well-documented theory of 'adaptation level' suggests something quite different. Judgments of heaviness, loudness, warmth, etc., are influenced by recent experiences. If, for example, one has been in a room where the temperature is above 100 °F, then 80 °F will seem positively cool. One adapts (within limits, of course) to changes. If inner states follow the same rules as judgments, one would adapt to increasing levels of resentment. If things do not get worse, one comes to consider them less serious than when they were first experienced. Thus one can adapt to one's own resentment, learn to live with it. In the same way, perhaps, one becomes adapted to one's level of offense behavior; what had been unthinkable becomes normal.

One can only speculate about the possibility that offense levels and resentment tend to increase or to decrease together. This relationship may be affected by individuals' tendencies to be 'self-justifiers'—'I had good reasons for what I did.' Persons who typically blame others are known as 'extrapunitive.' Such inmates would tend to be particularly resentful, and perhaps also to be frequent offenders. Conversely, those who are relatively intrapunitive might have relatively low levels of resentment, and probably low offense levels. If such reasoning is justifiable, there is a positive relationship between resentment and offense levels. At any rate, I suspect that both offense rates and resentment are related to personality variables. The published literature about youths in correctional institutions does not, typically, consider such variables, although demographic variables are often reported.

Can either resentment or offenses occur without the other? In the absence of a measure of resentment, no direct answer is available. One might assume that resentment increases with length of previous *and* current institutionalization. But, according to Slozar (1978) there is very little relationship between 'conformity' and previous offense history. This implies that resentment does not necessarily affect subsequent offenses. His index of conformity with rules in their present institutions is only slightly related to frequencies of previous offenses, the correlations being nonsignificantly negative. Perhaps resentment is *not* necessarily related to previous offenses and incarcerations. It seems reasonable that after several experiences, inmates become more or less adapted at a certain level of resentment, so that it does not increase after repeated incarcerations; they have learned to cope. It is possible, of course, that with increasing experience resentment decreases. This would be consistent with Helson's (1964) theory of adaptation level.

If this is indeed the case, what are the likely consequences of adapting to a certain level of resentment? One possibility is that adaptation to certain levels of offense commitment may parallel adaptation to resentment. The institution becomes a treadmill; monotony is broken by occasional offenses, for only some of which punishment follows. For some individuals the risk of punishment is outweighed by others' applause for bravado.

Such adaptation is surely influenced, for a considerable number of inmates, by a sense of hopelessness, maintained by the common belief of being stigmatized forever. With few or no marketable skills, except perhaps in the underworld, the stabilization of resentment together with hopelessness does not forebode success in 'going straight.' Such individuals are likely to find social support mostly from others like themselves. Such groups constitute the most formidable mini-contracultures. Their formation is, to an unknown extent, aided and abetted by their members' experiences in certain kinds of correctional institutions.

Group influences

There are probably few inmates whose behavior invites punishment who do not expect approval of that behavior from some of their peers. The fact that the frequencies of self-reported offenses inside the institution increase with length of time spent there may be, in part at least, a consequence of another fact: the veterans (all of whom have been in their institutions for long periods of time) have had ample opportunity (particularly in large programs) to form cliques whose members have in common an addiction to forbidden behaviors and who applaud such behaviors, especially if they 'get away with it.' Mutual reinforcement almost certainly contributes to the high offense rates on the part of the long-time residents.

Such groups, of which there may be several in large institutions, are mini-contracultures; that is, their values and their behaviors are opposed to those that are approved by the stated purposes of the institutions (learning to 'go straight,' and helping others to do so). The high frequencies of post-entry offenses in large institutions are presumably attributable, in large part, to such contracultures (see Slozar, 1978).

It is also of interest that 79% of the youths in large, heavily veteran institutions are 16 years of age, or older (Vinter *et al.*, 1976). In all the other programs only

46% were at those ages—a ratio of nearly 5 to 3. Nearly twice as many youths in the large veteran programs as in others had been in residence for at least 9 months and some of them as much as 2 years; many had previously been committed to other institutions. In view of the fact that adolescents tend to associate with their age-peers, it is likely that many of the older inmates form cliques of relatively frequent offenders.

One characteristic of most groups is consensus concerning the values and objectives that are related to the group's formation. But this is applicable to correctional institutions only in limited ways, since their purposes are not those of inmates, whose commonalities include mainly histories of breaking the law, and the desire to leave their institutions.

Whatever the commonalities of a group, they serve to solidify it, to keep its members together. Such 'sticking together' is commonly known as *cohesiveness*—a very general term which has been shown to include many distinguishable characteristics. For most purposes the most important of them are mutual attraction (liking each other), and sharing similar attitudes and values. A cohesive group thus develops norms about behaviors and beliefs that are shared.

The bases of cohesiveness and normativeness within correctional groups are quite limited, for several reasons. Except in small programs members of living groups are arbitrarily assigned—by staff and not by members themselves. They are constantly changing as some members leave and others replace them; in many large programs, members of different living groups are isolated from each other—partly, of course, in order to prevent 'trouble-makers' from forming cliques. Most important, however, is the likelihood that the dominant characteristic that is universally shared is resentment at being there. A phenomenon known as social facilitation comes into play; that is, there is 'an increase of response merely from the sight or sound of others acting in the same way (F. H. Allport, 1924). (This process, sometimes labeled as imitation, was originally used to explain crowd behavior, but its usefulness is not limited to crowds.) Insofar as inmates see or hear each other expressing resentment or hostility about their incarceration, they facilitate similar behavior on the part of others, although not necessarily all others.

In spite of limited opportunities to choose one's friends, there are possibilities for doing so. If friends tend to be birds of a feather who flock together, most inmates do find at least some others who wear the same plumage. Slozar (1978) reports that in each of two institutions for late-adolescent males about 25% report that they spend 'most of their free time with a group of guys who are together a lot;' and about the same proportion report 'mostly by myself' (Slozar, 1978, Table 20). To another question, 'How many of the guys you have met here would you like to see after you get out?' about two-thirds reply 'none' or a 'few' and just over 10% reply 'most' or 'almost all.' These findings do not suggest much congeniality among inmates. Indeed, individuals' strategies for 'earning' release are apt to be solitary rather than shared.

A crucial question is whether the most or the least 'hardened' individuals tend to flock together. Unfortunately the relevant data are sparse, and often not very informative. Slozar's (1978) conclusion is that inmates not having serious offense histories tend to choose as friends individuals like themselves in this respect, whereas those who had serious offense histories were less likely to choose others like themselves. But he also found that inmates most hostile to staff members 'more often stuck together.' Similarity of race was more conspicuous as a basis for friendship than similar offense histories. We can probably conclude that there is a tendency for both high-offense and low-offense birds to flock together. Institutional officials are of course more concerned about the former than about the latter.

Socialization—the tendency for new members of a family or of a society or a correctional institution to take on the ways of already established members—is a universal phenomenon. But previous members are not always very successful in their attempts to socialize newly arrived members. Families are usually more successful than correctional institutions. In both cases, but particularly in the large institutions, opposing influences may conflict with the approved socialization— a kind of contrasocialization. Its sources are apt to be from without (i.e. society at large) in the case of families, but from within in correctional institutions. This is their eternal dilemma.

It is important to understand inmates in terms of their previous histories. Those who have previously been incarcerated are usually the most 'hardened.' If, as seems likely, such inmates tend to become habitually resentful—as a way of life—then *re*socialization is not very likely. Such individuals are affected by psychological processes including those previously noted—justification, levels of frustration, adaptation, reactance, conflict, frustration. But such processes apply to all of us; the difference between 'hardened' inmates and most other people is the intensity, the continuity of resentment that is accompanied by such processes. It is a difference of degree rather than of kinds of psychological processes. Most of us live with fewer coercive restrictions than inmates do. Most of us also feel resentments from time to time, but we do not wake up every morning wondering how to cope with them for another day.

There is almost surely a relationship between contrasocialization and inmates' resentments. It is sometimes asserted that, using the analogy of hydraulic pressure, expressing one's anger reduces the tension. This of course may occur, but the opposite may be more frequent. That is, 'successful' retaliation may reinforce such behavior without reducing resentment. After all, such a 'success' does not ameliorate the fact of being incarcerated, and it may lead to punishment, which can only increase resentment. The hydraulic analogy probably does not fit the facts, in most cases. It is more likely that the sequence of resentment–offense behavior–increased resentment is typical.

All inmates have committed 'legal' offenses. Many but not all of them continue to be offenders during incarceration. Among important differences between those who do and those who do not, levels of resentment may be an important one. At one extreme are some individuals who are intrapunitive and have a tendency to blame themselves rather than others (Brown, 1947), and at the other extreme are extrapunitive individuals. Inmates of the latter kind are most likely to be resentful, to be offense-prone, and to justify their offenses by blaming others whom they see as hostile.

Such characteristics and such psychological processes as frustration or reactance are apt to be associated with resentment, and also with committing offenses. Coercion invites resentment, which may lead to offenses that invite punishments which perpetuates resentment. Too often, the cycle is repeated, over and over again.

Voluntary and coerced groups: overview

Most of the principles concerning group membership have been developed from studies of voluntary groups, or from those in which there is little or no coercion—as, for example, in families, or fraternities. Group influences within coerced groups have rarely been studied, and there are reasons for concluding that influences in groups created by coercion are not necessarily the same as those which are not coercive.

Collins and Raven (1969) note that 'Perhaps the most widely reported characteristic of cohesive groups is the greater tendency of individual members to influence and be influenced' (p. 123). This statement appears in a context of 'natural settings' and presumably refers to voluntary groups. Most living groups in correctional institutions are not voluntary—both because their members are there by *force majeure* and because they have not chosen each other—are not very cohesive, but they commonly include members who are influential by reason of size, strength, and capacities for bullying; and are feared by others. This kind of influence in coerced groups is consistent with Collins and Raven's position; little or no cohesion and only limited eagerness to be influenced go together.

Almost any textbook in social psychology notes several characteristics of groups that are typical, if not universal. These include such intragroup commonalities as *norms* and *consensus* about certain behaviors and beliefs, *roles* (expected behaviors, which may apply to different persons but are important for group functioning), *conformity* to certain rules, *cooperation* in certain activities, a considerable degree of mutual *trust*, and, overall, *cohesiveness*—an inclusive term implying 'sticking together.' All of these group characteristics imply unity or togetherness or oneness.

Such characteristics apply particularly to groups that tend to be rather small (divisiveness becomes more likely in large groups), relatively continuing membership over time, repeated face-to-face interaction, and membership that is voluntary, or at least is not externally compelled. (Children's membership in their families is a special case, usually, of compulsion that children take for granted: everyone belongs to a family.)

To what extent do these characteristics apply to living groups in correctional institutions, in which membership is *not* voluntary? How cohesive do these groups tend to be? The answers are not simple, or universal, but they can be enlightening. The complexities include the following facts.

1. Membership tends to be discontinuous. In a group of 10 inmates, for example, one member leaves and another one joins the group every month, on the average. The gain of one individual and the loss of another may result in a drastic change in group characteristics.

2. The major concern of almost every inmate is 'to get out of here.' But individuals can do little to hasten another's release; everyone, sooner or later, develops his or her own strategy for earning his or her way out. Sometimes group members may testify on behalf of a particularly well-liked individual, as worthy of release.

3. Resentment at being incarcerated is virtually unanimous in every living group, but degrees and forms of expressing it vary widely. Some individuals may be criticized by other group members for being 'chicken', too submissive, while others are annoyed by constant expressions of resentment ('you'll get all of us in trouble'). Some members may 'squeal on' fellow members—hardly a way of developing group unity—and some are afraid to do so.

4. Subgroups or cliques often develop in living groups. They may be in opposition about desirable behavior, or they may simply represent a lack of common interests. Cliques may represent ethnic differences, or differences in age, size, or 'toughness.' Staff members often discourage the formation of cliques, whose members may 'conspire' in various ways considered undesirable.

5. Finally, the rewards of developing a sense of group unity are dubious. After all, group members have not chosen each other; they will not be fellow members very long, and they may never meet again. It is difficult to know who is and who is not trustworthy. Superficial friendship with one or two fellow-members may be safe and very rewarding, for the time being. It is safer not to be too close, or to seem to be too close.

In sum, the coercive conditions of group membership in correctional institutions do not favor cohesiveness and unity. The shared characteristics of membership are negative—resentment of incarceration, offense histories, eagerness to 'get out,' uncertainty about the future (including stigmatization, and difficulties of finding jobs)—as opposed to the enjoyable aspects of being a member of a voluntary, cohesive group.

I find myself wondering about coercion and resentment outside of prisons and correctional institutions. Consider public (and perhaps private) schools, for example; no one knows how many of their 'inmates' feel coerced and resentful, but in some of them it must be a sizeable minority—especially including those who are in some sense handicapped. Such youths may be presumed to 'fight back' or retaliate in ways that resemble the tactics of incarcerated youths. Their retaliation—whether or not a consequence of limited capacity—is, in an important sense, normal. That is, it is a consequence of coercion and resentment. Perhaps Victor Hugo, long ago, said it best: 'He is a malicious animal; when attacked he defends himself' (my translation). Many an inmate feels that he is being attacked.

References

Allport, F. H. (1924). *Social Psychology*. Houghton-Mifflin, Boston.

Aronson, E. (1972). *The Social Animal*. Freeman, San Francisco.

Brehm, J. W. (1966). *A Theory of Psychological Reactance*, Academic Press, New York.

Brown, J. F. (1947). 'A modification of the Rosenzweig picture-formation test,' *Journal of Psychology*, **24**, 247–272.

Collins, B. E., and Raven B. H. (1969). 'Group structure: attraction, coalitions, communications, and power,' in G. Lindzey and E. Aronson *Handbook of Social Psychology*, 2nd ed., vol. 4, pp. 102–185, Addison-Wesley, Reading, Mass.

Dollard, J., Doob, L., Miller, N., Mowrer, V., and Sears, R. (1939). *Frustration and Aggression*. Yale University Press, New Haven.

Festinger, L. (1957). *A Theory of Cognitive Dissonance*, Harper & Row, New York.

Helson, H. (1964). *Adaptation Level Theory*, Harper & Row, New York.

Jones, E. E., and Gerard, H. B. (1967). *Foundations of Social Psychology*, Wiley, New York.

Miller, N. E. (1941). 'The frustration-aggression hypothesis,' *Psychological Review*, **48**, 337–342.

Miller, N. E. (1944). 'Experimental studies of conflict,' in *Personality and the Behavior Disorders*, in J. Mc. V. Hunt (ed.), Ronald Press, New York.

Newcomb, T. M. (1978). 'Characteristics of youths in a sample of correctional programs,' *Journal of Research in Crime and Delinquency* [January], 3–24.

Selo, E. (1976). 'The control function,' in R. D. Vinter, T. M. Newcomb, and R. Kisch (eds.), *Time Out*, National Assessment of Juvenile Corrections, University of Michigan, Ann Arbor.

Slozar, J. A., Jr (1978). *Prisonization, Friendship, and Leadership*, Lexington Books, Lexington, Mass.

Vinter, R. D., Newcomb, T. M., and Kisch, R. (eds.) (1976). *Time Out*, National Assessment of Juvenile Corrections, University of Michigan, Ann Arbor.

Small Groups and Social Interaction, Volume 1
Edited by H. H. Blumberg, A. P. Hare, V. Kent and M. Davies
© 1983 John Wiley & Sons Ltd

5.4 Minority or Majority Influences: Social Change, Compliance, and Conversion

Serge Moscovici and Geneviève Paicheler

École des Hautes Études en Sciences Sociales, Paris

'But the emperor has no clothes!'

The voice of a little child strikes the only discordant note among the chorus of praise that greet the emperor's procession. Everyone else is in agreement—the ministers, even the oldest and wisest among them; the courtiers, more or less prone to ingratiation; the attendants; the chamberlains holding an invisible, not to say imaginary, train; the townspeople—all agree to see the wonderful clothes, which attest to their intelligence . . . but do not exist.

You have probably recognized this as Andersen's fairy-tale; and though you must have forgotten the details, it illustrates perfectly two types of influence. Initially we see the first type of influence: conformity and the majority effect. At first the protagonists of the tale are faced with a conflict between what they see (none of them sees the clothes, and for good reason!) and what they are supposed to see, what they are told to see; and they agree together on an appropriate definition of reality. With accelerating rapidity, a majority effect then develops which becomes ever more powerful, and everyone 'sees' the emperor's new clothes. Their naive and wrong-headed reasoning runs like this: people cannot be collectively in error, therefore the clothes really exist, and if we can not see them, we had better keep quiet about it. So they all fall in with the pack and admire the emperor's beautiful new clothes.

But now a small voice can be heard: a minor voice, a minority voice so to speak; the voice of a little child. And however faint the voice may be, it expresses with marvellous precision the thought that lies suppressed in everyone's heart. It offers a perception of reality freed from contingent circumstances and freed from the requirements of submission. This sets in motion an excellent example of the process of *minority influence*. Once heard, the message is passed on first in an undertone, then amplified until the whole population laughs aloud at the fraud perpetrated on the emperor and his entire court; that is, on the whole structure of authority—a derided, decrepit authority which, for the sake of saving face, will go on to the bitter end pretending to believe in the fraud and refusing stubbornly to change.

It must be stressed that this allegory is very profound, being a remarkably apt paradigm of the process of social influence. But whereas the first effect (the conformity or majority effect) has been the central preoccupation of the theorists of influence, the second (the minority effect) has for long been eclipsed by it and has only recently gained a true theoretical status. For social influence was initially absorbed into conformity theory.

The bias of conformity

The psychology of social influence has long been a psychology of majority pressure. With rare exceptions it has concentrated on the phenomena of conformity and submission to norms. It has been studied in terms of three mechanisms: the social control of individuals; the extinction of differences between them; and the development of collective uniformities. Most examples of resistance to social control have been treated as deviant and/or pathological.

In this *functionalist model*, social systems (whether formal or informal) and the milieu are considered as pre-defined determinants for the individual and the group. Through them, everyone is provided with a role, a status and various psychological resources prior to any social interaction. The behaviour of individuals or groups serves to ensure their entry into the system and the milieu. Consequently, since the conditions to which the individual or group must adapt are given in advance, reality is uniform and the norms which must be observed apply equally to all. Deviance is seen as an obstacle to entry into the system, indicating a lack of resources or knowledge about the milieu, whereas normality is seen as a state of adaptation to the system and of equilibrium with the milieu. The process of influence aims at reducing deviance and stabilizing both interpersonal relations and exchanges with the outside world. Those who follow the norm are therefore acting in a functional and adaptive way, whereas those who depart from it or oppose it are acting in a dysfunctional or non-adaptive way. Thus conformity is seen as a requirement of the social system, leading to consensus and equilibrium. That being the case, the only changes which can be envisaged are those which make the system even more functional.

Let us reiterate the six fundamental propositions of this functionalist model (Moscovici, 1977).

1. *Influence is unequally distributed and unilaterally exercised.* Consequently the majority view derives prestige because it is correct and 'normal,' whereas any minority or divergent view is incorrect and deviant. One side is defined as active

and open to change—the majority and the authority structure—and the other as passive and resistant to change; but in that case, why have we not taken a closer look, for example, at the resistance to change evinced by company managers?

2. *The function of influence is to maintain and reinforce social control.* According to the functionalist model, before social control can occur, individuals must all have the same values, norms, and judgmental criteria, acceptable to all alike. Group members perceive differences as an obstacle, which leads to the exclusion of the offender.

Moreover norms are dictated by the majority and by authority; thus any divergence presupposes two things:

(a) a resistance, a non-conformity threatening the functioning of the group;
(b) an inadequacy or deficiency in the individual.

Divergence is therefore synonymous with inferiority and marginality; and in the interest of the group, influence becomes primarily a way of rehabilitating deviants. This mechanism serves to make everyone the same and to iron out peculiarities in individuals and subgroups. The cohesion of the group depends on the extinction of differences.

3. *Dependent relations determine the direction and magnitude of the social influence exercised within a group.* In the study of the process of influence, dependency is seen as a fundamental determining factor. Everyone accepts influence and conforms in order to win the approval of others. And everyone depends on others for the acquisition of information, since all individuals seek a correct and objective view of the world, and want their judgments to be validated. This is what Festinger (1950) argues in contrasting *physical reality* and *social reality*; people are obliged to call on others to validate their judgments for them when they feel unable to do so themselves.

4. *The forms which the process of influence takes are determined by states of uncertainty and by the need to reduce that uncertainty.* When ambiguity increases and objective criteria are undermined, a state of internal uncertainty arises in individuals which makes them open to the influence of others (Sherif, 1947). This uncertainty may affect skills and judgments both about oneself and about others.

5. *The consensus aimed at in the interchange of influence is based on the norm of objectivity.* When no objective reality is immediately to hand, people have no alternative but to look for a conventional wisdom to serve as substitute.

6. *All processes of influence must be understood in terms of conformity.* This conformity can take extreme forms: objective reality itself may be denied, as in Asch's (1956) experiment. And paradoxically, even the processes of innovation have been conceptualized within the framework of conformity. In Hollander's (1958) theory, innovation follows the following process: the individual, initially conformist, acquires thereby an elevated status and builds up an idiosyncrasy credit which allows him or her to diverge from the norms and to demand the same of others. Consequently (to recall one of our more whimsical examples) Lenin

would have had to become Czar of all the Russias as a prerequisite for making the revolution.

We must now show that this model is incomplete and that innovation and social change often originate at the periphery of society. We have for too long overlooked the attractive power of deviance, rule breaking, and refusal, and we must find theoretical ways of understanding these phenomena. We must, that is, admit that influence can flow from the minority to the majority.

The model of minority influence

The argument for its existence

This is based on the postulate that minorities and majorities can both exert influence, each in a privileged domain. The most surprising aspect of this proposition is that it should still appear novel and even incongruous despite the abundance of historical and sociological examples.

The functioning of all societies depends on agreements about fundamental principles, that is, *consensus*. Now the power of the minority derives precisely from its ability to refuse consensus. Of course the group will put pressure on the minority in order to re-establish homogeneity. But the sanction of exclusion is rare if not impossible: people must therefore be content to play for time with the stubborn minority; and it is this very attitude that sets in motion the process of influence. Moreover, unusual, marginal, and deviant behaviour possesses an undeniable power of attraction. Such behaviour gives other people access to the unknown, the original, and the surprising; these features attract attention, become 'visible' and can finally elicit approval.

One of the first experiments to demonstrate the minority effect, or at least the one which features in the literature as the classic experiment, is that of Moscovici *et al.* (1969). The experimental arrangement consisted of groups of six subjects, comprising two confederates and four naive subjects. They collectively underwent a colour perception test to establish their perceptual competence; they were shown a series of blue slides and the confederates consistently answered 'green' on each showing. The findings can be summarized under two headings:

1. The confederates—a minority—exercised a significant influence (8.42% green answers as against 0.25% in the control group);
2. The threshold of blue–green discrimination varied. Presented with the successive range of shades between pure blue and pure green, the experimental subjects detected green at an earlier stage than the controls.

Consistent behavioural style

Behavioural style depends on the organization, display, and expressive intensity of behaviour and opinions. It is the combination of behaviour and the context in which they are displayed that give them their instrumental and symbolic meaning. Consistency of behavioural style depends on its assurance, coherence, clarity, and internal logic: to be convincing one must obviously appear convinced of what one proposes. Thus a consistent behavioural style is assertive. It is proof of the commitment of the individual to it and of the individual's independence; thus even in hostile surroundings, such individuals will display their certainty and their determination to stick to their guns. The message of such a style is: '*I* do not intend to change; if you want to re-establish the consensus which you miss so badly, it's up to *you* to change.' Even when it is perceived as aggression, this style of behaviour exercises a considerable and (as we shall see) complex influence, and does not therefore necessarily function by mere force.

In the blue–green paradigm, consistency was realized in the reiteration of the same answer, signifying a refusal to change and an indifference to the answers of the others. In other experiments relating more specifically to attitudes (Paicheler, 1976, 1977; Mugny, 1974, Papastamou, 1979), consistency expressed itself in an assured and coherent exposition of an unchanging point of view, and in a refusal to submit to the influence of other people. These experiments demonstrate clearly the persuasive effect of consistency. But let us return to the familiar paradigm of the blue–green experiment (Moscovici *et al.*, 1969). In one experimental situation, the confederates, instead of constantly replying 'green,' answered 'green' in certain cases and 'blue' in others. Here the influence was negligible as there was no significant difference between the experimental group (1.25% 'green' answers) and the controls (0.25%).

This should obviously not be taken to imply that the consistency of the confederates made them appear any more likeable or competent.

Consistency can also be realized in an interpersonal agreement, such as unanimity among the confederates, as in the experiment of Asch (1956). Now in this paradigm, as soon as consistency visibly diminishes (that is, when a single confederate gives the same right answer as the naive subject) there is a considerable decrease in the influence exercised (between 10.4% and 5.5% wrong answers).

Social change

Social change and innovation, like social control itself, are objectives of influence.

It would be wrong to assume that social change can be instigated only by leaders, as it is precisely those leaders who manifest the greatest resistance to change, having the most to gain from stability. Two contradictory though also dialectically complementary theories coexist in social psychology. The first affirms that we like what we are used to and get used to what we like; the second argues that when habit becomes routine, it inevitably becomes a source of discontent and we are then attracted by change and novelty. What man has not shared the poet's dream of a woman who was 'never quite the same, nor yet entirely different' (and vice versa)?

Now, innovations often originate in deviant and powerless minorities, especially when they call into question the established order.

Let us examine the case of social norms. In the literature of social psychology, norms are generally defined as a majority code. The majority represents both what exists and what must inevitably exist. As a result it has no effective reason to change ... except at the instigation of a minority. Minority heterodoxy can get the upper hand over majority orthodoxy by rekindling buried and repressed desires latent in the majority.

To illustrate our argument let us examine an experiment by Nemeth and Wachtler (1973). Subjects were shown slides of 'Italian' or 'German' paintings (these attributions being random, of course). The controls showed a preference for 'Italian' paintings; thus the norm was 'pro-Italian.' In the experimental groups a confederate was introduced either as 'Italian' or as 'German' in origin. These confederates displayed a preference for the paintings for their own 'country of origin.' Whether in the presence of an 'Italian' or a 'German' confederate, the experimental subjects showed a greater preference for the 'German' pictures than the controls. Thus the less usual position was the more attractive.

One of us (Paicheler, 1974, 1976, 1977) has achieved similar findings after a series of experiments on the same lines. In a group discussion situation, it was demonstrated that a minority can accelerate the process of normative change, and the conditions under which this can happen were defined. Among the areas studied was the influence of an extreme and consistent confederate on attitudinal change—here attitudes towards women. Initially the subjects evinced a mildly feminist attitude, which accentuated itself during the discussion. Now historically and sociologically the norm is evolving towards the expression of more feminist attitudes. A consistent confederate, who was either very feminist (i.e. innovatory) or very antifeminist (i.e. reactionary), was therefore introduced into the groups. The feminist confederate had a considerable influence, whereas the antifeminist made it impossible for the subjects to reach agreement, provoking an effect of bipolarization. Here the feminist subjects became even more feminist; and the neutral or antifeminist subjects fell prey to old reactionary demons emerging from the woodwork, and became even more antifeminist. It would anyway be naive to suppose that minority effects work only in a positive or progressive direction; Fascism has provided us with many contrary proofs.

Conflict

The processes of influence are directly linked to the negotiation of conflict (production, avoidance, resolution).

When influence operates in the direction of change, discord is unavoidable. As soon as the latter is perceived, it is viewed as a threat and a source of anxiety. Let us, however, note that those who have deep convictions show no sign of tension in the face of discord.

Discord, like the threat of conflict, disturbs and engenders uncertainty. At such times the problem is not so much to reduce the uncertainty as to reduce the underlying discord or to persuade the other side that one is right, the more so if one is convinced of one's own opinion.

The origin of uncertainty is conflict: before trying to persuade people to believe us we must first try to make them doubt their own opinions. Conflict has an 'unfreezing' function; it forces individuals and groups to re-examine their own positions.

Without conflict nothing would ever wrinkle the smooth surface of social uniformity; and this conflict can be provoked by the majority and the minority alike. Resolution of conflict with the majority involves a phase of passive acceptance and compliance which manifests itself as a change in public response coupled with a retention of private beliefs on the part of the minority. On the other hand, conflict provoked by a minority attitude is a source of curiosity and a sort of social enigma for the majority. It accordingly requires a more active attitude of the individual, a process of validation and a re-examination of the substance of the conflict. This re-examination does not always manifest itself as a modification of the individual's public response, and may operate more indirectly and latently, whether via a halo effect or via a deep modification of the individual's response structure.

Indirect influence and latent influence

Frequently the influence of a minority deviant group is explicitly rejected, often along with the group itself, which is viewed negatively. Often, too, people try to escape this influence by looking for a psychological disturbance at the root of the unusual behaviour. An example is the process of psychologization described by Mugny (1980). Though rejected on a conscious level, this influence may nevertheless prosecute its subversive task in a somewhat more subterranean way, achieving results where they are least expected. This throws up an epistemological problem which may well have hindered previous investigations of these effects.

Direct or indirect influence. A celebrated French adage suggests that distance lends disenchantment (*les absents ont toujours tort*). This is not always so, as Moscovici and Neve (1971) have shown by demonstrating that an individual more readily accepts the opinion of another in the absence of the latter. For this purpose they once more employed the paradigm of the autokinetic effect (Sherif, 1947), placing the subject in the presence of a confederate who gave answers systematically exceeding the subject's estimates by 10 to 15 centimetres. In the experimental groups the confederate would then absent himself on some pretext, whereupon the subject's estimates tended to converge towards those of the departed confederate. In the control groups, however, the confederate remained in the subject's presence, and the latter's estimates tended to diverge from the confederate's.

The halo effect

The semantic halo.   Instead of affecting its ostensible target influence may affect contiguous areas, as has been demonstrated by Mugny and Papastamou (1976–77).

Subjects answered a questionnaire about the causes of pollution and the attribution of responsibility for it. Then they were asked to consider a message emanating from a minority group, in either a 'rigid' or a 'fair' style and with either a 'dissonant' or a 'consonant' content in terms of the general beliefs of the population. Then the subjects answered another questionnaire consisting both of the same items as the original (i.e. 'direct' items), and of related (i.e. 'indirect') items.

Changes in responses to the indirect items were proportionately greater than changes in responses to the direct items; that is, to those actually contained in the message. The 'fair' minority obtained the same amount of change on direct and indirect items. The 'rigid' minority, in contrast, had little influence on responses to the direct items, but its influence was far greater on the responses to the indirect items. Thus when minority pressure becomes too strong its influence becomes indirect.

The temporal halo: the minority sleeper effect.   In view of the complexity and profundity of minority influence, it was interesting to compare it with majority influence; such a comparison was realized in the experiment of Moscovici *et al.* (1980). The procedure was the same as in the experiment by Mugny and Papastamou already cited, with two differences:

1. An identical message was attributed either to a minority or to a majority source;
2. The influence of the message was measured both immediately afterwards and 3 weeks later, as in the sleeper-effect experiments. And the post-experimental questionnaire comprised not only direct and indirect items, but also questions testing memorization of the message and of the influence source.

The second post-experimental questionnaire, presented 3 weeks later, showed the minority to have become more influential than the majority. More precisely, the minority and the majority had the same effect on the direct items; but on the indirect items the majority's effect was negative, indicating that the subjects reacted *against* the attempt to influence them, whereas in this case the minority exercised a positive influence which was accentuated by a rigid behavioural style.

The after-effect.   The blue–green experiment had already demonstrated a change in subjects' *perceptual code*, brought about by a modification in their threshold of blue–green discrimination. Further investigation of this effect was required, and undertaken by Moscovici and Personnaz (1980).

The experimenters once again used the blue–green paradigm, with pairs of subjects: one naive and one confederate. The chromatic after-image was used to test the extent of perceptual change. As we know, if one fixates on a white screen after fixating on a colour for several seconds, one perceives its complementary colour: yellow–orange for blue slides and red–purple for green. The experiment comprised several phases which will not here be described in detail. The subjects were given to understand that their perception of the colour of each slide placed them either in a majority or in a minority. The essential findings were as follows: the influence of the confederate was the same (5% of green answers) whether the subject was alleged to belong to a minority or to a majority. It was in the subject's after-image perception that the effects were demonstrated: the subject's judgment in the minority influence condition shifted to the complement of green from the pre- to the post-interaction situations. Thus conversion behaviour takes place only if the influence source has a social meaning, which the mere simultaneous presence of two individuals fails to provide; these findings have been confirmed by Doms (1978) in an experiment which replicated the results of Moscovici and Personnaz.

Conclusion

The findings of researches into the influence of minorities constitute a system of growing coherence and completeness. In outline, they demonstrate—at the very least—that the body of theory arising from them is gaining in consistency. And that consistency comes at a very timely moment for those more recalcitrant spirits among us, who still need convincing that minority influence exists and that our comprehension of its mechanisms is improving all the time. The gaps in our understanding should be such as to encourage us to further progress in this field of research.

Fundamental progress in this area has necessitated something of a break with the paradigms previously associated with influence studies; for it has been necessary to try to go beyond the beautifully ordered artifice of appearances and beyond the evidence of facts whose meaning stems immanent within them, in order to illuminate the various layers of the process in all their richness, depth, and complexity. In this psychosocial 'archaeology of knowledge,' there is clearly still much digging to do; nonetheless we have already reached a solid foundation of understanding.

References

Asch, S. E. (1956). 'Studies of independence and conformity: A minority of one against a unanimous majority,' *Psychological Monographs*, **70**, (9, no. 416).

Deutsch, M., and Gerard, H. B. (1955). 'A study of normative and informational social influences upon individual judgment,' *Journal of Abnormal and Social Psychology*, **51**, 629–636.

Doms, M. (1978). 'Résultats de la réplication de l'effet consécutif,' Mimeo, Louvain.

Festinger, L. (1950). 'Informal social communication,' *Psychological Review*, **57**, 271–282.

Hollander, E. P. (1958). 'Conformity, status, and idiosyncrasy credit,' *Psychological Review*, **65**, 117–127.

Moscovici, S. (1977). *Social Influence and Social Change*, Academic Press, New York.

Moscovici, S., Lage, E., and Naffrechoux, M. (1969). 'Influence of a consistent minority on the response of a majority in color perception task,' *Sociometry*, **32**, 365–379.

Moscovici, S., Mugny, G. and Papastamou, S. (1980). 'Sleeper effect or minority effect,' Unpublished Ms.

Moscovici, S. and Nemeth, C. (1974). 'Social influence II: Minority influence,' in C. Nemeth (ed.), *Social Psychology: Classic and Contemporary Integrations*, Rand McNally, Chicago.

Moscovici, S. and Neve, P. (1971). 'Studies on social influence: I. Those who are absent are in the right. Convergence and polarization of answers in the cause of social interaction,' *European Journal of Social Psychology*, **1**, 201–213.

Moscovici, S., and Personnaz, B. (1980). 'Studies in social influence; V. Minority influence and conversion behaviour in a perceptual task,' *Journal of Experimental Social Psychology*, **16**, 270–282.

Mungny, G. (1974). 'Négociation et influence minoritaire,' Unpublished dissertation, Geneva.

Mugny, G. (1980). 'Le pouvoir des minorités,' Unpublished Ms.

Mugny, G., and Papastamou, S. (1976–77). 'Pour une nouvelle approche de l'influence minoritaire: les déterminants psychosociaux des stratégies d'influence minoritaires,' *Bulletin de Psychologie*, **328**, 573–579.

Nemeth, C. and Wachtler, G. (1973). 'Consistency and modification of judgment,' *Journal of Experimental Social Psychology*, **9**, 65–79.

Paicheler, G. (1974). 'Normes et changement d'attitude: de la modification des attitudes envers les femmes,' Unpublished dissertation, Paris.

Paicheler, G. (1976). 'Norms and attitude change: I. Polarization and styles of behaviour,' *European Journal of Social Psychology*, **6** (4), 405–427.

Paicheler, G. (1977). 'Norms and attitude change: II. The phenomenon of bipolarization', *European Journal of Social Psychology*, **7** (1), 5–14.

Papastamou, S. (1979). 'Stratégies d'influence minoritaires et majoritaires,' Unpublished dissertation, Geneva.

Sherif, M. (1947). 'Group influence on the formation of norms and attitudes,' in G. E. Swanson, T. M. Newcomb, and E. L. Hartley (eds.), *Readings in Social Psychology*, pp. 249–262, Holt, New York.

6 Helping and Hurting

Small Groups and Social Interaction, Volume 1
Edited by H. H. Blumberg, A. P. Hare, V. Kent and M. Davies
© 1983 John Wiley & Sons Ltd

6.1 Prosocial Behaviour and Small Group Processes

Valerie Kent   *University of London Goldsmiths' College*

If members of groups, small or large, are to coexist, they must sometimes act not only for their own immediate benefit, but also for each other's well-being. Research on benefiting others has been dominated by three issues: (1) Are people capable of altruism? (2) Do some people have characteristics which relate to a tendency to benefit others? (3) Are there situational factors which enhance or diminish such behaviour?

For both conceptual and methodological reasons, the measure of benefiting others has most frequently been in terms of unilateral acts by individuals who are not interacting with others. On conceptual grounds, as long as the focus of interest is 'altruism,' it is necessary to avoid the possibility of reciprocity between benefactor and beneficiary. Furthermore, since altruism embodies the idea of selfless, unrewarded, internally motivated behaviour, it is also logical to exclude contemporary social processes as far as possible, in order to look at altruism *in vacuo*. Studies aimed at identifying situational rather than internally motivating factors in benefiting others tended to adopt the 'altruistic' paradigm in order to challenge its assumptions.

The very notion of unrewarded behaviour is a problem for psychology, although it is demanded by a strict definition of altruism (see Rosenhan, 1978, for a discussion of the 'altruistic paradox'). Macaulay and Berkowitz (1970) defined altruism less strictly as 'behaviour carried out to benefit another without anticipation of rewards from external sources' (p. 3). However, as Staub (1978, 1979) points out, altruism is only one of many possible forms of benefiting others. These may vary with respect to the severity of the other's need, the degree of self-sacrifice involved in meeting it, whether or not it is a single act or part of a relationship. A more general term is 'prosocial behaviour,' of which altruism is only one form. It is defined by Staub as 'behaviour that benefits other people'

(Staub, 1978, p. 2). Unlike altruism, prosocial behaviour does not presuppose a particular motive, or that the behaviour has a single cause. To avoid confusion, though, one must assume that the benefit to others is deliberate and not accidental.

Where 'altruism' tended to obscure the relevance of small group processes, the term 'prosocial behaviour' opens up new issues and new approaches. At the same time, there have been methodological developments which also expand the scope of research and can include small group processes. While traditional experimental methods, exposing a single person to a standard stimulus, are no less important and proper, additional insights are available from research on groups of people in interaction. Such research is at present often carried out by developmental psychologists, and increasingly prosocial behaviour is receiving attention.

All the main approaches to prosocial behaviour, whether focusing on situational or individual variables, have a place for group processes, at least if these are defined so as to include the interaction of the ultimately small group of caregiver and child. However, although each approach implicates the group process, each in its own way fails to develop and extend research on the relationship between prosocial behaviour and small group processes. The aim of this paper is to discuss this relationship with respect to currently predominant 'individual' and 'situational' views of prosocial behaviour, and to suggest possible developments in research and theory.

Small group processes, personal variables, and prosocial behaviour

One approach to understanding prosocial behaviour is to seek to identify characteristics of people which relate to their prosocial behaviour. A characteristic, which might on theoretical or other grounds be expected to relate to prosocial behaviour, is measured to see if it correlates with the researcher's chosen measure of prosocial behaviour. In this section, the three variables which currently appear most frequently in the literature will briefly be discussed. They are (1) moral judgment: understanding what 'should' be; (2) role-taking ability: understanding someone else's perspective; and (3) empathy: vicariously experiencing someone else's feelings.

Each of these variables might plausibly be expected to relate to prosocial behaviour, but for each the evidence is conflicting. The study of small group interaction is relevant in three ways, each of which might illuminate the present contradictions. Firstly, the measure of prosocial behaviour or the postulated correlate, may be derived from observations of interaction. Secondly, contemporary group processes may affect the relationship between any of these 'characteristics' and prosocial behaviour—a possibility which remains virtually, although not entirely, unexplored. Thirdly, group processes may be involved in the development of the characteristics which purportedly relate to prosocial behaviour. Although this is an important part of the thinking about moral judgment, role taking, and empathy, discussed below, it has been the subject of very little systematic research.

Moral judgment

The study of moral judgment is most clearly identified with the cognitive–developmental approach of Piaget (1932) and Kohlberg (1976). Moral judgment is seen to progress through stages which are qualitatively different from one another and achieved in an invariant sequence, although the highest stages may not be reached at all. Kohlberg himself stresses the importance of the group in the development of moral judgment, arguing that it enhances role-taking ability which he sees as the bridge between cognitive and moral development.

'Extensive participation in any particular group is not essential to moral development but participation in some group is. Not only is participation necessary, but mutuality of role taking is also necessary. If, for instance, adults do not consider the child's point of view, the child may not communicate or take the adult's point of view' (Kohlberg, 1976, p. 50). However, despite this emphasis on the role of the group, there is surprisingly little research on the effect on moral development of different types of participation in different types of group.

Studies of preschool children in interaction, however, suggest that they are less egocentric and less hedonistic than Kohlberg's theory allows. Eisenberg-Berg and Neal (1979) found that preschoolers frequently gave empathic or pragmatic reasons for their spontaneous prosocial behaviour, but rarely gave hedonistic or social approval reasons. Damon (1977) also found 4-year-olds gave empathic rationales against stealing, in a study of social knowledge. Nucci and Turiel (1978) found preschoolers to be concerned about moral transgressions in their interactions, before social–conventional transgressions. The latter were emphasized by the adults rather than the children.

The study of interaction, then, may throw light on the nature of moral judgment, and might even be used to validate measures of moral judgment. Furthermore, and relevant to the whole of this paper, the measure of prosocial behaviour itself might be, in part at least, based on observations of people in interaction. This approach is increasingly being adopted, although mostly in studies of children. Additionally, observations of prosocial behaviour may be used as one criterion of the validity of a questionnaire on prosocial behaviour (Weir and Duveen, 1981), or some other prosocial measure.

Theories of moral development do not make explicit how judgment is translated into action. Studies of the relationship between level of moral judgment and prosocial behaviour have on the whole found positive correlations (see, for example, Emler and Rushton, 1974; Rubin and Schneider, 1973), but they have been criticized for using inadequate tests of moral judgment, and for inappropriately applying correlation techniques to a nonlinear variable (level of moral judgment). Both Krebs (1978) and Staub (1979) argue that the relationship between moral judgment and prosocial behaviour is mediated by the situation, but research on this is needed.

It would be interesting, too, to see if people's styles of interacting with others related to their levels of moral judgment. Do those who participate in many groups, especially where the groups have conflicting aims, have a consistent interaction style, or a variable one? According to Kohlberg, they should have a higher level of moral judgment, as should those who have opportunities to lead. Do such people in fact act more prosocially on one or more dimensions of prosocial behaviour when in interaction with others, and is this behaviour consistent with other measures of the various dimensions of prosocial behaviour?

Role-taking ability

Although role-taking ability is regarded as important by researchers with a cognitive–developmental orientation (see preceding section, and Selman, 1976), it is equally so for other approaches to prosocial behaviour, including both attribution and symbolic interaction theory perspectives. Moreover, it is on the face of it logical that one must be able to understand someone's perspective before meeting their perceived need. The evidence, however, is contradictory; for example, Emler and Rushton (1974) did not find a significant relationship between role taking and prosocial behaviour, but Buckley et al. (1979) did. Ianotti (1978), in an experimental study, found children in role-taking training conditions were more likely to donate candy than were control group children.

A problem here, as with studies of moral judgment, is that we are really talking about 'skills' related to benefiting others, and not the 'will' or motivation to do so. Skill does not presuppose or compel action; many factors, including perception of the current situation, may affect whether or not it is exercised. Furthermore, a relative lack of skill does not mean that there will be no prosocial behaviour. Zahn-Waxler et al. (1977) found, in a study of 3–7-year-olds, no relation between scores on a battery of perspective taking tests and prosocial interventions towards an adult, except in the 3-year-olds. As they suggest, this result may only mean that both perspective taking and prosocial behaviour demand at least some capacity to understand others. Given this minimal capacity, greater levels of role-taking ability may not increase the likelihood of prosocial behaviour.

It may be, however, that rather than looking at the incidence of prosocial behaviour in relation to role-taking ability, one should look at the *quality* of such behaviour, as Bar-Tal et al. (1980) have done with regard to age and prosocial behaviour. That is, one might expect increasing appropriateness of prosocial behaviour to relate to role-taking ability. The analysis of social interaction is a useful way of studying the different dimensions of prosocial behaviour, and different types of prosocial response, although this might only be used to provide a base for other types of test of the quality of response.

There is increasing evidence that young children are not as egocentric as the cognitive–developmental view had seemed to suggest. Children as young as 3 years, and certainly in the preschool age range, do modify their speech to others according to the listener's perspective (e.g. Menig-Peterson, 1975) and status (James, 1978); they take into account intention and consequences of behaviour (Peterson, 1980), including the social reactions, positive or negative, to behaviour (see, for example, Suls *et al.*, 1979; Keasey, 1977). However, as most of these researchers have found, the information is combined and used differently from older children and adults (see also Rogers, 1978; Berndt and Berndt, 1975; Karniol and Ross, 1979).

Surprisingly, there is little research on the factors affecting early role-taking ability. Light (1979) found that role-taking ability in 4-year-olds, measured on a battery of tests, related to their mothers' style of interacting with them; mothers who took a 'personal' rather than 'positional' approach had children with higher role-taking scores. The rationale for this study derived from Bernstein's work on linguistic styles, in which language is said to reflect and shape the child's role, and permits (elaborated code) or inhibits (restricted code) a differentiated view of self and others. Since a personal orientation should encourage a concern for intentions, Light's study is of interest on both theoretical and empirical grounds. The study looked only at the children's problem solving and not their prosocial behaviour. A somewhat similar study by Cook-Gumpertz (1973) looks at the issue of linguistic codes in relation to maternal controls, with implications for prosocial behaviour. What is needed is a study of this nature, but in which prosocial behaviour is also measured.

The problems of measuring role-taking ability have been reviewed by Ford (1979), and are mentioned in most papers on the subject of role taking. If we are to look at the early development of role taking ability, we may need to rely less on measures which depend on the child's comprehension of pictures, films or stories, or ability to respond to adult strangers, and more on the appropriateness of his/her behaviour in interaction with familiar others, whether peers, siblings or adults.

Although some of the conflicting data on the relation between role-taking ability and prosocial behaviour may be a consequence of the problems of measuring role-taking ability, they may also arise from different techniques of measuring prosocial behaviour. Emler and Rushton (1974) used donation of winnings to a charity, and Zahn-Waxler *et al.* (1977) used sharing, helping, and comforting initiations towards an adult confederate, while Strayer (1980) used prosocial behaviour scores based on interaction in a preschool. In this last study, conventional measures of role-taking ability (including empathic ability—see below) were unrelated to prosocial behaviour, and seemed also not to relate to the children's role taking and empathy as reflected in interaction.

Empathy

The many studies investigating a relationship between empathy, 'a vicarious affective response to others' (Hoffman, 1977a) and prosocial behaviour have produced more than usually conflicting results. Not only is there evidence of positive correlations (e.g. Murphy, 1937; Buckley *et al.*, 1979) or no correlation (Levine and Hoffman, 1975; Strayer, 1980), but also a negative correlation (Eisenberg-Berg and Lennon, 1980). Furthermore, several studies have reported a relationship between empathy and aggression, since Murphy (1937) first reported a relationship between 'sympathy' and aggression in her study of children in a nursery school. Barrett and Yarrow (1977) found a very complex relationship between aggression and empathy, and Light (1979) indirectly provides evidence in that children with high role taking ability, including affective role taking, were more likely to be reported as having temper tantrums. It may be that young children misattribute arousal, or that they do not act in the same ways as older children in order to reduce it, or that they are particularly subject to what Hoffman (1981) calls overarousal.

Part of the confusion may lie in the measurement of empathy (see Ford, 1979; Eisenberg-Berg and Lennon, 1980), and in the use of different measures of prosocial behaviour. It may also reflect a failure to distinguish between empathic ability and empathy as a state. A particular study may fail to arouse an empathic state, despite the subjects' empathic abilities. Alternatively, the situation may be sufficiently unambiguous as to arouse an empathic state in most subjects, masking differences in empathic ability. Studies of empathic ability, also known as affective role-taking ability, are akin to those of role taking and moral judgment, in that even if one 'has' this ability, it may not be the motive for action.

Hoffman (1977a, 1981) specifically concerns himself with empathy as a prosocial motive, taking a developmental approach. He argues that very young infants respond to the distress of others with 'primitive empathic distress,' and that this, interacting with a growing cognitive awareness of others, develops through a stage where there is increased accuracy of responding to the other's feelings in a situation, to a final stage when the child, having a sense of continuing identity, can perceive the problems of others in the broader context of their life histories. Although Hughes *et al.* (1981) have found age differences with respect to 'empathic understanding' which they feel provides some support for Hoffman's views, there is as yet no work relating developmental level of empathy to empathic response in a situation, or to prosocial behaviour.

A serious problem is how to measure empathy as a state. Leiman's (1978) work analysing videotapes of children's facial expressions is promising, but not yet developed. Batson and his colleagues have sidestepped the problem of direct measurement of empathic state by using a misattribution of arousal paradigm, in which some subjects are led to believe that their arousal is caused by something other than the need of the other person, (a 'drug'). They have interpreted their findings as evidence for a two-stage model of helping, in which taking someone else's perspective leads to an increase in empathic emotion, which leads in turn to helping (Coke *et al.*, 1978). Using the same approach, but varying the ease with which subjects could escape without helping, Batson *et al.* (1981) concluded that empathy led to an altruistic rather than egocentric motivation to help.

However, Archer *et al.* (1981) say that they were able to replicate the Batson *et al.* findings only for subjects who were high in dispositional empathy and in a 'high demand' condition, when they knew the experimenter was aware of their state. They argue that this implies a complex process in which 'helping is influenced by both empathic concern and personal distress' (p. 793). Hoffman's theory also implies an interaction between empathic ability and current state, but he does not see empathy as an egotistical motive.

Common to all these approaches is the view that the perception of need is part of the process of prosocial behaviour, and that empathy provides a motive—an altruistic motive—to relieve that need. Interaction with others has a place in Hoffman's scheme, in the elaboration of a cognitive awareness of others; this point is less explicit in Batson's approach (see also Batson and Coke, 1981). Additionally, Archer *et al.* suggest that the presence of another person, an 'aware' experimenter, affects prosocial responding. In the area of empathy, perhaps more than elsewhere, there are the glimmerings of a theory which would link individual 'skills', motivational dispositions and states to social interaction origins on the one hand and to prosocial responding, taking into account social context, on the other. At present, however, both the social interaction origins of empathy and the effects of contemporary group processes remain unexplored territory, and exploration will require more subtle measurement techniques than we now have.

Prosocial behaviour and socialization

Regardless of all the problems and issues raised so far in this paper, it does appear that there is a growing body of evidence, partly because of the increase in studies of social interaction, that children are less egocentric, more concerned about others, and more likely to engage in prosocial behaviour than was thought until quite recently. Indeed, Aronfreed has suggested 'that the basic cognitive and affective substance of moral value is formed fairly early in the socialization process and that it remains relatively stable thereafter. But it does become subordinated to increasingly differentiated structures and increasingly powerful operations of thought' (Aronfreed, 1976, p. 68). To what extent does the socialization process, and what aspects of it, enhance (or diminish) the ability to perceive someone's need, to feel concern, to act prosocially? As noted in earlier sections, there is little direct research on these problems; there is, though, a body of research on 'socialization techniques'.

Despite the many difficulties and indeed inadequacies of such research, noted by Hoffman (1977b) in his review, he nonetheless concluded that inductive techniques (using reasoning and explanation) were most effective in leading to 'moral internalization' when compared with physical punishment and love withdrawal. This seems to imply that mothers have a message to transmit, and incline to different procedures to do so. Three problems can be raised:

1. The 'technique' may be not only the medium, but also the message; for

example, in the case of induction, that causes and intentions are more important than actions *per se*. The Cook-Gumpertz (1973) study of maternal controls and Light's (1979) study of role taking are suggestive of possible lines of research.

2. The medium, or technique, may vary *with* the message rather than with the mother, as was found by Grusec and Kuczynski (1980).

3. Socialization may better be regarded as a two-way process, indeed, as the interaction between members of a dyad or the larger small group of the family (Bell, 1968; Keller and Bell, 1979; Mulhern and Passman, 1979; Schaffer and Crook, 1980).

The term socialization technique may be a shorthand, and misleading, way of referring to something very much more complex, which may be revealed by studies of interaction, such as many of those just cited. The study of social interaction is also important for testing specific hypotheses about its role in the development of prosocial behaviour and its correlates. A good example of such a study is the work reported by Zahn-Waxler in this volume. However, there is room for a theoretical position which relates style of interaction between caregiver and child *directly* to prosocial behaviour, without implying that the 'correlates' in fact mediate prosocial behaviour. Early sociability (see, for example, Hay, 1979; Rheingold, *et al.*, 1976; Eckerman, 1979; Vandell, 1980) may be extended and enhanced in a relationship between caregiver and child which shows *mutual* prosocial behaviour, rather than position-oriented (cf. Bernstein, 1972) 'care giving'. As with cognitive processes, what has gone on between two people may become internalized, the 'intermental' becomes 'intramental' (Vygotsky, 1962). In this view, moral judgment, role taking ability, and empathy would develop alongside and in interaction with prosocial behaviour: 'efficient practice precedes the theory of it' (Ryle, 1949; Shotter, 1974). This approach could accommodate both the early incidence of prosocial behaviour, and some of the anomalies in the correlational data. A test of this view is in progress (Kent, in preparation). It is interesting to note that Mueller and Brenner (1977) concluded from their study of toddlers' interaction that social interaction was not only a product of social skill, but also its source.

Generality

An important issue in the search for personal characteristics which correlate with prosocial behaviour is the generality of such behaviour across situations. While in general there is no more support for generality in this area than in any other (see Mischel, 1973), this may reflect an inadequate sampling of situations and types of prosocial behaviour on which to base and subsequently to test predictions (see Epstein, 1979, for a review). Not only is this a statistical point, but also one which recognizes the social nexus of action. There may be consistency across circumstances as perceived by the actor; perhaps behaviour depends on the view of the self which is engendered in the situation (see, e.g., Secord and Backman, 1961; Goffman, see Volume 2, sub-Chapter 7.11; Bem and Allen, 1974; Grusec and Redler, 1980). It may also depend on the personal norms (Schwartz, 1977) or values (Staub, 1979) evoked by the perception of the situation. The generality debate, too, may be informed by observational studies of interaction: Strayer *et al.* (1979) found that some of the preschoolers they observed were more prosocial towards adults, and some to peers. Types of prosocial behaviour also varied, according to child. In a study combining ethological and experimental methods, Ginsburg and Miller (1979) found some evidence of generality between intervention to give aid in the playground and sharing, both of which related to peer group social status.

Small group processes, situational variables, and prosocial behaviour

Studies designed to investigate the impact of situational variables on prosocial behaviour look for differential incidence of such behaviour across conditions to which subjects have been randomly assigned, either in the laboratory or in the field. Such a procedure necessarily highlights situational factors, but does not of course mean that individual differences are irrelevant or individuals necessarily inconsistent. Many situational variables have been identified (see Staub, 1978, for a review), and many theories have been advanced about the processes implied by their effects on prosocial behaviour.

Most of the explanations of the effects of situational variables on prosocial behaviour derive from theories closely connected with group processes, and indeed most of them relate to readings to be found elsewhere in these volumes. However, work on prosocial behaviour is not integrated with other work deriving from those same theories. Such an integration might shed more light on both. Furthermore, the place of group processes in work on situational variables tends to be obscured by: (1) the widespread use of only a narrow range of unilateral prosocial acts; (2) the lack of studies of prosocial behaviour by people interacting in groups; and (3) the lack of observational or experimental studies on the role of small group interaction in the facilitation or inhibition of prosocial behaviour. In this area, in contrast to the realm of personal correlates of prosocial behaviour, there is a wealth of theory about processes, which will briefly be mentioned below. However, prosocial behaviour is rarely studied as a facet of the group's behaviour, nor are measures of prosocial behaviour derived from observations of interaction.

The methodology is available to do so, not only the ethological techniques used in so many of the studies cited earlier in this paper, but also Bales's Interaction Process Analysis, and its developments, described in sub-Chapter 7.10 of Volume 2. Classifications of verbal and nonverbal behaviour of subjects towards a 'distressed' confederate have, however, been used, for example by Feinberg (1977) in a test of Staub's model of the interaction between personal and situational variables in resultant prosocial behaviour.

Latané and Darley (1970) found that intervention in a simulated emergency was more likely if the bystander was alone; and they proposed an information-processing model to explain this. Bystanders who are not alone may, as in other ambiguous situations, use each other to define social reality, and thus deduce from each other's inaction that the event is not in fact an emergency. If they do interpret it correctly, however, there may be diffusion of responsibility, with each person leaving it to someone else to respond for a variety of possible reasons, not simply an unwillingness to help.

Equity theory addresses itself to research on helping (see Hatfield, sub-Chapter 7.2, Volume 2), arguing that help may redress, or create, perceived inequity. Although a fundamental proposition of the theory refers to the role of the group in evolving and maintaining equity, this has not received much attention (although Homans (1976) on the basis of his work, questions the validity of this proposition). Studies of helping from an equity theory perspective derive from the fourth proposition of the theory, namely that individuals will strive to reduce perceived inequity. However, the study of the group in interaction, deciding to help or not to help a member or an outsider, might expose some of the processes underlying (a) at least some prosocial behaviour, and (b) the derogation of the victim as an alternative method of restoring equity (Lerner *et al.*, 1976).

Some studies are concerned with the rewards and costs of prosocial behaviour (Piliavin *et al.*, 1975), others explain their findings in terms of norms, such as social responsibility or reciprocity (Berkowitz, 1972). Do group members, though, talk to each other in terms of norms, reciprocity, rewards, coercion, equity or duty? Do their patterns of interaction imply any one or more of these?

Observations of interaction in naturally occurring and experimental groups would increase our understanding of the dimensions of prosocial behaviour and of the group processes which affect their incidence. Moreover, if interacting groups were studied, a wide range of issues would be opened up. For example, how do people try to influence each other when faced with taking a group decision to act prosocially? What would happen if a confederate took a minority stand on a prosocial issue (see Moscovici and Paicheler, sub-Chapter 5.4, this volume), perhaps challenging an intrinsic norm, or script (Milgram and Sabini, sub-Chapter 5.1, this volume; Langer, sub-Chapter 5.2, this volume)? Is there a group polarization effect for prosocial issues, and if so, what would it imply (see Burnstein and Schul, sub-Chapter 1.4, Volume 2)? One might look at the effect of feeding different information to the group on the style and content of their interaction and on their subsequent prosocial decision. How does group structure affect prosocial behaviour between members (and see Zander, sub-Chapter 7.6, Volume 2, on group achievement motivation)? Could it be used to enhance social skills? Do those who influence group members towards prosocial decisions behave in distinguishable ways, or have particular personal norms or values? What is the relationship of prosocial behaviour with emergence as a leader, and with the effectiveness of that leadership?

There have recently been several studies of the effect of situationally induced mood on helping, and both level of activation and focus of attention have been postulated as mediators of the effect of mood (Batson *et al.*, 1979; Thompson *et al.*, 1980, respectively). Both these variables are also studied with respect to the effects of the presence of others (see Chapter 4, this volume). This brings us back to the work of Latané and Darley; can their work be reinterpreted in terms of social facilitation? What would we learn from analyzing the interaction between members of groups in a simulated emergency?

Concluding comments

Despite this paper's constant exhortations that prosocial theory and research should focus more explicitly on social interaction, the study of social interaction cannot be construed as an easy route to answering our questions about prosocial behaviour. The methodological difficulties are considerable, from choosing which aspects of interaction to study, through recording, analysis, and interpretation of data. (See Cairns, 1979, for useful discussions of the issues and problems.)

Furthermore, caution must be exercised in relating interaction-based measures of prosocial behaviour to other studies using other measures, because there are important differences. The operational definition of prosocial behaviour is very different, and often includes several dimensions of such behaviour. The target of prosocial behaviour is also different, for the person in need may be one of the others in interaction. Additionally, studies of interaction and small group processes may simply observe natural groups, without an experimentally induced crisis; the sadness and tragedies are real and familiar.

The study of groups of people in interaction may indeed be valuable for our theories, descriptions, and measures of prosocial behaviour. Nonetheless, it remains but one method of approaching the subject—neither this nor any other single approach is likely to provide answers to the multitude of problems and issues. 'Any research problem that continues to rely exclusively on a single procedure ... will ultimately fall short of the mark of ideal methodological requirements' (Zahn-Waxler and Radke-Yarrow, 1982). While there is clearly a growing appreciation of the complexities of prosocial behaviour, and an increasing variety of research procedures directed towards them, the relevance of interaction in groups is underestimated and unelaborated in both personal and situational approaches. Each of these approaches has included different aspects of group process theory and methodology, but each could learn much from the other.

References

Archer, R. L., Diaz-Loving, R., Gollwitzer, P. M., Davis, M. H., and Foushee, H. C. (1981). 'The role of dispositional empathy and social evaluation in the empathic mediation of helping,' *Journal of Personality and Social Psychology*, **40**, 786–796.

Aronfreed, J. (1976). 'Moral development from the standpoint of a general psychological theory,' in T. Lickona (ed.), *Moral Development and Moral Behavior*, Holt, Rinehart and Winston, New York.

Barrett, D., and Yarrow, M. R. (1977). 'Prosocial behavior, social inferential ability, and assertiveness in children,' *Child Development*, **48**, 475- 481.

Bar-Tal, D., Raviv, A., and Leiser, T. (1980). 'The development of altruistic behavior: empirical evidence,' *Developmental Psychology*, **16**, 516–524.

Batson, C. D., and Coke, J. S. (1981). 'Empathy: a source of altruistic motivation for helping', in J. P. Rushton and R. M. Sorrentino (eds.) *Altruism and Helping Behavior*, Erlbaum, Hillsdale, NJ.

Batson, C. D., Coke, J. S., Chard, F., Smith, D., and Talliaferro, A. (1979). 'Generality of the "glow of goodwill": Effects of mood on helping and information acquisition,' *Social Psychology Quarterly*, **42**, 176–179.

Batson, C. D., Duncan, B. D., Ackerman, P., Buckley, T., and Birch, K. (1981). 'Is empathic emotion a source of altruistic motivation?' *Journal of Personality and Social Psychology*, **40**, 290–302.

Bell, R. Q. (1968). 'A reinterpretation of the direction of effects in studies of socialisation,' *Psychological Review*, **75**, 81–95.

Bem, D. J., and Allen, A. (1974). 'On predicting some of the people some of the time: the search for cross-situational consistencies in behavior,' *Psychological Review*, **81**, 506–520.

Berkowitz, L. (1972). 'Social norms, feelings and other factors affecting helping behavior and altruism,' in L. Berkowitz (ed.), *Advances in Experimental Social Psychology*, Vol. 6, Academic Press, New York.

Berndt, T. J., and Berndt, E. G. (1975). 'Children's use of motives and intentionality in person perception and moral judgment,' *Child Development*, **46**, 904–912.

Bernstein, B. (1972). 'Social class, language and socialisation,' in P. Giglioli (ed.), *Language and Social Context*, Penguin Books, Harmondsworth.

Buckley, N., Siegel, L. S., and Ness, S. (1979). 'Egocentrism, empathy, and altruistic behavior in young children,' *Developmental Psychology*, **15**, 329–330.

Cairns, R. B. (ed.) (1979). *The Analysis of Social Interactions: Methods, Issues and Illustrations*, Erlbaum, Hillsdale, NJ.

Coke, J. S., Batson, C. D., and McDavis, K. (1978). 'Empathic mediation of helping: a two-stage model,' *Journal of Personality and Social Psychology*, **36**, 752–766.

Cook-Gumpertz, J. (1973). *Social Control and Socialisation*, Routledge and Kegan Paul, London.

Damon, W. (1977). *The Social World of the Child*, Jossey Bass, San Francisco.

Eckerman, C. O. (1979). 'The human infant in social interaction,' in R. B. Cairns (ed.), *Social Interaction: Methods, Analysis and Illustrations*, Erlbaum, Hillsdale, NJ.

Eisenberg-Berg, N, and Lennon, R. (1980). 'Altruism and the assessment of empathy in the preschool years,' *Child Development*, **51**, 552–557.

Eisenberg-Berg, N., and Neal, C. (1979). 'Children's moral reasoning about their own spontaneous prosocial behavior,' *Developmental Psychology*, **15**, 228–229.

Emler, N. P., and Rushton, J. P. (1974). 'Cognitive-developmental factors in children's generosity,' *British Journal of Social and Clinical Psychology*, **13**, 277–281.

Epstein, S. (1979). 'The stability of behavior: 1. On predicting most of the people much of the time,' *Journal of Personality and Social Psychology*, **37**, 1097–1126.

Feinberg, H. K. (1977). 'Anatomy of a helping situation: some personality and situational determinants of helping in a conflict situation involving another's psychological distress,' Unpublished doctoral dissertation, University of Massachusetts, Amherst.

Ford, M. E. (1979). 'The construct validity of egocentrism,' *Psychological Bulletin*, **86**, 1169–1188.

Ginsburg, H. J., and Miller, S. M. (1979). 'The social context of altruism in elementary school children,' Paper presented at the annual meeting of the American Psychological Association, New York, September, 1979.

Grusec, J. E., and Kuczynski, L. (1980). 'Direction of effects in socialization: a comparison of the parent's versus the child's behavior as determinants of disciplinary techniques,' *Developmental Psychology*, **16**, 1–9.

Grusec, J. E., and Redler, E. (1980). 'Attribution, reinforcement and altruism: a developmental analysis,' *Developmental Psychology*, **16**, 525–534.

Hay, D. (1979). 'Cooperative interactions and sharing between very young children and their parents,' *Developmental Psychology*, **15** (6), 647–653.

Hoffman, M. L. (1977a). 'Empathy, its development and prosocial implications,' in *Nebraska Symposium on Motivation*, Vol. 15, University of Nebraska Press, Lincoln.

Hoffman, M. L. (1977b). 'Moral internalization: current theory and research,' in L. Berkowitz (ed.), *Advances in Experimental Social Psychology*, Vol. 10, Academic Press, New York.

Hoffman, M. L. (1981). 'Is altruism part of human nature?' *Journal of Personality and Social Psychology*, **40**, 121–137.

Homans, G. C. (1976). 'Commentary,' in L. Berkowitz and E. Walster (eds.), *Equity Theory: Toward a General Theory of Social Interaction* (Vol. 9 of *Advances in Experimental Social Psychology*), Academic Press, New York.

Hughes, R., Tingle, B. A., and Sawin, D. B. (1981). 'Development of empathic understanding in children,' *Child Development*, **52** (1), 122–128.

Iannotti, R. J. (1978). 'Effects of role-taking experiences on role-taking, empathy, altruism and aggression,' *Developmental Psychology*, **14**, 119–124.

Ickes, W. J., and Kidd, R. F. (1976). 'An attributional analysis of helping behavior,' in J. H. Harvey, W. J. Ickes, and R. F. Kidd (eds.), *New Directions in Attribution Research*, Vol. 1 Erlbaum, Hillsdale, NJ.

James, S. L. (1978). 'Effects of listener age and situation on the politeness of children's directives,' *Journal of Psycholinguistic Research*, **7** (4), 307–317.

Karniol, R., and Ross, M. (1979). 'Children's use of a causal attribution schema and the inference of manipulative intentions,' *Child Development*, **50**, 463–468.

Keasey, C. B. (1977). 'Children's developing awareness and usage of intentionality and motives,' in *Nebraska Symposium on Motivation*, Vol. 15, pp. 219–260, University of Nebraska Press, Lincoln.

Keller, B. B., and Bell, R. Q. (1979). 'Child effects on adult's method of eliciting altruistic behavior,' *Child Development*, **50**, 1004–1009.

Kohlberg, L. (1976). 'Moral stages and moralization: the cognitive–developmental approach,' in T. Lickona (ed.), *Moral Development and Behavior*, Holt, Rinehart and Winston, New York.

Krebs, D. (1978). 'A cognitive-developmental approach to altruism', in L. Wispé (ed.), *Altruism, Sympathy, and Helping*, Academic Press, New York.

Latané, B., and Darley, J. M. (1970). *The Unresponsive Bystander: Why Doesn't He Help?*, Appleton-Century-Crofts, New York.

Leiman, B. (1978). 'Affective empathy and subsequent altruism in kindergartners and first-graders,' Paper presented at the meeting of the American Psychological Association, Toronto, September 1978.

Lerner, M. J., Miller, D. T., and Holmes, J. G. (1976). 'Deserving and the emergence of forms of justice,' in L. Berkowitz and E. Wolster (eds.), *Advances in Experimental Social Psychology*, Vol. 9 [*Equity Theory*], pp. 133–162, Academic Press, New York.

Levine, L. E., and Hoffman, M. L. (1975). 'Empathy and cooperation in 4-year-olds,' *Developmental Psychology*, **11**, 533–534.

Light, P. (1979). *The Development of Social Sensitivity*, Cambridge University Press, Cambridge and London.

Macaulay, J., and Berkowitz, L. (1970). *Altruism and Helping Behavior*, Academic Press, New York.

Menig-Peterson, C. L. (1975). 'The modification of communicative behavior in preschool-aged children as a function of the listener's perspective,' *Child Development*, **46**, 1015–1018.

Mischel, W. (1973). 'Toward a cognitive social learning reconceptualization of personality,' *Psychological Review*, **80**, 252–283.

Mueller, E., and Brenner, J. (1977). 'The origins of social skills and interaction among playgroup toddlers,' *Child Development*, **48**, 854–861.

Mulhern, R. K., and Passman, R. H. (1979). 'The child's behavioral pattern as a determinant of maternal punitiveness,' *Child Development*, 1979, **50**, 815–820.

Murphy, L. B. (1937). *Social Behavior and Child Personality*, Columbia University Press, New York.

Nucci, L. P., and Turiel, E. (1978). 'Social interactions and the development of social concepts in preschool children,' *Child Development*, **49**, 400–407.

Peterson, L. (1980). 'Developmental changes in verbal and behavioral sensitivity to cues of social norms to altruism,' *Child Development*, **51**, 830–838.

Piaget, J. (1932). *The Moral Judgment of the Child*, Routledge and Kegan Paul, London.

Piliavin, I. M., Piliavin, J., and Rodin, J. (1975). 'Costs, diffusion and the stigmatized victim,' *Journal of Personality and Social Psychology*, **32**, 429–438.

Rheingold, H. L., Hay, D. F., and West, M. J. (1976). 'Sharing in the second year of life,' *Child Development*, **47**, 1148–1158.

Rogers, C. (1978). 'The child's perception of other people,' in H. McGurk (ed.), *Issues in Childhood Social Development*, Methuen, London.

Rosenhan, D. L. (1978). 'Toward resolving the altruistic paradox: affect, self-reinforcement and cognition,' in L. Wispé (ed.) *Altruism, Sympathy, and Helping*, Academic Press, New York.

Rubin, K. H., and Schneider, F. W. (1973). 'The relationship between moral judgment, egocentrism, and altruistic behavior,' *Child Development*, **44**, 661–665.

Ryle, G. (1949). *The Concept of Mind*, Hutchinson, London.

Schaffer, H. R., and Crook, C. K. (1980). 'Child compliance and maternal control techniques,' *Developmental Psychology*, **16**, 54–61.

Schwartz, S. H. (1977). 'Normative influences on altruism,' in L. Berkowitz (ed.), *Advances in Experimental Social Psychology*, Vol. 10, Academic Press, New York.

Secord, P. F., and Backman, C. W. (1961). 'Personality theory and the problem of stability and change in individual behavior,' *Psychological Review*, **68**, 21–32.

Selman, R. L. (1976). 'Social-cognitive understanding: a guide to educational and clinical practice,' in T. Lickona (ed.), *Moral Development and Behavior*, Holt, Rinehart and Winston, New York.

Shotter, J. (1974). 'The development of personal powers,' in M. P. M. Richards (ed.), *The Integration of a Child into a Social World*, Cambridge University Press, Cambridge.

Staub, E. (1978). *Positive Social Behavior and Morality: Social and Personal Influences*, Academic Press, New York.

Staub, E. (1979). *Positive Social Behavior and Morality: Socialization and Development*, Academic Press, New York.

Strayer, J. (1980). 'A naturalistic study of empathic behaviors and their relation to affective states and perspective-taking skills in preschool children,' *Child Development*, **51**, 815–822.

Strayer, F. F., Wareing, S., and Rushton, J. P. (1979). 'Social constraints on naturally occurring preschool altruism,' *Ethology and Sociobiology*, **1**, 3–11.

Suls, J., Gutkin, D., and Kalle, R. J. (1979). 'The role of intentions, damages, and social consequences in the moral judgment of children,' *Child Development*, **50**, 874–877.

Thompson, W. C., Cowan, C. L., and Rosenhan, D. (1980). 'Focus of attention mediates the impact of negative affect on altruism,' *Journal of Personality and Social Psychology*, **38**, 291–300.

Vandell, D. L. (1980). 'Sociability with peer and mother during the first year,' *Developmental Psychology*, **16**, 355–361.

Vygotsky, L. S. (1962). *Thought and Language*, Wiley, New York.

Weir, K., and Duveen, G. (1981). 'Further development and validation of the prosocial behaviour questionnaire for use by teachers,' *Journal of Child Psychology and Psychiatry*, **22**, 257–374.

Zahn-Waxler, C., and Radke-Yarrow, M. (1982). 'The development of altruism: alternative research strategies,' in N. Eisenberg (ed.), *The Development of Prosocial Behavior*, Academic Press, New York.

Zahn-Waxler, C., Radke-Yarrow, M., and Brady-Smith, J. (1977). 'Perspective-taking and prosocial behavior,' *Developmental Psychology*, **13**, 87–88.

Small Groups and Social Interaction, Volume 1
Edited by H. H. Blumberg, A. P. Hare, V. Kent and M. Davies
© 1983 John Wiley & Sons Ltd

6.2   Maternal Child Rearing Practices in Relation to Children's Altruism and Conscience Development

Carolyn Zahn-Waxler   *National Institute of Mental Health, Bethesda, Maryland*

Acts of sympathy and sharing first become manifest in children in the second year of life (Rheingold *et al.*, 1976; Yarrow and Waxler, 1977). Hence, this is a time when familial child-rearing practices might play an important role in the child's learning. This is a study of parental socialization practices and children's prosocial behavior toward victims of distress. Young children frequently observe others' distress emotions, both as bystanders and as causal agents. With few exceptions, research on children's prosocial and moral development has generally proceeded along two different conceptual paths, depending on whether the child is a bystander or a cause of another's distress. Children's aiding and comforting as bystanders has traditionally been considered to be altruism. Aiding or comforting when children have been responsible for the victim's distress has characteristically been seen as evidence of reparation for wrongdoing or conscience. A significant issue for research is to determine what are the common or different rearing conditions associated with early patterns in children's reparations and altruism.

The core of moral behavior can be conceptualized as the child's sense of concern and responsibility for the welfare of others. If altruism and reparation (conscience) share this core, then both can be investigated within the same research framework. Distinctions of cause and circumstance of distress may not be clear in the minds of very young children. They are struggling with self–other differentiations and attempting to decipher causal relations. When aroused by someone's emotions, young children may be unsure of whether it is their own or the other person's experience, and whether they or others have caused the harm. The actions taken by mothers in response to distress of either origin may affect how children interpret these situations and, also, how they behave toward distressed others.

Both experimental and naturalistic studies have suggested that the model of an adult who shares, helps, and comforts others contributes to children's altruism (e.g. Rosenhan, 1969; Yarrow *et al.*, 1973). Parental use of reasoning or explanations to convey to the child the nature of another person's distress circumstances may also aid altruistic behavior. Although theoretically relevant to children's altruism, reasoning more typically has been investigated as an antecedent of conscience and of guilt (e.g. Hoffman, 1970). Still other rearing practices have been suggested as antecedents of conscience development. Some studies have emphasized the role of parental warmth and withdrawal of love (e.g. Sears *et al.*, 1957) whereas others have investigated the effects of punishment and power assertion (e.g. Aronfreed, 1961).

Thus, the literature on moral development hints that both common and different rearing conditions may be determinants of the child's altruism and conscience. How the mother handles her child's transgressions against persons (i.e. distresses that the child causes to someone) is of special interest as a predictor of both altruism and conscience. In these circumstances mothers are especially likely to be aroused and, therefore, inclined to try to teach or otherwise influence the child. The purposes of this research are: (a) to study mothers and children in circumstances which theoretically provide the bases for altruism and reparations for wrong-doing; (b) to assess the kinds of child-rearing methods mothers use with $1\frac{1}{2}$- to $2\frac{1}{2}$-year-olds; and (c) to investigate the relations between mothers' methods and their children's manifestations of reparation and altruism.

There are limitations in attempting to address certain questions of socialization and prosocial development with experimental designs. Naturalistic observation methods insure greater ecological validity but the behaviors of interest may be infrequent and sporadic in occurrence. Therefore, an innovation of method was attempted in which mothers were the primary source of information (Goodenough, 1931). The research goal was to obtain data as similar as possible to the environmental contingencies in which the child is exposed to distress and in which the mother reacts (Zahn-Waxler and Radke-Yarrow, 1982).

Method

Sixteen white children, seven boys and nine girls, from intact families were studied over a 9 month period. Half the sample entered the study at 15 months and half at 20 months of age. The mothers, high school and college graduates, were volunteers from local organizations involving mothers with infants. They received financial reimbursement.

Mothers were trained to observe and report discrete sequences of behaviors in incidents of emotion. The training procedures consisted of two, 3 hour sessions with small groups of mothers, and one individual 2 hour session prior to data collection. Mothers were asked to tape-record incidents in which someone in the child's presence expressed distress (anger, fear, sorrow, pain, fatigue). Their narration was to include the emotional expression and who was expressing it, what preceded or caused the emotion, the child's reactions to the person in distress, and the mother's (and/or other's) response to the child and the person in distress. Events in which the child was the *cause* of someone's physical or psychological distress (e.g. hitting, snatching a toy), and in which the child was a *bystander* were reported. Mothers were asked to try to report and immediately record every relevant incident. Observing and reporting procedures were discussed in detail, examples of incidents were presented, practice observations were reviewed, and questions were answered. Mothers were also asked to simulate pain, acute physical discomfort (choking cough), fatigue, anger on the phone, and sorrow (crying) according to prescribed scripts. The simulation of each emotion was enacted five times during the 9 months of study.

Every third week an investigator spent 2 hours in the home to supervise the mother's data collection and to carry out a simulated emotional incident. On one visit the mother simulated an incident. The simulations provided an opportunity to obtain estimates of observer reliability. Mothers were also assessed on empathic caregiving of the child during the home visits. They were rated as high or low on: (a) anticipating dangers or difficulties; (b) responding promptly to child's hurts and needs; and (c) nurturant caregiving associated with specific hurts and needs. In the fourth month a second staff member accompanied the home visitor to obtain independent observations of the mother's empathic caregiving. Percents of agreement were 78%, 89%, 78% on the three dimensions of empathic caregiving. A summed measure across the three dimensions was used for data analysis.

Mothers' incident reports of children's responses to emotional distress provided data on children's altruism and reparation and on parental child-rearing practices. Excerpts of examples of incidents follow:

> John (92 weeks) had a friend over, Jerry. Today Jerry was kind of cranky; he just kept bawling. John kept coming over and handing Jerry toys, trying to cheer him up. He'd say: 'Here's a car, Jerry,' and I said to John, 'Jerry's sad; he doesn't feel good; he had a shot today.' John would look at me with his eyebrows kind of wrinkled together. He went over and rubbed Jerry's arm and said, 'Nice Jerry,' and continued to give him toys.

> Todd (96 weeks) and Susan (4 years) were in the bedroom playing. Susan started to cry and ran to her mother. Todd slowly followed after and watched. I said 'What happened?' and she said, 'He hit me.' I said, 'Well tell him not to hit you.' and I said 'Todd! Why did you hit Susan? Why would you hit Susan? You don't want to hurt people.' Later, there was a second run-in. That's when I said sternly, 'No, Todd. You mustn't hit people.' He just watched her sniffle as her Mom stroked her and said, 'He's just a little boy and boys do that sometimes.' He picked up the petal of a flower, smiled and handed it to her and said, 'Here.' She took it. Then he searched for other petals and gave them to her.

Mothers' child-rearing behaviors were coded in the following categories (percents of agreement between coders are given in parentheses):

1. *Explanations*
(a) Neutral explanation or linking of cause and consequence (86%). 'Tom's crying because you pushed him.' (b) Affective explanation with components of moralizing (67%). 'It's not nice to bite.' 'It was bad for Jim to hit Mary.' (c) Affective explanation with strong verbal prohibition (82%). 'Can't you see Al's hurt?' 'Don't push him.' (d) Affective explanation containing statements of absolute principles and values with high maturity demands on the child (78%). 'People are not for hitting.' 'You must *never* poke anyone's eyes.' (e) Affective explanation with components of love withdrawal (77%). 'When you hurt me, I don't want to be near you.' (f) Sum of affective explanations—a score of '1' was given for each affective technique (b and through e).
2. *Suggestion of positive action* (77%). 'Why don't you give Jeffy your ball?'
3. *Unexplained verbal prohibition* (82%). 'Stop that!'
4. *Physical restraint* (67%). 'I just moved him away from the baby.'
5. *Physical punishment* (91%). 'I swatted her a good one.'
6. *Modeling altruism to victim* (89%). Picks up and pats crying child.
7. *Reassurance, support of own child* (67%). 'Don't worry, it's okay.'
8. *No caregiver reaction* (85%).

Children's prosocial interventions with persons in distress took the following forms: physical or verbal sympathy (e.g. 'all better now?', hugs victim), providing objects (e.g. food, toys, bandaids), finding someone else to help, protecting the victim, giving physical assistance. Coder reliabilities for mothers' reports of children's prosocial interventions were 87% in natural incidents and 89% in simulated incidents. Observer agreement between mothers' and investigators' reports of simulated incidents in home visits was 86%. Separate summed scores were obtained on prosocial interventions that were reparations for distresses caused by the child and on altruistic interventions as bystanders in events of distress. The mothers' techniques and children's interventions were converted to ratio scores (i.e. the number of incidents in which a technique or intervention was reported in relation to total number of incidents). Children's prosocial interventions in natural and simulated bystander events were significantly intercorrelated ($r|15| = .63$, $p < .025$) and did not differ in mean frequency ($t < 1$). Therefore, the data from these incidents were combined. There were two sets of scores for each child and mother: one based on the first $4\frac{1}{2}$ months of observation, and the other based on the second $4\frac{1}{2}$ months. Primary analyses of relations between mother's techniques and child's interventions were based on the $4\frac{1}{2}$ months (20 through 24 months) in which the two cohorts overlapped in age. For a time lag replication, mothers' scores were based on the first half of the 9 months of observation in each cohort, and the children's scores, on the last half. For contemporaneous analyses, in order to rule out reporting differences by mothers as a function of length of time in the study, the two cohorts of mothers were compared, in 't' tests, on the average frequencies of each of the rearing dimensions. With one exception, the 't' values were less than one. For time lag analyses, in order to rule out differences in frequencies of children's interventions as a function of age, the average altruism and reparation scores of the two groups of children were compared (t's < 1).

Two analysis procedures were used to examine mother–child relations. (1) Mothers' scores on each rearing technique were dichotomized at the median and children's average scores on reparations and altruism were compared with 't' tests. (2) Stepwise multiple regression routines were also used to determine the relative power of different maternal techniques in predicting child behavior.

Results

Maternal techniques

Mothers had many means of conveying to the child the content and consequences of another person's distress experience, particularly when the child had caused the distress. Some mothers used as many as nine techniques, some as few as one (average 6.5). In the child-witnessed distresses, many fewer maternal interventions were reported and only rarely was more than one method used in the same incident. Mothers were significantly more likely to intervene when the child had caused the distress (56%) than when he or she had witnessed it (31%) ($t[12] = -3.84$, $p < .01$). Mothers provided much specific teaching and instruction in situations of child-caused distress. In 40% of the instances, mothers used explanations to communicate about child transgressions. This was often not calm, reasoned communication; in over half of the explanations there were affective messages with overtones of moralizing and judging. Mothers' use of explanations was less frequent (12% of occasions) when the child was witness to someone's distress, and virtually none of these explanations contained affective overtones ($t[12] = 4.72, p < .001$).

Mothers seldom modeled altruism to the child's victims (7% of occasions); they more often modeled altruism (21% of occasions) when the child witnessed distress ($t[12] = -2.63$, $p < .05$). The only other response that occurred with any frequency in bystander distress events was the mother's offering her own child reassurance (36% of occasions). This rarely occurred when the child had caused distress (8% of occasions ($|t|12| = -3.51, p < .01$). Only occasionally did mothers suggest positive actions by the child, and this was primarily when the child had caused distress (13% v. 1%, $t|12| = 4.69$, $p < .001$). Unexplained verbal prohibition (15%), physical restraint (13%), and physical punishment (9%) complete the mothers' repertoire of actions when the child had transgressed.

Maternal techniques in child-caused distress incidents and children's reparation

Children's reparations for transgressions occurred, on the average, in 32% of the incidents. Reparations in individual children ranged from none to 60%. In contemporaneous analyses, children of mothers who frequently explained the consequences of their hurtful behavior for the victim had reparation scores that were significantly higher than those of children whose mothers rarely used this technique. Only the neutrally communicated explanations did not significantly differentiate children on reparative acts. Whenever the basic explanation was affectively embellished with (a) judgmental, moralizing reactions ($t[12] = 2.60$, $p < .05$), (b) statements of principles and values ($t[12] = 5.93, p < .001$), (c) love withdrawal ($t[12] = 2.25, p < .05$) or (d) strong verbal prohibitions ($t[12] = 2.68$, $p < .05$), children's scores on reparation were significantly higher than when these affective accompaniments were infrequent (t values are listed in parentheses above). High frequencies of reparation occurred among children whose mothers often used multiple forms of affective explanations ($t[12] = 4.77$, $p < .001$). Mothers' unexplained prohibitions were associated with little reparative behavior ($t[12] = -3.37, p < .01$). Time lag analyses were directionally consistent with contemporaneous analyses but were of weaker magnitude. One consistent, significant finding was that children whose mothers expressed principles or rules about not hurting others were more likely to show reparation at a later time than children whose mothers tended not to use this technique ($t[12] = 2.44, p < .05$).

Multiple stepwise regression analyses corroborate the preceding findings by including some of those variables which, when taken singly, were most important. In contemporaneous analyses, the maternal variable most predictive of reparation was the use of statements of general rules about not hurting others ($F[1, 12] = 35.30, p < .001, R^2 = .75$). The addition, in the second step of the regression routine, of love withdrawal ($F[2, 11] = 28.44$), significantly increased the R^2 to .84. In time lag analyses the mothers' use of assertions of absolute principles was again a significant predictor of reparation ($F[1, 12] = 6.37, p < .05$ $R^2 = .35$).

Maternal techniques in child-caused distress incidents and children's altruism in bystander incidents

Children were altruistic, on the average, in 34% of the distress situations in which they were bystanders. The range of scores was 5% to 70%. Altruism and reparation scores were correlated ($r[12] = .55, p < .05$), in the contemporaneous time period. The children of mothers whose summed scores on affective explanations were high had significantly higher altruism scores than those children whose mothers were low on affective explanations, $t(12) = 2.60$, $p < .05$, in contemporaneous analyses, and $t(12) = 2.39$, $p < .05$, in time lag analyses. The mother's moralizing when the child caused distress was the major component of the affective explanation that carried over to children's altruism ($t[12] = 2.88$, $p < .05$) in contemporaneous analysis. The mother's suggestion to the child to make amends (in the time lag analysis) was another technique positively associated with altruism ($t[12] = 2.20, p < .05$).

Prohibitions without explanations were a deterrent to altruism, in contemporaneous analyses ($t[12] = -2.41$, $p < .05$) and time lag analyses ($t[12] = -2.25, p < .05$). Frequent use of prohibitions in the absence of clarifying information may result in the learning of a generalized inhibition, i.e. learning to stand back in the face of all kinds of distresses, thus minimizing altruistic as well as reparative efforts.

In multiple step-wise regression analyses, mothers' moralizing was the only dimension which predicted children's altruism in the contemporaneous analyses ($F[12] = 11.05$, $p < .01$, $R^2 = .48$). In time lag analyses, unexplained verbal prohibitions were the first significant (negative) predictor of altruism ($F[1, 12] = 7.28, p < .025, R^2 = .38$), and sum of affective explanatory techniques entered in the second step ($F[2, 11] = 6.68, p < .025, R^2 = .55$).

There is, then, a patterned set of relations between mothers' treatment of their children's transgressions against persons and children's altruism in bystander events. This suggests that what the child learns from the intense interaction with the mother when he or she transgresses may transfer to behavior in situations in which the child is witness to another person's distress. Cues in children's behavior provide a basis for the interpretation of generalized learning. There were instances of 'misplaced responsibility'; some children occasionally responded as if they had caused distress when, in fact, they had not. Upon seeing the mother cry, for example, they would ask apologetically, 'Did I make you sad?' or 'Sorry, I be nice.' Of the six children who showed misplaced responsibility, all were also observed to have used apology as a form of reparation for transgression. Of the eight children who did not show misplaced responsibility, seven had *not* learned to apologize for transgression, $\phi(12) = .87$, $p < .001$. It is inferred that apologies represent learned (not intrinsic) patterns of responding, inculcated during intense affective communications by caretakers in situations where the child has caused distress.

Maternal techniques in bystander incidents and children's altruism and reparation

In bystander events, mothers were relatively inactive. With one exception, no techniques were significantly associated with altruism or reparation, t's < 1. Mothers who frequently gave reassurances had children who were more likely to make reparation than children whose mothers were less reassuring, $t(12) = 2.36$, $p < .05$, in contemporaneous data.

Emotional accompaniments of altruistic interventions

Some of the prosocial behaviors that occurred in the bystander events had observable emotional overtones evidenced in facial or postural tension (e.g. 'she looked concerned,' or 'his body stiffened,' or 'her lips quivered as she patted the crying baby'). Altruism was accompanied by expressions of emotion in as many as one-third of the responses of some children; for others, there was little or no display of affect. Children whose mothers were high in use of explanations, a substantial number of which had affective overtones, displayed altruism with accompanying affect in 15% of their responses (on the average). Children whose mothers were low in this mode of teaching had accompanying affect in 7% of the responses ($t[12] = 1.86$, $p = .08$ in contemporaneous analysis). Comparable data in time lag analyses were 11% v. 6%, ($t[12] = 2.78$, $p < .05$).

Mothers' nurturant caregiving and children's altruism and reparation

Empathic caregiving by the mother conveys concern for her child and provides in her ministerings a model of altruism. Average altruistic responding was 46% among children whose mothers were rated high in empathic caregiving and 24% among those children whose mothers were rated low ($t[13] = 3.05$, $p < .01$, in contemporaneous analysis). Comparable time lag data were 45% v. 24% ($t[13] = 2.72$, $p < .02$). Altruism in children of empathic mothers was also more frequently accompanied by expressions of concern than was the altruism of children whose mothers were rated low on empathic caregiving (18% v. 7% respectively, $t[13] = 2.97$, $p < .02$ in contemporaneous data, and 12% v. 7% respectively, $t[13] = 2.33$, $p < .05$ in time lag data). There were similar relations between mothers' empathic caregiving and children's reparations in contemporaneous analyses only. The average percents of reparation, in relation to high v. low nurturance, were 47% v. 17% ($t[11] = 3.99$, $p < .01$); for emotional reparation in relation to high v. low nurturance, the percents were 21% v. 4% ($t[11] = 3.52, p < .01$).

Discussion

How children cope with emotions of distress in others is significantly related to specific maternal practices pertaining to children's encounters with distress. Prosocial interventions may be either reparations for children's own transgressions against someone or altruism toward an observed victim. Since maternal responses to the transgressions of their offspring are related to both children's reparative responses and also to their altruism, a kinship between early acts of altruism and some nascent forms of early conscience is suggested. Parental disciplinary practices may be helping to lay down the foundation not only for the child's responsibility for his/her own acts, but also for a more general sensitivity to others' feelings.

The prototypic mother of the prosocial child is one whose communications are both cognitively and affectively intense and clear when her child transgresses. Many consistent maternal influences with messages concerning expectations of socially responsible, interpersonal behavior, converge on the child. The mother brings the emotional stimulus events into focus. 'Look what you did!' 'Don't you see you hurt Amy—don't ever pull hair.' Her high expectations for the child's behavior are emotionally conveyed (e.g. 'A very disturbing thing happened today, Judy bit me.' 'I expected a hug or apology.') In other words, her affective 'inductive' techniques are also power assertive. The induction is not calmly dispensed reasoning, carefully designed to enlighten the child: it is emotionally imposed, sometimes harshly and often forcefully. These affective techniques coexist with empathic caregiving ($r = .70$, $p < .005$). Mother's nurturance may be an important condition for the success of her disciplinary techniques.

It is hypothesized that what is being taught by the mothers is a basic orientation toward others. In a context in which the child learns to perform caregiver functions at very early stages of development, there is evidence of emotional learning as well. The emotion that accompanies the child's prosocial acts may represent empathic arousal, fear, or guilt. Although difficult to interpret, the links between mothers' techniques and children's emotional altruism and reparation suggest possible different psychological processes: The mother's strong controlling and sometimes blaming techniques used in disciplinary encounters may arouse anxiety and guilt. If the child is made to feel apologetic and overly responsible for the grief caused to others, he or she may continue to feel responsibility in other situations. The young child may be especially vulnerable to the induction of guilt since he or she may be less able to distinguish clearly his or her causal role from the bystander role. On the other hand, the association between the mother's empathic caregiving and the child's concerned emotion in altruistic acts may reflect a process of developing empathic sensitivity. It would be valuable to explore how maternal practices influence the child's ability to distinguish distress for which he or she is responsible from distress to which he or she is an onlooker. These mothers did not extensively use for teaching, events in which their children were witnesses rather than causes of others' distresses. However, the use of bystander situations might be less guilt-inducing than the mothers' heavy concentration on the child's transgressions.

As with any research technique, the use of mothers as observers has special strengths and limitations. Parents have knowledge about significant naturally occurring events that are inaccessible to outside observers. At the same time, they may also find it difficult to maintain objectivity on some occasions. Therefore the thorough training of parents into a research role is a requirement of this methodology. We are continuing to increase methodological precision (a) by developing additional training procedures and reliability assessments for paraprofessional observers, (b) by comparing mothers' observation reports with videotape accounts of young children's responses to simulations of distress events enacted in the home environment, and (c) by comparing measures of child-rearing practices observed under laboratory conditions with those obtained from parental reports.

Research on familial socialization practices and children's altruism has characteristically focused on children's reactions to distresses of others that are of relatively brief duration. We have also begun to study children from a broader spectrum of affective environments in which distress is a more pervasive, chronic stimulus. Compassionate behaviors of 1- and 2-year-old children with a parent suffering from depression are assessed using procedures of parental report, along with home and laboratory observations of parent–child interaction. While depressed parents probably differ on the specific dimensions of expressions of their despair and hopelessness, their distress is undoubtedly characteristically conveyed with special intensity; one might expect their children to be aroused similarly with special intensity, for example, some children might become particularly avoidant of others' distresses while others might become especially empathic. Heightened affective sensitivity or extremes in prosocial behavior have been observed in some of the children with a depressed parent. The child's early nurturing or comforting of a depressed adult could reflect one means of coping with painful relationships. The development of compassion in certain children may be suggestive of the very early adoption of what are ordinarily conceived of as caregiver responsibilities. If the child is induced to feel responsible for the parent's sadness as well, guilt reactions also may make an early, forceful entry into the child's affective existence. Such examples serve to illustrate that the antecedents and motives for altruism, conscience and guilt are multiple and complex, and not always congruent with valued or idealized familial socialization practices.

References

Aronfreed, J. (1961). 'The nature, variety and social patterning of moral responses to transgression,' *Journal of Abnormal and Social Psychology*, **63**, 223–240.

Goodenough, F. (1931). *Anger in Young Children*, University of Minnesota Press, Minneapolis.

Hoffman, M. L. (1970). 'Moral development,' in P. H. Mussen (ed.), *Carmichael's Manual of Child Psychology*, Vol. 2, John Wiley and Sons, New York.

Rheingold, H. R., Hay, D. F., and West, M. J. (1976). 'Sharing in the second year of life,' *Child Development*, **47**, 1148–1158.

Rosenhan, D. (1969). 'Some origins of concern for others,' in P. H. Mussen, J. Langer, and M. Covington (eds.), *Trends and Issues in Developmental Psychology*, Holt, Rinehart & Winston, New York.

Sears, R. R., Maccoby, E. E., and Levin, H. (1957). *Patterns of Child Rearing*, Row, Peterson, Evanston, Ill.

Yarrow, M. R., Scott, P. M., and Waxler, C. Z. (1973). 'Learning concern for others,' *Developmental Psychology*, **8**, 240–260.

Yarrow, M. R., and Waxler, C. Z. (1977). 'The emergence and functions of prosocial behaviors in young children,' in R. C. Smart and M. S. Smart (eds.), *Readings in Child Development and Relationships*, 2nd edn, Macmillan Publishing Co., New York.

Zahn-Waxler, C., and Radke-Yarrow, M. (1982). 'The development of prosocial behaviors: Alternative research strategies,' in N. Eisenberg-Berg (ed.), *The Development of Prosocial Behavior*, Academic Press, New York.

Small Groups and Social Interaction, Volume 1
Edited by H. H. Blumberg, A. P. Hare, V. Kent and M. Davies
© 1983 John Wiley & Sons Ltd

6.3   Aggression as the Illegitimate Use of Coercive Power

James T. Tedeschi and Valerie Melburg

State University of New York at Albany

Introduction

The traditional approaches to the study of aggression have focused on biological and learning determinants. These views focus on internal states within the individual which tend to push out the relevant behaviors. This emphasis on internal determinants reveals itself in research on the effects of brain centers or circuits, endocrinological substances, instincts, internal tension states produced by frustration or psychic forces, and similar inferred processes. The causal status of these internal states is inferred from research on antecedent–consequent relationships. It is therefore important that clear observational terms be explicated. If the identification of an aggressive response is in doubt, then the operation of the cause would also be indeterminate.

In the absence of sophisticated theory, observational concepts in science are often defined in terms of the intuitive experiences of scientists and the ordinary language usage of the relevant terms. It is doubtful that anyone would claim the existence of a sophisticated theory of aggression. Hence, examinations of the definitions of aggression often take the form of ordinary language analysis. Inadequacies of definitions have been pointed out by almost every author who has written on the topic (e.g. Bandura, 1973; Baron, 1977; Buss, 1961; Fromm, 1973; Zillmann, 1979). There is general consensus that there is no adequate definition of aggression, but heretofore this judgment has not in any way affected the way the phenomena are conceptualized or studied.

A behavioristic definition of aggression as harm-doing behavior is inadequate because it does not allow for accidents or for ineptness on the part of a would-be harm-doer. Furthermore, even behavioristic proponents list exceptions such as accidents and normatively approved behaviors from the set of behaviors to be considered as aggression. Unfortunately, it is not possible without explicating the way we as scientists make attributions of intent (or accidental consequences). Furthermore, it would be necessary to state when judgments of good and bad should apply to behaviors so we can decide when to include or exclude a particular behavior from the set that is labeled as aggression. Clearly, the behavioristic definition of aggression does not allow for an unambiguous identification of a response as aggression.

The attempt to redefine aggression in terms of attribution of intent to do harm carries much the same problems for an observational concept as does the behavioristic definition. Theorists who adopt the attributional definition do not explicate how each scientist should make attributions of intent to do harm to actors. Furthermore, it seems clear that even when intent appears unambiguous, as when a fireman takes an axe to the front of someone's home, the actor is not perceived as aggressive. While the intent is to knock down and thus destroy or damage the door, the actor is considered justified for having such an intent by his role and the lofty objective behind the intent. Presumably, he has the goal of saving someone's life or of limiting the amount of damage done by the fire. Thus, attribution of intent and value judgments are required before one can observationally identify a response as an instance of aggression.

After examining problems with definitions of aggression Bandura (1973, p. 11) concludes that we should not be concerned about an abstract concept of aggression because in research we focus upon smaller sets of behaviors, such as homicides, destruction of property, and prejudicial practices. He believes each of these subsets of behavior has different determinants and that apparent inconsistencies in research are attributable to the use of the generic terms rather than the more specific observational concepts. This conclusion seems to preclude the development of a general theory of aggression and instead suggests that a rather sizable number of relatively unconnected smaller theories may be required to explain the phenomena of interest to those who study 'aggression.'

A different conclusion has been drawn by Tedeschi and his collaborators (Tedeschi et al., 1974; Tedeschi et al., 1977; Tedeschi et al., 1981). It is agreed that there are insuperable problems with the concept of aggression (see also Scott, 1977), but it is proposed that this implies a need for a more adequate conceptualization of the phenomena of interest. A coercive power formulation was proposed that de-emphasized biological and learning processes, focuses on social psychological determinants of behavior, and is the basis of a general theory of the relevant behaviors. This conceptualization also proposes to separate the description and explanation of action from the labeling of observers. Thus, use of coercive power might or might not be labeled as aggression by observers, depending on a number of circumstances, including the kinds of attributions that are made and the values of the observers. We will now consider these ideas in more detail.

A theory of coercive power

Definitions

When one person does something that affects the intentions, attitudes, motives, or actions of another, social influence has occurred. It is not necessary for the influencer to know that influence has occurred. There are of course many forms of influence, including controlling the environment, reinforcements, and information, promises, moral suasion, modeling, and so on. Coercive power refers to forms of influence involving the use of threats and punishments.

Tedeschi (1970) offered observational definitions for various kinds of threats and punishments. Threats are communications in which the source states an intention to administer punishments. A contingent threat makes a demand from the target and offers punishment for noncompliance. In a noncontingent threat communication the source merely announces an intention to punish the target. In the parlance of learning theory a contingent threat offers the target an avoidance opportunity, whereas a noncontingent threat is more like escape conditioning.

The threatener may make his demands specific or leave them to be inferred by the target, and he may be specific about the punishment to be administered or it may be left to the imagination of the target. Thus, it is possible to identify threats in which demands are specific but the punishments are not, ones in which demands are nonspecific but punishments are specific, and so on. Of course it is possible for threats to be communicated nonverbally, and it is also possible for a target to perceive threats that were not intended as transmissions by the source. These latter more implicit or tacit threats and threat perceptions have not been satisfactorily identified by any clear observational criteria, but presumably with the development of a taxonomy of nonverbal behaviors and linguistic theory such observational criteria will eventually be developed. In the meantime more explicit verbal threats are easily identifiable, can be coded by computers (cf. Holsti, 1968) and can be manipulated in the laboratory (cf. Tedeschi et al., 1973). The identification of threats does not involve an attributional analysis of the intentions of the source, nor is it necessary to consider the values that would approve or condemn them. Thus, the problems associated with developing an adequate definition of aggression are resolved by redefining the phenomena of interest as various forms of threats and punishments.

Thorndike's (1913) law of effect included an empirical definition of punishment as any stimulus the organism will work to avoid or escape and will do nothing to attain. Tedeschi (1970) suggested that it may be important to distinguish between different forms of punishments and proposed a simple intuitive typology.[1] Noxious stimulation refers to any stimulus which produces discomfort, pain, or tissue damage when applied to an individual's body and may include shock, noise, acid, punching, and many other stimuli. Deprivation of resources involves taking away from an individual something of value or which can mediate value, such as money, material objects, and friends. *Withholding expected gains* produces volatile reactions from a victim because it appears to be quite unjust and immoral to break promises. To withhold a reward when the victim has done or believes he or she has done something to earn it, is particularly maddening. *Social punishments* include name calling, the spreading of malicious information, stigmatizing, degradation ceremonies, denial of access to social groups, and so on, and are considered harmful because they damage the target's identity in the eyes of others. *Political retribution* refers more to the way in which punishment is decided upon and administered than on the form it takes. A punishment may be considered a form of political retribution when it is administered through some formalized process or institution, such as a jury trial, grievance proceeding, congressional hearing, and so on. Of course a person can lose his job, be incarcerated, lose a hand or head, be excommunicated or expatriated, or almost anything else as a function of political retribution. These forms of punishments are not mutually exclusive and they may or may not be forecast by preceding threats.

The use of coercive power

According to Tedeschi and Bonoma (1977, p. 228) 'if a person cannot persuade, bribe, manipulate, or otherwise induce another person to comply with his wishes ... then his power may ultimately depend on his ability to threaten, restrain, immobilize, injure, punish, or destroy the target.' Of course in addition to the attempt to gain compliance punishment may be administered for purposes of revenge or rehabilitation of the victim. The scientific questions to be answered concern why, when, how, and against whom coercive power will be used.

The first stage of decision making for a source of influence is to choose a target. Typically, though not always, the source contemplates influencing a target to gain reinforcement or to avoid punishment. In many instances there are a number of alternative targets all of whom possess the ability to mediate the relevant goal. It is presumed that the source will consider how each potential target will respond to each mode of influence, including persuasion, promises, and threats, and chooses the target and influence mode with the highest probability and value of success and the least probable costs.[2]

The question we are concerned with here is why the source chooses to use coercive power rather than some other form of influence. Among the factors proposed by Tedeschi *et al.* (1977) are lack of self-confidence, failure to consider the future costs of behavior, fear, self-presentation and face-saving, the attempt to maintain legitimate authority, conflict over scarce resources, norms of self-defense and reciprocity, relative deprivation and unjust distribution of rewards, and modeling and learning. We will consider each of these factors in more detail.

Lack of self-confidence.   When a source does not believe that control over information or positive reinforcements will induce a target to engage in the desired behavior (or refrain from an undesirable behavior), he may use coercion. In this sense coercion is the influence mode of last resort. The source may believe he does not possess relevant characteristics that would make noncoercive means of influence successful. Thus, he must choose between giving up interpersonal goals or using coercion. Inadequate education, lack of expertise and status, inarticulateness, and a general sense of powerlessness are associated with the use of coercion (Lindskold and Tedeschi, 1970; Ransford, 1968). Once the source uses coercion a vicious cycle may be started. Targets (and other observers) develop a distrust and enmity toward sources who threaten and punish them. Yet, positive forms of influence, such as promises and persuasion, require trust if they are to be successful in bringing about the desired responses from a target. This brings about a situation in which the source must once again use coercion if he wants to influence the target. A person of low self-esteem finds it difficult to extricate himself from this vicious cycle and may become locked in to a coercive influence style.

Failure to consider future costs of behavior. Theories of aggression propose factors inhibiting the organism from performing the relevant behaviors. Nuclear strategists and criminologists have examined the logic and effectiveness of various forms of deterrence. Essentially, these theories examine the role of prospective costly consequences of behavior on eliminating or suppressing it. Among such costs are those imposed by the target, those associated with gaining access to the target, and opportunity costs derived from influence, such as paying off promises or backing up threats. If it is presumed that the source is concerned with maximizing gains and minimizing costs, then each increment of expected costs for using coercion should decrease the likelihood of its use. However, if the source does not consider the potential costs of his or her behavior, then they cannot affect the decision to use coercion. Among the factors known to have the effect of contracting the individual's time perspective to the existential moment and to ignore the potential costs of behavior are strong emotions, alcohol consumption, and the use of certain drugs. All of these conditions are strongly associated with the incidence of homicides, suicides, child abuse, physical assaults, and automobile fatalities.

Fear. People react to fear by avoiding, escaping, or removing the source of anticipated harm. Coercive power may be used to control, destroy, or deter another person who may be perceived as intending to harm the source. People cannot usually tolerate fear for extended periods of time and are motivated to terminate it. This dynamic may lead the individual to make a pre-emptive attack on a victim. That is, when the person is sure that another is about to attack her she may attack first and gain whatever advantage such a first strike provides.

When a person is in a heightened fear state he may be prone to interpret cues emitted from others as indicating danger and imminent attack. According to Toch

(1969) prison inmates who had a history of violent behavior tended to display violence in the presence of specific cues emitted from others. That is, various kinds of verbal and nonverbal cues reliably elicited violence by these men. Perhaps they had learned that such cues represented danger to them and their violence may be directed toward controlling others considered dangerous to them.

Impression management.   A concern for maintaining high credibility for one's communications may lead to the use of punishments. If a person issues threats to a target and the target does not comply with the source's demands, the source is placed in a put-up or shut-up situation. The failure to back-up one's threats undermines the source's credibility. If a target does not believe the source's communications, the latter will not be an effective influencer. Thus, in order to maintain a reputation for credibility and to bolster the ability to influence others, it is necessary to punish a target's failure to comply with a threat (even when the source is reluctant to do so).

Coercive power might also be used to build or maintain other kinds of identities. Fighting and violence on the street or on the playground may be directed toward building a reputation for being manly and tough. In order to build a macho image young men may start fights with strangers, deface property, steal cars, and otherwise engage in coercive activities. A macho image may be very functional for a person in a ghetto where such a reputation may deter others from using coercion against him and may also enhance the effectiveness of his own attempts to influence others.

Defense of a positive identity against the assaults of others may lead to extremely violent behavior. Deliberate insults, sarcasm, jokes, and other forms of embarrassment have been shown by Felson (1981) to be important in cases of homicide and physical assaults. Coercion may be used to terminate the verbal assaults of the other person and to restore a positive identity by controlling or defeating the offending person. Concern for one's face and self-respect may lead to an acceptance of great costs to mend a spoiled identity. Thus, costs that would normally deter use of coercion may not do so when the person's face is under deliberate attack by others.

An ineffectual and powerless person may engage in an uncharacteristic act of violence as a means of affirming his existence and gaining the attention of an audience. Just as a child may risk a spanking so as to gain attention from visitors to the home, so the unnoticed and unloved person may harm a highly visible other person. The attempt by Arthur Bremer to assassinate Governor George Wallace appeared to be motivated by a need to bolster self-esteem and sense of importance. The assassination of John Lennon may have been similarly motivated.

Maintenance of authority.   Defiance of legitimate authority often leads to some form of punishment for the subordinate. Disobedience endangers the authority's legitimate base of power by providing a disobedient model for others. Such disobedience, if rewarded or left unpunished, may reveal a basic weakness of the authority. As Tedeschi and Lindskold have indicated, 'Punishing disobedience serves notice to other subordinates that authority cannot be flouted with impunity, restores the high status person's sense of power, and either causes the recalcitrant to submit to authority or removes him from a position where he can continue to defy authority' (1976, p. 176).

To some extent the tendency of authorities to punish disobedience is associated with the kinds of resources that are available and with characteristics of the recalcitrant subordinate. Police officers, for example, display tools for delivering noxious stimuli (guns, clubs, etc.) and when their authority is challenged are prone to use them (Toch, 1969). Few others in society are provided with such discretion in the use of these kinds of resources. Of course officials in a corporation may use other kinds of penalties for insubordination. Characteristics of the subordinate, such as sex, race, and age may affect the probability of punishment and its form. Quiet disobedience may bring less punishment than noisy defiance.

Conflict over scarce resources. A conflict exists between two or more persons when each desires what only one can have. Two men who desire the same woman, or two children who want to watch different television programs experience conflict. In such situations the person can withdraw and allow the other person to have his or her way, seek some form of compromise through bargaining and persuasion, or attempt to make the other person withdraw. The more intense the conflict between the parties, the more likely it is that coercion will be used to make the other person withdraw. Conflict intensity is associated with the value of the goals. When goals are interdependent, vital to each party, and incompatible, suspicion and distrust render more positive forms of influence, such as promises and persuasion, ineffective. Threats and counterthreats may lead to an escalating cycle of hostilities that may get out of control. Each party may up the ante in an attempt to make the other withdraw from the conflict. The possibilities for misperception and miscalculation are quite good in the course of escalation and both parties lose control over the consequences that eventually occur.

Norms of self-defense and reciprocity. Rules of conduct often mandate that an individual use coercive power. A person may be believed to have the right to harm others under certain conditions. For example, in American society there is a strong norm of self-defense. According to a study by Blumenthal *et al.* (1972) a majority of adult American males believe they have the right to kill another human being in defense of property, self, and family. This norm is reflected in law which allows for justifiable homicide. Of course most coercion used in self-defense falls far short of such catastrophic consequences.

Gouldner (1960) has examined a universal norm of reciprocity, which in its negative form legitimates harming those who harm the person. The harm that is legitimated is proportional to the provocation. Such revenge is not automatic but is affected by the capability, attractiveness, and sex of the provoker. If the harm-doer is especially powerful, the person may be inhibited with regard to direct forms of reciprocity, although more subtle forms may be invoked. Thus, one might not directly attack a bully, but one may use influence to harm anonymously his interests. There also appears to be a tendency to reciprocate with less harm when the provoker is socially attractive rather than unattractive. Furthermore, norms in some cultures prohibit males from using noxious stimuli against females, although other forms of punishment may be used.

An individual's interpretation of the norm of reciprocity may lead to illegitimate conduct. For example, a Californian woman who had been raped by two men invited them to her house where she greeted them with a shotgun. One of the men was killed and the other escaped harm. Under the law the judicial authorities are the only ones who have the legitimate right to punish the offenders. The victim does not have such a right, although had she shot the rapists at the time of the rape, she would have been justified by a norm of self-defense. On occasion a person will undertake to punish an actor who has carried out what is considered a socially reprehensible action when the action did no direct harm to the offended party. This kind of vigilante action is often modeled for viewers of television programs in the United States. What may appear to be bizarre harm-doing actions may be interpreted in terms of individuals who use their own value systems to condemn actions of others and then take it upon themselves to punish the wrong-doers. Jack-The-Ripper apparently was engaged in a private war against prostitutes, who epitomized one of the worst kinds of evils in his moral schemata.

Relative deprivation and unjust distribution of rewards.   When people cooperate with one another to achieve collective goals, there is a problem of how these rewards should be distributed to individuals in the group. Whatever standard of distribution is adopted, the individual will feel relatively deprived when he or she gets less than his or her prescribed allocation. Perceptions of unjust division of rewards may serve to justify otherwise illegitimate means for remedying the situation. In American society which continually espouses principles of equal opportunity and equitable distribution of wealth, those who feel excluded from legitimate means of achievement may attempt to achieve rewards through illegitimate actions. Robbery, theft, assault, rape, arson, blackmail, and murder may be justified by deviant individuals who experience relative deprivation.

On occasion a person who feels relatively deprived may administer costs to an advantaged other person. When the advantaged person has done nothing to provoke or harm the disadvantaged person, as when a supervisor has allocated the rewards to both, the episode may appear to be irrational and unmotivated. The choices open to a relatively disadvantaged person who wants to restore justice to the world are: (a) to get more for self; (b) to impose costs on the advantaged person; (c) to seek a change in the rules of distribution; (d) to attack the authority who distributes the rewards and undermine his authority. Of course these remedies are not mutually exclusive.

Modeling and learning. Persons probably learn influence styles through observation of adult models. If every conflict is resolved through discussion and compromise, the person may learn to approach such situations in a conciliatory manner. However, if coercion is typically used by adults in the home to resolve disputes the individual may adopt similar tactics as the preferred means of solving his conflicts with persons outside the home. Thus, a child who frequently experiences corporal punishment and thus loses in conflicts with adults, may adopt threats and bodily harm as means of imposing his will upon peers and others outside the home. Coercive influence styles derive to some extent from the parents' mode of socialization and are inextricably linked with the child's system of values and moral thought (Hoffman, 1963).

Modeling effects on audiences of the mass media are not well documented. Our view is that the mass media do influence viewers by introducing, maintaining, and reinforcing social norms and values that support the use of coercion. Norms of justice, self-defense, and reciprocity, vigilantism, legitimation of grievances, and desensitization of emotional reactions to violence may be conveyed and reinforced. Each of these factors may serve to increase the probability that the viewer will use coercion against other persons. Thus, the effects of the mass media are not attributable to the direct imitation of rewarded models but rather to the regulation of behavior by social rules that are taught or reinforced by them.

Perceived aggression and interaction

The study of coercive power focuses upon actions taken by a source of influence. The conditions under which coercive action is labeled by observers as aggression is a subject for those who study person perception and implicit personality theory. According to Tedeschi *et al.* (1974) an actor is perceived as aggressive when an observer attributes, to him or her, intention to do harm and the action undertaken is considered to be illegitimate or unjustified. Thus, the use of coercion is an objectively determinable event, whereas the labeling of an actor as aggressive is a subjective event dependent upon the observer's perceptions and values.

Being labeled as an aggressor typically is associated with costs for the actor. To be considered an aggressor is to be blamed for a wrong action. Observers negatively evaluate an aggressor, may tend to avoid him or her in the future, and may support or carry out retribution against him or her. Anticipation of being labeled as an aggressor is associated with expectation of costs and may serve to inhibit or deter the actor from using coercion. It is for this reason that systems of legitimation are so important for the occurrence of violence in society. If a behavior is judged to be legitimate or justifiable, the actor will not be labeled as aggressive and no costs will be imposed on him; but if the action is considered to be illegitimate and unjustified, the actor will be labeled as aggressive and can anticipate costs will follow his behavior. Of course it is possible that the actor believes his action to be justified when few others concur so that there may be no anticipation of being labeled as an aggressor. In such cases education about the values and standards of conduct approved by others could serve to reduce the incidence of violence.

The actor may engage in prior legitimation of an action in order to preclude observers from labeling him as aggressive, or the actor may provide accounts for behavior afterward to change in a more favorable direction the perceptions and evaluations of observers. The post-transgression responses of actors intended to influence observers include excuses, justifications, expressions of remorse and guilt, and self-punishment (see Tedeschi *et al.*, 1981 for more detail about these tactics).

Implications for research

The paradigms developed to study human aggression in the laboratory have similar characteristics. Subjects are attacked, insulted, or angered by a confederate and are then given an opportunity to harm the provoker. The delivery of noxious stimulation to the confederate is legitimized by the experimenter as a scientifically valuable contribution. Thus, while factors that contribute to a subject's use of coercion are studied, the action is typically defensive, retaliatory, directed toward eliminating a state of inequity, and legitimated by the experimenter. Unfortunately, most of the phenomena of interest to investigators of 'aggression' involve offensive, unprovoked, and illegitimate coercive actions. Inadvertantly, investigators have generalized the principles learned from laboratory paradigms involving defensive and legitimate uses of coercion to real-world situations typified by offensive and illegitimate coercive actions. Those actions which are labeled as aggression by most people in a society have largely escaped laboratory investigation. Whether subjects will engage in such actions while under the surveillance of a scientist is questionable. It may be necessary to apply our research ingenuity to developing ways of studying illegitimate uses of coercion in field settings.

Conclusion

A social influence perspective provides an alternative conceptualization of the phenomena heretofore referred to as aggression. Observational concepts of threat and punishment avoid the problems of developing an unambiguous definition of aggression. The language of coercive power focuses the investigator's attention on the social causes of interpersonal behaviors. In a social context the use of coercion can be interpreted as one way the individual has of influencing others, resolving conflicts, and conforming to social norms. To a large extent systems of legitimation are viewed as facilitators or inhibitors of coercive behavior. When coercive power is perceived as illegitimate its wielder is labeled as an aggressor, is held morally responsible for the negative action, is blamed, and considered deserving of retribution. Those coercive actions which are legitimated are not considered as acts of aggression and are generally accepted or approved by observers. The distinctions made in the language of coercive power make it clear that there are serious limitations to laboratory studies which typically focus on defensive and legitimated actions. Future research will help us to further develop a theory of coercive power and will be especially interested in studying factors that lead individuals to engage in illegitimate coercive actions.

Notes

1. For a more complex theory of reinforcements see Foa (1971).
2. See Tedeschi *et al.* (1972) or Tedeschi *et al.* (1973) for a more detailed presentation of a subjective expected value theory of social influence.

References

Bandura, A. (1973). *Aggression: A Social Learning Analysis*, Prentice-Hall, Englewood Cliffs, NJ.
Baron, R. A. (1977). *Human Aggression*, Plenum, New York.
Blumenthal, M., Kahn, R. L., Andrews, F. M., and Head, K. B. (1972). *Justifying Violence: Attitudes of American Men*, Institute for Social Research, Ann Arbor, Mich.
Buss, A. H. (1961). *The Psychology of Aggression*, Wiley, New York.
Felson, R. B. (1981). 'An interactionist approach to aggression,' in J. T. Tedeschi (ed.), *Impression Management Theory and Social Psychological Research*, Academic Press, New York.
Foa, U. G. (1971). 'Interpersonal and economic resources,' *Science*, **171**, 345–351.
Fromm, E. (1973). *The Anatomy of Human Destructiveness*, Holt, Rinehart & Winston, New York.
Gouldner, A. W. (1960). 'The norm of reciprocity: A preliminary statement,' *American Sociological Review*, **25**, 161–178.
Hoffman, M. L. (1963). 'Child-rearing practices and moral development,' *Child Development*, **34**, 295–318.
Holsti, O. R. (1968). 'Content analysis,' in G. Lindzey and E. Aronson (eds.) *Handbook of Social Psychology*, 2nd edn, Addison-Wesley, Reading, Mass.
Lindskold, S., and Tedeschi, J. T. (1970). 'Self-confidence, prior success, and the use of power in social conflicts,' *Proceedings of the 78th Annual Convention of the American Psychological Association*, **5**, 425–426 (Summary).
Ransford, H. E. (1968). 'Isolation, powerlessness, and violence: A study of attitudes and participation in the Watts riot,' *American Journal of Sociology*, **73**, 581–591.
Scott, J. P. (1977). 'Agonistic behavior: Function and dysfunction in social conflict,' *Journal of Social Issues*, **33** (1), 9–21.
Tedeschi, J. T. (1970). 'Threats and promises,' in P. Swingle (ed.), *The Structure of Conflict*, Academic Press, New York.
Tedeschi, J. T., and Bonoma, T. V. (1977). 'Measures of last resort: Coercion and aggres-

sion in bargaining,' in D. Druckman (ed.), *Negotiations: Social Psychological Perspectives*, Sage, Beverly Hills, CA.

Tedeschi, J. T., Gaes, G. G., and Rivera, A. N. (1977). 'Aggression and the use of coercive power,' *Journal of Social Issues*, **33** (1), 101–125.

Tedeschi, J. T., and Lindskold, S. (1976). *Social Psychology: Interdependence, Interaction, and Influence*, Wiley, New York.

Tedeschi, J. T., Melburg, V., and Rosenfeld, P. (1981). 'Is the concept of aggression useful?' in P. Brain and R. Benton (eds.), *Aggression: A Multidisciplinary View*, Academic Press, London.

Tedeschi, J. T., Schlenker, B. R., and Bonoma, T. V. (1973). *Conflict, Power, and Games*. Aldine, Chicago.

Tedeschi, J. T., Schlenker, B. R., and Lindskold, S. (1972). 'The exercise of power and influence: The source of influence,' in J. T. Tedeschi (ed.), *The Social Influence Processes*, Aldine, Chicago.

Tedeschi, J. T., Smith, R. B., III., and Brown, R. C., Jr. (1974). 'A reinterpretation of research on aggression,' *Psychological Bulletin*, **81**, 540–563.

Thorndike, E. L. (1913). *The Psychology of Learning*, Teachers College, New York.

Toch, H. H. (1969). *Violent Men: An Inquiry into the Psychology of Violence*, Aldine, Chicago.

Zillmann, D. (1979). *Hostility and Aggression*, Lawrence Erlbaum Associates, Hillsdale, NJ.

Small Groups and Social Interaction, Volume 1
Edited by H. H. Blumberg, A. P. Hare, V. Kent and M. Davies
© 1983 John Wiley & Sons Ltd

6.4 Collective Aggression: The Group–Individual Paradigm in the Study of Collective Antisocial Behavior

Yoram Jaffe and Yoel Yinon   *Bar-Ilan University, Israel*

It is unfortunate, but in our daily lives we are constantly reminded that groups are capable of far greater violence and aggression than persons who act alone. Events of collective aggression in which we are involved as participants, victims, or spectators frequently present themselves to us in various forms and degrees of severity. The present paper is concerned with the question of how group aggression compares with individual aggression and with the processes underlying this contrast.

The historic work of Le Bon (1903) on crowd behavior and his pivotal assumption about the 'disappearance of conscious personality' and the emergence of a '. . . collective mind which makes them (crowd members) feel, think, and act in a manner quite different from that in which each individual of them would feel, think, and act were he in a state of isolation' (p. 27) have inspired much of contemporary theory and research on phenomena of collective antisocial behavior. In particular Le Bon's further assertions that, 'In the life of the isolated individual it would be dangerous for him to gratify these instincts while his absorption in an irresponsible crowd in which in consequence he is assured of impunity gives him entire liberty to follow them' (p. 57), and '. . . having lost his conscious personality . . . (the crowd member) commits acts in utter contradiction with his character and habits' (p. 31), have been most influential and are reflected in the more recent analyses of phenomena of collective aggression (Bandura, 1973; Diener, 1980; Milgram and Toch, 1969; Zimbardo, 1969).

Bandura's (1973) social learning theory addresses the release of aggressive behavior in terms of a process of *disinhibition* of antisocial behavior—behavior which is usually restrained by fear of adverse consequences mediated externally (punishment) or internally (guilt). Conditions that reduce anticipated risk of punishment or guilt disinhibit aggressive actions. Social psychologists, following

Festinger, *et al.* (1952), have used the term *deindividuation* to refer to disinhibition occasioned in group contexts. Festinger *et al.* (1952) defined deindividuation from the external, group perspective and characterized it as a condition in which group members are '. . . not seen or paid attention to as individuals' (p. 382). Focusing on an internal, subjective state, Singer *et al.* (1965) defined deindividuation as a '. . . subjective state in which people lose their self-consciousness' (p. 356). More recently, Diener (1980) conceptualized this construct as follows: 'A deindividuated person is prevented by situational factors present in a group from becoming self-aware. Deindividuated persons are blocked from awareness of themselves as separate individuals and from monitoring their own behavior' (p. 2). Diener (1980) presents a model of deindividuation which purports to represent an improvement over Zimbardo's (1969) three-component model. Deindividuation is construed as a highly complex construct and as yet, as Diener (1977, p. 143) concludes, '. . . research has failed to confirm the causal role of deindividuation in releasing antisocial behavior.' Consequently, the purpose of the series of three studies presented here was to provide empirical documentation for the phenomenon of collective aggression and investigate some of the processes assumed to mediate it, without commitment to the complex construct of deindividuation in its entirety.

The purpose of the first experiment (Study 1: Jaffe and Yinon, 1979) was to provide empirical evidence for the expectation that groups would retaliate more severely than individuals. The second experiment (Study 2: Jaffe *et al.*, 1981) examined differences between group and individual conditions in escalation of aggression and also the cross-cultural generality of heightened group versus individual aggression. In addition, the study assessed the contribution of diffusion of responsibility in groups to the group aggression effect. Study 3 (Yinon *et al.*, 1981) investigated the role of anonymity in group versus individual aggression and the contribution of additional, internal variables to this social phenomenon.

All three studies employed a modification of the aggression machine paradigm developed by Buss (1961) for the measurement of physical aggression. Study 1 used Israeli male college students as subjects, and its procedure was based on the original bogus learning experiment used by Buss. The subjects in Study 2 were adult male workers, including Isreali natives and immigrants to Israel from three ethnic groups of the Soviet Union—European Russians, Georgians, and Caucasians. The procedure followed the bogus ESP experimental paradigm reported in Jaffe *et al.* (1974) and, as in the original Buss aggression machine procedure, 10 levels of electric shock were used as the aggressive measure. Study 3 employed adolescent males (13–14 years old) who attended junior high school. Aversive noise replaced electric shock as the aggressive measure and the procedure was based on the modification developed by Baron (e.g. Baron and Bell, 1977) in which instructions concerning an experiment on physiological responses to aversive stimuli serve as the cover story.

In all group conditions of the three experiments, there were groups of three members each who were required to reach jointly a unanimous decision as to the level of aversive stimulus to be delivered to the victim (confederate). In Studies 1 and 2, use of electric shock presumably served to punish incorrect responses on a learning or an ESP task, and in Study 3 noise was used presumably to stimulate psychophysiological reactions.

Physical aggression

Consistently in all three studies, a highly significant main effect was found according to which groups acted considerably more aggressively than individuals, as can be seen in Table 1. The obtained effect seems to be a robust one, holding across variations in demographic characteristics of subjects, nature of aversive stimulus serving as the aggressive measure, and experimental design and procedure.

Escalation

In Studies 2 and 3, where escalation of aggression over repeated trials was measured, the results demonstrated a strong main effect for this phenomenon. As Figure 1 shows, in Study 2 there was a clear difference between groups and individuals: While groups escalated their aggressive responses over trials, individuals did not. In Study 3, however, escalation was consistent for both group and individual conditions. This difference between studies may be attributed to variations in the populations sampled.

Provocation

As far as motivation for aggression is concerned, the findings summarized here

Table 1   Mean physical aggression scores for individual and group conditions in the three experiments

	Social condition	
Study	Individual	Group
1. Jaffe and Yinon (1979)	3.84 $n = 10$	6.88 $n = 10$
2. Jaffe, Shapir, and Yinon (1981)	5.37 $n = 40$	6.93 $n = 40$
3. Yinon, Jaffe, and Ginzburg (1981)	5.22 $n = 40$	5.95 $n = 40$

Note: All comparisons between individual and group conditions were significant at the $p < .001$ level.

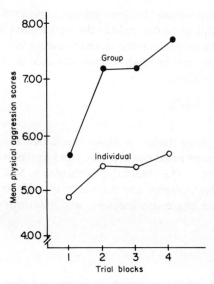

Figure 1 Escalation of physical aggression as a function of the interaction between trial blocks and social condition (Study 2)

make it apparent that while physical or verbal provocation facilitates aggressive behavior in general, it is not a necessary condition for heightened group over individual aggression. Study 2 obtained this effect without induction of aggressive motivation, and Study 3 found groups to be more aggressive than individuals under no-anger as well as under anger-arousal conditions. This difference, however, was more pronounced for the angered subjects. In Study 1, the substantial increase of group as compared with individual aggression was obtained following a common provocation procedure in which *all* subjects were attacked both physically, by means of electric shock, and verbally through an insulting communication.

Mediating variables

Anonymity

A number of variables are discussed in the literature as mediating the influence of group conditions on antisocial behavior of individuals. The releasing influence of anonymity typical of crowd members is fundamental to early (Le Bon, 1903) as well as recent theories of crowd behavior (see review by Milgram and Toch, 1969); a number of empirical investigations have supported this effect of the anonymity of the individual in a group (e.g. Mathes and Guest, 1976; Zimbardo,

1969). A distinctive feature of Study 3 is its manipulation of anonymity conditions for the assessment of the role of this presumably important variable in effecting heightened group as compared with individual aggression. Anonymity from the experimenter was assessed separately from anonymity from the victim. Subjects in a low anonymity, i.e. identifiability, condition were asked by the experimenter to give him personally identifying information including name, address, and telephone number; this information was also passed on to the victim as part of the provocation manipulation used. No such identifying data were collected in the anonymity condition. The results indicated a strong main effect for the anonymity variable ($p < .01$). Subjects in the anonymity condition administered on the average a noise intensity of 5.80 (on the 10-point noise intensity scale) as compared with 5.38 of the identifiable subjects. It is important to note that the external conditions of anonymity v. identifiability were accompanied (according to responses on 7-point self-rating scales in a postexperimental questionnaire) by the respective internal feelings of greater or lesser anonymity from the experimenter ($M = 5.00$ and 3.35, $p < .001$, respectively) and from the victim ($M = 4.71$ and 3.60, $p < .001$, respectively). The apparent contribution of feelings of anonymity to the heighted aggression found in groups as compared with individuals is further highlighted by results showing that group members reported greater feelings of anonymity from the experimenter ($M = 4.67$) and from the victim ($M = 4.92$) than their individual counterparts ($M = 3.70$ and 3.42, respectively, $p < .001$, for both kinds of anonymity).

Diffusion of responsibility

In addition to anonymity, the role of the mechanism of diffusion of responsibility as a disinhibitor of aggressive and other forms of antisocial conduct has been frequently demonstrated in experiments (e.g. Bandura *et al.*, 1975; Diener *et al.*, 1975) and underscored in reviews pertinent to group aggression (Bandura, 1973; Milgram and Toch, 1969). As compared with the individual who acts alone, members of groups are likely to perceive themselves as less personally accountable for negative consequences of collective actions in which they participate. This process was tested directly in a study by Mynatt and Sherman (1975). They showed that group members who jointly gave someone advice that led to failure attributed less responsibility to themselves personally than isolated individuals who gave such advice. No differences in felt responsibility between group members and individuals were found when advice led to success. Mathes and Kahn (1975) found that group members who collaborated in reaching group decisions concerning how much an ostensible learner should be fined for incorrect responses reported feeling significantly less personal responsibility for the punishment they gave than did isolated subjects. It is important to note that groups tended to exact higher fines than did isolated subjects.

In Studies 2 and 3, subjects responded to the question: 'To what extent did you feel personally responsible for the shock (noise) you administered?' The answer was given on a 7-point scale on a postexperimental questionnaire. In Study 2, there was a significant main effect ($p < .001$), in the expected direction, for the social condition variable: group members received a mean personal responsibility score of 3.98, whereas individuals received a mean score of 6.30. In Study 3, however, there was no main effect for social condition ($F < 1$) but, surprisingly enough, its interaction with the provocation variable was significant ($p < .001$): under anger arousal group members reported a mean of 3.56 compared with 4.95 reported by individuals ($p < .01$), whereas under no-anger arousal this group–individual difference was reversed, with group members reporting a mean of 5.18 and individuals a mean of 4.25 ($p < .01$). This pattern of findings stresses the possible importance of aggressive motivation for the process of diffusion of responsibility among group members. When such motivation was lacking and apparently due to the fact that present group members were schoolmates, their sense of personal responsibility received salience in the collective as contrasted with the isolated situation.

Fear of retaliation

Closely related to feelings of anonymity and reduced personal responsibility is fear of punishment or retaliation. The presence of fear of punishment was assessed by asking the subjects to respond (on the postexperimental questionnaire) to an item dealing with his fear of retaliation by the victim of his aggression. The scores on the 7-point scale yielded a mean of 3.00 for group members and 4.37 for individuals ($p < .001$). This difference supports observations in the literature (Bandura, 1973) that fear of punishment is a major inhibitor of aggressive behavior, and that participation in collective antisocial acts often reduces such fear, thereby allowing for disinhibition of aggressive and other forms of socially disapproved behavior.

Self-awareness and restraint

In an attempt to expand investigation of internal, subjective variables presumed to influence restraint of antisocial aggressive conduct (cf. Diener, 1980; Scheier et al., 1974), subjects in Study 3 were further questioned (in the same postexperimental format noted above) about their sense of self-awareness and freedom from restraints. The question: 'To what extent were you aware of yourself in the course of the experiment?' yielded an interaction ($p < .001$) between social condition and provocation which, as far as group–individual differences are concerned, paralleled the interaction just noted for diffusion of responsibility. Subsequent to being annoyed by the victim (confederate), group members showed a tendency to report less self-awareness than individuals (means were 2.60 and 3.15, respectively). With no such provocation, however, this tendency was reversed and group members reported a greater sense of awareness of themselves than did individuals (means were 3.35 and 2.00, respectively, $p < .01$). Again, this may be explained by the observation that without justification for the aggressive act, the group situation apparently highlighted personal distinctiveness for subjects who were at least superficially acquainted with one another and thereby inhibited this kind of antisocial action. With the apparent justification for retaliation, i.e. prior provocation, reduction in self-awareness tended to be facilitated among the group members, but not in subjects acting in isolation. What is more, for the isolated subject, anger arousal was associated with increased self-consciousness as compared with no-anger arousal, and this can explain why these angered subjects were inhibited and did not retaliate physically. (Their physical aggression scores were 5.31 and 5.14 for the anger-arousal and no-anger-arousal conditions, respectively.)

The direct inquiry as to the subjective state of restraint reduction (cf. Festinger *et al.*, 1952) via the question: 'To what extent was your behavior in the course of the experiment free of restraints?' sheds further light on the issue at hand. Table 2 presents in the format of the full $2 \times 2 \times 2$ experimental design employed in Study 3 the means for reduction of restraints scores on the 7-point postexperimental rating scale and for comparison, the means for physical aggression as measured by the 10-point aversive noise scale of the modified Buss aggression machine used in this experiment. The similarity in the pattern of results for these two variables is striking. Both patterns set in relief one cell against all the others—the cell representing group action under conditions of anonymity coupled with aggressive

Table 2 Freedom from restraints and physical aggression scores as a function of social condition, anonymity, and provocation

		Provocation		No provocation	
		Anonymity	Identifiability	Anonymity	Identifiability
Group	Freedom from Restraints	5.80_b	4.56_a	4.26_a	4.50_a
	Aggression	6.94_b	5.74_a	5.66_a	5.47_a
Individual	Freedom from Restraints	4.50_a	4.70_a	4.40_a	4.40_a
	Aggression	5.41_a	5.21_a	5.17_a	5.11_a

Note: For each dependent variable separately, means with a common subscript are not significantly different from each other by *a posteriori* tests.

provocation. Subjects partaking in collective action under these conditions reported the highest level of freedom from restraints and contributed to the highest level of aggressive behavior manifested in the experiment.

Phenomenology of the collective aggressor

As stated earlier, in carrying out the present studies we have been particularly interested in contrasting the collecive aggressor with the isolated aggressor. By generalization and integration of the findings from this series of investigations, it is possible to draw a partial, overall outline of the phenomenology of the individual who joins others and collaborates with them in perpetrating acts of antisocial nature such as aggression and violence.

Our collective aggressor is the individual subject who arrived at the experimental room and by random assignment happened to become a member of a triad rather than being asked to follow the experimental procedure alone. He then experienced or did not experience an attack by a confederate of the experimenter who later became victim of collective aggression. Our group member proceeded to participate with his fellow members in a series of joint discussions which always terminated in a consensual collective decision as to the intensity of aversive stimulation to be delivered to the victim. He apparently perceived responsibility for these decisions and their execution to be shared with his fellow group members, and viewed himself as less personally accountable for whatever negative consequences and implications might have accrued from this collaborative, aggressive action.

As compared with his isolated counterpart, our typical group member seemed also to feel less identifiable and detectable by outsiders, particularly when no personally identifying information was collected from him and divulged to his victim. Feeling relatively anonymous and less liable for punishment and retaliation, he apparently experienced a lessened fear of punishment and sensed himself to be freer from this and other inhibitions which normally restrain antisocial behavior. There is also some evidence to suggest that when angered he might have felt less self-conscious, less aware of himself as a separate distinct human entity.

This representing at least in part his internal subjective state, the collective aggressor, whether angered by prior provocation or not, contributed to elevation of the aggression manifested by his group as a whole as well as to its accelerated pace of escalation over repeated trials—all in comparison with the aggression of the individual who acted alone. Considering the complexity of the phenomenon concerned, the phenomenology described here for the collective aggressor calls for refinement and completion in further research.

References

Bandura, A. (1973). *Aggression: A Social Learning Analysis*, Prentice-Hall, Englewood Cliffs, NJ.

Bandura, A., Underwood, B., and Fromson, M. E. (1975). 'Disinhibition of aggression through diffusion of responsibility and dehumanization of victims,' *Journal of Research in Personality*, **9**, 253–269.

Baron, R. A., and Bell, P. A. (1977). 'Sexual arousal and aggression by males: Effects of type of erotic stimuli and prior provocation,' *Journal of Personality and Social Psychology*, **35**, 79–87.

Buss, A. H. (1961). *The Psychology of Aggression*, Wiley, New York.

Diener, E. (1977). 'Deindividuation: Causes and consequences,' *Social Behavior and Personality*, **5**, 143–155.

Diener, E. (1980). 'Deindividuation,' in P. Paulus (ed.), *The Psychology of Group Influence*, Erlbaum, Hillsdale, NJ.

Diener, E., Dineen, J., Endresen, K., Beaman, A. L., and Fraser, S. C. (1975). :'Effects of altered responsibility, cognitive set, and modeling on physical aggression and deindividuation,' *Journal of Personality and Social Psychology*, **31**, 328–337.

Festinger, L., Pepitone, A., and Newcomb, T. (1952). 'Some consequences of deindividuation in a group,' *Journal of Abnormal and Social Psychology*, **47**, 382–389.

Jaffe, Y., Malamuth, N., Feingold, J., and Feshbach, S. (1974). 'Sexual arousal and behavioral aggression,' *Journal of Personality and Social Psychology*, **30**, 759–764.

Jaffe, Y., Shapir, N., and Yinon, Y. (1981). 'Aggression and its escalation in individuals and groups,' *Journal of Cross-Cultural Psychology*, **12**, 21–36.

Jaffe, Y., and Yinon, Y. (1979). 'Retaliatory aggression in individuals and groups,' *European Journal of Social Psychology*, **9**, 177–186.

Le Bon, G. (1903). *The Crowd: A Study of the Popular Mind*, Unwin, London.

Mathes, E. W., and Guest, T. A. (1976). 'Anonymity and group antisocial behavior,' *Journal of Social Psychology*, **100**, 257–262.

Mathes, E. W., and Kahn, A. (1975). 'Diffusion of responsibility and extreme behavior,' *Journal of Personality and Social Psychology*, **31**, 881–886.

Milgram, S., and Toch, H. (1969). 'Collective behavior: Crowds and social movements,' in G. Lindzey and E. Aronson (eds.), *The Handbook of Social Psychology*, Vol. 4, 2nd edn, Addison-Wesley, Reading, Mass.

Mynatt, C., and Sherman, S. J. (1975). 'Responsibility attribution in groups and individuals: A direct test of the diffusion of responsibility hypothesis,' *Journal of Personality and Social Psychology*, **32**, 1111–1118.

Scheier, M. F., Fenigstein, A., and Buss, A. H. (1974). 'Self-awareness and physical aggression,' *Journal of Experimental Social Psychology*, **10**, 264–273.

Singer, J. E., Brush, C. A., and Lublin, S. C. (1965). 'Some aspects of deindividuation: Identification and conformity,' *Journal of Experimental Social Psychology*, **1**, 356–378.

Yinon, Y., Jaffe, Y., and Ginzburg, S. (1981). *Physical Aggression in Individuals and Groups: Effects of Anonymity*. Manuscript submitted.

Zimbardo, P. G. (1969). 'The human choice: Individuation, reason, and order versus deindividuation, impulse, and chaos,' in W. J. Arnold and D. Levine (eds.), *Nebraska Symposium on Motivation, 1969*, University of Nebraska Press, Lincoln.

7 Friendship and Attraction

Small Groups and Social Interaction, Volume 1
Edited by H. H. Blumberg, A. P. Hare, V. Kent and M. Davies
Published by John Wiley & Sons Limited, 1983.

7.1 Similarity and Propinquity: Making Friends with 'Different' People*

Lucille Nahemow   *West Virginia University*

and

M. Powell Lawton   *Philadelphia Geriatric Center*

Introduction

The concept of social space was first articulated by Emile Durkheim (1893/1933) and developed by the geographer Maximilian Sorre (1943), who envisioned a collection of physical areas defined in terms of the perceptions of the inhabitants of the area. Social space was perceived in terms of visible features of the environment such as theaters and schools, by a group living in close physical propinquity.[1] Sorre conceived of the density of social space in terms of the interaction and consequent perceptual overlap between groups. Paul-Henri Chombart de Lauwe, a French sociologist, enlarged the concept of social space by distinguishing diverse dimensions such as geographic, economic, cultural, religious, and legal space (Chombart de Lauwe, 1966). The limit of the area comprising the individual's social space could be identified as the place in which groups of individuals could interact and move about with a feeling of comfort; beyond this area an individual would feel 'lost.'

Chombart de Lauwe conceived of a hierarchy of spaces within which certain kinds of interactions were likely to occur. These can be seen as a series of roughly concentric circles that constitute the differentiated social space of the individual (see Figure 1). First there is the *family space*, the area in which domestic interactions usually take place, then the *neighboring space*, involving local movement, then *economic space*, the area within which people move to and from work, and finally the *urban regional space*. These areas are seen as roughly corresponding to frequencies of occupancy. Family space is typically occupied on a daily basis,

---

*From L. Nahemow and M. P. Lawton (1975). 'Similarity and propinquity in friendship formation,' *Journal of Personality and Social Psychology*, **32**, 205–213. © 1975 by the American Psychological Association. Adapted by the authors; by permission of the publisher.

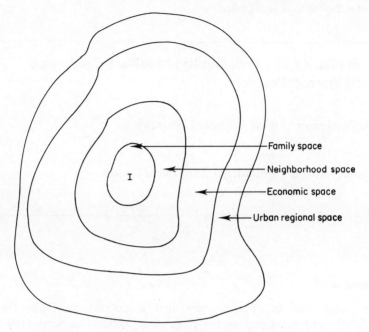

Figure 1   Chombert de Lauwe's model of social space

neighborhood and employment space on a regular but not necessarily daily basis, and finally urban regional space on an occasional basis (Buttimer, 1969).

Nahemow and Kogan (1971) developed an operational definition of the range of an individual's social space that encompassed the area within which people spent most of their lives. Social space was measured in terms of an individual's longest customary trip, *customary* meaning once a month or more. Thus the range of an individual's social space was defined as the longest trip taken each month averaged over a period of a year. Since it was found that people rarely knew the distance to a destination in miles, but almost always knew how long it took to get there, time spent in transit became the yardstick for measurement. Those with the most restricted social space took less than a 10 minute trip each month; those with an extended social space took at least one hour-long trip each month over the course of a year.

The concept of an individual's social space thus operationalized is very similar to Stea's (1969) 'home range,' and closely related to Hall's (1966) 'personal space' and Gelwick's (1970) 'life space.' We prefer the term *social space* because the concept developed from studies of human groupings in urban neighborhoods and does not imply a relationship to the instinctive behavior of other animals.

Several investigators found the range of social space to be limited for working-class people (Fried, 1963; Gans, 1962) and more extended for those with higher socioeconomic status (Adams, 1968; Wilmott and Young, 1960). In constrast, Nahemow and Kogan (1971) found that among retired persons in New York City, socioeconomic status was not related to the range of social space. This seemed to be due to the unusually low relationship between income and socioeconomic status based on previous occupation. With a few notable exceptions, elderly city dwellers are all poor. On the other hand, a major portion of the social space variance was predicted simply by the distance that the individual lived from his or her children and other relatives. Distance to children alone predicted nearly 10% of the social space variance.

This finding led us to think of social space as variable rather than fixed, and we began to ask questions about the factors that would serve to extend an individual's social space. We have all had the experience of 'moving out' toward the limits of our subjective comfort range. What are the things that make a person move out? For retired New Yorkers, visiting with children seems to be one. Children who have moved away from home attract parents to them.

What makes people attractive to one another? Over many years Byrne and his associates have found a linear relationship between attitudinal similarity and interpersonal attraction (Byrne, 1961b; Byrne and Griffitt, 1969; Byrne et al., 1969; Byrne and McGraw, 1964). They have also found evidence of remarkable sensitivity to the attitudes of others on relevant dimensions (Byrne et al., 1967). We postulate that when people are unacquainted they are likely to be more attracted to others whom they perceive as being like themselves. Status similarity usually bespeaks common fate as well as like-mindedness. Once we get to know another person we often find ourselves feeling less different from him or her than we did previously. Older people will frequently tell you that 'old friends are the best friends,' The question that we are posing is: Under what circumstances do people make friends of strangers? All things being equal there is a tendency to select friends among those of our own age and ethnic group.

In a national study of elderly people residing in public housing in the United States it was found that racially segregated sites were more conducive to on-site friendship formation than were racially integrated sites. The effect was greater for non-white than for white tenants, which could be explained simply by the fact that in racially integrated buildings non-whites were likely to be in the minority. When those integrated buildings in which the distribution of races was approximately equal were examined separately, it was found that black and white tenants made approximately the same number of friends. There were also interracial friendships in these buildings (Nahemow et al., 1976).

In his classic study of the acquaintance process in a college dormitory, Newcomb (1961) found the development of friendship highly dependent on common attitudes. Priest and Sawyer (1967), who studied developing friendships in four college residence towers, found that the better acquainted students became, the more likely they were to appreciate one another. Both investigators explained the interrelationship between attitudinal similarity, frequency of contact, and friendship in terms of balance theory. Brown (1968) conducted another study of friendship formation in a college dormitory. Students with either science or humanities majors were assigned rooms on floors in such a way that half were on floors in which four out of five students shared their college major and the other half were on floors in which only one in five shared their major. He found that those in the majority were more satisfied with both the college and their own major than those in the minority. Thus, residential closeness with like-minded others was found to make the adjustment to college life easier.

Newcomb found that proximity in the dormitory was important as a precursor to friendship only insofar as it promoted readiness of communication. However, there is considerable evidence from other investigations that propinquity is a very important determinant of friendship formation (Athanasiou and Yoshioka, 1973; Byrne, 1961a; Festinger, et al., 1960; Lawton and Simon, 1968). In a homogenous 'university village' Caplow and Forman (1950) found the proximity effect so marked that they noted 'the almost mechanical effect of accessibility on intimacy' (p. 366). People often reside in homogeneous neighborhoods where they perceive their neighbors as being like themselves. Lee (1968) found that people often defined their neighborhood as an area that contained 'people like us.' We posit that similarity attracts, particularly in the beginning stages of a friendship. The more attractive an individual finds another person, the further he will be willing to go to see him.

Figure 2 represents a theoretical model of the friendships an individual is expected to form with people perceived as being like himself or herself and people perceived as different. The individual is indicated by the letter I, those perceived as similar by a ●, and those perceived as dissimilar by a ○. The social space that is occupied on a daily basis is the *daily living space*; beyond that lies the *selected activity space*. D' represents the distance that an individual will travel to interact with persons like himself or herself; D represents the distance he or she will travel to meet those who are different. Within the daily living space I would be expected to make the acquaintance of both similar and dissimilar people. Beyond this range he or she will be more selective. In Figure 2 I would be expected to become acquainted with thirteen people—eleven similar and two dissimilar (all four people within the daily living space, but only those nine perceived as similar in the selected activity space). Both D and D' will vary from person to person. Both are expected to decrease when individual competence declines.

Let us formalize our expectations:

1. The greater the attractiveness of an other, the farther I will be willing to travel to meet him or her.
2. The shorter the distance between I and the other person, the less attractive that person must be for the trip to be undertaken.
3. Attractiveness increases as a function of perceived similarity.

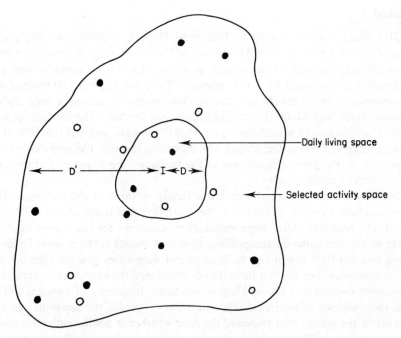

Figure 2   Differentiated social space. *I*, individual; ●, someone like himself; ○, someone unlike himself; *D*, distance *I* will travel to ○ (someone perceived as similar); *D'*, distance *I* will travel to ● (one perceived as dissimilar)

Thus the probability of contact is a function of the attractiveness of the other person and the distance separating the two. Typically, when people become elderly their social space constricts. When this occurs, the attractiveness/distance ratio must increase for contact to be made. This may result in the isolation of elderly persons who seem to be surrounded by potential friends.

In neighborhoods in which a small minority of the population is elderly, older people are likely to become isolated (Rosow, 1967) and unhappy (Bultena and Marshall, 1969). This is exacerbated by poor health (Gubrium, 1970) or low income (Rosenberg, 1970). Those who are old, poor, and sick are most likely to become cut off from others, particularly if they are surrounded by people who are different from themselves. In our society, where best friends are usually of the same age from nursery school on, it is very important that older people have easy access to age peers. However, this does not mean that they must be surrounded by nothing but age peers. It is hypothesized that as the boundaries of both daily living space and selected activity space constrict, in order for the older person to associate with *anyone* who is different from himself, the other person must reside in very close physical proximity.

Method

This study was conducted in Dyckman Houses, a public housing project located on the northern tip of Manhattan in New York City. It consists of seven 14-story buildings with 12 apartments to a floor. Each floor contains three one-bedroom units occupied by elderly persons. There are about 1,150 families with approximately three people per family. The project is almost evenly divided between black and white. It is for middle-income families: The average reported income per household was slightly over $7,000 per year, and less than 3% of the tenants received welfare. The project was about 20 years old. The interviewers were impressed by the general cleanliness of the buildings, the absence of graffiti, and the absence of noxious odors.

Interviews were attempted with every family in three of the buildings. They were conducted on the threshold of the apartment and required about 10 to 15 minutes to complete. After some introductory questions the interviewer said, 'I'm going to ask you some questions about your best friends in the project. I'd like to know whether they live in this building or not, how often you get together, and where you meet,' For the first three friends mentioned the interviewer recorded the apartment number and the building of residence, frequency of contact, and the age, race, and sex of the friend. The interviewer recorded the apparent age, race and sex of the person who answered the door whether or not the individual agreed to be interviewed. When people were not at home, interviewers called back at least four times at different times of the day. The interviewers were young white adults from the Philadelphia Geriatric Center and Sarah Lawrence College.

The identifying features of the tenants who were selected as friends were obtained in several ways. If a person had identified a friend who was interviewed, the friend's age, race, and sex were known. If the friend could not be interviewed and the apartment was identified, age of the occupant could be obtained from the management files, but not race, because of the confidentiality of those files. Sex could not usually be ascertained. If the friend was seen by an interviewer, even if he or she refused an interview, his or her age and race were recorded. Despite methodological difficulties, the approximate age and race of those reported as friends were more often known than unknown. As expected, there were fewer unknowns for age than for race. Age was known for 87% of the first-chosen friends and race for 72%. In all three buildings the number of reported friends for whom this information was available exceeded the number for whom it was unavailable. Sex of the friend chosen was known only when specifically mentioned by the chooser. In only one building did this exceed 50%. Consequently, analysis for this variable was limited to one building.

In all, 270 people were interviewed: 67% of the residents in each of two buildings and 47% of those in another. The distributions were approximately even across floors and apartment lines. When those who were interviewed were compared to those who were not interviewed with regard to number in household and age of head of household, no major differences were found.

Approximately the same number of people were considered old and young by the interviewers, with somewhat fewer labeled middle-aged. This was partly because of the nature of the tenants and partly because of the bias of the interviewers, who were instructed to favor the extreme categories. The interviewer's estimate of old, middle-aged, or young was compared with the actual ages of these people, using date of birth from the management records as the basis for comparison. The correspondence was very high. Those considered old had a mean age of 71 ($SD = 7.4$), the middle-aged averaged 45 years ($SD = 8.5$), and the young averaged 28 years ($SD = 7.3$).

About half of the residents were black, one-third white, and the remainder predominantly Puerto Rican.[2] There was a tendency for white people to be older and Puerto Ricans to be younger, which is characteristic of the city as a whole. However, nearly half of the old people were black, and at least some young people were white. In fact, Dyckman Houses were selected for study because there was a mixture of ages and races. Fifty-six percent of the interviews were conducted with women; the remaining 44% were with men or with a man and a woman. The ratio corresponds to that of tenants in Dyckman Houses.

Tenants had resided in Dyckman Houses for anywhere from a few months to 22 years. The mean length of residence was 10 years, reflecting a highly stable occupancy. However, in the last year the turnover was more than double that of any previous year, and the residents reflected a consequent feeling of discomfort. Several of the older white residents complained to the interviewers that the project was deteriorating, and more often than not such complaints had racial overtones.

Results

Friendship

The correlation between length of occupancy and number of reported friends was trivial after the first year. When asked where friendships were originally made, 52% volunteered that they met their current friends in the hallways, elevators, and entrance area of their own building, and 30% met on project grounds. Twenty-five percent met through their children or while actively engaged in child care. Only 11% met through an organized activity such as a senior citizens' club. From direct observation of people in outdoor spaces, it seemed as though contacts made there would be likely to occur within age categories. Typically, young mothers sat near the playground, whereas older people sought sunlit areas.

Frequency of contact was high. Nearly half of the sample visited the first-chosen friend daily. One-third visited the second-chosen friend daily, and a quarter visited the third-chosen friend daily as well. In 85% of the cases, friends met at least once a week; no differences were found between young, old, and middle-aged in this regard.

Old people averaged 1.9 friends ($SD = 1.5$), middle-aged 2.5 ($SD = 2.0$), and young people 2.4 ($SD = 1.6$); the difference did not reach statistical significance. Had we inquired about friendship beyond project grounds, we expect that this discrepancy would have been considerably greater. Nonetheless, it is noteworthy that older people, who are usually isolated in age-integrated housing, seem to have friends and know their neighbors in Dyckman Houses.

Proximity

Proximity proved to be a critical factor in the selection of friends. Of all first-chosen friends, 88% lived in the same building as the respondent, and nearly half lived on the respondent's own floor. The tendency to choose nearby friends diminished slightly for subsequent choices. (Forty-two percent of the second-named and 38% of the third-named friends resided on the respondent's floor.)

Contrary to our expectation, the proximity effect did not increase significantly with age, although there was a trend in that direction. Fifty percent of the old and 37% of the young chose first friends on the same floor: $\chi^2(2) = 2.65$. This was equally true for blacks and whites and for men and women. Thus the proximity effect appears to be a powerful force in friendship formation and operates for people of all ages, races, and for both sexes.

Similarity

Similarity proved to be an equally powerful predictor of friendship formation. Residents of Dyckman Houses usually chose friends within their own status category. Of all reported friends, 60% were of the same age category as the chooser and as many as 72% of all reported friends were of the same race. In the building where this information was available, 73% of reported choices were of the same sex. People's tendency to choose friends of their 'own kind' is so pronounced that it would be easy to lose sight of the important fact that a substantial minority of friendships did cross age and racial lines.

Table 1 Percentage of each age group choosing like, mixed, or different friends

Similarity of first-chosen friends (in age and race)	Percentage of choosers		
	Old ($n = 74$)	Middle-aged ($n = 45$)	Young ($n = 83$)
Alike	55	29	60
Mixed	30	47	25
Different	15	24	15

Note Old v. middle-aged: $\chi^2(2) = 7.56$, $p < .05$; young v. middle-aged: $\chi^2(2) = 11.50$, $p < .01$; old v. young: $\chi^2(2) = .62$. *ns*.

Table 1 shows the age and race characteristics of friendship choices by the three age groups. (If either age or race of the friend was unknown, the classification was based on the one that was known.) Once again the expected differences between young and old did not emerge. Old people were no more likely to choose friends like themselves than were young people. Both old and young people were more likely to select people like themselves as friends than were middle-aged people, which would be expected because the middle-aged are in between and therefore closer to both young and old than either are to each other. Consequently, the middle-aged served as an integrating force in the project.

Interaction between similarity and proximity

Table 2 compares friendship within age categories with those that occur between age categories. When a person chose a friend of a different age, the chances were that the person lived very close to the chooser. When the friend was of the same age, there was not as great a likelihood that their apartments were nearby.

When race was considered (Table 3), similar findings were obtained. Not only did whites tend to make friends with whites, blacks with blacks, and Puerto Ricans with Puerto Ricans, but they would go farther from home base to do so.

Table 2 Percentage of first-chosen friends by age and proximity

	Proximity of friend		
Similarity of age	Same floor	Different floor, same building	Different building
Same ($n = 119$)	43	42	13
Different ($n = 75$)	60	36	4

Note $\chi^2(2) = 7.18, p < .05.$

Table 3 Percentage of first-chosen friends by race and proximity

	Proximity of friend		
Similarity of race	Same floor	Different floor same building	Different building
Same ($n = 122$)	47	41	12
Different ($n = 39$)	69	31	0

Note $\chi^2(2) = 8.23, p < .05.$

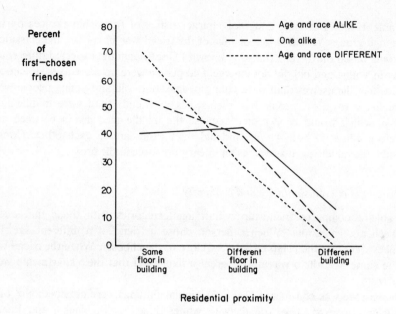

Figure 3   Similarity of age and race by residential proximity

In contrast, no significant relationship was found between the sex of friends and how close to one another they resided. This seems to reflect the obvious: when interpersonal attractiveness is an issue, gender operates differently from age and race.

When age and race were combined into an index of similarity (Figure 3), the inverse relationship between similarity and residential propinquity was even more pronounced and statistically highly significant, $\chi^2(4) = 14.26, p < .01$. Friendships between people of different ages and races existed almost exclusively among those who lived very close to one another. These people resided on the same floor 70% of the time. Friendships between people of the same age and race involved immediate neighbors less than half the time. Conversely, friends of different ages and races never resided in different buildings, but friends of the same age and race were in different buildings 12% of the time. This strong inverse relationship between similarity and proximity was demonstrated for second- and third-chosen friends as well.

Discussion

This study provided support for a differentiated theory of social space. It was demonstrated that friendship between dissimilar people was common only under conditions of close residential proximity, whereas friendship among people of the same age and race occurred at a greater distance. Thus the daily activity space proved to be the region within which people were likely to know everyone, whereas in the more extended selected activity space people were likely to reach out only to those whom they perceived as similar to themselves.

We are aware of the fact that age, race, and sex are not the only attributes that people have, nor are they by any means the most important basis for perceived similarity. Lee (1968) suggested that what people really mean when they define their neighborhood as containing 'people like myself' is that it is the region in which others 'live in houses like mine.' This may well be. It may also be true that most people define a similar other as a person who shares their values and attitudes, and the visible attributes of age, sex, and race are seen as a clue that a person will probably share these values. Thus, when blacks refer to another black as 'white under the skin,' they mean that the individual does not share the values of the black community.

Deutsch and Collins (1951) found that close physical proximity to members of another race under conditions of residential equality made for more positive attitudes towards members of the other group. Festinger and Kelley (1951) found that when a town had a black project forced on it, with no ameliorating social contact provided, attitudes toward blacks in general and project residents in particular remained negative. When community action programs were provided that (among other things) put people into closer physical contact with one another, attitudes improved. Proximity seems to be a necessary but not sufficient condition for people who initially perceive one another as different to begin to break down the resulting barriers. 'Different' people will most likely be ignored unless they are within the individual's daily living space.

The question arises concerning the appropriateness of the word *friend* to describe the associations between neighbors. Admittedly, *friend* means different things to different people. Nonetheless, the residents of Dyckman Houses were asked about their best friends in the project. A correlate of intimacy in friendship is frequency of contact, and in this case people usually saw one another several times a week. Using this as a criterion, there was no indication that similar persons were more intimate friends than dissimilar persons. Moreover, similar people were no more likely than others to be the first-chosen friend. It looks as though status similarity is important in making initial contact with people; thereafter, it diminishes in importance. Old friends come to see one another as less different, and in the most important sense, they become less different as they learn to understand one another's point of view.

The study did not provide support for the predictions that were based on the anticipated consequences of constriction of social space with aging. Within the project, there was little evidence that older people had fewer friends, that they had proportionately more friends who were like themselves, or that they had proportionately more proximal friends. Since the median age of the group was 72 years, this can not be attributed to relative youth. Therefore we must look for other personal or environmental considerations to explain these unexpected findings. We know that social space generally constricts with aging (Rawles, 1978).

However, a solid environmental support structure would be expected to have more impact on the maintenance of a rich lifestyle for elderly persons than for others who are less dependent on their immediate surroundings (Lawton and Simon, 1968).

One possible ameliorating factor is the stability and history of the project, in which the average length of residence is over 10 years.[3] Rosow (1967) found that when older people in an age-integrated community had long tenure and an established network of associations, they were likely to retain their social ties in that community. Another factor is the high proportion of elderly in the project, which seems to be near optimal for the maintenance of a network of social interaction.

It is important to note that young people were at least as likely to choose the elderly as friends as the elderly were to choose them. No evidence emerged to support the contention that older people will be ignored by the young. There was interaction between young and old and between black and white. It does not appear to be twice as difficult to overcome two difference barriers as it is to overcome one. This has enormous implications for housing elderly persons as well as for racially integrating communities.

Conclusion

People will travel greater distances and generally put themselves out to see those who are like themselves. However, social contacts with different kinds of people, which is one aspect of an enriched lifestyle, will only occur in the presence of environmental supports. Dyckman Houses appears to have some of those supports; there is a good age, race, and gender mix, and there are enough apartments in close propinquity so that each person has the possibility of running into at least 11 others on the way to the elevator.

Notes

1. A similar point of view is expressed by Lynch (1960).
2. For those who are bothered by the obvious illogic of this categorical breakdown, let us note that it is the one used by the management and readily comprehended by the tenants, who think of themselves in this way. Interviewers found it easy to use, though no doubt some errors were made.
3. This is typical of the elderly residents of New York City (Nahemow and Kogan, 1971) but it is not typical of most of the studies of elderly housing.

References

Adams, B. (1968). *Kinship in an Urban Setting*, Markham, Chicago.
Athanasiou, R., and Yoshioka, G. A. (1973). 'The spatial character of friendship formation,' *Environment and Behavior*, **5**, 43–65.
Brown, R. D. (1968). 'Manipulation of the environmental press in a college residence hall,' *Personnel and Guidance Journal*, **46**, 555–560.

Bultena, G. L., and Marshall, D. G. (1969). *Structural effects on the morale of the aged: A comparative analysis of age-segregated and age-integrated communities.* Paper presented at the meeting of the American Sociological Association, Chicago, September.

Buttimer, A. (1969). 'Social space in interdisciplinary perspective,' *Geographical Review*, **59**, 417–426.

Byrne, D. (1961a). 'The influence of propinquity and opportunities for interaction on classroom relationships,' *Human Relations*, **14**, 63–69.

Byrne, D. (1961b). 'Interpersonal attraction as a function of affiliation need and attitude similarity,' *Human Relations*, **14**, 283–289.

Byrne, D., and Griffitt, W. (1969). 'Similarity and awareness of similarity of personality characteristics as determinants of attraction,' *Journal of Experimental Research in Personality*, **3**, 179–186.

Byrne, D., Griffitt, W., Hudgins, W., and Reeves, K. (1969). 'Attitude similarity–dissimilarity and attraction: Generality beyond the college sophomore,' *Journal of Social Psychology*, **79**, 155–161.

Byrne, D., Griffitt, W., and Stefaniak, D. (1967). 'Attraction and similarity of personality characteristics,' *Journal of Personality and Social Psychology*, **5**, 82–90.

Byrne, D., and McGraw, C. (1964). 'Interpersonal attraction toward Negroes,' *Human Relations*, **17**, 201–213.

Caplow, T., and Forman, R. (1950). 'Neighborhood interaction in a homogeneous community,' *American Sociological Review*, **15**, 357–366.

Chombart de Lauwe, P. H. (1966). *Paris Essais de Sociologie, 1952–1954*, Éditions Ouvrières, Paris.

Deutsch, M., and Collins, M. E. (1951). *Interracial Housing: A Psychological Evaluation of a Social Experiment*, University of Minnesota Press, Minneapolis.

Durkheim, E. (1933). *The Division of Labor in Society*, Free Press, New York. (Originally published: Paris: Alcan, 1893.)

Festinger, L., and Kelley, H. H. (1951). *Changing Attitudes through Social Contact*, University of Michigan Press, Ann Arbor.

Festinger, L., Schachter, S., and Back, K. W. (1950). *Social Pressures in Informal Groups*, Harper, New York.

Fried, M. (1963). 'Grieving for a lost home,' in L. J. Duhl (ed.), *The Urban Condition*, Basic Books, New York.

Gans, H. (1962). *The Urban Villagers: A Group and Class in the Life of Italian–Americans*, Free Press, New York.

Gelwicks, L. E. (1970). 'Home range and use of space by an aging population,' in L. A. Pastalan and D. H. Carson (eds.), *The Spatial Behavior of Older People*. University of Michigan Institute of Gerontology, Ann Arbor.

Gubrium, J. F. (1970). 'Environmental effects on morale in old age and the resources of health and solvency,' *Gerontologist*, **10**, 294–297.

Hall, E. T. (1966). *The Hidden Dimension*, Doubleday, New York.

Lawton, M. P., and Nahemow, L. (1973). 'Ecology and the aging process,' in C. Eisdorfer and M. P. Lawton (eds.), *The Psychology of Adult Development and Aging*, American Psychological Association, Washington, DC.

Lawton, M. P., and Simon, B. B. (1968). 'The ecology of social relationships in housing for the elderly,' *Gerontologist*, **8**, 108–115.

Lee, T. (1968). 'The urban neighborhood as a socio-spatial schema,' *Human Relations*, **21**, 241–268.

Lynch, K. (1960). *The Image of the City*, MIT Press, Cambridge.

Nahemow, L., and Kogan, L. S. (1971). *Reduced fare for the elderly*, Mayor's Office for the Aging, (New York). (Mimeo).

Nahemow, L., Fulcomer, M., and Lawton, M. P. (1976). 'The effects of race and racial integration on the well-being of residents in elderly housing,' Paper presented at the 29th Annual Meeting of the Gerontological Society, New York City.

Newcomb, T. M. (1961). *The Acquaintance Process*, Holt, Rinehart & Winston, New York.

Priest, R. F., and Sawyer, J. (1967). 'Proximity and peership: Bases of balance in interpersonal attraction,' *American Journal of Sociology*, **72**, 633–649.

Rawles, G. D. (1978). *Prisoners of Space?* Westview Press, Boulder, CO.

Rosenberg, G. S. (1970). *The Worker Grows Old*, Jossey-Bass, San Francisco.

Rosow, I. (1967). *Social Integration of the Aged*, Free Press, New York.

Sorre, M. (1943). *Les Fondements de la Geographie Humanie* (3 vols.), Colin, Paris.

Stea, D. (1969). 'Environmental perception and cognition: Toward a model for "mental maps",' in G. J. Coates and K. M. Moffett (eds.), *Response to Environment*. Raleigh: School of Design, North Carolina State University, Raleigh.

Wilmott, P., and Young, M. (1960). *Family and Class in a London Suburb*, Routledge & Kegan Paul, London.

Small Groups and Social Interaction, Volume 1
Edited by H. H. Blumberg, A. P. Hare, V. Kent and M. Davies
Published by John Wiley & Sons Limited, 1983.

7.2 The Skills of Friendship*

Zick Rubin   *Brandeis University, Massachusetts*

I began this book [from which this extract is taken] with an account of two boys in the same preschool class—Ricky, who made many friends, and Danny, who made none. Ricky's greater ability to make friends could not have been predicted from the two boys' physical or intellectual characteristics. But Ricky had mastered to an impressive degree the social skills needed to establish and maintain friendships. These skills include the abilities to gain entry into group activities, to be approving and supportive of one's peers, to manage conflicts appropriately, and to exercise sensitivity and tact. They are subtle skills, by no means easy to learn, and the fact that most children ultimately succeed in acquiring them is itself one of the most remarkable aspects of social development.

Consider, first, the immediate problem confronting a child who enters a new group and wants to join other children in their play. During their first days in a new preschool setting, children frequently avoid their peers and instead hover nervously on the sidelines (McGrew, 1972; see also Putallaz and Gottman, 1981). As they become more familiar with their environment, the newcomers may try to approach other children. But these attempts—like Danny's—are not likely to succeed until the child has accumulated a repertoire of tactics for entering groups, complete with implicit rules about how and when a certain ploy can be used most effectively.

William Corsaro offers the following example of the 'access strategies' of 4-year-olds in nursery school:

> Two girls, Jenny and Betty, are playing around a sandbox in the

*Reprinted with permission from Zick Rubin (1980). *Children's Friendships*, Harvard University Press.

outside courtyard of the school. I am sitting on the ground near the sandbox watching. The girls are putting sand in pots, cupcake pans, bottles and teapots ... Another girl, Debbie, approaches and stands near me observing the other two girls. Neither Jenny nor Betty acknowledges her presence. Debbie does not speak to me or the other girls, and no one speaks to her. After watching for some time (5 minutes or so) she circles the sandbox three times and stops again and stands near me. After a few more minutes of watching, Debbie moves to the sandbox and reaches for a teapot in the sand. Jenny takes the pot away from Debbie and mumbles, 'No.' Debbie backs away and again stands near me observing the activity of Jenny and Betty. Then she walks over next to Betty, who is filling the cupcake pan with sand. Debbie watches Betty for just a few seconds, then says: 'We're friends, right? We're friends, right, Betty?'

Betty, not looking up at Debbie and while continuing to place sand in the pan, says, 'Right.'

'I'm making coffee,' Debbie says to Betty.

'I'm making cupcakes,' Betty replies.

Betty turns to Jenny and says, 'We're mothers, right, Jenny?'

Jenny replies, 'Right.'

The three 'mothers' continue to play together for twenty more minutes, until the teachers announce cleanup time (Corsaro, 1979).

Debbie's persistent effort to join the group illustrates a variety of strategies. At first Debbie merely places herself in the area of the interaction, a strategy that Corsaro calls 'nonverbal entry'. When this tactic gets no response, Debbie proceeds to 'encircle' the area. When this strategy, too, is ignored, she enters the area directly and produces 'similar behaviour' (she picks up a teapot). And when this attempt is rebuffed, Debbie switches to a verbal strategy, making a direct 'reference to affiliation' ('We're friends, right?'). After Betty responds positively to this move, Debbie once again produces behaviour similar to that of the others, this time explicitly describing it ('I'm making coffee'). At this point, Debbie's attempt to join the group finally succeeds. Betty responds in a way that includes Debbie in the activity ('We're mothers'), and the three now play together for some time.

Corsaro notes that nursery school children rarely use more direct verbal access strategies, such as saying 'Hi', 'What ya doing?' or 'Can I play?' One likely reason is that such direct approaches call for a direct response by the approached children, and this response is very likely to be negative. Once two or more children have structured and defined for themselves a particular activity, whether it is making cupcakes or blasting off in a spaceship, they often 'protect' their activity by excluding any outsiders who might dare to request entry. Sometimes this exclusive stance is established even before the activity begins. For example:

(David, Josh, and Jonah are in the sandbox together.)
David (to Josh): Will you help me make some soup?
Josh: Yea—and Jonah can't play, right?

Unless the 'outsider' is already a highly accepted group member who has special rights of entry, young children will frequently refuse him admission. A 'Hi' may be ignored, a 'What ya doing?' responded to with 'We're making cupcakes and you're not', and a direct 'Can I play?' answered with an equally direct 'No'. To enter the activity, therefore, the child may have to be cautious and subtle, like Debbie. By first reconnoitring the situation unobtrusively, then quietly joining in the ongoing activity, and finally making direct verbal statements—including the ingratiating 'We're friends, right?'—Debbie was able to include herself in Betty and Jenny's activity without mobilizing their resistance.

On the other hand, direct approaches may be more effective when the child wants to engage a single other child who is not already involved in a group activity. And as children grow older, specific verbal formulas for initiating interaction become more important. In a study of eight- and nine-year-olds, John Gottman and his co-workers asked children to pretend that the researcher was a new child in the class with whom they wanted to make friends (Gottman *et al.*, 1975). From the children's performance in this role-play situation, the researchers were able to assess their knowledge of friendship-making tactics. Offering greetings ('Hi, Mary'), offering appropriate information ('My favourite sport is basketball'), requesting information ('Where do you live?'), and extending invitations ('Wanna come over to my house some time?') were all scored as reflecting the child's knowledge of how to make friends. The researchers then compared these social-knowledge scores with popularity ratings derived from questions asked of all class members. They found, not surprisingly, that popular children knew more about how to make friends than unpopular children did.

'Knowing how' to make friends is no guarantee of social success, however. Some children may excel on a role-play test of social skills but at the same time may be unable or unwilling to put these skills to practical use. For example, an experience with rejection may lead some children to avoid approaching others for long periods of time; other children will bounce back from rejection much more easily. As Carol Dweck and Therese Goetz suggest, the difference in reactions may depend on the child's personal explanation of a rejection (Dweck and Goetz, 1978). Some children tend to blame any rejection on their own inadequacies ('I'm just a shy person') and, as a result, do not feel that the problem can be overcome. Other children will attribute the same rejection to temporary moods or misunderstandings ('Maybe her mother yelled at her that morning') and will persist in their efforts to gain acceptance. In this comparison, it is the resilient child who is more likely to establish friendships.

The skills of friendship include not only the ability to gain entry into group activities, but also the ability to *be* a friend—an attentive, approving, and helpful playmate and associate. Even in the first year of life, children have distinctive styles of interaction that can make them agreeable or disagreeable to their peers. Lee C. Lee observed a daycare group of five infants in Ithaca, New York, for a period of six months, beginning when the infants were all about nine months old (Lee, 1973). She found that one of the infants, Jenny, was by far the best-liked member of the group; throughout the six-month period, each of the other four babies approached her most often. Patrick was the least-liked group member; he was approached least often by three of the other four infants. On the basis of detailed observations of each baby, Lee was able to paint a picture of their contrasting styles of interaction. Jenny was a responsive, adaptive social partner. She displayed a range of emotions in her social encounters. And she seldom terminated social contacts that had been initiated by others. Patrick, on the other hand, was a belligerent and unfriendly baby. He frequently grabbed others and was reluctant to end encounters that he had initiated. But when others initiated contacts with him, he was passive and unresponsive. Patrick did not smile, laugh, or otherwise display positive feelings in a single one of the occasions in which he was contacted by another baby. To put it bluntly, Patrick was no fun. Not surprisingly, in light of their differing styles of response, Jenny continued to be approached by other babies while Patrick was shunned.

There is no strong reason to believe that such differences in the 'likeability' of infants are likely to persist past the second year of life. As children grow older, however, they become capable of producing a wider range of behaviour that may be either rewarding or unrewarding to their peers. In extensive observations of nursery school children, Willard Hartup and his colleagues at the University of Minnesota found that the most popular children—those whom their classmates enjoyed playing with most—were also the ones who most often paid attention to other children, praised them, showed affection, and willingly acceded to their requests. Children who frequently ignored others, refused to cooperate, ridiculed, blamed, or threatened others were most likely to be disliked by their classmates (Hartup *et al.*, 1967). In short, for a child to be included and accepted, he must also include and accept.

Again, Ricky epitomizes such an inclusive and accepting child. He is an engaging, supportive boy who goes out of his way to involve others in his activities. When Caleb comes out to the big rotating swing, which already has four children on board, Ricky immediately shouts to him, 'You can get on it!' 'It's crowded,' Caleb shouts back. In Ricky's view of things, however, there is always room for one more. 'Someone else wants to get on,' he informs his fellow riders. Then he takes charge of slowing down the swing and shows Caleb where he can climb on. Ricky is a skilful social facilitator, and others like him for it.

It is important to stress, however, that 'friendly' behaviour does not always win friendship. Whether an affectionate act is in fact experienced as rewarding will depend on *how* the affection is expressed and, most important, how it is interpreted by the recipient. While some children must learn to be more outgoing, others must learn to stop 'coming on too strong.' At the beginning of the year, Fiona would regularly run up to other children and hug them effusively. She discovered, to her dismay, that this display of affection usually frightened off the others. She eventually learned that she could do better by approaching others more subtly—for example, by patting them on the arm and suggesting an activity.

What may be, for one child, a show of friendship is not necessarily viewed that way by another. Even gift giving can backfire, if the recipient attributes ignoble motives to the giver. Ann, who began to interact with other children only late in the school year, gave Craig a paper envelope she had made, as a gesture of friendship. Later Craig tells me, 'I'm not going to take it home because it doesn't have a drawing.' 'Why do you think Ann gave it to you?' I ask. 'I don't know. Maybe she doesn't like it either.' Moreover, the same overt behaviour can be regarded as rewarding if it comes from a child one already likes and unrewarding if it comes from a child one already has doubts about. 'I'll tell you why I don't like David,' Rachel explains to me. 'Because he screams around all sorts of places. But I don't mind if Steven screams because he just screams a little bit.'

Studies of nursery school children have also indicated that the best-liked children are not highly dependent on teachers (Moore, 1967). Ricky often chatted amiably with teachers and generally followed their instructions, but only rarely went to a teacher for help in dealing with routine matters. Danny, in contrast, frequently called for help in a whiny tone of voice and would cry for the teacher whenever he received a minor injury or rebuff. Ricky's lesser dependence on teachers was almost certainly related to his greater ability to be supportive of his classmates. When a child must constantly turn to adults for support and assistance, he is unlikely to have the emotional resources necessary to be rewarding to his peers.

The skills of friendship also include the ability to manage conflicts successfully. Children learn that it is often valuable to talk out their hurt feelings in order to restore goodwill. While playing fireman, for example, Josh and Tony managed to offend each other. After a period of sullen silence, the following conversation ensued:

Josh: I'm not going to be your friend, Tony. You're talking mean to me so I'm not going to be your friend.
Tony: You're talking mean to *me*.
Josh: You're calling me names—Bloody Boy, Fire Boy.
Tony: Well, you're not letting me and David play by ourselves.

Once they put these feelings on the table, Josh and Tony quickly restored harmony. 'I can be a fireboy in the fireman game,' Josh declares. 'Let him spray out fires,' Tony orders his other fireman.

In order to maintain friendships in the face of the disagreements that inevitably arise, children must learn to express their own rights and feelings clearly while remaining sensitive to the rights and feelings of others. They must be able to suggest and to accept reasonable compromises, even as they stand up against unreasonable demands. As S. Holly Stocking and Diana Arezzo note, different children may start in different places in their quest for the ability to manage conflict appropriately:

> The overly aggressive child ... may need to learn how to listen to others without interrupting or putting them down, and how to accept reasonable disagreement gracefully, without anger or attack. The overly submissive child, in turn, may have to learn how to stand up for himself with a definite posture and a calm tone of voice that communicates conviction [Stocking and Arezzo, 1979].

As children become more sensitive to the feelings of their peers, they also learn the subtle skills of tact that are needed to maintain friendships. Even four-year-olds may begin to display such tact, especially in the context of close friendships. When Tony took his pants off to go swimming, for example, his best friend David inadvertently burst into laughter. But a moment later, David turned to Tony and assured him, 'I'm not laughing at you, Tony. I'm laughing at Neil.' Although this explanation may have involved a white lie on David's part, it also illustrates his sensitivity to his friend's feelings and his ability to act in such a way as to protect them.

I observed a particularly striking example of tact among four-year-olds in the following conversation between David and Josh, who were walking together and pretending to be robots:

> *David*: I'm a missile robot who can shoot missiles out of my fingers. I can shoot them out of everywhere—even out of my legs. I'm a missile robot.
> *Josh* (tauntingly): No, you're a fart robot.
> *David* (protestingly): No, I'm a missile robot.
> *Josh*: No, you're a fart robot.
> *David* (hurt, almost in tears): No, Josh!
> *Josh* (recognizing that David is upset): And I'm a poo-poo robot.
> *David* (in good spirits again): I'm a pee-pee robot.

As in the case of the interaction between David and Tony, Josh realized that he had said something ('you're a fart robot') that greatly distressed his friend. He handled the situation resourcefully by putting himself down as well ('I'm a poo-poo robot'), thus demonstrating that his insult was not to be taken seriously. David's response to Josh's move ('I'm a pee-pee robot') indicates that Josh had appraised the situation accurately and had successfully saved his friend's feelings.

Acquiring the skills of friendship can be a difficult struggle for the pre-school child, especially if he has not had much previous experience in interacting with other children of his own age without direct adult supervision. Nursery schools often serve as valuable proving grounds for the development of such skills. Although the learning may sometimes be painful or frustrating, children gradually develop both more sophisticated concepts of friendship and more sophisticated techniques for establishing and maintaining such friendships for themselves. The development of communication skills through interaction with one's peers may itself be an important prerequisite for the acquisition of skills specifically related to friendship. In this connection, Danny, who had doting parents but little experience with children of his own age before entering nursery school, probably suffered in his attempts at making friends because of his relatively undeveloped powers of communication. Ricky, in contrast, lived in the same household as several cousins of varying ages and had developed communication skills of an unusually high order. With additional experience, as it turned out, Danny, too, became more successful at making friends. When I revisited him a year after I had concluded my observations of the class, I found that he was interacting much more successfully and was sought out by several of his classmates.

Children, then, acquire social skills not so much from adults as from their interaction with one another. They are likely to discover through trial and error which strategies work and which do not, and later to reflect consciously on what they have learned. While playing with blocks one day, four-year-old Alex remarked to his teacher, 'Remember that day when I gave Colin a truck he needed? That was a very nice thing to do, don't you think, Miss Beyer?' (Beyer, 1956). Children also learn social skills from the direct tutelage or examples provided by their peers. When David whines, 'Gary pushed me,' for example, Josh firmly advises him, 'Just say stop.' In other instances, children introduce their friends to one another, help others to launch joint activities, or show others how to resolve their conflicts. Rachel is one child who is successful, in her own soft-spoken way, in promoting good feelings among other children. For example, she serves as timekeeper while several other children take turns standing in a special hiding place. When Claudia occupies the space before it is her turn, Rachel calls her back to the table where the timekeeper's hourglass is kept and gently explains, 'Here, Claudia—when it goes all the way through there it's your turn, all right?' When all the sand has trickled through, Rachel happily informs Claudia that her turn has come, and lets Alison know that her time has run out. One suspects that such advice and assistance from respected peers may often be more effective than similar interventions by teachers or parents.

There are also cases, however, when children need help from adults in mastering particular skills of friendship. When children wish to make friends but lack the skills to do so, vicious circles can be set in motion. The friendless child must interact with his peers in order to develop the self-confidence and skills needed for social success. But his lack of social skills—for example, the inability to approach other children or the tendency to scare them off—may cut him off from just such opportunities. In such cases, intervention by parents or teachers may be necessary. One approach is to steer a friendless child to a particular other child—sometimes one who also lacks friends—with whom the adult thinks the child might hit it off. In at least some cases, such matchmaking can help to give two withdrawn children an initial and valuable experience of social acceptance. Another tactic, ... is to pair an older child who is too competitive or aggressive with a younger child to whom he can relate as a 'big brother'—and, in the process, learn that he can win the approval of others without being a bully (see Furman *et al.*, 1979).

Psychologists have also developed a variety of training programmes for both pre-school and school-age children. In such programmes, children who have been identified as isolates or outcasts are given a series of sessions which may include demonstrations of specific social skills, opportunities to practise them, and feedback on their performance. In at least some cases, these programmes have been notably successful in increasing the social acceptance of initially isolated children (for a review of such programmes, see Combs and Slaby, 1977; see also Oden and Asher, 1977).

Because training programmes tend to be focused on increasing 'social acceptance' or 'popularity', they bring up some troublesome questions of values. Do the programmes really help children develop the capacity for friendship, or are they geared to some 'American' ideal of glib sociability and congeniality that has little to do with real friendship at all? The answer to this question depends both on the details of the programme and on the values of the adults who administer it. In the view of at least some leading practitioners, however, 'The objective of social skills instruction is not to create "popular" or "outgoing" children, but to help youngsters, whatever their personality styles, to develop positive relationships ... with at least one or two other children.' (Stocking and Arezzo, 1979). One can also ask whether it is ethically acceptable to impose social skills training on children who have little choice in the matter and who in some instances may not really want to be changed into 'friendlier' people. In the last analysis, though, the most compelling defence for such programmes is that they may be able to increase the child's degree of control over her own life. As Melinda Combs and Diana Arezzo Slaby note, 'A child who has the skills to initiate play and communicate with peers may still choose to spend a good deal of time alone. But that child will be able to interact effectively when she (he) wants to or when the situation requires it. On the other hand, a socially unskilled child may be alone or "isolated" out of necessity rather than by choice.' (Combs and Slaby, 1977, p. 165).

Even without instituting formal training, parents and teachers can make use of similar demonstrations, explanations, and feedback in order to teach the skills of friendship in school or home settings. In making use of such procedures, however, adults must be sensitive to the fine line that exists between help and interference.

Although adults have a role to play in teaching social skills to children, it is often best that they play it unobtrusively. In particular, adults must guard against embarrassing unskilled children by correcting them too publicly and against labelling children as shy in ways that may lead the children to see themselves in just that way (see Zimbardo, 1977, especially Ch. 4 'Parents, Teachers, and Shy Children').

Rather than 'pushing' social skills indiscriminately, adults should respect the real differences between children that motivate some to establish friendly relations with many others, some to concentrate on one or two close friendships, and some to spend a good deal of time by themselves. Children's friendships take many forms and involve different styles of interaction. In our efforts to help children make friends, we should be more concerned with the quality of these friendships than with their quantity.

Adults must also recognize that there are many personal attributes, some of them relatively immutable, which are likely to affect the way a child is viewed by his peers in a particular setting, including physical appearance, athletic prowess, intellectual abilities, and family background (see, for example, Dion and Berscheid, 1974; McCraw and Tolbert, 1953; Asher et al., 1977). As a result, different children may be best equipped with somewhat different skills of friendship. Finally, adults must be sensitive to events in children's lives that may underlie problems with making and keeping friends. Moving to a new school or neighbourhood may create special difficulties, and so may stressful family events such as divorce (see Hetherington et al., 1979). For the most part, as we have seen, children learn the skills of friendship not from adults but from each other. But parents and teachers who are sensitive to individual children's distinctive needs and circumstances can play a crucial role in facilitating this learning.

References

Asher, S. R., Oden, S. L., and Gottman, J. M. (1977). 'Children's friendships in school settings,' in L. G. Katz (ed.), *Current Topics in Early Childhood Education*, Vol. 1, Ablex, Norwood, NJ.

Beyer, E. (1956). 'Observing children in nursery school situations,' in L. B. Murphy, *Personality in Young Children*, Basic Books, New York.

Combs, M. L., and Slaby, D. A. (1977). 'Social-skills training with children,' in B. B. Lahey and A. E. Kazdin (eds.), *Advances in Clinical Child Psychology*, Vol. 1, Plenum, New York.

Corsaro, W. A. (1979). ' "We're friends, right?": Children's use of access rituals in a nursery school,' *Language in Society*, **8**, 315–336.

Dion, K. K., and Berscheid, E. (1974). 'Physical attractiveness and peer perception among children,' *Sociometry*, **37**, 1–12.

Dweck, C. S., and Goetz, T. E. (1978). 'Attributions and learned helplessness,' in J. H. Harvey, W. Ickes, and R. F. Kidd (eds.), *New Directions in Attribution Research*, Vol. 2, Lawrence Erlbaum Associates, Hillsdale, NJ.

Furman, W., Rahe, D. F., and Hartup, W. W. (1979). 'Rehabilitation of socially-withdrawn preschool children through mixed-age and same-age socialization,' *Child Development*, **50**, 915–922.

Gottman, J. M., Gonso, J., and Rasmussen, M. (1975). 'Social interaction, social competence, and friendship in children,' *Child Development*, **46**, 709–718.

Hartup, W. W., Glazer, J. A., and Charlesworth, R. (1967). 'Peer reinforcement and sociometric status,' *Child Development*, **38**, 1017–1024.

Hetherington, E. M., Cox, M., and Cox, R. (1979). 'Play and social interaction in children following divorce,' *Journal of Social Issues*, **35**(4), 26–49.

Lee, L. C. (1973). 'Social encounters of infants: The beginnings of popularity,' paper presented to the International Society for the Study of Behavioral Development, Ann Arbor, Michigan, August, 1973.

McCraw, L. W., and Tolbert, J. W. (1953). 'Sociometric status and athletic ability of junior high school boys,' *The Research Quarterly*, **24**, 72–80.

McGrew, W. C. (1972). *An Ethological Study of Children's Behavior*, Academic Press, New York.

Moore, S. (1967). 'Correlates of peer acceptance in nursery school children,' *Young Children*, **22**, 281–297.

Oden, S., and Asher, S. R. (1977). 'Coaching children in social skills for friendship making,' *Child Development*, **48**, 495–506.

Putallaz, M., and Gottman J. M. (1981). 'Social skills and group acceptance,' in S. R. Asher and J. M. Gottman (eds.), *The Development of Children's Friendships*, Cambridge University Press, New York.

Stocking, S. H., and Arezzo, D. (1979). *Helping Friendless Children: A Guide for Teachers and Parents*, Boys Town Center for the Study of Youth Development, Boys Town, Nebraska.

Zimbardo, P. G. (1977). *Shyness*, Addison-Wesley, Reading, Mass.

Small Groups and Social Interaction, Volume 1
Edited by H. H. Blumberg, A. P. Hare, V. Kent and M. Davies
Published by John Wiley & Sons Limited, 1983.

7.3 Men and Women*

Carlfred B. Broderick   *University of Southern California*

We live today in a ferment of conflicting views about how men and women ought to relate to each other. Traditional marriage has been under attack as not well suited to the times, as inconsistent with contemporary life. Many explanations are offered for these changes, but at least one of the larger social and intellectual movements of our time, what might be called the existential revolution, has played a major role. Existential thought has swept through this century like a tidal wave. It has fueled the civil rights movement, the women's movement, the sexual revolution, the peace movement, the environmental movement, and the phenomenal growth of interest in Oriental religions. It has probably contributed to some less constructive social developments, such as the widespread use of drugs. It has profoundly influenced every aspect of our culture: philosophy and theology, political theory and therapy, arts and literature.

Few contemporary Americans are untouched by the existential perspective, and many couples have adopted existential values with wholehearted enthusiasm. Others, fearing they may be destructive of familial and societal stability, reject them. The majority of people are probably somewhere in the middle; they incorporate elements selectively into their own versions of the ideal relationship. As I survey the mountains of rhetoric that have been generated by the confrontation between these conflicting views, it seems to me that the general dispute can be broken down into three different but related subissues:

1.   Ought man–woman relationships to have as their chief aim the protection and

*This is a revised version of Carlfred B. Broderick, *Marriage and the Family*, © 1979, pp. 27–48 (Ch. 3). Adapted by permission of Prentice-Hall, Inc., Englewood Cliffs, NJ. The original version of this paper deals with two additional issues: child-free v. child-centered and role-free v. role-bound relationships.

enhancement of the partner's freedom, growth, and personal fulfillment, or is the greatest good served when the partners invest rather in the relationship itself, sacrificing, if necessary, their own needs for the good of the union?

2. Is the best relationship one which leaves the partners a relatively painless exit should they change their feelings, or is it best to value long-term commitments and security?

3. Is it more desirable to strive to extend love, affection, and intimacy to the widest possible circle or to jealously guard an exclusive, lifelong relationship?

Every couple can probably place themselves somewhere on a continuum between the existential and traditional viewpoints with respect to each of these issues. Let us look in greater detail at several positions along this continuum.

Personal growth versus sacrificial commitment

The self-actualizing couple

Growth-oriented couples have as their chief object the sponsoring of each member's achievement of his or her greatest human potential. This is also called the pursuit of self-actualization. The relationship itself is valued only so long as it contributes to this goal. It is understood from the beginning that if either partner feels that the relationship has become stifling, oppressive, or stagnant, it should be dissolved and the members freed to pursue their separate destinies.

In a society such as ours, which puts a great premium on marriage, these couples face something of a dilemma. They may deal with the pressures in various ways. For the sake of parents and friends of more traditional orientation, they may submit to a conventional wedding ceremony but make it clear between themselves that they take their vows with existential reservations. Another option is to write their own ceremony, incorporating into it their own philosophy of marriage. They may, for example, promise to live together as long as they both shall love.

A more thoroughly existential option is to live together without any formal vows at all. The increasing popularity of this option warrants a separate discussion here.

Living together. The notion that the best of all possible arrangements between a man and a woman is one involving the fewest possible conditions or commitments is not new. At one time the chief advocates of this view were bohemians of either sex and independent-minded men. Today, this view is much more broadly based. Many people see an open-ended relationship as more honest and sincere, since neither partner is constrained to stay any longer than he or she want to. It avoids involving third parties (ministers, county registrars, lawyers, courts) in decisions to live together or to leave. It anticipates that individuals may grow at different rates and in different directions, so that a great 'fit' at one point may become a great 'misfit' at another. Moreover, many individuals are in situations in school or work where they may need to be ready to move at short notice in order to take advantage of job openings in distant places. Or the people involved may simply not be ready to 'settle down.'

In many cases, couples who begin with this philosophy eventually change their minds and marry. Others, however, appear to be deeply committed to this position and unlikely to change (Macklin, 1978).

On the face of it, living together represents an acting out of existential values by a substantial minority of men and women in our society. In reviewing all the studies of cohabiting college students, however, Macklin (1978) notes that these apparently liberated relationships are likely to be conducted according to more traditional values than one might expect. For example, most reported limiting their sexual life to the relationship as a token of their commitment to each other even though they did not feel obligated to do so. The same review suggests that breaking up long-term cohabitation is only marginally less painful than breaking up a marriage. Thus even living together is often a mixed position, exhibiting elements of both existential and traditional values.

Marriage as an enduring institution

Those who are committed to a traditional view of marriage are less concerned with marital enrichment and individual self-actualization than with marital success. Success, in turn, is defined as fulfilling one's expectations for being a 'good' wife and mother, a 'good' husband and father. Naturally, there are some variations in the criteria for 'good,' but we can sketch a rough outline of the traditional successful marriage.

The successful husband is, first of all, a good and responsible provider. He supplies his family with all the advantages his socioeconomic status permits: a good home equipped with a reasonable number of labor-saving devices and recreational equipment, a car, adequate medical and dental care, a good education for the children. As a husband he is strong and capable of making decisions but also gentle, emotionally supportive, and personally devoted to his wife. For her part, the wife should be a first-class homemaker, practical nutritionist, and therapist–nurse to her family. She should provide the members with a physical environment which is neither compulsively neat nor irresponsibly messy. She is supposed to be a good manager of time, space, and money. As a mother, she is informed about the essentials of child development and practical psychology. She is warm and loving, but not permissive. As a wife she is equally warm and supportive—and also sexy. Both husband and wife place the family, its welfare and future, above any self-centered considerations. Sacrifice is the ultimate virtue; the ultimate failure is divorce.

There are, of course, many versions of the traditional model for the ideal man–woman relationship. But, because it is so integral a part of our culture, for the most part the traditional view is reflected in quite ordinary ways. For example, the same family section of the Sunday paper may have an article on the new liberated woman, one on how to teach children to read, one on how to prepare duck *à l'orange* for 14, another on how to get old wax up with the least effort, and still another on how to keep your husband interested even though you may have reached that 'certain age.' Traditional values, despite the inroads of competing views and all the changes, are still very much a part of American life.

Permanent availability versus permanent commitment

The American marital system, compared to systems in other cultures, has been described by sociologist Bernard Farber (1973) as typified by permanent availability. In America the divorce rate is so high that married people are not permanently, or even currently, out of the courtship market. Farber argues that contemporary US marriages are so fragile that anyone is fair game, married or not. He or she can always get a divorce and be available to marry in a few months. If the object is not marriage but some less demanding relationship, there are even fewer obstacles. But like all other positions on relationships, there is more than one current and common view. Let us look at three possibilities: open options, disposable marriage, and lifelong commitment.

Open options

Everyone goes through periods in life when he or she is 'footloose and fancy free'—and many believe this is also the best way to stay. These are not social isolates but those who feel that man–woman relationships are best when they are open, without any promises for the future. This keeps all one's options open, avoids encumbering one's life with obligations, and yet does not preclude intimacy or love. It does require that each partner live each moment for itself and not permit him or herself the luxury of planning the future around the relationship. Aldous Huxley conceived of such a world in his classic anti-Utopian novel, *Brave New World* (1937), but in this case more permanent liaisons were seen as a threat to the all-powerful state and so were actively discouraged. Clearly this is not what contemporary advocates of this position have in mind; they see open options as enhancing individual freedom.

It has been suggested that short-term (for example 3- or 5-year) marriage contracts with an option for renewal might serve our society well. Such an arrangement would reduce the uncertainty of no-commitment relationships and yet avoid both the emotionally costly experience of a long-term empty marriage or a painful and financially devastating divorce. One variant suggestion is that if the short contract arrangement worked out well, the couple might exercise the option for a lifelong contract.

Disposable marriage: serial monogamy

In our society, anybody who wishes to can end one marriage and try another. And as we have seen, about two out of five do just that. There is much evidence that this is rapidly becoming the officially approved position in our culture. For one thing, the divorce rate keeps climbing and has already reached a level that puts us in a class by ourselves among the nations of the world. For another, a growing number of states have followed California's lead and instituted no-fault divorce laws. In those states, virtually anyone who wants a divorce for any reason can have one. Even states with traditional divorce laws that technically require one partner to have committed a sin against the marriage (such as adultery, desertion, or cruelty) have established grounds such as mental cruelty or incompatibility which make divorce relatively easy to get. Increasingly, the judge's main function is to preside over the division of property according to some predetermined formula and to assign custody of the children.

In some ways serial monogamy combines the best of both extremes. It begins with a promise to stay together forever and actually delivers on that promise much of the time. But everyone knows, even as he or she promises to 'love, honor, and cherish till death do us part,' that there is a relatively easy exit close at hand. This is not to suggest that divorce is ever painless, but that many people find it less painful than staying married.

Lifelong commitment

This traditional position is still the ideal of most Americans, even those who divorce. It is also the actual experience of most people, for the idea of relationships enduring forever is deeply embedded in our culture and in legend and myth. Roman Catholics and members of some other religious groups are formally committed to lifelong marriage as the only acceptable position, and in those faiths divorced persons are prohibited from remarriage so long as their former spouse is living. So far as I know only one religious group, the Mormons, teach that marital and family ties extend beyond death.

Those who hold the view that marriage is or should be permanent are likely also to hold that the belief itself is one of the strongest motivators for marital endurance. They believe that if a couple knows they will be together for the duration, they will compromise more readily, forgive more quickly, and work harder at solving problems. Such couples also have a greater feeling of security and a willingness to take on long-term projects such as having or adopting children, investing in joint business ventures or in each other's education, and so forth. On the negative side, their sense of permanence might also result in taking each other for granted, since there is little fear of one's partner leaving the relationship.

Inclusivity versus exclusivity

One of the most hotly contested issues in the debates between existentialists and traditionalists is the question of how exclusive the marital relationship ought to be. On one side are those who feel that the most demanding, rewarding, and growth-producing arrangements are the most open ones. On the other side are those who value privacy, fidelity, and exclusivity. It appears that while there may be relatively few ways to be exclusive, the number of ways to be inclusive are limited only by the resourcefulness of the couple. Let us look at a few.

Multilateral marriage

Marriage among three or more persons is held by its practitioners to be the ultimate expression of interpersonal maturity and openness. Everyone in a group is not married to everyone else, but each person is married to at least two other persons (Constantine and Constantine, 1971, 1973). This arrangement is seen as providing a broader base of intimate companionship within marriage. In particular, it includes unusual opportunity for closeness with adult members of one's own sex. Sexual life is enriched with variety in the context of commitment, and children receive the benefits of multiple parenting. Finally, the whole group can function as an ongoing encounter session with a unique combination of group support and group pressure for change.

The trouble with group marriage is that it makes heavy demands on individuals' discipline and selflessness. Out of 20 that were followed in a 2-year study, only 6 survived that time period. Apparently pleasing two or three husbands or wives, when compounded with trying to get along with two or three co-husbands or co-wives, is demanding in the extreme. Studies have indicated that the toughest problems faced by multilateral spouses are (1) communication, (2) friction in personalities, (3) jealousy, and (4) commitment (Ramey, 1975). In some urban areas such as Los Angeles, where this lifestyle is sufficiently practiced to provide a pool of similarly situated families, organizations of such groups have grown up. The topics discussed at meetings and in newsletters are most often the same four listed above.

Marriage in communes

Some couples believe that communal life offers the most attractive setting for marriage. Although communes take many forms, all are an attempt to establish face-to-face intimacy with a larger circle of close associates. Most communes are more conventional in their sexual arrangements than multilateral marriages, but a few are based on open sexual patterns. Close association is always demanding, and the communes that survive are those based on common religious or ideological commitment and discipline. Another stable communal form described by James Ramey (1972) is based on a formal social contract that often includes legal incorporation. These groups band together to enable members to succeed better in the competitive American system through pooling their resources. The least stable are the revolutionary or Utopian communes, which tend to resist organization and structure and thus fail to sustain themselves or their boundaries.

One study of 35 urban cooperative communes (Kanter *et al.*, 1975) found that the chief problems encountered were (1) loss of privacy, (2) interference, and (3) political jockeying among commune members. In compensation, they experienced a broader base of support and alternative resources in times of stress.

Marriage in an intimate network

Ramey (1975) reports that in our new, more open society many couples choose to have a contract which defines sex as an acceptable part of friendship. Couples who have adopted this style tend gradually to exclude couples with more traditional views from their close circle of friends. Unlike multilateral marriage, there is no thought in these networks of living together or pooling resources. The relationships are, nevertheless, continuing and emotional as well as sexual. As with other types of networks, a couple's close friends may not all be friends of each other. The difference between this position and the more demanding multi-lateral marriage are reflected in the differences in the most troublesome difficulties they report, namely: (1) lack of time to pursue these relationships and scheduling difficulties; (2) babysitting; (3) sleeping arrangements; (4) situational complexities; and (5) sharing (Ramey, 1975). On the positive side, they listed greater personal freedom and variety and the opportunity to strengthen friend-ships with a sexual bond.

Open marriage

Open marriage, as described by the O'Neills in their best-selling book by that title (1972), involves a commitment to openness in the relationship along many dimensions, including sex. The emphasis, however, is on the freedom of each spouse to have separate as well as joint sectors in their lives. Friends, nights out, vacations, hobbies, and even sex partners may be separate without threatening the primary relationship. No particular one of these options needs to be exercised to make it an open marriage; it is open by virtue of the nondemanding quality of the bonds. Judging by the number of books sold, this idea appeals to a great number of Americans. Perhaps it should be noted that one of the original authors of *Open Marriage*, Nena O'Neill (1977), has recently re-evaluated the viability of this concept based on her own experience with it and negative feedback from other couples who have found it more difficult to live than they had at first imagined.

Constantine (1977) has argued that principles of openness ought to apply to parent–child relationships as well, but as yet this view has not received the same popular response.

Swinging

Swinging couples are, for the most part, exclusive in every other aspect of their marriages except sex. That is, their living and child care arrangements, vacations, and so on are all conventionally pair-oriented except that they are involved in recreational sexual exchanges with other couples. Since they swing as a couple and by mutual consent, they do not view this lack of exclusivity as a threat to the relationship. Many, in fact, claim their marriages have been strengthened by this style of life. One study indicates that most swingers return to a more traditional marital format after 2 or 3 years simply because it is such an emotionally taxing style of life (Bartel, 1971).

One study surveyed marriage and family counselors to learn whether they had seen any dropout from swinging and if so what their problems with it had been. In this very special sample of 1,175 ex-swingers, the most common problems cited were jealousy (109 couples), guilt (68), a threat to the marriage (68), development of outside emotional attachments (53), boredom and loss of interest (49), disappointment (32), divorce or separation (29), and wife's inability to 'take it' (29). The same study showed that those who stayed in did so because of the excitement, sexual freedom, greater appreciation of mate, the learning of new sex techniques, sexual variety, and better communication or openness among the partners (Denfeld, 1974).

Estimates of how many couples swing have varied tremendously from a few hundred thousand to millions. One national sample of college students found that about 10% thought they might try this lifestyle, 10% were uncertain, and 80% were certain they would not (Edwards and Stinnett, 1974).

Traditional monogamy

Research shows that 'Forsaking all others, till death do us part' is still a popular position despite all the competing positions described above. The Edwards and Stinnett survey found that this lifestyle was believed to be the most fulfilling by 70% of the students; 22% were uncertain and only 8% were sure there was a better way.

Kinsey (Kinsey et al., 1948, 1953) was the first researcher to ask how many Americans actually kept their commitment to marital exclusivity. He reported that about half of the men and a quarter of the women had admitted at least one extramarital experience. As might be expected, more recent surveys show a shift toward a greater frequency of extramarital involvement, especially among women, but many of those who have extramarital experiences may nevertheless be committed to the monogamous ideal. The double standard, under which husbands were allowed outside relationships but the family remained sacred, may be becoming a single standard, with the fundamental values unchanged.

Summing up

Traditional views toward marriage have been challenged in recent decades by an alternative set of values generated in part by the existential revolution. Among the contested issues are personal growth v. sacrificial commitment, permanent availability v. permanent commitment, and inclusivity v. exclusivity. In our pluralistic society, all these alternatives now compete; there is no one right way to manage a relationship. As a result, each couple is faced with the challenge of finding an individual style.

References

Bartel, Gilbert. (1971). *Group Sex: A Scientific Eyewitness Report on the American Way of Swinging*, Wyden, New York.

Constantine, Larry L. (1977). 'Open family: A lifestyle for kids and other people,' *Family Coordinator*, **26**, 113–121.

Constantine, Larry L., and Constantine, Joan M. (1971). 'Sexual aspects of multilateral relations,' *Journal of Sex Research*, **7**, 204–225.

Constantine, Larry L., and Constantine, Joan M. (1973). *Group Marriage: A Study of Contemporary Multilateral Relations*, Macmillan, New York.

Denfeld, Duane. (1974). 'Dropouts from swinging,' *The Family Coordinator*, **23**, 45–49.

Edwards, M., and Stinnett, N. (1974). 'Perceptions of college students concerning alternate life styles,' *Journal of Psychology*, **87**, 143–156.

Farber, Bernard. (1973). *Family and Kinship in Modern Society*, Scott, Foresman, Glenview, Ill.

Huxley, Aldous Leonard. (1958). *Brave New World*. Harper & Row, New York. (Originally published in 1937.)

Kanter, Rosabeth Moss, Jaffe, Dennis, and Weisberg, D. Kelly. (1975). 'An analysis of communes and intentional communities with particular attention to sexual and genderal relations,' *The Family Coordinator*, **24**, 433–452.

Kinsey, Alfred C., Pomeroy, Wardell B., and Martin, Clyde E. (1948). *Sexual Behavior in the Human Male*. Saunders, Philadelphia.

Kinsey, Alfred C., Pomeroy, Wardell B., Martin, Clyde E., and Gebhard, Paul H. (1953). *Sexual Behavior in the Human Female*. Saunders, Philadelphia.

Macklin, Eleanor. (1978). 'Nonmarital heterosexual cohabitation,' *Marriage and Family Review*, **1**, 1–12.

O'Neill, Nena. (1977). *The Marriage Premise*, Evans, New York.

O'Neill, Nena, and O'Neill, George. (1972). *Open Marriage*, Evans, New York.

Ramey, J. W. (1972). 'Communes, group marriage and the upper middle class,' *Journal of Marriage and the Family*, **34**, 647–655.

Ramey, James W. (1975). 'Intimate groups and networks: Frequent consequences of sexually open marriage,' *The Family Coordinator*, **24**, 515–530.

Part III

Nature of the Group: Structure and Function

Introduction

Even a cursory examination of different types of groups such as a playgroup versus a committee reveals that the kinds of task performed and the social interaction engaged in are central to an understanding of the nature of a group.

Argyle's paper (sub-Chapter 8.1) describes the tasks and forms of interaction typically associated with five kinds of small group. Such a comparative review serves to point out the importance of certain group processes which may be overlooked or underemphasized in research based on only one type of social group.

Hackman and Morris's paper (sub-Chapter 8.2) deals with the impact of interaction processes on the performance of groups. Their analysis identifies three summary variables which contribute substantially to group effectiveness according to the type of task involved, and shows how these variables are in turn affected by group interaction processes. These authors note, however, that methodological improvements are required to advance our understanding of how to maximize the effectiveness of groups.

One such area of improvement is in the analysis of the interaction process. In order to analyze and interpret the 'flow' of social interaction, researchers have adopted coding systems, such as Bales's (1950) Interaction Process Analysis, which divides up the behavioral stream into acts or action sequences—usually based on verbal utterances. At the simplest level, this analysis yields a frequency count of different types of acts occurring in a given interaction. Further analysis is required before anything can be said about the sequential nature of the interaction however, and, as can be seen from Krokoff and Gottman's paper (sub-Chapter 8.3), fairly sophisticated methods are required to obtain information about this. Clearly, such sequential analysis may uncover important processes that could not be identified by analysis of overall frequencies of actions alone. Further research on issues related to the task and interaction in groups can be found in Jacob (1975), Sorenson (1971), Steiner (1972), Zander (1971).

In Chapter 9, we turn to the patterning of interpersonal behavior.

Hinde (sub-Chapter 9.1) stresses the importance of developing a sound descriptive base on which to build 'an integrated science of interpersonal relationships.' Although he is here specifically dealing with dyads, the important issues which he raises are relevant, generally, to the study of small groups. The paper might equally well have been placed in the 'Theory' section (Volume 2, Part III), but it appears here for two reasons. Firstly, its wide scope makes it an excellent bridge between earlier topics, such as personality, impressions of the group, social influence and attraction, and later ones such as group processes (e.g. Volume 2: Part I and much of Part III) (especially Harrison and McCallum on Kelley and Thibaut's Interdependence Theory). Secondly, as Hinde himself makes clear, the concept of role is only one way of approaching the description of relationships so that his paper places the subsequent discussion of role in a broader context.

The concept of role is more often used by sociologically rather than psychologically oriented social psychologists. This is a pity, because although it had a long history defined as the dynamic aspect of status (cf. Linton, 1945), it is now widely used in a much more active sense, as part of our construction of social reality. As the person's concept of norms, rights, obligations, and expectations with respect to some other(s), it can be seen to deserve a place in psychology which it has not yet been accorded.

Cicourel (sub-Chapter 9.2), in his closely argued paper, discusses the interpretative procedures and summarization principles through which people derive, from interaction, negotiated roles, norms, and status on which to base future interaction. He comments that we need to know more about how children acquire interpretative and summarization abilities.

In a very different approach, Jacklin and Maccoby (sub-Chapter 9.3) have studied the effects of same-sex and mixed-sex pairings on the social behavior of children at 33 months old. Their finding of higher rates of social behavior in same-sex dyads does not need to be interpreted as a consequence of innate compatibility, but might reflect the self-roles learned in other interactions (Smith and Lloyd, 1978), or the children's own sex-typed concepts. As Jacklin and Maccoby say, while the reasons for the differences in social behavior are not resolved, it is clear that a pattern has been established very early, which is likely to be reinforced in subsequent social experience.

In the paper by Zimbardo (sub-Chapter 9.4), we turn to the impact of formal role upon behaviour, or role enactment. Zimbardo describes his well-known prison simulation study, and also addresses the potential role of the social psychologist as an advocate. For a consideration of the value of simulations, see Banuazizi and Movahedi, 1975; Spencer, 1978.

For further reading on roles, see Biddle's important integration of Role Theory (Biddle, 1979) and Heiss, 1981. For relationships, see Burgess and Huston, 1979.

In Chapter 10 we consider the group when some members have acquired more influence than others, and some may be deemed, formally or informally, to be leaders. In reading leadership research, it is important to note carefully the nature of the research question. Is it concerned with the differences between leaders and followers, or between effective and ineffective leaders? Is the leader in question imposed on the group, or did one member (or more) emerge from the group, with the corollary in the latter case that most if not all the group actively or passively endorsed this.

Stein and Heller's piece (sub-Chapter 10.1) addresses the frequent research finding that the relative extent to which members participate in groups correlates with their emergence as leaders. At first, such a finding might suggest that groups members are unable to distinguish quality from sheer quantity. Does it perhaps suggest pluralistic ignorance ('The others are listening so it must be more intelligent than I think it is'), or does it reflect a rational decision to be silent and let the most able person do the talking? In this paper, Stein and Heller examine the reports in the literature, discussing both explanations for the findings and ways of improving the research.

Fiedler's research on the differences between effective and ineffective leaders in different situations is well known. This paper by Fiedler and Potter (sub-Chapter 10.2) describes recent work in which his contingency model has been used to predict changes in leadership performance as a consequence of changes in situational control. For example, experience may increase a leader's situational control; the model therefore predicts that task-motivated leaders will become more effective, while relationship-motivated leaders will become less effective.

Fiedler has mainly studied formal groups with appointed leaders, and in most cases his subjects have been males. Schneier and Goktepe (sub-Chapter 10.3) describes their extension of the contingency model to emergent leadership, using sexually heterogeneous groups, and go on to discuss possible developments in emergent leadership research.

Hollander (sub-Chapter 10.4) specifically addresses the issue of women leaders in both formal and informal groups, concluding his review of the recent literature on a fairly optimistic note.

The work of Soviet psychologists seldom appears in books edited in the West, and it may seem somewhat unfamiliar in style and content to the Western reader. The paper written by Krichevskii (sub-Chapter 10.5) describes recent work on leadership which he has done with his colleagues. His studies of the differentiation of leadership roles developed from Bales's work, but are extended within a different theoretical framework based on the concept of 'activity.' The word 'activity' has particular and important connotations in Soviet psychology, and the concept is the subject of a book translated by Wertsch (1981). It is interesting to compare Fiedler's analysis of effective leadership with Krichevskii's approach to leadership role differentiation. Their work appears to proceed along separate lines, yet each seemingly has ideas which might interest the other. For further reading on Soviet social psychology, see Strickland (1979).

For further reading on leadership, see Stogdill, 1974; Hunt and Larson, 1979; Hollander, 1978.

References

Bales, R. F. (1950). *Interaction Process Analysis*, Addison-Wesley, Cambridge, Mass.

Banuazizi, A., and Movahedi, S. (1975). 'Interpersonal dyanmics in a simulated prison,' *American Psychologist*, **30**, 152–160.

Biddle, B. J. (1979). *Role Theory: Expectations, Identities, and Behaviors*, Academic Press, New York.

Burgess, R. L. and Huston, T. L. (eds.) (1979). *Social Exchange in Developing Relationships*, Academic Press, New York.

Heiss, J. (1981), 'Social Roles,' in M. Rosenberg and R. H. Turner (eds.), *Social Psychology: Sociological Perspectives*, Basic Books, New York.

Hollander, E. P. (1978). *Leadership Dynamics*, Free Press, New York.

Hunt, J. G. and Larson, L. L. (eds.) (1979). *Crosscurrents in Leadership*, Southern Illinois University Press, Carbondale, Ill.

Jacob, T. (1975). 'Family interaction in disturbed and normal families: A methodological and substantive review,' *Psychological Bulletin*, **82**, 33–65.

Linton, R. (1945). *The Cultural Background of Personality*, Appleton-Century-Crofts, New York.

Smith, C., and Lloyd, B. (1978). 'Maternal behavior and perceived sex of infant: revisited,' *Child Development*, **49**(4), 1263–1265.

Sorenson, J. R. (1971). 'Task demands, group interaction and group performance,' *Sociometry*, **34**, 483–495.

Spencer, C. D. (1978). 'Two types of role playing: Threats to internal and external validity,' *American Psychologist*, **33**, 265–268.

Steiner, I. D. (1972). *Group Process and Productivity*, Academic Press, New York.

Stogdill, R. M. (1974). *Handbook of Leadership*, Free Press, New York.

Strickland, L. H. (ed.) (1979). *Soviet and Western Perspectives in Social Psychology*, Pergamon Press, Oxford.

Wertsch, J. (Tr.) (1981). *The Concept of Activity in Soviet Psychology*, M. E. Sharpe, White Plains, NY.

Zander, A. (1971). *Motives and Goals in Groups*, Academic Press, New York.

Reference Note

The reader may wish to consult the following papers in other Parts of Volumes 1 and 2 which seem particularly relevant to the chapters in Part 3:–

Chapter 8. See Volume 1: Shaw (2.4), Broderick (7.3).
See Volume 2: Tindale and Davis (1.1), Janis (1.2), Deutsch (2.1), Schmitt and Marwell (2.2), Lindskold (2.4), Chapter 4, Harrison and McCallum (7.3), Hare (7.4), Hoffman and Stein (7.5), Bales (7.10).

Chapter 9. See Volume 1: Milgram and Sabini (5.1), Newcomb (5.3), Chapter 7.
See Volume 2: Murton (6.7), Hatfield (7.2), Harrison and McCallum (7.3), Hare (7.4), Hoffman and Stein (7.5), Holmes (7.9), Bales (7.10), Goffman (7.11).

Chapter 10. See Volume 1: Webster and Driskell (2.1), Nemeth (2.2), Shaw (2.4).
See Volume 2: Hare (7.4), Hoffman and Stein (7.5), Holmes (7.9), Bales (7.10).

8 Social Interaction and Task

Small Groups and Social Interaction, Volume 1
Edited by H. H. Blumberg, A. P. Hare, V. Kent and M. Davies
Published by John Wiley & Sons Limited, 1983.

8.1   Five Kinds of Small Social Group*

Michael Argyle   *University of Oxford*

The concentration of research on laboratory groups has diverted attention away from the very varied kinds of interaction taking place in real-life groups. We shall describe interaction in the three most important types of group—the family, work-groups, and groups of friends (we shall concentrate on adolescent friendship groups). In addition an account will be given of some other kinds of group which have been extensively studied—committees, T-groups, and therapy groups. . . .

The family as a small group

There is something like a family in all species of mammals: the mother has to care for the young, and the father often provides food and protection during this period. Only in humans does the father become an enduring member of the family, and only in humans is there a life-long link between children and parents. What is probably the most important kind of small group in human society is often overlooked by small group researchers—and consequently there are important features of the family group which have never been embodied in small group experiments or theorising.

The nuclear family consists of two parents, sons and daughters, and can thus be regarded as a four-role system, divided by generation and sex (Parsons and Bales, 1955). There are also characteristic relations between older and younger brothers, and between older and younger sisters, so that it may be better to see the family as potentially a six-role system, though not all the positions may be filled

---

*Abridged from Michael Argyle (1969). *Social Interaction*, Methuen, London and Atherton, New York, pp. 240–263. Reprinted by permission of the author and Methuen & Co Ltd. Copyright © Michael Argyle 1969, 1973.

(Murdock, 1949). The basic features of the relationship between each pair of positions are much the same in all human societies. For example between older and younger brothers there is a 'relationship of playmates, developing into that of comrades; economic co-operation under leadership of elder; moderate responsibility of elder for instruction and discipline of younger' (Murdock, op. cit.). The family has some of the features of a formal organisation—a set of positions, each associated with a role, including patterns of interaction with occupants of other positions. . . .

Unlike groups of friends, family members have tasks to perform. In primitive societies these are mainly the growing and preparation of food, the rearing and education of children, and maintenance of the house. In modern society some of these activities are performed by outside agencies, but there are still the domestic jobs connected with eating, sleeping, and the care of young children. In addition there are leisure activities such as TV, gardening, games, and family outings. Some of these are like activities of friends in that they are performed because of the interaction involved. Interaction in the family is closely connected with these joint activities—eating, watching or playing together. Interaction is also brought about through the members pursuing their private goals under conditions of physical proximity, and where their joint activities have to be more or less closely coordinated—this is an extension of the necessity for meshing. The physical environment and technology have an important effect on family life. Overcrowding of other animals results in aggression, and the murder rate is greater in overcrowded areas (Henry and Short, 1954). The family tasks include looking after one another, in particular caring for the bodily needs of members: in addition to close physical proximity there is also intimacy and interdependence. . . .

What goes on inside the family is private and not readily subject to external control. Models of how families should behave are, however, provided by magazines and TV, and by the previous families of the parents. The actual elements of interaction of which family life consists differ from all other groups, in that greater intimacy, aggression, affection, and emotional violence occurs. Family members see each other undressed, or naked, and there is almost no attempt at self-presentation; they know each other's weaknesses and understand each other extremely well; family life is very much 'off-stage,' in Goffman's terminology (1956). There is physical aggression, mainly of parents towards children, but also between children; there is aggression between parents, but it is mainly verbal. Affection is equally violent and often takes the form of bodily contact, between parents, and between parents and children until they 'get too old for it.' Members of laboratory groups do not usually take their clothes off, laugh uproariously, cry, attack or kiss each other, or crawl all over each other, as members of families commonly do. Interaction in the family is more complex and subtle than most other interaction because of the intense and complex relationships between members, and their long history of previous interaction. Spiegel (1956) describes cases of tense mother–daughter interaction, and suggests that various unconscious fantasies and projections are taking place in addition to what seems to be occurring. This is similar to the interpersonal behaviour found in some neurotics. The subtler nonverbal communications may be very important—as in the possible effect of 'double-bind' parents in making children schizophrenic. The dimensions of parent behaviour which have the greatest effect on children, however, are probably warmth *v.* rejection, strictness *v.* permissiveness, and type of discipline (Sears, Maccoby and Levin, 1957). . . .

Adolescent groups

Friendship groups are one of the basic forms of social grouping in animals and men; they are distinguished by the fact that members are brought together primarily through interpersonal motivations and attractions, not through concern with any task. Of all friendship groups, adolescent groups are the most interesting. During adolescence work and family attachments are weak and the strongest attachments are to friends. These groups are formed of young people between the ages of 11–12 up to 21–23, when the members marry and settle down in jobs, and other kinds of group become more important to them.

The motivations of members are partly to engage in various joint activities, but more important are interpersonal needs—sexual, affiliative, and the establishment of identity. It has been suggested that there are certain 'developmental tasks' during this period of life to develop an identity independent of the family, and to establish a changed relation with adults (Erikson, 1956; Muuss, 1962). . . .

The activities of adolescent groups vary with the culture: in the USA groups of boys are concerned with cars, entertainment, sport, and girls (Sherif and Sherif, 1964). There is avoidance of the tasks of home and school. Many group activities are invented, whose chief point is the social interaction involved—such as dancing, listening to records, and drinking coffee. The forms of social interaction involved are rather different from those in other groups—there is more bodily contact, joking, aggressive horseplay, and just being together, less problem-centred discussion. Schmuck and Lohman (1965) observe that 'adolescents in a group often engage in infantile behaviour and pranks, while giggling and laughing hilariously; and are encouraged to feel silly together, and to withhold evaluation from such experiences' (p. 27). They suggest that this behavioural abandon has a regressive element. There is an easy intimacy and social acceptance of those who wear the right uniform. Conversation is mainly about other adolescents, parents, interpersonal feelings and social interaction. These are probably the only natural groups that discuss social interaction (T-groups do it too). Such topics are discussed because adolescents have problems to solve in this area—as well as working out an identity and establishing a changed relationship with adults, they have to acquire the social skills of dealing with the opposite sex, to come to terms with the difficulty of playing different roles on different occasions, and having relationships of different degrees of intimacy with different people (Fleming, 1963).

Adolescent groups are of interest to us because a number of special processes can be seen, which are not present in laboratory groups. (1) There is no specific task, but joint activities are devised which entail the kinds of interaction which meet the needs of members. (2) One of these needs is the establishing of an ego-identity, independent of the family of origin (Erikson, 1956). This explains the emphasis on clothes, the great self-consciousness, and the concern about acceptance by members of these groups. (3) Sexual motivation is a major factor in adolescent groups, and is partly responsible for the intensity of attraction to the groups, and for their pairing structure. (4) There is a group task of acquiring together the social skills of dealing with the opposite sex and dealing with adults.

Work-groups

In groups of animals the work of gathering food and building homes is often carried out by males. In ants it is a specialised and highly organised group activity. In primitive society this work may be carried out by males or females, and follows a seasonal cycle. In modern communities work outside the home has become a highly specialised activity, mainly performed by adult males, for financial reward, and is done in special social organisations. Work is performed in groups for several reasons—(1) One man alone may not be able to perform the task; in primitive societies this is the case with hunting and building; (2) there can be division of labour, so that different people can use or develop specialised skills; this is a central feature of work in modern communities; (3) people prefer to work together because of their social motivations; (4) another factor is social facilitation; the presence of others is arousing, so more work is done. Even ants work harder when there is more than one of them on the job (Zajonc, 1965).

Work-groups are at the opposite pole from adolescent groups in that their primary concern is with carrying out a task. They are the other main kind of group outside the family in which adults spend most of their time. They are not so well defined as the other two kinds, and often have no clear membership. It is sometimes difficult, in a factory for example, to decide which are the group—all that can be seen are a lot of people, some of whom collaborate over work or interact informally from time to time. Such groups can be defined in terms of the formal organisation—having the same supervisor or being paid jointly, or in terms of informal group-formation—sociometric cliques, or people who think of themselves as a group. Much research in this area has been on groups of manual workers—gangs of men engaged in the maintenance of railway track, men on assembly lines. There has also been research on the more technically skilled men in charge of automated plant, and recently attention has turned to the work of engineers, accountants, scientists and managers. In these latter cases much of the social interaction is between people two at a time, so there is a network rather than a group. They may also meet in committees and similar talking and decision-taking groups, which will be discussed separately in the following section. In this section we are concerned with groups which have a definite task to do, and where the social interaction arises out of the task activity. . . .

What form does interaction take in work-groups? In the first place the task performance may partly consist of interaction. If A passes a brick to B this is both task behaviour and interaction; if A likes B, more bricks will be passed (Van Zelst, 1952). He will pass them with accompanying verbal and non-verbal signals, not strictly necessary for the task, but which sustain the social relationship. If A talks to B, where B is his supervisor, or colleague, it is impossible to disentangle the task and the informal interaction elements of the conversation. Much work in fact consists almost entirely of social interaction—the work of supervisors, interviewers, teachers, and many others. In addition to interaction linked to the task, interaction may take place during coffee-breaks, in the lunch hour, after hours, and during unauthorised pauses from work. Non-verbal communication, such as gestures, may occur during the work process. Social interaction of the usual kind is perhaps more limited in work-groups than in groups of other kinds. The relationships established may only operate in the work situation—as when good working relations exist between members of different racial and social class groups. Only part of the personality is involved, but it is an important part, and work-relations can be very important to people. Friendships are made at work, especially between people of equal status in the organisation; many of the links joining family members to the outside world are made in the work situation. Relationships at work may also, on occasion, resemble the relaxed informality of the family. This is most common among young people, who know each other very well, and have shared emotional experiences. Life in the services has something of this quality. There is often considerable intensity of feeling in work-groups, because the economic position, the career, the self-image and sometimes the safety of members is at stake. . . .

What special interaction processes are found in work-groups? (1) Interaction arises out of cooperation and communication over task activity, and can be regarded as a secondary or informal system that sustains working relationships and satisfies interpersonal needs. (2) Social relationships at work differ from those in the family or in adolescent groups in that they are based on concern for the task, tend to be less permanent and less intimate, and often do not operate outside the work situation. (3) The boundaries of work-groups are vague, and these groups may in fact consist of networks. (4) In addition to one or more informal leaders, there may be a leader of the opposition.

Committees, problem-solving and creative groups

This kind of group does its work entirely by talking, and consequently is not found in any species apart from man. Committees are concerned with taking decisions and solving problems; there are other kinds of working group, for example groups of research workers, who are more concerned with the creative solution of problems. There is no sharp division between the two kinds of group.

Committees are small groups of a rather special kind; while their devotion to problem solving and their degree of formality make them different from other groups, these features are found to some extent in most other groups too. . . .

Interaction in committees is unlike interaction in most other groups. It is primarily verbal; furthermore it consists of a number of carefully delivered utterances, in the formal mode of speech. The 12 categories of the Bales system (Bales, 1950) were devised to record interaction in groups of this kind. As well as pure task categories—asking for and giving opinions and suggestions, it includes socioemotional categories—agreeing and disagreeing, showing tension, showing antagonism and solidarity. As with work-groups interpersonal relations are established and maintained during the execution of the task. There is considerable use of non-verbal signals. To speak it may be necessary to catch the chairman's eye, and the regulation of who speaks and for how long is achieved by eye-movements, head-nods and smiles. Comments on what A is saying may be indicated by B's facial and gestural signals; these may be directed to A, or to another listener C. When the non-verbal channel proves inadequate, written messages may be passed along the table. To be an effective committee member requires special skills. These include squaring other people before the meeting, studying the papers before the meeting, and the usual social skills of persuasion and handling groups. There also appear to be skills unique to committees: a member should not seem to be emotionally involved with an issue, but be concerned with what will be acceptable to the others. A chairman should do his [or her] best to come to solutions which are acceptable to all members, rather than coming to majority decisions.

The activities of a committee are problem solving and decision taking. These terms refer to two different elements—arriving at new solutions to problems, and coming to agreements. These are rather different matters which are, however, closely bound up together in committee work. Coming to an agreement has . . . been considered in connection with conformity; each agenda item produces in miniature a norm-formation situation. The item will be more or less closely related to more general norms held by the group, and to issues on which subgroups have their own views. The problem-solving process can be divided into two stages—information exchange and the study of hypotheses. Thibaut and Kelly (1959) discuss the conditions under which information is offered and accepted in groups, and what happens when the information is complementary, conflicting or simply heterogeneous. A number of experiments have been carried out in which the task of the group consists in putting together information related in these ways. In real committees this is certainly part of the story, but information exchange is usually followed by the study of suggestions and is affected by conformity processes. There is a great deal of experimental work in this area, of which one sample will be given. Freedman and Sears (1965), reviewing experiments by themselves and others, show that people do *not* just seek information that supports their existing views, as dissonance theory would seem to predict, but actually want to find out the facts. Thibaut and Kelley (op. cit.) argue that both individuals and groups start to engage in problem-solving activity when they think that they may be able to deal with the external world to better advantage. . . .

T-groups and therapy groups

Finally we turn to a kind of group which did not exist until psychologists invented it. Just as physicists study particles created by special experimental techniques so it is of interest to study the forms social interaction *can* take under quite new conditions. In fact the processes of feedback and analysis of the group found in this setting also take place, although with less intensity, in other groups too. On the other hand these groups are very different from natural groups in a number of ways, so that the findings cannot simply be generalised to other kinds of group. There has been a certain shift of interest away from laboratory groups towards T-groups (cf. Mann *et al.*, 1967), simply because the latter last longer and can be studied in greater detail. Apart from the limited generality of the findings it should be pointed out that most of these studies are essentially clinical investigations of a rather small number of groups (cf. Stock, 1964).

In most T-groups, about 12 trainees meet with a trainer for a number of 2 hour sessions; they may meet once a week, or more frequently for up to two weeks. The Harvard version has 20-30 members. The leader introduces himself, explains that he is there to help the members study the group, and then takes a passive role and leaves the group to get on with this task as best it can. From time to time he will intervene in various ways: (1) he shows how to make constructive and nonevaluative comments on the behaviour of members; (2) he shows how to receive such comments non-defensively, and learn from them; (3) he makes interpretations, i.e. explains what he thinks is happening, interpersonally, in the group; (4) he discusses the relevance and application of the group experiences to behaviour in real-life situations; (5) he tries to teach the members a more cooperative and less authoritarian attitude to people in authority. In addition to the T-group sessions proper there are sometimes lectures, role-playing and other ancillary training experiences (cf. Bradford, Gibb and Benne, 1964).

Therapy groups consist of a psychiatrist and usually 6-9 mental patients. The main differences from T-groups are that: (1) the members are emotionally disturbed and at a lower level of social competence, often suffering from real interpersonal difficulties; (2) the content of conversation is the actual symptoms or difficulties of group members; (3) the therapist creates an atmosphere of acceptance for sexual and aggressive material, but makes sure that the tension level does not get too high; (4) there is a greater gap between leader and group members—the former is not simply a more experienced member of the group; (5) the behaviour of members in the group situation is used to diagnose basic personality disturbances, rather than indicating their level of social competence (Powdermaker and Frank, 1953; Foulkes and Anthony, 1957)....

The 'task' of T-groups, like that of committees, consists of conversation, and is difficult to separate from 'interaction.' However, some kinds of conversation are regarded as more relevant to the task—conversation which is concerned with the interaction and relationships of members of the group, and about the symptoms of members of therapy groups. The goal to be attained is insight and understanding of group processes and emotional problems respectively. An important sub-goal is the formation of a sufficiently cohesive group for this understanding to develop in the group setting—i.e. the internal and external goals are closely intertwined (Tuckman, 1965). Unlike committees, however, these groups have no agenda, and proceed in a largely undirected and rambling manner, the leader taking whatever opportunities he can for explaining various phenomena. The content of the conversation is most unusual; language in the natural world is usually about external matters, and other people, rather than about relations between speaker and hearer, or about embarrassing personal matters. This kind of task is emotionally arousing and awkward, and for these reasons is often avoided in periods of 'flight' from the task—by making jokes, talking about other matters, and silence....

The social interaction in T-groups can be thought of as including the task activity. Various classification schemes have been devised to deal with it, which between them provide some account of the forms interaction takes.... It should be added that the general atmosphere and flow of interaction are very different in these groups from those in the other groups which we have considered. While committees are formal, and groups of adolescents are relaxed and intimate, T-groups and therapy groups are tense and awkward. Both T-group and therapy group practitioners maintain that some degree of emotionality is necessary for any fundamental changes of behaviour to occur. Interaction sequences are reported in these groups which may be unique to them, for example: (a) an intensification of the process of becoming aware of the self-image from the reactions of others—which are here unusually frank and uninhibited; (b) obtaining insight into oneself through the close observation and study of another person with similar attributes or problems; (c) the 'condenser' phenomenon, in which interaction loosens group resistances, and common emotions, normally repressed, are suddenly released (Foulkes and Anthony, 1957)....

References

Bales, R. F. (1950). *Interaction Process Analysis*, Addison-Wesley, Cambridge, Mass.
Bradford, L. P., Gibb, J. R., and Benne, K. D. (1964). *T-group Theory and Laboratory Method*, Wiley, New York.
Erikson, E. H. (1956). 'The problem of ego-identity,' *American Journal of Psychoanalysis*, **4**, 56–121.
Fleming, C. M. (1963). *Adolescence*, Routledge & Kegan Paul, London.
Foulkes, S. H., and Anthony, E. J. (1957). *Group Psychotherapy: The Psychoanalytic Approach*, Penguin, London.

Freedman, J. L., and Sears, D. O. (1965). 'Selective exposure,' in L. Berkowitz (ed.), *Advances in Experimental Social Psychology*, Vol. 2, Academic Press, New York.

Goffman, E. (1956). *The Presentation of Self in Everyday Life*, Edinburgh University Press, Edinburgh.

Henry, A. F., and Short, J. F. (1954). *Suicide and Homicide*, Free Press, Glencoe, Ill.

Mann, R. D., *et al.* (1967). *Interpersonal Styles and Group Development*, Wiley, New York.

Murdock, G. P. (1949). *Social Structure*, Macmillan, New York.

Muuss, R. E. (1962). *Theories of Adolescence*, Random House, New York.

Parsons, T., and Bales, R. F. (1955). *Family, Socialization, and Interaction Process*, Free Press, Glencoe, Ill.

Powdermaker, F. B., and Frank, J. D. (1953). *Group Psychotherapy*, Harvard University Press, Cambridge, MA.

Schmuck, R., and Lohman, A. (1965). Peer relations and personality development. Institute for Social Research, University of Michigan, Ann Arbor, MI. Unpublished manuscript.

Sears, R. R., Maccoby, E. E., and Levin, H. (1957). *Patterns of Child Rearing*, Row, Peterson, New York.

Sherif, M., and Sherif, C. W. (1964). *Reference Groups*, Harper, New York 1964.

Spiegel, J. P. (1956). 'Interpersonal influences within the family,' in B. Schaffner (ed.), *Group Processes*, Josiah Macy Foundation, New York.

Stock, D. (1964). 'A survey of research on T-groups,' in L. P. Bradford, J. R. Gibb, and K. D. Benne (eds.), *T-Group Theory and Laboratory Method*, Wiley, New York.

Thibaut, J. W., and Kelley, H. H. (1959). *The Social Psychology of Groups*, Wiley, New York.

Tuckman, B. W. (1965). 'Developmental sequence in small groups,' *Psychological Bulletin*, **63**, 384–399.

Van Zelst, R. H. (1952). 'Validation of a sociometric regrouping procedure,' *Journal of Abnormal and Social Psychology*, **47**, 299–301.

Zajonc, R. B. (1963). 'Social facilitation,' *Science*, **149**, 269–274.

Small Groups and Social Interaction, Volume 1
Edited by H. H. Blumberg, A. P. Hare, V. Kent and M. Davies
© 1983 John Wiley & Sons Ltd

8.2   Group Tasks, Group Interaction Process, and Group Performance Effectiveness[1]

J. Richard Hackman   *Yale University*

and

Charles G. Morris   *University of Michigan*

When decision makers in public and private institutions in this society are faced with genuinely important tasks, it is likely that they will assign those tasks to groups for solution. Sometimes the reason is simply that one individual could not be expected to handle the task by himself [or herself] (e.g. formulating a new welfare policy, which requires a diversity of knowledge and skills). Other times it is because decision makers assume that the added human resources available in a group will lead to a higher *quality* product—or will at least lessen the chances that the product will be grossly defective.

Given current knowledge about group effectiveness, the state of affairs described above is not an occasion for optimism. Although literally thousands of studies of group performance have been conducted over the last several decades (Hare, 1972; McGrath and Altman, 1966), we still know very little about why sόme groups are more effective than others. We know even less about what to do to improve the performance of a given group working on a specific task. Moreover, the few general findings that have emerged from the literature do not encourage the use of groups to perform important tasks (cf. reviews by Collins and Guetzkow, 1964; Davis, 1969; Steiner, 1972).

It is tempting to conclude that the 'group effectiveness problem' will not be solved in the foreseeable future, and to recommend to decision makers that in the meantime they use groups as infrequently as possible. The present paper explores the possibility that this viewpoint is unduly pessimistic—that the human resources present in groups can, in fact, be harnessed and directed toward more effective performance than would·be obtained from individuals alone. We suggest that the key to understanding the 'group effectiveness problem' is to be found in the on-going *interaction process* which takes place among group members while they are working on a task. At one extreme, for example, group members may work together so badly that members do not share with one another uniquely held information that is critical to the problem at hand; in this case, the quality of the group outcome surely will suffer. On the other hand, group members may operate in great harmony, with the comments of one member prompting quick and sometimes innovative responses in another, which then leads a third to see a synthesis between the ideas of the first two, and so on; in this case, a genuinely creative outcome may result.

The challenge is to identify, measure, and change those aspects of group interaction process that contribute to such obvious differences in group effectiveness. Toward this end, we offer the following ideas about the features of group interaction that may be especially powerful in influencing group performance.

The performance-relevant functions of group interaction

As Katzell *et al.* (1970) note, the number of factors that can affect group output is so great that managing more than a few factors at a time, either conceptually or experimentally, is nearly impossible. As a strategy for dealing with this manifold, they suggest using 'a single set of mediating variables in order to link conceptually and functionally all kinds of group inputs ... with various kinds of group outputs' (p. 158). Consistent with this strategy, we propose that a major portion of the variation in measured group performance is proximally controlled by three general 'summary variables': (a) the *effort* brought to bear on the task by group members; (b) the *task performance strategies* used by group members in carrying out the task; and (c) the *knowledge and skills* of group members which are effectively brought to bear on the task. It is proposed that, if one could somehow control or influence these three summary variables, one would be able to affect substantially the level of effectiveness of a group working on almost any task.

Each of the summary variables can be substantially affected (both positively and negatively) by what happens in the group interaction process. The interaction among group members can, for example, either increase or decrease the level of effort members exert in doing the task, and can affect how well the efforts of individual group members are coordinated. Similarly, group interaction can lead to either effective or ineffective task performance strategies, and to efficient or wasteful use of the knowledge and skills of group members. The specific roles that group interaction plays in a given situation depend substantially on the task being performed.

Different summary variables (or combinations of them) are operative for different types of group tasks. For some tasks, for example, how hard group members work (member effort) will almost entirely determine their measured effectiveness; Ringlemann's group tug-of-war (Ingham *et al.*, 1974) is an example of such a task. For other tasks, effort will be mostly irrelevant to performance effectiveness, and other summary variables will be operative. For example, on a vocabulary test which is taken collaboratively by group members with no time limit, performance is unlikely to be affected by how hard members 'try,' but it will be dependent on their collective knowledge of the meanings of words (member knowledge and skill). For some group tasks, of course, measured performance effectiveness may depend on two or on all three of the summary variables. The point is simply that which of the summary variables will 'make a difference' in measured group effectiveness is heavily determined by the type of group task on which the group is working.

Member effort

The first summary variable to be considered is also the most ubiquitous: how hard group members work on a task should be an important determiner of group effectiveness on many different types of group tasks. And, while many personal and situational factors can influence the level of effort the group brings to bear on its task activities, it is proposed that group interaction affects effort primarily in two ways: (a) by affecting the *coordination* of the efforts of individual group members, and (b) by affecting the *level* of effort members choose to expend working on the group task (their task motivation).

Coordination of member efforts. If effectiveness on a given group task is influenced by the amount of effort group members apply to it, then it is important that members coordinate their activities so that efforts of individual members are minimally 'wasted.' On the Ringlemann tug-of-war, for example, a group will do quite poorly unless the group devises some means of ensuring that members pull at the same time (Ingham *et al.*, 1974). Whatever coordination is achieved among members should be evident in the group interaction process; that is, examination of interaction should at least reveal the nature of the coordination scheme being used by the group, and (especially for tasks unfamiliar to group members) it may show exactly how the group came up with whatever coordination devices it is using.

Steiner (1972) shows that, when the efforts of individual group members must be coordinated to accomplish the task, there will always be some slippage which can only serve to keep a group from achieving its potential productivity (i.e. that which would be obtained if the efforts of each group member were fully usable by the group in the service of task effectiveness). Moreover, the larger the group, the greater will be the process loss (which Steiner calls 'coordination decrement'), simply because the job of getting all members functioning together in a coordinated fashion becomes increasingly difficult as the number of members gets larger. Therefore, attempts to increase productivity by helping group members coordinate their activities more effectively can be construed as working toward minimizing inevitable process losses, rather than as creating 'process gains.'

Enhancing or depressing the level of member effort. While individual members usually approach a given group task with some notion about how hard they expect to work on it, what happens in the group can radically alter that expectation in either direction. Presumably individuals will increase their level of effort to the extent that working hard with the other group members leads to the satisfaction of personal needs or the achievement of personal goals. If their task-oriented efforts are reinforced, individuals should work harder on the task; but if these efforts are ignored or punished, effort should decrease. The point here is that social interaction can importantly affect how much effort an individual chooses to expend in work on the group task, and that the level of effort can easily change over time as the characteristics of the group interaction change.

The depression of member effort has been explored by Steiner (1972) in terms of a 'motivation decrement.' He suggests, for example, that member effort declines as group size increases. If our paradigm is valid, then the explanation for the relationship between group size and member effort will be found in the patterns of interaction that characterize small v. large groups. Conceptual and empirical attention recently has been directed toward such group process aspects of motivation decrements (see Steiner, 1972, Ch. 4). As yet, however, systematic attention has not been given to ways in which patterns of interaction might be created in groups which would result in a 'motivation increment,' encouraging members to work especially hard on the group task. The feasibility of creating such increments in task-oriented groups is explored later in this chapter.

Task performance strategies

As used here, 'strategy' refers to the collective choices made by group members about how they will go about performing the task. Included are choices group members make about desirable performance outcomes and choices about how the group will go about trying to obtain those outcomes. For example, group members might elect to try to make their product funny or elegant or practical; or they might decide to free-associate for a period of time to get ideas about the task before evaluating any of the possibilities that they generated. These all are examples of performance strategies under the voluntary control of group members, and they are related. How we proceed to carry out the task depends in part on what we are trying to achieve, and vice versa.

A number of researchers have demonstrated that the performance effectiveness of a group can be affected markedly by the strategies members use in working on the task (e.g. Davis, 1973; Maier, 1963; Shiflett, 1972; Shure *et al.*, 1962; Stone, 1971). What specific strategies will be effective or ineffective in a given performance situation, however, depend on the contingencies built into the task itself. As was the case for effort, there are some tasks for which differences in performance strategies will have relatively little impact on the ultimate effectiveness of the group. The group vocabulary test described earlier, for example, would seem minimally responsive to differences in task performance strategies; almost any strategy that ensures that group members who know the answer will communicate it to their peers will suffice. Strategy would be considerably more important for a task requiring the solution of complicated algebra problems. In this latter case, the approach a group takes to the task (e.g. breaking the problem into parts v. trying to solve the problem in one step) could have a considerable impact on the probability of successful performance. Because of such differences in 'what works' for different tasks (or at different stages of work on a single complex task), it has been suggested that perhaps the only universally effective strategy may be an ability and willingness to switch from one specific strategy to another as the need arises (Shiflett, 1972, pp. 454–455).

There are two ways in which group interaction process can affect the performance strategies that a group brings to bear on its task: (a) through implementing pre-existing strategies that are shared among group members; and (b) through reformulating existing performance strategies or generating new ones. These two functions of group interaction are examined below.

Implementing existing, shared strategies. As people gain experience with particular kinds of tasks in the course of their everyday lives, particular strategies for working on these tasks become well-learned. When an individual is given a new task from some familiar, general class of tasks, he or she need not spend time actually deciding how to work on the task or selecting appropriate outcomes. Instead, the individual can simply begin to do the new task. The same process occurs when a group of individuals works on a task that is familiar to them. Everyone in the group may know very well the 'obviously right' way to go about working on the task, and no discussion of strategy need take place in the group at all.

In such cases, group interaction serves mainly to implement existing strategies already well learned by group members, and no evidence of the group's 'working on its performance strategy' may be visible in the overt interaction among members. This phenomenon is demonstrated clearly in data collected by the present authors (Hackman, 1968; Morris, 1966). The characteristics of the written products prepared by groups in the study were quite strongly affected by the type of task being worked on. 'Production' tasks led to highly original products; 'discussion' tasks prompted products high in issue involvement; and 'problem solving' tasks led to products high in action orientation. In a follow-up study, individuals working by themselves indicated, when asked, that they were confident that a response to a production task 'ought' to be original, a response to a discussion 'ought' to be heavily issue-involved, and so on.

Yet analysis of interaction transcripts from the original study revealed that these apparently well-learned strategies were rarely discussed in the experimental groups. One hundred of the 432 transcripts (each of a single group working on one task) were randomly selected and analyzed for strategy comments by two judges. A total of only 143 comments about strategy were found—less than 1.5 comments per group. Only 25 of the comments prompted further discussion among group members, and on 36 of the transcripts there was no strategy-relevant interaction at all during the 15 minute work period.

These data support the notion that, at least in some circumstances, group members are both capable and desirous of implementing implicitly-agreed-upon performance strategies without explicit discussion of what they are doing. In these circumstances, the interaction process serves primarily as a *vehicle* for implementing the pre-existing performance strategies. As in the case of coordination of member efforts, group members may encounter interpersonal difficulties which impair the efficiency with which such implementation is actually carried out—in other words, a process loss occurs which results in suboptimal group effectiveness.

Developing or reformulating strategic plans.   While most tasks do not constrain a group from overtly discussing and reformulating its performance strategies (or from developing new strategies from scratch), there appears to be a pervasive norm in groups *not* to address such matters explicitly (Weick, 1969, pp. 11–12). The low incidence of strategic discussion noted above in the Morris–Hackman data is one possible example of this norm in operation. Another is reported by Shure *et al.* (1962). In that study, it was found that 'planning' activities tended to be generally lower in priority than actual task performance activities—even when group members were aware that it was to their advantage to engage in planning before starting actual work on the task, and when it was possible for them to do so without difficulty. A closely related phenomenon is the tendency for group members to begin immediately to generate and evaluate solutions when they are presented with a task, rather than to take time to study and analyze the task itself (Maier, 1963; Varela, 1971, Ch. 6).

To the extent that norms against strategy planning exist, the chances are lessened that the pre-existing strategies members bring to the group will be altered and improved upon, or that new (and possibly more task-effective) strategies will be generated by group members. This obviously can limit the effectiveness of the group on many types of tasks.

To explore whether group task effectiveness can be *improved* by explicit attention to matters of performance strategy, an additional analysis was made of the interaction transcripts collected by the present authors. The relationship between the frequency of strategy comments and the judged creativity of group products was analyzed for the 100 transcripts described above. Only comments made during the first third of the performance period were included in the analysis, since those made later would be unlikely to have much effect on the final product. Even though relatively little interaction about strategy took place in these groups, the relationship between the number of strategy comments and group creativity was significantly positive ($p < .05$), as shown in Figure 1.

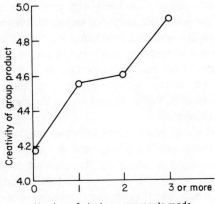

Figure 1   Relationship between amount of
interaction about performance strategy and
group product creativity

The data in Figure 1 are correlational, and they do not permit a conclusion that strategy discussion 'caused' increased group creativity.[2] Nevertheless, to search for possible reasons for the positive relationship obtained, all transcripts in which relatively full-fledged exchanges about strategy took place were reviewed. The transcripts suggest that one function of strategy discussion is to 'unfreeze' individuals from traditional, well-learned approaches to the task, and thereby open the possibility of discovering a more task-effective way of proceeding. Strategy discussion often began, for example, after one group member made a suggestion that was deviant from shared ideas about 'appropriate' strategy for the task at hand (e.g. suggesting a bizarre solution to a routine problem-solving task). In some cases, in the process of explaining to the deviant why the idea was faulty, members began to explore new ways of proceeding, some of which subsequently were adopted.[3]

In sum, it appears that the functions of interaction guiding the implementation and reformulation of performance strategies may be of considerable importance in understanding and predicting group performance effectiveness. Moreover, the data suggest that overriding existing norms which often discourage explicit strategy planning may be a useful way to help groups improve their performance effectiveness in some circumstances.

Member knowledge and skill

The knowledge and the skills of group members—and the way these are brought to bear on the group task—are the third general summary variable which may be impacted by group interaction process. Once again, there are some tasks that require only a minimal level of knowledge or skill for effective performance, and there are others for which performance measures will be substantially affected by the level of knowledge and skill group members bring to bear on the task. A task requiring the group to assemble a number of very simple mechanical devices with no time limit should not be very responsive to differences in the knowledge and skill members apply to the task; the group vocabulary test described earlier, on the other hand, should be highly responsive to the way group members assess and apply their knowledge.

It is proposed that group interaction serves two major functions in influencing the effectiveness with which the knowledge and skill of group members are applied to the task: (a) assessing and weighting the possible contributions of different group members—who presumably vary in the level of task-relevant talent they have brought to the group; and (b) creating conditions within the group which will lead to a change (presumably an increase) in the overall *level* of knowledge and/or skill group members have and are able to apply to the task.

Assessing and weighting member knowledge and skill.   For tasks on which knowledge or skill is important in determining performance, it often is possible to predict how well the group will do solely on the basis of the talents of its members (Davis, 1969; Haythorn, 1968; Kelley and Thibaut, 1969; Steiner, 1972). The specific predictive model required, of course, depends on the task: for some tasks, the group should operate at the level of its most competent member (e.g. as in Steiner's 'disjunctive' model); for others, the group would be expected to perform at the level of the 'average' member; for still others, group performance should be determined by the least competent member (e.g. Steiner's 'conjunctive' model).

In general, empirical tests of such predictive models have been reasonably successful. Of special interest for present purposes, however, is the recurrent finding that, when actual group productivity is at variance with predictions, it is usually because the model has *over*-predicted group performance. That is, given the level of member talent in the group, the group 'should' have performed better than it actually did. The implication is that the interaction process of the group, through which the talents of members are assessed, weighted, and brought to bear on the task, must have been in some way inadequate.

For some tasks, such process losses should not be substantial. For example, when the specific knowledge or skill required is obvious, and when obtaining the solution does not involve complex teamwork among members, sophisticated or subtle social processes are not required to identify the necessary talents and to apply them to the task. Instead, group interaction may serve merely as a vehicle for exchanging data, and for informing other members that one 'knows the answer.' There is little opportunity here for process foul-ups.

Such apparently was the case in a study reported by Laughlin et al. (1969) which used the Terman Concept Mastery Test as the group task. A large number of students were given the Terman test, and were trichotomized on the basis of their tests scores. Triads were formed with different combinations of member talent (i.e. high-high-high, high-high-medium, high-high-low, etc.). All 10 possible combinations of talent were used. The Terman test was then readministered, but this time it was taken collaboratively by triad members. The relative level of performance of triads could be predicted quite accurately from the overlap of member talent within each type of triad. All predictions were made solely from the preinteraction test scores of triad members; group interaction processes within triads did not enter into the data or theorizing at all, and apparently would have contributed little to predictions of group effectiveness on this particular task. Similar findings predicting group performance from member knowledge or skills with minimal attention to matters of interpersonal process have been noted by numerous other researchers.

On other tasks, however, the mediating role of group process may be more substantial and the risk of process losses substantially greater. Consider, for example, tasks on which the knowledge or skills required for successful performance are complex and subtle, and on which considerable teamwork is required to coordinate and apply member talents. In such circumstances, our ability to predict group effectiveness simply from measures of individual talent without knowledge of group process should be diminished.

A novel case in point is the prediction of the performance of professional athletic teams from data about the skills of individual team members (Jones, 1974). As would be expected, Jones found substantial relationships between measures of individual skill and team performance; teams with better athletes did better. However, the *level* of prediction attained was higher for some sports than for others. For example, nearly 90% of the variation in baseball team effectiveness was predictable from measures of team member skill, as compared to only about 35% for basketball teams. As the author notes, success in basketball is especially dependent upon personal relations and teamwork among players. Thus, process losses might be more likely to impair basketball team effectiveness than would be the case for other team sports.

We have suggested above that, when the primary functions of group interaction are to assess, weight, and apply member talent, process losses are inevitable. For some tasks (i.e. those involving complex skills and high levels of teamwork) the potential losses are greater than for others. In every case, however, group process considerations will determine to some degree how near a group comes to its potential performance, given the capabilities of its members.

Affecting the level of talent available to the group.   Group interaction process can, at least potentially, serve as a means for actually increasing the total amount of member talent available to the group for work on the task. The issue here is *not* the simple exchange or coordination of existing knowledge and skill, as discussed above; that function of group interaction (while relatively easy to observe and document) does not result in a net increase in the total supply of talent available to the group. Instead, the present focus is on how group members can do more than merely share among themselves what they already know—and instead work as a group to gain knowledge or generate skills that previously did not exist within the group.

Virtually no controlled research has been carried out on this latter function of group interaction. The 'training group' approach to the development of interpersonal skills (Argyris, 1962; Bradford *et al.*, 1964; Schein and Bennis, 1965) postulates that group members can effectively use one another as resources to increase member interpersonal competence and thereby increase the level of competence in the group as a whole. But the social processes through which such learning takes place are only beginning to be illuminated (cf. Argyris and Schon, 1974), and additional research on the talent-enhancing functions of group interaction is much needed.

Summary

In this section, we have examined the impact of group interaction process on each of three summary variables: (a) the level of effort brought to bear on the

Table 1   Summary of the proposed functions of group interaction

Summary variables postulated as important in affecting performance outcomes	Impact of interaction process on the summary variables	
	(A) Inevitable process losses	(B) Potential for process gains
Member effort brought to bear on the task	Interaction serves as the less-than-perfect means by which member efforts are coordinated and applied to the task	Interaction can serve to enhance the level of effort members choose to expend on task work
Performance strategies used in carrying out the task	Interaction serves as a less than-perfect 'vehicle' for implementing pre-existing strategies brought to the group by members and (often) shared by them	Interaction can serve as the site for developing or reformulating strategic plans to increase their task appropriateness
Member knowledge and skills used by the group for task work	Interaction serves as a less-than-perfect means for assessing, weighting, and applying member talents to the task	Interaction can serve as a means for increasing the total pool of knowledge and/or skill available to the group (i.e. when the group is the site for generation of new knowledge or skill by members)

task; (b) the task performance strategies implemented by group members in carrying out the task; and (c) the level of knowledge and skill at the disposal of the group for task work. The impact of group interaction on each of the three summary variables is summarized in Table 1.

The table emphasizes that the functions interaction process serves are quite different for each of the three summary variables. The implication is that a researcher who is attempting to understand the process determinants of group performance will have to examine different aspects of the group process, depending on which of the summary variables is operative in his particular task situation. By the same token, the approach an interventionist would take in attempting to help group members create more task-appropriate patterns of interaction would vary, depending on the summary variables operative for the task being performed.

As noted in column A of Table 1, there are inevitable process losses associated with each of the three summary variables. A group can never handle the process issues in column A perfectly; the group's performance therefore will depend in part on how successful members are in finding ways to minimize these process losses. At the same time (column B) there are potentially important (but often unrecognized) process *gains* associated with each of the summary variables. That is, at least the possibility exists for group members to find and implement new, task-effective ways of interacting which will make it possible for them to achieve a level of effectiveness which could not have been anticipated from knowledge about the talents and intentions of group members prior to the start of work on the task.

Conclusions and implications

In the introductory section of this chapter, we pointed out that many social psychologists have reached rather pessimistic conclusions about the efficiency and performance effectivenesss of interacting groups. A working assumption of this chapter, however, has been that it is in fact possible to conduct research that will demonstrate how groups can be designed and managed so that they perform much more effectively than they would 'naturally.' To design and carry out such research, we believe the following will be required:

1. It will be necessary to attempt to *create* effective groups in order to understand their dynamics. Merely describing what happens in existing, natural groups is unlikely to generate knowledge useful for improving group effectiveness because some of the most critical ingredients of truly effective groups may never appear spontaneously in groups allowed to develop naturally. As a start toward the design of such research, we have proposed several ways in which 'input' factors might be experimentally modified to see if they generate more task-effective group processes and higher quality outputs. In particular, we have suggested that by appropriate alteration of group task design, of group norms, and of the way groups are composed, it may be possible to increase the coordination and level of member effort, the task-appropriateness of group performance

strategies, and the utilization and development of the task-relevant knowledge and skill of group members.

2. It will be necessary to design experiments in which group processes are allowed to vary more widely than typically is the case either in laboratory experimental groups or in naturally occurring groups in field settings. We have suggested that, while group interaction process is a crucial mediator of input–output relationships in groups, its functions often are not visible because group tasks and group norms tend powerfully to constrain the richness of the patterns of interaction which can emerge. Fuller understanding of the determinants and effects of group interaction will require both 'opening up' or revising the norms people bring to the group about what is and is not appropriate behavior in task-oriented groups, and more attention to the sampling and experimental variation of group tasks than heretofore has been the case in experimental research.

3. Finally, it will be necessary to adopt a more differentiated view of the functions of group interaction as a mediator of input–performance relationships than previously has been the case. Given that group interaction may serve quite different functions in affecting performance effectiveness for different kinds of tasks, methods of coding and analyzing interaction process will have to be developed which are specifically appropriate to the kind of group task on which the group is working.

If research is to be carried out according to the suggestions outlined above, a number of new methodological tools and techniques will have to be developed, especially in the areas of task description and group process measurement.

Interaction coding systems. Interaction coding systems, to be useful for tracing how group processes mediate between input conditions and group effectiveness, should have two attributes. First, they should be capable of dealing with interaction process as it develops and changes over time, rather than generating simple frequency tallies or summaries averaged over an entire performance period. And second, they should address at a relatively molar level those aspects of interaction which are uniquely important in affecting performance outcome for the class of task being performed. In terms of the summary variables outlined in the present chapter, for example, one should use systems that assess the activities of group members (a) to coordinate and increase member efforts, or (b) to select and implement appropriate performance strategies, or (c) to assess, weight, and develop the knowledge and skills of members. Which of these aspects of the interaction process would actually be measured, of course, would depend on which (or which combination of) summary variables is operative for the task being performed. While systems having the attributes described above do not presently exist, we believe that their development would be a most useful addition to the set of tools available to researchers interested in studying small group effectiveness.

Task classification systems. The problem of task description is heavily intertwined with the problem of measuring group interaction, as Roby pointed out in 1963:

> The thesis will be argued here, first, that any major advance in theory and research on small group problems will depend very heavily on progress in measuring task properties and group processes. Second, it will be argued that these measurement problems are closely interrelated—that is, a clarification of the essential attributes of group tasks will contribute significantly to a better understanding of the important aspects of group process, and conversely (pp. 1–2).

Despite repeated calls for increased attention to task description and classification—and despite a number of attempts to develop schemes for differentiating among group tasks—no satisfactory methodology for describing group tasks has yet emerged (cf. Davis, 1969, Ch. 3; Hackman, 1969; Roby and Lanzetta, 1958; Shaw, 1971, Ch. 9; Zajonc, 1965). One of the difficulties in describing tasks is that they serve, simultaneously, at least two functions which must be described in different terms.

(1) *Task as stimulus.* Through direct instructions about what is to be done, and through cues present in the task materials, tasks affect member behavior in the group setting. Examples earlier in this paper have shown that task design can prompt high or low effort on the part of group members, attention to matters of performance strategy or ignoring these issues, and so on. The stimulus properties of group tasks can be described on an almost endless number of dimensions, in terms ranging from the molecular (e.g. the way lights in a stimulus display are configured) to the molar (e.g. the overall judged challenge of a task). The job of task description is difficult, and will inevitably involve a good deal of 'bootstrapping,' because a strictly empirical/inductive approach is too large and cumbersome, and because theories that can specify *a priori* the most critical stimulus characteristics of tasks for given research questions are not yet available.

(2) *Task as moderator.* As is noted throughout this paper, tasks moderate process–performance relationships in groups; that is, what kinds of behaviors serve to increase or decrease task effectiveness depend, often to a substantial extent, on the nature of the task itself. Thus, any attempt to understand process effects on performance must take account not only of group interaction, but also of the *contingencies in the task* that determine the kinds of behaviors that contribute to effectiveness for that task (cf. Hackman, 1969).

Such contingencies can be referred to as 'critical task contingencies'—i.e. they specify what types of behavior are critical to successful performance on the task in question. Which of the three summary variables discussed in this paper are relevant to performance effectiveness on a given task depends on these task-based contingencies. Thus, if a researcher were attempting to understand or change group effectiveness in a given instance, he or she would deal only or mainly with those summary variables that were objectively important in determining effectiveness for the task at hand.

In practice, it often is possible to determine which of the three summary variables is likely to be most important for a given task simply by inspection—e.g. by asking, 'If greater effort (or different performance strategies, or different levels of knowledge and skill) were brought to bear on this task, would performance effectiveness be likely to change markedly?' But ultimately it will be necessary to know what it is in the *task itself* that determines whether such questions are answered affirmatively or negatively. For only when critical task contingencies can be described in terms of the task itself will it become possible to generate unambiguous and objectively operational propositions about the interactions among task characteristics, group processes, and group effectiveness.

Notes

1. This article is an excerpt (adapted by the authors) from J. R. Hackman and C. G. Morris, 'Group tasks, group interaction process, and group performance effectiveness: A review and proposed integration.' In L. Berkowitz (ed.) (1975). *Advances in Experimental Social Psychology* (Vol. 8). Academic Press, New York. For a more current statement of these ideas (and application of them to task-oriented groups in organizations), see Chs. 7 and 8 of J. R. Hackman and G. R. Oldham (1980). *Work redesign.* Addison-Wesley, Reading, Massachusetts.

2. Experimental confirmation that strategy discussion does enhance group performance when the optimal performance strategy is not immediately obvious subsequently has been provided by Hackman *et al.* (1976).

3. Increased group effectiveness as a consequence of explicit planning activities also has been reported by Shure *et al.* (1962). Davis (1973), on the other hand, suggests that social decision schemes that remain *implicit* may have some adaptive advantages—such as minimizing intermember divisiveness.

References

Argyris, C. (1962). *Interpersonal Competence and Organizational Effectiveness,* Irwin-Dorsey, Homewood, Ill.

Argyris, C., and Schon, D. (1974). *Theory in Practice,* Jossey-Bass, San Francisco.

Bradford, L. P., Gibb, J., and Benne, K. (eds.) (1964). *T-Group Theory and Laboratory Method,* Wiley, New York.

Collins, B. E., and Guetzkow, H. A. (1964). *A Social Psychology of Group Processes for Decision-Making,* Wiley, New York.

Davis, J. H. (1969). *Group Performance,* Addison-Wesley, Reading, Mass.

Davis, J. H. (1973). 'Group decision and social interaction: A theory of social decision schemes,' *Psychological Review,* **80,** 97–125.

Hackman, J. R. (1968). 'Effects of task characteristics on group products,' *Journal of Experimental Social Psychology,* **4,** 162–187.

Hackman, J. R. (1969). 'Toward understanding the role of tasks in behavioral research,' *Acta Psychologica*, **31**, 97–128.

Hackman, J. R., Brousseau, K. R., and Weiss, J. A. (1976). 'The interaction of task design and group performance strategies in determining group effectiveness,' *Organizational Behavior and Human Performance*, **16**, 350–365.

Hare, A. P. (1972). 'Bibliography of small group research: 1959–1969,' *Sociometry*, **35**, 1–150.

Haythorn, W. W. (1968). 'The composition of groups: A review of the literature,' *Acta Psychologica*, **28**, 97–128.

Ingham, A. G., Levinger, G., Graves, J., and Peckham, V. (1974). 'The Ringlemann Effect: Studies of group size and group performance,' *Journal of Experimental Social Psychology*, **10**, 371–384.

Jones, M. B. (1974). 'Regressing group on individual effectiveness,' *Organizational Behavior and Human Performance*, **11**, 426–451.

Katzell, R. A., Miller, C. E., Rotter, N. G., and Venet, T. G. (1970). 'Effects of leadership and other inputs on group processes and outputs,' *Journal of Social Psychology*, **80**, 157–169.

Kelley, H. H., and Thibaut, J. W. (1969). 'Group problem solving,' in G. Lindzey and E. Aronson (eds.), *The Handbook of Social Psychology*, 2nd edn, Addison-Wesley, Reading, Mass.

Laughlin, P. R., Branch, L. G., and Johnson, H. H. (1969). 'Individual versus triadic performance on a unidimensional complementary task as a function of initial ability level,' *Journal of Personality and Social Psychology*, **12**, 144–150.

McGrath, J. E., and Altman, I. (1966). *Small Group Research: A Synthesis and Critique of the Field*, Holt, New York.

Maier, N. R. F. (1963). *Problem Solving Discussions and Conferences: Leadership Methods and Skills*, McGraw-Hill, New York.

Morris, C. G. (1966). 'Task effects on group interaction,' *Journal of Personality and Social Psychology*, **5**, 545–554.

Roby, T. B. (1963). 'Process criteria of group performance,' Paper presented as part of the Task and Criterion work group of the Small Groups in Isolation project of the Neuropsychiatric Division, NMRI, Bethesda, Maryland.

Roby, T. B., and Lanzetta, J. T. (1958). 'Considerations in the analysis of group tasks,' *Psychological Bulletin*, **55**, 88–101.

Schein, E. H., and Bennis, W. (1965). *Personal and Organizational Change through Group Methods*, Wiley, New York.

Shaw, M. E. (1971). *Group Dynamics*, McGraw-Hill, New York.

Shiflett, S. C. (1972). 'Group performance as a function of task difficulty and organizational interdependence,' *Organizational Behavior and Human Performance*, **7**, 442–456.

Shure, G. H., Rogers, M. S., Larsen, I. M., and Tassone, J. (1962). 'Group planning and task effectiveness,' *Sociometry*, **25**, 263–282.

Steiner, I. D. (1972). *Group Process and Productivity*, Academic Press, New York.

Stone, T. H. (1971). 'Effects of mode of organization and feedback level on creative task groups,' *Journal of Applied Psychology*, **55**, 324–330.

Varela, J. A. (1971). *Psychological Solutions to Social Problems*, Academic Press, New York.

Weick, K. E. (1969). *The Social Psychology of Organizing*, Addison-Wesley, Reading, Mass.

Zajonc, R. B. (1965). 'The requirements and design of a standard group task, *Journal of Experimental Social Psychology*, **1**, 71–88.

Small Groups and Social Intreraction, Volume 1
Edited by H. H. Blumberg, A. P. Hare, V. Kent and M. Davies
© 1983 John Wiley & Sons Ltd

8.3 The Structural Model of Marital Interaction

Lowell J. Krokoff and John M. Gottman

University of Illinois, Urbana-Champaign

Our research on marriage is organized by the question, 'What, if anything, is different about interaction in satisfying and unsatisfying marriages?' To answer this question we have studied couples' conflict resolution along three dimensions: (1) positiveness–negativeness, (2) reciprocity, and (3) dominance. Although these variables had occupied a place in previous theories of marital functioning, their conceptualization and assessment in our research were guided by developments in coding nonverbal behaviors (e.g. Mehrabian, 1972), ideas from information theory (e.g. Attneave, 1959; Shannon and Weaver, 1949), and some recent innovations in the analysis of sequences of observational data (e.g. sequential analysis, Sackett, 1974, 1977; spectral time series analysis, Granger and Hatanaka, 1964). These innovations, and the findings from the investigations that form the cornerstone of the Structural Model of Marital Interaction, have been described in detail by Gottman (1979). In this chapter we will present an overview of the Structural Model.

First, we will discuss the hypothesis that a consideration of the nonverbal rather than the verbal component of couples' conflict resolution will increase the empirical relationship between marital interaction and marital satisfaction. Thus, while interaction in unsatisfying marriages is expected to be characterized by higher proportions of negative behaviors and lower proportions of positive behaviors than in satisfying marriages, it is also predicted that these differences will be greater for nonverbal behaviors than verbal behaviors. Second, we will describe the application of sequential analysis to assess the hypothesis that the reciprocation of negative behaviors, and not positive behaviors, will best discriminate between the interactions of maritally satisfied and unsatisfied couples. Third, we will discuss the application of some recent developments in spectral time series analysis to test the idea that interaction in unsatisfying marriages will show greater asymmetry in predictability than in satisfying marriages.

Because the evaluation of the above hypotheses requires an objective and meaningful way of both selecting criterion groups and describing marital interaction, we will begin our presentation with a discussion of these issues.

Selecting criterion groups

The first step in assessing the hypothesis presented in the introduction to this chapter is to specify a method for selecting criterion groups, i.e. a group of couples experiencing satisfaction in their marriages and another group of couples that is not. In the remainder of this chapter two distinctions are made. The first is called the clinic–nonclinic distinction. Clinic couples were those who were seeking marriage counseling, and nonclinic couples were those who answered an advertisement calling for couples with a mutually satisfying marriage. The second distinction, the distressed–nondistressed differentiation, was based in part on spouses' responses to the Locke–Williamson (1958) Marital Relationship Inventory (MRI). Distressed couples were those clinic couples in which at least one spouse's MRI score fell below a criterion of 85, whereas nondistressed couples were those nonclinic couples in which both spouses' MRI scores fell above a criterion of 102. The selection of the above cutoff scores was based on a recommendation provided by Burgess et al. (1971). The idea that the MRI taps a dimension of marital satisfaction has been widely supported by findings from both sociological investigations of marital adjustment and observational studies of marital interaction (Gottman, 1979).

Once criterion groups have been identified, the next task for researching differences between distressed (or clinic) couples and nondistressed (or nonclinic) couples' interaction is to determine an objective and meaningful way of describing couples' communication. This issue will be addressed in the next section of this paper.

Describing marital interaction: the Couple's Interaction Scoring System

Before we can assess differences between distressed (or clinic) and nondistressed (or nonclinic) couples' interactions, we need to decide what aspects of their interaction to base this comparison on, as well as to specify a method for objectively measuring these behaviors. In our research with married couples, we usually look at the way spouses discuss and resolve their disagreements. We decided to study couples' conflict resolution after reviewing the research literature on the variables that predict marital adjustment and happiness. These findings support the general conclusion that a couple's ability to arrive at a consensus in resolving differences may be of central importance in predicting their marital satisfaction (Gottman, 1979).

The task of comparing conflict resolution in satisfying and unsatisfying marriages requires an objective and meaningful way of measuring those behaviors that are presumed to be involved in both successful and unsuccessful communication. For instance, a review of the research findings on marital and family interaction suggests that communication in social relationships can be characterized along a dimension of positiveness–negativeness, as interaction in distressed relationships is less positive and more negative than in nondistressed relationships (e.g. Alexander, 1973a,b; Birchler et al., 1975; Caputo, 1963; Jacobson, 1977; Mishler and Waxler, 1968; Riskin and Faunce, 1970, 1972; Stuart, 1971; Weiss et al., 1973; Wills et al., 1974). Furthermore, a method for operationalizing positiveness in the *verbal component* of communication, namely, the ratio of agreement to disagreement statements, was implicated by Riskin and Faunce's (1972) decade review of research on marital interaction. In addition to agreement and disagreement, our early work with couples identified several other important dimensions to problem-solving. These include mindreading, expressing feelings or attitudes about a problem, summarizing other, summarizing self, proposing a solution to a problem, and communication talk. To measure the above, we developed the Couple's Interaction Scoring System (CISS). Because these behaviors are revealed by the verbal or literal component of couples' communication, we refer to the above as 'content codes.'

Research on nonverbal behavior suggests that positiveness can also be reliably coded from vocal, facial, and postural cues (e.g. Ekman and Friesen, 1975; Mehrabian, 1972; Zahn, 1975). Therefore, the CISS contains provisions for coding the nonverbal behavior of both the speaker (called 'affect code') and the listener (called 'context code') as either positive, negative, or neutral using a hierarchical decision rule based in part on Mehrabian's (1972) regression equation. CISS coders scan for specific nonverbal cues involving facial expressions, voice tone, body position, and movement (in that order).

The main advantages of the CISS over other coding systems previously used in this area include the independent assessment of the verbal and nonverbal components of communication, the preservation of the sequential flow of marital interaction, and the assessment of behaviors directly involved in couples' conflict resolution (Notarius and Markman, 1981).

The CISS also meets three important conditions for demonstrating reliability with observational methods: (1) generalizability across coders, as measured by Cronbach's Alphas, (2) demonstrating interobserver agreement beyond that which would be expected by chance alone, as measured by Cohen's Kappa, and (3) the maintenance of interobserver agreement over time, i.e. the issue of 'reliability decay' (Gottman, 1979). The reader is referred to reviews by Gottman (1979) and Notarius and Markman (1981) for a more detailed discussion of the CISS.[1] In the discussion that follows, we will describe how the CISS has been used in our research to assess interaction in satisfying and unsatisfying marriages.

Positiveness–negativeness and nonverbal behavior

Research on marital and family interaction (e.g. Jacobson, 1977; Riskin and Faunce, 1970, 1972), as well as common sense, suggests that interaction in satisfying and unsatisfying marriages can be differentiated along a positive–negative dimension. While previous investigations of marital interaction have assessed positiveness in the verbal component of communication alone or by combining verbal and nonverbal messages into one code (e.g. Birchler *et al.*, 1975; Riskin and Faunce, 1972), it is likely that a consideration of the nonverbal component of couples' communication will increase the empirical relationship between marital interaction and marital satisfaction. With this in mind, Gottman (1979) independently assessed the proportion of positive and negative verbal and nonverbal behaviors in the interactions of a group of distressed and nondistressed couples. To measure positiveness in the verbal dimension of communication, the proportion of agreement statements to agreement plus disagreement statements was calculated for couples' conflict resolution discussions. Positiveness was operationalized in the above manner in light of Riskin and Faunce's (1972) conclusion that the ratio of agreement to disagreement was the most consistent discriminator across studies between distressed and nondistressed families.

By summing positive, neutral, and negative CISS affect codes over all content codes a separate index of the nonverbal component of positiveness in marital interaction was also revealed. The results of the above study indicate that compared to nondistressed couples, the interactions of distressed couples were characterized by higher proportions of negative behaviors and lower proportions of positive behaviors, and that these differences were greater for nonverbal than verbal behaviors, and greater for negative than positive behaviors.

A more meaningful analysis of the role of nonverbal behavior in couples' communication is revealed by looking at the nonverbal behaviors that accompany particular verbal messages. For example, an agreement statement such as 'sure, anything you say,' may convey enthusiastic agreement when spoken in a positive tone of voice; however, the same verbal message may reflect either sarcasm or defeated acquiescence when accompanied by negative affect. In fact, Gottman (1979) found that the interactions of distressed and nondistressed couples were differentiated by this latter characteristic, as distressed couples were more likely than nondistressed couples to express verbal agreement accompanied by negative nonverbal behaviors. Additional analyses revealed that distressed couples were also more likely to express their feelings about a problem, to mindread, and to disagree, all with negative effect.

The findings presented in this section have shown that interaction in satisfying and unsatisfying marriages can be differentiated by couples' respective proportions of positive and negative verbal and nonverbal behaviors. Furthermore, the assessment of the nonverbal component of couples' communication represents a significant development in research in this area. In the next section on reciprocity in marriage, we will introduce a methodology for assessing the connectedness of husbands and wives' behaviors during conflict resolution discussions.

Reciprocity

An interest in the sequential or reciprocal nature of social interaction has characterized much of the theoretical and empirical work in this area (e.g. behavior exchange theory, Thibaut and Kelley, 1959; the double bind hypothesis, Bateson *et al.*, 1956; the 'quid pro quo' arrangement, Jackson, 1965, Stuart, 1969; social learning theory and reinforcement models, Patterson and Reid, 1970). This implies that in addition to assessing overall levels of positive and negative behaviors, as we described in the previous section on positiveness, we can also look at how a husband is likely to respond to his wife's positive and negative behaviors, and vice versa. In fact, the idea that compared to interaction in satisfying marriages spouses in unsatisfying marriages are more likely to reciprocate negative behaviors and less likely to reciprocate positive behaviors is a widely accepted concept, particularly among social learning theorists and behavior therapists (e.g. Stuart, 1969).

However, previous empirical work in this area has often been flawed by the application of inappropriate methods for analyzing sequences of observed behaviors, as well as a neglect of the nonverbal component of couples' communication (Gottman, 1979). Testing the above hypothesis on positive and negative reciprocity requires statistical tools that—unlike those used to evaluate overall levels of positive and negative behaviors—preserve the sequential flow of marital interaction and assess contingent relationships in a husband and wife's verbal and nonverbal behaviors over time.

A statistical procedure that meets the above conditions is sequential analysis (Notarius *et al.*, 1981). Sequential analysis is derived from a view of communication, known as information theory, whose basic premise is that a behavior of one organism has communicative value in a social sense if it reduces uncertainty in our ability to predict the behavior of another organism. Uncertainty reduction is assessed by comparing a behavior's conditional probability and its simple or unconditional probability using Sackett's (1977) z-statistic.

The information theory approach to describing communication is illustrated by Gottman's (1979) example, involving the interaction of spider crabs presented below:

> Spider crabs have a relatively simple behavioral repertoire . . . and for the purpose of this illustration I shall further simplify that repertoire. These crabs can move or remain fixed in one place, and they can move their chilepids (arms) in a single side chilepid raise (right or left

chilepid), a double chilepid raise, or by a forward chilepid extension. They also occasionally, but rarely, fight or flee. Let us denote these behaviors as *Move, Single Chilepid Raise, Double Chilepid Raise, Forward Chilepid Extension, Fight,* and *Flee.*

Suppose we want to discover the 'language' of the spider crab; that is, we want to know what, if anything, these behaviors 'mean' or communicate socially to other spider crabs in the vicinity. We need to know the communicative value of each of the crab's behaviors . . . We notice, for example, that the probability of a crab's moving is very low; that is, it rarely moves. Let us assume we discover that p (Move) = .06. This means that the average crab in our tank was observed to have moved in 6% of our observational coding units.

Now we look at the proportion of times that Crab B moved after Crab A did a Single Chilepid Raise. This is a conditional probability, written p (B moved | A's Single Chilepid Raise), and it is verbalized as 'the conditional probability that B moved given that A did a Single Chilepid Raise.' We note in our data that A raised a single chilepid 100 times and that, of those, B moved 6 times. The conditional probability was thus 6% (6/100), and it is, therefore, no different from the unconditional probability of a move. As a result, we have gained no information, that is, no reduction of uncertainty in B's having moved by prior knowledge of A's Single Chilepid Raises. . . . Suppose we look at the double chilepid raises of A and again find that p (B moved | A's Double Chilepid Raise) = .07. We would probably conclude that, again, the double chilepid raise did not reduce uncertainty in our ability to predict B's having moved. However, if we were to look at all the times A performed a Forward Chilepid Extension, we would see that p (B moved | A's Forward Chilepid Extension) = .65. If the two crabs were facing one another, we would then wonder if the Forward Chilepid Extension means, 'Get out of my way, you crab.'

We might investigate further by looking at what happens to the 35% of the occasions when A did a Forward Chilepid Extension and B did not move. We notice that a fight occurred on 60% of those occasions. Suppose that the unconditional probability of a fight is .02 (it would have to be lower than the unconditional probability of a move). We are beginning to detect an elaborate sequence. This latter probability p (Fight | B did not move after A did a Forward Chilepid Extension), is called a 'lag-2 conditional probability with A's Forward Chilepid Extension as the criterion behavior,' because something else intervened between Flight and A's Forward Chilepid Raise. We can continue in this manner to conditional probabilities of lag 3, lag 4 and so on, in each case comparing conditional to unconditional probabilities (pp. 31–32).

Gottman (1979) describes the application of Sackett's (1974, 1977) lag analysis to assess reciprocity in conflict resolution. Videotapes of couples discussing a troublesome marital issue were first coded for affect using the CISS. Results indicated that the reciprocation of negative affect, and not positive affect, best discriminated between the interactions of clinic and nonclinic couples, with more reciprocity of negative behavior in clinic couples than in nonclinic couples. These findings failed to support a popular idea in the clinical folklore, namely, the 'quid pro quo' arrangement (e.g. Stuart, 1971). The quid pro quo concept presumes that the reciprocation of positive behaviors over time is a defining characteristic of a stable and well-functioning marriage, and thus by implication, an essential target for clinical interventions with couples in unsatisfying marriages.

In addition to the reciprocation of negative affect, detailed sequential analysis of CISS content codes revealed additional patterns of interaction that differentiated between the interactions of clinic and nonclinic couples. These sequences, which are described in detail by Gottman (1979), are as follows.

1. *Cross-complaining and validation sequences.* Clinic couples are more likely to enter into cross-complaining interactional sequences and are less likely to enter into validation sequences than are nonclinic couples. Cross-complaining sequences involve a temporal exchange of complaints about a relationship problem, i.e. one complaint is met with a counter-complaint by the other spouse. However, in validation sequences a spouse follows his or her partner's complaint about a relationship problem with agreement or acknowledgement. It is important to note that what we call 'agreement or acknowledgement' is also called 'back-channeling' by Duncan and Fiske (1977). These brief acknowledgements appear to communicate that the listener is tracking the speaker and understands the point or the speaker's point of view. Validation does not imply that the listener agrees with the speaker's point of view.

2. *Contract and counter-proposal sequences.* Clinic couples are less likely to enter into contract sequences and more likely to enter into counter-proposal sequences than are nonclinic couples. That is, nonclinic spouses are more likely to follow their partner's proposals for resolving a relationship problem with agreement, whereas clinic couples are more likely to offer counter-proposals. The form of agreement here is substantially different than in validation sequences. It involves direct agreement with the other person's point of view or accepting modification of one's own point of view.

3. *Communication talk.* Communication talk statements involve comments on the process of communication. An old issue in the marital and family interaction literature is whether metacommunication characterizes good relationships (Goodrich and Boomer, 1963) or poor relationships (Jackson, 1965). Results reported in Gottman (1979) revealed that the frequency of communication talk was about the same in clinic and nonclinic couples' interactions; however, these two groups utilized communication talk in different ways. Clinic couples entered into long chains involving the reciprocation of communication talk, whereas these

sequences were brief in nonclinic couples, and easily exited by one spouse following *his or her* partner's communication talk with agreement.

This section has demonstrated how one statistical innovation, namely, sequential analysis, can have important conceptual implications for our understanding of marital interaction. In the next section we will introduce an additional technique for assessing the pattern of social interaction.

Dominance

In addition to positiveness and reciprocity, social relationships have also been described along a dimension of dominance (e.g. Jacob, 1975; Watzlawick *et al.*, 1967). In previous investigations of family interaction, dominance has been operationalized as an asymmetry in the frequency of a particular variable presumed to measure power between family members. For instance, measures of dominance have included talk time, the number of communications, and successful interruptions (Jacob, 1975). Unfortunately, the widespread use of these measures has not resulted in unambiguous empirical support for the idea that interaction in distressed and non-distressed families can be differentiated along a dimension of dominance (Gottman, 1979). This conclusion is not surprising, as clinical folklore and common experience teach us that the person doing the least amount of talking or overt decision making is often the 'real power behind the throne.' In these instances, the dominant spouse's 'power' may only be revealed by the more subtle aspects of the interaction.

Therefore, as an alternative to operationalizing dominance as an asymmetry in the frequency of a particular variable, we propose that dominance may instead involve an asymmetry in patterns of interaction, perhaps involving a complex array of nonverbal signals. Consistent with the information theory definition of communication described in the previous section on reciprocity, dominance is conceptualized as an asymmetry in the predictability of behavior between a husband and wife. Thus, if a wife's future behavior is more predictable from her husband's past behavior than conversely, then the husband is said to be dominant. Asymmetry in predictability can be assessed with a spectral time series model recommended for economic data by Granger and Hatanaka (1964). In the discussion that follows, we will present a brief overview of time series terminology and its applicability to the study of dominance in marriage.

Spectral time series analysis assesses lead–lag relationships between two time series. For example, for the two time series X_t and Y_t, where $X_t =$ observations of the wife's affect over time, and $Y_t =$ observations of the husband's affect over time, this model determines whether or not changes in X_t follow changes in Y_t at some fixed lag (in which case we'd say the husband's behavior leads and the wife's behavior lags), and vice versa.

In frequency domain analysis, the component oscillations of a time series (called 'frequency components') are revealed by the spectral density function. The Granger and Hatanaka model identifies two frequency components: (1) a slow component and (2) a fast component. When this model is applied to CISS affect codes, the above components can be viewed as reflecting slow variations in affect (such as those characteristic of longer lasting mood states), (called 'mood fluctuations') in the case of the slow component, and as rapidly changing emotional expressions (such as the momentary raised eyebrow accompanying surprise), (called 'expression fluctuations') in the case of the fast component. The phase spectrum reveals lead–lag relationships between a frequency component in one series and a frequency component in another series; e.g. the lead–lag relationship between the slow frequency component in the husband's series (husband's mood fluctuations) and the slow frequency component in the wife's series (wife's mood fluctuations). Because nine different dominance patterns are possible with this model (Gottman, 1979), the phase spectrum has important implications for the study of dominance and emotional responsiveness in marriage. For example, a husband may be dominant for mood fluctuations (i.e. the slow component in the wife's series lags behind the slow component in the husband's series, although the converse is not true), while the wife may be dominant for expression fluctuations (i.e. the fast component in the husband's series lags behind the fast component in the wife's series, although the converse is not true).

In a study described in detail by Gottman (1979), the Granger and Hatanaka (1964) model was used to test the idea that interaction in unsatisfying marriages is characterized by more asymmetry in predictability than in satisfying marriages. The findings from the above study revealed that clinic and nonclinic couples' interactions were differentiated along a dimension of dominance only during discussions of high conflict issues (and not low conflict issues), and only for rapid fluctuations in affect (and not mood fluctuations). Thus, on high conflict tasks, clinic husbands' expression fluctuations were more predictive of their wives' subsequent behavior than conversely. The interactions of nonclinic couples were characterized by more equalitarian dominance patterns on both low and high conflict tasks for both mood and expression fluctuations.

The above findings suggest that in unsatisfying marriages, husbands drive or dominate the affective climate of the couples' interaction. Another way of interpreting these findings is that in unsatisfying marriages, husbands are less responsive to their wives' affect than their wives are to theirs. This idea is consistent with the findings from two recent studies—one with couples in the United States (Gottman and Porterfield, 1981) and the other with Australian couples (Noller, 1980)—which suggest a deficit in the ability of husbands in unsatisfying marriages to accurately read their wives' nonverbal cues. Furthermore, the results of a series of intervention studies suggest that a husband's emotional responsiveness is an important variable for predicting the outcome of clinical interventions with the maritally unsatisfied (Gottman, 1979).

Summary

We introduced this chapter by posing the following question about marital interaction: 'What, if anything, is different about interaction in satisfying and unsatisfying marriages?' Three dimensions have been implicated by the present review: positiveness–negativeness, reciprocity, and dominance—which when taken together make up the Structural Model of Marital Interaction. Compared to interaction in satisfying marriages, interaction in unsatisfying marriages is characterized by more negative behaviors and less positive behaviors, more reciprocity of negative behaviors, and a greater asymmetry in the predictability of behavior between a husband and wife. When taken together, these findings make up the Structural Model of Marital Interaction.

The findings reported here have been seplicated across studies differing in the demographic characteristics of participating couples, criterion groups (the clinic/nonclinic and the distressed/nondistressed distinctions), tasks (high and low conflict issues, enjoyable conversations), and settings (conflict resolution in the home and the laboratory). Furthermore, spouses' perceptions of their interactions parallel those patterns revealed by the ratings of trained coders using the CISS (Gottman, 1979).

To be meaningful, the findings reported in this chapter must have implications for clinical interventions with the maritally unsatisfied. Gottman et al. (1976) describe a couple's communication program that was derived in part from the Structural Model variables. In a series of investigations reported in detail by Gottman (1979), Structural Model variables were related to both the process and outcome of clinical intervention. The couple's communication program produced a significant increase in marital satisfaction, and decrease in both overall levels of negative affect and negative affect reciprocity. The above changes transferred to home interactions and were maintained at follow-up assessments. Furthermore, changes in Structural Model variables were able to predict changes in marital satisfaction, as decreases in wives' negative affect were correlated with increases in the couple's marital satisfaction.

In addition to the substantive findings presented in this paper, the present chapter has also highlighted the importance of assessing nonverbal aspects of couples' communication and the interface between theoretical concepts and statistical methods. Developments in sequential analysis and spectral time series analysis have added to our understanding of the patterning of marital interaction, and in the process have shed new light on some old issues in this area.

Note

1. Coding manuals are currently available from either author at the following address: Department of Psychology, University of Illinois, Champaign, Illinois, 61820, USA. Recently, Gottman (1979) developed a voice tone coding system that reliably codes affect from audio-tapes. This coding manual is also available.

References

Alexander, J. F. (1973a). 'Defensive and supportive communications in family systems,' *Journal of Marriage and the Family*, **35**, 613–617.

Alexander, J. F. (1973b). 'Defensive and supportive communication in normal and deviant families,' *Journal of Consulting and Clinical Psychology*, **40**, 223–231.

Attneave, F. (1959). *Applications of Information Theory to Psychology*, Holt, New York.

Bateson, G., Jackson, D. D., Haley, J., and Weakland, J. (1956). 'Toward a theory of schizophrenia,' *Behavioral Science*, **1**, 251–264.

Birchler, G., Weiss, R., and Vincent, J. (1975). 'Multimethod analysis of social reinforcement exchange between maritally distressed and nondistressed spouse and stranger dyads,' *Journal of Personality and Social Psychology*, **31**, 349–360.

Burgess, E. W., Locke, J. J., and Thomes, M. M. (1971). *The Family*, Van Nostrand Reinhold, New York.

Caputo, D. V. (1963). 'The parents of schizophrenics,' *Family Process*, **2**, 339–356.

Duncan, S. Jr., and Fiske, D. W. (1977). *Face-to-face Interaction: Research, Methods, and Theory*, Lawrence Erlbaum Associates, Hillsdale, NJ.

Ekman, P., and Friesen, W. V. (1975). *Unmasking the Face*, Prentice-Hall, Englewood Cliffs, NJ.

Goodrich, D. W., and Boomer, D. S. (1963). 'Experimental assessment of modes of conflict resolution,' *Family Process*, **2**, 15–24.

Gottman, J. M. (1979). *Marital Interaction: Exerpimental Investigations*, Academic Press, New York.

Gottman, J., Notarius, C., Gonso, J., and Markman, H. (1976). *A Couple's Guide to Communication*, Research Press, Champaign, Ill.

Gottman, J. M., and Porterfield, A. L. (1981). 'Communicative competence in the nonverbal behavior of married couples,' *Journal of Marriage and the Family*, **43**, 817–824.

Granger, C. W. J., and Hatanaka, M. (1964). *Spectral Analysis of Economic Time Series*, Princeton University Press, Princeton, NJ.

Jackson, D. D. (1965). 'Family rules: Marital quid pro quo,' *Archives of General Psychiatry*, **12**, 1535–1541.

Jacob, T. (1975). 'Family interaction in disturbed and normal families: A methodological and substantive review,' *Psychological Bulletin*, **82**, 33–65.

Jacobson, N. S. (1977). 'Problem solving and contingency contracting in the treatment of marital discord,' *Journal of Consulting and Clinical Psychology*, **45**, 92–100.

Locke, H. J., and Williamson, R. C. (1958). 'Marital adjustment: A factor analysis study,' *American Sociological Review*, **23**, 562–569.

Mehrabian, A. (1972). *Nonverbal Communication*, Aldine-Atherton, New York.

Mishler, E. G., and Waxler, N. E. (1968). *Interaction in Families: An Experimental Study of Family Process in Schizophrenia*, Wiley, New York.

Noller, P. (1980). 'Marital misunderstandings: A study of couples' nonverbal communication,' Unpublished doctoral dissertation, University of Queensland.

Notarius, C. J., Krokoff, L. J., and Markman, H. J. (1981). 'Analysis of observational data,' in E. E. Filsinger and R. A. Lewis (eds.), *Marital Observation and Behavioral Assessment: Recent Developments and Techniques*, Sage Publications, Beverly Hills, Calif.

Notarius, C. J., and Markham, H. J. (1981). 'The couple's interaction scoring system (CISS): An observational coding system for marital interaction,' in E. E. Filsinger and R. A. Lewis (eds.), *Marital Observation and Behavioral Assessment: Recent Developments and Techniques*, Sage Publications, Beverly Hills, Calif.

Patterson, G. R., and Reid, J. B. (1970). 'Reciprocity and coercion: Two facets of social systems,' in J. Michaels and C. Neuringer (eds.), *Behavior Modification for Psychologists*, Appleton-Century Crofts, New York.

Riskin, J., and Faunce, E. E. (1970). 'Family interaction scales, III. Discussion of methodology and substantive findings,' *Archives of General Psychiatry*, 22, 527–537.

Riskin, J., and Faunce, E. E. (1972). 'An evaluative review of family interaction research,' *Family Process*, 11 (4), 364–455.

Sackett, G. P. (1974). 'A nonparametric lag sequential analysis for studying dependency among responses in observational coding systems,' Unpublished manuscript, University of Washington.

Sackett, G. P. (1977). 'The lag sequential analysis of contingency and cyclicity in behavioral interaction research,' in J. Osfsky (ed.), *Handbook of Infant Development*, Wiley, New York.

Shannon, C. E., and Weaver, W. (1949). *The Mathematical Theory of Communication*, The University of Illinois Press, Urbana.

Stuart, R. B. (1969). 'Operant-interpersonal treatment for marital discord,' *Journal of Consulting and Clinical Psychology*, 33, 675–682.

Stuart, R. B. (1971). 'Behavioral contracting within the families of deliquents,' *Journal of Behavior Therapy and Experimental Psychiatry*, 2, 1–11.

Thibaut, J. W., and Kelley, H. H. (1959). *The Social Psychology of Groups*, Wiley, New York.

Watzlawick, P., Beavin, J. H., and Jackson, D. D. (1967). *Pragmatics of Human Communication: A Study of Interactional Patterns, Pathologies, and Paradoxes*, W. W. Norton, New York.

Weiss, R. L., Hops, H., and Patterson, G. R. (1973). 'A framework for conceptualizing marital conflict: A technology for altering it, some data for evaluating it,' in L. A. Hamerlynch, I. C. Handy, and E. J. Mash (eds.), *Behavior Change: The Fourth Banff Conference on Behavior Modification*, Research Press, Champaign, Ill.

Wills, T. A., Weiss, R. L., and Patterson, G. R. (1974). 'A behavioral analysis of the determinants of marital satisfaction,' *Journal of Consulting and Clinical Psychology*, 42, 802–811.

Zahn, L. G. (1975). 'Verbal-vocal integration as a function of sex and methodology,' *Journal of Research in Personality*, 9, 226–239.

9 Roles and Relationships

Small Groups and Social Interaction, Volume 1
Edited by H. H. Blumberg, A. P. Hare, V. Kent and M. Davies
© 1983 John Wiley & Sons Ltd

9.1 Dyadic Relationships

Robert A. Hinde   *MRC Unit on the Development and Integration of Behaviour, Madingley, Cambridge, CB3 8AA*

The study of interpersonal relationships

The study of interpersonal relationships comes within the provinces of several of the social sciences, yet it has provided the central focus of none. Social psychologists, for instance, have provided much interesting material on short-term interactions, and on the dynamics of groups, but, with certain notable exceptions, have provided relatively little material on interpersonal relationships. It has been suggested elsewhere (Hinde, 1979) that an integrated science of interpersonal relationships, so obviously of great practical importance, has not so far flourished because of the absence of an adequate descriptive base: what follows is a summary of the views there expressed.

We may start with certain presuppositions.

1. *Social phenomena must be studied at a number of different levels, each of which has properties not relevant to those subordinated to it.* The first level in the present context is that of social behaviour, but this is normally studied in the context of interactions between two or more individuals. An interaction has properties that are simply not relevant to the behaviour of individuals in isolation: for instance the behaviour of the participants may or may not be coordinated each with that of the other, and they may be competitive or cooperative. The next level is that of the interpersonal relationship. A relationship involves a series of interactions over time between two individuals who are known to each other, such that each interaction may be influenced by those that have preceded it. Relationships involve properties that emerge from the relative frequency and patterning of the constituent interactions. Beyond this are yet further levels of complexity, such as that of group structure: the structure of a group depends on the nature and patterning of the relationships within it, and has properties that are emergent from that patterning.

2. *Considering first behaviour, description must specify both content and quality.* Thus to describe an interaction, it is necessary to say what the participants are doing together, and how they are doing it: they may be kissing, but are they kissing dutifully, passionately or politely? To describe a relationship, it is necessary to specify not only the content and quality of the component interactions, but also qualities that depend on their frequencies or relative frequencies, and/or how they are patterned in time. We shall return to this issue later.

3. *Description must involve not only behaviour, but also affective/cognitive aspects.* A relationship may continue over periods during which the participants do not meet. What happens in an interaction may be less important than what the participants believe to have happened. Individuals evaluate their relationships, and those evaluations may affect the future course of the relationship. Thus while relationships involve a series of interactions in time, description only of those interactions provides an inadequate picture of the relationship.

We may also note here that the social behaviour shown by an individual may provide little guide to the extent to which he has formed or has the capacity to form social relationships. Individuals may be sociable and yet direct their social behaviour promiscuously: they may be devoted, yet too shy to express their devotion.

4. *The relationships affect, and are affected by, the personalities of the participating individuals.* That the nature of any relationship is affected by the natures of the participating individuals does not need to be said. Conversely, as stressed by Sullivan, Mead, Cooley, and others, personalities of individuals are influenced by the important relationships in their lives. This of course does not mean that those relationships are the sole determinants of personality, but only that they are important influences. Earlier relationships are of course of special importance here, primarily because the range of possible courses that development could take is then widest: subsequent influences can act only within the potentialities left by earlier ones. Both the constant threads that run through our lives, and the often surprising flexibility that social behaviour can show, must be seen in terms of a range of possibilities determined in large part by earlier experience.

5. *Relationships affect, and are affected by, their social setting.* Every relationship is set within a social nexus, whose nature is determined by the nature of and relations between its constituent (dyadic and higher order) relationships. But reciprocally every relationship is influenced by its social setting. The latter influence may operate through other relationships engaged in by the participants, or by social norms which are transmitted and transmuted through the agency of the social group and affect the relationships within it.

6. *An integrated science of interpersonal relationships will require both a descriptive framework related to each of the levels of complexity mentioned above, and a series of principles which 'explain' the patterning observed at each level.* We shall discuss these further in a moment, but it is worth while emphasizing the word

'integrated.' Much work in the several social sciences has involved attempts to establish the range of applicability of one paradigm, or to pit one theory or paradigm against its rivals. This has led to considerable progress in certain isolated areas, but has not been conducive to the development of overall understanding. In the study of interpersonal relationships integration is perhaps of special importance. Relationships involve interactions, yet involve more than interactions. They have both behavioural and affective/cognitive aspects. They must be related to the personalities of the participants, and to the social network within which they exist. Their understanding requires diverse concepts, and an integrated science of interpersonal relationships demands that the relations between those concepts be understood.

The description of interpersonal relationships

Successful description involves selectivity guided by the problems to be solved and by the theories thought likely to be useful in solving them. Description of relationships must involve dimensions relevant to a wide range of relationships, and be capable both of discriminating between gross categories of relationships (e.g. between parent–child and teacher–pupil relationships) and between relationships within those broad categories (how this teacher–pupil relationship differs from that, for example). Description must be concerned both with what actually happens in the relationship, and with how the participants see what happens. One powerful approach is to study a wide range of relationships, measure their characteristics, and reduce the data by factor analysis to a limited number of dimensions. Such an approach has been used with considerable success (e.g. Wisch *et al.*, 1976). However, what emerges from such an analysis must be in part influenced by the dimensions selected for measurement initially. At present it seems wise to acknowledge that we do not yet know precisely what to describe and measure if we are to understand the dynamics of relationships, and it is better to attempt to specify merely what sorts of issues are likely to be helpful. In the following paragraphs I have listed eight categories of criteria that seem valuable for describing relationships. They concern the properties of the relationship itself, and not the personality characteristics of the participants. Each category may later be refined into one or many dimensions, with each dimension assessable in terms of one or a number of intercorrelated measures. The list moves from aspects of behavior more useful in differentiating gross types of relationships to those concerned more with their affective/cognitive aspects.

Content of interactions

The initial categorization of relationships which we make usually refers primarily to what the participants do together. It is on this basis, for instance, that we distinguish mother–child, doctor–patient, and teacher–pupil relationships.

These labels are useful because, within any one culture, there are regularities in the ways in which interactions are grouped within relationships. These regularities are in part biological, in part utilitarian and conventional. Thus the interactions expected within father–child or husband–wife relationships are biologically influenced, but differ considerably from those usually found a few decades ago. The contents of the interactions within relationships may be used to differentiate not only major classes of relationships but also to distinguish between relationships within classes.

Diversity of interactions

Some relationships involve many types of interactions, while others involve only one or a few. This distinction depends in part on the level of analysis: a mother–infant relationship could be called uniplex, involving only maternal–filial responses, or multiplex, involving all the things mother and child do together. Clearly, the greater the variety of interactions, the more diverse ways there are for interactions to affect interactions, and the more diverse the aspects of their personalities that the participants will reveal to each other.

Qualities of interactions

What two individuals do together may be less important than how they do it. However, we do not yet know just how many qualities of interactions should be recognized. The difficulties of measurement are obvious, but the following categories of characters have proven useful:

1. Intensity. For example, do the participants touch, hit, or clout each other?
2. Content and presentation of verbal material. This includes both the locutionary meaning, and its illocutionary or perlocutionary force (Austin, 1962).
3. Nonverbal communication. This may be an important indicator of the quality of an interaction even in the absence of verbal communication.
4. The extent to which the behaviour of the two participants is coordinated or meshes each with that of the other.

While a given quality may apply to one or many of the types of interactions in a relationship, and to the behaviour of one or both partners, we must remember that all behaviour in interaction is made with respect to the other partner and is thus to some extent a property of both.

It must also be noted that the content of an individual's behaviour may be dissociated from the quality or style with which it is expressed. This issue is emphasized in the distinction between the expressions an individual gives and those he gives off (Goffman, 1959), or between the explicit and the command or metacommunicational aspect of messages (Bateson et al., 1956).

Relative frequency and patterning of interactions

Here we are concerned with several different issues:

1. Clusters of co-varying properties. Many judgments we make about relationships depend not on just one type of interaction, or one quality, but on a number. Thus we would not label a mother–child relationship as involving maternal warmth merely on the grounds that the mother frequently kissed the child, but would also take into account how often she cuddled it, how sensitive she was to its needs, and so on.
2. Ratio and derived measures. Relative frequencies often tell us something different from, or something more than, absolute frequencies. Thus it may be more important to know how often a couple made love relative to how often each partner wanted to make love than to know the absolute frequency.
3. Relations between heterologous interactions. Some properties of relationships depend on the relative frequencies of interactions of different sorts. For instance a mother who kept her child near her would be regarded as restrictive, but a mother who some times kept the child near her and at other times sent it away would be regarded as controlling.
4. Patterning of interactions. The sequencing of interactions may have an importance that is independent of their absolute frequencies.

Reciprocity versus complementarity

A reciprocal interaction is one in which the participants show similar behaviour, either simultaneously or alternately, as when one child chases another and then the other chases the one. A complementary interaction is one in which the behaviour of each participant differs from but complements that of the other. Relationships in which all interactions are complementary are common—for instance in hierarchical organizations such as businesses. Relationships in which all interactions are reciprocal are rare, but those between peers or colleagues may approach this condition. In close personal relationships there need be no congruence in the degree or direction of complementarity in different aspects of the relationship, and the interactions may show complex patterns of imbalance. Complementarity may involve many different properties—maleness–femaleness, dominance–subordinance, achievement–vicariousness, etc.

Similarity or complementarity in behaviour is likely to be related to similarities or differences in personal characteristics. Unfortunately much earlier work involved the supposition that either overall similarity or overall differences, measured along one or more dimensions in tests outside the relationship, is of primary importance for friendship choice or for long-term relationships. This is now seen to be a gross oversimplification. Not only may similarities be important in some contexts and differences in others, but what is important may change as a relationship progresses (e.g. Duck and Craig, 1978).

Intimacy

This concerns the extent to which the participants reveal all aspects of themselves to each other (see e.g. Altman and Taylor, 1973).

Interpersonal perception

This concerns the extent to which the participants in a relationship see each other as they really are (important for behavioural meshing), how far each sees the other as the other sees himself (i.e. understands him) and perceives the other to perceive him as he sees himself (i.e. feels understood), how far each construes the world in a similar way to that in which the other construes the world (as assessed, for instance, by a repertory grid technique), and how far each sees the other as approximating to his ideal partner in a relationship of the type in question (i.e. feels satisfied).

Commitment

This refers to the extent to which each partner accepts the relationship as continuing indefinitely, or directs his or her behavior toward ensuring its continuance or optimizing its properties. Commitment arises naturally from the processes inherent in the formation of a relationship, though it may become overtly recognized by the participants in a private pledge, or more widely in a public one. It is useful to distinguish between commitment imposed from the outside, as in arranged marriages and kin relationships, and endogenous commitment which arises within the dyad. It is also useful to distinguish between commitment for continuity (i.e. for continuation of the relationship), and commitment concerning consistency in, or the quality or content of, the relationship. A crucial issue is, of course, not only the degree of commitment of the two partners, but the extent to which each believes in the other's commitment. The latter is necessary if each partner is to incur the costs which inevitably arise in the course of a relationship, and absence of faith in the other's commitment to continuity in spite of limited change could inhibit personal growth.

These eight categories are merely a convenient way to pigeon hole data, and are not to be regarded as absolute. The precise characteristics that will prove useful, and the ways in which those characteristics are best measured, remain to be worked out. Furthermore it is not suggested that these are the only ways in which aspects of interpersonal relationships could be classified. For instance many more global properties of relationships, such as the extent to which a relationship is seen as affectionate or competitive, depend on dimensions from a number of the categories mentioned above.

Principles of dynamics

Description is of course only a means to an end, and we need also principles for understanding how relationships work. All the principles at present available have a limited range of usefulness, and it is essential that they should be considered in relation to a system for describing relationships in order that the limits of their applicability can be specified. This may be illustrated by considering the explanatory principles available under four headings.

Social issues

The way individuals behave within relationships is profoundly affected by cultural norms relating to relationships of the type in question. For example, what husband and wife expect from their marriage differs greatly between cultures, and with time in any one culture. The norms that determine behaviour within relationships lie along continua from those that are obligatory to those that merely convey expectations, and from those that are general throughout the whole society to those that are limited to a subculture or group within the society: indeed they may even be virtually idiosyncratic.

Now the course of interindividual relationships depends on evaluations of the relationships by the participant. These evaluations are relative to the standards they have brought to the relationship by virtue of their past experience. Thus understanding of the dynamics of interpersonal relationships must depend on adequate descriptions of the relationship, of how each participant perceives the relationship, and of what he expects from it as determined by the social norms that he accepts.

Interpersonal perception

Each participant in a relationship assesses his own behaviour, his partner's behaviour, and the relationship. In doing so, he attributes enduring dispositions to his partner, and on the basis of these predicts possible future courses for the relationship and acts appropriately (Kelley, 1979). Principles concerned with how partners attribute qualities to each other, and the bases by which they respond negatively or positively to each other, are therefore crucial for understanding the dynamics of relationships. Theories of attribution (Kelley, 1971), balance, and dissonance (Heider, 1958; Newcomb, 1961; Festinger, 1957) are of course crucial here. But such theories must be linked to a descriptive base. For instance balance theories would predict that if John loves football he would be more prone to like Jack if Jack likes football. But balance theories would also predict that if John loves Jill he would be more prone to like Jack if Jack likes Jill. The latter is not necessarily the case. Newcomb (1971) points out that attraction will vary with how the participants see the nature of the relationship in which they are involved. Once again, a descriptive base is essential: in its absence, the limits of relevance of balance theories cannot be specified.

Exchange and interdependence theories

These theories share the assumption that social behaviour is in large measure determined by the rewards and costs, or expectations of rewards and costs, consequent upon it (e.g. Homans, 1961; Thibaut and Kelley, 1959; Kelley, 1979; Walster et al., 1978). However, for a number of reasons the utility of such theories must be linked with an adequate means for describing relationships. For one thing, the problem of measuring the rewards and costs exchanged in real-life situations is crucial to any exchange theory. But the value of many of the resources exchanged in interpersonal interactions, such as social approval or gestures of affection and love, varies with the nature of the relationship in question. Profits and costs must be assessed in relation to their meanings to the individual concerned in the context of the relationship. The words 'I love you' mean something very different in relationships of different sorts, or at different stages in the same relationship.

Again what is considered fair exchange by the participants in a relationship will vary with its nature. In some cases the participants will require equal outcomes, in others they will require that outcomes should be related to costs incurred, and in yet others that they should be related to needs. Again, specification of the nature of the relationship is essential.

Furthermore the properties of the rewards used in interpersonal exchange differ. Foa and Foa (1974) claim that the rewards exchanged can be classified into six classes of meanings assigned to actions—money, goods, services, love, status, and information. They suggest that these categories can be arranged in a circular order, with those adjacent to each other more similar than those on opposite sides of the circle. Among the dimensions they discuss are the extent to which the reward is concrete, and the extent to which it matters from whom the resource is received. As an example of the latter, the value of money is not usually affected by whom it comes from, but it matters very much who it is who says 'I love you.'

A categorization of rewards related to a system for describing relationships is therefore also essential for the exchange theorists.

Description in terms of positive and negative feedback

Many aspects of the dynamics of interpersonal relationships can be described as involving positive or negative feedback. For instance loving promotes loving, competitiveness promotes competitiveness, intimacy promotes intimacy, and so on. However, intimacy can lead to repugnance, and giving can lead merely to selfish acceptance, rather than to reciprocation. It is thus important to specify in what circumstances positive feedback will occur. Such questions demand an adequate description of the relationships in question.

Similarly some relationships have homeostatic or self-stabilizing properties. A mother–infant relationship may be disturbed in the short term by a period of separation, but regain its original course in the longer term. However, such stabilizing properties, which can be described in terms of negative feedback, operate only within limits. If the relationship is too much disturbed, it never regains its original course. It is thus necessary to have an adequate description of the relationship in order to understand the extent to which positive or negative feedback can operate.

These examples illustrate the ways in which an adequate descriptive base is necessary before principles concerned with the dynamics of interpersonal relationships can be successfully applied. The discussion has been concerned only with the relationships themselves, and not with the effects of personality on relationships or of relationships on personality. Clearly it is there that the really important questions lie. But this chapter is based on the view that a better understanding of the dynamics of dyadic relationships is essential before those questions can be tackled successfully. And for that, a descriptive base is essential.

References

Altman, I., and Taylor, D. A. (1973). *Social Penetration*, Holt, Rinehart and Winston, New York.
Austin, J. L. (1962). *How to do Things with Words*, Oxford University Press, London.
Bateson, G., Jackson, D. D., Haley, J., and Weakland, J. (1956). 'Toward a theory of schizophrenia,' *Behavioral Science*, 1, 251–264.
Duck, S. W., and Craig, G. (1978). 'Personality similarity and the development of friendship: A longitudinal study,' *British Journal of Social and Clinical Psychology*, 17, 237–242.
Festinger, L. (1957). *Theory of Cognitive Dissonance*, Row, Peterson, Evanston.
Foa, U. G., and Foa, E. B. (1974). *Societal Structures of the Mind*, Thomas, Springfield, Illinois.
Goffman, E. (1959). *The Presentation of Self in Everyday Life*, Doubleday Anchor, New York.
Heider, F. (1958). *The Psychology of Interpersonal Relations*, Wiley, New York.
Hinde, R. A. (1979). *Towards Understanding Relationships*, Academic Press, London.
Homans, G. C. (1961). *Social Behaviour: Its Elementary Forms*, Routledge and Kegan Paul, London.
Kelley, H. H. (1971). *Attribution in Social Interaction*, General Learning Press, Morristown, NJ.
Kelley, H. H. (1979). *Personal Relationships*, Erlbaum, Hillsdale, NJ.
Newcomb, T. M. (1961). *The Acquaintance Process*, Holt, Rinehart and Winston, New York.
Newcomb, T. M. (1971). 'Dyadic balance as a source of clues about interpersonal attraction,' in B. J. Murstein (ed.), *Theories of Attraction and Love*, Springer, New York.
Thibaut, J. W., and Kelley, H. H. (1959). *The Social Psychology of Groups*, Wiley, New York.

Walster, E., Walster, G. W., and Berscheid, E. (1978). *Equity Theory and Research*, Allyn and Bacon, Boston.

Wisch, M., Deutsch, M., and Kaplan, S. J. (1976). 'Perceived dimensions of interpersonal relations,' *Journal of Personality and Social Psychology*, **33**, 409–420.

Note

Since the above was written, a number of important books on dyadic relationships have appeared. Particular mention must be made of

Duck, S., and Gilmour, R. (eds.) (1981). *Personal Relationships*, Volumes 1, 2 and 3. Academic Press, London.

Small Groups and Social Interaction, Volume 1
Edited by H. H. Blumberg, A. P. Hare, V. Kent and M. Davies
Published by John Wiley & Sons Limited, 1983.

9.2 Interpreting Normative Rules in the Negotiation of Status and Role*

Aaron V. Cicourel *Department of Sociology University of California, San Diego*

Environmental settings create informational resources necessary for logical and practical inference and action in small groups. But participants of social interaction are constrained by limited capacity processing in their use of memorial knowledge and different forms of reasoning in order to interpret sources of information that emerge from everyday social settings.

The interplay between memorial knowledge, the informational resources that are part of local, emergent social interaction, and the larger social organization or institution, informs the negotiated aspects of notions like role and status. The idea of 'role' as the dynamic aspect of 'status' or the 'less' institutionalized class of statuses (Goode, 1960), implies a problematic or innovational element in behavior. Goffman's remark that 'Life may not be much of a gamble, but interaction is' (1959, p. 243), underscores the problematical elements of 'role.' The term 'status' has become a normative ideal for structuring the way participants of social interaction subsume initial impressions, based on appearances, and verbal identifications and introductions, to establish some preliminary basis for assessing each other. Ritualized introductions can support or detract from the appearances displayed (Goode, 1960). The range of elements that are included under the term 'status' is used by participants of social interaction as practical language games to simplify the task of summarizing complex stimuli making up the perceived environment (Wittgenstein, 1953). Hence we should not expect to have a single or unitary description or set of features for all members of a group or society who are subsumed under the same status. Instead there should be a family resemblance among the separate descriptions or exemplars for various members of a group viewed as occupying the same status.

*Based on a revision of a brief portion of a larger paper called 'Interpretive procedures and normative rules in the negotiation of status and role,' in *Cognitive Sociology*, Penguin, London, 1973.

The labels designating a range of elements we call 'statuses' do not recover the appearances and imputations subsumed by participants unless imagined details are supplied by our model of the participant. Our model of the participant or actor must specify this elaboration process—an elaboration not subject to direct verification—because the elaboration serves the actor's practical interests. We must model the tacit elaborations that our theory presumes take place in actual social interaction. We must distinguish between the actor's 'logic-in-use' versus his or her reflections or 'reconstructed logic' after leaving the scene (Kaplan, 1964). During social interaction the actor engages in a form of reasoning termed 'abductive' by Peirce (1931–35) in which the observation and interpretation of facts and ambiguous information lead to inferences or hypotheses that are embedded in the particular circumstances that exist at the time of interaction. Inferring the role of the other participant of an exchange requires a theory of comprehension. The researcher can conceive of this comprehension process as an interaction between the selection and verification of conceptual schemata or knowledge of concepts in memory (Rumelhart, 1975), and the use of informational resources from the setting and larger organizational context.

When we say that someone takes the role of the other, or infers the role of the other, we assume a theory of comprehension. The idea of enacting a role includes developing and pursuing a goal by using a communicative competence and strategies that are appropriate to the situation of interaction. We need a model of interactional settings that permits the researcher to infer someone's comprehension of role taking by their use of speech acts, prosodic information, paralinguistic details, and nonverbal behavior. Interpretation, comprehension, and summarization are meta-terms that refer to cognitive and linguistic processes that can clarify notions like 'role expectation' and the 'definition of the situation.'

Several authors (Mead, 1938; Goffman, 1959; Turner, 1962) have called attention to the idea that a role is a construction by the actor over the course of interaction. Mead stresses the problematic aspects of the way two participants evoke a kind of cooperative exchange. Goffman refers to the idea that participants of social interaction will possess many motives for seeking to control what they infer about a situation while employing different techniques for sustaining impressions. Turner discusses the way the actor creates and modifies roles while making them known to others. There is a role taking and role making. The actor's relationships to others and the identification of the roles reflected in the actions of others means that the actor's role definition and performance always retain a tentative quality that is tested over the course of interaction.

One implication of the preceding remarks is that while current theories of role and status recognize the emergent nature of role construction, they often lack explicit statements about how the actor recognizes relevant stimuli and manages to locate the stimuli in a socially meaningful context such that an organized response can be made that will be recognized as relevant to others. The comprehension process presumes the acquisition of interpretative and summarization procedures (Cicourel, 1973; Rumelhart, 1975) that enable the actor to identify the tacit meanings and 'appropriate' norms that are associated with a given setting over the course of interaction.

The idea of rules or normative ideals that are invoked during social interaction in specific settings presumes that these rules are shared with others in a group. But we must distinguish between an abstract or ritual collective recognition and acknowledgement of rules, and the ways in which an actor is aware of or employs normative rules when making inferences while taking or creating roles. The idea of interpretative procedures refers to the actor's memorial knowledge base and reasoning abilities when using beliefs and mental models in settings where several sources of (cognitive–emotional, interactional or ecological, and organizational) information interact. Information about a rule can also be embedded in the setting because of printed signs, the physical arrangement of furniture and walls or windows, the existence of audible loudspeakers or other props, and the modes of dress and communication utilized.

The actor's interpretative procedures are basic in the sense that they enable the participants of interaction to go beyond the information given by a rule and to generate appropriate (often innovative) responses in changing settings. Normative rules provide a more general institutional or historical validity to the meaning of social interaction when they are described retrospectively in summary fashion or as an account. But interpretative procedures enable the actor to sustain a culturally relevant sense of social structure over the course of changing social settings. The Meadian (Mead, 1934) dialectic of the 'I' and the 'me' presupposes mechanisms or reasoning abilities that are abductive (interpretative) and basic for what Peirce (1931–35) describes as a linking of retrospectively present and projected consequent conditions (verbal and nonverbal displays) to antecedent information. An implicit interpretative procedure in Mead's theory (Stone, 1962, p. 88) is the notion that participants of social interaction assume that their use of verbal and nonverbal signs or symbols refer to the 'same' objects and events, or that this 'sameness' is assumed to hold in some ideal sense.

The preceding discussion has sought to clarify some problems associated with traditional views of 'role taking' or 'role making' by calling attention to the way that the notion of role can mask the inductive or interpretative procedures that enable participants of social exchanges to produce behavioral displays that others and some observer can label 'role behavior.' Theorists often seek to link a structural notion like status with a behavioral notion like role to stress the assumed relationship between a person's position or status in a group or organization and the kinds of expectations that are said to be organized around roles (Sarbin, 1953). The idea here is that roles are learned in everyday life. We must clarify the way that such learned roles are represented in memory, the extent to which their enactment is contingent on information emanating from the interactional setting and institutional constraints perceived by the actor, and the way that beliefs and reasoning strategies assign significance to the different sources of information.

We can summarize this section by calling attention to two problems that contribute to our ambiguous use of the concept 'role.'

1. Little empirical clarification exists for understanding how the actor and observer are able to recognize 'statuses' or 'positions' and the role taking and role enactment to which they are supposed to be intimately linked. The significance of 'non-role' behavior, social action that is not identified with or that does not follow some recognized 'status,' remains unclear as a residual category because such a notion would presumably include considerable verbal and nonverbal behavior that is culturally understandable but is not viewed as criterial or as exemplary of an identifiable 'status.' Such information may prove to be essential for making inferences that a particular social exchange is part of a normal cultural environment. A person's status may not be the most important information associated with the setting.

2. The literature on 'status' and 'role' does not clarify how our understanding of conduct, attributed to some label of 'role,' presumes that we are clear about the actor's perception of 'norms.' Many writers seem to shift their structural discussion of 'status' as institutionalized to the idea of 'role' as a set of implicit 'norms.'

The literature on 'status' and 'role' seldom goes beyond Mead's (1938) important notion of the actor directing his or her acts by monitoring the corresponding acts of others and following 'the rules of the game.' How many 'games' are there? How do actors and an observer come to treat some sequence of events as a 'game' or legitimate and socially sanctioned activity? What 'rules' or 'norms' are involved? To what extent are they implicit or explicit or negotiated by the participants of social exchanges?

Norms and problematic aspects of everyday life

Role taking or role enactment is said to be inextricably linked to 'norms' or 'rules.' But 'roles' are tied to 'statuses' and the latter term implies stable meaning about a 'position' with respect to others in a network of social relationships. There is an implied consensus about the 'rights and obligations' of actors occupying a commonly known and accepted 'status.' The variability attached to 'role' (its innovative or 'less institutionalized' character) appears to be attributable to the fact that various actors may come to occupy a given 'status.' These actors presumably engage in differential perception and interpretation of their 'statuses' vis-à-vis the sources of knowledge available, thus creating the possibility of ambiguity or misinterpretation for participants of social interaction.

I want to call attention to the contrast between the common view of 'norms' as providing for stable features of society (regardless of differences between the mores and folkways), evoking consensus in groups, and the notion that norms are problematic to all social interaction.

Our thought or reasoning can be reflexive or self-conscious because of having to pursue goals within settings that can often produce competing or contradictory sources of information and incompatible courses of action. Mead's distinction between the 'I' and the 'me' is relevant here. Interaction can be a gamble for all concerned because there is competition between an 'I' that leads the way with potentially impulsive, innovative, spontaneous interpretations of the situation, and the 'me' that reflects on what is happening and reinterprets perceptions and actions. The 'me' is the link to some wider group or community. The 'I' seems to be more responsive to the immediate action scene. The more general point is that the actors must attend to a particular action scene while simultaneously identifying emergent (constructed) meanings that can be linked to a wider context of general rules or policies (Rawls, 1955). The actors must negotiate the way that emergent or constructed information and action can be subsumed under or be made compatible with general rules or policies we call norms.

Statuses are like general rules or policies. They both require recognition and interpretation during social interaction. Participants must elicit and search appearances for relevant information about each other's status. Actors may or may not be self-conscious about the significance of their own status or that of others, but role taking and role making require an articulation between statuses or general rules or policies (norms), and an emergent or constructed action scene in order to make inferences about one's behavior or that of some other.

The notion of interpretative procedures consists of a cultural sense of membership that is reflected in various competencies, particularly a communicative competence that is developmental in origin and permits the actor to assign meaning or relevance to different and changing environments. Knowledge of normative rules enables the actor to link his or her views of the world to that of others during social exchanges, and to presume that the interaction will be governed by consensus or shared agreement about what is happening. Recognizing the existence of conflict and differences in the interpretation of normative rules calls attention to the fact that the presumption of consensus or shared agreement is only one aspect of social interaction.

The constructed or negotiated nature of consensus or shared agreement is clearly stated in work by Goode (1960) and Shibutani (1961) in their discussions of normative behavior. Goode stresses the necessity of viewing normative behavior as including variations in the way general rules are interpreted. Shibutani notes the importance of tacit assumptions employed by ego and alter when they trust their environment despite the absence of cumbersome and redundant details about the meaning of 'familiar' activities such as waiting in line at a grocery store. We recognize the grocery store queue as a particular instance of a general case. We ordinarily would not ask a clerk or other persons standing in line if the 'general rule' holds 'in this grocery store' that we will be waited on when our turn comes up (Shibutani, 1961).

We cannot speak of interpretative abilities without referring to a normative order for they interact continually and one cannot exist without the other. The idea of interpretative procedures is intended to motivate a conception of status and role in which we can specify how the actor negotiates and constructs *possible* action, and summarizes and evaluates the results of *completed* action.

We need to know more about the way general rules or norms are invoked to justify or evaluate a course of action during social interaction or in some post-accounting session. How do innovative constructions that occur in local contexts of interaction influence or alter general rules or norms, providing the basis for social change?

Terms like 'internalized norms' and attitudes and beliefs appear inadequate unless we can address their representation in memory, the way they are shaped by socialization experiences, and the way they are influenced by linguistic construc- tions and displays that reflect personal and group experiences over real time. The child employs discourse to resolve misunderstandings or conflicts, to understand property rights during peer play, and to re-create adult roles during play. These processes enable the child to adjust gradually to an increasingly more complex form of social structure, learning to get along with others under conditions of stress, conflict, and cooperation. Research on discourse teaches us that the local context of social interaction plays a central role in the way language is used to convey power, deference, agreement, disagreement, and social status differences. The study of language use can help us understand role taking and role making by examining utterances that have functional significance in directing interaction, requesting information or confirmation about what is happening, and talking about the mental states of the speaker or others. The teacher's role may be clarified by noting his or her use of specific forms of interrogation (Corsaro, 1977; Mehan, 1979) to 'control' what children will say. For example, if a child and an adult are playing 'restaurant' and the child is explaining how to cook something, the adult may ask:

Adult: What are you going to do now, Bobby?
Child: Put some of *that* |pointing| 'stuff' on it.
Adult: What's that 'stuff' called, Bobby?

The educational process is designed to teach children how to think abstractly and exercise particular forms of literacy when organizing and describing experiences and observations. The child's family background, peer encounters, and educational experiences must be studied if we are to understand the child's gradually acquired ability to negotiate the everyday world that we think is associated with notions like status and role.

Social theory refers to structural arrangements that are said to provide boundary conditions by trading on knowledge the actor takes for granted about ecological settings, common linguistic usage, and bio-physical conditions. Particular constellations of buildings, space, signs, and the like, create sources of knowledge in the environment that orient actors in their daily round of activities. These arrangements help the actor to invoke knowledge or beliefs as organized schemata that appear to be congruent with the setting. Hence these structural conditions, along with normative rules and fixed linguistic expressions such as idioms, metaphors, similes, help to reduce surprise, convey complex knowledge, and create the sense of a normal environment. These structural conditions help us understand the reference to status as a more institutionalized notion while the problematic aspects of actual social interaction are linked to the more fragile notions of role taking and role making.

An understanding of terms like status, role, and norms has been proposed that insists on the prominence of interpretative procedures and summarization principles as part of a model of social interaction that would necessitate explicit assumptions about the cognitive and linguistic aspects of social organization. The interpretation of normative rules is tied to the attribution of membership in social groups and the ability to exhibit particular and general competencies. The actor's ability to recognize status and role activities presumes memorial knowledge and a communicative competence that is absent from existing theories of small group structure. Terms like status, role, and norms cannot be clarified until we recognize the necessity of studying the way children acquire the interpretative and summarization abilities to integrate their experiences in social settings with an understanding of abstract normative rules. On the adult side this means understanding the way interpretative and summarization abilities enable us to invoke general rules or policies to account for or to explain the meaning of different courses of action and the sources of information we experience in specific settings.

References

Cicourel, A. V. (1973). *Cognitive Sociology: Language and Meaning in Social Interaction*, Penguin, London.

Corsaro, W. (1977). 'The clarification request as a feature of adult interactive styles with young children,' *Language in Society*, **6**, 183–207.

Goffman, E. (1959). *The Presentation of Self in Everyday Life*, Doubleday, New York.

Goode, J. G. (1960). 'Norm commitment and conformity to role-status obligations,' *American Journal of Sociology*, **66**, 246–58.

Kaplan, A. (1964). *The Conduct of Inquiry*, Chandler, San Francisco.

Mead, G. H. (1934). *Mind, Self and Society*, University of Chicago Press, Chicago.

Mead, G. H. (1938). *The Philosophy of the Act*, University of Chicago Press, Chicago.

Mehan, H. (1979). *Learning Lessons: Social Organization in the Classroom*, Harvard University Press, Cambridge, Mass.

Peirce, C. S. (1931–35). *Collected Papers*, Harvard University Press, Cambridge, Mass.

Rawls, J. (1955). 'Two concepts of rules,' *Philosophical Review*, **64**, 3–32.

Rumelhart, D. (1975). 'Notes on a schema for stories,' in D. Bobrow and A. Collins (eds.), *Representation and Understanding: Studies in Cognitive Science*, Academic, New York.

Sarbin, T. R. (1953). 'Role theory,' in G. Lindzey (ed.), *Handbook of Social Psychology*, Addison-Wesley, Cambridge, Mass.

Shibutani, T. (1961). *Society and Personality*, Prentice-Hall, Englewood Cliffs, NJ.

Stone, G. P. (1962). 'Appearance and self,' in A. Rose (ed.), *Human Behavior and Social Process*, Houghton Mifflin, New York.

Turner, R. H. (1962). 'Role-taking: Process versus conformity,' in A. Rose (ed.), *Human Behavior and Social Process*, Houghton Mifflin, New York.

Wittgenstein, L. (1953). *Philosophical Investigations* (trans. by G. E. M. Anscombe), Blackwell, Oxford.

Small Groups and Social Interaction, Volume 1
Edited by H. H. Blumberg, A. P. Hare, V. Kent and M. Davies
Published by John Wiley & Sons Limited, 1983.

9.3 Social Behavior at 33 Months in Same-Sex and Mixed-Sex Dyads*

Carol Nagy Jacklin and Eleanor E. Maccoby   *Stanford University*

In the present study, 90 unacquainted children were brought together in a laboratory playroom in same-sex or mixed-sex pairs. The children were all within 2 weeks of 33 months of age.

The study is primarily intended to answer the following questions:

1. Do children of this young age play in a different manner with partners of different sexes?
2. If the answer to (1) is positive, is it the absolute or relative sex of the partner that makes a difference? (That is, do boy–boy and girl–girl pairs play similarly, with mixed pairs being different, or is there a simple sex-of-child or sex-of-partner effect?)

Procedure

Mothers were asked to bring the children in play clothes, and specifically *not* to have the girls wear dresses. Children were not told each other's names or sexes. The mothers were present throughout the session, filling out questionnaires. Mothers were asked not to intervene with the children and very few did so. They did often talk to each other. Observations were made from behind one-way mirrors. The session lasted approximately 30 minutes.

Several toys in series were presented to the children. At certain portions of the session, only one toy was present, an arrangement designed to maximize interaction.

*Reprinted by permission of the author and the Society for Research in Child Development, Inc. Unabridged article appears in *Child Development*, 1978, **49**, 557–569.

Behaviors coded for each child were: proximity to mother (within 2 feet), look at mother, vocal prohibition (e.g. 'No,' 'don't'), vocal command (e.g. 'give me'), nonsocial (solitary) play with toy, hold toy, touch other child's toy, attempt to take toy from other child, successfully take toy, withdraw toy from other child's reach, offer toy, accept offer, reject offer, look at other child, look at other child's toy, proximity to other child (going to within 2 feet), fuss/cry, aggress (hit, other physical assault—such as choke or physically threaten other child—or physical anger), tease, imitate other child, away–distract (i.e. engage in nonplay behavior such as investigating door knob). The interobserver reliabilities (measured with a subsample of eight children) ranged from .82 to 1.00 (Pearson r correlation coefficients). Scores for each category reflect the number of 10 second intervals in which the behavior occurred (maximum: 156).

As an approach to the problem of interdependence of subject and partner scores, a new statistical procedure has been devised to correct for between-pair correlation. It parallels the logic of a t-test between matched pairs, but is more general, and permits the evaluation of both main effects and interactions (see Kraemer and Jacklin, 1979). The statistic yielded by the procedures is a z which can be evaluated as a standard normal deviate in the same way that the probability levels for a t would be ascertained.

Results

The summary score *total social behavior* reflects the total number of social actions of all kinds—both initiations and responses, both positive overtures and aversive behaviors—by each child of the pair directed toward the other. Figure 1

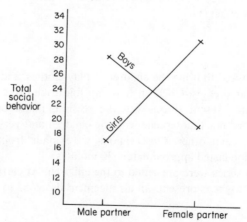

Figure 1 Higner rates of social behavior
shown by children with same-sex partners

shows that there are higher rates of such social behavior for children playing with like-sex partners. The classical analysis of variance shows a highly significant interaction, but there are high subject–partner correlations in some pairs (particularly girl–girl pairs), so the Kraemer–Jacklin test is more appropriate. For girls particularly, social behavior is reduced when playing with an opposite-sex partner. Girls playing with girls show a high rate of social behavior, and boys playing with boys have very nearly as high a rate.

In Figure 2 a different kind of pattern may be seen. Children of both sexes are more likely to cry or remain close to their mothers when paired with a boy. The analysis of variance shows a significant sex of partner effect and this test is appropriate since subject and partner scores on Social Withdrawal are virtually uncorrelated. The effect of being paired with a boy is much stronger for girls, however. Girls not only show more crying and seeking of proximity to mother when with a boy, but they also show more 'passive' behavior in this pairing: they stand or sit quietly watching their partner play, sometimes simply holding a toy but not playing with it. When girls are paired with girls, however, they show less passivity than children in any other pairing (see Figure 3).

We cannot resolve the issue as to whether the tendency for our subjects to show higher levels of social behavior in same-sex than in mixed-sex dyads rests upon behavioral compatibility, upon identifying the sex of self and other and applying sex-typed concepts accordingly, or upon some combination of the two. It is clear, however, that by the age of 33 months, the foundations have already been laid for children to select same-sex playmates when they enter nursery school (usually at the age of 36 months or later). Pressures from nursery school teachers may strengthen these already-existing tendencies. Sex-typed preferences for certain

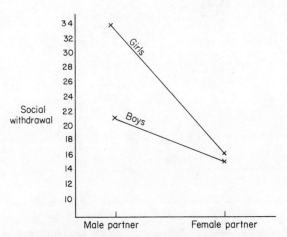

Figure 2   Effect of sex of partner when children paired with same-sex partners

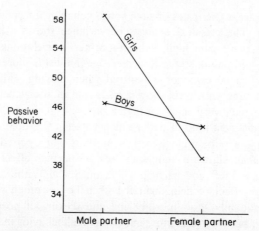

Figure 3 Relative passivity of children when playing with children of the same or opposite sex

kinds of activities may also serve to draw children into same-sex friendships, and maintain them once initiated. But we have found that even in the absence of such factors, young children's initial reactions to agemates point to the existence of greater compatibility in same-sex pairs.

Reference

Kraemer, H. C. and Jacklin, C. N. (1979). 'Statistical analysis of dyadic social behavior,' *Psychological Bulletin*, **86**, 217–224.

Small Groups and Social Interaction, Volume 1
Edited by H. H. Blumberg, A. P. Hare, V. Kent and M. Davies
Published by John Wiley & Sons Limited, 1983.

9.4 Transforming Experimental Research into Advocacy for Social Change*

Philip G. Zimbardo   *Stanford University*

How do men adapt to the novel and alien situation in which those called 'prisoners' lose their liberty, civil rights, and privacy, while those called 'guards' gain power and social status? What is responsible for the alleged brutality and violence in American prisons—is it the nature of the prison population, alleged to be filled with 'sociopathic' criminals and 'sadistic' guards, or is it the quality of the social psychological environment of the prison experience itself? (Here we pitted *dispositional* against *situational* determinants of behavior to see which would emerge victorious, i.e. come out with the largest slice of explained variance attributable to it.)

Under what conditions can role-playing simulation achieve a sufficient level of reality to become more than just a game (in this instance, one of 'cops and robbers'), so that it is both a source of new self-knowledge for the participants and one of socially relevant knowledge for the researchers studying it?

On the basis of our observations, we have been able to give answers, or partial ones at least, to these questions, and in addition have discovered new issues we were unaware of before being directly confronted by them. But most significantly, as a consequence of this study of imprisonment I and my research associates have experienced a major transformation in some of our basic values, attitudes, and cognitive orientation. Unknown to us at the time, we were as much 'subjects' imprisoned in our roles of prison staff as we were experimenters directing the events of the study. ... We became subject to the same forces which were responsible for the metamorphosis of a group of average, healthy, intelligent

*Abridged from Philip G. Zimbardo (1975). 'Transforming experimental research into advocacy for social change,' in *Applications of Social Psychology* (eds. M. Deutsch and H. A. Hornstein), pp. 33–66, Erlbaum, Hillsdale, New Jersey. Abridged and reprinted by permission of the copyright holder (Social Science Research Council, Washington, DC) and the publishers (Lawrence Erlbaum Associates, Inc.) as well as the author.

individuals into a mass of pathetic prisoners and a block of guards perverted by the pathology of power which dominated that prison environment. So intense were these forces that I reluctantly terminated the experiment prematurely, closing down the prison after only six days and nights of its operation.

It had become too real, too unpredictable and beyond the control of any one person. This play we had staged became one in which the characters refused any direction except from each other and insisted on their own constantly improvized scenario. It no longer even mattered whether or not the scenes had an audience; the characters were playing their roles only for each other. At that point, differences dissolved between 'role' and 'identity,' between 'experiment' and 'experience,' between 'play' and 'business,' and finally, between 'illusion' and 'reality.'

Let us first describe the experiment within the traditional format for communicating research to colleagues via professional journals.

Method

Overview

The effects of playing the role of 'guard' or 'prisoner' were studied in the context of an experimental simulation of a prison environment. The research design was a relatively simple one, involving as it did only a single treatment variable, the random assignment to either a guard or prisoner condition. These roles were enacted over an extended period of time (nearly one week) within an environment that was physically constructed to resemble a prison. Central to the methodology of creating and maintaining a psychological state of imprisonment was the functional simulation of significant properties of 'real prison life.'

The guards were free within certain limits to implement the procedures of induction into the prison setting and maintenance of custodial retention of the prisoners. These inmates, having voluntarily submitted to the conditions of this urgency of mundane decisions forced upon me as 'superintendent' of the Stanford County Prison made me ever more remote from the reality of the detached, intellectual stance of 'experimenter.'

We became subject to the same forces which were responsible for the metamorphosis of a group of average, healthy, intelligent individuals into a mass total institution in which they now lived, coped in various ways with its stresses and its challenges. The behavior of both groups of subjects was observed, recorded, and analyzed. The dependent measures were of two general types: (1) transactions between and within each group of subjects, recorded on video and audio tape as well as directly observed; (2) individual reactions on questionnaires, mood inventories, personality tests, daily guard shift reports, and post-experimental interviews.

Subjects

The 22 subjects who participated in the experiment were selected from an initial pool of 75 respondents who answered a newspaper ad asking for male volunteers to participate in a psychological study of 'prison life' in return for payment of $15 per day. Each respondent completed an extensive questionnaire concerning his family background, physical and mental health history, prior experience, and attitudinal propensities with respect to sources of psychopathology (including their involvements in crime). Each respondent also was interviewed by one of two experimenters. Finally, the 24 subjects who were judged to be most stable (physically and mentally), most mature, and least involved in antisocial behaviors were selected to participate in the study. On a random basis, half of the subjects were assigned the role of guard, half were assigned to the role of prisoner.

The subjects were normal, healthy, male college students who were in the Stanford area during the summer. They were largely of middle class socioeconomic status and Caucasians (with the exception of one Oriental subject). Initially they were strangers to each other, a selection precaution taken to avoid the disruption of any pre-existing friendship patterns and to mitigate against any transfer into the experimental situation of previously established relationships or patterns of behavior.

This final sample of subjects was administered a battery of psychological tests on the day prior to the start of the simulation, but to avoid any selective bias on the part of the experiment—observers, scores were not tabulated until the study was completed.

Procedure

Physical aspects of the prison

The prison was built in a 35 ft section of a basement corridor in the psychology building at Stanford University. It was partitioned by two fabricated walls; one was fitted with the only entrance door to the cell block and the other contained a small observation screen. Three small cells (6 × 9 ft) were made from converted laboratory rooms by replacing the usual doors with steel barred, black painted ones, and removing all furniture.

A cot (with mattress, sheet, and pillow) for each prisoner was the only furniture in the cells. A small closet across from the cells served as a solitary confinement facility; its dimensions were extremely small (2 × 2 × 7 ft), and it was unlighted.

In addition, several rooms in an adjacent wing of the building were used as guards' quarters (to change in and out of uniform or for rest and relaxation), a bedroom for the warden and superintendent, and an interview-testing room. Behind the observation screen at one end of the 'yard' (small enclosed room representing the fenced prison grounds) was video recording equipment and sufficient space for several observers.

Operational details

The prisoner subjects remained in the mock prison 24 hours per day for the duration of the study. Three were arbitrarily assigned to each of the three cells; the others were on standby call at their homes. The guard subjects worked on 3-man, 8-hour shifts; remaining in the prison environment only during their work shift and going about their usual lives at other times.

Role instructions

All subjects had been told that they would be assigned either the guard or the prisoner role on a completely random basis and all had voluntarily agreed to play either role for $15 per day for up to two weeks. They signed a contract guaranteeing a minimally adequate diet, clothing, housing, and medical care as well as the financial remuneration in return for their stated 'intention' of serving in the assigned role for the duration of the study.

It was made explicit in the contract that those assigned to be prisoners should expect to be under surveillance (have little or no privacy) and to have some of their basic civil rights suspended during their imprisonment, excluding physical abuse. They were given no other information about what to expect nor instructions about behavior appropriate for a prisoner role. Those actually assigned to this treatment were informed by phone to be available at their place of residence on a given Sunday when we would start the experiment.

The subjects assigned to be guards attended an orientation meeting on the day prior to the induction of the prisoners. At this time they were introduced to the principal investigators, the 'superintendent' of the prison (the author), and an undergraduate research assistant who assumed the administrative role of 'warden.' They were told that we wanted to try to simulate a prison environment within the limits imposed by pragmatic and ethical considerations. Their assigned task was to 'maintain the reasonable degree of order within the prison necessary for its effective functioning,' although the specifics of how this duty might be implemented were not explicitly detailed. They were made aware of the fact that, while many of the contingencies with which they might be confronted were essentially unpredictable (e.g. prisoner escape attempts), part of their task was to be prepared for such eventualities and to be able to deal appropriately with the variety of situations that might arise. The warden instructed the guards in the administrative details, including: the workshifts, the mandatory daily completion of shift reports concerning the activity of guards and prisoners, the completion of 'critical incident' reports which detailed unusual occurrences, and the administration of meals, work, and recreation programs for the prisoners. In order to begin to involve these subjects in their roles even before the first prisoner was incarcerated, the guards assisted in the final phases of completing the prison complex—putting the cots in the cells, signs on the walls, setting up the guards' quarters, moving furniture, water coolers, refrigerators, etc.

The guards generally believed that we were primarily interested in studying the behavior of the prisoners. Of course, we were as interested in the effects which enacting the role of guard in this environment would have on their behavior and subjective states.

To optimize the extent to which their behavior would reflect their genuine reactions to the experimental prison situation and not simply their ability to follow instructions, they were intentionally given only minimal guidelines for what it meant to be a guard. An explicit and categorical prohibition against the use of physical punishment or physical aggression was, however, emphasized by the experimenters. Thus, with this single notable exception, their roles were relatively unstructured initially, requiring each guard to carry out activities necessary for interacting with a group of prisoners as well as with other guards and the correctional staff.

Uniforms

In order to promote feelings of anonymity in the subjects each group was issued identical uniforms. For the guards, the uniform consisted of plain khaki shirts and trousers, a whistle, a police nightstick (wooden batons), and reflecting sunglasses which made eye contact impossible. The prisoners' uniform consisted of a loose fitting muslin smock with an identification number on front and back, no underclothes, a light chain and lock around one ankle, rubber sandals, and a cap made from a nylon stocking. Each prisoner also was issued a toothbrush, soap, soapdish, towel, and bed linen. No personal belongings were allowed in the cells.

Induction procedure

With the cooperation of the Palo Alto City Police Department all of the subjects assigned to the prisoner treatment were unexpectedly 'arrested' at their residences. A police officer charged them with suspicion of burglary or armed robbery, advised them of their legal rights, handcuffed them, thoroughly searched them (often as curious neighbors looked on), and carried them off to the police station in the rear of the police car. At the station they went through the standard routines of being fingerprinted, having an identification file prepared, and then being placed in a detention cell. Each prisoner was blindfolded and subsequently driven by one of the experimenters and a subject-guard to our mock prison.

Throughout the entire arrest procedure, the police officers involved maintained a formal serious attitude, avoiding answering any questions of clarification as to the relation of this 'arrest' to the mock prison study.

Upon arrival at our experimental prison, each prisoner was stripped, sprayed with a delousing preparation, . . . and made to stand alone naked for a while in the cell yard. After being given the uniform described previously and having an ID picture taken . . . the prisoner was put in his cell and ordered to remain silent.

Administrative routine

When all the cells were occupied, the warden greeted the prisoners and read them the rules of the institution (developed by the guards and the warden). They were to be memorized and to be followed. Prisoners were to be referred to only by the number on their uniforms, also in an effort to depersonalize them.

The prisoners were to be served three bland meals per day, were allowed three supervised toilet visits, and given 2 hours daily for the privilege of reading or letter writing. Work assignments were issued for which the prisoners were to receive an hourly wage to constitute their $15 daily payment. Two visiting periods per week were scheduled, as were movie rights and exercise periods. Three times a day all prisoners were lined up for a 'count' (one on each guard workshift). The initial purpose of the count was to ascertain that all prisoners were present and to test them on their knowledge of the rules and their ID numbers. The first perfunctory counts lasted only about 10 minutes, but on each successive day (or night) they were spontaneously increased in duration until some lasted several hours. Many of the pre-established features of administrative routine were modified or abandoned by the guards, and some privileges were *forgotten* by the staff over the course of study.

Results

There is a body of results pertaining to those events and behaviors we measured and recorded which shall be outlined briefly so we can turn to consider what we discovered through the medium of this experimental paradigm.

1. An analysis of the pattern of interaction between prisoners and guards on 25 occasions, recorded on video tape (presented in Figure 1), clearly reveals the dramatic difference between these two groups. Guard behavior was characterized as: issuing commands, insults, threats, verbal and physical aggression, and deindividuating references towards prisoners. Prisoners resisted, answered when queried, and asked questions. But prisoner behavior is most notable not for its specific qualities, but for its low base level of emission. With each successive day, prisoners did less and less, rarely initiated actions, and at best reacted to demands imposed by guards.

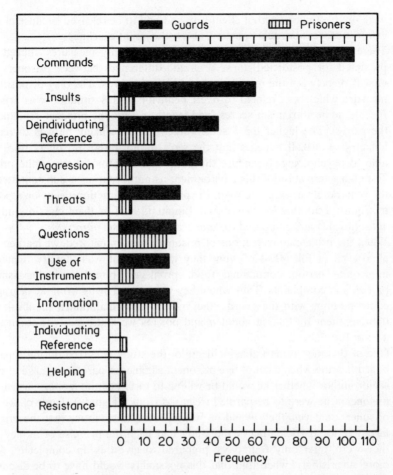

Figure 1   Interaction profile of guard and prisoner behavior derived from video tape analyses of 25 occasions over 6 days in the simulated prison environment

2. The level of verbal and physical aggression of the guards escalated systematically over time. Every guard behaved at one time or other in abusive, dehumanizing ways toward the prisoners, some did so only occasionally, while about a third of them were so consistently hostile and degrading as to be described sadistic. They appeared to take pleasure in the prisoners' suffering.

3. Prisoner affect showed a marked tendency toward ever increasing negativity, depression, and intention to harm others.

4. Every prisoner suffered considerable mental anguish, half of them (5 subjects)

were unable to cope with it effectively and had to be released because of their extreme depression, acute anxiety, or psychosomatic sickness.

5. There were no differences on any of the personality measures utilized that predicted (or postdicted) these dramatic differences between prisoners and guards or between the most brutal and lenient guards. The only dispositional measure which was related to overt behavior in this situation was prisoner F-scale authoritarianism scores (and length of time the prisoner remained in the study). The higher the F-scale value, the more likely he was to remain longer ($r = .90$). It appears that the most authoritarian prisoners were best able to psychologically endure the authoritarian atmosphere of the prison. The characterization of this environment as authoritarian is substantiated by the remarkable analogy between the pattern of interaction behavior reported in Figure 1 to that of White and Lippitt (1960) in their classic study of autocratic leaders compared to democratic and *laissez-faire*.

6. When the private conversations of prisoners were monitored, we learned that almost all (a full 90%) of what they talked about was directly related to immediate prison conditions, food, privileges, punishment, harassment, parole, and complaints. Thus when they were alone, away from the degrading confrontations with the guards, they nevertheless maintained the illusion of imprisonment by talking about *it* and not (as we had expected) about their past or future lives.

7. One of the most remarkable incidents of the study occurred during a parole board hearing when each of five prisoners eligible for parole was asked by the senior author whether he would be willing to forfeit all the money earned as a prisoner if he were to be paroled (released from the study). Three of the five prisoners said yes, they would be willing to do this. Notice that the original incentive for participating in the study had been the promise of money and they were, after only four days, prepared to give this up completely. And, more surprisingly, when told that this possibility would have to be discussed with the members of the staff before a decision could be made, each prisoner got up quietly and was escorted by a guard back to his cell. If they regarded themselves simply as subjects participating in an experiment for money, there was no longer any incentive to remain in the study and they could have easily escaped this situation which had so clearly become aversive for them by quitting. Yet, so powerful was the control which the situation had come to have over them, so much a reality had this simulated environment become, that they were unable to see that their original and singular motive for remaining no longer obtained, and they returned to their cells to await a 'parole' decision by their captors.

8. In terms of the original questions posed it seemed evident that pathology was rampant in this prison environment; for the guards it was through abuse of power, for the prisoners it was manifest in their pervasive display of learned helplessness. It seems reasonable to conclude that in the contest between the

forces of good men and evil situations, the situation triumphed. Individuals carefully selected for their normality, sanity, and homogeneous personality traits were, in a matter of days, acting in ways that *out of this context* would be judged abnormal, insane, neurotic, psychopathic, and sadistic. Their behavior was role dependent and not attributable to pre-existing traits or so-called 'premorbid' history.

Discovery

Power

Power is the most important variable in social psychology and the most neglected. Because psychologists are credentialed, generally middle-class citizens enjoying modest security and affluence, they have ignored the significance of power as the moderating variable in all social interactions. This would not have been so had they been suppressed by its abuse as are the poor, the deviants, the uncredentialed of every society, or had they been equally in positions of power where most decisions rested on securing and extending power. They have just enough not to notice its existence.

The exercise of power was at first instrumental—to gain control of rebellious prisoners, to manage more efficiently administrative routines, and so on—but it soon acquired inherently rewarding properties. Power was used not to get something but as a political statement of how the existing *status quo* was to be recognized and accepted. For example, the use of force, harassment and aggression by the guards steadily escalated from day to day although prisoner resistance—its original justification—declined and dissolved. Not only did direct acts of power by the guards increase, but so too the indirect use of the symbols of power, such as rapping the nightsticks (billy clubs) into their hands or against the furniture, assuming tough, swaggering walks and postures, enforcing trivial meaningless demands. As the dominant guards stood taller, the submissive prisoners literally began to assume less stature, shoulders slouched, heads down. At the end of the study when we inquired of all subjects what they thought was the basis for deciding who would be the guards and who the prisoners, the guards thought there was no systematic rationale; to the contrary, from the prisoners' perception it was clearly 'because the guards were bigger.' So ultimately differential power was conferred on the guards by the prisoners themselves; they helped to create their own feared guardians.

But there were also power confrontations within some of the three-man guard shifts for who would be the 'boss,' among prisoners for leadership in their plans to rebel and escape, as well as among the administrative staff for who was in charge of which activities and who was accountable to whom and who got credit for what. (The latter conflicts continued for months afterwards and strained formerly good social relationships among us.)

Time

Time is the greatest of all human inventions, the masterpiece of imagination, and the illusion that makes adversity bearable and the absurdity of life meaningful. Through developing a temporal perspective in which the abstractions of past and future form a trilogy with the empirical reality of the present, we transcend the animal level of existence. Awareness of our origins and our eventual death, of what was and what will be has incredibly profound effects on what *is*.

It became evident to me that time was an independent variable and not merely a constant or dependent variable in our psychological formulation. It could be manipulated by circumstance to expand or contract past, present, or future, and in each case the consequence would be more extreme than by manipulating any other variable known to us. (Research is in progress using hypnosis to study the effects of systematic alterations in this temporal orientation; see Zimbardo, Marshall, and Maslach, 1972.)

Institutionalization breaks the continuity of life by separating the imprisoned from their past, distancing the future, and by imposing as the dominant temporal frame of reference a limited, immediate present. The endless routines and undifferentiated daily activities create a seeming circularity of time; it flows not in discriminable meaningful linear units, but like an ant's journey along the Möbius strip of life. It does not matter who you are or where you've been, or even where you are going. All that matters is how much protection and power you have *now*. In an atmosphere where survival is paramount, the future is a luxury one cannot afford. Similarly, the past is a dangerous place to return to too often—if nostalgic, you might not want to come back to the ugly present, or you might not be vigilant and prepared for an ever-present assault upon your person.

Where there is fear, limited resources, power relationships, and no exit, one's survival depends upon sensitivity to all potentially important cues. No event is trivial until proven so. Every action may have a counteraction, unless it does not. Every prisoner and guard must become an instant personality diagnostician under such circumstances, since a false positive diagnosis of misplaced trust may cost them dearly.

This immediate present time focus necessitated by a perception of the survival nature of imprisonment also causes men to lose their perspective on life—to overreact to minor stimuli and to fail to plan for major events, such as what to do after the parole date finally comes.

Anonymity

Conditions that reduce a person's sense of uniqueness, that minimize individuality, are the wellsprings of antisocial behaviors, such as aggression, vandalism, stealing, cheating, rudeness, as well as a general loss of concern for others (Zimbardo, 1970). Conversely, prosocial behaviors are encouraged by environmental and interpersonal conditions which enhance one's sense of social recognition and self-identity. The feeling that no one knows who you are, nor does anyone care to, becomes reciprocated by not bothering to notice or be concerned about others. The golden rule of 'doing unto others as you would have them do unto you' is tarnished as anonymity eliminates the motivational basis for monitoring one's social behavior.

Prisons are designed to maximize anonymity. They do so by putting everyone in uniforms which categorize individuals as guards or prisoners. Numbers may replace names or become more administratively important than names. Uniqueness is reduced by having hair shaved off new prisoners, by insisting on standard hair lengths for prisoners and guards, and by having standard meals in standard plates and glasses eaten with standard silverware at standard times. Loss of individuality is furthered by limits on personal possessions and restrictions on personalizing one's home cell, and more so by unannounced body and cell searches.

The physical structure of the prison conveys a very direct, immediate, and constantly repeated message to all within its walls. This place is different from all others where you have lived, and from where respectable, trustworthy, normal people live. But is this not equally true of our mental hospitals, old age homes, and low-rent, high-rise housing projects where the poor are quartered? The ecology of dehumanization is also apparent in the design of the prison which furthers the anonymity process by minimizing the possibility for any privacy, except in solitary confinement. Mass eating in cafeterias, mass exercise in the yard or corridors, cells with bars instead of doors, and animal cage cells which can be looked in from all sides mean the prisoner has lost the right of privacy, solitude, and individual treatment. Prisoners must begin psychologically to detach themselves, to daydream or fantasize privacy in order to be alone in a crowd, or to be unseen, though constantly watched by guards and other prisoners. In our mock prison some of the prisoners made trouble precisely so they could be put into solitary, the Hole, which they defined as their escape to a place of quiet and privacy.

Finally we must acknowledge that not only do prisons and other aspects of our life engender a state of anonymity, but that people may seek the protective camouflage of anonymity when they perceive their environment is threatening. Thus we may also judge the human quality of environments by the extent to which there are social indicators of preferred anonymity. As the crime rate rises, as obscene phone calls come in, as killings become indiscriminate and prominent individuals are kidnapped for ransom, citizens *want* to melt into the crowd, to be ground and not figure. Names are unlisted in phone books and addresses are removed from official files (as many students did at the University of California, Berkeley, after Patricia Hearst was abducted). People will also dress and live in a style that will not call undue attention to themselves—that is, they will live without 'style.'

Emotions

When people lose the capacity to experience emotions, or when their emotional expression is flattened, that is taken as a sign of major psychological disturbance, as in autism or schizophrenia. Without emotions there is little basis for empathy, for attachment to others, for love, for caring, for fear of the consequences to oneself of one's actions. A person without emotions becomes a robot, an automaton, an animal, and potentially the most dangerous enemy of mankind. Instead of promoting a fuller, more normal expression of emotions among the inmates, prisons do exactly the reverse by creating conditions that distort, inhibit, and suppress emotions. Emotions in institutional settings must be contained to the extent that they represent spontaneous, impulsive, often unpredictable, individual reactions. In institutions charged with the management of deviant individuals, such emotional expression is seen as a source of potential danger and must be held in check.

Rules

'If you follow all of these rules . . . you and I will get along just fine.' If you do not, the final rule always describes how you will be punished.

We have learned that rules are the backbone of all institutionalized approaches to managing people. Institutions vary only in how many rules they have, and how explicit and detailed they are—never in whether or not they have rules. Rules impose an impersonal, externalized structure on interpersonal relationships. They remove ambiguity from social interaction. They make human conduct more predictable by reducing idiosyncratic reactions and individualized interpretations of how to behave. Rules obviate the need for personal explanations or justifications for any desired course of action. 'It's the rule' is sufficient reason. Rules proliferate in institutional settings. They come to have a life of their own, continuing to be enforced even after they are obsolete and their original purpose can no longer be remembered by the rule enforcers. Coercive rules automatically force power relationships upon people; somebody must have the power to enforce the rules, and somebody must have to obey them. Those who obey often come to expect, and even respect, the structure which a rule-governed environment provides.

A final word about rules is the insidious way in which some of them become so ingrained in our social programming that they continue to influence our behavior for a lifetime in situations bearing only remote resemblance to the original one. In some instances observance of the rule may even be counterproductive or antisocial because the fundamental character of the situation is not fully appreciated while attention to its rule-relevant aspects are being obeyed.

Milgram's now classic research on obedience (1974) should be viewed in this light. It is less curious to me after my experience in the Stanford County Prison that the majority of Milgram's subjects showed blind obedience to authority than it is to speculate about what the disobedient minority did *after* they refused to shock the innocent victim. Given the enormity of their disobedience in the face of compelling situational forces, did they exercise the next smaller option which should rationally follow from their refusal to injure and perhaps kill a fellow man so obviously in distress? Did they get up out of their seat and go to the aid of the victim? Milgram in a personal conversation verified my prediction that not one of his subjects did so! The silent rule still operating even after complicity with the authority was rejected was that drilled into every school child: 'Stay in your seat until you are given permission to leave it' (and by its extension, 'Know your place in every social situation and stay put in it.')

Paradigms for advocacy and action

Acceptance by the scientific community of this research has come about because the minimal criteria for establishing causal attributions have been satisfied. We are not dealing solely with personal observations, however perceptive the observer may be, but with an *experiment*. It is the random assignment to treatments of subjects drawn from an initially homogeneous population which is the scientific essence of this study. It allows the researchers to separate what the prison environment brings out in the men from what the men bring into the prison. When systematic record keeping and data collection are added, along with some attempts at methodological control, a valid experimental paradigm is the consequence.

The heuristic value of such a paradigm is extolled by Helmreich and his associates in their 1973 annual review of small group research. They argue that the power of such experiments 'lies precisely in their demonstration of how strong situational determinants are in shaping behavior. No resort to a correlation between "those" people who do "evil" things is allowed: the subjects were randomly assigned. It is the experimental method, not a fascination with the artificial, that convinces' (Helmreich, Bakeman, and Scherwitz, 1973, p. 343).

Two other features of this research which make it appealing to both the public and the purveyors of mass media news and entertainment are its 'mundane realism' and its tragic design. Our prison setting, with all its attention to props, costumes, roles, and cast of characters, permits instant translatability of its essential features to real-world analogues. This confers intuitive appreciation of the implications and relevance of this simulation not only to better understanding of real prisons, but also for insight into the psychological prisons of the mind in which Everyman may be guard, or prisoner, or both. The use of normal, average, healthy, intelligent young men as subjects also served to make possible the tragic conclusion when the forces of evil conquered the goodness of the hero.

Advocacy

Suddenly I'm an advocate

It was my invited appearance before a subcommittee of the House of Representatives conducting hearings on prison reform (25 October, 1971) that made my transformation from academic social psychologist to advocate for social change a reality. They wanted not only analysis but recommendations for reform. This statement in the *Congressional Record* clearly advocates intervention into the existing prison structure to bring about improvements in conditions for the inmates as well as for the correctional personnel.

My advocacy has been largely in the form of consciousness raising about the necessity for terminating 'the social experiment of prisons' because of its failures, while also trying to understand the reasons for those failures, alternative solutions, and sources of resistance to meaningful prison reform.

Most notable has been my participation in the Federal Court trial of Spain *et al.* versus Procunier *et al.* The 'San Quentin Six' have been in solitary confinement for over three years for their supposed involvement in the deaths of the prison guards during the alleged escape attempt of George Jackson on 21 August, 1971. As an expert witness, I toured the facilities of San Quentin's maximum adjustment center and interviewed each of the six prisoners over four occasions. My prepared statement and two days of trial testimony concluded with the opinion that the totality of these conditions of involuntary, prolonged, indefinite confinement constitutes cruel and unusual punishment (the Court arrived at a similar verdict). In addition, I served throughout the trial as a psychological consultant to the team of lawyers for the plaintiffs.

[See also, Abelson and Zimbardo, 1970.]

The Stanford Slide Show

We have been able to reach hundreds of college, high school, civic, and prison-related groups with our message by means of the slide show Greg White and I prepared.

We have accepted speaking engagements to disseminate the message of this research at national psychological and science conventions, to Chamber of Commerce groups, law school groups, to parole officer units, and many others.

. . . And then action

Institutions resist change and outlive their critics. Prisons are a low-priority item in our current world of economic upheaval and rising crime. Prison reform is also a transient social cause.

So the final question is where to go from here? The three directions in which I plan to move are:

1. Discovering the sources of power and resistance to change in the California prison structure with an eye toward then developing action proposals for change. With a grant from the Abelard Foundation, James Newton and I are heading a team of researchers investigating the interlocking systems which

support the prison *status quo*—the political machinery, labor unions, lobbies, businesses, etc.—as well as public opinion on prisons and the specific repositories of power at various points in the chain of command;

2. Writing a popular account of this experience in a new nonfiction form to educate and raise the consciousness of a new audience while entertaining them with prison stories;

3. Acting politically to support candidates and legislation which may provide meaningful alternatives to incarceration, and the incarcerated in being released as quickly as possible, and make the time spent in prison less filled with injustice and pathology than it is now.

And when prisons are no more, then we may study not only how to right wrongs, but how to extend human joy and understand the dynamics of happiness. It would be wonderful to be a social advocate for love and goodness, but would anybody want an advocate if there were no problems?

References

Abelson, R. P., and Zimbardo, P. G. (1970). *Canvassing for Peace; a Manual for Volunteers*, Society for the Psychological Study of Social Issues, Ann Arbor, MI.

Helmreich, R., Bakeman, R., and Scherwitz, L. (1973). 'The study of small groups,' in P. H. Mussen and M. R. Rosenzweig (eds.), *Annual Review of Psychology*, **24**, 337–354.

Milgram, S. (1974). *Obedience to Authority*, Harper and Row, New York.

White, R., and Lippitt, R. (1960). *Autocracy and Democracy*, Harper & Row, New York.

Zimbardo, P. G. (1970). 'The human choice: Individuation, reason, and order versus deindividuation, impulse, and chaos,' in W. J. Arnold and D. Levine (eds.), *1969 Nebraska Symposium on Motivation*, University of Nebraska Press, Lincoln, Nebraska, pp. 237–307.

Zimbardo, P. G. (1971). 'The power and pathology of imprisonment,' *Congressional Record*. Serial No. 15, October 25, 1971. Hearings before Subcommittee No. 3 of the Committee on the Judiciary, House of Representatives, 92nd Congress, First Session on Corrections, Part II, Prisons, Prison Reform and Prisoners' Rights: California. US Government Printing Office, Washington, DC. (Reprinted in J. J. Bonsignore *et al.* (eds.), *Before the Law: An Introduction to the Legal Process*, 2nd edn, pp. 396–398, Houghton Mifflin, Boston, 1979.)

Zimbardo, P. G., Marshall, G., and Maslach, C. (1972). 'Liberating behavior from time-bound control: Expanding the present through hypnosis,' *Journal of Applied Social Psychology*, **1**, 305–323.

10 Leadership

Small Groups and Social Interaction, Volume 1
Edited by H. H. Blumberg, A. P. Hare, V. Kent and M. Davies
© 1983 John Wiley & Sons Ltd

10.1 The Relationship of Participation Rates to Leadership Status: A Meta-Analysis

R. Timothy Stein   *A. T. Kearney, Inc.*

and

Tamar Heller   *University of Illinois, Chicago*

Numerous investigators have reported a positive relationship between the verbal participation rates and leadership status of members of lab and classroom groups. In reviewing the literature, the authors found 77 correlations between participation rates and leadership status. The mean was .65; the range was −.48 (Gustafson and Harrell, 1970) to .98 (Bates, 1952). Only four correlations were negative. Other lab studies report higher mean leadership ratings for high participants (e.g. Gintner and Lindskold, 1975) and an increase in leadership scores through the reinforcement of participation (e.g. Zdep and Oakes, 1967).

The covariation of leadership status and participation rates has been attributed to: (a) the performance of task leadership acts, (b) task skill and knowledge, (c) social status characteristics, (d) the presence of observers, and (e) motivation.

First, both empirical and theoretical studies in the small group literature suggest that leadership status is based, at least in part, on the group members' performance of a number of discrete leadership acts. Comparisons of leaders and non-leaders indicate that leaders perform more task-related behaviors (e.g. Morris and Hackman, 1969; Kirscht *et al.*, 1959; Carter *et al.*, 1950). These behaviors include identifying problems, proposing solutions, and giving or seeking information, opinions, or structure. The development of task-related roles is the major thesis of emergent leadership theories (see Stein *et al.*, 1979 for a review). For example, the leadership valence theory of emergence (see Hoffman and Stein in Volume 2) holds that a force for implicitly adopting a group member as leader builds with each successive task leadership act and each acceptance of such acts by others. A member is accepted as leader after making a threshold number of successful leadership attempts.

If the performance of task leadership behaviors is the source of common variance between leadership status and participation, then two hypotheses follow. *Hypothesis 1a*: The leadership–participation rate correlations in which task leadership measures are used are higher than those in which maintenance leadership measures are used. Task-leadership behaviors are behaviors related to helping the group achieve its goals. Group maintenance behaviors are aimed at establishing and maintaining cordial and socially satisfying relations (Bales, 1958). *Hypothesis 1b*: The more general the task leadership measure, the higher is the correlation with participation rates.

Task competence has been related to emergent leadership in both field (e.g. Crockett, 1955) and lab studies (e.g. Heinicke and Bales, 1953). It is possible that both leadership status and participation rate differences occur because those who offer better solutions make more attempts to influence others. *Hypothesis 2*: The value of the correlation between leadership status and participation is directly related to the skill requirements of the task.

Third, according to Blau (1964), members who impress others as being capable of providing task assistance are initially permitted more participation time. The personal characteristics which have been tied to these judgments include intelligence, personality traits, and social status (race, sex, and income). Of these variables, only sexual status seems to be strongly related to both participation rates and leadership. Men have been shown to be more verbose and more influential (e.g. Strodtbeck *et al.*, 1957), and more proactively involved in performing the task (e.g. Strodtbeck and Mann, 1956). *Hypothesis 3*: The correlation between leadership status and participation is higher in mixed-sex than in same-sex groups.

Finally, Wilson (1971) has suggested that the leadership–participation rate relationship is an artefact. Members with high assertiveness and ascendancy needs participate more and act in an ingratiating manner in the presence of observers. Because the other members assume that the observer identifies leadership with dominance, influence, and high participation rates, the ingratiating members receive higher peer ratings. *Hypothesis 4*: The correlation between leadership and participation is lower in groups not aware that they are being observed.

The literature suggests that a stronger relationship between participation and leadership will be present under two additional conditions: (1) when the groups are large; and (2) when an observer rates the members on leadership. Greater size is associated with an increase in role differentiation (Thomas and Fink, 1963) and sharper differences in participation rates (Hare, 1976). Other research (e.g. Stein, 1977) has found that observers, but not group members, fail to distinguish between task and maintenance functions. Observers may use a more global criterion, which includes a greater proportion of the total participation, in evaluating leadership. Additional independent variables were included to explore their association with the leadership–participation rate relationship.

Method

Seventy-two correlations reported in the literature between verbal participation rates and leadership status were used as the dependent variable (see Stein and Heller, 1979, for a list of the correlations and a more extensive report on this research). Fisher scores were used for all statistical tests. The correlations were not weighted by sample size because the error variance due to differences in sample size was randomly distributed. Sample size was uncorrelated with the value of the leadership–participation rate correlations ($r = -.12$, n.s.).

The study involved 28 independent measures related to (a) the type of task, (b) the characteristics of the task, (c) the nature of the group, and (d) the nature of the leadership measure. A number of these measures simply involved coding the investigators' reports (e.g. whether or not the group was comprised of all males). Other measures, such as the skill requirements of the task, involved ratings by two judges. The Pearson correlations between the two judges' ratings on these dimensions ranged from .79 to .97 (see Stein and Heller, 1979). The raters did not know the values of the leadership–participation rate correlations.

Results

Leadership behaviors

The data support the contention that the performance of task leadership behaviors is a common source of both high participation and leadership status. The mean value of the leadership–participation rate correlations with task leadership measures was .69, whereas the mean for the maintenance measures was only .16, $t(70) = 6.37$, $p < .001$.

Since the leadership–participation rate relationship was limited to measures of task leadership, all other analyses were performed separately on the total sample of 72 correlations and on the 57 correlations that involved task leadership measures.

As hypothesized (1b), the association between leadership and participation was significantly correlated with ratings of the breadth of the task leadership measures, $r = .36$, $p < .01$. However, the correlation was only .13 when the entire sample of 72 values was used. This lower value is consistent with the notion that the maintenance behaviors are not the source of the leadership–participation rate relationship.

Task skill

A positive relationship was predicted (Hypothesis 2) between task skill required and the association between the participation and leadership. The variables were correlated .27 ($p < .01$) for the total sample, and .35 ($p < .01$) for the task sub-sample.

Sexual status

A significantly higher leadership–participation correlation mean was found for mixed-sex groups than for same-sex groups in the total sample, $t(70) = 3.18$,

$p < .01$, and the subsample of task measures, $t(55) = 5.68$, $p < .001$. The means for all male and all female groups were almost identical. Unfortunately, the mixed-sex variable is confounded with type of task. Thirty-one of the 34 correlations for mixed-sex groups were from groups assigned opinion tasks (see below).

Demand characteristics

The leadership–participation correlations based on data from subjects aware of being observed were not significantly higher than those from unaware subjects for either the total sample, $t(70) = .88$, or for the subsample, $t(55) = .61$.

Situational variables

Group size was correlated with the dependent measure, for both the total sample ($r = .39$, $p < .01$) and the subsample ($r = .45$, $p < .01$). Contrary to expectations, the leadership–participation rate correlations based on observer ratings were not significantly higher than those based on peer-ratings or self-ratings.

Exploratory analyses

Other measures of the groups, tasks, and leadership measures were related to the dependent measure. Participation–leadership correlations were higher when the tasks were judged to be more interesting, task performance was tied to rewards such as grades or money, tasks required more intellectual operations and fewer mechanical operations, and when the leadership measure was taken later in the group's history. The correlations were also significantly higher in discussion groups which did not require consensual decision making. As pointed out above, these 'opinion' groups were predominantly mixed-sex groups. Finally, the correlations were lower when leadership ratings gave the leader some future power over the group members.

Multiple regression analysis

A stepwise multiple regression was performed to determine the relative importance of the 28 independent measures. With a multiple R of .792, the four independent measures included accounted for 63% of the variance in the leadership–participation rate correlations. The measures were added in the following order: maintenance functions (with a negative weight, 37% of the variance accounted for), mixed-sex groups versus same-sex groups (15%), leadership ratings by observers versus group members (6%), breadth of the leadership measures (5%). The negative weight given to the correlations based on maintenance leadership and the positive weight given to the breadth of the leadership measure strongly indicate that the performance of task leadership behaviors is a source of the common variance between leadership and participation.

Conclusions

The data support three of the explanations for the leadership–participation rate relationship: (1) task leadership behaviors are a component of total participation and a basis for leadership status; (2) those with superior task ability make more task-related contributions to the group which increases their participation; and (3) males are permitted both greater influence and higher participation rates (though the sex differences are confounded with task differences).

These explanations can be integrated if the performance of task-leadership behaviors is viewed as the major source of the variance common to leadership status and participation rates. Competency and sexual status seem to moderate the performance of such behaviors. Behavioral manifestations of competency (such as giving information, proposing solutions, procedures, and structure) are in themselves task-leadership behaviors. In addition, members of new groups who feel they are competent make more influence attempts, while members who realize that they are less competent make fewer leadership attempts (Hemphill, 1961). The literature on sex differences indicates that males are considered to be more influential, talk more often, and perform more task leadership acts.

Sorrentino and Boutillier (1975) have suggested that high motivation is the underlying cause of both high participation and high leadership status. Their hypothesis could not be tested in this study because measures of differences among group members were not available.

Past research on the relationship of participation to leadership has been restricted by the narrow range of methods and populations used. The typical study involved a group of students or military personnel working in a short term group of strangers to complete a task assigned by the experimenter. Rarely did the leadership ratings elect a formal leader. The leadership–participation relationship needs to be tested in real-world groups of people motivated to accomplish goals they value. Some possibilities are temporary work groups, committees, and *ad hoc* groups in businesses and non-profit organizations, and new autonomous groups such as condominium associations, neighborhood clubs, and study groups.

References

Bales, R. F. (1958). 'Task roles and social roles in Problem-solving groups,' in E. E. Maccoby, T. M. Newcomb and F. L. Hartley (eds.), *Readings in Social Psychology*, 3rd edn, Holt, Rinehart & Winston, New York.

Bates, A. P. (1952). 'Some sociometric aspects of social ranking in a small, face-to-face group,' *Sociometry*, **15**, 330–341.

Blau, P. M. (1964). *Exchange and Power in Social Life*, Wiley, New York.

Carter, L., Haythorn, W., Shriver, B., and Lanzetta, J. (1950). 'The behavior of leaders and other group members,' *Journal of Abnormal and Social Psychology*, **46**, 589–595.

Crockett, W. H. (1955). 'Emergent leadership in small decision-making groups,' *Journal of Abnormal and Social Psychology*, **51**, 378–383.

Gintner, G., and Lindskold, S. (1975). 'Rate of participation and expertise as factors influencing leader choice,' *Journal of Personality and Social Psychology*, **32**, 1085–1089.

Gustafson, D. P., and Harrell, T. W. (1970). 'A comparison of role differentiation in several situations,' *Organizational Behavior and Human Performance*, **5**, 299–312.

Hare, A. P. (1976). *Handbook of Small Group Research*, 2nd edn, Free Press, New York.

Heinicke, C., and Bales, R. F. (1953). 'Developmental trends in the structure of small groups,' *Sociometry*, **16**, 7–38.

Hemphill, J. K. (1961). 'Why people attempt to lead,' in L. Petrullo and B. M. Bass (eds.), *Leadership and Interpersonal Behavior*, Holt, Rinehart & Winston, New York.

Kirscht, J. P., Lodahl, T. M., and Haire, M. (1959). 'Some factors in the selection of leaders by members of small groups,' *Journal of Abnormal and Social Psychology*, **58**, 406–408.

Morris, C. G., and Hackman, J. R. (1969). 'Behavioral correlates of perceived leadership,' *Journal of Personality and Social Psychology*, **13**, 350–361.

Sorrentino, R. M., and Boutillier, R. G. (1975). 'The effect of quantity and quality of verbal interaction on ratings of leadership ability,' *Journal of Experimental and Social Psychology*, **11**, 403–411.

Stein, R. T. (1977). 'Accuracy of process consultants and untrained observers in perceiving emergent leadership,' *Journal of Applied Psychology*, **62**, 755–759.

Stein, R. T., and Heller, T. (1979). 'An empirical analysis of the correlations between leadership status and participation rates reported in the literature,' *Journal of Personality and Social Psychology*, **37**, 1993–2002.

Stein, R. T., Hoffman, L. R., Cooley, S., and Pearse, R. W. (1979). 'Leadership valence: Modeling and measuring the process of emergent leadership,' in J. G. Hunt and L. L. Larson (eds.), *Crosscurrents in Leadership*, University of Southern Illinois Press, Carbondale, Ill.

Strodtbeck, F. L., James, R. M., and Hawkins, C. (1957). 'Social status in jury deliberations,' *Journal of Abnormal and Social Psychology*, **22**, 713–719.

Strodtbeck, F. L., and Mann, R. D. (1956). 'Sex role differentiation in jury deliberations,' *Sociometry*, **19**, 3–11.

Thomas, E. J., and Fink, C. F. (1963). 'Effects of group size,' *Psychological Bulletin*, **60**, 371–384.

Wilson, S. R. (1971). 'Leadership, participation and self-orientation in observed and non-observed groups,' *Journal of Applied Psychology*, **55**, 433–438.

Zdep, S. M., and Oakes, W. F. (1967). 'Reinforcement of leadership behavior in group discussion,' *Journal of Experimental and Social Psychology*, **3**, 310–320.

Small Groups and Social Interaction, Volume 1
Edited by H. H. Blumberg, A. P. Hare, V. Kent and M. Davies
© 1983 John Wiley & Sons Ltd

10.2   Dynamics of Leadership Effectiveness

Fred E. Fiedler   *University of Washington*

and

Earl H. Potter, III   *US Coast Guard Academy*

Most leadership theories now accept the principle that the effectiveness of the leader is dependent (or contingent) on the situation as well as on the leader's personality or behavior. The Contingency Model (Fiedler, 1964, 1978) further predicts the specific effects of situational changes on the leader's performance and behavior, and it has led to empirical studies supporting these predictions. The present paper briefly describes some of the dynamic interpretations of the Contingency Model and empirical studies which test their validity.

The Contingency Model postulates two interacting elements in any leadership situation. The first of these is the leader's underlying goal of motivational structure; the second is the leader's situational control and influence. Motivational structure is measured by the Least Preferred Coworker (LPC) scale, on which the individual describes the characteristics of the one person with whom he or she has been able to work least well. The scale classifies people into those whose primary motivation is the maintenance or development of close interpersonal relations (high LPC or relationship motivated), and those whose primary motivation is the accomplishment of the task (low LPC or task motivated).

The second major element, situational control (or favorableness) indicates the degree to which the leader feels secure and confident that the task will be accomplished (Beach *et al.*, 1975). The leader's situational control is defined by three factors: the degree to which (a) the leader's group is loyal, supportive, and reliable; (b) the task is structured and clearly defined as to goals, methods, and expected outcomes; and (c) the leader is given power to reward and punish, to reprimand and praise in controlling group members' efforts. A highly accepted foreman of a production crew tends to have high situational control; a disliked chairman of a volunteer committee to develop a new school policy will have low situational control. Moderate control is illustrated by a respected leader of a research team or a rejected commander of an army tank crew.

The theory postulates that task-motivated (low LPC) leaders will be most effective in situations in which they have very high or else very low control and influence; relationship-motivated (high LPC) leaders will be most effective in situations which provide moderate control.

The theory has been the subject of strong criticism, mostly on the basis that the predictor measure, LPC, is insufficiently stable and uninterpretable, and that the validation evidence does not support the theory's predictions. Both of these points have now been adequately addressed by extensive reviews of the literature and meta-analyses of existing studies. Rice (1978a) summarized the results of 23 studies in which the LPC score had been obtained at two different times. This enabled the investigator to obtain test–retest correlations of LPC to estimate its stability over time and, therefore, also its status as a personality variable. Rice reported a median test–retest correlation of .67 ($n = 23, p < .001$) and a mean of .64. The magnitude of these correlations compares with other personality tests as, for example, a test–retest correlation of .65, obtained for the California Personality Inventory (Mehrens and Lehmann, 1969) or the Minnesota Multiphasic of .60 (Sax, 1974). Rice (1978b) also summarized 66 studies on LPC, randomly selected from among 114 he could locate in the literature. He concluded that the results fully support the interpretation of LPC as indicating, in Rice's terms, a value orientation concerned with the task or interpersonal relations.

In a meta-analysis of all available studies, Strube and Garcia (1981) recently computed the joint probability of all statistical tests, positive and negative, of the Contingency Model. The authors reported the probability level supporting the Contingency Model as $p = 2.02 \times 10^{-14}$ ($z = 7.56$), requiring over 2,500 nonconfirmatory studies before it could be concluded that the Contingency Model is invalid.

Changes in situational control and performance

The theory is graphically represented on Figure 1, with situational control shown on the horizontal, and performance on the vertical axis. The effectiveness of relationship-motivated (high LPC) leaders is represented by the solid line and that of task-motivated leaders by the dashed line. As indicated before, task-motivated leaders perform best in high and in low control situations, and relationship-motivated leaders are more effective in moderate control situations. However, the graph also shows that a change in situational control will have opposite effects on the performance on these two types of leaders. As situational control increases from low to moderate, and from moderate to high (going from right to left on the graph), performance should decrease as the task-motivated leader moves from low to the moderate control zone and again increase as he moves into the high control zone. The relationship-motivated leader's performance should increase when moving into moderate control, and decrease in the high control zone. Similar effects should, of course, occur as the leader's control decreases from high to moderate, and from moderate to low.

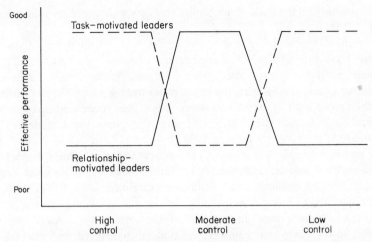

Figure 1 Situational control and performance

These non-obvious and rather complex predictions have been supported by a number of studies. A few of these are here described to illustrate the point (see also Fiedler, 1978).

Experience and leadership performance

Common sense, as well as empirical evidence (e.g. Bons and Fiedler, 1976), tells us that experience generally increases the leader's control; the job becomes more routine and, therefore, more structured, relations with group members become stabilized and usually better, and the leader becomes more secure in using authority. Experience should, therefore, benefit the task-motivated leader when moving from a moderate to a high control zone; it should decrease the performance of relationship-motivated leaders under the same conditions.

This hypothesis was tested by Fiedler *et al.* (1975) in a study of 39 army infantry squad leaders who were evaluated by the same superior officers shortly after their unit was formed, and again approximately 8 months later. Situational control had been judged as moderate at the time of the first rating and high at the time of the second rating, when the leaders had become more experienced in handling their units.

As the Contingency Model predicts, in the first evaluation (moderate control) the relationship-motivated leaders were rated as performing better than the task-motivated leaders, while the task-motivated leaders received higher ratings in the second evaluation (high control situation).

A study of a large consumer sales cooperative federation yielded similar results. The various companies in the federation sold the same products, followed highly uniform procedures, and kept identical records, permitting an objective evaluation of each company on the basis of net profits and operation expenses/total sales (see Fiedler, 1978).

The general managers of these companies were divided into those with relatively high and relatively low experience, and into task- and relationship-motivated persons. As in the infantry squad leader study, among the inexperienced general managers, the relationship-motivated individuals performed better than those who were task motivated, while the experienced task-motivated managers outperformed the experienced relationship-motivated managers. (For other studies of this type, see Fiedler, 1978.)

In a rather dramatic test of the Contingency Model, Chemers *et al.* (1975) experimentally increased task structure (and, therefore, situational control) through leadership training. The laboratory experiment used ROTC cadets as leaders of four-man groups, which were given the task of diciphering simple coded messages, i.e. cryptograms. In one-half of the groups the leaders were task motivated, in the other half they were relationship motivated, and the task- and relationship-motivated leaders were randomly assigned to a task training or a control condition. The task training was designed to make the coding task, which was unstructured for the untrained leader, structured for the leaders in the training condition. Since the leaders rated their relations with group members as poor and the position power was low, the untrained leaders were in a low control situation and the trained leaders in a moderate control situation. According to the Contingency Model, and Figure 1, task-motivated leaders *without* training should perform better than task-motivated leaders with training, while relationship-motivated leaders should improve with training. This hypothesis was supported, indicating that training, which improved situational control, was dysfunctional for task-motivated leaders. These and other studies demonstrated, therefore, that changes in situational control increase or decrease the performance of task- and relationship-motivated leaders in predictable ways. The obvious next question was whether we could teach leaders how to improve their performance by modifying their own situational control.

Leader match training

A training program was developed which instructs leaders how to diagnose their situational control, and then modify the situation if necessary to match their motivational structure, indicated by the LPC score. Since motivational structure is a personality attribute, as already shown by the stability of LPC scores, it would be very difficult to change at will. In fact, most leaders cannot even tell how they appear to their subordinates (e.g. Mitchell, 1970). On the other hand, most leaders find it relatively easy to change their leader–member relations, their task structure, and position power.

For example, leader–member relations can be changed by making oneself more or less available to subordinates, by more or less face-to-face contact, by more or less socializing. Task structure can be increased by dividing the task into smaller components, by carefully programming the procedure, or decreased by volunteering for more challenging tasks or by becoming expert on the task or by controlling information channels, and decreased by sharing decision-making functions or being one of the gang. The 6–8 hour training, which provides detailed instructions along this line, is available in the form of a self-paced programmed manual, or it can be administered in lecture–discussion format.

The effectiveness of leader match training has been successfully tested in 17 different studies. In all of these studies leaders were randomly assigned to a training or control condition and superiors' ratings, obtained 2 to 12 months after training, served as performance criteria. In several of these studies, evaluators did not know that certain individuals had received training while others had received no training or an alternative training program. In one study, leaders were randomly assigned to groups as well as to leadership tasks (Fiedler and Mahar, 1979).

Two studies are here described for illustrative purposes. The first of these was conducted by Csoka and Bons (1978) and involved cadets who had completed their third year at the military academy. One-third of these cadets were randomly chosen for leader match training. They were handed the programmed manual with instructions to read it carefully. All cadets were then assigned to various field units in which they served as acting platoon leaders. At the end of the summer's field assignment, all cadets were rated by their battalion leaders who had no information about the study. Cadets with Leader Match were given substantially and significantly higher performance evaluations than those in the control group. The study is of particular significance since all cadets had been immersed in a leadership training environment for 3 full years. The fact that an additional 6 hour self-paced training program could improve performance still further speaks to the power of the leader match approach.

Another illustration of this type is an executive training program by a large department store chain. College graduates are assigned to one of five training stores where they serve as assistant managers and rotate through various service departments. At the conclusion of the 9 month training, they become managers of various retail sales departments in stores throughout the country, and organizational policy requires that the former trainees be evaluated by the store's manager and his staff 7 months after arrival.

Two of the five training stores were randomly chosen for leader match training. The other stores devoted an equivalent amount of time to role playing and management lectures. Trainees who had received leader match instruction were subsequently rated as significantly more effective than those who had received alternative training.

Finally, it seems worthy of note that trainees in one study were given a test to determine how well they had understood the principles of the training program, and they were also asked how frequently they used these principles (Fiedler and

Mahar, 1979). Those who understood leader match and those who applied it more frequently by making changes in their situational control were rated as more effective by their superiors and their peers than those who had received low comprehension test scores or had not applied leader match principles in their leadership positions.

In summary, we have attempted to show that deliberate, as well as incidental, changes in situational control affect leadership performance in ways which can be predicted on the basis of the Contingency Model. The theory, thus, represents a first step toward understanding the effects of a changing environment on the effective performance of the leader.

References

Beach, B. H., Mitchell, T. R., and Beach, L. R. (1975). 'Components of situational favorableness and probability of success,' University of Washington, Organizational Research Group Technical Report No. 75–66, Seattle.

Bons, P. M. and Fiedler, F. E. (1976). 'Changes in organizational leadership and the behavior of relationship- and task-motivated leaders,' *Administrative Science Quarterly*, **21**, 433–472.

Chemers, M. M., Rice, R. W., Sundstrom, E., and Butler, W. (1975). 'Leader esteem for the least preferred coworker score, training, and effectiveness: An experimental examination,' *Journal of Personality and Social Psychology*, **31**, 401–409.

Csoka, L. S. and Bons, P. M. (1978). 'Manipulating the situation to fit the leader's style—two validation studies of Leader Match,' *Journal of Applied Psychology*, **63**, 295–300.

Fiedler, F. E. (1964). 'A contingency model of leadership effectiveness,' in L. Berkowitz (ed.), *Advances in Exerpimental Social Psychology*, Vol. 1, pp. 149–190, Academic Press, New York.

Fiedler, F. E. (1978). 'The contingency model and the dynamics of the leadership process,' in L. Berkowitz (ed.), *Advances in Experimental Social Psychology*, Vol. 11, pp. 59–112, Academic Press, New York.

Fiedler, F. E., Bons, P. M., and Hastings, L. (1975). 'The utilization of leadership resources,' in W. T. Singleton and P. Spurgeon (eds.), *Measurement of Human Resources*, pp. 233–244, Taylor and Francis, London.

Fiedler, F. E. and Mahar, L. (1979). 'The effectiveness of contingency model training: A review of the validation of Leader Match,' *Personnel Psychology*, **32**, 45–62.

Mehrens, W. A. and Lehmann, I. J. (1969). *Standardized Tests in Education*, Holt, Rinehart and Winston, New York.

Mitchell, T. R. (1970). 'The construct validity of three dimensions of leadership research,' *Journal of Social Psychology*, **80**, 89–94.

Rice, R. W. (1978a). 'Psychometric properties of the esteem for least preferred coworker (LPC) scale,' *Academy of Management Review*, **3**, 106–117.

Rice, R. W. (1978b). 'Construct validity of the least preferred coworker score,' *Psychological Bulletin*, **85** (6), 1199–1237.

Sax, G. (1974). *Principles of Education Measurement and Evaluation*, Wadsworth Publishing Company, Belmont, Calif.

Strube, M. J. and Garcia, J. E. (1981). 'A meta-analytic investigation of Fiedler's contingency model of leadership effectiveness,' *Psychological Bulletin*, **90**, 307–321.

Small Groups and Social Interaction, Volume 1
Edited by H. H. Blumberg, A. P. Hare, V. Kent and M. Davies
© 1983 John Wiley & Sons Ltd

10.3 Issues in Emergent Leadership: The Contingency Model of Leadership, Leader Sex, and Leader Behavior

Craig Eric Schneier and Janet R. Goktepe

University of Maryland

Leadership research and theory

Leadership has been studied in terms of traits, behavioral styles, and situations (see e.g. Stogdill, 1974). Two overriding impressions conveyed by a survey of leadership in the last two decades are a dissatisfaction with the results of these approaches (e.g. Dansereau *et al.*, 1975) and a need to redirect interests in leadership toward the view that it is an ongoing *process* rather than an *outcome* or result (e.g. Hollander and Julian, 1969; Lord, 1977).

Leadership theory and research are essentially built on studies of appointed or elected leaders (Stogdill, 1974). Leaders are hence viewed in static terms, with an emphasis on the outcomes of their influence assertions. Relatively little work has been done with leaders who *emerge* from the group as a result of the group process itself. By redirecting research toward the study of emergent leadership, the process issues of leadership may be more adequately addressed and understood.

Most theoretical and conceptual leadership models are built upon the assumptions that the formal position (be it appointed or elected) provides the leader with legitimacy and power and that the leader impacts group performance. This view may neglect the fact that many groups have no formal leaders; that leaders can be challenged, deposed, or ignored, with new leaders emerging to deal with new situations and filling needs not met by formal leaders. It also diminishes the role of the needs and perceptions of followers and ongoing interactions within groups.

Understanding the evolutionary process or the progressive series of actions and interactions leading to ascendance or emergence of a leader can provide a rich basis for future leadership research. There are numerous leaderless situations, such as informal meetings, teams, and task forces (Galbraith, 1977) which provide opportunities for individuals to emerge as leaders. Organizations which rely upon project teams, committees, or temporary work groups where there is no appointed leader also permit informal leaders to emerge and to avoid structural barriers to bureaucratic lines of authority. Whatever is gleaned from research with emergent leaders also has applicability to the maintenance of status by those who are appointed leaders (Lord, 1977). The acceptance of influence, which is conditional upon the consent of followers, produces 'emergent' leadership (Hollander, 1964).

A fuller understanding of the emergent leadership process can facilitate the personnel selection and career development process and enhance upward mobility programs within organizations. For example, as the variables which bring emergent status in terms of potential influence are identified, they can be useful to persons seeking election or appointment to leadership positions or those seeking to develop programs to aid progress toward upward mobility for others.

By identifying the selection criteria that members of groups use in their interpretations and attributions concerning each other's behavior, we can better understand what variables interact to yield leadership status (Stein, 1975). Applying these criteria to specific situations can be valuable. Women, minorities, and other groups who may have been previously denied leadership status because of certain stereotyping may gain access to leadership roles as people in organizations recognize erroneous perceptions and biases implicit in instruments such as personnel performance appraisals (Carroll and Schneier, 1982; Landy and Farr, 1980), and base personnel decisions on more situation-specific criteria.

Individuals are attributed leadership status by displaying certain verbal and nonverbal behaviors (Stein, 1975) within groups. Once a person becomes 'labeled' a leader, the transition to additional leadership positions is facilitated. To a great extent, individuals control or shape the impressions others make of them through certain behavioral tactics (Goffman, 1959; Jones, 1975). Lord (1977) concluded that in most situations, interpersonal perceptions are based on stereotypes rather than situation-specific criteria (see also Schein, 1975).

A capsule review of emergent leadership literature

A most prominent theory of emergent leadership is Hollander's (1958) 'idiosyncrasy credit' concept. A person's potential to be influential arises out of the positive dispositions others hold toward him or her. Reinforcement theories have been developed by Bales (1953), Stogdill (1959), and Bormann (1969). According to Bales (1953), the emergence process begins with a member making proactive statements he or she feels contribute to the immediate task. Bormann (1969) provided a description of the overall process of emergence consisting of the following three general phases: the elimination of those who are unsuitable; the selection of one of the potential leaders; and a probationary period during which the leader must continue to demonstrate necessary capabilities.

Stogdill (1959) sees the leadership role emerging as a result of mutually reinforced intermember expectations, suggesting that the primary reinforcer is the success or failure of the influence attempt to help the group attain its goals. A social exchange theory of emergent leadership views the leader as a provider of benefits which the group cannot easily do without or obtain from other members (Jacobs, 1971). The valence model of leadership emergence (Stein *et al.*, 1978), describes a process by which members of newly forming groups become 'differentiated' until one becomes the leader. This process is one facet of the developmental sequence by which a group establishes an interpersonal structure as the tool for task performance. Each of these conceptual views of emergent leadership has received some support in research (see Stein *et al.*, 1978; Lord, 1977).

The extension of Fiedler's contingency model of leadership to emergent leadership

Given the prevailing trends in leadership research toward contingency (e.g. House and Baetz, 1979) and process-oriented approaches (e.g. Lord, 1977; Stein, 1975), a logical synthesis of the two seems appropriate and timely. Extending the contingency model (e.g. Fiedler and Chemers, 1974) to emergent leadership situations (neglected in previous contingency research) meets Ashour's (1973) criticism that the model is static. Since the contingency model is built upon research using appointed leaders, it is valuable to know if the leadership style predicted by the traditional model for appointed leaders is equally predictable for emergent leaders. It is also important to assess the impact of emergent (versus appointed) leaders on group performance or effectiveness.

A study was designed by Schneier (1978) to assess the validity of Fiedler's (1967) contingency model for emergent leadership situations, taking into account both conceptual and methodological criticisms of the contingency model.

The study's design met the criteria for conditions of a field situation deduced to be Octant II in Fiedler's (1967) model. Octant II is defined as a situation which is favorable to the leader, due to a positive group atmosphere. In addition, the tasks have a high degree of structure and the leader's position power is weak due to the failure to designate a formal leader *a priori*. Subjects were 207 undergraduate students in 42 sexually heterogeneous groups working together for a 15 week period to complete assignments of 10 experiential exercises. All persons in groups were given the Least Preferred Coworker (LPC) questionnaire early in the period. Group performance was measured by adding the points each group earned on each of 10 separate projects assigned throughout the 15 week period. Each assignment was evaluated by two graders, whose scores were averaged. Emergent leaders were identified *post hoc* sociometrically.

The results of mean LPC score comparisons from the Schneier (1978) research are shown in Table 1. The leaders had LPC scores significantly lower than non-leaders' scores, leaders' scores were significantly lower than the mean score of the other members of their groups, and the emergent leader's LPC score was the lowest of *any* member in the group in almost 74% of the groups. These findings

Table 1   Mean LPC score comparisons[a]

Subsamples compared	Mean LPC scores compared	t Value
Nonleaders ($N = 165$)	74.40	
vs. leaders ($N = 42$)	vs. 59.64	3.095*
Mean of all members of each		
group except leader ($N = 42$)	73.47	
vs. group's leader ($N = 42$)	vs. 59.64	5.775*
Male nonleaders ($N = 112$)	72.88	
vs. male leaders ($N = 26$)	vs. 60.27	1.715**
Female nonleaders ($N = 53$)	74.79	
vs. female leaders ($N = 16$)	vs. 58.63	1.174***
Male leaders ($N = 26$)	60.27	
vs. female leaders ($N = 16$)	vs. 58.63	.506

*$p < .001$
**$p < .05$
***$p < .10$
[a]From Schneier (1978). Reprinted by permission of Academic Press, New York.

support the validity of the contingency model for predicting leadership style for emergent leaders as the model predicts low LPC scores for leaders in Octant II.

The results also indicate no difference between LPC scores for male and female leaders. However, there is a significant difference between male leaders and male nonleaders.

The study also assessed the relationship between LPC and group performance. According to the model, there should be a negative relationship between LPC and group performance in Octant II, characterized as a favorable leadership situation. A significant, negative correlation was obtained between leaders' LPC scores and group performance, as reflected in Table 2.

This finding represents the only *statistically* significant correlation reported to date between LPC and group performance in Octant II of the contingency model. Neither the research cited to develop the model nor research conducted to test it after its formulation found a statistically significant result in Octant II.

Table 2 shows that the relationship between LPC and male and female leaders, when assessed separately, is of the same negative magnitude as when sex is not distinguished. The results, therefore, hold equally well for emergent male and female leaders in Octant II of Fiedler's model.

An additional analysis in the Schneier (1978) study revealed that leaders were cognitively simple (i.e. saw their LPC in a unidimensional light, such as either positive or negative), but remained task oriented. This directly conflicts with

Table 2 Relationship between LPC and group performance for entire sample and male and female subsamples[a]

Sample	Pearson correlation coefficient	N
All leaders	−.55*	42
Male leaders	−.49**	26
Female leaders	−.54***	16

*$p < .001$
**$p < .005$
***$p < .05$
[a]From Schneier (1978). Reprinted by permission of Academic Press, New York.

Fiedler's (1972) behavioral explanation of LPC scores (i.e. that leaders should vary their behavior and adapt to the situations in which they find themselves).

Male versus female emergent leaders

Sex of leaders has been largely ignored in Fiedler's (e.g. 1971) work, as well as in subsequent research testing the model, with few exceptions. Tasks used by contingency model researchers often have not been sex-neutral. That is, because of past experience and social conditioning, males and females are not able to identify with the task with equal ease. Performance may then become a function of social conditioning due to sex-role stereotyping (see e.g. Terborg, 1977; Rice *et al.*, 1980).

Many recent studies have compared leadership styles of males and females (see Brown, 1979). Most, however, are based on research with appointed or elected, as opposed to emergent, leaders. The bulk of research addressing emergent issues in leadership has not addressed sex as a variable (e.g. Stein *et al.*, 1978).

A recent study by Schneier and Bartol (1980) was undertaken to investigate sex differences in emergent leadership among 52 task groups during a 15 week period. Group member ratings based on modified Bales's (1950) interaction process analysis (IPA) categories were used. Results indicated that a similar proportion of females and males emerged as leaders, conflicting with Lockheed and Hall's (1976) study revealing that men emerge much more often than women in mixed-sex groups.

Results also showed that there was little difference in actual behaviors of male and female leaders, as perceived by members in their groups. This finding is consistent with numerous studies indicating that leadership differences between males and females may be minimal (see e.g. Bartol, 1978). Performance was the same in the groups regardless of the emergent leader's sex, supporting other research showing similar performance from groups led by females versus males (e.g. Eskilson and Wiley, 1976).

Future research needs in emergent leadership

Future leadership research could benefit from addressing the issue of emergent leadership in organizations. Research could: (1) apply various existing leadership models and theories to situations and environments other than those for which they were developed; (2) identify other settings and circumstances where models hold; (3) use male and female leaders in research, investigating further any process differences; and (4) address experimental design and methodological criticisms identified in the literature.

While emergent leadership attends to the process issues neglected in many static models of leadership, there are still basic needs to be addressed. There should be an effort to reduce semantic ambiguities in the literature, perhaps by beginning to address the lack of precision in definitions and measurement of variables (Lord, 1977). The contingency model (Fiedler, 1971) could be tested further in field settings. Attribution research (e.g. Green and Mitchell, 1979) addresses process issues by explaining how individuals make inferences and subjective interpretations about what causes certain behavior of others. If the process described in this work accurately reflects how leadership is situationally defined and inferred from observing behaviors, and predicts the attribution of leadership, then it has tremendous implications for emergent leadership. The vertical dyadic linkage approach (e.g. Dansereau *et al.*, 1975), argues that a leader's style could vary with each subordinate. Each superior–subordinate dyad might thus require different behaviors of a leader. This approach offers a fruitful area for future emergent leadership work. Vertical dyads of emergent leaders could be studied across different situations, identifying the type of influence prevailing in different organizational structures and environments.

Many organizations, perhaps stimulated by legislation, are struggling to cope with numerous problems associated with the movement of women into management. Research has focused on predicting or explaining male versus female leader (and follower) satisfaction, style, behavior and/or performance (e.g. Bartol and Butterfield, 1976), neglecting for the most part dynamic, process issues of leadership. Understanding the ascendance process and identifying those specific behaviors which yield emergent leadership status can be tremendously valuable for women. Those who seek power or wish to be appointed or elected as leaders may emulate those behaviors which others attribute to emergent leaders within groups. Brown (1979) found that results of most studies reviewed showed statistically significant differences in leadership style by sex. Most of the studies, however, focused on outcomes and did not address dynamic process issues.

The potential of incorporating new variables and conceptual models in emergent leadership research

The results of available emergent leadership research should be organized into a meaningful conceptual framework. Using an existing model (e.g. the attribution or valence models noted above), identifying deficiencies, and investigating additional variables would be useful. From that point, a close examination of internal (person-centered) factors and external (situation-centered) elements may shed light on the emergent leadership process. The circumstances surrounding the selection of a leader can influence the leader's effectiveness and group members' behavior and attitudes (Knight and Weiss, 1980). External (situational) factors may include environmental pressures (e.g. legislation), group composition, tasks, rewards, group atmosphere, cohesion, cultural and societal norms, and job assignments.

Internal factors may include personality traits, physical attraction, androgyny, behavioral characteristics, decision-making style, social power, values, attitudes, and self-perceptions. Recent research (e.g. Wolters and Bell, 1977) has already addressed a few of these factors. Others, such as physical attraction, have received little or no attention but seem to be important (see e.g. Heilman and Saruwatari, 1979; Berscheid and Walster, 1974).

The notion of emergent leadership provides an approach to understanding how leader status and influence are attained, used, and become effective. Research to date provides some excellent clues to the workings of this complex process bound up in an intricate web of group processes, interpersonal relations, and individual characteristics. Further conceptual and empirical work can make significant contributions to our understanding.

References

Ashour, A. S. (1973). 'Further discussion of Fiedler's contingency model of leadership effectiveness,' *Organizational Behavior and Human Performance*, **9**, 369–376.

Bales, R. F. (1950). *Interaction Process Analysis*, Addison-Wesley, Reading, Mass.

Bales, R. F. (1953). 'The equilibrium problem in small groups,' in T. Parsons, R. F. Bales, and E. A. Shils (eds.), *Working Papers in the Theory of Action*, Free Press, Glencoe, Ill.

Bartol, K. M. (1978). 'The sex structuring of organizations: A search for possible causes,' *Academy of Management Review*, **3**, 805–815.

Bartol, K. M., and Butterfield, D. A. (1976). 'Sex effects in evaluating leaders,' *Journal of Applied Psychology*, **61**, 446–454.

Berscheid, E., and Walster, E. H. (1974). Physical attractiveness,' in L. Berkowitz (ed.), *Advances in Experimental Social Psychology*, Vol. 7, Academic Press, New York.

Bormann, E. G. (1969). *Discussion and Group Methods: Theory and Practice*, Harper & Row, New York.

Brown, S. M. (1979). 'Male versus female leaders: A comparison of empirical studies,' *Sex Roles*, **5**, 595–611.

Carroll, S. J., and Schneier, C. E. (1982). *Performance Appraisal and Review (PAR) Systems*, Scott Foresman, Glenview, Ill.

Dansereau, F., Graen, G., and Haga, W. (1975). 'A vertical dyad linkage approach to leadership within formal organizations,' *Organizational Behavior and Human Performance*, **13**, 46–78.

Eskilson, A., and Wiley, M. G. (1976). 'Sex composition and leadership in small groups,' *Sociometry*, **39**, 183–194.

Fiedler, F. E. (1967). *A Theory of Leadership Effectiveness*, McGraw-Hill, New York.

Fiedler, F. E. (1971). 'Validation and extension of the contingency model of leadership effectiveness: A review of empirical findings,' *Psychological Bulletin*, **76**, 128–48.

Fiedler, F. E. (1972). 'Personality, motivational systems and the behavior of high and low LPC persons,' *Human Relations*, **25**, 391–412.

Fiedler, F. E., and Chemers, M. M. (1974). *Leadership and Effective Management*, Scott Foresman, Glenview, Ill.

Galbraith, J. R. (1977). *Organization Design*, Addison-Wesley, Reading, Mass.

Goffman, E. (1959). *The Presentation of Self in Everyday Life*, Anchor, New York.

Green, S. G., and Mitchell, T. R. (1979). 'Attributional processes of leaders in leader-member interactions,' *Organizational Behavior and Human Performance*, **23**, 429–458.

Heilman, M. E., and Saruwatari, L. R. (1979). 'When beauty is beastly: The effects of appearance and sex on evaluations of job applicants for managerial and nonmanagerial jobs,' *Organizational Behavior and Human Performance*, **23**, 360–372.

Hollander, E. P. (1958). 'Conformity, status and idiosyncrasy credit,' *Psychological Review*, **65**, 117–127.

Hollander, E. P. (1964). *Leaders, Groups and Influence*, Oxford University Press, New York.

Hollander, E. P., and Julian, J. W. (1969). 'Contemporary trends in the analysis of leadership processes,' *Psychological Bulletin*, **71**, 387–397.

House, R. J., and Baetz, M. L. (1979). 'Leadership: Some empirical generalizations and new research directions,' in B. M. Staw (ed.), *Research in Organizational Behavior*, pp. 341–423, JAI Press, New York.

Jacobs, T. O. (1971). *Leadership and Exchange in Formal Organizations*, Human Resources Research Organization, Alexandria, Va.

Jones, E. E. (1975). *Ingratiation*, Irvington Publishers, New York.

Knight, P. A., and Weiss, H. M. (1980). 'Effects of selection agent and leader origin on leader influence and group member perceptions,' *Organizational Behavior and Human Performance*, **26**, 7–21.

Landy, F. J., and Farr, J. L. (1980). 'Performance rating,' *Psychological Bulletin*, **87**, 72–107.

Lockheed, M., and Hall, K. (1976). 'Conceptualizing sex as a status characteristic: Applications to leadership training strategies,' *Journal of Social Issues*, **32**(3), 111–124.

Lord, R. G. (1977). 'Functional leadership behavior: Measurement and relation to social power and leadership perceptions,' *Administrative Science Quarterly*, **22**, 114–133.

Rice, R. W., Bender, L. R., and Vitters, A. G. (1980). 'Leader sex, follower attitudes toward women, and leadership effectiveness: A laboratory experiment,' *Organizational Behavior and Human Performance*, **25**, 46–78.

Schein, V. E. (1975). 'Relationships between sex role stereotypes and requisite management characteristics among female managers,' *Journal of Applied Psychology*, **60**, 340–344.

Schneier, C. E. (1978). 'The contingency model of leadership: An extension to emergent leadership and leader's sex,' *Organizational Behavior and Human Performance*, **21**, 220–239.

Schneier, C. E., and Bartol, K. M. (1980). 'Sex effects in emergent leadership,' *Journal of Applied Psychology*, **65**, 341–345.

Stein, R. T. (1975). 'Identifying emergent leaders from verbal and nonverbal communications,' *Journal of Personality and social psychology*, **32**, 125–135.

Stein, R. T., Cooley, S., Hoffman, L. R., and Pearse, R. W. (1978). 'Leadership valence: Modeling and measuring the process of emergent leadership,' *Conference Proceedings of Fifth Biennial So. Ill. Univ. Leadership Symposium*, Carbondale, Ill.

Stogdill, R. M. (1959). *Individual Behavior and Group Achievement*, Oxford Univ. Press, New York.

Stogdill, R. M. (1974), *Handbook of Leadership*, Free Press, New York.
Terborg, J. R. (1977). 'Women in management: A research review,' *Journal of Applied Psychology*, **62**, 647–664.
Wolters, R., and Bell, R. R. (1977). 'Some relationships between managerial value profiles and sex, age, and supervisory experiences,' *Proceedings of Southeastern American Institution for Decision Sciences.*

Small Groups and Social Interaction, Volume 1
Edited by H. H. Blumberg, A. P. Hare, V. Kent and M. Davies
© 1983 John Wiley & Sons Ltd

10.4   Women and Leadership

Edwin P. Hollander   *State University of New York at Buffalo*

Despite some notable cases of women who have become leaders in business, politics, and elsewhere, leadership has been and still is largely a male domain. In a parallel way, the study of leadership in groups has been done mainly with men (Borgatta and Stimson, 1963). Hare's revised *Handbook of Small Group Research* (1976) indicates that the situation had not changed much with regard to group composition. Evidently, our knowledge about leadership in groups has largely been founded on studies with men and far less with studies of women, or of men and women in groups of mixed composition.

Gender differences in social behavior

Conventional wisdom accepts that women and men differ in certain aspects of their social behavior. While there are data to support that view, as Deaux (1976) and O'Leary (1977) have noted, they have to be interpreted cautiously because of a good deal of confusion about femininity and masculinity based on social roles *or* on characteristics of gender (see Heine, 1971). Moreover, the basis used to establish so-called 'sex differences' in social behavior often rests on stereotypes rather than on observations of interaction. For example, McKee and Sherriffs (1957) found that men were more favorably rated than women on a variety of evaluations by both women and men. Heilbrun (1968) looked at differences in instrumental and expressive behaviors of men and women and found that women were seen as more expressive than instrumental in their behavior by both sexes. However, men were rated by both women and men as being expressive *and* instrumental. Broverman *et al.* (1972) found that the male stereotype was laden with competence items and the female stereotype with a cluster of warmth and expressiveness items.

A second area of comparative research on gender has investigated the responses of women and of men who have been in interaction. Many of these studies have included groups of two (dyads), or of three (triads). Dyads are a particularly special group because the departure of either member effectively destroys it. Among the classic experiments in this vein are those by Bond and Vinacke (1961) and by Strodtbeck and Mann (1956). Overall, they found that the performance of men tended to be exploitative and competitive in these groups, and that of women tended to be more accommodative. Although such results neatly fit the Bales and Slater (1955) distinction between the father's task role, and the mother's socioemotional role, they are not conclusive on the point because of the effects of social learning and society's expectations. Women, for instance, have long been discouraged from too openly displaying competitive behavior with men, given the anticipation of men's negative attitudes toward such displays (see Tavris and Offir, 1977, Ch. 6).

Furthermore, the existence of such gender differences does not substantiate a predetermined quality of masculinity and femininity. Instead, gender distinctions in leadership behavior can be attributed to role expectations, style, and the task demands in the group (Hollander and Yoder, 1980).

As suggested earlier, dyads are special groups because accommodation is so important to their persistence. Therefore, the family's continuity as a parental unit depends upon it, which may account for the traditional expectation that women be oriented toward harmonious relations to keep the unit intact. The Bales and Slater (1955) distinction also overlooks the reality that married women perform tasks, even if they are not working at a job, in being a housewife and mother.

The point goes still further. The distinction between the mother and father roles in the family seems to underpin the usual findings in the experimental vein. This may well be because the stereotype of the father as the task specialist and mother as supporter is still relatively entrenched among experimenters and subjects alike.

In fact, the comparative activity of women and men is not so clearly divergent. In modern society, the altered pattern of women at work is something which demands a re-examination of the stereotypic view. According to the 1979 *Statistical Abstract of the United States*, almost half of American married women *with husband present* hold jobs outside the home. That does not include women who are widowed, separated, or divorced, and who work *and* also are heads of households. There are more of these than ever before (see Hollander, 1981, pp. 187–196).

Although there have been observed differences in the aggression and dominance shown by women in groups versus men in groups, the nature of the activity and its context are important. If physical aggressiveness is what is meant, then women show less of it, bearing in mind of course that there is considerable cultural encouragement for boys to engage in physically aggressive contact sports as testimony to their 'manliness,' as Mead (1949) has long since noted. Girls may be 'aggressive,' but not so much in physical ways.

Indeed, Deaux (1976) contends that women are as active as men, but that the areas in which they strive to achieve are different. With respect to being dominant or assertive, women in mixed-sex company tend to be less obviously so than men. However, the social context matters, with respect to who is present and for what purpose. A masculine orientation in traditional culture has been associated with 'taking charge,' while the feminine orientation has been traditionally associated with 'harmonious interpersonal relations' (cf. Eagly, 1978).

Taking the leader role

Associated with dominance, and aggressiveness in the assertive sense, is the emergence of leaders in groups. Members who participate more are likely to be more influential and to be seen as leaders.

In groups composed of men and women, a standard finding is that women generally are less likely to become the leader, and are less inclined than men to seek that role (Eskilson and Wiley, 1976). In another experiment, Megargee (1969) showed further that, regardless of the dominance of the women paired with a man, she was unlikely to become leader. Interestingly, a dominant woman was more inclined to assign the leader role to the man than the reverse.

Recognizing that there are individual differences, and that groups and their activities vary widely, women generally do participate less in the presence of men than men do with men. For example, in their classic study of jury deliberations, Strodtbeck and Mann (1956) found that men talked significantly more than women. A more recent study by Aries (1976) found that men initiated and received 66% of the communications in the group. Aries also examined participation rates over time, which are considered to indicate the stability of the group's dominance hierarchy, or status ladder (Bales, 1950). Men in both all-male and mixed-sex groups were found to have more stable rates than did women. But women *did* have an impact insofar as men in mixed-sex groups increased their expressive remarks, which is more characteristic of the content of women's communications (Aries, 1976).

The differences in the participation rates of women and men in groups can be explained, where found, by the task ability which is required, and what is perceived to be expertise, and not by a gender-specific attribute. As Maccoby and Jacklin (1974) have observed, the choice of a task can itself create a biased condition for men or for women.

There is also the factor of expectations. A good deal of research evidence indicates or implies that people generally expect the leader role to be filled by a man. For instance, in a study by Schein (1973), male middle managers rated women in general, men in general, or successful middle managers on their overall characteristics, attitudes, and temperaments. On 60 of these 86 items, men and successful managers were rated similarly, while on only eight items were women and successful managers rated similarly.

As O'Leary (1974) has pointed out, a basic concern exists among women and men about whether or not the leader role is appropriate for a woman in a mixed-sex setting. The success of women therefore may be inhibited not only by external expectations, but by attitudes held by the woman herself. While an ineffectual male leader may have to cope with a stronger sense of failure for mismanaging his role, a successful female leader might have to face the fact that societal attitudes do not readily recognize her success in the leader role (cf. Jacobson and Effertz, 1974).

There are still comparatively few studies of women who serve as leaders of mixed-sex groups, whether through appointment, election, or some informal process of emergence. In one attempt to rectify this, Fallon and Hollander (1976) studied 32 groups, each of two men and two women undergraduate students, who were able to elect a leader in a discussion task concerned with urban problems. Each group talked about the first two problems for about 10 to 15 minutes, and made a group ranking of the alternative action programs for each. A secret ballot was then distributed. Of the 32 groups, 14 elected men and 10 women as leaders; 2 men tied and a coin toss yielded the choice. In 6 groups a woman and a man tied and the woman was made the winner to offset what was an overall tilt to elect men. However, by the process used, the leader was *always* the most or equal to the most chosen person in the group. Following the first two phases, half the groups were given success feedback and half failure feedback on performance. Regardless of the type of feedback, we found that the men leaders were significantly more influential than women leaders in the last phases. There was, however, no difference by the sex of the leader in the satisfaction item of the post-interaction questionnaire, although men as leaders were seen by both men and women as having significantly *more task leadership ability*. It may be that we had a sex-biased task, but our pretesting certainly did not reveal it. Therefore, we must take seriously the fact that men evidently fared better than did the women as leaders, and that the women generally joined men in seeing women leaders as less able on the task.

In a recent study at the US Military Academy at West Point (1980), my colleagues Robert Rice and Lisa Richer Bender, together with Captain Alan Vitters of the staff there, compared men and women cadets as leaders of three-man cadet groups. They had previously measured the attitudes toward women of those men, using the Spence–Helmreich Attitudes Toward Women Scale (1972). While the sex of the leader did not appear to affect performance and morale, these attitudes proved to be quite decisive in determining the attributions made about the women as compared to the men leaders. When the group was 'successful' with a woman leader, both the leader and men followers tended to attribute it to 'luck.' With a man leader they attributed success more to the leader's ability.

Performance as a leader

As indicated, the factors that affect the leadership behavior of women and men are quite often complex and interactive. There also are subtle differences which go unnoticed. For instance, in a recent analysis I did with Jan Yoder (Hollander and Yoder, 1980), we concluded that there appear to be two distinct approaches to studying differences between women and men as leaders: assign women or men to the role of leader, keeping other factors constant; or, examine the leader's and group's reactions to women or men who are already in place as leaders, for example, those who are managers. The first procedure addresses the general question of whether women *assigned* to be leaders can be as effective as men. The second asks if women who *choose* to be leaders are as effective as men who choose the leader role.

Not surprisingly, when one reflects on it, these two approaches produce conflicting research findings. Studies supporting sex differences in leadership behavior tend to take a sample from the general population of women, and to thrust those into the leader role. Studies finding few differences between women and men leaders tend to sample the population of actual leaders. The factor which appears to be critical is whether the individual has the initiative in assuming the leader role.

What happens if a woman is put in charge of a group or an organization as an executive or a manager? For one thing, she is likely to be at an initial disadvantage. However, in her book *Men and Women of the Corporation*, Rosabeth Kanter (1977) concludes that individual differences matter more than a woman's gender in managerial roles. This is despite the fact that women will often face the extra burden of overcoming negative attitudes in managing mixed-sex groups, as Virginia O'Leary (1974) has indicated. On this point, Florence Denmark (1977) has said:

> Many of the assumptions that women managers are basically different from men are just not supported by data. The one difference investigators generally agree upon is women's greater concern for relationships among people; this should be considered a plus in terms of leadership effectiveness. Alleged sex differences in ability, attitudes, and personality have been based on sex-role stereotypes, rather than empirical observations of women leaders (pp. 110–111).

Nevertheless, women in managerial and executive roles are likely to be treated differently by their male associates. For example, there are instances of attempted or actual sexual harassment which present a social problem that has gained increased attention. In another vein, there is a tendency for women's comments to be interrupted, overlooked, ignored, or 'unheard' by men not used to paying attention to what women say in mixed-sex groups (Bunker and Seashore, 1975). Unfortunately, women may themselves ignore other women.

It seems true, in sum, that serving as a leader of a group made up of men and women presents extra difficulties for a woman. As noted here, this is usually considered to be an outgrowth of the stereotype associating masculinity with dominance and leadership (see McGregor, 1967; Lockheed, 1977). However, viewed as a transactional process between a leader and followers, leadership basically depends upon competence and a sense of fairness (Hollander, 1978). Therefore, even with the impediments presented to women, they can be effective in these functions if the primary task is not sex-biased. Indeed, recent evidence from two organizations suggests that the leader's gender was not related either to leader behavior or subordinates' satisfaction (Osborn and Vicars, 1976).

The overall picture is therefore not quite so disheartening as might appear, especially since many of the studies which show women at a disadvantage may become increasingly dated. As more women move into leader roles, and perform capably, their numbers may well reduce the disadvantages they have encountered.

References

Aries, E. (1976). 'Interaction patterns and themes of male, female, and mixed groups,' *Small Group Behavior*, **7**, 7–18.

Bales, R. F. (1950). *Interaction Process Analysis: A Method for the Study of Small Groups*, Addison-Wesley, Reading, Mass.

Bales, R. F., and Slater, P. E. (1955). 'Role differentiation in small decision-making groups,' in T. Parsons, *et al.* (ed.), *Family, Socialization, and Interaction process*, Free Press, Glencoe, Ill.

Bond, J. R., and Vinacke, W. E. (1961). 'Coalitions in mixed-sex triads,' *Sociometry*, **24**, 61–75.

Borgatta, E. F., and Stimson, J. (1963). 'Sex differences in interaction characteristics,' *Journal of Social Psychology*, **60**, 89–100.

Broverman, I., Vogel, S. R., Broverman, D. M., Clarkson, F. E., and Rosenkrantz, P. S. (1972). 'Sex-role stereotypes: A current appraisal,' *Journal of Social Issues*, **28** (2), 59–78.

Bunker, B. B., and Seashore, E. W. (July, 1975). 'Breaking the sex role stereotypes,' *Public Management*, **57**, 5–11.

Deaux, K. (1976). *The Behavior of Women and Men*, Brooks/Cole, Monterey, Calif.

Denmark, F. L. (1977). 'Styles of leadership,' *Psychology of Women Quarterly*, **2** (2), 99–113.

Eagly, A. H. (1978). 'Sex differences in influenceability,' *Psychological Bulletin*, **85**, 86–116.

Eskilson, A., and Wiley, M. G. (1976). 'Sex composition and leadership in small groups,' *Sociometry*, **39**, 183–194.

Fallon, B. J., and Hollander, E. P. (1976). 'Sex-role stereotyping in leadership: A study of undergraduate discussion groups,' Paper presented at the Annual Convention of the American Psychological Association.

Hare, A. P. (1976). *Handbook of Small Group Research*, 2nd edn, Free Press, New York.

Heilbrun, A. B., Jr (1968). 'Influence of observer and target sex judgments of sex-typed attributes,' *Perceptual and Motor Skills*, **27**, 1194.

Heine, P. J. (1971). *Personality in Social Theory*, Aldine, Chicago.

Hollander, E. P. (1978). *Leadership Dynamics: A Practical Guide to Effective Relationships*, Free Press/Macmillan, New York.

Hollander, E. P. (1981). *Principles and Methods of Social Psychology*, 4th edn, Oxford University Press, New York and Oxford.

Hollander, E. P., and Yoder, J. (1980). 'Some issues in comparing women and men as leaders,' *Basic and Applied Social Psychology*, **1**, 267–280.

Jacobson, M. B., and Effertz, J. (1974). 'Sex roles and leadership perceptions of the leaders and the led,' *Organizational Behavior and Human Performance*, **12**, 383–396.

Kanter, R. M. (1977). *Men and Women of the Corporation*, Basic Books, New York.

Lockheed, M. E. (1977). 'Cognitive style effects on sex status in student work groups,' *Journal of Educational Psychology*, **69**, 158–165.

Maccoby, E. E., and Jacklin, C. N. (1974). *The Psychology of Sex Differences*, Stanford University Press, Stanford, Calif.

McGregor, D. (1967). *The Professional Manager*, McGraw-Hill, New York.

McKee, J. P., and Sherriffs, A. C. (1957). 'The differential evaluation of males and females,' *Journal of Personality*, **25**, 356–371.

Mead, M. (1949). *Male and Female*, Morrow, New York.

Megargee, E. I. (1969). 'Influence of sex roles on the manifestation of leadership,' *Journal of Applied Psychology*, **53**, 377–382.

O'Leary, V. E. (1974). 'Some attitudinal barriers to occupational aspirations in women,' *Psychological Bulletin*, **81**, 809–826.

O'Leary, V. E. (1977). *Toward Understanding Women*, Brooks/Cole, Monterey, Calif.

Osborn, R. N., and Vicars, W. M. (1976). 'Sex stereotypes: An artifact in leader behavior and subordinate satisfaction analysis?' *Academy of Management Journal*, **19**, 439–449.

Rice, R. W., Bender, L. R., and Vitters, A. G. (1980). 'Leader sex, follower attitudes toward women, and leadership effectiveness: A laboratory experiment,' *Organizational Behavior and Human Performance*, **25**, 46–78.

Schein, V. E. (1973). 'Relationship between sex role stereotypes and requisite management characteristics,' *Journal of Applied Psychology*, **57**, 95–100.

Spence, J. T., and Helmreich, R. (1972). 'The attitudes toward women scale: An objective instrument to measure attitudes toward the rights and roles of women in contemporary society,' *Journal Supplement Abstract Service*, **2**, 66.

Statistical Abstract of the United States. (1979). Table No. 660. Government Printing Office, Washington, DC, p. 400.

Strodtbeck, F. L., and Mann, R. D. (1956). 'Sex role differentiation in jury deliberations,' *Sociometry*, **19**, 3–11.

Tavris, C., and Offir, C. (1977). *The Longest War: Sex Differences in Perspective*, Harcourt, Brace, Jovanovich, New York.

Small Groups and Social Interaction, Volume 1
Edited by H. H. Blumberg, A. P. Hare, V. Kent and M. Davies
© 1983 John Wiley & Sons Ltd

10.5 The Phenomenon of the Differentiation of the Leadership Role in Small Groups

R. L. Krichevskii *Scientific Research Institute of General and Pedagogic Psychology of the USSR Academy of Pedagogic Sciences, Moscow*

Summarized in this article are the results of the research that we have conducted over the course of a number of years with the aim of studying the phenomenon of the differentiation of the leadership role in small groups (Krichevskii, 1977; Kovalev and Krichevskii, 1978; Krichevskii, 1980; Krichevskii and Antonova, 1980; Krichevskii and Smirnova, 1981). A brief description will be presented of the theoretical approach that we use, empirical data obtained on the basis of this will be set out, and a comparison will be made of the results of our research and their interpretation with theoretical positions and experimental data contained in other authors' investigations, in particular in the works of Bales and Slater (1955) and Burke (1972) which constitute important landmarks in the study of the problem of the differentiation of the leadership role. Through the efforts of these and other researchers two important leadership roles have been revealed and studied by means of laboratory experimentation: the role of the instrumental or task-directed leader and the role of the expressive or social–emotional leader. In our work we have undertaken the next step in investigating the phenomenon of the differentiation of the leadership role—considering it in conditions of the functioning of genuine (non-laboratory) human groups.

Our approach to investigating the group and its phenomena is based upon the principle of the so-called activity methodology (Andreeva, 1980; Leont'ev, 1975; Petrovskii, 1979). According to this methodology an adequate description of group phenomena, their genesis and functioning, is not possible outside a thematic analysis of group activity. In speaking of group activity, however, we are utilizing the concept in the most general and collective of its meanings. 'But in reality, we always deal with particular activities' (Leont'ev, 1975, p. 102). This issue leads us to the idea of the diversity of human activities, realized by individuals as *members of some concrete group*, i.e. in other words the analysis of the *diversity* of group activities becomes the starting point for our research.

Group activities may be examined in their most general form in two very important aspects:

1. from the point of view of solving the tasks confronting the group, of achieving a certain group product;
2. from the point of view of maintaining an internal balance and stability within the group, of keeping it as an intact unity.

Activities relating mainly to the first of the above aspects we characterized as instrumental (we conditionally call activities of this kind 'productive'), and activities connected predominantly to the second of them as social–emotional or expressive (to these we attribute the group members' interpersonal intercourse, whether it be in the form of their independent activity or in connection with realizing the 'productive' activity). It goes without saying that activities of both types are closely connected with each other and coordinated (depending upon the dominant type), they mutually influence one another and in a number of cases their strict differentiation is only possible in theoretical analysis.

The approach set out above permits us to interpret the nature of the role differentiation of leadership in the following way. We examine the roles of the instrumental and expressive leader in connection with the presence of the two above-mentioned types of group activities. It is in the process of realizing group activities that the functional specification of the group's members takes place and the basic functional units—the group roles—are identified. The parameters for accomplishing these are given by the content of the appropriate type of group activity, by means of the role requirements that it (the content) generates (i.e. by means of the requirements made by the content of the activity for filling the role)—by means of distinctive systems of activity—role norms, or in the narrow sense that interests us more, by means of the norms of leadership that correspond to a certain type of group activity (instrumental or expressive). In other words, the acceptance or non-acceptance of one or other member of the group in the role of leader is brought about, as a specially conducted investigation (Krichevskii, 1977) reveals, by the degree of his correspondence from his partners' point of view to the norms of group leadership. This position also applies, according to our data, to the group's ranking organization as a whole, being realized in the strict, normative determination of the positions taken by the group's members.

The above are some of the results of the first stage in the investigation of the role differentiation of leadership carried out (Krichevskii, 1977) on real groups with a type of dominant activity that is highly personally significant for the members of these groups. Seventeen sports teams served as the object of the study, in each of which the structures of instrumental and expressive leadership were revealed by means of the sportsmen ranking their partners according to their contribution (a) to the teams's success at games and (b) to the development of friendly relationships within it, while the team members' degree of correspondence to the norms of leadership were determined by their responses on a specially worked out scale of norms.

Further analysis confronts us with the following problem. Although the presence of the two above-mentioned types of group activity may be examined as the decisive condition for the origin of the differentiation of the leadership role, this circumstance in itself, however, is not yet enough to explain the differences relating to the group members' personal achievements within the structure of instrumental and expressive leadership. We have in mind both the results that characterize the rank positions of the same group members in the various structures of group leadership and the status indices, when compared with each other, of the various group members. Suffice it to say that in the overwhelming majority of groups that we have studied, the roles of instrumental and expressive leaders have been realized by different people.

This circumstance demanded an extension of the initial theoretical scheme to include personality as one of the additional determinants of the role differentiation of leadership. We investigated the role of this variable at the next stage of the empirical work (Kovalev and Krichevskii, 1978; Krichevskii, 1979).

Taking account of the complexity and questionability of selecting some particular personality trait as the factor for determining leadership we relied upon an approach to understanding personality founded on its most essential, basic parameters (Leont'ev, 1975). One of these in particular is personality structure, conceived of as 'a relatively stable configuration of the main motivational lines, hierarchicalized within themselves. The question is that it is incompletely described as a "tendency of the personality"' (Leont'ev, 1975, p. 221). It was precisely this parameter—a description of the personality in terms of its tendency—that we chose as the necessary aim of our investigation of the personality variable. Let us additionally note that in accordance with contemporary ideas and methods of working (Bozhovich and Blagonadezhna, 1972; Bass, 1967) we have taken account of three types of personality tendency, task oriented, personal, and interpersonal.

The basic part of the empirical work at this stage of the investigation (Kovalev and Krichevskii, 1978) was carried out on 20 genuine small groups, in 12 sports teams and 8 student groups. Both leadership structures were defined by means of the ranking method, the personality tendency of the members of the groups was measured with Bass's orientation inventory (Bass, 1967).

The data obtained show that personality undoubtedly determines the structure of group leadership, but it is, however, manifest in different ways in the one type of group or the other. So, in the majority of sports teams there were revealed high positive links between indices of the sportsmen's task-directed and personal tendencies and their positions in the structure of instrumental leadership. and an almost total absence of significant correlations between emotional leadership and the interpersonal tendency. A different trend was revealed in the student groups: here the personal tendency does not achieve any significant realization (we have in mind negative correlations of this type of tendency with both structures of leadership). But, to make up for it, there were clear-cut, positive links between task-directed and interpersonal tendencies on the one hand, and correspondingly the structures of instrumental and emotional leadership on the other. The above-mentioned differences we explain mainly by the specific character of the activities realized by the members of the groups studied, a specificity that caused the significance and value of a certain kind of personality tendency in the group.

An additional investigation (Krichevskii, 1979) that we carried out on 10 sports teams have analogous results, although the method of measuring personality variables was changed. Instead of the orientational inventory a specially worked out 'motivational questionnaire' was used, revealing individual's level of aspiration to act for the benefit of the collective well-being. There were revealed high linear links between individuals' useful contributions to the task-directed and emotional spheres of the group's vital activity, measured by the 'motivational questionnaire,' and their positions within the structures of correspondingly instrumental and emotional leadership.

As for the results of direct empirical fixation, strictly the phenomenon of the differentiation of the leadership role, then one should note that the differentiation of leadership roles in our research, i.e. their realization by different people, was observed in more than 80% of the groups studied. At the same time we did not confine ourselves to establishing this fact but tried to make a further step in analysing the phenomenon of the role differentiation of leadership. Its crux comprises not only identifying within genuine groups two leadership roles that do not coincide with each other, but also revealing the structures of instrumental and emotional leadership as a whole, i.e. in the revelation of the fact of their differentiation. In particular, the complete differentiation of leadership structures (i.e. the negative, zero, or near-zero correlation between both structures) has been found by us in approximately 30% of the groups studied.

Let us also note some other manifestations that we have revealed of the phenomenon under discussion. So, in a series of investigations (Krichevskii, 1980; Krichevskii and Antonova, 1980) we observed evidence to identify situational leadership roles, arising as a rule in connection with solving some frequent group problems. In so far as in the overwhelming majority of the situations of group life, according to our observations, it is the high-status members of the groups who lead, there is a basis for considering the situational leadership roles as being predominantly the two fundamental and dominant leadership roles. Moreover, depending upon the specificity of the group activity and the completeness of the theoretical analysis, one may describe the roles of the instrumental or emotional leader as a multidimensional formation (Krichevskii and Smirnova, 1981).

In general, arising out of the principles of the activity methodology and based upon the empirical evidence presented here, that we obtained in the study of real human groups, it is possible to conclude that activity brings about, as it were, a twofold determination of the differentiation of the leadership role:

1. It provides the different roles and structures of leadership, determining their general 'outline'.
2. It selects personality variables that are more relevant from the point of view of its realization and which in their turn influence the rank organization of the leadership structures.

How then is all the aforesaid linked to earlier results obtained in works in this field? Like the authors of these works (for example, Bales and Slater, 1955; Burke, 1972), we can establish the presence in small groups of the phenomenon of the differentiation of the leadership role as an indubitable fact. Our interpretation of the reasons for the origin of the given phenomenon, however, turns out to be different in principle, stemming from the theoretical approach presented here, which proposes the study of the genuine human group as it realizes real social activity in a system of real human relations. Such an approach permits us, so it seems to us, to consider the phenomena of human groups far more fully and richly than in cases of laboratory experimentation.

It goes without saying that an exhaustive description of the structure of group leadership (that is the structure, and not just the two separate leadership roles) is a matter for further research, but even now one may pose a number of questions the solution of which is of undoubted interest in connection with the problem under discussion. What is the optimal degree of differentiation of leadership roles and structures? How do the situational leadership roles relate to the two fundamental roles of group leadership? To what extent do the latter complement each other? What is the interconnection between the degree of the differentiation of the leadership role and the effective functioning of the group? The answers to these questions will make for a better understanding of the complex social organization that the human group turns out to be.

References

Andreevna, G. M. (1980). *Sotial'naya psikhologiya (Social Psychology)*, Moscow State University Press, Moscow.

Bales, R. F., and Slater, P. E. (1955). 'Role differentiation in small decision-making groups', in T. Parsons and R. F. Bales (eds.), *Family: Socialization and Interaction Process*, Free Press, Glencoe, Ill., pp. 9–306.

Bass, B. M. (1967). 'Social behaviour and orientation inventory,' *Psychological Bulletin*, **68**, 260–292.

Bozhovich, L. I., and Blagonadezhna, L. V. (*eds.*) (1972). *Izuchenie motivatsii povendeniya detei i podrostkov (A Study of the Behaviour of Children and Adolescents)*, Pedagogika, Moscow.

Burke, P. J. (1972). 'Leadership role differentiation,' in C. G. McClintock (ed.), *Experimental Social Psychology*, pp. 514–546, Holt, Rinehart and Winston, NY.

Kovalev, C. V., and Krichevskii, R. L. (1978). 'Faktory differentsiatsii liderstva' (Factors in the differentiation of leadership), *Vestnik MGU (Moscow State University Bulletin)*, Series XIV Psychology (2) 26–36.

Krichevskii, R. L. (1977). 'Determinanty rolevoi differentsiatsii liderstva v malykh gruppakh' (Determinants of the role differentiation of leaderships in small groups), *Voprosy psikhologii (Questions of Psychology)*, (1) 28–38.

Krichevskii, R. L. (1979). 'Motivatsiya grappovoi prinadlezhnosti i mechanism vydvizheniya v pozitsiyu lidera' (The motivation of group membership and the mechanism of promotion to the position of leader), *Novye issledovariya v psikhologii (New Research in Psychology)*, (1) 95–101.

Krichevskii, R. L. (1980). 'Dinamika gruppovogo liderstva' (The dynamics of group leadership), *Voprosy psikhologii (Questions of Psychology)*, (2) 42–52.

Krichevskii, R. L., and Antonova, I. B. (1980). 'Ob odnoi iz funktsii gruppogo liderstva' (On one of the functions of group leadership), *Novye issledovaniya v psikhologii (New Research in Psychology)*, (2) 87–93.

Krichevskii, R. L., and Smirnova, M. M. (1981). 'Udovletvorennost' gruppovym chlenstvom kak funktsiya sootnosheniya fenomenov liderstva i rukovodstva' (The satisfaction of group membership as a function of the phenomena of leadership and direction), *Voprosy psikhologii (Questions of Psychology)*, (3) 109–113.

Leont'ev, A. N. (1975). *Deyatel'nost'. Sloznanie, Lichnost' (Activity, Consciousness, Personality)*, Politiziat, Moscow.

Petrovskii, A. V. (*ed.*) (1979). *Psikhologicheskaya teoriya kollektiva (A Psychological Theory of the Collective)*, Pedagogika, Moscow.

Name Index

If a name is not on an indicated page, it could be part of an 'et al.' - check the references (on pages indicated) at the end of the sub-chapter.

Abelson R P   134, 135, 396, 397
Ackerman P   232, 233, 238
Adams B   281, 290
Adinolfi A A   135, 136
Adler A   43, 52
Aiello J R   33, 37
Alexander J'F   349, 357
Alker H R   70, 76
Allen A   235, 238
Allen V   5, 125, 128, 172, 179
Allen W R   94, 95
Allport F H   209, 213
Allport G   100, 106, 120, 122, 128, 165, 179
Alpert R   147, 150
Altman I   17 — 41, 43, 52, 79, 87, 137, 331, 345, 366, 369
Anderson H C   215
Andreevna G M   431, 435
Andrews F M   261, 265
Ansel M   166, 180
Anthony E J   328, 329
Antonova I B   431, 433, 436
Appleman J A   70, 76
Appley M H   102, 107
Appleyard D   13, 14
Archer R L   27, 39, 233, 237
Arezzo D   298, 300, 302
Argyle M   10, 13, 14, 32, 33, 36-38, 315, 321-329
Argyris C   340, 344

Aries E   93, 94
Aronfreed J   233, 238, 244, 252
Aronoff J   4, 79-88
Aronson E   4, 119-130, 137, 206, 213
Asch S E   172, 179, 217, 219, 223
Asher S R   300-302
Ashour A S   415, 419
Assor A   86, 87
Athanasiou R   282, 290
Atkinson J W   147, 150
Attneave F   347, 357
Austin J L   364, 369
Austin W G   5
Averill J R   45, 51, 52

Back K W   18, 39, 90, 94, 282, 291
Backman C W   235, 240
Baetz M L   415, 420
Baird J E   76
Bakeman R   395, 397
Bales R F   57, 66, 71-73, 76, 79, 81, 87, 235, 315, 317, 318, 321, 326, 328, 329, 402, 405, 406, 414, 417, 419, 424, 425, 428, 431, 435
Ballachey E   172, 180

437

Bandura A   255, 256, 265, 267,
    271, 272, 274, 275
Banuazizi A   316, 317
Bardwick J   70, 76
Barefoot J   25, 33, 38, 40
Barker R G   18, 38, 105, 106
Barnard J J   70, 76
Baron R   43, 52
Baron R A   255, 265, 268, 275
Baron R S   141, 142, 148, 152,
    153, 155, 156, 158, 162, 163
Barrett D   232, 238
Bar-Tal D   230, 238
Bartel G   310, 311
Bartol K M   417-420
Bass B M   433, 435
Bates A P   401, 405
Bateson G   351, 357, 363, 369
Batson C D   232, 233, 237,
    238
Baum A   3, 5, 31, 38, 41, 43,
    53
Beach B H   407, 412
Beach L R   407, 412
Beaman A L   271, 275
Beavin J H   354, 358
Beck H P   146, 150
Becker F D   25, 38, 40
Becker H S   103, 106
Becker S W   11, 14
Beery R G   126, 129
Bell P A   268, 275
Bell R Q   234, 238, 239
Bell R R   419, 421
Bem D J   235, 238
Bender L R   417, 420, 426, 429
Benne K   327, 328, 340, 344
Bennis W   340, 345
Benware C   125, 128
Berger D E   33, 39
Berger J   58-60, 62, 67
Berger P   192, 193
Berger S M   149, 150
Berkey A S   147, 150
Berkowitz L   90, 91, 94, 102,
    106, 134-136, 227, 236, 238,
    240
Bernard N   143, 144, 152
Berndt E G   231, 238
Berndt T J   231, 238
Bernstein B   231, 234, 238
Berscheid E   102, 107, 135,
    136, 301, 368, 370, 419
Berser J   4, 5

Beyer E   299, 301
Biddle B J   316, 317
Billig M   101, 106, 108, 111
Birch K   232, 233, 238
Birchler G   349, 350, 357
Blagonadezhna L V   433, 435
Blake R R   18, 38
Blaney N   124, 128
Blank A   196, 198
Blank T O   149, 150
Blau P M   402, 405
Blumenthal A   43, 53
Blumenthal M   261, 265
Boffa J   43, 52
Bond J R   424, 428
Bonoma T V   257, 258, 265, 266
Bons P M   409, 412
Boomer D S   353, 357
Booth A   4, 5
Borden R J   142, 153
Borgatta E F   81, 82, 87, 423,
    428
Borkovec T D   142, 153
Bormann E G   414, 419
Bovard E W   90, 94
Bozhovich L I   433, 435
Bradford L P   327, 328, 340,
    344
Brady-Smith J   230, 241
Branch L G   93, 95, 338, 345
Bray R M   143, 150
Breed G   33, 38
Brehm J W   206, 213
Bremer A   260
Brenner J   234, 240
Bridgeman D   124, 125, 128,
    129
Brock T C   168, 179
Broderick C   135, 303-311, 318
Brousseau K R   344, 345
Broverman I   423, 428
Brown   119, 129
Brown B B   32, 38
Brown J F   211, 213
Brown R C   256, 263, 266
Brown R D   282, 290
Brown S M   417-419
Bruning J L   148, 150
Brush C A   268, 275
Buchanan R W   31, 39
Buckley N   230, 232, 238
Buckley T   232, 233, 238
Budd L G   22, 40
Bultena G L   283, 291

Bundy R P 111
Bunker B B 427, 428
Burgess E W 348, 357
Burgess R L 316, 317
Burke P J 431, 435
Burnstein E 135, 137, 172,
  179, 236
Buss A H 255, 265, 268, 272,
  275
Butler W 410, 412
Buttimer A 280, 291
Byers D A 158, 163
Byrne D 11, 14, 281, 282, 291
Byrnes A 92, 95

Cacioppo J T 133, 165-181
Caharack G 160, 162
Cairns R B 237, 238
Calder B J 172, 179
Callahan-Levy C M 93, 96
Campbell A 171, 179
Campbell D T 5, 102, 107
Capage J E 148, 150
Caplow T 18, 38, 282, 291
Cappell H 142, 152
Caputo D V 349, 357
Carli L L 149, 150
Carment D W 146, 150
Carr S J 33, 38
Carroll S J 419
Carter L 401, 406
Carver C S 105, 107
Catalano J F 145, 152
Chaikin A L 26, 39
Chamberlain A S 24, 39
Chandler M 126, 129
Chanowitz B 105, 107, 196-198
Chapman A J 142, 143, 150
Chapman M 134, 136
Chapple E D 24, 39
Chard F 237, 238
Charlesworth R 296, 302
Chemers M M 410, 412, 415,
  420
Chombart de Lauwe P H 279,
  280, 291
Chomsky N 192, 193
Cicourel A V 6, 134, 137,
  316, 371-378
Clark K B 120, 129
Clarkson F E 423, 428
Cofer C N 102, 107
Cohen A R 92, 94, 168, 179

Cohen B P 59, 67
Cohen E G 63, 65, 67, 122,
  129
Cohen J L 142, 150
Cohen R 4, 5
Cohen S 106, 107
Coke J S 232, 233, 237, 238
Collins B E 33, 39, 79, 86,
  87, 211, 213, 331, 344
Collins M E 18, 39, 289, 291
Combs M L 300, 301
Constantine J M 309, 311
Constantine L L 309-311
Converse P 171, 179
Cook S W 120, 129
Cook-Gumpertz J 231, 234, 238
Cooley C H 362
Cooley S 401, 406, 415, 417,
  420
Cooper J 168, 181
Corah N 43, 52
Cornish W R 69, 76
Cororan C 143, 152
Corsaro W 293, 294, 301, 376,
  377
Corsaro W A 293, 294, 301
Coser L A 110. 118
Cottrell N B 141-144, 149,
  150, 156, 162
Coutts A M 33, 38
Covington M V 126, 129
Cowan C l 237, 241
Cox M 301, 302
Cox R 301, 302
Craig G 363, 369
Crandall R 144, 150
Crockett W H 402, 406
Cronbach L 349
Crook C K 234, 240
Crutchfield R 172, 180
Csoka L S 411, 412

Dabbs J M 33, 38, 166, 180
Damon W 229, 238
Dansereau F 413, 418, 419
Darley J 166, 180, 236, 237,
  239
Darrow C 70, 76
Davis J H 6, 137, 142, 150,
  315, 318, 331, 334, 338,
  343, 344
Davis K 126, 129
Davis M H 233, 237

Dean J   10, 13, 14, 32, 33,
  36-38
Deaux K   133, 136, 423, 424,
  428
Deffenbacher K A   142, 150
Delbecq A L   94
DeLong A J   25, 39
Denfeld D   310, 311
Denmark F L   427, 428
Derlega V J   26, 39, 135, 136
Desor J A   30, 39
DeSoto C B   27, 41
Deutsch M   6, 18, 39, 122,
  129, 224, 289, 291, 318,
  363, 370
Diamond S G   33, 40
Diaz-Loving R   233, 237
Diener E   267, 268, 271, 272,
  275
Dineen J   271, 275
Dion K K   301
Dodson   147
Dollard J   123, 129, 205, 206,
  213
Doms M   223, 224
Donath C H   149, 150
Doob A N   100, 101, 106, 107
Doob L   205, 206, 213
Dore S R   33, 40
Douvan E   70, 76
Driskell J E   3, 4, 57-67, 318
Droppleman L F   142, 151
Dua J K   149, 151
Duck S   135, 136, 363, 369,
  370
Duncan B D   232, 233, 238
Duncan B L   11, 14
Duncan S   353, 357
Duren   70, 77
Durkheim E   279, 291
Duveen G   229, 241
Dweck C S   295, 301
Eagly A H   72, 77, 425, 428
Eatman J   4, 6, 94, 95
Eckerman C O   234, 238
Edney J J   3, 5, 22, 25, 39
Edwards M   310, 311
Effertz J   426, 429
Eisenberg N   134, 136
Eisenberg-Berg N   134, 136,
  232, 238
Ekman P   349, 357
Ellertson N   90, 96
Emler N P   229-231, 238

Empey J   33, 40
Endicott J   71-77
Endler N S   4, 5, 79, 87
Endresen K   271, 275
Entin E   147, 151
Epley S W   157, 158, 162
Epstein S   234, 238
Epstein Y   3, 5, 51, 52
Erickson B   31, 40
Erikson E H   323, 324, 328
Eskilson A   93, 94, 417, 419,
  425, 428
Esser A H   24, 28, 30, 39
Etcoff N L   106, 108
Evans G W   10, 14
Exline R   33, 39, 91, 95

Fallon B J   426, 428
Farber B   306, 311
Farber J   105-107
Farr J L   414, 420
Faunce E E   349, 350, 358
Feinberg H K   235, 238
Feingold J   268, 275
Felipe N J   11, 14, 33, 39
Fell D   166, 180
Felson R B   255, 265
Fenigstein A   272, 275
Ferguson   119, 129
Feshbach S   268, 275
Festinger L   13, 14, 18, 39,
  89, 95, 168, 179, 206, 213,
  217, 224, 268, 273, 275,
  282, 289, 291, 367, 369
Fiedler F E   317, 407-412,
  415, 417-419
Fink B   166, 180
Fink C F   402, 406
Firestone I J   31, 39
Fisek M H   60, 67
Fisher J D   11, 14
Fisher R B   125, 129
Fiske D W   353, 357
Fiske S T   105-108
Flament C   111
Fleming C M   323, 329
Foa U G   265, 368, 369
Ford M E   231, 232, 238
Forman R   18, 38, 282, 291
Foulkes S H   328, 329
Foushee H C   233, 237
Frank J D   328, 329
Franks D D   126, 129

Fraser S C 271, 275
Freedman J L 43, 52, 100,
  101, 106, 107, 326, 329
Fried M 280, 291
Friedman R 33, 39
Friesen W V 349, 357
Fromm E 255, 265
Fromson M E 271, 275
Fry C L 92, 95
Fulcomer M 281, 291
Furman W 300, 301

Gaes G G 256, 258, 266
Gagnon J 128, 130
Galbraith J R 413, 420
Gange J 133, 141-153, 155,
  162
Gans H 280, 291
Ganzer V J 147, 151
Garcia J E 408, 412
Garfinkel H 134, 136, 185,
  186, 193
Gartner A 125, 129
Gastorf J W 147, 148, 151
Gebhard P H 310, 311
Geen R G 133, 135, 136,
  141-153, 155, 162
Geffner R 124, 129
Gelwicks L E 280, 291
Gerard H 121, 129, 134, 136,
  168, 180, 206, 213, 224
Gergen K J 105, 107
Gibb J 327, 328, 340, 344
Giby R G 126, 129
Gilmour R 370
Ginsburg H J 235, 239
Gintner G 401, 406
Ginzburg S 268, 269, 275
Glaser A N 133, 136
Glass D C 43, 44, 52,
  105-107, 142, 143, 151
Glazer J A 296, 302
Goetz T E 295, 301
Goffman E 99, 100, 103-105,
  107, 127, 129, 192, 193,
  235, 318, 322, 329, 364,
  369, 371, 372, 377, 414, 420
Goktepe J R 6, 317, 413-421
Goldberg G N 33, 39
Goldberg M L 92, 95
Goldman M 93, 95
Goldstein I 70, 77
Gollwitzer P M 233, 237

Gonick M R 105, 106
Gonso J 295, 302, 356, 357
Gonzalez A 124, 129
Good K J 144, 151
Goodacre D M 91, 95
Goode J G 371, 377
Goodenough F 244, 252
Goodrich D W 353, 357
Gorman C 137
Gottman J M 293, 295, 301,
  302, 315, 347-358
Gouldner A W 261, 265
Gove W R 103, 104, 107
Graen G 413, 418, 419
Grandmaison P S 149, 150
Granger C W J 347, 354, 355,
  357
Graves J 166, 180, 332, 333,
  345
Graves T D 33, 41
Gray D 33, 39
Greeley A M 123, 129
Green S G 418, 420
Greenberg G N 33, 39
Greene M S 25, 39
Gregory D 90, 96
Griffitt W 50, 52, 281, 291
Gross E 91, 95
Grusec J E 234, 235, 239
Guardo C J 10, 15
Gubrium J F 283, 291
Guest T A 270, 275
Guetzkow H A 331, 344
Gullahorn J 13, 14
Gump P 18, 38
Gustafson D P 401, 406
Gutkin D 231, 241

Haas J 143, 151
Haber R N 147, 150
Hackman J R 6, 315, 331-345,
  401, 406
Haga W 413, 418, 419
Haire M 401, 406
Haley J 351, 357, 363, 369
Hall E T 9, 10, 13, 14, 280,
  291
Hall J 4, 5
Hall K 64, 67, 417, 420
Hampton K L 149, 150
Hare A P 318, 331, 345, 423,
  428
Harkins S 133, 136, 165-181

Harrell T W 401, 406
Harrison A A 179, 180
Harrison W 6, 315, 318
Hartup W W 296, 300-302
Harvey J H 133, 136
Hassan R K 145, 153
Hastings L 409, 412
Hatanaka M 347, 354, 355, 357
Hatfield E 236, 318
Hatfield. See also Walster
Hawkins C 71, 74, 77, 402,
    406
Hay D 234, 239
Hay D F 234, 240, 243, 252
Hayduk L A 3, 5
Haythorn W W 5, 19, 20, 25,
    38, 338, 345, 401, 406
Head K B 261, 265
Hearst P 393
Hebb D O 101, 107
Hecken M H 149, 150
Heider F 100, 107, 122, 129,
    367, 369
Heilbrun A B 423, 428
Heilman M E 419, 420
Heine P J 423, 428
Heingartner A 143, 153, 158,
    163
Heinicke C 402, 406
Heiss J 316, 317
Heller T 6, 316, 401-406
Helmreich R 71, 76, 77, 395,
    397, 426, 429
Helson H 207, 208, 213
Hemphill J K 405, 406
Henchy T 142, 143, 151
Henley N M 3, 5
Henry A F 322, 329
Herman E M 143, 153, 158, 163
Heshka S 10, 14
Hetherington E M 301, 302
Hillery J M 142, 148, 151,
    160, 162
Hinde R A 137, 315, 361-370
Hirst W 160, 162
Hoffman L R 94, 95, 318, 401,
    406, 415, 417, 420
Hoffman M L 231-233, 239,
    244, 252, 263, 265
Holdsworth W 69, 77
Hollander E P 6, 133, 136,
    217, 224, 317, 413, 414,
    420, 423-429
Holmes J G 236, 239

Holmes R 318
Holsti O R 257, 265
Homans G C 236, 239, 368, 369
Hoogstraten J 90, 95
Hook L H 12, 15
Hoople H 25, 38
Hoppe R A 25, 39, 147, 150
Hops H 349, 358
House R J 415, 420
Howard R B 10, 14
Howe M D 69, 77
Howells L T 11, 14
Hoyt 70, 77
Hudgins W 281, 291
Hughes E C 59, 67
Hughes R 232, 239
Hugo V 213
Hull C 141, 160
Humphreys P 62, 67
Hunt J G 317, 318
Hunt P J 142, 148, 151, 160,
    162
Huston T L 135, 136, 316, 317
Huxley A L 306, 311

Iannotti R J 230, 239
Ickes W J 143, 152, 239
Imber L 196-198
Ingham A G 166, 180, 332,
    333, 345
Innes J M 146, 151
Insham R 33, 38
Insko C A 172, 179, 180
Ittleson W H 3, 6

Jack the Ripper 260
Jacklin C N 137, 316,
    379-382, 425, 429
Jackson D D 351, 353, 354,
    357, 358, 363, 369
Jackson G 396
Jacob T 315, 318, 354, 357
Jacobs T O 415, 420
Jacobson M B 426, 429
Jacobson N S 349, 350, 357
Jaffe D 309, 311
Jaffe Y 135, 267-275
Jahoda G 101, 108
James R M 71, 74, 77, 402,
    406
James S L 231, 239
Janis I 137, 197, 198, 315, 318

Johnson H H   93, 95, 338, 345
Jones E E   126, 129, 134, 136,
    168, 180, 206, 213, 414
Jones M B   339, 345
Jones S E   33, 37
Jordan-Edney N L   25, 39
Jourard S M   33, 39
Julian J W   413, 420
Justman J   92, 95

Kagan S   4, 5
Kahn A   271, 275
Kahn R L   261, 265
Kalle R J   231, 241
Kanter R M   5, 6, 137, 309,
    311, 427, 429
Kaplan A   372, 377
Kaplan S J   94, 363, 370
Karlin R A   51, 52
Karniol R   231, 239
Katz I   4, 63, 67, 94, 95,
    99-108
Katzell R A   332, 345
Kawamura-Reynolds M   147, 151
KcKee J P   423, 429
Keasey C B   231, 239
Keating J P   3, 6
Keil L J   6
Keller B B   234
Kelley H H   156, 163, 289,
    291, 315, 326, 327, 329,
    338, 345, 351, 358, 367-369
Kennedy J   126, 130
Kenney J W   25, 39
Kent V   134, 227-241
Kidd R F   239
Kiesler C A   33, 39, 172, 180
Kiesler S B   158, 163, 172,
    180
Kinsey A C   310, 311
Kinzel A F   11, 14
Kirscht J P   401, 406
Kisch R   200, 208, 213
Kitsuse J I   103, 107
Kleck R E   11, 14, 105, 107
Kleinke C L   33, 39
Klemp, G   43, 52
Kline D   128, 130
Kline N W   24, 39
Klinger E   146, 152
Knight P A   419, 420
Knower F H   166, 180
Knowles E S   3, 5, 11, 14, 15

Kogan L S   280, 281, 290, 291
Kohfeld D L   146, 152
Kohlberg L   229, 230, 239
Kohler M C   125, 129
Kovalev C V   431, 433, 436
Kozuh J F   148, 150
Kraemer H C   380, 382
Krebs D   135, 136, 229, 239
Krech D   172, 180
Krichevskii R L   317, 431-436
Krokoff L J   315, 347-358
Kuczynski L   234, 239
Kuethe J L   11, 14

Ladwig G W   94, 95
Lage E   218, 219, 224
Lamy M W   127, 129
Landers D M   146, 152
Landy F J   414, 420
Langer E   43, 52, 53, 105,
    107, 134, 195-198, 236
Lanzetta J   343, 345, 401, 406
Larsen I M   334, 336, 344, 345
Larson L L   317, 318
Latane B   133, 136, 142, 152,
    158, 163, 166-168, 179, 180,
    236, 237, 239
Latchford M   146, 150
LaTour S   172, 180
Laughlin P R   93, 95, 338, 345
Lawton M P   6, 135, 279-292
Layton B   31, 40
Lazarus R S   45, 51, 52
Leavitt H J   12, 14
LeBon G   267, 270, 275
Lee L C   296, 302
Lee T   282, 289, 291
Lefcourt H M   94, 95
Lehmann I J   408, 412
Lehrer T   119, 129
Leiman B   232, 239
Leiser T   230, 238
Lemert E M   103, 107
Lenerz K   143, 152
Lenin   217
Lennon J   260
Lennon R   229, 232, 238
Leont'ev A N   431, 433, 436
Lerner M J   102, 107, 236, 239
Levin H   244, 253, 323, 329
Levine A G   70, 77
Levine J M   142, 153, 152
Levine L E   232, 239

Levine R A 5
Levinger G 135, 136, 166,
    180, 332, 333, 345
Levy A S 31, 39
Levy P 166, 180
Lewin K 79, 87
Lewis M 135, 136
Lickona T 134, 135
Lieb R 27, 41
Light P 231, 234, 240
Lind E A 172, 180
Linderer D 168, 181
Lindskold S 259, 261, 265,
    266, 318, 401, 406
Lintell M 13, 14
Linton R 316, 318
Lipper S 142, 152
Lippitt R 79, 87, 390, 397
Little K B 10, 15
Lloyd B 316, 318
Locke H J 348, 357
Locke J J 348, 357
Lockheed M 64, 66, 67, 417,
    420, 427, 429
Lodahl T M 401, 406
Lohman A 323, 329
Lombardo J P 145, 152
Loo C M 31, 39
Lord R G 413-415, 418, 420
Lott A J 90, 95
Lott B E 90, 95
Lott D 10, 15
Lublin S C 268, 275
Lucido D J 105-107
Lucker G 124, 129
Luckmann T 192, 193
Lundgren D 166, 180
Lynch K 290, 291

Macaulay J 227, 240
MacBridge P 93, 96
Maccoby E E 137, 244, 253,
    316, 323, 329, 379-382, 425,
    429
Macklin E 305, 311
Madsen M C 4, 5
Magnusson D 4, 5, 79, 87
Mahar L 411, 412
Maier N 76, 77
Maier N R F 94, 95, 334, 336,
    345
Malamuth N 268, 275
Mann L 166, 180

Mann R D 4, 5, 57, 58, 67,
    71, 72, 74, 77, 327, 329,
    402, 406, 424, 425, 429
Manstead A S R 133, 136
Marcus A 147, 152
Maritindale D A 22, 39
Markman H 356, 357
Markman H J 349, 357
Markus H 143, 152
Marolla J 126, 129
Marshall D G 283, 291
Marshall G 392, 397
Martens R 142, 146, 147, 152
Martin C E 310, 311
Martindale D A 22, 39
Marwell G 6, 318
Maslach C 392, 397
Maslow A H 80, 87
Mathes E W 270, 271, 275
Matlin M W 148, 152
Matter C F 11, 15
Mayo C 25, 38
McBride D 90, 96
McCallum R 6, 315, 318
McClay D 25, 38
McClintock C G 6
McDavid J 72, 77
McDavis K 232, 238
McDowell K V 33, 39
McGrath J 79, 87, 166, 180,
    331, 345
McGraw C 281, 291
McGraw L W 301, 302
McGregor D 427, 429
McGrew W C 293, 302
McNair D M 142, 151, 152
McNeel S P 146, 153
Mead G H 362, 372-375, 377
Mead M 424, 429
Meeker B F 4, 5, 64, 65, 67
Megargee E I 425, 429
Mehan H 376, 377
Mehrabian A 33, 40, 347, 349,
    357
Mehrens W A 408, 412
Meisels M 10, 15
Melburg V 134, 255, 266
Menig-Peterson C L 231, 240
Messe L A 4, 79-88, 93, 96
Metcalf J 3, 43-53
Meyerson L 105, 106
Middlebrook P N 133, 136
Middlemist R D 11, 15
Milgram S 30, 40, 133,

185-193, 236, 267, 270, 271, 275, 318, 394, 395, 397
Miller C E 332, 345
Miller D T 236, 239
Miller F G 144, 153
Miller N 121, 129, 205, 206, 213
Miller S M 235, 239
Miller W 171, 179
Mills E S 70, 77
Mills T M 57
Mischel W 234, 240
Mishler E G 349, 357
Mitchell T R 407, 410, 412, 418, 420
Monty R A 3, 6, 43, 52
Moore D L 141, 148, 152, 155, 156, 162, 163
Moore D M 158, 163
Moore S 297, 302
Morris C G 6, 315, 331-335, 401, 406
Moscovici S 134, 215-224, 236
Mouton J S 18, 38
Movahedi S 316, 317
Mowrer V 205, 206, 213
Mueller E 234, 240
Mueller J H 148, 152
Mugny G 219, 221, 222, 224
Mulhern R K 234, 240
Mullens S 33, 40
Murdoch P 143, 152
Murdock G P 322, 329
Murphy L B 232, 240
Murton T 137, 318
Mussen P 134, 136
Muuss R E 323, 329
Mynatt C 271, 275

Naffrechoux M 218, 219, 224
Nahemow L 6, 135, 279-292
Neal C 229, 238
Neisser U 160, 162
Nelson Y 10, 14
Nemeth C J 4, 69-77, 220, 224, 318
Nesbitt P D 10, 15
Ness S 230, 232, 238
Newcomb T M 134, 199-213, 268, 273, 275, 281, 292, 318, 367, 369
Newman H 198
Newman O 18, 40

Newton J 396
Newton J W 166, 180
Nezlek J 4, 6
Nida S 133, 136
Noller P 355, 357
Norman R Z 60, 67
Notarius C 349, 351, 356, 357
Nucci L P 229, 240

Oakes W F 401, 406
Oden S 300, 302
Oden S L 301
Offir C 424, 429
Okun M 143, 152
O'Leary V E 423, 426, 427, 429
O'Neal E C 135, 136
O'Neill N 309, 311
Osborn R N 428, 429
Osgood C E 101, 107

Page J 24, 40
Page R 105, 107
Paicheler G 215-224, 236
Paivio A 147, 152
Papastamou S 219, 222, 224
Parsons T 321, 329
Passman R H 234, 240
Passow A H 92, 95
Patterson A H 31, 40
Patterson G R 349, 351, 357, 358
Patterson M L 13, 15, 33-36, 40
Paulus P B 3, 6, 143, 146, 152, 153
Pearse R W 401, 406, 415, 417, 420
Peckham V 166, 180, 332, 333, 345
Peirce C S 372, 373, 377
Pellegrini R J 33, 40
Penrod S 6
Pepitone A 268, 273, 275
Perlmuter L C 3, 6, 43, 52
Pervin L 43, 52
Peterson L 231, 240
Petrovskii A V 431, 436
Pettigrew T F 110
Petty R E 133, 169, 179
Piaget J 125, 129, 229, 240
Piliavin I M 105, 107, 236, 240

Piliavin J   236, 240, 105, 107
Pinner B   18, 41
Platt G J   142, 150
Plessy   119, 129
Pomeroy W B   310, 311
Pope J   69, 70, 77
Porterfield A L   355, 357
Potter E H   317
Powdermaker F B   328, 329
Powell E R   125, 130
Presser N   126, 130
Price J   31, 39
Priest R F   13, 15, 281, 292
Proshansky H M   3, 6
Pugh M D   65, 67
Purkey W W   126, 129
Putallaz M   293, 302

Quarter J   147, 152

Radke-Yarrow M   134, 136, 230,
   237, 241, 244, 253
Rahe D F   300, 301
Rajecki D W   143, 152
Rall M   18, 41
Ramey J W   308, 309, 311
Ransford H E   259, 265
Rasmussen M   295, 302
Raven B H   79, 86, 87, 211,
   213
Raviv A   230, 238
Rawles G D   289, 292
Rawls J   375, 377
Ray M H   105, 107
Reaves C   160, 162
Reddy W B   92, 95
Redler E   235, 239
Reeves K   281, 291
Reid J B   351, 357
Reis H T   4, 6
Reitan H T   93, 95
Rhead C C   18, 38
Rheingold H L   234, 240, 243,
   252
Rice R W   408, 411, 412, 417,
   420, 426, 429
Ridgeway C   65, 67
Riessman F   125, 129
Ringlemann   332, 345
Riskin J   349, 350, 358
Risner H T   146, 153
Rittle R H   142, 143, 144,

   149, 150, 152
Rivers A N   256, 258, 266
Rivlin L G   3, 6
Roberts E   128, 130
Roberts G C   143, 151
Roberts S O   94, 95
Robinson J M   94, 95
Roby T B   343, 345
Rodin J   3, 43-53, 105, 107,
   197, 198, 236, 240
Rogers C   231, 240
Rogers M S   334, 336, 344, 345
Rohe W   31, 40
Romano J   33, 40
Roper S   122, 129
Rosen S   125, 130
Rosenberg G S   283, 292
Rosenberger M   43, 52
Rosenblatt P C   22, 40
Rosenblum L A   135, 136
Rosenfeld P   256, 264, 266
Rosenfield D   124, 128, 129
Rosenhan D L   227, 237, 240,
   241, 244, 253
Rosenkrantz P S   423, 428
Rosow I   283, 290, 292
Ross E A   57
Ross M   31, 40, 231, 239
Rotter J B   46, 53
Rotter N G   332, 345
Rubin K H   229, 240
Rubin Z   27, 40, 135, 293-302
Ruderman A J   106, 108
Ruhe J A   4, 6, 94, 95
Rumelhart D   372, 373, 378
Rushton J P   134, 136,
   229-231, 235, 238, 240
Russell J A   3, 6
Russo N F   33, 40
Rutter D R   33, 40
Ryan W   102, 107
Ryle G   234, 240

Sabini J   133, 185-193, 236,
   318
Sackett G P   347, 351, 353,
   358
Sadow J S   149, 150
St John N   120, 121, 130
Sakurai M M   90, 95
Sales S M   142, 153
Sanders G   133, 141, 147,
   148, 151, 152, 155-163

Sapolsky A 92, 95
Sarason I G 147, 152
Sarbin T 103, 107
Sarbin T R 125, 130, 373, 378
Saruwalari L R 419, 420
Sasfy J 143, 152
Sawin D B 232, 239
Sawyer A 179, 180
Sawyer J 13, 15, 281, 292
Sax G 408, 412
Schachter S 18, 32, 39, 40,
   90, 96, 282, 291
Schaffer H R 234, 240
Scheff T 185, 188, 193
Scheff T J 103, 107
Scheier M F 272, 275
Schein E H 340, 345
Schein V E 414, 420, 425, 429
Scherwitz L 395, 397
Schiavo S R 135, 136
Schiffenbauer A 135, 136
Schkade J K 146, 153
Schlenker B R 257, 265, 266
Schmidt D E 3, 6
Schmitt D R 6, 318
Schmuck R 323, 329
Schneider C E 415-417, 420
Schneider F W 33, 38, 229,
   240
Schneier C E 6, 317, 413-421
Schon D 340, 344
Schopler J 18, 31, 40, 41
Schubot D B 125, 130
Schuette D 33, 39
Schul Y 135, 137, 236
Schulz R 33, 40
Schur E M 103, 107
Schutz W C 91, 92, 96
Schwartz G 45, 53
Schwartz H 134, 136
Schwartz S H 235, 240
Schweber-Koren C 70, 77
Scott J F 186, 191-193
Scott J P 256, 265
Scott P M 244, 253
Scott R A 104, 107
Sears D O 326, 329
Sears R 205, 206, 213
Sears R R 244, 253, 323, 329
Seashore E W 427, 428
Seashore S E 91, 96
Secord P F 235, 240
Segal M W 135, 136
Sekerak G J 143, 150

Selman R F 230, 240
Selo E 200, 213
Semin G R 133, 136
Seta J J 145, 146, 150, 153
Shannon C E 347, 358
Shapir N 268, 269, 275
Shaver P 149, 150
Shaw L M 90, 91, 96
Shaw M E 4, 79, 87, 89-96,
   135, 318, 343, 345
Sheatsley P B 123, 129
Shepher J 137
Sheppard B H 147, 153
Sherif C W 102, 107, 323, 329
Sherif M 102, 107, 123, 130,
   217, 221, 224, 323, 329
Sherman S J 271, 275
Sherriffs A C 423, 429
Sherrod D R 44, 52, 53
Shibutani T 375, 376, 378
Shiflett S C 334, 335, 345
Short J F 322, 329
Shotter J 234, 240
Shriver B 401, 406
Shure G H 334, 336, 344, 345
Siegel L S 230, 232, 238
Sigall H 22, 41, 105, 107
Sikes J 124, 128, 129
Simmel G 30, 40
Simon B B 282, 290, 291
Simon C K 70, 77
Singer J E 32, 40, 43, 44,
   52, 268, 275
Singerman K J 142, 153
Sistrunk F 72, 77
Skinner B F 191, 193
Slaby D A 300, 301
Slater P E 57, 424, 428, 431,
   435
Slozar J A 207-210, 213
Smelser W T 92, 96
Smirnova M M 431, 433, 436
Smith C 316, 318
Smith D 237, 238
Smith R B 256, 263, 266
Smith W P 133, 136
Snapp M 124, 128
Snoek J D 135, 136
Solomon S K 3, 43-53
Sommer R 3, 6, 9-15, 18, 25,
   33, 39, 137
Sorenson J R 315, 318
Sorre M 279, 292
Sorrentino R M 22, 41, 134,

136, 147, 153, 405, 406
Spelke E 160, 162
Spence J T 71, 76, 77, 426, 429
Spence K W 141
Spencer D D 316, 318
Spiegel J P 322, 329
Spielberger C D 147, 153
Spinner B 26, 40
Staff I 149, 150
Staneski R A 33, 39
Statistical Abstract ... 424, 429
Staub E 45, 53, 227-229, 235, 240
Stea D 280, 292
Stefaniak D 281, 291
Stein R T 6, 316, 318, 401-406, 414, 415, 420
Steiner I D 80, 85, 87, 315, 318, 331, 333, 334, 338, 345
Stephan C 124, 126, 128, 130
Stephan W 120, 130
Stephenson G M 33, 40
Steven G 10, 15
Stimson J 423, 428
Stinnett N 310, 311
Stock D 327, 329
Stockdale J 3, 6
Stocking S H 298, 300, 302
Stogdill R M 317, 318, 413, 414, 420
Stokes D 171, 179
Stokols D 3, 6, 18, 28, 30, 40, 41, 43, 44, 53
Stone G P 373, 378
Stone T H 334, 345
Stotland E 43, 53
Strayer F F 235, 240
Strayer J 231, 232, 240
Strickland L H 317, 318
Strodtbeck F L 12, 15, 57, 58, 67, 71, 72, 74, 77, 402, 406, 424, 425, 429
Strube M J 408, 412
Stuart R B 349, 351, 353, 358
Suci G H 101, 107
Sugarman R 143, 150
Sullivan H S 362
Suls J 147, 151, 231, 241
Sundstrom E 25, 31, 41, 51, 53, 410, 412
Szasz T S 103, 107

Tajfel H 4-6, 101, 106, 108-118
Takooshian H 186, 192, 193
Talliaferro A 237, 238
Tannenbaum P H 101, 107
Tarte R D 142, 153
Tassone J 334, 336, 344, 345
Tavris C 424, 429
Taylor 70, 77
Taylor D A 3, 17, 41, 137, 366, 367
Taylor R B 27, 41
Taylor S E 105-108
Teddlie C 18, 32, 35, 41
Tedeschi J T 134, 255-265
Teevan R C 148, 151
Terborg J R 417, 421
Terman L C 338, 339, 345
Thayer S 33, 41
Thibaut J W 156, 163, 315, 326, 327, 329, 338, 345, 351, 358, 368, 369
Thomas E J 402, 406
Thomes M M 348, 357
Thompson W C 237, 241
Thorndike E L 257, 266
Tiger L 137
Tindale R S 6, 137, 318
Tingle B A 232, 239
Toch H 259, 261, 266, 267, 270, 271, 275
Tolbert J W 301, 302
Triplett N 141, 153
Tuckman B W 328, 329
Tuddenham R D 93, 96
Turiel E 229, 240
Turner R H 372, 378
Tursky B 45, 53

Underwood B 271, 275

Valins S 31, 38, 41
Vallacher R R 93, 96
Vandell D l 234, 241
Van Tuinen M 146, 153
Van Zelst R H 91, 96, 325, 329
Varela J A 336, 345
Veitch R 50, 52
Venet T G 332, 345
Vicars W M 428, 429
Vinacke W E 424, 428

Vincent J 349, 350, 357
Vinokur A 172, 179
Vinsel A M 32, 38
Vinter R D 200, 208, 213
Vitters A G 417, 420, 426, 429
Vogel S R 423, 428
Vorst H C M 90, 95
Vygotsky L S 234, 241

Wachtler G 220, 224
Wachtler J 71-77
Wack D L 142, 143, 149, 150
Wahrman R 65, 67
Walker J W 142, 153
Walkere E L 142, 153
Wallace G 260
Walster E H 102, 107, 135-136, 368, 370, 419
Walster G W 368, 370
Walster. See also Hatfield
Wankel L M 147, 153
Ward L 86, 87
Wareing S 235, 240
Watson O M 33, 41
Watzlawick P 354, 358
Waxler C Z 243, 253
Waxler N E 349, 357
Waxler. See also Zahn-Waxler
Weakland J 351, 357, 363, 369
Weaver W 347, 358
Webster M 3, 4, 57-67, 318
Wedge B 18, 38
Weick K E 336, 345
Weinman C 196, 198
Weir K 229, 241
Weisberg D K 309, 311
Weiss H M 419, 420
Weiss J A 344, 345
Weiss R 349, 350, 357, 358
Weiss R M 144, 153
Weitzel W 146, 152
Weitzel-O'Neill P A 4, 5, 64, 65, 67
Wertsch J 317, 318
West M J 234, 240, 243, 252
Wheeler L 4, 6, 18, 19,, 21, 25, 30, 38
White D 172, 181
White G 396
White R 51, 53, 390
White W P 3, 6
Whyte W F 13, 15

Whyte W H 14, 15
Wicklund R A 168, 181
Wilder D A 5, 101, 106, 108, 168, 177, 181
Wiley M G 93, 94, 417, 419, 425, 428
Williams K 133, 136, 166, 167-170, 179. 180
Williams M A 142, 150
Williams M S 4, 5
Williamson R C 348, 357
Willis F N 10, 15
Wills T A 349, 358
Wilmott P 281, 292
Wilson J P 4, 79-88
Wilson S R 402, 406
Wine J 148, 153
Wirth L 30, 41
Wisch M 363, 370
Wispe L 134, 136
Wittgenstein L 371, 378
Wohlwill J F 30, 41
Wolfer J 197, 198
Wolosin R J 148, 153
Wolters R 419, 421
Worchel S 5, 18, 22, 25, 32, 35, 41
Wright B A 100, 105, 106, 108
Wright H T 18, 38
Wrightsman L 133, 136
Wyer R S 90, 96

Yandell B 172, 179
Yarrow M R 232, 238, 244, 253
Yates S 4, 119-130, 137
Yerkes 147
Yinon Y 135, 267-275
Yoder J 424, 427, 428
Yohai S 32, 41
Yoshioka G A 282, 290
Young M 281, 292
Young P F 148, 150
Young W E 148, 150

Zahn L G 349, 358
Zahn V 93, 96
Zahn-Waxler C 134, 136, 230, 237, 241, 243-253
Zajonc R B 133, 136, 142, 143, 148, 149, 152, 153, 155, 158, 163, 324, 329, 343, 345

Zander A   137, 236, 315, 318
Zdep S M   401, 406
Zelditch M   4, 5, 59, 60, 67
Zentall T R   142, 152, 153

Zillmann D   255, 266
Zimbardo P G   137, 168, 181,
    267, 268, 270, 301, 302,
    316, 383-397

Subject Index

This index is based partly on author-specified terms; some entries might not be exhaustive for the work as a whole

Abductive 372, 373
Abilities of group members – homogeneity/heterogeneity 92, 93
Achievement (academic) 121-128
Achievement motivation 147, 236
Acquaintanceship 18, 22, 26, 281, 282
Adolescent groups 323, 324
Adolescent groups – social interaction in 323
Advocacy 383-397
Advocacy and action 395, 397
Affect in marital interaction 348-351, 353, 355
Affiliation motivation 147
After effect (visual) – minority influence 222, 223
Age – effect on norm behaviour 190
Age differences and friendship choices 281, 283-290
Aggression 232, 255-275, 388, 389
Aggression – behaviouristic definition 255, 256
Aggression – displacement of 102
Aggression – perceived 263, 264

Agreement – shared 375, 376
Altruism. See also: Helping; Prosocial behaviour
Altruism 227, 228, 243-253
Anonymity 268, 270, 271, 273, 387-392
Antisocial behaviour 267-275
Appointed leaders 414, 415
Arousal and spatial behaviour 11, 31, 32, 36
Asymmetry in predictability in marriage 347, 354, 355
Attentional processes 155-163
Attentional processes model of social facilitation 159
Attitude change. See also Social influence
Attitude change 165-181
Attitude moderation 168-172
Attitude polarization 168-172
Attitudes – intergroup 109-111
Attraction 277-311
Attraction – in children 293-301
Attribution – and dyadic relationships 367
Attribution – and leadership 418
Audiences 155-163
Authority – coercion 260, 261
Automaticity and social

cognition 196

Bales categories 71-75, 81-83
Bales group 57, 58, 63
Behavioural style 218, 219
Behavioural style - sex
  differences 71-76
Behaviouristic definition of
  aggression 255, 256
Boundaries - dyadic 19, 20,
  24-28
Boundaries - interpersonal
  19, 20, 24-28, 30, 32, 33,
  35, 37
Boundaries - self 25-28, 37
Burden of proof and status
  expectations 58-63, 66
Bystanders and emergencies
  236

Categorization into groups
  100-102, 106, 111-118
Child rearing. See also
  Socialization
Child rearing 243-253
Child rearing practices
  243-253
Children - play in mixed dyads
  379-382
Children's friendship skills
  293-301
Classroom performance 119-130
Closedness of self to others
  25-27, 32, 36
Coercion. See also:
  Compliance; Social influence
Coercion - authority 160, 261
Coercion - legitimation 263,
  264
Coercion in correctional
  institutions 199-213
Coercive power 255-266
Cognition - social 195-198
Cognitive activity and
  mindfulness 195-198
Cognitive effort and attitude
  change 165-181
Cohesiveness in groups 89-91
Collective aggression 267-275
Commitment and dyadic
  relationships 366
Committees 325-327

Commodity theory 168
Communes - and marriage 308, 309

Communication in marital
  interaction 349-356
Communicative competence 372,
  375-377
Compatibility of group members
  19, 20, 23, 89, 91, 92
Competition in the classroom
  122-124, 126
Competition between groups
  110, 123, 124
Complementarity 365
Compliance. See also Social
  influence
Compliance 215-224
Composition of group 55-96
Comprehension and roletaking
  372-373
Conflict and social influence
  220, 221, 261
Conflict between groups
  109-111, 117
Conflict in marriage 347-351,
  355, 356
Conflict resolution in
  marriage 347-351, 355, 356
Conformity. See also Social
  influence
Conformity 172-175, 215-224
Conformity and cohesiveness
  90
Conformity and homogeneity of
  group members 93
Conscience development
  243-253
Consciousness and mindfulness
  195, 196
Consensus 217, 218
Consistency 218-220
Content of interactions
  362-364
Contingency model of
  leadership 407-422
Control 43-52, 197
Conversion 215-224
Cooperation 119-130
Coordination of members'
  efforts 333, 339
Correctional institutions. See
  also Imprisonment
Correctional institutions
  199-213
Costs and use of coercion 259
Costs in social exchange
  22-24, 30, 36

Coworkers 155-163
Creativity 332, 337
Crowding 17-52
Crowding - two-factor theory
  32, 35
Crowding and density 43-52
Cue utilization and social
  facilitation 148
Cues to status 58, 59

Decision making 69-77, 197
Decision making - in juries
  71-76
Decision making - sex
  differences 71-76
Deindividuation. See also
  Anonymity
Deindividuation 267, 388
Deindividuation theory 168
Density - perceptions 43-52
Density and crowding 30, 31,
  35, 43-52
Density and perceived control
  43-52
Density-intensity 31
Deprivation 262, 263
Deprivation of resources 257
Derogation of victims 102,
  106, 236
Desegregation 119-121, 123
Deviance 196, 197, 216-224
Deviance and labeling theory
  103
Differentiation between groups
  111-118
Differentiation of leadership
  role 431-436
Diffusion of responsibility
  268, 271, 272
Discipline and young children
  243-253
Discrimination between groups
  99-106, 109-118
Dissonance theory 168
Distraction - drive theory of
  social facilitation 141,
  156-163
Distributive justice 262, 263
Divorce 306, 307
Dominance in marriage 347-356
Drive theory of social
  facilitation. See also
  Social facilitation
Drive theory of social

facilitation - distraction
  141, 156-163
Drive theory of social
  facilitation - evaluation
  apprehension 141, 143-146
Drive theory of social
  facilitation - mere presence
  of others 141, 143, 144
Drive theory of social
  facilitation -
  psychophysiological
  reactions 142
Dyadic interaction in infants
  379-382
Dyadic relationships. See also
  Interpersonal relationships
Dyadic relationships -
  approaches to the study of
  361-370

Effort justification 168
Egocentrism. See also
  Roletaking
Egocentrism 125, 126, 229-231
Elderly persons 197
Elderly persons and friendship
  choices 281, 283-290
Emergencies - helping in 236
Emergent leaders - male vs.
  female 413-421
Emergent leadership 413-422
Emergent leadership - research
  needs 418, 419
Emotional leadership. See also
  Socio-emotional leadership
Emotional leadership 431-436
Empathy. See also Roletaking
Empathy 125-127, 231-233
Enforcement of norms 185,
  186, 188-193
Environment and behaviour
  17-37
Environment and interpersonal
  behaviour 9-14, 17-37
Environment and interpersonal
  relationships 279-290
Environmntal knowledge
  374-377
Equal status contact 121, 122
Equity theory and helping
  behaviour 236
Escalation of aggression 269,
  270
Ethnic relations 119-122, 124

Ethnocentrism   102
Evaluation apprehension –
  drive theory of social
  facilitation   141, 143–146,
  156–160
Exchange (social) in dyadic
  relationships   368
Existential revolution   303
Expectation states   58–66
Expectation states theory
  58–62, 122
Expectations – aggregate
  61–63, 66
Expectations – for performance
  57–66
Expectations and status   57–66
Experiments in subway   187–189
Eye contact and gaze   10, 17,
  33–35, 37

Failure – effects on social
  facilitation   144–146
Fairness and intergroup
  discrimination   114, 115,
  117, 118
Family (as a small group)
  321–323
Family – social interaction in
  322, 323
Family – structure   321–322
Family – tasks   322
Fear and aggression   259
Feedback   368, 369
Friendship   277–311
Friendship – in children
  293–301
Friendship – social skills of
  293–301
Friendship choices and age
  differences   281, 283–290
Friendship choices and elderly
  persons   281, 283–290
Friendship choices and
  integration   281, 290
Friendship choices and race
  281, 284–290
Friendship in adolescent
  groups   323, 324
Functionalist model   216–218

Gender roles   423–429
Group ... See also under
  second word
Group – and personality

variables   80–86
Group – egalitarian   80–86
Group – hierarchical   80–86
Group activity   431–436
Group atmosphere   415
Group composition   55–96
Group dynamics in juries
  71–76
Group effectiveness   331–344
Group function   313–436
Group leadership structure
  431–436
Group maintenance behaviours
  402
Group performance   90, 91, 94,
  331–344, 415–417
Group polarization   236
Group process. See Interaction
  process
Group productivity   80, 81,
  83–85, 91, 333
Group satisfaction and
  cohesiveness   91
Group satisfaction and
  compatibility   92
Group size   165–181, 402
Group size effects   165–181
Group structure   79–86,
  313–436
Guards. See Prison guards
Guilt in young children
  243–253

Halo effect   222
Helping. See also: Altruism;
  Prosocial behaviour
Helping   225–275
Homogeneity/heterogeneity of
  group members 89, 92, 93
Hostility between groups   102,
  104, 105, 109–111
Hurting   225–275

Identification. See social
  influence
Idiosyncrasy credit   414
Impression management   260
Impression management and
  social facilitation   148,
  149
Impressions   414
Impressions of group   97–130
Imprisonment. See also:
  Correctional institutions;

Prisons
Imprisonment 383-397
Indirect minority influence
221, 222
Inequality (in small groups)
57, 58, 63, 64, 66
Infants - and altruism
243-253
Infants - and conscience
243-253
Infants - and maternal
behaviour 243-253
Infants - in mixed sex dyads
379-382
Influence. See also Social
influence
Influence - acceptance of 414
Influence of others 131-302
Influence processes - in
juries 71-76
Influence processes - sex
differences 71-76
Information overload and
crowding 28, 30
Ingroup 109, 111-118
Innovation and minority
influence 219, 220
Institutions. See:
Correctional institutions;
Imprisonment
Instrumental leadership
431-436
Integration and friendship
choices 281, 290
Interaction - approaches to
the study of 361-370
Interaction - in juries 71-76
Interaction and cohesiveness
90
Interaction coding systems
342, 348, 349
Interaction disability 62-66
Interaction in adolescent
groups 323
Interaction in committees 326
Interaction in infant dyads
379-382
Interaction in married couples
347-356
Interaction in T groups 328
Interaction in the family
group 322, 323
Interaction in work groups
325

Interaction process 331-345
Interaction processes -
coordination of effort 333
Interaction zones 9-10
Interactions - content
362-364
Interdependence 123, 368
Interethnic relations 119-130
Intergroup - attitudes
109-111
Intergroup categorization
100-102, 106, 111-118
Intergroup competition 110
Intergroup conflict 109-111,
117
Intergroup differentiation
111-118
Intergroup discrimination
101, 106, 109-118
Intergroup fairness 114, 115,
117, 118
Intergroup friendship choices
281-290
Intergroup hostility 102,
104, 105, 109-111, 123
Intergroup relations 99-106,
109-111, 119-122, 124
Internalization. See Social
influence
Interpersonal attraction
281-283
Interpersonal attraction and
group composition 89-90
Interpersonal behaviour and
environment 9-14, 17-37
Interpersonal boundaries 19,
20, 24-28, 30, 32, 33, 35,
37
Interpersonal distance 9, 10,
20, 21, 32, 33
Interpersonal perception 366,
367, 414
Interpersonal relationships -
and marriage 303-311
Interpersonal relationships -
and personality 362
Interpersonal relationships -
between men and women
303-311
Interpersonal relationships -
in children 293-301
Interpersonal relationships -
patterning of 361, 362
Interpersonal relationships -

principles of dynamics
367-369
Interpersonal relationships
and environment 9-14,
17-37, 279-290
Interpersonal relationships
and proximity/propinquity
13, 18, 33
Interpersonal similarity
281-290
Interpersonal spacing 11-12
Interpretative procedures
371-378
Interventions (to overcome
status generalization)
63-66
Intimacy 17-37, 366
Intimacy equilibrium 32-36
Intimacy-arousal 34-36
Intragroup communication and
group cohesiveness 90
Intrusions and invasions of
personal space 10, 11, 19,
24, 25, 30, 31, 32

Jigsaw Cooperative Learning
Method 123-128
Juries 69-77
Juries - qualifications for
69, 70
Justice 262, 263
Juvenile correctional
institutions 199-213

Kinds of group 321-329, 403,
405
Knowledge and performance
effectiveness 337-340
Knowledge and process losses
337-340
Knowledge of group members
337-340

LPC scale 415, 416
LPC scores 407-412
Labeling 103, 104
Labeling - and stigmatization
103, 104
Laboratory paradigms -
aggression 264
Latent influence 221, 222
Law of effect 257
Leader sex 413-429
Leaderless situations 413, 414

Leaders vs. nonleaders 416
Leadership 80, 84, 86, 236,
401-436
Leadership - and member
motivation 80, 84, 86
Leadership - measures 403
Leadership - observer ratings
401-403
Leadership - related to
participation rates 401-406
Leadership and seating
arrangements 12
Leadership effectiveness
407-412
Leadership experience 407-412
Leadership role
differentiation 431-436
Learning and modeling of
aggression 263
Least Preferred Co-worker
(LPC) Scale 407-412, 415,
416
Legitimation of coercive
actions 263, 264
Limited capacity processing
375-377
Living together 304, 305

Mainstreaming 127
Maintenance of norms 185,
186, 188-193
Majority influence. See also
Social influence
Majority influence 215-224
Man-woman relationship 303-311
Marital enrichment 304, 305
Marital interaction 347-356
Marital satisfaction 347-356
Markers of territory 25
Marriage 303-311, 347-356
Marriage - exclusivity
308-311
Marriage - in an intimate
network 309
Marriage - in communes 308,
309
Marriage - inclusivity
308-310
Marriage - interaction in
347-356
Marriage - multilateral 308
Marriage - open 309-310
Marriage - permanent
availability 306

Marriage – traditional 305,
  306, 310, 311
Marriage contracts 306, 307
Marriage options 303–311
Marriage roles 305, 306
Mass media 263
Maternal child rearing
  practices 243–253
Media 263
Mere presence. See Presence of
  others
Mere presence of others –
  drive theory of social
  facilitation 141, 143, 144
Meshing 366
Methodological issues 379–382
Methodological issues –
  prosocial behaviour 228,
  229, 231, 232, 234–237
Mindfulness. See also Script
Mindfulness 195–198
Mindlessness 195–198
Minority groups 99–106,
  120–122, 127
Minority influence. See also
  Social influence
Minority influence 215–224
Mock prison 383–397
Modeling and learning 263
Monogamy 305–307, 310, 311
Mood and prosocial behaviour
  237
Mood (prisoners) 389, 390
Moral judgment 229, 230
Motives 79–86
Motives – and interaction with
  group structure 80–86
Motives – esteem needs 80–86
Motives – of group members
  79–86
Motives – safety needs 80–86

Nature of group 313–436
Needs – and group structure
  79–86
Needs – esteem 80–86
Needs – group compatibility
  91
Needs – interpersonal 91
Needs – safety 80–86
Negotiation of status 371–378
Nonverbal behaviour 9–11, 13,
  14, 17, 26, 27, 33–37
Nonverbal behaviour in marital

interaction 347, 349–356
Norm 236
Normalization of violations
  186
Normative rules 371–378
Norms. See also Rules
Norms – and deviance 103, 104
Norms – and the description of
  relationships 362
Norms – enforcement of 185,
  186, 188–193
Norms – maintenance of
  185–193
Norms of self-defence and
  reciprocity 261, 262
Noxious stimulation 257

Objectivity of social world
  192, 193
Observational methods in
  marital interaction 348–356
Observers and leadership roles
  401, 402
Old age and mindfulness 197
Onlookers and subway norm
  violations 189
Open marriage 309, 310
Openness of self to others
  25–27, 32, 36
Operant conditioning 185–191
Organizational effectiveness
  407–412
Outgroup 109, 111–118
Overlearning 196

Parental discipline. See
  Socialization
Participation rates – related
  to leadership 401–406
Participation rates – sex
  differences in juries 71–75
Peer tutoring 124, 125, 128
Peer tutoring – in children's
  friendship skills 299
Perceived aggression 263, 264
Perceptions of density 43–53
Performance. See Group
  performance
Performance and member effort
  333, 334
Performance and task
  strategies 334–337
Performance decrements 196
Performance effectiveness 331–344

Performance expectationss
57-66
Personal characteristics and
prosocial behaviour 228-235
Personal growth in woman-man
relationships 304, 305
Personal space 9-11, 19, 24,
25, 30-32, 280
Personality 55-96, 362
Personality - and group
structure 79-86
Personality variables 79-86
Personality variables - group
performance and homo-
/heterogeneity 94
Persuasion. See also: Social
influence; Attitude change
Persuasion 168-178
Physical attraction 419
Physical situation 7-53
Planning strategies 336, 337
Political retribution 258
Power 255-266, 391
Power and prestige structure
57-59, 63-66
Pre-attentive processing 196
Prejudice 99-106, 109-111,
119-121, 123, 127
Premature cognitive commitment
195, 197
Preschool. See Infants
Presence of others. See also
Social facilitation
Presence of others 139-181
Prison 383-397
Prison guards' behaviour
388-390
Prison guards' roles 386-388
Prisoner behaviour 388-390
Prisoners' mood 389, 390
Prisoners' roles 386-388
Prisons. See also Imprisonment
Prisons 199-213
Privacy 17-41
Privacy desired/achieved
26-28, 30, 37
Privacy maintenance 26-28
Privacy regulation 17, 25-28,
32, 36
Problem-solving in groups
326, 327
Process. See Interaction
processes
Process losses 80, 86, 333,

334, 337-340
Processing - limited capacity
375-377
Productivity. See: Group
productivity; Performance
effectiveness
Propinquity/proximity and
interpersonal relationships
13, 18, 33, 279-290
Prosocial behaviour. See also:
Altruism; Helping
Prosocial behaviour 227-241
Prosocial behaviour - and
personal characteristics
228-235
Prosocial behaviour - and
situational variables
235-237
Prosocial behaviour - and
social interaction 227-241
Prosocial behaviour -
generality of 234, 235
Prosocial behaviour -
methodological issues 228,
229, 231, 232, 234-237
Prosocial development 243-253
Provocation 269-274
Proximity/propinquity and
interpersonal relationships
13, 18, 33, 279-290
Psychophysical reactions -
drive theory of social
facilitation 142
Punishment - deprivation of
resources 257
Punishment - noxious
stimulation 257
Punishment - political
retribution 258
Punishment - social
punishments and aggression
258
Punishment - withholding
expected gains 258

Quality of interactions 364, 365

Race (as status
characteristic) 59, 62-64
Race and friendship choices
281, 284-290
Race relations 119-122, 124
Racial composition and group
behaviour 94

Ratio measures 365
Reactions to norm violations –
  experimenters 190
Reactions to norm violations –
  onlookers 189
Recipients (of a persuasive
  message) 165, 166
Reciprocity 261, 262, 365
Reciprocity in marital
  interaction 351–354
Reciprocity in social exchange
  17, 34–37
Reduction of restraints 272,
  274
Relations between groups
  109–111, 119–122, 124
Relationship – dyadic 361–370
Relationships 359–397
Relationships – interpersonal.
  See Interpersonal
  relationships
Relative deprivation 262, 263
Resentment – of juveniles in
  corrections 199–213
Residual rules 185, 186
Resource deprivation 257
Resources – scarce 261
Retaliation 268, 272, 274
Retribution, political 258
Rewards and individual motives
  79, 86
Rewards in social exchange
  22–24, 30, 36
Role 371–378
Roleplaying simulation of
  prison 383–397
Roles 191, 192, 359–397
Roles in marriage 305, 306
Roletaking. See also Empathy
Roletaking 125, 126, 128
Roletaking ability. See also
  Egocentrism
Roletaking ability 230, 231
Rules. See also Norms
Rules – interpretation of, in
  interaction 371–378, 394,
  395
Rules – in prisons 394, 395
Rules – residual 185, 186

Sanction by authority 121
Scapegoat model (of
  stigmatization) 102–104,
  106

Scarce resources 261
Schemata 372, 377
Script 236
Scripts. See Mindlessness
Seating arrangements 11, 12,
  18, 21, 25
Self-actualization 304, 305
Self-awareness 272–274
Self-confidence 258, 259
Self-consciousness 375
Self-defence 261, 262
Self-disclosure 19, 22,
  25–28, 31, 33, 35–37
Self-esteem 119–128
Self-image 118
Self-perceptions 419
Sequential analysis 347, 349,
  351–356
Sex (as status characteristic)
  58, 59, 64–66
Sex composition and effects on
  group behaviour 93
Sex differences – in
  conformity 72
Sex differences – in juries
  69–76
Sex differences – in
  participation rates 71–75
Sex education 128
Sex role socialization (v.
  status) 64, 65
Sex roles 423–429
Sex segregation. See also Sex
  roles
Sex segregation 379–382
Sexual status 403–405
Shared agreement 375, 376
Similarity 281–290, 365
Simulations – reality of 384,
  390
Situation (physical) 1–130
Situational control 407–412
Situational variables and
  prosocial behaviour 235–237
Size of group 165–181, 402
Skill of members 337–340
Sociability 234
Social ... See also under
  second word
Social action 395, 397
Social change 215–224,
  383–397
Social characteristics 55–96
Social cognition and

automaticity 196
Social comparison 118
Social exchange 17, 22-24, 34-37
Social facilitation. See also Presence of others
Social facilitation 141-163, 237
Social facilitation - cue utilization 148
Social facilitation - drive theory of 141-153
Social facilitation - effects of success and failure 144-146
Social facilitation - individual differences 146-148
Social facilitation - practical significance 161, 162
Social facilitation and impression management 148, 149
Social identity 118
Social influence. See also: Attitude change; Coercion; Compliance; Conformity; Influence; Majority influence; Minority i
Social influence 183-224
Social influence and group cohesiveness 90
Social inhibition 166, 167
Social interaction 315-338, 371-382
Social interaction and prosocial behaviour 227-241
Social isolation 19, 20, 22-25, 28, 30
Social norms 185-193
Social penetration 17-37
Social power and group cohesiveness 90
Social punishments and aggression 258
Social skills - and friendship 293-301
Social skills - in children 293-301
Social space 279-290
Social world - objectivity 192, 193
Socialization. See also Child

rearing
Socialization 233, 234
Sources (of a persuasive message) 172-177
Spatial behaviour 9-15, 17-37
Status - combining of 59-64
Status - diffuse 59-63, 66
Status - inequality 57, 58, 63, 64, 66
Status - negotiation of 371-378
Status - specific 59-64, 66
Status and seating arrangements 13
Status characteristics 57-66, 401
Status generalization 57-66
Status generalization - to overcome 63-66
Status inequalities 57, 58, 63, 64, 66, 121, 122
Status struggle 63, 65
Stereotypes 100, 109
Stereotypes of males and females 70, 71, 76
Stigma 99-106
Stigmatization 99-106
Stress 19, 28, 30-32, 35, 36
Stress and crowding 43-45, 51, 52
Structural model 347-358
Structure 313-436
Subway 185-193
Subways - experiments in 185-193
Subways - rules of behaviour 185-187
Success and failure - effects on social facilitation 144-146
Summarization abilities 373, 376, 377
Swinging 310
Sympathy. See Empathy

T groups 327, 328
T groups - social interaction in 328
T groups - structure 327
T groups - tasks of 327, 328
Tacit meanings 372, 373
Task 315-338
Task factors in committees 326, 327

Task factors in problem
   solving groups   326, 327
Task factors in T groups   327,
   328
Task factors in the family
   group 322
Task factors in work groups
   324

Task leadership behaviours
   401-403, 405
Task performance   155-163
Task skill   401
Tasks - group effectiveness
   331-344
Tasks - performance strategies
   334-337
Territoriality   18-25, 28, 30,
   36
Threats   257
Time   392
Time series analysis   347,
   354-356
Trait anxiety   146, 147
Two-factor theory of crowding
   32, 35
Type A behaviour pattern   147,
   148

Types of group   321-328, 403,
   405
Types of punishment. See
   Punishment

Urban norms   185-193
Use of coercion   259

Valence model (of emergent
   leadership)   415
Vertical dyads   418
Victim denigration   102, 106,
   236
Violence. See Aggression

Withholding expected gains
   258
Woman-man relationships
   303-311
Women and leadership   413-429
Women as leaders   423-429
Women in juries   69-76
Work groups   324, 325
Work groups - interaction
   processes in   325
Work groups - organisation in
   324
Work groups - tasks of   324